First World War
and Army of Occupation
War Diary
France, Belgium and Germany

56 DIVISION
Headquarters, Branches and Services
General Staff
1 September 1916 - 31 December 1916

WO95/2932

The Naval & Military Press Ltd
www.nmarchive.com
Published in association with The National Archives

Published by

The Naval & Military Press Ltd

Unit 10 Ridgewood Industrial Park,
Uckfield, East Sussex,
TN22 5QE England
Tel: +44 (0) 1825 749494

www.naval-military-press.com

www.nmarchive.com

This diary has been reprinted in facsimile from the original. Any imperfections are inevitably reproduced and the quality may fall short of modern type and cartographic standards.

© **Crown Copyright**
Images reproduced by permission of The National Archives, London, England, 2015.

Contents

Document type	Place/Title	Date From	Date To
Heading	56th Division General Staff Sep-Dec 1916		
Heading	War Diary General Staff 56th Division September 1916		
War Diary	St Riquier	01/09/1916	03/09/1916
War Diary	Corbie	04/09/1916	05/09/1916
War Diary	Forked Tree	06/09/1916	06/09/1916
War Diary	Billon Copse	07/09/1916	14/09/1916
War Diary	A.10.b.3.8	14/09/1916	21/09/1916
War Diary	Billon Copse	21/09/1916	29/09/1916
War Diary	Billon Copse A.10.b.3.8	30/09/1916	30/09/1916
War Diary	Billon Copse	28/09/1916	28/09/1916
Heading	56th Divisional Account Of Operation During September & October 1916		
Miscellaneous	Account Of Operation Carried Out By 56th Division	29/10/1916	29/10/1916
Miscellaneous	Notes On Operations Of 56th (London) Division	29/10/1916	29/10/1916
Miscellaneous	Casualties		
Miscellaneous	With Reference To O.G.59. Account Of Operations	02/11/1916	02/11/1916
Heading	Appendix VI 56th Division General Staff Operation Order September 1916		
Operation(al) Order(s)	56th Divisional Order No. 28	01/09/1916	01/09/1916
Miscellaneous	March Table	01/09/1916	01/09/1916
Operation(al) Order(s)	56th Divisional Order No. 29	02/09/1916	02/09/1916
Miscellaneous	Move Of Units 56th Division Into Corbie Area	02/09/1916	02/09/1916
Operation(al) Order(s)	56th Divisional Order No. 30	05/09/1916	05/09/1916
Operation(al) Order(s)	56th Divisional Order No. 31	06/09/1916	06/09/1916
Operation(al) Order(s)	56th Divisional Order No. 32	07/09/1916	07/09/1916
Operation(al) Order(s)	Special Instructions Issued In Continuation Of 56th Divisional Order No. 33	08/09/1916	08/09/1916
Operation(al) Order(s)	56th Divisional Order No. 33	07/09/1916	07/09/1916
Operation(al) Order(s)	56th Divisional Order No. 36	12/09/1916	12/09/1916
Operation(al) Order(s)	56th Divisional Order No. 37	12/09/1916	12/09/1916
Operation(al) Order(s)	Artillery Instructions	12/09/1916	12/09/1916
Operation(al) Order(s)	Preliminary Instructions For The Employment Of Tanks	12/09/1916	12/09/1916
Map	Map		
Operation(al) Order(s)	56th Divisional Order No. 35	10/09/1916	10/09/1916
Operation(al) Order(s)	56th Divisional Order No. 34	10/09/1916	10/09/1916
Map	Map		
Operation(al) Order(s)	56th Divisional Order No. 38	13/09/1916	13/09/1916
Miscellaneous	The Following Amendments Are Made To 56th Divisional Order No. 37	14/09/1916	14/09/1916
Miscellaneous	Instructions For The Employment Of R.E. And Pioneers	13/09/1916	13/09/1916
Map	Map		
Operation(al) Order(s)	56th Divisional Order No. 39	16/09/1916	16/09/1916
Operation(al) Order(s)	56th Divisional Order No. 40	17/09/1916	17/09/1916
Operation(al) Order(s)	56th Divisional Order No. 41	18/09/1916	18/09/1916
Operation(al) Order(s)	56th Divisional (Warning) Order No. 42	19/09/1916	19/09/1916
Operation(al) Order(s)	56th Division Order No. 43	22/09/1916	22/09/1916
Miscellaneous	Instructions As To Employment Of Smoke Mortars	22/09/1916	22/09/1916
Miscellaneous	Instructions As To Employment Of Tanks	22/09/1916	22/09/1916
Miscellaneous	Key		
Map	Map		

Operation(al) Order(s)	56th Divisional Order No. 44	23/09/1916	23/09/1916
Operation(al) Order(s)	56th Divisional Order No. 45	26/09/1916	26/09/1916
Miscellaneous	A Form Messages And Signals.		
Operation(al) Order(s)	56th Divisional Order No. 47	27/09/1916	27/09/1916
Operation(al) Order(s)	56th Divisional Order No. 48	28/09/1916	28/09/1916
Operation(al) Order(s)	56th Divisional Order No. 49	29/09/1916	29/09/1916
Operation(al) Order(s)	56th Divisional Order No. 50	30/09/1916	30/09/1916
Map	Sketch Map		
Heading	Appendix I 56th Division General Staff September 1916		
Map	Map		
Miscellaneous	List Of Appendices To 56th Divisional War Diary		
Miscellaneous	Extract From 56th Division Order No. 556.	29/08/1916	29/08/1916
Miscellaneous	Scheme For Operation		
Miscellaneous	Extracts From 56th Divisional Order No. 557	02/09/1916	02/09/1916
Heading	Appendix II 56th Division General Staff September 1916		
Miscellaneous	Provisional Billeting Areas	02/09/1916	02/09/1916
Miscellaneous	Dispositions Of Units In 56th Division		
Miscellaneous	Appendix II		
Heading	Appendix III 56th Division General Staff September 1916		
Map	Map E2		
Map	Map		
Map	Map E.3		
Map	Map		
Map	Map F		
Map	Map		
Miscellaneous	Map G		
Map	Map		
Miscellaneous	Map E.4		
Map	Map		
Miscellaneous	Location Map		
Map	Map		
Miscellaneous	Map D		
Map	Map		
Miscellaneous	Trench Map		
Heading	Appendix III 56th Division General Staff September 1916		
	Map A		
Map	Map		
Miscellaneous	Glossary		
Map	Map		
Miscellaneous	Glossary		
Map	Map		
Miscellaneous	Glossary		
Map	Map		
Miscellaneous	Glossary		
Map	Map		
Miscellaneous	Trench Map Map A Guillemont		
Map	Map		
Miscellaneous	Glossary		
Map	Map		
Miscellaneous	Glossary		
Map	Map		
Miscellaneous	Map Z Dvnl Area 1st To 3rd Sept 1916		
Heading	Appendices IV & V 56th Division General Staff September 1916		

Miscellaneous	Reference 56th Divisional Order No. 36	12/09/1916	12/09/1916
Miscellaneous	Amendments To Operation Order No. 1	24/09/1916	24/09/1916
Operation(al) Order(s)	Operation Order No. 1 by Brigadier-General R.J.G. Elkington C.M.G. Commanding Right Divisional Artillery	23/09/1916	23/09/1916
Miscellaneous	French Liaison Officer	24/09/1916	24/09/1916
Miscellaneous	No. S/CRA/344/15	24/09/1916	24/09/1916
Miscellaneous	Copy Of Letter received from Captain Boillot by C.R.A. Right Artillery	22/09/1916	22/09/1916
Miscellaneous	Extract		
Miscellaneous	Reference 5th Division Operation Order No. 127		
Miscellaneous	Captain Boillot. 2nd French Div		
Miscellaneous	Priority To French Liaison Officer		
Miscellaneous	56th Divn. O.G 47		
Miscellaneous	To Capt. Boillot		
Miscellaneous	56th Div S.G 158/5	06/10/1916	06/10/1916
Miscellaneous	Capt. Boillot		
Miscellaneous			
Miscellaneous	Copy Of Wires		
Miscellaneous	Copy Of Messages		
Operation(al) Order(s)	Operation Order No. 3 by Brigadier-General R.J.G. Elkington C.M.G. Commanding Right Divisional Artillery	08/10/1916	08/10/1916
Miscellaneous	Appendix No.1. To Right Artillery Operation Order No. 3		
Miscellaneous	Amendment		
Miscellaneous	Copy Of Wire		
Operation(al) Order(s)	4th Division Operation Order No. 68	11/10/1916	11/10/1916
Operation(al) Order(s)	4th Division Operation Order No. 67	10/10/1916	10/10/1916
Miscellaneous	XIV Corps No. S.76/134	08/09/1916	08/09/1916
Miscellaneous	56th Division 'G' (For Liaison Officer French Army)	11/09/1916	11/09/1916
Miscellaneous	Casualties		
Miscellaneous	Prisoners And Material Captured By 56th Division		
Heading	Appendix VII 56th Division General Staff September 1916		
Miscellaneous	Appendix VII		
War Diary		01/10/1916	09/10/1916
War Diary	Citadel	10/10/1916	10/10/1916
War Diary	Belloy Sur Somme	11/10/1916	20/10/1916
War Diary	Hallencourt	20/10/1916	23/10/1916
War Diary	Lestrem	23/10/1916	28/10/1916
War Diary	La Gorgue	28/10/1916	31/10/1916
Heading	Appendix III Divnl Orders For October 1916		
Operation(al) Order(s)	56th Divisional Order No. 51	02/10/1916	02/10/1916
Operation(al) Order(s)	56th Divisional Order No. 62	03/10/1916	03/10/1916
Miscellaneous	56th Division OC 43	04/10/1916	04/10/1916
Operation(al) Order(s)	56th Divisional Order No. 53	06/10/1916	06/10/1916
Map	Map		
Operation(al) Order(s)	56th Divisional Order No. 54	07/10/1916	07/10/1916
Operation(al) Order(s)	56th Divisional Order No. 55	08/10/1916	08/10/1916
Miscellaneous	March Table	06/10/1916	06/10/1916
Operation(al) Order(s)	56th Divisional Order No. 56	09/10/1916	09/10/1916
Miscellaneous	March Table	09/10/1916	09/10/1916
Operation(al) Order(s)	56th Divisional Order No. 57	18/10/1916	18/10/1916
Miscellaneous	March Table	17/10/1916	17/10/1916
Operation(al) Order(s)	56th Divisional Order No. 58	21/10/1916	21/10/1916

Operation(al) Order(s)	56th Divisional Order No. 59	24/10/1916	24/10/1916
Miscellaneous	Dispositions Of Brigade	24/10/1916	24/10/1916
Miscellaneous	List Of Appendices To 56th Divisional War Diary October 1916		
Heading	Appendix IV Tactical Progress Reports October 1916		
Map	Map		
Miscellaneous	Trench Map Guillemont		
Miscellaneous	56th Division Tactical Report No.1 from 8.0 a.m. 28th October to 8.0 a.m. 29th October	29/10/1916	29/10/1916
Miscellaneous	56th Division Tactical Report No.2 from 8.0 a.m. 29th October to 8.0 a.m. 30th October	30/10/1916	30/10/1916
Miscellaneous	56th Division Tactical Report No.3 from 8.0 a.m. 30th October to 8.0 a.m. 31st October	31/10/1916	31/10/1916
Miscellaneous	Map E Dvnl Area "Area D" 11th To 20 Oct 1916		
Map	Map		
Miscellaneous	Map C1		
Map	Map		
Map	Location Map		
Miscellaneous	Location Map 011016		
Map	Map		
Map	Location Map		
Miscellaneous	Location Map		
Map	Location Map		
Map	Administrative Map		
Miscellaneous	Map F		
Map	Map C3		
Map	Map		
Miscellaneous	Map C2		
Map	Map		
Map	Map D		
Map	Map		
Map	Situation Map		
Miscellaneous	Fourth Army Trench Map B		
Miscellaneous	Account Of Operations	29/10/1916	29/10/1916
Miscellaneous	Notes On Operations	29/10/1916	29/10/1916
Miscellaneous	Casualties		
Heading	War Diary General Staff 56th Division 1st To 30th November 1916 Vol X		
War Diary	La Gorgue	01/11/1916	30/11/1916
Miscellaneous	Location Table For Infantry Brigades		
Operation(al) Order(s)	56th Divisional Order No. 60	24/11/1916	24/11/1916
Miscellaneous	Addressed To All Recipients Of 56th Div. Order No. 60	25/11/1916	25/11/1916
Miscellaneous	56th Division Tactical Progress Report No.4 From 8.0 am 31st October to 8.0 am 1st November	01/11/1916	01/11/1916
Miscellaneous	56th Division Tactical Progress Report No.5 From 8.0 am 1st November to 8.0 am 2nd November	02/11/1916	02/11/1916
Miscellaneous	56th Division Tactical Progress Report No.6 From 8.0 am 2nd November to 8.0 am 3rd November	03/11/1916	03/11/1916
Miscellaneous	56th Division Tactical Progress Report No.7 From 8.0 am November 3rd to 8.0 am November 4th	04/11/1916	04/11/1916
Miscellaneous	56th Division Tactical Progress Report No.8 From 8.0 am 4th November to 8.0 am 5th November	05/11/1916	05/11/1916
Miscellaneous	56th Division Tactical Progress Report No.9 From 8.0 am 5th November to 8.0 am 6th November 1916	08/11/1916	08/11/1916
Miscellaneous	56th Division Tactical Progress Report No.10 From 8.0 am 6th November to 8.0 am 7th November	07/11/1916	07/11/1916

Miscellaneous	56th Division Tactical Progress Report No.11 From 8.0 am 7th November to 8.0 am 8th November	08/11/1916	08/11/1916
Miscellaneous	56th Division Tactical Progress Report No.12 From 8.0 am 8th November to 8.0 am 9th November	09/11/1916	09/11/1916
Miscellaneous	56th Division Tactical Progress Report No.13 From 8.0 am 9th November to 8.0 am 10th November	10/11/1916	10/11/1916
Miscellaneous	56th Division Tactical Progress Report No.14 From 8.0 am 10th November to 8.0 am 11th November	11/11/1916	11/11/1916
Miscellaneous	56th Division Tactical Progress Report No.15 From 8.0 am 11th November to 8.0 am 12th November	12/11/1916	12/11/1916
Miscellaneous	56th Division Tactical Progress Report No.16 From 8.0 am 12th November to 8.0 am 13th November	13/11/1916	13/11/1916
Miscellaneous	56th Division Tactical Progress Report No.17 From 8.0 am 13th November to 8.0 am 14th November	14/11/1916	14/11/1916
Miscellaneous	56th Division Tactical Progress Report No.18 From 8.0 am 14th November to 8.0 am 15th November	15/11/1916	15/11/1916
Miscellaneous	56th Division Tactical Progress Report No.19 From 8.0 am 15th November to 8.0 am 16th November	16/11/1916	16/11/1916
Miscellaneous	56th Division Tactical Progress Report No.20 From 8.0 am 16th November to 8.0 am 17th November 1916	17/11/1916	17/11/1916
Miscellaneous	56th Division Tactical Progress Report No.21 From 8.0 am 17th November to 8.0 am 18th November	18/11/1916	18/11/1916
Miscellaneous	56th Division Tactical Progress Report No.22 From 8.0 am 18th November to 8.0 am 19th November 1916	19/11/1916	19/11/1916
Miscellaneous	56th Division Tactical Progress Report No.23 From 8.0 am 19th November to 8.0 am 20th November	20/11/1916	20/11/1916
Miscellaneous	56th Division Tactical Progress Report No.24 From 8.0 am 20th November to 8.0 am 21st November 1916	21/11/1916	21/11/1916
Miscellaneous	56th Division Tactical Progress Report No.25 From 8.0 am 21st November to 8.0 am 22nd November 1916	22/11/1916	22/11/1916
Miscellaneous	56th Division Tactical Progress Report No.26 From 8.0 am 22nd November to 8.0 am 23rd November 1916	23/11/1916	23/11/1916
Miscellaneous	56th Division Tactical Progress Report No.27 From 8.0 am November 23rd to 8.0 am November 24th	24/11/1916	24/11/1916
Miscellaneous	56th Division Tactical Progress Report No.28 From 8.0 am 24th November to 8.0 am 25th November 1916	25/11/1916	25/11/1916
Miscellaneous	56th Division Tactical Progress Report No.29 From 8.0 am 25th November to 8.0 am 26th November	26/11/1916	26/11/1916
Miscellaneous	56th Division Tactical Progress Report No.30 From 8.0 am 26th November to 8.0 am 27th November 1916	27/11/1916	27/11/1916
Miscellaneous	56th Division Tactical Progress Report No.31 From 8.0 am 27th November to 8.0 am 28th November 1916	28/11/1916	28/11/1916
Miscellaneous	56th Division Tactical Progress Report No.32 From 8.0 am 28th November to 8.0 am 29th November 1916	29/11/1916	29/11/1916
Miscellaneous	56th Division Tactical Progress Report No.33 From 8.0 am 29th November to 8.0 am 30th November 1916	30/11/1916	30/11/1916
Heading	War Diary General Staff 56th Division December 1916 Vol II		
War Diary	La Gorgue	01/12/1916	31/12/1916
Operation(al) Order(s)	56th Divisional Order No. 61	05/12/1916	05/12/1916
Operation(al) Order(s)	56th Divisional Order No. 62	17/12/1916	17/12/1916
Miscellaneous	All Recipients Of 56th Div. Order No. 62	19/12/1916	19/12/1916
Miscellaneous	Location Table		
Miscellaneous	56th Divisional Tactical Progress Report No 34	01/12/1916	01/12/1916
Miscellaneous	56th Divisional Tactical Progress Report No 35	02/12/1916	02/12/1916
Miscellaneous	56th Divisional Tactical Progress Report No 36	03/12/1916	03/12/1916

Miscellaneous	56th Divisional Tactical Progress Report No 37	04/12/1916	04/12/1916
Miscellaneous	56th Divisional Tactical Progress Report No 38	05/12/1916	05/12/1916
Miscellaneous	56th Divisional Tactical Progress Report No 39	06/12/1916	06/12/1916
Miscellaneous	56th Divisional Tactical Progress Report No 40	07/12/1916	07/12/1916
Miscellaneous	56th Divisional Tactical Progress Report No 41	08/12/1916	08/12/1916
Miscellaneous	56th Divisional Tactical Progress Report No 42	09/12/1916	09/12/1916
Miscellaneous	56th Divisional Tactical Progress Report No 43	10/12/1916	10/12/1916
Miscellaneous	56th Divisional Tactical Progress Report No 44	11/12/1916	11/12/1916
Miscellaneous	56th Divisional Tactical Progress Report No 45	12/12/1916	12/12/1916
Miscellaneous	56th Divisional Tactical Progress Report No 46	13/12/1916	13/12/1916
Miscellaneous	56th Divisional Tactical Progress Report No 47	14/12/1916	14/12/1916
Miscellaneous	56th Divisional Tactical Progress Report No 48	15/12/1916	15/12/1916
Miscellaneous	56th Divisional Tactical Progress Report No 49	16/12/1916	16/12/1916
Miscellaneous	56th Divisional Tactical Progress Report No 50	17/12/1916	17/12/1916
Miscellaneous	56th Divisional Tactical Progress Report No 51	18/12/1916	18/12/1916
Miscellaneous	56th Divisional Tactical Progress Report No 52	19/12/1916	19/12/1916
Miscellaneous	56th Divisional Tactical Progress Report No 54	20/12/1916	20/12/1916
Miscellaneous	56th Divisional Tactical Progress Report No 55	21/12/1916	21/12/1916
Miscellaneous	56th Divisional Tactical Progress Report No 56	22/12/1916	22/12/1916
Miscellaneous	56th Divisional Tactical Progress Report No 57	23/12/1916	23/12/1916
Miscellaneous	56th Divisional Tactical Progress Report No 58	24/12/1916	24/12/1916
Miscellaneous	56th Divisional Tactical Progress Report No 60	26/12/1916	26/12/1916
Miscellaneous	56th Divisional Tactical Progress Report No 61	27/12/1916	27/12/1916
Miscellaneous	56th Divisional Tactical Progress Report No 62	28/12/1916	28/12/1916
Miscellaneous	56th Divisional Tactical Progress Report No 63	29/12/1916	29/12/1916
Miscellaneous	56th Divisional Tactical Progress Report No 64	30/12/1916	30/12/1916
Miscellaneous	56th Divisional Tactical Progress Report No 65	31/12/1916	31/12/1916
Miscellaneous	56th Divisional Tactical Progress Report No 66	01/01/1917	01/01/1917
Miscellaneous	56th Divisional Tactical Progress Report No 67	02/01/1917	02/01/1917
Miscellaneous	Central Registry		
Miscellaneous	XI Corps 56th Division	07/12/1916	07/12/1916
Miscellaneous	56th Division	07/12/1916	07/12/1916
Miscellaneous	The Rangers Report On Raid		
Miscellaneous	The Rangers Operation Order No. 3	05/12/1916	05/12/1916
Heading	Appendix I Location Tables		
Miscellaneous	Location Table-56th Division	21/10/1916	21/10/1916
Miscellaneous	Location Table-58th Division	25/10/1916	25/10/1916

56TH DIVISION

GENERAL STAFF
SEP - DEC 1916

56TH DIVISION

WAR DIARY

GENERAL STAFF

56th DIVISION

SEPTEMBER 1916.

Appendices under separate cover

WAR DIARY or INTELLIGENCE SUMMARY

Army Form C. 2118.

HRGS/52 Vol 5

Place	Date	Hour	Summary of Events and Information	Remarks and references to Appendices
ST RIQUIER	FRI 15th SEPT	noon	For areas allotted to unit while in ST RIQUIER training area see Appendix. Orders received for units from 3rd Army for 33rd Divl. Artillery. It was during the day so follow R.G. Hqrs. and 2 Brigades to LE MEILLARD, one Brigade to OUTREBOIS, one Brigade to NEUF PLESIS, LE QUESNOY FARM, and COQUREL - D.A.C. to BOIS BERGUES. During the morning a Military Salute was carried out by the visiting over by 15 P.O.s brigade in conjunction with the 1st (?) evolution of H.S.M.C.G. Amongst those present was H.R.H. Prince/Wales. G.O.C. 2.S.S and C.R.A. attended conference at Hqrs. 14th Corps MFAULTE at 4.30 p.m. Divl Order No 28 with reference to the move again there issued. See appendix.	Appendix III Map Z Appendix I (?) Appendix D

WAR DIARY or INTELLIGENCE SUMMARY

Army Form C. 2118.

Place	Date	Hour	Summary of Events and Information	Remarks and references to Appendices
ST RIQUIER	2nd SEPT		Troops detailed in General Order No 28 to 2nd inst. carried out a tactical scheme under the Divl. Commander and over the Corps as yesterday. Was carried out by 168th Inf Brigade in conjunction with 1 Coy. H.S.M.G. Coy. Cooperation between the two Brigades and with better than hitherto and the 6 Tanks concerned carried out the scheme without mishap. Amongst the spectators was G.O.C. 4th Army. Bryn Campbell, Gordon Highlanders from 3rd Army Infantry School returned for bayonet fighting to 157th Inf Bde at 12 noon and 168 and 169 Inf. Bdes at 3pm. Divisional Order No 29 issued to all concerned. See appendix For location of units on arrival in CORBIE area on Sept 3/4.	See APPENDIX I (a). Appendix VI Appendix II (a)

Army Form C. 2118.

WAR DIARY
or
INTELLIGENCE SUMMARY
(Erase heading not required.)

Instructions regarding War Diaries and Intelligence Summaries are contained in F.S. Regs., Part II. and the Staff Manual respectively. Title Pages will be prepared in manuscript.

Place	Date	Hour	Summary of Events and Information	Remarks and references to Appendices
ST RIQUIER	SUN 3rd SEPT.		168 and 169 Inf. Brigades proceeded to CORBIE area by tactical trains during the day. Those ordered in Order No. 29 carried out. A tactical scheme was carried out during the afternoon in the training area in order that the Commanders in Chief of the French Army might see the working of H.S.M.G. Coys. This scheme was carried out by 167 Inf. Bde; in conjunction with two sections 1/6 (Ashn) M.S.M.G.C. Owing to the spectators arriving late the scheme did not commence until 3.51 pm instead of 3 pm. General Joffre was accompanied by Sir Douglas Haig, C-in-C, C.G.S., + D.M.G. of the British Army, during the day AA + QMG, G.S.O.2 and G.S.O.1. G.S.O.2 and Lt R Horn left ST RIQUIER for C ORBIE	See Appendix I (b)
		9pm	56th Division transferred to XIV Corps from midnight 3/4/3. Order received from XIV Corps for divisional artillery to take over position in the line of 5th and 6th divns.	

Army Form C. 2118.

WAR DIARY
or
INTELLIGENCE SUMMARY
(Erase heading not required.)

Place	Date	Hour	Summary of Events and Information	Remarks and references to Appendices
CORBIE	MON 4 SEPT	10 a.m.	Move carried out in accordance with Divisional Order No. 29 and AQ.S/1146. Divisional HQrs. closed at ST. RIQUIER and opened at CORBIE at 10 a.m.	See Appendix VI
		10.20 a.m.	XIV Corps Operation Order received stating that division of the Corps on the line moved continued to progress well and that division of the Corps on the line moved continued to attack at 3.10 p.m. today.	
		11.9 a.m.	Operation order received by wire from XIV Corps that two brigade groups would move forward today to HAPPY VALLEY and the CITADEL, N. and N.W. respectively of BRAY-SUR-SOMME. Divisional stoppages to move forward but destination not yet fixed.	See Appendix III MAP A Sheet 62 D.N.E.
		12.25 p.m.	Orders issued for 168 Inf. Bde. Group and 169 Inf. Bde. Group to move forward to THE CITADEL 2 miles N. of BRAY-SUR-SOMME and HAPPY VALLEY 1 mile N.N.W. BRAY-SUR-SOMME respectively starting from at 2 p.m.	"
		2.30 p.m.	Instructions received by telephone from XIV Corps that Divn. HQrs. will move to the CITADEL tomorrow morning. 167 Inf. Brigade returned detrained at CORBIE during the morning and early part of the afternoon and proceeded to bivouacs in BOIS DES TAILLES of Cheshire Regt. (Army Halts) detrained at CORBIE on arrival from ST. RIQUIER and was billeted by about midnight 4/5th.	"

2449. Wt. W14957/M90 750,000 1/16 J.B.C. & A. Forms/C.2118/12.

Army Form C. 2118.

WAR DIARY
or
INTELLIGENCE SUMMARY
(Erase heading not required.)

Instructions regarding War Diaries and Intelligence Summaries are contained in F. S. Regs., Part II. and the Staff Manual respectively. Title Pages will be prepared in manuscript.

Place	Date	Hour	Summary of Events and Information	Remarks and references to Appendices
CORBIE	TUES 5th SEPT.	9 a.m.	XIV Corps telephoned that Genl. Hqrs. were not to move from CORBIE at present.	
		9.15 a.m.	G.O.C. accompanied by G.S.O.1, 2 and Brigadier went out to reconnoitre treat area.	
		11 a.m.	5th Cheshire Regt. warned to be ready to move up to forward area today.	
		12.5 p.m.	XIV Corps telephoned that the move should be made accordingly and at about 2.30 p.m. more. 168 Inf. Bde. were warned to move to MARICOURT SIDING.	See Appendix III MAP A (Sheet 62c. N.W.)
	About 5.30 p.m.		Received orders direct from XIV Corps to come under orders of 5th Division. Division is to be in readiness to move tomorrow for the Division being now received from F.A.A. The French today. B Echist every to the division gained by	See Appendix III MAP A (Sheet 62c. S.N.E.)
	About 6 p.m.		Orders issued to 5th Cheshire Regt. to move to BOIS ???S tomorrow.	
	7 p.m.		Orders issued for 167 Inf. Bde. to move to CITADEL at 7 a.m. tomorrow.	See Appendices V
	7.30 p.m.		Genl. Orders No. 30 issued to all concerned	

WAR DIARY or INTELLIGENCE SUMMARY

Army Form C. 2118.

Place	Date	Hour	Summary of Events and Information	Remarks and references to Appendices
FORKED TREE	WED. 6 SEPT	10 a.m.	Divl. Hqrs. closed at CORBIE and opened FORKED TREE at this hour. Taking over from 20'S.Div.	See Appendix III MAP A. Ref 62 D.N.F.
		10.15 a.m.	Information received from XIV Corps that 5th Division would relieve 5th Div. in the line during night 6/7.	
		11.55 p.m.	Orders issued for 169th Infy Brigade to march as soon as possible to GERMANS WOOD with a view to relieving 13th (Right) Inf. Bde of 5th Div. in the line tonight. Inf. Bn of 5th Div. near BRONFAY FARM to find our relieving and examine maps, papers etc. and a man is taking over tomorrow.	See Appendix III MAP A Ref 62 D.N.F.
		5.30 p.m.	Received order M31 issued at all concerned during the afternoon	See Appendix
		7.30 p.m.	167 Inf. Bde moved up to find reserve in 2 Divl. encampts. G.O.C. & G.S.O. went up to 5th Divl. Hqrs. for the night. Heavy bombardment on the front.	See Appendix III MAP A Ref 62 D.N.F.
BILLON COPSE	THURS 7 SEPT	9 a.m.	Divl. Hqrs. closed at FORKED TREE and opened at BILLON COPSE. Taken over command from G.O.C. 5th Div.	"
		9.30 a.m.	Corps commander held conference at Divl. Hqrs: G.O.C., G.S.O., G.O.C. 5th Dvn., G.O.C. 16th Dvn. were present.	
		6.15 p.m.	A quiet day on this front. From Reliefs shelling along S.W. face of LEUZE WOOD G20 & G803 united Mgn of 118 and 169 Inf. Bdes in CHIMPANZEE TRENCH and SUPPORTING TRENCH in direction of LEUZE WOOD from HARDECOURT CAZMAZ.	See Appendix III MAP B. Ref 572.5. See Appendix III MAP B. See Appendix III MAP B.

Place	Date	Hour	Summary of Events and Information	Remarks and references to Appendices

BILLON COPSE

FRI: 8: SEPT 12:30 a.y.

Bomb. station 32 wired to all concerned. See Appendix.
A prisoner of 28 R.I.R. 185 A Div: was taken by 118 Inf. Bde in LEUZE WOOD about 12 Noon.

During night 7/8: the division extended its line about 500ʸ further W along COMBLES/GUILLEMONT road, relieving the right brigade (49ᵗʰ) of 16ᵗʰ Division.

9:30 p.m. Bomb. Order 33 issued. See appendix.

Relief reported to have now completed. 167 Inf. Bde. holding LEUZE WOOD, 118 Inf. Bde holding from N.W. corner of LEUZE WOOD to a point about 500ʸ due W on COMBLES/GUILLEMONT road where they join 16ᵗʰ Divn. Regts. 169 Inf. Bde in touch with 2ⁿᵈ French Division.

During night 7/8 hostile artillery was active against our front, support and reserve line trenches.

During afternoon and night 8/9: there was intermittent hostile shelling throughout the area held by the Division.

During the afternoon reconnaissance of LEUZE WOOD showed that trenches along N.E., S.W., and W. edges and W. exit, the positions of which were occupied...

Appendix VI
Sec. Appendix III M.M.P.B. M.M.M.M. 57 C.S.M.
Appendix VI

Army Form C. 2118.

Instructions regarding War Diaries and Intelligence Summaries are contained in F.S. Regs., Part II. and the Staff Manual respectively. Title Pages will be prepared in manuscript.

WAR DIARY
or
INTELLIGENCE SUMMARY

(Erase heading not required.)

For map reference in connection with the operations on this date see APPENDIX III Map E.1.

Place	Date	Hour	Summary of Events and Information	Remarks and references to Appendices
BILLON COPSE.	9th Sept.		During the night 8/9th the 5th London Regt. (L.R.B.) moved up to the vicinity of LEUZE WOOD. A bombing attack carried out by the 9th London Regt. (Q.V.R.) and 5th London Regt. along COMBLES Trench from LEUZE WOOD gained some ground but was eventually driven back by a counter bombing attack by the enemy.	
		7.0am.	Bombardment of enemy's positions preparatory to this afternoon's attack. (See Divnl. Order No. 33) The 169th Infantry Brigade had assembled in LEUZE WOOD and the 168th Infantry Brigade in the assembly trenches which had been dug just South of LEUZE WOOD - GINCHY ROAD with units assembled as follows:- 168th Bde. Hdqrs. CHIMPANZEE TRENCH - 4th London Regt. and 12th London Regt. (Rangers) in the front line - 13th London Regt. (Kensingtons) in reserve about A.4.d.4.0. 14th London Regt. (London Scottish) in support A.5.d.9.9. The 169th Bde. Hdqrs. CHIMPANZEE Trench - 5th London Regt. and 9th London Regt. front line - 2nd London Regt. (R.F.) in support B.2.c.3. - 16th London Regt. (Q.W.R.) in reserve about A.5.d.5.5. The whole of the 167th Inf. Bde. was in reserve about BILLON WOOD.	see Appendix VI.
		4.45 pm.	At this hour the assault commenced and was soon followed by a heavy hostile barrage, rifle and machine gun fire was opened on the assaulting troops of the 168th Inf. Bde.	
		5.56pm.	Both assaulting battalions of the 168th Inf. Bde. reported to have reached their first objectives. Shortly afterwards the 4th London Regt. was reported to have reached its second objective and the 9th London Regt. (169th Bde) their first objectives. This was the first information received from 169th Infa. Bde. The situation opposite the 5th London Regt. on the extreme right was still obscure, but subsequent information showed that during our bombardment parties of enemy snipers had entered the edge of LEUZE WOOD and had delayed the launching of the assault.	
		7.7pm.	The 169th Inf. Bde. reported that the enemy were counter-attacking against LEUZE WOOD along the SUNKEN ROAD running North from COMBLES. This counter-attack was dealt with by our Artillery.	
		7.20 pm.	The 169th Inf. Bde. ordered to secure right flank and if necessary use reserve battalions for this purpose.	
		7.50 pm.	The G.O.C., 169th Inf. Bde. reported that the 5th Lond. Regt. had been re-inforced by one company of the 2nd London Regt. and were attacking S.E. of LEUZE WOOD.	
		7.59 pm.	The 167th Inf. Bde. ordered to place one battalion at the disposal of 169th Inf. Bde.	
		8.30 pm.	Information received as to the position of the 16th Division on our left. Their Left Bde. had reached its final objective East of GINCHY but the Right Bde. had failed to make progress and was approximately on the line of the road from T.29.a.1.4. to T.20.c.1.5. to T.20.d.3.2. where they connected up with our own troops. It was also reported that their was a large number of Germans still about T.20 central. The 168th Inf. Bde. was accordingly /ordered	

WAR DIARY
or
INTELLIGENCE SUMMARY

Army Form C. 2118.

Place	Date	Hour	Summary of Events and Information	Remarks and references to Appendices
			ordered to put in its reserve battalion from about the North corner of LEUZE WOOD in an N.W. direction so as to surround the Germans in T.20. central by joining up with the Left Bde. of the 16th Division along the GINCHY - 141.7 Road. In order to carry this out the 168th Bde. ordered the 13th London Regt. to reinforce the 12th London Regt. and the 14th London Regt. to move forward on their left to the line of the GINCHY/141.7 Road.	
		10.16 pm.	The following message was received from 168th Inf. Bde.:- "Report received from Rangers in final objective" timed 9.0 pm. 'Rangers 4th Londons and Q.V.R's are in their final objectives and are in touch and holding the line fairly strongly. Rangers left is in the air." Reports ends. London Scottish seen moving forward to departure trench about T.20.d. The 16th London Regt. (169th Brigade) seen moving forward at northern edge LEUZE WOOD."	See APPX. III not "B"
		10.22	7th Middlesex Regiment ordered forward from 167th Brigade have reported at H.Q.. 169th Brigade.	
		10.30	A prisoner of the 161st Regiment, 185th Division stated that there was about 1 Battalion of his Regiment in T.20.a. He thought that their morale was low and that there should be little difficulty in capturing them. This information was sent to the Brigades concerned.	
		11.10	9th London Regiment still hold their objectives, but on the right of 169th Brigade the enemy was pressing hard, but was being dealt with by bombers of 5th London Regiment and 2nd London Regiment in LEUZE WOOD.	
BILLON COPSE	10th Sept.	12.30 am.	No further INFORMATION had been received as to progress on the extreme right and left flanks of the Division, but materials for establishing Strong Points about T.15.c.0.5. and T.21.a.6.4. had been sent forward by 168th Brigade.	
		1.9 am.	The 16th London Regt. had reached LEUZE WOOD and were distributed as follows :- 2 Company's in the WOOD 1 Coy. moving to reinforce N. of the WOOD and 1 Coy. lining the East face of the WOOD. The 9th London Regiment reported as holding T.21.a.e.e.a.65.40 to T.21.b.0.9. The 16th London Regiment had been ordered to attack. (Time for the attack to start had not yet been fixed) T.27.b.0.6. to T.21.d.5.2. By this time the 14th London Regiment were moving North towards their objective. Copy of orders issued by 16th Division shewed that their right brigade had been ordered to co-operate with the attack of the London Scottish by bombing forward along trench and road running Eastwards through T.14.c. and d. to point 141.7.	
		5.5.	In B. 61 & A. posns. C.2118/120f. 16th Londons along S.E. side of LEUZE WOOD was not /clear	

WAR DIARY
or
INTELLIGENCE SUMMARY

(Erase heading not required.)

Army Form C. 2118.

Place	Date	Hour	Summary of Events and Information	Remarks and references to Appendices
		5.27.	clear, and the General Officer Commanding 169th Brigade considered their attack should be withheld till dawn.	
		6.15	168th Brigade hold their final objectives and consolidation proceeding. Enemy hold trench running in N.W. direction from T.20.b.9.6. but we were occupying South end of this trench as far as the road, the Brigade boundary. London Scottish ordered to capture the hostile portion of this trench and join up with the right of the 16th Division.	
		8.40	The 169th Brigade reported that the attack by the 5th London Regiment against the original objective of the 5th Londons would take place at 7.0 a.m.	
			The 14th Londons were disposed as follows at this hour from North corner of LEUZE WOOD along GUILLEMONT - LEUZE WOOD ROAD and moving North to prolong our line to the North of final objective. Q.W.R. at this time reported that one company had siezed a part of the objective successfully, that the other was held up by rifle fire but was being pushed on. The situation during the rest of the day was never very clear chiefly owing to the misty weather which prevented confirmation by reports from air. During the morning reports were received that the London Scottish had succeeded in reaching the GINCHY 141.7 road and where extending Westwards so as to obtain touch with the Guards and were REPORTED supposed to be in position in trenches due East of GINCHY. Eventually the London Scottish that they had failed to obtain touch with the Guards about T.14.c. At one time S.O.S. signals were put up on the greater part of the Divisional front, and it was reported that the enemy was massing in BOULEAUX WOOD but no vigorous attack developed.	
		10.18	Attack by Q.W.R. had evidently failed, one company had reached a point within fifty yards of its objective in T.21.d., but were forced to withdraw by x heavy rifle fire from a trench which was strongly held by the enemy. Attempts to bomb up the trench in T.27.a. proved ineffectual.	See App. VI
		12.45 pm.	Divisional Order No. 34 issued to all concerned. This order dealt with the relief of 169th Inf. Bde. and the front line by a Composite Brigade of the 5th Division and the relief of the 168th Inf. Bde. by the 167th Bde. on the left of the Divisional line. This relief to take place on the night 10/11th.	
		2.15 pm.	Brigadier 169th Bde. after personal reconnaissance in LEUZE WOOD had arranged for a FRESH attack from the S.E. side of the WOOD to commence at 3.0 pm.	
		3.45 pm.	An Operation Order was received from the 14th Corps detailing the 6th Division to relieve the left of the 56th Divisional front by the evening of the 12th instant. During the afternoon, the Guards Division on our left was heavily attacked by the enemy and in some places had been forced to give ground.	
		6.26	Wire received from 169th Bde. that the second attack by the Q.W.R. on trenches round T.21.d.0.0. /which	

Army Form C. 2118.

WAR DIARY
or
INTELLIGENCE SUMMARY

(Erase heading not required.)

Instructions regarding War Diaries and Intelligence Summaries are contained in F. S. Regs., Part II. and the Staff Manual respectively. Title Pages will be prepared in manuscript.

Place	Date	Hour	Summary of Events and Information	Remarks and references to Appendices
		8.10 pm.	had started at 3.0 pm. had failed chiefly owing to the very heavy hostile shelling. A message was sent to the 167th Bde. with reference to Divisional Order No. 34, para. 1 (b), stating that the exact point of junction with the Guards Division could not be ascertained at present but that the 167th Bde. would take over all ground at present held by the London Scottish, and establish a strong point T.14.d.5.3. In addition strong patrols to push out in direction of GINCHY and every effort made to obtain touch with the 3rd Guards Brigade. Strong point at T.15.c.1.2. was also to be consolidated and wired.	
		8.25 pm.	The following situation report was sent to H.Q. 14th Corps - "The 169th Bde. attack by Q.W.R. on trench T.27.a.9.6. to T.21.d.6.3. failed: line runs from T.21.d.2.5. to TRIANGLE T.14.d.8.3. London Scottish had attacked in T.14.a. and present position obscure. 167th Bde. which is taking over this front tonight has arranged to establish strong point T.14.d.5.4. and has been instructed to push out strong patrols in direction of GINCHY with the object of linking up with 3rd Guards Brigade".	See App. VI
		11.0 pm.	Divisional Order No. 35 issued as a result of an order received from 14th Corps stated that the left of the Divisional front would be relieved by the 6th Division during the night of the 11/12th. During the whole day the enemy had maintained a heavy artillery fire along the whole of the Divisional front, but this lessened considerably during the evening.	
BILLON COPSE	11th Sept.	12.30 am.	Guards Division reported that they held along road T.20.d.0.5. - T.20.c.0.5. to 0.3 and that the enemy held trench running N.E. from about T.20.c.4.5. This information was repeated to 168th Bde.	
		1.0 am.	The G.O.C., 168th Inf. Bde. telephoned that the situation as regards the London Scottish appeared to be as follows :- "The battalion had apparently lost direction in its attack on the previous day and were not holding the line of the GUINCHY/141.7 but were apparently occupying trench in T.15.c.25.07. running towards BOULEAUX WOOD with one company in the COPSE at T.21.b.2.7. and that the strong point about T.15.c. (The QUADRILATERAL) was held by the enemy. This was the situation as handed over to the relieving (167th) Brigade. This situation was definitely confirmed by conference later in the day.	See App. II and App. III and photo B
		1.30 am.	The relief of 169th Bde. by the Composite Brigade of the 5th Division was complete. The relief of 168th Bde. by 167th Bde. reported complete. The location of units was as follows: 167th Inf. Bde. holding left sub-sector of Divisional front - Hdqrs. CHIMPANZEE TRENCH - 3rd London Regt. in the front line on the right - 8th Middlesex in the front line on the left 4th Middlesex in support North of WEDGE WOOD - 1st Londons in reserve in MALTZ HORN HILL TRENCHES. Composite Brigade of the 5th Division holding the Right subsector of the Divisional front -	
		3.15 am.	Hdqrs. CHIMPANZEE TRENCH. 2nd K.O.S.B's in the front line on the right - 14th R. Warwicks Centre - 1st R.W. Kents on the left. 1st Devon and East Surrey Regts. in support at FALFEMONT Farm /15th R.W's.	

WAR DIARY
or
INTELLIGENCE SUMMARY

(Erase heading not required.)

Army Form C. 2118.

Place	Date	Hour	Summary of Events and Information	Remarks and references to Appendices
	11th Sept.	4. am.	15th Royal Warwicks in reserve CHIMPANZEE TRENCH - 168th Infantry Bde. in the vicinity of BILLON WOOD. 169th Inf. Bde. at the CITADEL. Situation report sent to XIVth Corps Hdqrs. stated that the reliefs were completed, and that except for heavy shelling of LEUZE WOOD during the early part of the night, the night of the 10/11th had passed comparatively quietly. Corps Headquarters were also informed of what was presumed to be the situation on the left flank of the left Brigade.	See App. III Map "A" Sheet 62 d. NE.
		6 am.	At this hour the Germans attempted a bombing enterprise supported by Flammenwerfers against the blocks of the left Brigade at T.21.a.2.8. and T.21.d.2.5. This was repulsed, the enemy leaving three dead on our side of the block.	See App. III Map "F"
		9.15am	A conference was held by the Corps Commander at Headquarters Guards Division at MINDEN POST at which the General Officer Commanding, G.S.O.1 and C.R.A. were present.	
		10.5am	The following air report was recived by wire from Corps Headquarters:- "Pilot of contact aeroplane saw no troops or movements in the following trenches at 7 am. this morning T.15.c.3.3. - T.14.d.9.3. and T.14.d.9.3. - T.21.a.7.3". The Intelligence Officer of the 167th Infantry Brigade who visited the front line during the early part of the morning reported that the left Battalion (8th Middlesex Regiment) was just south of trench junction T.15.c.3.1. and that a trench which had been partially dug during the night of the 10/11th from T.15.c.3.1. to about T.20.b.7.3. was held by this Battalion. During the morning the enemy continued to shell LEUZE WOOD and the Valley in T.26.c.	
		12.22pm	An airman's report stated that no troops could be seen in the trench GINCHY - T.14.d.9.3. to T.14.a.9.3. T.21.a.5.5. None of our troops could be seen on the S.E. side of BOULEAUX or LEUZE WOODS, but it was thought that we held the trench T.27.a.7.8. - T.21.c.4.7. in strength. New trenches were observed from T.20.d.9.1. - T.20.d.7.2. and from T.19.b.5.6. - T.13.c.8.2. During the afternoon an attack was organised by the 167th Brigade to take place against the QUADRILATERAL in conjunction with the Guards Division commencing at 7.45 p.m. Countersign for the 56th Division was "LONDON" and for the Guards Division "WINDSOR". During the evening it was decided that the Zero hour for this attack should be 12 midnight instead of 7.45 p.m. and that owing to this operation the relief of the 167th Infantry Brigade by the 16th Infantry Brigade of the 6th Division detailed in Divisional Order No. 35 would be postponed for 24 hours. During the remainder of the day there was no change in the situation. Enemy artillery shewed increased activity during the afternoon, especially against the Northern end of LEUZE WOOD.	
BILLON COPSE.	12th Sept.	3.0am	Guards Division reported that 1 of their Companies operating in conjunction with 167th Brigade in the attack on the QUADRILATERAL had lost direction and was proceeding S.E. instead of E. /The	

13.

Army Form C. 2118.

WAR DIARY
or
INTELLIGENCE SUMMARY

(Erase heading not required.)

Place	Date	Hour	Summary of Events and Information	Remarks and references to Appendices
		5.15am	The 167th Brigade was informed accordingly. Verbal report received from 167th Brigade that the 8th Middlesex Regiment were half way up to the QUADRILATERAL, and having met with stiff resistance were consolidating their position.	See App. III /MN/ "F"
		5.50am	Guards Division reported having reached T.14.d.9½.4½ where they were consolidating.	
		6.17am	The first definite reports of progress made by the 8th Middlesex Regt. were received. They had gained and were holding trench from the German block at T.15.c.2.0. to the GINCHY Road at T.15.c.1.4. The trench to the West of this was reported as having been obliterated by artillery fire, and unoccupied by the enemy. A Strong Post was being consolidated at T.15.c.1.4. Germans were strongly holding the road running into GINCHY VILLAGE, and the 8th Middlesex Regt. had suffered many casualties from machine gun fire which appeared to come from a party of the enemy in shell holes S.W. of the GINCHY Road. This situation was forwarded to Corps H.Q. in the Morning Report.	
		9.55am	An air report timed 7.58 am; was received shewing that the 8th Middlesex had not progressed further than T.21.a.4.8. where bombing was in progress. The enemy were strongly holding all ground North of this point. No signs of our troops could be seen along GINCHY Road, and it appeared that the enemy's means of communication with the QUADRILATERAL was by trench running due North from the north side of the GINCHY Road. During the morning, Corps Heavy Artillery commenced a steady bombardment of the QUADRILATERAL and ground in the vicinity which was known to be held by the enemy. Divisional Artillery co-operated with shrapnel on BOULEAUX WOOD and enemy positions opposite the Divisional front.	
		12.30pm	Divisional Order No. 36 issued. This ordered the relief of the 167th Infantry Brigade by the 16th Infantry Brigade, 6th Division, to be carried out during the night of the 12th/13th and the relief of the Composite Brigade of the 5th Division by troops of the 56th Division on the night 13th/14th. In order to enable this to be carried out the following adjustments were to be made on the Divisional front; - 167th Brigade to take over the line North of Point T.27.a.2.4. (the Southern Corner of LEUZE WOOD) and 169th Brigade on the right from Point T.27.a.2.4. Southwards.	See App. VI
		3.40 pm	Guards Division reported that they were gaining ground towards the QUADRILATERAL and were meeting with little opposition. 167th Brigade were ordered to co-operate by bombing vigorously Northwards so as to obtain touch with the 3rd Guards Brigade. To enable this to be carried out the Heavy Artillery bombardment was lifted from the QUADRILATERAL. During the afternoon an air report was received shewing definitely that we held trench up to road East of GINCHY as far as T.14.d.8.3. at which point there was a block. Our position at T.21.a.5.8. was confirmed and the enemy still held ground North of this point in force. The chief hostile shelling during the day had been directed against LEUZE WOOD, the Southern half of the Divisional Front having been comparatively quiet	

Army Form C. 2118.

WAR DIARY
or
INTELLIGENCE SUMMARY

(Erase heading not required.)

Instructions regarding War Diaries and Intelligence Summaries are contained in F. S. Regs., Part II. and the Staff Manual respectively. Title Pages will be prepared in manuscript.

Place	Date	Hour	Summary of Events and Information	Remarks and references to Appendices
BILLON COPSE	13th Sept.	6.0pm	Divisional Order No. 37 issued. This dealt with operations to be carried out by the 56th Division in co-operation with the general attack by the Fourth Army against the enemy's front between COMBLES RAVINE and MARTINPUICH.	See App. VI "" "" III Appx "A"
		1.0am	The relief of the 167th Infantry Brigade by the 16th Infantry Brigade, 6th Division, completed. The composite Bde. holding the right of the Divisional Line had taken over a post from the French at B.3.a.8.2. Patrols reported no movement outside the enemy trenches, but a post had been established about 150 yards from the S.E. edge of LEUZE WOOD in COMBLES TRENCH at T.27.a.8.6. On receipt of this latter information the General Officer Commanding Composite Brigade was instructed to make further progress by bombing down COMBLES Trench and secure trench junction at T.27.a.9.6. with a view to assisting future operations. Divisional Order No. 38 was issued containing further details with regard to the forthcoming attack referred to in DIVISIONAL ORDER No.37.	Sheet 57c. SW. See App. III Appx "F"
		5.15pm	Evening Reports contained no information except usual shelling of LEUZE WOOD and BOULEAUX WOOD, and increased activity against the ANGLE WOOD VALLEY. During the night 13th/14th 169th Brigade relieved the Composite Brigade 5th Division in the Right of the Divisional Front as ordered in Divisional Order No. 36 and 167th Infantry Brigade handed over a portion of the line to the 16th Infantry Brigade 6th Division.	See App. VI
BILLON COPSE	14th Sept.	3.0am	The distribution of troops was as follows :- 167th Infantry Brigade holding the left of the Divisional Front H.Q. CHIMPANZEE TRENCH. 1st London Regiment in front line. 7th Middlesex Regt. in Support WEDGE WOOD. 3rd London Regiment Reserve GERMANS WOOD. 8th Middlesex Regt. Reserve about A.12.a. 169th Brigade on the right of the Divisional Front H.Q. HARDECOURT. 9th London Regiment in the front line. 2nd London Regiment in Support at FALFEMONT FARM. 16th London Regiment in Reserve near HARDECOURT and the 5th London Regiment in Reserve at A.10.d. 169th Infantry Brigade in Reserve with H.Q. and all four Battalions at BILLON COPSE. The Morning Report shewed that the night of the 13th/14th had passed quietly and without incident. During the night of the 13th/14th three Tanks attached to the Division for the forthcoming operation (see Divisional Orders No. 37 and 38) proceeded from their H.Q. near BILLON COPSE to rendezvous in CHIMPANZEE TRENCH where they arrived at 2.48 a.m. It was originally intended that they should proceed as far as the Valley West of HARDECOURT and remain hidden there during the day but owing to engine trouble and the bad condition of the ground this was impossible.	See App. II

Army Form C. 2118.

WAR DIARY
or
INTELLIGENCE SUMMARY

(Erase heading not required.)

Instructions regarding War Diaries and Intelligence Summaries are contained in F.S. Regs., Part II. and the Staff Manual respectively. Title Pages will be prepared in manuscript.

Place	Date	Hour	Summary of Events and Information	Remarks and references to Appendices
A.10.b.3.8	14th	3.0 am. Contd.	Morning reports showed that the night of the 13/14th had passed quietly with less hostile artillery activity than usual.	See Appendix III N/p 12.
		3.20 pm.	Divisional Headquarters closed at BILLON COPSE and opened at point A.10.b.3.8. on the East of the MARICOURT - BRIQUETERIE Road.	See Appendix III.
		8.0 pm.	The three tanks commenced to move forward from CHIMPANZEE Trench to their assembly points South and West of LEUZE WOOD. During the night 13/14th a special route had been taped for them from about 400 yards East of the HARDECOURT CRUCIFIX to just South of LEUZE WOOD.	See Map D × The middle
A.10.b.3.8	15th	12.45 am.	Report received from O.C. "Tanks" that one machine had broken down at ANGLE WOOD, and that the other two had reached the South end of LEUZE WOOD and were proceeding to their points of departure.	See Appendix IV post Corner 37, p.76
		4.25 am.	Instructions were sent to 167th Infantry Bde. to give orders for the left tank to act as follows:- On reaching blue objective at T.16.c. central to proceed at once from this point to the German main line about T.16.a.7.7. where it would cut wire from that point point Northwards through T.16.a., T.10.c.; T.9.d., which points lay opposite the front to be attacked by the Division on our left. This order cancelled previous instructions issued to O.C. "Tanks".	See Appendix VI
		5.30 am.	Brigades were in position as follows:- 167th Inf. Bde. on the left of the Divisional front: Hdqrs. at FALFEMONT FARM. 7th Middlesex Regt. on the right, 1st London Regt. on the left of the front line, 8th Middlesex in support at LEUZE WOOD, 3rd London Regt. in reserve at FALFEMONT FARM. 169th Inf. Bde. on the right of the Divisional front. 9th London Regt. on the right, 2nd London Regt. on the left of the front line. 5th and 16th London Regts. in divnl. reserve at FALFEMONT FARM. 168th Inf. Bde. in reserve with headquarters and all four battalions in the ANGLE WOOD VALLEY. In the attack due to commence at 6.20 am., the task of the 56th Division on the right of the Corps front was the clearing of BOULEAUX WOOD and the formation of a protective flank covering the hostile lines of advance from COMBLES, and the valleys running N.E. from COMBLES. The main attack of the XIVth Corps included the capture of MORVAL and LES BOEUFS which was to be undertaken by the 5th and Guards Divisions.	See Div. Order 37.
		5.50 am. 6.20 am. 7.10 am.	The tanks started from their departure points for their first objective followed by the infantry assaulting at 6.20 am. The Liaison Officer with the 2nd French Division on our right telephoned asking if we required any assistance from the French Artillery and was informed that if possible the General Officer Commanding would like them to fire on the Northern exits from COMBLES and the enemy's third line trench running from MORVAL through T.17.d., but not further North than the point where the road crossed the trench at T.17.d.2.5. /8.0 am.	

2449 Wt. W4957/Mgo 730,000 1/16 J.B.C. & A. Forms/C.2118/12.

Army Form C. 2118.

WAR DIARY
or
INTELLIGENCE SUMMARY

(Erase heading not required.)

Instructions regarding War Diaries and Intelligence Summaries are contained in F. S. Regs., Part II. and the Staff Manual respectively. Title Pages will be prepared in manuscript.

Place	Date	Hour	Summary of Events and Information	Remarks and references to Appendices
		8.0am.	No reports were received until nearly 8.0 am., at which hour information was received that the assault of the 167th Inf. Bde. had started and that one company of the 1st London Regt. was reported to have reached its first objective. On the front of the 169th Inf. Bde. the 2nd London Regt. were believed to have taken their first objective with little loss and were working up the communication trench running North East from T.27.b.2.4. assisted by the tank. An air report telephoned from Corps Headquarters showed that the left tank had been seen working along the North side of BOULEAUX WOOD and had reached T.15.d.9.1. Contact patrol reported that the 6th Division were held up from the QUADRILATERAL to T.14.b.9.9., and that this line was strongly held by the enemy. The 168th Inf. Bde. was informed of this and ordered not to move forward without further orders from the Division.	
		8.30am.	Reports at this hour tended to show that the 169th Inf. Bde. had gained their first objective, and that a company of the 2nd London Regt. was fighting hard in the ORCHARDS at T.21.d.8.4. As regards the 167th Inf. Bde., the 1st London Regt. was believed to have reached its first objective and the 7th Middlesex Regt. had started for the second objective. Owing to the situation of the Division on our left the 167th Inf. Bde. was ordered to extend its left on reaching the blue objective and work in the direction of T.15.central and co-operate with the 16th Infantry Brigade of the 6th Division.	
		9.24 am	An Artillery Observing Officer reported that the right tank had stopped at T.27.b.4.7. An airman's report timed 8.45 am. shewed that our troops were still in the advanced trench about T.21.a.8.5. that the tank on the North side of BOULEAUX WOOD was in the vicinity of MIDDLE COPSE, and that none of our troops could be seen in advance of our front line N.W. of BOULEAUX WOOD. This information was passed to 167th Infantry Brigade with instructions to ascertain the exact situation and report. About this time 169th Brigade reported that they were definitely at T.27b.4.7.	
		9.30.am	Enemy were still holding the QUADRILATERAL. The situation on the front of the 167th Infantry Brigade was reported to be as follows :- 7th Middlesex Regt. advancing to their second objective had been held up by Machine Gun fire between our front line and the German line. The first objective was however in our possession. Situation at Trench Junction T.21.d.2.4. obscure - 2 Companies of 8th Middlesex were being moved into Trench T.27.a.6.8. to T.21.c.4.7..	
		10.0 am	Message received from Corps Headquarters that the Heavy Artillery had been ordered to shell the ORCHARD T.18.b. and the Trench running East from there to T.17.b.2.3. with a view to assisting the advance on to the second and third objective.	
		10.17am	167th Brigade ordered to act vigorously in order to clear BOULEAUX WOOD and to obtain the second objective, at the same time extending their left to T.15.Central in conjunction /with

Army Form C. 2118.

WAR DIARY
or
INTELLIGENCE SUMMARY
(Erase heading not required.)

Place	Date	Hour	Summary of Events and Information	Remarks and references to Appendices
			with the 16th Infantry Brigade.	
		10.30 am	The following message was sent to the 167th and 169th Brigades :- "Air Report, timed 10.10 am showed 167th Brigade on Green Objective with Tank outside wood at T.21.d.1.2. 169th Brigade's objective is not shown as held by us - enemy are not shown as holding trench opposite our objectives. Act vigorously, employ your reserves to obtain objectives" Message received from 6th Division showed that the 16th Infantry Brigade had been ordered to carry out a fresh attack against the South and South West faces of the QUADRILATERAL at 1-30 pm and the 71st Infantry Brigade would attack simultaneously from the West and North West. This attack was to be assisted by two Tanks.	See APP. VI Div. Order No. 37.
		10.57 am	Report received from 169th Brigade that one of their Stokes Mortars had managed to get into SUNKEN ROAD Trench at T.21.d.4.4. This Brigade had received no reports as to the progress made by the 167th Brigade towards the S.E. Face of BOULEAUX WOOD.	
		11.0 am	167th Brigade ordered to move 3rd Londons from the trenches North of FALFEMONT FARM so as to make room for the Battalions of the 169th Brigade in Divisional Reserve which were being moved forward under the command of Lt.Col. Shoolbred C.M.G. with orders to remain in these trenches until further instructions were issued, the intention being to use these two Battalions to reinforce the 167th Brigade if necessary before putting the 168th Brigade into the line. A Pigeon message was received from 2nd Lt.Arnold in command of the Tank operating on the North side of BOULEAUX WOOD stating that his Tank had broken down and was being attacked by hostile bombing parties. The 167th Brigade were informed of this and ordered to render any assistance they could.	
		11.10 am	Message received from the 168th Brigade that a Tank had passed ANGLE WOOD on its way back to CHIMPANZEE TRENCH. It had come from the QUADRILATERAL were one Machine Gun and a number of Germans were stated to have been dealt with.	
		11.15 am	167th Infantry Brigade informed of the fresh attack to be carried out against the QUADRILATERAL during the afternoon and instructed to arrange cooperation direct with the General Officer Commanding 16th Infantry Brigade.	
		11.30 am	Message received from 167th Brigade showed that the assaulting Companies of the 7th Middlesex when advancing to the second objective had been met with a heavy Machine Gun fire from the direction of the SUNKEN ROAD running from COMBLES to LEUZE WOOD. This Road was still apparently strongly held by the enemy. 7th Middlesex had been ordered to hold MIDDLE COPSE as a strong point.	See APP. III Map "F".
		11.35 am	A Pigeon Message addressed to the 169th Brigade - telephoned from Corps Headquarters stated that the 2nd Londons had bombed up LOOP TRENCH almost as far as SUNKEN ROAD but were short of bombs and men. Enemy Snipers very active in COMBLES TRENCH. This information was /telephoned	

Army Form C. 2118.

18

WAR DIARY
or
INTELLIGENCE SUMMARY

(Erase heading not required.)

Instructions regarding War Diaries and Intelligence Summaries are contained in F.S. Regs., Part II. and the Staff Manual respectively. Title Pages will be prepared in manuscript.

Place	Date	Hour	Summary of Events and Information	Remarks and references to Appendices.
			telephoned to the Brigade concerned WHICH WAS also notified that a party of 100 men (this was detailed by 5th Londons) from the Divisional Reserve had been placed at their disposal for the purpose of carrying Grenades. They were also informed as to the movement of Battalions in Divisional Reserve and instructed to get into touch with the Officer Commanding and inform him of the place where carrying party was required.	
		12.3 pm	Report from 169th Brigade that the Tank in T.27.b.4.6. had been put out of action by a direct hit by a German Shell and was on fire. This information was sent to Officer Commanding "C" Coy. H.S.M.G.Corps.	
		12.20pm	Situation of 167th Brigade appeared to be as follows :- 1st Londons had gained their objective with the exception of that part which lay outside an along S.E. face of BOULEAUX WOOD. 7th Middlesex who were considerably mixed with the 1st Londons had been ordered to push forward to the second objective at 1.30.pm under a creeping barrage and to move outside the Divisional Boundary in a North Westerly direction to assist the attacks of the 6th Division. 8th Middlesex to proceed to the second objective at the same hour North of the 1st Londons. The 3rd Londons were ordered to be in support in LEUZE WOOD by 1.30.pm and assist the 1st Londons at T-21.d.2.5. with their bombers. The left of the 7th Middlesex was in touch with the 16th Infantry Brigade about T.21.b.0.9. As regards the 169th Brigade the attack down COMBLES TRENCH from T.21.d.2.5. was to be reinforced. The 2nd Londons had progressed up LOOP TRENCH to within 40 yards of the SUNKEN ROAD. A strong point was being consolidated at T.27.b.1.5. and progress made 200 yards down COMBLES TRENCH in a S.E. Direction where a block had been established.	See App.III Map "F".
		1.49.pm	The following order was received from XIV Corps :="6th Division HAVE been ordered to prepare a fresh attack on the QUADRILATERAL and Trench running West of it. You will simultaneously clear BOULEAUX WOOD. Necessary bombardment will be arranged direct between you and G.O.C. Heavy Artillery, time of attack will be arranged between you and the 6th Division but it is not to be made without a thorough Artillery preparation." This was shortly followed by another message from the Corps stating that the latest Air Report did not confirm previous information as to the progress made by the 56th and Guards Divisions. It was therefore considered by the Corps Commander that the Operation against the QUADRILATERAL and BOULEAUX WOOD would probably not be practicable. The 6th Division was therefore ordered to attack the Trench running from the QUADRILATERAL from a West or N.W. direction.	/2.15 pm
		2.3.pm	Enemy put a very heavy barrage between assembly trenches and trenches captured by the 169th Brigade.	
		2.10.pm	Divisional Reserve Battalions arrived at FALFEMONT FARM.	

WAR DIARY or INTELLIGENCE SUMMARY

Army Form C. 2118.

Place	Date	Hour	Summary of Events and Information	Remarks and references to Appendices
		2.15 pm.	Message received from 167th Inf. Bde. that the 8th Middlesex Regt. had been launched to their attack before they could be stopped. A post with Lewis Guns had been by this time established in MIDDLE COPSE. XIVth Corps informed of this. During the day a party of Engineers and Pioneers had been working on a track up to LEUZE WOOD; this was now completed as far as T.20.d.5.0.	
		3.0 pm.	Message sent to 167th Inf. Bde. that the situation on their front must be definitely ascertained and report rendered immediately if the attack of the 8th Middlesex Regt. had not been successful, so that the artillery barrage might be brought back and BOULEAUX WOOD re-bombarded.	
		3.39 pm.	167th Inf. Bde. reported that none of the first objective in BOULEAUX WOOD was then held by them. First objective to T.21.b.3.2. - T.21.a.8.5. and MIDDLE COPSE was in their possession. This information was definite and the barrage could be brought back.	
		4.0 pm.	The Corps Commander telephoned to the General Officer Commanding that the 56th Division would not make a fresh attack against BOULEAUX WOOD but would consolidate its present position. This was confirmed by a written order shortly afterwards, which showed that the situation was as follows:- The Guards Division advanced line stretched more or less continuously T.9.b.1.6. through T.9.a.3.4. - T.2.d.8.3. - T.2.c.9.5. 6th Division still held up in front of first objective. 56th Division in possession of first line trench in BOULEAUX WOOD but held up beyond that by machine guns. MORVAL and LES BOEUFS strongly held by the enemy. Previous orders as to fresh attacks by the 56th Division were definitely cancelled. The attack by the 6th Division against the trench running North from the QUADRILATERAL was to be carried out as previously ordered at a time to be selected by the General Officer Commanding, 6th Division, and was to be assisted by an attack to be made by the 56th Division from the South as far as was considered practicable by the commander on the spot. /Addressed to 167th and 169th Inf. Bdes. and the C.R.A.:-	See App. III. Map "A" Sh.57c.SW.
		4.38 pm.	The following air report timed 3.10 pm. showed our troops holding first objective from trench T.21.a.7.7. to S.E. edge of BOULEAUX WOOD also original front line to trench junction T.21.d.2.5. 167th Inf. Bde. reports MIDDLE COPSE held by us. Divisional Artillery have been ordered to search BOULEAUX WOOD as far S.W. as the line 140 contour. The Heavy Artillery are shelling valley E. of MIDDLE COPSE. The attack on blue objective will not be expected. Positions gained to 1 to be consolidated and the following minor operations undertaken :- 1st line of captured trench and right of our original line to 1 be joined up and trench junction at T.21.d.2.5. consolidated - 2nd. Trench parallel to the SUNKEN ROAD T.21.d.2.5. to T.21.d.6.2. to 1 be captured by 167th and 169th Infantry Brigades working from Northwest and Southwest. Point of junction to 1 be consolidated. C.R.A. to arrange to bombard this trench with Field Artillery until time selected by 167th and 169th Brigades for attack. Airman reports 169th Brigade in German communication trench 100 yards South of SUNKEN ROAD. Half of the 2nd /1st London	

WAR DIARY
or
INTELLIGENCE SUMMARY
(Erase heading not required.)

Army Form C. 2118.

Instructions regarding War Diaries and Intelligence Summaries are contained in F.S. Regs., Part II. and the Staff Manual respectively. Title Pages will be prepared in manuscript.

Place	Date	Hour	Summary of Events and Information	Remarks and references to Appendices
		5.15 pm	2/1st London Field Coy. at present attached to the 168th Inf. Bde. and one company of pioneers will be attached to each Brigade to assist in consolidation. Acknowledge and notify zero time selected". About this time considerable movement of enemy troops was reported in the vicinity of MORVAL and LES BOEUFS.	
		5.37 pm	The O.C., Divisional Reserve ordered to place 16th London Regt. at the disposal of the 169th Inf. Bde. and the 5th London Regt. at the disposal of the 167th Inf. Bde. These battalions were not to be used the line for purposes of relief, but were to be reserved for work and carrying parties. 167th Inf. Bde. instructed to bring fire from as many machine guns as possible to bear on the track running N.E. from point 141.7 in order to assist the operations of the 6th Division. G.O.C., 167th Inf. Bde. to get in touch with right brigade of 6th Division and arrange for time and limits of machine gun fire.	
		7.15 pm	167th and 169th Inf. Bdes. notified that half of Field Company R.E. and one company pioneers had been placed at the disposal of the former and one Field Company R.E. and one company pioneers at the disposal of the latter. R.E. officers had been sent up to report to Brigade Headquarters and Brigadiers were to ensure that they were allotted definite tasks to be carried out during the night.	
		8.0 pm	XIVth Corps Order No. 54 received stating that the attack on LES BOEUFS - GUEDECOURT would be carried out tomorrow at zero (9.25 am.) XIVth Corps attacking the former and the XVth Corps the latter, the attack of the XIVth Corps to be carried out by Guards Division, Guards Division to form a protective flank facing MORVAL which would be protected by the Heavy Artillery of the XIVth Corps and the Field Artillery of 6th and 56th Divisions.	See App. III Map "A" Sheet 57c. SW.
		8.30 pm	Instructions issued for the 167th Infantry Brigade to ascertain definitely the position of the tank N.E. of BOULEAUX WOOD and to ensure its protection by fire if it proved to be in advance of trenches held by the Brigade. A reply to this message was received later stating that the right was derelict about T.27.b.3.9. and could best be covered by fire from 169th Inf. Bde. The position of the tank at the North side of BOULEAUX WOOD was not known. The position of this latter tank had however been ascertained by an airman at 6.0. pm. but this report was not received until 9.47pm. He stated that the tank was at T.21.b.2.2. and had been bombed by the enemy. 167th Inf. Bde. were informed of this and ordered to give all assistance they could. They were also informed that the same airman reported that he had seen our troops at T.21.d.4.4. at 6.20 pm.	
		10.45 pm	Orders received from the XIVth Corps that in the event of the 6th Division's attack on the QUADRIKATERAL the 56th and 6th Divisions would consolidate themselves in their present positions. No further news as to the situation was received up to 12 midnight 15/16th.	

Army Form C. 2118.

WAR DIARY
or
INTELLIGENCE SUMMARY
(Erase heading not required.)

Instructions regarding War Diaries and Intelligence Summaries are contained in F. S. Regs., Part II. and the Staff Manual respectively. Title Pages will be prepared in manuscript.

Place	Date	Hour	Summary of Events and Information	Remarks and references to Appendices
A.10.b.3.8	16th Sept.	12.20 am.	167th Brigade informed that the right Brigade of the 6th Division had been ordered to establish itself facing North with its right at MIDDLE COPSE and to connect up with the 56th Division.	
		1.5 a.m	6th Division reported that the attack against the QUADRILATERAL would not take place but that the 16th and 71st Brigades had been ordered to endeavour to improve their positions by working round the enemy's flanks with a view to a possible subsequent attack on the QUADRILATERAL.	
		1.15 am	169th Brigade reported that the bombing attack towards the SUNKEN ROAD timed for 11.0 p.m. had failed owing to a heavy barrage having been put up by the enemy at once. Another attack was being organised. News as to the position of the 167th Brigade had not been received. This information was repeated to the 167th Brigade.	See Appendix III Map F.
		2.0 am.	A report received from the 167th Brigade shewed that two bombing attacks were made on German trenches at T.21.b.3.2. and that both of them had failed. Attacks on T.21.d.2.5. had also been made and that heavy casualties had been sustained by our troops in each case.	"
		2.47 am.	The second bombing attack carried out by the 2nd and 5th London Regiments of the 169th Brigade had failed. Germans were reported to be holding the SUNKEN ROAD strongly. Our consolidation was progressing satisfactorily. Trench running N.E. from T.27.b.1.4. up to and including LOOP TRENCH had been wired. The construction of a Strong Point at T.27.b.1.4. was progressing well. The communication trench from T.27.b.1.4. in a Southwesterly direction to the 2nd London Regt. assembly trenches about T.27.a.7.0. was being dug. The third bombing attack was organised to commence at 5.0 a.m. It was thought that the failure of the two previous attacks had been chiefly due to the lack of trained bombers nearly all of whom had become casualties. With the exception of the consolidation of our position the Morning Report shewed no change in the situation from the previous evening.	See Appendix IV Map E.2
		5.35 am.	The 1st London Regt. holding first objective as far as point T.21.b.2.2. where the tank which was stuck on the previous day served as a bombing block for both our troops and the enemy. Unfortunately owing to the position of the tank its machine guns were unable to be used. Brigades were notified of the intention of the Corps to resume the attack by the 6th and Guards Divisions against LESBOEUFS during the day.	
		6.0 am.		
		7.28am.	Message received from 167th Brigade that for the third time since 2.0 a.m. our infantry in captured German trenches N.W. of LEUZE WOOD complained of being shelled by our own artillery. C.R.A. was informed accordingly.	
		9.21 am.	Wire received from Corps H.Q. ordering the 56th Division to make every effort to isolate /the	

Army Form C. 2118.

22.

WAR DIARY
or
INTELLIGENCE SUMMARY

(Erase heading not required.)

Instructions regarding War Diaries and Intelligence Summaries are contained in F. S. Regs., Part II. and the Staff Manual respectively. Title Pages will be prepared in manuscript.

Place	Date	Hour	Summary of Events and Information	Remarks and references to Appendices
			the enemy occupying the QUADRILATERAL by pushing out small parties of selected men Northwards from BOULEAUX WOOD to establish posts in N.E. corner of T.21.a. and S.E. corner of T.15.c. It was essential that the QUADRILATERAL should be cleared of the enemy as soon as possible as it had been holding up our attacks since the 9th inst. This message was repeated to 167th and 168th Infantry Brigades with a view to the 167th Brigade carrying out the operation. The fighting condition reports received from 167th and 169th Brigades shewed that the battalions in the front line were only fit for defensive action having lost heavily in the attack of the previous day but the battalions of the latter Brigade had not suffered so heavily and were still fit to resume the offensive.	(See Ap.III Map E2.)
		1.43 pm.	XIVth Corps telephoned that an airman reported enemy advancing from T.27.a.9.5. to T.26.d.5.5 but as no reports to this effect had been received from 169th Brigade, and both points lay in our own lines this information was disregarded.	(See Ap. III Map E2.)
		1.50 pm.	Orders issued for the 169th Infantry Brigade to arrange to dig a fire trench during the night 16/17th from LOOP TRENCH T.27.b.4½.9½ to LEUZE WOOD about T.21.c.9.3. One Company of Pioneers were placed at their disposal for this purpose and the General Officer Commanding was informed that the battalion in Brigade Reserve could be used to supplement the labour. The pioneer company to be at Brigade Headquarters at HARDECOURT CRUCIFIX at 6.0 p.m. Another report received from 167th Brigade stated that trenches taken by us yesterday North of BOULEAUX WOOD were again being shelled by our own artillery.	
		2.2 pm.	The defence of the Divisional Front was allotted to the 167th and 169th Infantry Brigades as follows :- 167th Brigade to be responsible for the defence of the face of BOULEAUX and LEUZE WOODS as far South as T.27.a.5.8. (where COMBLES TRENCH enters the WOOD). 169th Brigade to be responsible for the face of LEUZE WOOD from that point Southwards.	(See Ap.III Map "F")
		2.15 pm.	A/t Observer reported that at 1.0 p.m. he had seen considerable movement of motor and horse transport in rear of the enemy's lines, also troops marching along the LIGNY to BEAULENCOURT ROAD.	(See Ap.III. Map "A". Sheet 57c. SW.)
		2.18 pm.	Battalions which had been in Divisional Reserve yesterday and were attached to the 167th and 169th Brigades were ordered to rejoin their own Brigades.	
		2.55 pm.	Message received from XIVth Corps stated definitely that we had occupied trench running North from the QUADRILATERAL as far South as T.14.d.9.7. Divisions ordered to consolidate all ground gained during the last 24 hours and establish lines within assaulting distance of any portions of their objectives which were still held by the enemy.	
		4.0 pm.	C.R.E. ordered to place 1 Company Pioneers at the disposal of the 167th Brigade for work /during	

Army Form C. 2118.

WAR DIARY
or
INTELLIGENCE SUMMARY

(Erase heading not required.)

Instructions regarding War Diaries and Intelligence Summaries are contained in F. S. Regs., Part II. and the Staff Manual respectively. Title Pages will be prepared in manuscript.

Place	Date	Hour	Summary of Events and Information	Remarks and references to Appendices
		4.25 pm.	during the night. Officer in charge of the Company to report to 167th Brigade H.Q. at 7.0 pm. The following message sent to the 167th Brigade:- "You will arrange to push out a strong Patrol or Patrols tonight from MIDDLE COPSE northwards to the track between T.15.d.2.3. and T.15.c.9.1. Points occupied will be consolidated. You will inform 16th Brigade *(who is to cover the operation)* 6th Division is being asked to arrange for artillery barrage to be clear of these points. They will endeavour to connect with you from advanced trench of 16th Brigade". The old German second line running through FALFEMONT FARM was allotted as follows :- To Brigades in the front line for the use of Reserve and Supporting troops that portion of the line North of FALEEMONT FARM to 167th Brigade, and the portion South of the FARM to the 169th Brigade.	
		5.35 pm.	Situation was unchanged on the Divisional Front. Usual hostile shelling of LEUZE WOOD and our trenches in the vicinity had been in progress throughout the day. 167th Brigade reported that the post at MIDDLE COPSE had been consolidated to hold 25 men and LEWIS GUNS.	
		9.30 pm.	Divisional Order No. 39 issued. This dealt with the necessity for connecting up detached post and making a continuous line on the Divisional Front.	See Ap.VI.
		9.40 pm.	It had been decided by the General Officer Commanding during the afternoon to send a battery of medium trench mortars to assist 169th Brigade against the Germans occupying the SUNKEN Road. 168th Brigade were ordered to detail carrying party for the purpose of moving up the guns and ammunition during the night of the 16/17th. XIVth Corps were informed of this intention and requested to issue four Temple Silencers for use with these Mortars. During these operations identifications had been obtained of the 28th Regiment. 167th Brigade informed that commencing at 7.0 a.m. heavy artillery would be bombarding the QUADRILATERAL and that they had been informed of the position our patrols would be occupying if they had succeeded in pushing out Northwards as had been ordered the previous evening.	
A.10.b.3.8.	17th Sept.	1.0 am.		

Army Form C. 2118.

WAR DIARY
or
INTELLIGENCE SUMMARY

(Erase heading not required.)

Instructions regarding War Diaries and Intelligence Summaries are contained in F. S. Regs., Part II. and the Staff Manual respectively. Title Pages will be prepared in manuscript.

Place	Date	Hour	Summary of Events and Information	Remarks and references to Appendices
Avd.G.S.P.	17th Contd.	6.0 am.	No work was done during the night 16/17th on the trench which was to be dug from LOOP TRENCH to LEUZE WOOD parallel to the SUNKEN ROAD owing to the company of the pioneer battalion who were to have carried out the work being led close to the German line by their guide who lost his way. The company was heavily fired on from the German trenches and dispersed.	see appendix II
			The night of the 16/17th passed quietly except for shelling by our own Heavy Artillery of our trenches about T.29.b.5.9. This very seriously impeded the work of consolidation and caused a number of casualties amongst the 5th London Regt. During the night the 8th Middlesex had relieved the 7th Middlesex and 1st London Regts; and the 3rd London had relieved the 8th Middlesex Regt. in LEUZE WOOD.	
		8.40 am.	Warning Order was received from Corps saying that preparations had to be made for continuing the attack on the 18th instant. The objectives of the XIVth Corps were MORVAL and LESBOEUFS. The relief of the 169th by the 168th Inf. Bde. ordered in Divisional Order No. 39 was accordingly cancelled. Headquarters of these Brigades were ordered to remain in their present positions. Later in the morning more detailed instructions were received from the Corps with regard to the operations to be carried out on the 18th. The task assigned to the 56th Division was the capture of a line running from trench junction from T.21.d.7.2. to BOULEAUX WOOD T.21.d.1.5. thence along the S.E. face of BOULEAUX WOOD to T.21.b.7.3. thence to MIDDLE COPSE inclusive. The 6th Division on our left was to continue the line from MIDDLE COPSE to T.15.a.7.9..	see appendix III Map No 3
		11.30 am.	Orders sent to the 169th Inf. Bde. that the trench parallel to the SUNKEN ROAD must be dug without fail during the night of the 17/18th instant as it would be required as an assembly trench for the attack on the 18th.	
		2.50 pm.	4th London Regt. was placed at the disposal of the 167th Inf. Bde. In accordance with the Corps Warning Order which had been received on the evening of the 16th ordering certain re-adjustments of the line to be made by mutual consent of G.O.C's of Divisions, the 6th Division were asked to evacuate the trench running from T.21.c.4.7. to T.21.a.6.4. as it was required by us for assembly purposes by the morning of the 18th.	
		3.30 pm.	Warning Order sent to the Brigades and C.R.A. notifying them of the forthcoming operations and alloting objectives as follows:- 169th Inf. Bde. SUNKEN ROAD only from T.21.d.7.2. to BOULEAUX WOOD T.21.d.1.3. The objective of the 167th Inf. Bde. with 4th London. Regtz attached S.E. face of BOULEAUX WOOD from SUNKEN ROAD to T.21.b.7.3. and thence to MIDDLE COPSE inclusive. C.R.A. to visit Brigadier-s during the afternoon to arrange the necessary barrages. One section of medium trench mortars placed at the disposal of each brigade. Evening report showed no change in the situation exceept that a patrol of 169th Inf. Bdez had progressed down COMBLES TRENCH for two hundred yards as far as T.27.b.7.0. where a number of dead Germans of the 26th Regiment were seen / 6.0 pm.	see appendix III Map No 3.

25.
Army Form C. 2118.

WAR DIARY
or
INTELLIGENCE SUMMARY
(Erase heading not required.)

Instructions regarding War Diaries and Intelligence Summaries are contained in F.S. Regs., Part II. and the Staff Manual respectively. Title Pages will be prepared in manuscript.

Place	Date	Hour	Summary of Events and Information	Remarks and references to Appendices
A.10.b.3.8.	18th	6.0 pm.	The 169th Inf. Bde. reported that the enemy were working on a new trench W. of COMBLES TRENCH about line T.27.d.7.3. to 6.5.. The Brigade was ordered to take steps at once to make the enemy stop working.	
		7.0 pm.	Divisional Order No. 40 issued containing full instructions for the operations to take place on the 18th instant. The French on our immediate right reported very violent hostile bombardment of their front line in progress and they were expecting a counter-attack. This was shortly afterwards followed by a message from our right battalion saying that their front was also being heavily bombarded.	(See Ap.VI)
		8.10 pm.	London Scottish placed at the disposal of the 167th Inf. Bde.. Brigade Major 168th Bde. attached to the 167th Bde. for tomorrow's operations.	
		8.20 pm.	The battalion Hdqrs. in the trench just S. of FALFEMONT FARM recently used by 167th Bde. as Bde. Hdqrs. were allotted to the 169th Bde. for night 17/18 for use as a Bde. Hdqrs. again. During the evening heavy rain fell which caused the tracks and the trenches underfoot to become very muddy making progress up to LEUZE WOOD a matter of great difficulty. Night of the 17/18th passed very quietly except for intermittent shelling.	(See Ap.III Map "B")
		5.50 am.	This was the zero hour fixed for the assault.	
		6.40 am.	Telephone message from 167th Inf. Bde. that the battalions moving up the assembly trenches had arrived late and therefore the attack on the left had not started. The late arrival of the battalions was due to the impossible state of the ground. This information was at once sent on to Corps headquarters with a further report that no news had arrived from 169th Inf. Bde. as to the progress of their attack, but it was known that battalions had reached all their assembly trenches.	
		7.0 am.	Instructions sent to 167th Inf. Bde. to withdraw one of the battalions detailed for the assault, to a position in rear. All trenches which had been vacated prior to our bombardment were to be re-occupied and every endeavour made to avoid congestion of troops in LEUZE WOOD.	
		9.0 am.	First report received from 169th Inf. Bde. of the progress of their attack which was now stated to have failed. The right company of the 16th Londons had nearly reached its objective, but had failed to get in and had suffered very heavy casualties. The supports had also lost heavily. The 5th London Regt. failed to make progress up LOOP TRENCH and both these battalions were occupying the new trench (afterwards known as Cheshire Trench) running parallel to and S.W. of the SUNKEN ROAD.	
		10.20 am.	More definite report received as to the situation on the front of the 169th Inf. Bde. - 16th London Regt. holding the new trench from T.27.b.5.8. to T.21.c.5.2. with 90 men. None of our troops in front of this. 9th London Regt. over 200 yards down COMBLES trench from our /strong	For map refs. in connection with the operations on this date see App. III, Map B3.

2449 Wt. W14957/M90 750,000 1/16 J.B.C. & A. Forms/C.2118/12.

Army Form C. 2118.

WAR DIARY
or
INTELLIGENCE SUMMARY

(Erase heading not required.)

Instructions regarding War Diaries and Intelligence Summaries are contained in F. S. Regs., Part II. and the Staff Manual respectively. Title Pages will be prepared in manuscript.

Place	Date	Hour	Summary of Events and Information	Remarks and references to Appendices
		10.40 am.	strong point at T.27.b.2.4., enemy 30 yards further down the trench. The attack appeared to have failed owing to very heavy hostile machine gun fire from the ORCHARDS at T.21.d.8.2. Warning Order issued to Brigades for the relief of 167th Inf. Bde. by 168th Inf. Bde. in the left sector during the night 18/19th. 169th Inf. Bde. was ordered to consolidate all ground occupied and to continue the work down COMBLES TRENCH.	
		11.10 am.	The following order was sent to 167th Inf. Bde. "6th Division reports their advanced posts on line of the railway T.15.d.5.8. Patrol has reached N.E. Corner of BOULEAUX WOOD and reports no enemy there. No enemy in railway cutting at T.15.a. French report prisoners state that enemy has evacuated COMBLES but this is not yet confirmed. Push out strong patrols at once to ascertain the situation in BOULEAUX WOOD and occupy ground gained." 169th Inf. Bde. was informed of this situation and ordered to continue pushing down COMBLES TRENCH in order to ascertain whether reports as to the enemy's evacuation were correct.	
		11.40 am.	XIVth Corps were notified of the action being taken by the patrols of the 167th Inf. Bde. with a view to co-operating with the patrols sent out by the 6th Division on our left.	
		12.6 am.	Message received from the Corps timed 11.32 am. stated that, the 6th Division had captured the QUADRILATERAL and the trench to the North of it. This message confirmed the position of patrols at T.15.d.5.8. and the N.E. Corner of BOULEAUX WOOD. All Divisions were ordered to patrol actively to their front with the object of establishing a line of posts as far forward as possible. Zones for patrols were allotted as follows:— 20th Division from T.14.b.9.9. to road junction T.16.a.7½.6½; the 6th Division thence to MIDDLE COPSE; the 56th Division thence to S.E. edge of BOULEAUX WOOD. This information was repeated to Brigades with an order for 167th Inf. Bdez to patrol actively to their front in the zone from S.E. edge of BOULEAUX WOOD from a line drawn from MIDDLE COPSE to T.16. central. 14th London and 4th London Regts. were placed at the disposal of the G.O.C., 167th Inf. Bde. for providing patrols if required.	
		1.30 pm.	Both Brigades in the front line were notified that a squadron of our Cavalry was moving forward via LEUZE WOOD towards MORVAL to clear up the situation and had left the headquarters of the 6th Division at 1.0 pm.	
		2.30 pm.	Divisional Order No. 41 was issued containing instructions for the relief referred to in Warning Order and the action to be taken by Brigades in the front line.	
		2.45 pm.	Situation report from 169th Inf. Bde. stated that 80 yards more of COMBLES TRENCH had been occupied by us, bombing parties being assisted by a Stokes mortar. Hostile rifle fire from the SUNKEN ROAD still continued. COMBLES TRENCH was still occupied by the enemy to the South of our block.	
		3.0 pm.	A Corps Conference was held at MINDEN POST at which the G.O.C. and G.S.O.2 were present /530 pm.	

WAR DIARY
or
INTELLIGENCE SUMMARY

(Erase heading not required.)

Army Form C. 2118.

Place	Date	Hour	Summary of Events and Information	Remarks and references to Appendices
		5.30 pm.	Patrol reports showed that the S. end of BOULEAUX WOOD was still held by the enemy. No reports had been received from the patrol of 167th Inf. Bde. which went out further to the North. A party of about two hundred of the enemy had been seen West of MORVAL and had been effectively dealt with by five batteries of artillery.	
		6.20 pm.	XIVth Corps and 6th Division informed that patrol reports showed W. side of BOULEAUX WOOD to be held from T.21.b.2.3. to T.21.b.6.6. A patrol which had left MIDDLE COPSE and proceeded towards the Northern end of BOULEAUX WOOD had been met by heavy rifle fire and rifle grenades from the enemy holding the end of the wood.	
		8.15 pm.	Patrol reports received from both Brigades confirmed the previous reports that the Western face of BOULEAUX WOOD was held by the enemy; that a trench mortar had come into action in the wood at about T.21.b.7.6. and had fired on the front line of the 167th Inf. Bde.. That during the afternoon the enemy did not hold the trench T.21.b.3.2. - T.21.b.4.8. in force and that parties of the enemy had been seen in BOULEAUX WOOD in shell holes N.E. of this trench and also in the Northern end of the wood. Enemy was still occupying the trench running along Northern side of the SUNKEN ROAD.	
A.10.b.3.8.	19th Sept.	5.10 am.	Relief of 167th Brigade by 168th Brigade in the left sector Divisional front reported complete. Battalion reliefs were also carried out on the front of the 169th Brigade, so that at this hour the disposition was as follows :- 167th Brigade in reserve, with Headquarters in CHIMPANZEE TRENCH - 1st Londons and 7th Middlesex Regiments in trenches at MALTZHORN FARM, and the 3rd/and 8th Middlesex Regiments in CASEMENT TRENCH - 168th Brigade in the left sector of the Divisional line - Headquarters at ANGLE WOOD. The London Scottish in the front line, 4th Londons in support at LEUZE WOOD - 12th and 13th Londons in Reserve at ANGLE WOOD - 169th Bde. on the right of the Divisional front, Headquarters at THE CRUCIFIX, HARDECOURT - 9th Londons in the front line on the right - L.R.B. in the front line on the left - 2nd Londons in support in trenches South of FALFEMONT FARM. 16th Londons in reserve at ANGLE WOOD. The 5th Divn. had also relieved the 6th Division on our left. The night of the 18/19th had passed quietly and our reliefs had not been interfered with by the enemy. During the early hours of the morning G.S.O. 2 with the Brigade Major of the 168th Brigade reconnoitred the ground N. of BOULEAUX WOOD with a view to fixing approximately the siting of a new front line trench which was to be dug by the 168th Brigade parallel to the N.W. side of BOULEAUX WOOD.* It subsequently transpired that the officer of the 8th Middlesex in charge of the post at MIDDLE COPSE had withdrawn before the arrival of the relieving post of the London Scottish. The COPSE had been visited by an officer and a party of men from the London Scottish, but on finding it un-occupied the officer returned. The G.O.C. 168th Brigade was informed of this by telephone and ordered to re-occupy the COPSE as soon as possible.	See Ap. II. * Drawing the reconnaissance they found that MIDDLE COPSE was unoccupied.

/ 10.0 am.

Army Form C. 2118.

WAR DIARY
or
INTELLIGENCE SUMMARY

(Erase heading not required.)

Instructions regarding War Diaries and Intelligence Summaries are contained in F. S. Regs., Part II. and the Staff Manual respectively. Title Pages will be prepared in manuscript.

Place	Date	Hour	Summary of Events and Information	Remarks and references to Appendices
		10.0 am.	Report was received from the 168th Infantry Brigade that a company of pioneers which had been attached to the Brigade for work during the night of the 18/19th had been ordered to dig a communication trench from T.21.a.6.4. to MIDDLE COPSE. The Company had reached the S.W. edge of LEUZE WOOD where the O.C. Coy stated they had been heavily shelled and dispersed, he had accordingly marched them back to Brigade Headquarters without carrying out the task which had been allotted to the company. This explanation was not considered satisfactory in view of the fact that both battalions in the line had reported quiet night.	
		11.30 am.	The following order was sent to the 168th Brigade and repeated C.R.E. and Pioneer Battalion:- "In confirmation of instructions issued verbally MIDDLE COPSE is to be re-occupied as soon as conditions of light admit of movement. MIDDLE COPSE (BEEF TRENCH) as near to the derelict tanks as possible. A strong point is to be made at about T.15.d.5.5. selected by G.S.O.2 and the Brigade Major 168th Brigade. This point is to be connected up to MIDDLE COPSE by fire trench. All this will be done tonight. R.E. and Pioneers will move up to front line before dark so as to start work immediately it is possible. 168th Brigade will provide covering parties. In order to get maximum amount of work done 50% of R.E. and Pioneers will carry rifles and one bandolier with ammunition, the remainder will be unarmed" During the morning a warning order was received from the Corps stating that Fourth Army would renew the attack on September 21st, the objectives of the XIVth Corps included the villages of MORVAL and LESBOEUFS. The attack to be carried out by the Guards Division on the left and the 5th Division on the right, 56th Division forming a protective flank facing South. Division (Warning) Order No. 42 was issued giving the outline of the operations to be carried out on the 21st.	See Ap. III Map "F" See Ap. VI.
		5.0 pm.	Situation on Divisional front was unchanged. During the day there had been intermittent bombing in BOULEAUX WOOD and shelling of the N. and N.W. faces of LEUZE WOOD. Three hostile aeroplane bombs had been dropped outside the S. Corner of LEUZE WOOD about 5.0 pm. without causing any damage.	
		5.30 pm.		
		6.30 pm.	The G.O.C., 168th Brigade had decided not to sent patrols into BOULEAUX WOOD during the night 19/20th for fear of them becoming engaged with the enemy and causing a hostile barrage to be put on our lines, which might seriously interfere with the work of digging the new trench.	
		7.0 pm.	Wire received from XIVth Corps that the operations ordered for the 21st instant had been postponed for 24 hours. Brigades and C.R.A. were notified accordingly.	
		9.0 pm.	MIDDLE COPSE had been re-occupied by the London Scottish.	

/20th

Army Form C. 2118.

WAR DIARY
or
INTELLIGENCE SUMMARY

(Erase heading not required.)

Instructions regarding War Diaries and Intelligence Summaries are contained in F.S. Regs., Part II. and the Staff Manual respectively. Title Pages will be prepared in manuscript.

Place	Date	Hour	Summary of Events and Information	Remarks and references to Appendices
A.10.b.3.8.	20th	1.30 am.	The following wire was received from 168th Infantry Brigade:- "New trench successfully laid out by 9.0 pm. First company started work by 9.20 pm., last company by 10.20 pm. At 11.30 situation strong posts of trench was continuous from T.21.b.½.3½. in front of MIDDLE COPSE to T.15.d.8.7. strong posts being dug close to tram way cutting and overlooking valley - old German gun position T.15.d.8.7. Some casualties from rifle fire in T.21.b. otherwise quiet. MIDDLE COPSE was occupied at 8.20pm."	(See App. Map F.)
		5.30 am.	The morning report showed a quiet night with intermittent bursts of rifle fire from BOULEAUX WOOD. New trench had been dug and occupied - T.15.c.7.7. to T.21.b.0.4.	
		7.0 am.	Detailed report received from 168th Brigade in regard to the new trench which had been dug during the night. A good trench had been dug from about T.21.b.0.4. to MIDDLE COPSE where a strong point had already been made, from thence the trench was continuous to junction of tramway line at T.15.d.7.7. where the strong point remained to be dug. The new trench which was everywhere 3'6" to 5' deep was provided with fire steps and had been garrisoned before 4.30 am. The garrison had been given orders to improve the trench as much as possible during the day. During the night a German deserter of the 74th Reserve Regiment had walked into our covering party N.E. of MIDDLE COPSE about T.21.b.4.8.	
		9.15 am.	Report was received from the Corps that a French aeroplane reconnaissance made the previous evening reported great activity on all railways in rear of the enemy's lines.	
		9.30 am.	Conference was held at Corps Headquarters G.O.C., G.S.O.1 and C.R.A. were present. During the morning hostile artillery was active over the greater part of the Divisional front and several German aeroplanes flew over our lines.	
		1.20 pm.	Orders issued to 168th Brigade for the following work to be carried out during the night of the 20/21st:- MIDDLE COPSE to be connected up to a trench which had been dug by the 5th Division about T.15.d.2.3. strong posts to be established and wired about T.15.d.7.2. to T.15.d.9.4., also on the tramline at T.16.c.1.6. and the cutting at T.15.b.9.0. special care to be taken to protect and strengthen the left flank of the new line. G.O.C. 168th Brigade to arrange direct with the C.R.E. for such R.E. personnel as was necessary to carry out this work. Two companies of pioneers were also attached to the Brigade. Order received from the Corps that previous warning orders with reference to the forthcoming operations were cancelled. The attack was now decided on for the 23rd instant, any further postponements which might be necessary would be made by periods of 48 hours. It had been decided at the Corps Conference held during the morning that the attack would be made by the 5th, 6th and Guards Divisions, the 56th Division forming a defensive flank facing the South as previously ordered. During the remainder of the day new trench N.W. of BOULEAUX WOOD was continually shelled by the enemy as were also most of the other trenches on our front. /Enemy	

Army Form C. 2118.
30

WAR DIARY
or
INTELLIGENCE SUMMARY

(Erase heading not required.)

Instructions regarding War Diaries and Intelligence Summaries are contained in F.S. Regs., Part II. and the Staff Manual respectively. Title Pages will be prepared in manuscript.

Place	Date	Hour	Summary of Events and Information	Remarks and references to Appendices
A.10.b.3.8.	21st Sept.	5.30 am.	Enemy was still in force South of our block in COMBLES TRENCH. During the evening an Operation Order was received from the Corps giving the full orders for the attack which had been decided on for the 23rd inst. The night had passed quietly. A new trench had been dug by the 168th Brigade from MIDDLE Copse T.15.d.1½.0. also four new posts established at T.15.d.7.2 - 9.4. T.16.c.1.8. - T.15.b.9.1. During the night a patrol of the enemy had been engaged by a covering party of the 168th Brigade just North of the tram line at T.15.d.8.8. Two MEN of the enemy's patrol escaped but a Feldwebel of the 2nd Battalion 235th Reserve Regiment, 51st Reserve Division was captured.	See App. III. Map F.
BILLON COPSE		9.30 am.	Report from the 168th Brigade showed that the post which was dug at T.16.c.1.8. during the night had not been occupied, all the other posts were occupied. Divisional Hdqrs. closed at A.10.b.3.8. and re-opened at BILLON COPSE at the same hour. Remainder of the day passed without incident. Two men of the 168th Brigade succeeded in moving into the post at T.16.c.1.8. by 4.30 pm., the remainder of the garrison had been ordered to occupy the post at dusk.	"
do.	22nd	1.45 am.	Notification received from Corps Headquarters that the operations ordered for the 23rd inst. had been postponed until the 25th on account of the wet weather.	"
		4.0 am.	O.C. Company pioneers working with 168th Brigade reported that heavy shells from our own Artillery (thought to be 6") were falling about post at T.16.d.1.8. A large number of rounds had failed to explode, but a certain number of casualties had been sustained by the working party. Situation report received from 168th Brigade stated that one of our patrols moving N.E. during the night from post T.15.d.9.3. had been challenged and fired on at a range of about thirty yards. Working party at post T.16.c.1.8. had been continuously fired on and bombed by the enemy. A space of thirty yards between post T.16.c.1.8. and the most Northerly end of the new trench had been connected. Hostile artillery had been active. Two Stokes mortars had been moved into position in BULLY Trench. Company of the Rangers had been relieved in trench T.15.d.2.2. to T.15.d.0.5. by the right company of the 5th Division. Prisoner of the 1st Battalion 236th Reserve Regiment, 51st Reserve Division had been captured by 168th Brigade at T.21.b.4.5. at 4.0 am. During the morning aeroplane photographs were received showing the new trenches which had been dug on the N.W. side of BOULEAUX WOOD. These proved to be well traversed and to form a very good front line. This was commented on by the Corps Commander who directed that every effort should be made to join the new trench dug by the 5th Divn. from T.15.b.5.2 to our new line.	"

Army Form C. 2118.

WAR DIARY
or
INTELLIGENCE SUMMARY

(Erase heading not required.)

Instructions regarding War Diaries and Intelligence Summaries are contained in F.S. Regs., Part II. and the Staff Manual respectively. Title Pages will be prepared in manuscript.

Place	Date	Hour	Summary of Events and Information	Remarks and references to Appendices
(Contd.)	22nd Sept.	11.0 a.m.	During the night of the 21/22nd the following work had been done by the 168th Inf. Bde. - The post at T.15.d.7.2. joined to the post at T.15.d.9.3. by a continuous fire trench. T.15.d.9.3. joined to T.16.c.1.8. except for a gap of about thirty yards near the latter post. Communication trench had been dug joining post T.15.d.7.2. to the trench running through MIDDLE COPSE (GROPI TRENCH). MIDDLE COPSE, T.15.b.9.1., T.15.b.9.7., T.15.b.9.1., T.15.b.7.2. had all been wired. The post at T.16.c.1.8. had not been wired, this and the gap in the new front line trench were due to hostile bombing and rifle fire which had continued throughout the night. During the last 24 hours the enemy had dug a trench from the Northern Corner of BOULEAUX WOOD to about T.16.c.5.6. This was reported to have been held by him during the night of the 21/22nd. During the morning enemy working parties were seen at the Northern end of LOOP TRENCH and were satisfactorily dealt with by our Stokes mortars.	See App. III Map F.
		12.0 Noon.	169th Brigade reported an attack in progress opposite the French left on the heights above COMBLES, but whether the French or the Germans had assumed the offensive, was not known. The G.O.C., 169th Inf. Bde. was instructed to cover possible hostile movement from COMBLES with machine gun fire from S. of LEUZE WOOD. A reconnaissance carried out during the afternoon by officers of the 12 and 13th London Regts. showed that the wire in front of the main German 3rd. line S. and W. of MORVAL was comparatively thin. From T.16.b.6.3. to T.16.b.2.5. wire appeared to be very thick and it was thought that this was a strong point.	do.
		6.15 pm.	Divnl. Order No. 43 issued. This contained orders for the attack to take place on the 25th instant. The main task of the 56th Division was to form a protective flank facing S. and to secure firing positions to prevent hostile movement along the valley running N.E. from COMBLES; to obtain touch with the 5th Division about T.16.c.4½.7. and to neutralise German detachments occupying BOULEAUX WOOD. Certain re-adjustments of the front were to be carried out on the night 24/25th so as to bring all three brigades into the front line. Two tanks had been allotted to the Division for these operations. They were ordered to rendezvous in the QUARRY W. of LEUZE WOOD on the night of the 24/25th. These tanks would not be used until the main operations had succeeded when it was intended that they should proceed along the SUNKEN ROAD towards COMBLES to clear certain trenches, and finally block the N.E. exits from COMBLES.	See App. II and Map attached to Div.O. No. 43. (See App III Map "A" Sh.57 S.W.
		12.0 midnight.	Enemy fired gas shells for the first time on the Divisional front. These were bursting over the trenches S. of FALFEMONT FARM.	
BILLON COPSE.	23rd Sept.		During the night of the 22/23rd 167th Inf. Bde. had relieved 168th Inf. Bde. on the left of the Divisional front. Night had passed quietly except for the usual intermittent shelling. During the last two nights the 169th Inf. Bde. had dug the following trenches - a communication /trench	

2449 Wt. W14957/M90 750,000 1/16 J.B.C. &A. Forms/C.2118/12.

WAR DIARY or INTELLIGENCE SUMMARY

Army Form C. 2118.

(Erase heading not required.)

Place	Date	Hour	Summary of Events and Information	Remarks and references to Appendices
			trench from T.27.b.1.4. to T.27.c.3.5. connecting the portion of COMBLES TRENCH in our hands to LEUZENAKE TRENCH. Length of trench from T.27.c.6.9. to T.27.d.0.7. and from T.3.b.0.2. to 0.8. It was intended that these two lengths should be connected so as to form a continuous fire trench.	See Ap. III Map "F"
		10.15 am.	Information was received that the French had taken about 150 yards of the trench running from B.4.b.2.2. to T.28.c.0.0. - this was the continuation of COMBLES TRENCH. 169th Infantry Brigade were informed of this and ordered to organise vigorous bombing and trench mortar attacks down COMBLES TRENCH from the North with a view to connecting up with the French. Reports received at midday shewed that there had been considerable increase in hostile artillery fire during the morning. Our front line trenches, LEUZE WOOD and ANGLE WOOD VALLEY received the most attention. At one time it appeared that the enemy was shelling his own trenches in BOULEAUX WOOD as a great number of green lights were sent up from his line.	See Ap. III Map "F" sheet 57.c.SW.
		4.0 pm.	167th Brigade ordered to hand over to the right Brigade of the 5th Division during the night of the 23rd/24th. The remainder of the day passed without incident, hostile artillery becoming quiet during the evening. Divisional Order No. 44 issued containing further instructions for the forthcoming operations.	See Ap. III Map "F" See Ap. VI
	24th Sept.	5.0 am.	Morning Report shewed hostile artillery activity over the whole front especially South of LEUZE WOOD where a number of gas shells had been fired over LEUZENAKE TRENCH.	
		8.55 am.	Report received from the 169th Brigade with reference to the bombing operations carried out in COMBLES TRENCH in conjunction with the French. The French reported that their first attack had failed owing to the German trench being very strongly held; another attack was being organised. Q.V.R. had made considerable progress down trench from the north until attacked on their left flank from communication trench running from COMBLES which had not been previously located. This attack had forced them to withdraw. Germans were in considerable force about the roads in T.27.b.8.3. Our net gains in this attack was consisted of the German barricade which was being consolidated. G.O.C. 169th Brigade instructed that as much as of COMBLES TRENCH as possible must be occupied and fresh blocks made. 167th Brigade reported that during the night 23/24th the Strong Point at T.16.c.1.8. and a communication trench constructed from RANGER TRENCH back to Battalion Headquarters at T.15.d.6.6.	See Ap. III Map "F"
		1.50 pm.	Notification received from Corps Headquarters that Zero hour for the attack on the 25th would be 12.30 p.m. The French were attacking on our right at the same hour. All those concerned were notified.	

Army Form C. 2118.

WAR DIARY
or
INTELLIGENCE SUMMARY

(Erase heading not required.)

Instructions regarding War Diaries and Intelligence Summaries are contained in F. S. Regs., Part II. and the Staff Manual respectively. Title Pages will be prepared in manuscript.

Place	Date	Hour	Summary of Events and Information	Remarks and references to Appendices
FALCON COPSE	25th	10.48.pm.	O.C., Section, Tanks, reported that both tanks had safely reached WEDGE WOOD at 10.50.pm. en route for the QUARRY West of LEUZE WOOD where they had been ordered to rendezvous. They had proceeded along the track which had been taped during the night of the 23/24th by the Pioneers from HARDECOURT to Quarry West of LEUZE WOOD.	
		12.24 am.	Information received from the Corps that prisoners captured by the French stated that the houses on the N.W. and S.E. sides of COMBLES were organised for defence and were strongly held by machine guns. They also reported that one company was in reserve in dug-outs near the station which had not been damaged by our artillery fire. The artillery were informed of the position of these dug-outs with a view to destroying them.	
		4.10 am.	Report received that the relief of the left portion of the 167th Brigade by the 168th Brigade was complete. The position of Brigades in the line now was :- 167th Brigade on the left - 168th Brigade in the centre and 169th Brigade on the right. During the night 24th/25th the right of our line had been fairly heavily shelled otherwise the night passed quietly and without incident.	
		10.6 am.	169th Brigade informed that the enemy had extended the trench East of LOOP TRENCH so as to join up with COMBLES TRENCH at T.27.b.6.3. As this trench lay within the area reported as being held by 169th Brigade, the G.O.C. was instructed to take steps immediately to ascertain the exact point which had been reached by his troops in COMBLES TRENCH, and active measures taken to prevent the enemy carrying on work on this new trench.	
		12.35 pm.	Zero hour for the assault.	
		1.10 pm.	B.G., G.S. XIVth Corps telephoned that the Guards and the 5th Division had taken all their first objectives, the latter with practically no opposition.	
		1.14 pm.	Aeroplane report received at this hour shewed that 168th Brigade had taken its objective and that our troops were in the trench at the North end of BOULEAUX WOOD as far as the railway. Report received from the 5th Division shewed that their right battalion had gained its first objective but was slightly too much to its left but that it was working down to its right to the cross roads in T.16.a.8.8.6.	
		1.25 pm.	Report was received from O.C. Tanks that the tanks had safely reached the QUARRY West of LEUZE WOOD.	
		1.38 pm.	Message received that air reports shewed that XIVth Corps had captured the whole of its first objective with the exception of about 150 yards of trench from T.3.a.1.7. to T.3.d.3.4. There was some doubt about situation from T.16.c.4.8. to T.16.a.7.6.	
		1.45 pm.	French on our right reported the capture of FREGICOURT. /2.20 p.m.	

28. XI. 34.

Army Form C. 2118.

WAR DIARY
or
INTELLIGENCE SUMMARY

(Erase heading not required.)

Instructions regarding War Diaries and Intelligence Summaries are contained in F.S. Regs., Part II. and the Staff Manual respectively. Title Pages will be prepared in manuscript.

Place	Date	Hour	Summary of Events and Information	Remarks and references to Appendices
		2.20 p.m	Air reports shewed that the whole of the second objective had been captured, and that parties had seized one or two houses just in front of the second objective in LESBOEUFS. Enemy was holding trenches at T.16.b.3.5. Observer reported that the attack appeared to have been carried out excellently and without a hitch.	
		2.40 p.m	Message received from the Cavalry Corps Observation Balloon stated that no enemy movement was visible behind LESBOEUFS and MORVAL or towards LE TRANSLOY and SAILLY-SAILLISEL. No French attack on SAILLY-SAILLISEL had been observed. The French advance appeared to have stopped at RANCOURT.	See appendix 27 Map ↑ Sheet 52c NW and 57.C.S.W.
		3.10 pm.	Report from the 4th London Regiment timed 1.5 p.m. shewed that the assault had been successful and that they had two companies in BOULEAUX WOOD which were digging in - touch obtained with the London Scottish on the left.	
		3.30 pm.	F.O.Os. reported parties of Germans seen leaving COMBLES in an Easterly direction about T.28.c.	
		3.45 pm.	Message received from the 168th Brigade that the London Scottish on the left had gained their objective and that they were in touch with the 4th London Regiment on their right but not with the 5th Division on their left. They had been ordered to get touch by visual with the 5th Division.	
		3.55 p.m.	Telephone message from the Corps stated that LESBOEUFS and the northern half of MORVAL had been captured by us, and FREGICOURT by the French. Thus at this hour the whole of the objectives allotted to the XIVth Corps had been captured with the exception of the southern half of MORVAL which was being dealt with by the French Division according to their programme.	
		4.0 p.m.	Message received from 167th Brigade stated that 1st London Regiment reported that hostile machine gun fire from the southern corner of BOULEAUX WOOD had ceased, but the enemy were still holding the Wood in the vicinity of the disabled tank from which point they were sniping vigorously. XIVth Corps and the 5th Division informed of the situation on our front.	
		4.15	An aeroplane map received at this hour shewed that the whole of the third objective was now in our hands. Message received from the 169th Brigade stated that the French on their right had asked for counter-battery assistance on German batteries at T.17.a.9.1., T.17.b.2.2. and T.17.d.1.8. All of these had been previously located and at the time of the report could be seen active. C.R.A. informed.	
	4.20p.m.			
		5.7 p.m.	Message received from Corps Headquarters shewed that there was some doubt as to whether the French held FREGICOURT. All three Brigades and C.R.A. informed.	
		5.25 p.m.	Instructions issued to 167th and 168th Brigades to push out strong patrols at dusk to /ascertain	

Army Form C. 2118.

WAR DIARY
or
INTELLIGENCE SUMMARY

(Erase heading not required.)

Instructions regarding War Diaries and Intelligence Summaries are contained in F. S. Regs., Part II. and the Staff Manual respectively. Title Pages will be prepared in manuscript.

Place	Date	Hour	Summary of Events and Information	Remarks and references to Appendices
		5.40 pm.	ascertain the position of the enemy East of the trench captured by us to-day, and in BOULEAUX WOOD; any ground gained was to be held. All artillery barrages on BOULEAUX WOOD were to cease at 6.30 pm.. This message was repeated to the C.R.A.	
			A message received from the French Liaison Officer at 5.40 pm. showed that the French held the line on our right as follows:- Elements of the 43rd Divisions working round end of the spur running S.W. from T.21.a.35.65; right of this division was about T.10.a.80.80. 42nd Division on the line U.25.c.55.80. to U.26.c.15.75. A telephone message from the same source stated that the French intended to make a further attack on FREGICOURT at 6.0 pm. This information was repeated to Brigades and C.R.A.	See Appendix Map F.
		7.27 pm.	168th Inf. Bde. stated that the bombing on their left flank had ceased but that a gap of 300 yards existed between them and the 5th Division, whose right was North of the tramline. 168th Brigade had a machine gun in position to cover this gap	
		7.35 pm.	Instructions sent to the 168th Brigade with reference to their previous report that if contact had not already been obtained with the 5th Division in the neighbourhood of LEMCO TRENCH touch must be obtained as soon as possible under cover of darkness.	
		7.41 pm.	The following situation report received from the 168th Brigade :- "This Brigade now holds line of trench T.16.c.35.00. to T.16.c.5.4. thence line of trenches to N. end of RANGER TRENCH, strong points being made at T.16.c.0.1., T.16.c.35.00., also two on the tramline. Patrols ordered to move N.E. and S. from the line held. Certain amount of sniping from BOULEAUX WOOD." This report was repeated to Corps Headquarters.	
		9.0 pm.	O.C. Tanks ordered to remain at the QUARRY W. of LEUZE WOOD until receipt of further instructions. Move of the tanks was to depend on the success attained by the French when the result of their second attack against FREGICOURT was ascertained.	
		8.5 pm.	Report timed 6.15 pm. received showing that the left battalion (168th Brigade) was in touch with the 5th Division T.15.c.45.70. The total captures of this brigade amounted to 4 machine guns, three officers and about 80 men. Of these 15 men had been captured by a patrol in a dug-out at T.16.c.8.2. By this time a post had been established on the railway at T.16.c.65.25. Two machine guns had been ordered to this post to command the COMBLES VALLEY.	
		8.25 pm.	Patrols of the 168th Brigade reported that the valley in T.16.c. and T.22.a. were clear of the enemy.	
		10.15 pm.	German officer captured by the 5th Division stated that the garrison of COMBLES intended to break out to the East during the night. 168th Brigade was ordered to send strong patrols to T.22.a. central and 167th Brigade to send patrols from BOULEAUX WOOD in order to get instant information of any move of this nature on the part of the enemy and to prevent it. Defensive /barrage	

Army Form C. 2118.

WAR DIARY
or
INTELLIGENCE SUMMARY

(Erase heading not required.)

Instructions regarding War Diaries and Intelligence Summaries are contained in F.S. Regs., Part II. and the Staff Manual respectively. Title Pages will be prepared in manuscript.

Place	Date	Hour	Summary of Events and Information	Remarks and references to Appendices
BILLON COPSE	26th	1.0 a.m.	The situation of the front of the 168th Brigade at this hour was as follows :- Strong Point was being constructed at T.23. Central to block the road running northwards from COMBLES through this point. Another post was being constructed T.16.c.6.5. so as to be ready for occupation by daylight. Two Posts to support these were being made at T.22.a.7.6. and on the embankment at T.22.a.4.7. which were also to be ready for occupation by daylight. The intention being to cover the exits from COMBLES by fire during the daylight in case the garrison should not come out during the night.	See Ap."III" Map "F"
		2.30 a.m.	Constant pressure had been kept by the 167th Brigade on the enemy behind the tank on the N.W. side of BOULEAUX WOOD. At 2.25 a.m. we had established a post inside the Wood behind the tank, the Germans having left BEEF TRENCH.	"
		6.30 a.m.	The following situation report was sent to the XIVth Corps " Constant pressure kept on the enemy with bombing parties and patrols during the night. On the North side of BOULEAUX WOOD we have established a post inside of BOULEAUX WOOD behind the derelict tank and enemy have left the trench running N. from T.21.b.25.15. Hostile Artillery inactive. The German blocks in COMBLES TRENCH and LOOP TRENCH bombed during the night. Touch maintained with the enemy at these points.	"
		6.55 a.m.	169th Brigade reported minor grenade actions during the night. By 6.30 a.m. the London Rifle Brigade had occupied the whole of LOOP TRENCH and the new trench dug by the enemy to connect up with COMBLES TRENCH. A barricade and Lewis Gun had been established on the SUNKEN ROAD at T.21.b.5.2. where the enemy was still making some opposition. Trench junction T.27.b.5.3. had been occupied and the London Rifle Brigade were pushing down COMBLES TRENCH. French reported capture of the trench running northwards to T.28.c.5.3. 2nd London Regiment were patrolling along the railway towards COMBLES.	"
		7.10 a.m.	Report received that a strong patrol from 167th Brigade had pushed forward to the Orchards in T.21.d.9.6. which had been reached as far as was known by 3.15 a.m., at which hour the enemy was stated to have been shelling COMBLES.	"
		7.40 a.m.	Telephone report received that the French had taken FREGICOURT and were pushing patrols into COMBLES on the East and N.E. Shortly afterwards 169th Brigade reported the capture of the whole of COMBLES TRENCH as far South as the railway and that patrols were moving into the N.W. of COMBLES.	/7.53 a.m.

Army Form C. 2118.

WAR DIARY
or
INTELLIGENCE SUMMARY

(Erase heading not required.)

Instructions regarding War Diaries and Intelligence Summaries are contained in F. S. Regs., Part II. and the Staff Manual respectively. Title Pages will be prepared in manuscript.

Place	Date	Hour	Summary of Events and Information	Remarks and references to Appendices
		7.53 a.m.	168th Brigade reported that they believed COMBLES to be practically clear of the enemy. A strong patrol from this Brigade was moving down the tramline towards T.22. Central. All the posts dug during the night of the 25th/26th were occupied.	Cc. Appendix B Page F.
		8.40 a.m.	Brigades informed that the artillery barrage east of COMBLES had been stopped in order to allow of free movement of patrols.	
		8.45 a.m.	8th Middlesex Regiment were being moved forward to the trenches at WEDGE WOOD.	
	9.5		A belated report was received from the 168th Brigade that BOULEAUX WOOD was definitely clear of the enemy, and that one company had been pushed forward to the S.E. edge, in touch with the left battalion of the 169th Brigade. 167th Brigade were informed of this situation.	
		9.30	In accordance with orders received from the Corps, 168th Brigade was ordered to send out strong patrols immediately to gain touch with the 5th Division about T.17.c.7.7. These patrols were to ascertain if MUTTON TRENCH from T.17.c.7.7. to T.23.d.5.5. had been vacated by the enemy. If possible this trench was to be occupied and a junction effected with the French about T.23.d. About this time a message was received from the Corps stating that as it appeared that the enemy had retired from the ground east of the line held by the 5th Division small cavalry patrols were to be sent out under orders of the 5th Division to ascertain by reconnoitring the positions held by the enemy. The Corps was informed of these instructions, issued to 168th Brigade, and also that patrols of the 167th Brigade had gained touch with the French patrols in COMBLES.	
		9.55 a.m.	An Officers' patrol of the 168th Brigade had obtained touch with a French patrol on the northern outskirts of COMBLES. 168th Brigade reported the capture of two bomb throwers of the 49th Artillery Regiment. 169th Brigade were made responsible for sending troops into COMBLES to search dugouts and collect material. 167th Brigade informed of this. The C.R.E. instructed to commence work on the road running up the SEVERNAKE VALLEY to COMBLES. Prisoners taken by the 167th Brigade up to this time belonging to the 234th R.I.R. and Machine Gun Company of the 235th R.I.R., both of the 51st Division.	
		10.50 a.m.	16th London Regiment ceased to be in Divisional Reserve and was placed under the orders of the 169th Brigade. An Advanced Divisional Report Centre was established at the CRUCIFIX HARDECOURT (A.12.b.2.2.), Advance Report Centre of 169th Brigade moving to FALFEMONT FARM.	
		11.46 a.m.	Two Companies of the 12th London Regiment ordered forward to occupy the SUNKEN ROAD from T.16.d.9.0. to T.22.b.95.00. From there patrols were to be pushed forward to the German third line between MORVAL and FREGICOURT. If found unoccupied this trench would be occupied by the two companies and their place taken by two support companies in the SUNKEN ROAD. This was found to be occupied by the enemy our patrols were to dig as close to it as possible. This was in accordance with the orders which had been previously issued from Divisional Headquarters with reference to the occupation of MUTTON TRENCH.	/12.40 p.m.

Army Form C. 2118.

WAR DIARY
or
INTELLIGENCE SUMMARY

(Erase heading not required.)

Instructions regarding War Diaries and Intelligence Summaries are contained in F.S. Regs., Part II. and the Staff Manual respectively. Title Pages will be prepared in manuscript.

Place	Date	Hour	Summary of Events and Information	Remarks and references to Appendices
		12.40 p.m.	168th Brigade and O.C. Tanks were informed that airman reported MUTTON TRENCH to be occupied by the enemy. The two tanks at the QUARRY T.20.d.1.3. were placed at the disposal of 168th Brigade with a view to their being employed to clear this trench.	
		1.0 p.m.	The following was the situation on the French front :- French were holding the line from T.22.d.3.0. to T.23.a.1.5. thence along trench to T.23.d.9.2. and were advancing up the trench towards T.24 central. At 4.0 p.m. they had arranged to dig the line between T.24.a.9.0. and T.23.b.8.2. At this time an aeroplane report was received stating that the whole of COMBLES and MORVAL were in our possession.	See appendix D & F
		1.22 p.m.	Brigades informed that active patrolling was to be carried out against MUTTON TRENCH but it was not the G.O.C's intention for any attack on a large scale to be launched against this trench. The intention was for our infantry to occupy it after it had been dealt with by the tanks.	
		2.30 p.m.	The following situation report was sent to the XIVth Corps:- "Two companies of infantry are now assembled in SUNKEN ROAD T.16.d.9.0. to T.22.d.7.5. Two tanks are now proceeding to MORVAL with the intention of working down MUTTON TRENCH. Do not expect tanks to reach MUTTON TRENCH before 4.30 p.m. but they will deal with trench as soon as they arrive there. Do not wish any French Artillery to fire on MUTTON TRENCH T.23.b.7.4. after 4.0 p.m.	
		3.15 p.m.	Patrols of 168th Brigade reported that the Germans in MUTTON TRENCH opened a heavy fire on any of our troops shewing themselves East of the road T.22.b.9.0 to T.16.d.8.5.	
		3.30 p.m.	The situation of Brigades along the Divisional front was as follows :- 167th Brigade in touch with the 5th Division at T.17.a.1.9. and holding the line thence to T.22.b.2.7. and joining up with the French at T.22.d.9.4. 168th Brigade - two companies in SUNKEN ROAD T.22.b.9.0. to T.22.d.9.4. Remainder of the Brigade in the trench system West of the line held by 167th Brigade. 169th Brigade - two companies of the 5th London Regiment and two companies of the 4th London Regiment in the North part of COMBLES. The remainder of the Brigade in the trenches West of COMBLES.	
		4.26 p.m.	An aeroplane report was received stating that at 1.25 p.m. there were no signs of the enemy in MUTTON TRENCH between T.17.a.9.0. and the French left. It was also stated that the French had been seen moving up the trench leading from COMBLES towards FREGICOURT. THUNDER TRENCH appeared to be unoccupied.	
		5.18 p.m.	Advanced Divisional Report Centre closed at the CRUCIFIX, HARDECOURT.	
		5.55 p.m.	Corps informed that the tanks had been seen to have reached MORVAL at 5.5 p.m. and that the latest instructions which had been issued to them were to deal with MUTTON TRENCH at 5.30 p.m. instead of at 4.30 p.m. as previously ordered.	
		6.0 p.m.	Divisional Order No. 45 issued. This order dealt with the relief of the 169th Brigade by the 167th Brigade	See Appendix W

'2449 Wt. W14957/Mgo 750,000 1/16 J.B.C. & A. Forms/C.2118/12.

Army Form C. 2118.

WAR DIARY
or
INTELLIGENCE SUMMARY
(Erase heading not required.)

Instructions regarding War Diaries and Intelligence Summaries are contained in F. S. Regs., Part II. and the Staff Manual respectively. Title Pages will be prepared in manuscript.

Place	Date	Hour	Summary of Events and Information	Remarks and references to Appendices
		6.15 p.m. 6.26 8.15p.m.	167th Brigade during the night of the 26/27th. Message was received from O.C. Tanks that the female tank was stuck at the corner of SUNKEN ROAD (T.17.a.65.80.) South of MORVAL, and that efforts were being made to dig it out. French reported that they had reached MUTTON TRENCH, and that their left was at T.23.b.9.5. Orders received from the XIVth Corps that in the event of the 56th Division gaining touch with the French in MUTTON TRENCH on the South, and the 5th Division on the North, the 5th Division would relieve the 56th Division in that portion of the line as early as possible. The 56th Division providing any troops required by the 5th Division for the support of this line. Warning Order received from the Corps that the French would probably take over the XIVth Corps front from the present right up to the Northern End of MORVAL during the night 27/28th and that the 56th Division would probably be withdrawn to the rear area.	See Appendix III May F.
		8.37 p.m.	Report received from 168th Brigade that the tanks had failed to reach MUTTON TRENCH, consequently the infantry did not go forward. We were now holding the SUNKEN ROAD from T.16.d.9.8. to T.22.b.8.6. At the latter point we were in touch with the 5th Division on our right left.	
		8.45 p.m.	The following message was sent to 168th and 167th Brigades "Situation of MUTTON TRENCH not clear. Tanks had not arrived and G.O.C. 168th Brigade reports he had made no move. Right battalion of 5th Division report they are in touch with troops of 56th Division in MUTTON TRENCH who are in touch with the French at BOIS de la HAIE. No confirmation of this has been received. 168th Brigade will push out strong patrols Eastwards towards MUTTON TRENCH and down MUTTON TRENCH from the North. Ascertain and report exactly what the situation is. 168th Brigade will occupy MUTTON TRENCH when gained until arrangements can be made to hand over to 5th or 20th Divisions."	
		10.45 pm.	Position of tanks was, the female tank T.17.a.6.5. and the male tank at T.16.c. 168th Bde. ordered to give O.C. Tanks any working parties required for digging out both these tanks, which were reported to be stuck, so that they might be available for active operations under command of G.O.C., 168th Brigade, who would use them the following morning to complete the capture of MUTTON TRENCH which was to be occupied as soon as cleared by the tanks.	
		11.0 pm.	Message received from the Corps stating that three tanks which had been placed at the disposal of the 20th Division would be used by them for clearing MUTTON TRENCH on the morning of the 27th.	
		11.45 pm.	169th Brigade reported that the 2nd London Regt. and 5th London Regt. had been withdrawn from the line which had been handed over to the 167th Brigade.	

Army Form C. 2118.

WAR DIARY
or
INTELLIGENCE SUMMARY

(Erase heading not required.)

Instructions regarding War Diaries and Intelligence Summaries are contained in F.S. Regs., Part II. and the Staff Manual respectively. Title Pages will be prepared in manuscript.

Place	Date	Hour	Summary of Events and Information	Remarks and references to Appendices
BILLON COPSE	27th Sept.	12.35 a.m.	Report received from 169th Infantry Brigade that progress was being made with the collection of material captured from the enemy in COMBLES.	See Appendix III MAP F
		12.45 a.m.	20th Division reported that the three tanks at TRONES WOOD would arrive early in the morning at road and trench junction T.16.a.7.6. These tanks had been placed at the disposal of the 60th Infantry Brigade for the clearance of MUTTON TRENCH. 168th Brigade were notified of this.	See Appendix III MAP A Sheet 62 d N.E.
		2.35 a.m.	168th Brigade enquired as to whether they or the 60th Infantry Brigade would be required to carry out the operations against MUTTON TRENCH which they reported to be strongly held and well wired. On receipt of this message they were ordered to get in touch with the 60th Brigade and ascertain the time at which their attack was due to commence. G.O.C., 168th Brigade was ordered to carry out the attack if the tanks allotted to him were ready before those of the 60th Brigade. He was further ordered to report by wire to Divisional Headquarters when he obtained touch with G.O.C. 60th Inf. Bde. Reports received shewed that the night had passed quietly with the exception of some hostile shelling with lachrymatory shells on the SUNKEN ROAD running N.W. from COMBLES. This was included in the information sent to the Corps in the Morning Report, also situation with regard to MUTTON TRENCH.	"
		9.23 a.m.	Warning Order was sent to all 3 Brigades stating that Headquarters of 167th Brigade and 2 battalions would probably move to MEAULTE during the night 27th/28th and that the Divisional front would be taken over by the French, with 168th Brigade and 2 battalions of 167th Brigade in support.	
		9.56 a.m.	The following extract from a wire was received from Corps H.Q. "56th Division will withdraw to-day 6 battalions and as many details as possible to the area MEAULTE - SAND PITS - these troops to move as soon as possible after receipt of this order."	
		11.0 a.m.	169th Brigade Group ordered to move to MEAULTE at once proceeding via THE CITADEL by cross country tracks.	
		11.15 a.m.	The following moves were ordered to take place at once as a preliminary measure to handing over the Divisional front to the French :- 3rd Londons and 8th Middlesex with the Machine Guns of the 167th Brigade actually in the line and one Staff Officer of the 167th Brigade placed under orders of the 168th Brigade. 167th Brigade, less 4 battalions and machine guns actually in the line, Pioneer Battalion and 1/1st Edinburgh Field Co. R.E. to move to the SAND PITS E.18.d. Billeting party of 169th Brigade group to report to a Divisional Staff Officer at the cross roads LE CHAILLOT E.18.Central. Billeting party of 167th Infantry Brigade Group to report at the CITADEL. All movements to be by cross country tracks with ten minutes interval between battalions and 2 minutes between companies. Brigades in the line to leave behind burying parties of 2 Officers and 80 O.Rs. to bury all bodies in their areas.	/12.27 p.m.

Army Form C. 2118.

WAR DIARY
or
INTELLIGENCE SUMMARY

(Erase heading not required.)

Instructions regarding War Diaries and Intelligence Summaries are contained in F. S. Regs., Part II. and the Staff Manual respectively. Title Pages will be prepared in manuscript.

Place	Date	Hour	Summary of Events and Information	Remarks and references to Appendices
BILLON COPSE.	29th Sept.	11.25 a.m.	Operation Order received from the Corps stating that the 56th Division would relieve the Guards and 6th Divisions in the line on the night 30th/1st October. The Divisions to be relieved were holding the line East of LESBOEUFS.	See App. VI.
		3.0 p.m.	There was a Corps Conference at MINDEN POST at which the G.O.C. and G.S.O.1 were present. This dealt with a relief which was to take place on the night of the 30th September/1st October. The line to be taken over extended approximately from T.10.b.9.9. to N.34.a.0.5. 169th Brigade was to relieve the 71st Infantry Brigade of the 6th Division in the right sub-sector South of the LESBOEUFS - LE TRANSLOY road. 167th Brigade was to relieve the second Guards Brigade in the left sector from the left of 169th Brigade to N.34.a.0.5. 168th Brigade to be in Divisional Reserve.	See App. III. Map A Sh.57c S.W.
		8.0 p.m.	Divisional Order No. 48 issued.	
		11.0 a.m.	Divisional Conference held at Headquarters 169th Brigade MEAULTE at which Brigadiers and C.Os. were present.	See App. VI.
		3.0 p.m.	Divisional Order No. 49 issued containing further instructions with reference to the move of the Division in the line. After the preliminary move detailed in Divisional Order No. 48 had been carried out brigades and battalions were distributed as follows :- 167th Brigade H.Q. at TRONES WOOD. 1st Londons, 7th Middlesex, Machine Gun Coy. and Trench Mortar Battery all in TRONES WOOD. 3rd Londons and 8th Middlesex at MORLANCOURT. 168th Brigade H.Q. 4th Londons, 14th Londons and Trench Mortar Battery at VILLE sur ANCRE.- 12th and 13th Londons at MORLANCOURT. 169th Brigade H.Q. at A.3. 3.5. Battalions in the area A.8.a. and b. and A.3.d.	See App. II.
			A Warning Order was received from the Corps stating that the 4th Army would renew the attack on or about the 10th October. In order to ensure the success of this attack Divisions holding the line were to gain a certain line of ground commanding the LE TRANSLOY line by October 5th. This order was shortly afterwards confirmed by an Operation Order containing instructions for operations to be carried out on the 1st October.	
BILLON COPSE. A.19.b.3.8	30th Sept.	9.30 a.m.	Divisional Order No. 50 issued containing the orders for the operations to be carried out on the 1st October.	
			Moves detailed in Divisional Order No. 49 were carried out at 6.0 p.m. Divisional H.Q. closed at BILLON COPSE and re-opened at A.10.b.3.8.	
			The following Appendices should be noted :- Appendix II,III,IV, V and VII.	

Army Form C. 2118.

WAR DIARY
or
INTELLIGENCE SUMMARY

(Erase heading not required.)

Instructions regarding War Diaries and Intelligence Summaries are contained in F. S. Regs., Part II and the Staff Manual respectively. Title Pages will be prepared in manuscript.

Place	Date	Hour	Summary of Events and Information	Remarks and references to Appendices
	28th Sept.	12.27 p.m.	Message received from 168th Infantry Brigade stating that one tank at T.15.c. was reported to have been ready to move at 9.45 a.m., also that 3 other tanks had passed the tram line proceeding to MORVAL at 10.15 a.m. 169th Brigade reported that their rear battalion would leave ANGLE WOOD en route for MEAULTE at 1.0 p.m., and that the Brigade H.Q. would close at the CRUCIFIX, HARDECOURT, at 1.30 p.m.	See appendix III Map F.
		1.0 p.m.	The location of troops on the Divisional front was as follows :- 167th Brigade on the right with 8th Middlesex Regt. holding the front line from the railway running through COMBLES to T.28.b.5.5. 3rd Londons continuing line to T.22.b.8.7. 7th Middlesex Regiment in trenches at MALTZHORN FARM and 1st Londons at ANGLE WOOD. 168th Brigade on the left with 12th Londons holding the line from the left of 3rd Londons, to T.17.a.0.0. 13th Londons in support at the northern end of BOULEAUX WOOD. 14th Londons in reserve at ANGLE WOOD. H.Q. of 167th Brigade at CHIMPANZEE TRENCH and Headquarters of 168th Brigade in LEUZE WOOD T.26.b.3.3. 169th Brigade in process of moving to MEAULTE.	See appendix III Map G.
		1.18 p.m.	Message received from XIVth Corps stating that the French would relieve the Infantry of the 56th and 20th Divisions in the line during the night 27/28th, also the 6th Division as far as southern end of LESBOEUFS; details of relief to be arranged direct between G.Os' Commanding Divisions and French Commanders concerned. 56th Division would relieve the Guards and 6th Divisions on the night of the 30/1st October.	See appendix W
		2.0 p.m.	An aeroplane report shewed that MUTTON TRENCH was held by the enemy throughout its entire length.	
		3.55 p.m.	Divisional Order No. 55 issued dealing with the relief of battalions in the line by the French.	
		5.0 p.m.	A report from the Corps shewed that a patrol of the 20th Division had pushed down MUTTON TRENCH for about 400 yards. It was also stated that the attack on MUTTON TRENCH had not taken place during the morning owing to heavy machine gun fire from the direction of SAILLY-SAISSEL. It was hoped that this attack might be carried out during the evening so as to hand MUTTON TRENCH over to the French on relief. (for situation of DIVISIONAL front on relief by the French see Map)	See appendix III Map G.
		9.30 p.m.	Divisional Order No. 47 issued. This dealt with the billeting areas allotted to Brigades on being withdrawn to the back area.	See appendix V
BILLON COPSE		/11.25 a.m.	The moves detailed in 56th Divisional Order No. 47 were carried out. 168th Brigade, plus 3rd Londons and 8th Middlesex Regt. moved out to the forward area during the morning to VILLE sur ANCRE and TREUX.	

56th DIVISIONAL ACCOUNT OF OPERATIONS

DURING SEPTEMBER & OCTOBER & 1916.

SECRET

UNOFFICIAL: L&N   169

GENERAL STAFF,
56th DIVISION.
No. 0G.59
Date................

ACCOUNT OF OPERATIONS CARRIED OUT BY 56th DIVISION DURING SEPTEMBER and OCTOBER, 1916.

1. On the 23rd August the 56th Division arrived in the St. RIQUIER Training area and remained there until September 3rd, when the Division moved partly by road and partly by rail to CORBIE.

   During the stay of the Division at St. RIQUIER information was received that the Division would take part in offensive operations in co-operation with the Heavy Section Machine Gun Corps, and each Brigade had an opportunity of practising with the Tanks during its stay at St. RIQUIER.

   On the arrival of the Division at CORBIE orders were received for the Division to proceed at once to the forward area with a view to going into the line to relieve the 5th Division on the extreme right of the British front.

   On the afternoon of the 5th September the 168th Infantry Brigade proceeded to MARICOURT SIDING and came under the orders of the 5th Division, the remainder of the Division moving up to the CITADEL and HAPPY VALLEY.

   Divisional Headquarters opened at the FORKED TREE (L.2 b.0.9.) at 10 a.m. on 6th September.

   On the night of the 6th/7th the 56th Division relieved the 5th Division in the line in accordance with 56th Divisional Order No. 31. Divisional Headquarters was established at BILLON FARM on the morning of the 7th September.

2. On the 6th September a Warning Order was received from the XIVth Corps that it was intended to renew the offensive with the 16th and 56th Divisions on the line T.27.b.3½.4½ - 141.7 East of GINCHY. This operation was to be carried out in co-operation with the XVth Corps, and was originally intended to take place on the 8th but was postponed to the 9th September.

3. In view of the offensive operations mentioned in the preceding paragraph, 56th Divisional Order No. 33 was issued ordering the attack to be carried out by the 169th Infantry Brigade on the right and the 168th Infantry Brigade on the left with the 167th Infantry Brigade in Divisional Reserve.

   The 169th Infantry Brigade assembled in LEUZE WOOD and the 168th Infantry Brigade in assembly trenches that were dug just South of the LEUZE WOOD - GINCHY ROAD. The hour for the assault was fixed for 4.45 p.m. By 6.0 p.m. the 168th Infantry Brigade were reported to have reached all their objectives also the left battalion (Q.V.R.) of the 169th Infantry Brigade. The situation as regards the 5th Londons (L.R.B.) on the extreme right was obscure. Information was also received that the left Brigade of the 16th Division had reached its final objective East of GINCHY, but that the right brigade had not made progress and was approximately on the line of the road from T.29.a.1.4. T.20.c.1.5. to T.20.d.3.2. where they connected up with our own troops. It was also reported that there was a fair number of Germans still about T.20 central.

   The 169th Infantry Brigade was instructed to clear up the situation on its right flank by putting in its reserve battalion if necessary, and the 168th Infantry Brigade was ordered to put in its reserve battalions from about the Northern corner of LEUZE WOOD in a North Westerly direction so as to surround the Germans in T.20 central by joining up with the left brigade of the 16th Division along the GINCHY - 141.7 road.

   In order to carry this out the 168th Brigade ordered the Kensingtons to reinforce the Rangers and the London Scottish to move forward on 9th their to the line of the GINCHY - 141.7 road.

4. 10th SEPTEMBER.
   Reports were received during the morning that the left brigade had occupied all its final objectives and that consolidation was proceeding; also that the London Scottish had
   /succeeded

succeeded in reaching the GINCHY - 141.7 road and were extending Westward so as to obtain touch with the Guards who had relieved the 16th Division and were supposed to be in position in trenches due East of GINCHY.

The day was misty and no confirmation of our situation could be obtained from the air. The London Scottish reported that they had failed to obtain touch with the Guards about T.14.c.. On the right of the divisional front the Q.W.R's carried out an attack at 7.0 am with the object of gaining the QUADRILATERAL due East of LEUZE WOOD, but this attack failed.

5. On the evening of the 10/11th, arrangements were made for the 167th Infantry Brigade to take over the line held by the 168th Infantry Brigade, and a composite brigade of the 5th Division relieved the 169th Infantry Brigade on the Southern half of the 56th Divisional front. During the morning of the 11th, reports were received that our troops holding the QUADRILATERAL had been driven out previous to the relief taking place, and that the Northern extremity of our line now rested at T.21.a.4.8. It also transpired that the London Scottish were not holding the line of the GINCHY-141.7 road but that they had on the previous day apparently lost direction in the mist and were occupying the trench facing North East in T.21.a. This situation was definitely confirmed by air reconnaissance during the afternoon which showed that the QUADRILATERAL in T.15.c. was in German hands. The 167th Bde. made several attempts to gain a footing in the QUADRILATERAL but met with no success, chiefly owing to machine gun fire from T.20.b.

As the efforts to surround the Germans in T.20 had not proved successful, the Corps decided that an attack against the enemy in this neighbourhood would be carried out as a separate operation by the 6th Division on the 13th instant, and the front held by the Division was consequently altered in accordance with 56th Divnl. Order No. 35. This operation however, did not meet with success. On the night of the 13/14th the Composite Brigade of the 5th Division was relieved by the 169th Infantry Brigade.

6. Orders were now received from the Corps that the main offensive would be renewed on the 15th instant, and that the main task of the 56th Division on the right would be the clearing of BOULEAUX WOOD and the formation of a protective flank covering all the lines of advance from COMBLES and the valleys running N.E. from COMBLES. The capture of MORVAL and LESBOEUFS was to be undertaken by the 6th and Guards Divisions.

7. Orders and instructions for the attack on the 15th instant were contained in 56th Divisional Orders No. 37 and 38 which included instructions for the use of tanks, three of which were allotted to this Division. The 169th Infantry Brigade were again formed up on the right with the 167th Brigade on the left and the 168th Brigade in the rear, with orders to pass through 167th Brigade and to secure the right flank of the 6th Division in its attack on MORVAL. The attack was fixed for 5.50 am. and was carried out according to time-table. As regards the three tanks allotted to the Divisions, the male tank broke down on its way to the point of assembly owing to engine trouble, and this tank never came into action. One female tank rendezvoused at the S.W. corner of LEUZE WOOD and got as far as T.27.b.4.7., but was unable to proceed any further. The third tank cruised about the Northern side of BOULEAUX WOOD, but finally stuck at T.21.b.2.2.

The attack of the 169th Infantry Brigade failed to make much progress, and the bombing attacks of the 167th Infantry Brigade on the same objective were also held up. The attack of the 167th Infantry Brigade was successful as regards its first objective, but the 7th Middlesex, who were ordered to advance to the second objective were held up in BOULEAUX WOOD by hostile machine gun fire.

/ All

All efforts to make further ground were without avail. About 8.30 am. reports from our patrols indicated that the attack of the Division on our left was not progressing favourably. Consequently, orders were sent to the 168th Infantry Brigade that they would not keep to the time-table issued with Divisional Orders, but would await instructions from Divisional H.Q. before attempting to pass through the 167th Brigade.

The situation on the evening of the 15th September was, therefore, that the 169th Brigade had only obtained a portion of their objective. They had progressed up the LOOP TRENCH as far as T.20.b.8.8., and they were in possession of the COMBLES TRENCH from LEUZE WOOD down as far as the track at T.27.b.4.4.

The 168th Infantry Brigade were holding the main German line running through BOULEAUX WOOD from T.21.b.2.2. to T.21.d.2.7., and had joined up with the 6th Division on our left on the LEUZE WOOD - MORVAL track at T.21.d.8.8.

The 167th Brigade had pushed forward posts into MIDDLE COPSE at T.21.b.2.8.

8. **16th SEPTEMBER.** Was spent in consolidating our present position, and beyond a few isolated bombing attacks, no attack on any large scale was carried out to gain further ground.

Owing to the considerable success attained by the Fourth and Reserve Armies on the 15th instant, further attacks were carried out by the Guards Division and by the XVth Corps against LES BOEUFS and GUEUDECOURT. Attacks were timed to start at 9.25 am.

9. **17th SEPTEMBER.** Instructions were received from the Corps that minor operations were to be carried out on the following day with a view to obtaining a satisfactory line for a further advance in the near future. The 56th Division were to capture the line T.21.b.7.3. - MIDDLE COPSE, where touch was to be obtained with the 6th Division. This attack was to be carried out at 5.50 am. on the 18th instant. The objectives of the 56th Division were allotted as follows. 169th Infantry Brigade to complete the capture of the QUADRILATERAL East of LEUZE WOOD. General direction of attack, S.W. to N.E. The 167th Infantry Brigade were to make good the S.E. face of BOULEAUX WOOD up to T.21.b.7.3., and secure a line thence to MIDDLE COPSE inclusive. The general direction of attack was to be from W. to E. The 4th Londons and the 14th London Scottish were attached to the 167th Infantry Brigade for this operation.

Rain started to fall on the evening of the 17th instant, so that the whole country very soon became a mass of mud, and progress over the ground near LEUZE WOOD, which was badly pitted with "crump" holes, became a matter of extreme difficulty.

The result was, that by 5.50 am., the time arranged for the attack, the troops of the left (167th) Brigade attack had failed to reach their rendezvous. This attack, accordingly never materialised. The right (169th Brigade) attack was carried out under an artillery barrage but it again failed to make good its objectives. The attack was not renewed. The attack of the 6th Division on the QUADRILATERAL was completely successful.

On the evening of the 18th, the 167th Brigade was relieved by the 188th Brigade, while the 169th Brigade continued to hold its present front with orders to consolidate the ground gained and to push down the COMBLES Trench.

A Warning Order had now been received from the XIVth Corps that the general offensive would again be resumed on the 21st September, and that the task of the 56th Division was again to form a protective flank on the line from the N.E. Corner of BOULEAUX WOOD to the Southern end of MORVAL.

/ With

With this object in view the ground in the vicinity of MIDDLE COPSE was reconnoitred, and instructions were issued for a trench to be dug on the night 19/20th running from the tramline at T.15.d.8.7. through MIDDLE COPSE on to BEEF TRENCH in the vicinity of the Tank at T.21.b.2.2. This trench was successfully dug by the 1/5th Cheshire Regiment and was occupied by troops of 168th Infantry Brigade on the 20th instant, and on the night of the 20/21st strong points at T.16.c.1.8., T.15.d.9.4., and T.15.d.8.2. were connected up, and this system of trenches was used as assembly trenches for the next offensive.

Information was now received from the Corps that the attack arranged for the 21st inst. had been put off until the 22nd; it was again postponed until the 23rd, and finally postponed until the 25th September.

During this time the Division was busily employed in consolidating the line. On the 23rd instant, a change in the weather occurred and the ground rapidly dried in the fine weather that ensued.

Orders for the attack on the 25th September were issued in 56th Divisional Order No. 43, which also contained instructions for the employment of two tanks, and instructions to the Special Brigade R.E., who had orders to create a smoke barrage across the Northern end of BOULEAUX WOOD.

On the 25th September, the task allotted to the 56th Division was the capture of the trench running from the Northern corner of BOULEAUX WOOD up to the tram line at T.16.c.4.6., and the construction of a strong post at the Northern extremity of BOULEAUX WOOD. This was carried out successfully by two battalions of the 168th Infantry Brigade - London Scottish on the left. 4th Londons on the right, who were assembled in RANGER and GROPI Trenches.

The assault of the 168th Brigade was timed seven minutes after zero to allow the troops on our left to come up into line, as we occupied trenches well in advance of the Division on our left. The Royal Fusiliers on the right and the London Scottish on the left advanced to their objectives close under a most efficient enfilade artillery barrage. The Royal Fusiliers reached their objective and cleared the Northern end of BOULEAUX WOOD without great opposition, but they killed a number of Germans who were occupying shell craters on the Western side of the Wood. This battalion suffered from snipers in the Southern part of the Wood, while they were establishing and consolidating the two strong points allotted to them. The London Scottish captured their objective the first German trench running N.E. from the end Corner of BOULEAUX WOOD without much opposition. The Germans were very strongly posted in the railway embankment N. of this trench, and for some time a hot bombing fight took place here. The left assaulting company put out of action and captured four hostile machine guns, but in spite of this suffered severe losses from the enemy posted in the embankment. This was finally cleared by 1.30 pm. and 80 prisoners were taken and sent back. Meanwhile, the leading company of London Scottish found the trench objective to have a poor field of fire, and also observed Germans driven out of BOULEAUX WOOD by the Royal Fusiliers withdrawing to a second trench running N.E. from the Eastern corner of BOULEAUX WOOD. This was captured, being cleared with the bayonet.

At a low estimate 150 Germans were killed in these operations a certain number escaped in the direction of COMBLES.

Eight prisoners were taken with four machine guns and five medium Minnenwerfer.

The strong points ordered to be made were sited further S.E. to conform with the greater extent of ground captured.

At 5.50 pm. the 2/1st Field Company, R.E. and "C" Company, 5th Cheshire Regiment were ordered forward to consolidate the ground won. Each section R.E. and each platoon of pioneers had a definite job allotted to it, and the details of stores required had been worked out, and forward dumps

5.

had been formed at BILLON COPSE and at North end of GROPI Trench.
Touch was obtained with the 5th Division on our left after the embankment was cleared at 1.30 p.m., the 5th Division having exactly obtained the objectives allotted to them. The forward trench captured by the London Scottish was of great value in that it commanded a good view of the valley between MORVAL and COMBLES. Patrols were ordered to move Eastwards but could not at first be pushed far forward owing to our own barrage in this valley, but in spite of the barrage our patrols moved several hundred yards East and cleared some dug-outs and captured a few more prisoners.

The Lewis Guns were invaluable in these operations as the dugouts and caves in the embankment were cleared by bombs, the Lewis Guns obtained many good targets as the Germans strived to escape eastwards.

At 10.40 p.m. orders were issued for the blocking of the COMBLES - MORVAL Road to prevent the exit of the garrison of COMBLES. One Officer, 40 O.R. and two Lewis Guns of the London Scottish were moved South along the tram line and established themselves at T.22. Central before dawn. Other posts were established to support them. At dawn our patrols moved down to COMBLES and met French patrols in T.22.d. coming from the Town. From this time on touch was maintained with the French North of COMBLES, and with the 5th Division in the MORVAL-LESBOEUFS Trench line.

10. **26th SEPTEMBER.**
During the night of the 25/26th information was received from the French that the enemy proposed to evacuate COMBLES during the night. Brigades were directed to keep constant pressure on the enemy wherever they were in touch, and to patrol actively towards COMBLES from the S.W. N.W. and N. 168th Brigade was directed to block the roads leading from COMBLES towards MORVAL. A heavy barrage was placed across the valley N.E. of COMBLES and the French were asked to continue the barrage to the South, in their own barrage area.

The events of the night can be traced from the following :-
at 12.30 a.m.   the enemy was working at his end of LOOP TRENCH.
at 3.0 a.m.   his bombing blocks opposite our right Bde. were still active.
at 2.55 am.   the enemy evacuated his post behind the derelict tank at T.21.b.2.1. and the 1st Londons had established a post there.
at 3.0 am.   patrols from our centre brigade entered the ORCHARDS West of COMBLES.
at 5.30 am.   The London Rifle Brigade who had worked down COMBLES TRENCH, obtained touch with the French on the railway.
at 7.0 am.   the French occupied the portion of COMBLES south of the railway.
at 7.20 am.   reports were received that BOULEAUX WOOD was clear of the enemy.
at 8.0 am.   reports were received at 167th Brigade H.Q. that our patrols were in touch with the French along the railway through COMBLES.

It is thought that the bulk of the garrison of COMBLES escaped by the trench running through T.29.a. and b. and N. of FREGICOURT which was not in French hands until early on the 26th. A few small parties who tried to break away north were shot and dispersed by the posts of the London Scottish about T.22 central.

The trophies found in COMBLES were very few -
3 small Minnenworfer
7 small Flammenworfer
1 large do.

Large quantities of rifles, grenades and ammunition were abandoned there by the enemy.

Progress was made throughout the 26th by all Brigades and the situation on the evening of the 26th was that the 168th and 169th Brigades kept touch with the 5th Division at about T.16.d.9.9.

/and

and were holding the line of the road from that point through
T.22.b.1.9. joining up with the French at T.22.d.9.2.   Two
Companies of the Rangers were situated in SUNKEN ROAD between
T.22.b.9.0 and T.22.d.9.0 ready to seize MUTTON TRENCH which
runs through T.17.c. and d. as soon as that trench had been
dealt with by Tanks.   The situation of this trench was that
the French were reported at T.23.b.8.3. and that the 5th Divn.
were as far down as T.17.c.8.6.   This trench in between,
which was strongly wired on its Western side, was held by the
Germans.

Instructions were issued for two Tanks to proceed to MORVAL
on the afternoon of the 26th with orders to work down in front
of MUTTON TRENCH and destroy the wire, and the Rangers who were
in the SUNKEN ROAD were to occupy the trench, as soon as the
Tanks were seen to have accomplished their object.   One tank,
however, stuck at the southern corner of MORVAL and the second
tank stuck near the tram line in T.16.c. so the attack of the
Rangers from the SUNKEN ROAD never materialised.

On the 27th inst., another three tanks were allotted to
the 20th Division for the purpose of clearing up the situation
as regards MUTTON TRENCH.   This task was, therefore, handed
over to the 20th Division and the 56th Division took no further
part.

On the evening of the 27/28th the whole of the front was
taken over by troops of the 1st and 2nd French Divisions and the
56th Division withdrew to the MEAULTE - SAND PITS and TREUX
area.

11.   On the morning of the 29th September, Brigades were disposed as follows:-

167th Inf. Bde.   In the area of SAND PITS & MORLANCOURT.
168th   "   "   "   "   " VILLE-sur-ANCRE & MORLANCOURT.
169th   "   "   "   "   " MEAULTE.
Divnl. Hdqrs.   BILLON COPSE.

There was a conference of Brigadiers and Commanding Officers at H.Q. 169th Inf. Bde. MEAULTE during the morning.

In the afternoon, the preliminary moves as detailed in 56th Divnl. Order No. 48 were carried out, the 167th and 169th Brigades moving up into the forward area.

A warning order had been received from the XIVth Corps stating that the Fourth Army would renew the attack on the line LE TRANSLOY - THILLOY - WARLENCOURT - FAUCOURT on or about October 10th; and to enable this to be carried out successfully it was necessary to gain by the 5th October, certain tactical points from which observation of the enemy's main positions could be obtained.

During the afternoon Divisional Order No. 48 was issued for the relief on the night of the 30/1st October of the 6th and Guards Divisions in the Sector E. of LESBOEUFS.

12.   On the 30th September moves detailed in Divisional Order No. 49 were carried out, and at 6.0 pm. Divnl. Hdqrs. closed at BILLON COPSE and opened at A.10.b.3.8. on the MARICOURT - BRIQUETERIE Road.

On the night of the 30/1st relief was carried out as ordered without incident, and on the morning of the 1st October Brigades were disposed as follows:-

169th Inf. Bde.   holding the right subsector, with
                   H.Q. at GUILLEMONT QUARRY.
167th   "   "   holding the left subsector, with
                   H.Q. GUILLEMONT STATION.
168th   "   "   in reserve in the area TRONES WOOD -
                   BERNAFAY WOOD, with two battalions at
                   the CITADEL and the Brigade H.Q.
                   at the BRIQUETERIE

At 7.0 am., with a view to co-operating with operations further N., a heavy bombardment of the LE TRANSLOY line and other selected points commenced and lasted until 3.15 pm. when the XIVth Corps opened an intense barrage on the enemy's defences on its front. Under cover of this barrage patrols were pushed out with a view to establishing themselves on a line running approximately parallel to the Divisional front at a distance varying from 500 to 300 yards from it.

The patrols left our trenches and advanced apparently without difficulty. It was not until the evening that the left battalion of the left brigade reported all objectives gained and parties digging in. The right battalion of the left brigade reported RAINY TRENCH occupied by one platoon with posts pushed forward to the Crest - The report about the posts was not correct. The position of the patrols of the right brigade was obscure because although the patrols got forward, it was definitely reported by airmen that the trenches in T.5.c. central were strongly held by the enemy. A further air report showed our occupation of RAINY TRENCH doubtful, but subsequent events proved that it was undoubtedly in our possession.

13.   During the night 1/2nd the 139th Infantry Brigade dug a trench parallel to and E. of FOGGY TRENCH, but it was some days before its position could be accurately determined owing to lack of aeroplane photographs.

14. On the morning of the 2nd October, 167th Brigade reported that they were uncertain as to whether RAINY TRENCH was held by them, but they had joined up a line of posts from N.34.b.0.9. to N.34.d.3.7.
During the night 2nd/3rd the right brigade took over 500 yards of the front line from the left brigade so that on the morning of the 3rd the Divisional front was held by 2 Battalions of the right brigade and 1 Battalion of the left brigade. This move was preparatory to relieving the 169th Brigade by the 168th during the night of the 3rd/4th the intention being to reduce the left brigade to a one battalion front in order to avoid the necessity for relief.

15. <u>3rd October</u> By this time it had been ascertained definitely that we were in occupation of RAINY TRENCH, and that DEWDROP immediately East of it was strongly held by the enemy.
During the night 3rd/4th the relief of the 169th Brigade by the 168th Brigade was carried out. Before the relief took place, the London Rifle Brigade seized and occupied at 8.30 p.m. the length of isolated trench T.5.c afterwards known as GERMAN TRENCH. This was connected up the same night by a communication trench to the trench immediately West of it (MUGGY TRENCH), and thence to our front line at FOGGY TRENCH.

16. <u>4th October</u>. GINCHY and the area immediately North of it were frequently shelled throughout the day. A flight of 5 Hostile Aeroplanes over our lines preceded the commencement of the shelling.
On account of the extremely wet weather the renewal of the attack which had been arranged to take place on the 5th was definitely postponed for 48 hours

17. <u>5th October</u> - was uneventful except for the usual shelling of our trench system and valleys to the West of LESBOEUFS.

18. <u>6th October</u> - intermittent shelling of our front line trenches by the enemy with occasional heavy bursts of 77 mm. fire. No enemy movement was observed but his snipers were active throughout the day. During the evening, a flight of four enemy aeroplanes reconnoitred over LE TRANSLOY LESBOEUFS and MORVAL, and were fired on by our anti-aircraft guns and infantry.
From the 1st up to this date a considerable amount of digging had been done by our troops, so as to make a connected trench system which was necessary for launching the attack due to take place on the 7th. This work was greatly impeded by the wet weather which also prevented the taking of aeroplane photographs. Consequently it was exceedingly difficult to obtain correct information as to the position of our own troops and those of the enemy. It was known that the latter was occupying a number of short lengths of trench and gun pits between his main line in front of LE TRANSLOY and our own front system. Reports received from patrols indicated that the whole of RAINBOW and SPECTRUM TRENCHES were wired through; this was contradicted by a special aeroplane reconnaissance. The only definite positions known to be held by the enemy were RAINBOW, SPECTRUM, DEWDROP, Gun Pits in T.5.a. and HAZY TRENCH. It was suspected that DEWDROP and SPECTRUM had been connected by a trench.
The wet weather made living conditions extremely bad, this added to the length of time the troops had been engaged in offensive operations, and the hostile shelling had considerably lowered the fighting efficiency of the Division.
During the night 6th/7th the Divisional front had been readjusted to allow of two battalions of 167th Brigade and three battalions of 168th Brigade being in the front line.

19. <u>7th October</u> - shewed improved weather conditions. The task of the 56th Division in the attack which was to take place at 1.45 pm. was divided into two portions, the first objective was the capture of the Southern portion of RAINBOW TRENCH, SPECTRUM, DEWDROP and HAZY TRENCHES; the second was to push forward a further 500 yards and establish a line within assaulting distance of the enemy's main TRANSLOY line. This second position was to be strengthened by numerous strong points, communication was to be obtained with the 20th Division on the left, and our right flank slightly advanced to gain and keep touch with the 56th French Division on the right.

A heavy bombardment of the enemy's position was maintained throughout the morning; this was not to be increased before zero hour for fear of disclosing our intention to attack. The assault under cover of a standing and a creeping barrage was so arranged that troops which were farthest away from their objectives started at Zero hour and the remainder at varying times according to the distances to be covered so that all assaulting waves should reach their first objectives simultaneously along the Divisional front. This expedient was necessary owing to the fact that it had been impossible to construct a continuous line parallel to that held by the enemy, and a barrage conforming exactly to our irregular line of departure trenches would have been dangerous.

The first reports received showed that the infantry went forward well, and it was shortly afterwards reported that they had gained their first objective. However, this later proved to be incorrect. The left battalion of the left brigade (7th Middlesex Regt.) having reached its first objective and occupied it after some minutes of hand to hand fighting in which they succeeded in capturing a number of prisoners (70 odd). The right battalion (1st London Regt) of the left brigade was not so successful although it was repeatedly reported that it had taken SPECTRUM trench. Actually the left company of the 1st London Regt reached its objective in SPECTRUM, bombed up to the left, where it obtained touch with the 7th Middlesex Regiment. Several Germans were killed and a machine gun captured. The right brigade were reported as having captured all their first objectives and at 2.15 pm. observers reported seeing troops move forward to their final objective. The first definite information received was from an aeroplane report at 4.3 pm. which stated that the situation at HAZY TRENCH was doubtful but it was thought that this trench was in our hands. The enemy could be seen in occupation of the gun pits at T.5.a.4.7. The attack on DEWDROP and SPECTRUM TRENCHES had failed, but we had gained and were holding RAINBOW TRENCH. The observer stated that owing to the strong wind that was blowing he was unable to vouch for the accuracy of his report. Shortly afterwards the right brigade reported that the advance of their left battalion was being held up by two machine guns in the gun pits T.5.a.4.7. Reserve companies were pushed forward with a view to assisting the advance, but they in their turn failed to dislodge the enemy from this point. Up to nightfall, no further definite information was received. At 6.45 pm the following orders were issued:- Right Brigade (i) to push out a company from RAINBOW TRENCH and establish a strong point at N.35.a.3.9. and round up the enemy occupying SPECTRUM and connect up with a post which was reported to have reached N.35.a. central (ii) to dig a trench 200 yards W. of SPECTRUM from which a further attack could be launched if necessary. One battalion from the reserve brigade (169th Infantry Brigade) was placed at the disposal of the 167th Brigade. 168th Brigade was to ascertain whether or not DEWDROP was held by the enemy. (1) If found empty it was to be occupied and posts established to connect between N.35.a. central and HAZY TRENCH. The battalion from the reserve brigade which had been sent up earlier in the afternoon could be used for this purpose. (11) If DEWDROP was held by the enemy a new trench was to be dug 200 yards to the West to admit of bombardment should a new attack be launched. The organisation of a fresh attack was to depend on the reports received from the 168th Brigade as to whether DEWDROP was held by the Germans.

On receipt of information as to the position of the right
/flank

flank of the 20th Division our left brigade was ordered to obtain touch with it about the Southern end of MISTY TRENCH. About 7.30 pm. a report was received that we had a footing in the Northern end of SPECTRUM TRENCH where a machine gun had been captured and further progress was being made by bombing.

At 9.10 pm. a message was received stating that the French on our right had fallen back to their line of departure, that the right battalion of the right brigade had been counter-attacked and forced to withdraw from HAZY TRENCH, and the gun pits in T.5.a. central to the trenches from which they had delivered their assault in the morning. By this hour it was definitely ascertained that the Germans were in occupation of DEWDROP.

20. On receipt of instructions from Corps Headquarters orders were issued for the attack to be renewed on HAZY, DEWDROP and that portion of SPECTRUM not in our hands on the morning of the 8th. The night which was comparatively quiet was spent in digging the necessary trenches and re-organising troops for the attack on the forthcoming day.

Owing to our proximity to the objective it was necessary to withdraw from the Northern end of SPECTRUM TRENCH and from RAINY TRENCH so as to allow of the bombardment of SPECTRUM and DEWDROP Trenches.

21. To enable the attack to be carried out, two battalions of the reserve brigade were placed at the disposal of 168th Brigade and one battalion at the disposal of 167th Brigade. These were to be employed either for carrying out the attack or for assisting in the digging of the necessary trenches. As it was unavoidable that the order should be issued very late at night, great difficulty was experienced in getting the troops into position and it was not until daylight that the last battalion reached its assembly trenches. Arrangements for the bombardment and the artillery support were similar to those of the previous day except as regards the barrage. On the 7th RAINY TRENCH was occupied by our troops, and the barrage on DEWDROP was provided by Stokes Mortars. On the 8th in order to allow the artillery barrage to reach DEWDROP, RAINY TRENCH had to be evacuated. Several adjustments of the barrage had to be made, as many batteries owing to the short range were unable to clear LESBOEUFS and hit DEWDROP TRENCH. This readjustment of lines of fire may have been responsible for the thinness of the barrage on the 8th. The assaulting troops, however, left their assembly trenches at Zero hour irrespective of the distances from their objectives. The bombardment by the heavy artillery was not successful, chiefly owing to the difficulty of observation caused by the weather conditions, and many shells were reported to be falling very short. Shortly after Zero a report from an F.O.O. stated that our infantry were advancing along our whole front and that the enemy could be seen leaving their trenches and running back over the rise. This, however, was not the case and at 3 55 pm. a message was received from the left brigade which stated that their attack had been held up by heavy German barrage and machine gun fire and had definitely failed. On the other hand, the left battalion of the right brigade were reported to be progressing favourably. No definite reports were received as to progress of the right and centre battalions of the right brigade until later in the afternoon when a report was received from a wounded officer of the battalion on the extreme right that he had seen his company go through the gun pits in T.5.a. central and enter HAZY TRENCH. At this time reports from wounded tended to show that the extreme right had got to its final objective. No definite news, however, was to hand as regards DEWDROP TRENCH until a message was received that the situation of the right battalion as discovered by the personal reconnaissance of the Commanding Officer was as follows :- His battalion were digging in just West of HAZY TRENCH which was held by the Germans. His left was in touch with the centre battalion about T.5.a.5.9. and his right at T.5.a.7.3. The centre battalion appeared to be East of DEWDROP. The position of the French on the right was unknown.

22. <u>9th October.</u> At 12.10 am. the O.C. of the centre battalion returned from personal reconnaissance and reported that DEWDROP and RAINY TRENCHES were held by the enemy and that his battalion was back in its departure line having been heavily counter-attacked at dusk from the direction of DEWDROP. It was also ascertained that this same counter-attack succeeded in dislodging the right battalion which appeared to have been digging in in prolongation of RAINY TRENCH, in a Southerly direction, bringing back with them 17 prisoners and a machine gun.

On the morning of the 9th the situation was that with the exception of our gains in SPECTRUM trench, we were back in our departure line, RAINY TRENCH apparently having been occupied by the enemy during our bombardment of the 8th.

During the early hours of the morning 167th Brigade had succeeded in digging a continuation of WINDY TRENCH for several hundred yards in a S.E. direction thus forming a more or less continuous line along the Divisional Front.

23. During the night of the 9th/10th the Division was relieved in the line by the 4th Division and withdrawn to the back area.

Head Qrs. 56th Divn.
29th October, 1916.

C. Hull

Major-General,
Commanding 56th Division.

NOTES on OPERATIONS of 56th (LONDON)
DIVISION on the SOMME 7.9.16 to 10.10.16.

The results of the operations carried out by the Division during September and October 1916 have led to the following deductions:-

Direction of Advance.

1. To give an attack a fair chance of success it must be launched from departure trenches as nearly as possible parallel to the objectives. Complicated manoeuvres, such as a wheel or change of direction during an assault prejudice the chances of success of present-day troops.

Distance of departure trenches from objective.

2. The system of departure trenches should not be nearer than 200 yards from the first objective; otherwise trenches may have to be evacuated to enable the Artillery to bombard. An evacuated trench may be occupied by the enemy; and even if it is not, it is liable to be mistaken during an assault for the enemy's first line.

In order to ensure the success of an assault, a proper scheme of assembly trenches must be thought out, and sufficient time must be given for their construction. To enable this to be done, accurate information must be available as to the position of our own troops and trenches, and the enemy's troops and trenches.

Woods.

3. An attack through or from a wood is to be avoided, if it is possible to work round it. If the wood has been heavily shelled it is impossible to dig assembly trenches in it, and troops get disorganised directly they try to move in it.

Selection of Objective.

4. The selection of objectives should be as definite as possible – i.e. they should be recognisable on the ground. Considering the heavy casualties which occur among officers, and the partially trained state of many of the N.C.O's and men, it is seldom of any use leaving the site of the objective to the judgment of the assaulting troops.

Flank in the Air.

5. Too much attention is apt to be paid to the "bogey" of the flank in the air. Commanders should never be deterred from seizing and occupying valuable ground for fear of having a flank exposed. Such a flank is comparatively easily protected, at any rate for a time, by machine or Lewis Guns, or a bombers post, and one knows from experience that it is no easy matter, and usually a costly one, to attack an enemy trench in flank. For example, the left flank of the 56th Division was entirely in the air from September 9th until the QUADRILATERAL was captured by the 6th Division on the 18th; and again (in GROPI and RANGER Trenches in T.15.d. and T.13.c.) from the night of the 20th to the 24th September. The right flank of the Division in the COMBLES, BULLY and BEEF Trenches was continuously in touch with the enemy.

Information as to Situation.

6. Experience has shewn that the first reports received from units and from F.O.O's as to the position of advanced troops are generally unreliable. Air photos and air reports are the only reliable sources of information, and both are dependent on the weather. Airmen also complain that troops in the front line frequently neglect to show their positions when called on. This is due to ignorance and want of training. It is suggested that a time should be fixed at which troops in the front line should always indicate their position, on fine days by flares or mirrors, to air observers, and on dull or cloudy days by shutter or some other signal to F.O.O's. In active operations a fixed board is dangerous as it is apt to be left on the parados when our troops advance or withdraw

- 2 -

Air Photos and Maps.

7. The air photos are excellent but the issue is so small that they scarcely ever reach units below brigades.

The Army, Corps, Divisions and Brigades all produce sketch maps, all of which vary considerably. A clear and reliable map is wanted, in sufficient numbers to be issued down to platoon commanders. It is of course impossible to issue sufficient maps showing daily changes on this scale. A weekly issue of a 1/10,000 map (on paper and similar in style to the GUILLEMONT Trench Map) in sufficient numbers to allow of all commanders down to battalion commanders issuing them with their orders, would meet the case, provided the periodical corrections were issued on a sufficiently large scale to reach battalions and batteries. At present there are too many different maps. Fewer maps and a larger issue would improve matters.

Liaison with R.F.C.

8. It would be an advantage if rather closer liaison could be established between the R.F.C. and Divisions. If the observer detailed to reconnoitre a divisional front were in personal touch with the G.S. of the division concerned, particular points about which further information is wanted could be discussed with the observer overnight.

It is understood that duplicate copies of reports to divisions by contact patrols are always dropped at Corps Headquarters. It would save unnecessary congestion of the telephone and telegraph lines if observers could state on their reports when similar reports are dropped at neighbouring divisions.

Barrages

9. All battalions have realised the importance of working close up under the creeping barrage. The simpler the task set to the Artillery, the more effective will be the barrage. The task for the Artillery is simple when the front departure trench of our own troops is parallel to the enemy's first line trench, and not less than 200 yards from it. An enfilade creeping barrage is most effective, and should be employed whenever possible.

To avoid complications for the Artillery, it is most important after the capture of a village or wood to push troops forward well beyond it; otherwise the trees will interfere with the creeping barrage when the next advance is attempted (e.g. it was difficult to arrange a good creeping barrage on the German trenches just E. of LESBOEUFS on October 7th and 8th)

The system of dividing the barrages into a creeping and standing barrage is sound; but the standing barrage must stand on something definite, such as a line of trenches, or a road known to be held. A standing barrage on an indefinite system of defended shell holes, gun-pits, and short lengths of trench, is likely to result in waste of ammunition unless very careful registration can be carried out beforehand. Under these circumstances it is better to have two creeping barrages.

An effective creeping barrage in a wood is very difficult to arrange, and unobserved bombardment by howitzers is frequently very disappointing. In spite of considerable bombardment GRAPHIC Trench in BOULEAUX WOOD was found to be almost untouched. The same cannot be said of IRISH Trench in LEUZE WOOD, which was most effectively and accurately bombarded by the German Artillery. This was partially due to the fact that IRISH Trench was originally dug by the Germans and was no doubt accurately marked on their maps.

Liaison with Hy Artillery.

10. The liaison between Heavy Artillery and units of the Division is not sufficiently close. Many batteries of Heavy guns are newly raised and more than one case has occurred of our Heavy Artillery shelling our own trenches. It is quite realised that an occasionally short round is unavoidable, but the delay that occurred in discovering

/and

and stppping the offending battery is avoidable. The present procedure is cumbrous when a message from a company commander that his trenches are being shelled by our own guns has to pass through battalion, brigade, Divisional H.Q., thence from the Heavy Artillery Liaison Officer to Corps Heavy Artillery H.Q., and down through similar channels to the offending battery. It is not suggested that Liaison Officers should be multiplied, as trained officers are too valuable. I think, though, that matters would be improved whenever a heavy battery was detailed to bombard any points in the enemy's line in close proximity to our own trenches, if that battery were placed (temporarily) under the orders of the Field Artillery Group Commander who was responsible for that sector of the front. The battery would then be in close liaison with the infantry brigade, through the Group Liaison Officer, and would have better information regarding, and access to, the best positions from which to observe.

Bombing Attacks. 11. Bombing attacks should not be undertaken lightly. An unsuccessful bombing attack is very wasteful of specially trained men. They are frequently necessary in order to gain some tactically important point, and every means must then be employed to ensure the success of the operation. This means obtaining the co-operation of the Artillery, who must know the exact point the bombers are to start from, and the point they are expected to reach, and the operation must be conducted according to the time table. The bombers must work up close to the barrage, and be able to indicate their position to the supporting guns.

Stokes Gunners, Lewis Gunners and Bombers, must be trained to work together. The training of bombers in the Mills Rifle Grenade is most important.

Pole Patrols. 12. Considerable ground was made on occasions by patrols, who were ordered to work their way forward and dig themselves in. A definite "objective" for these patrols is most essential; otherwise it is most difficult to arrange a suitable defensive barrage.

Digging. 13. Much ground was made at night by digging lines of trenches; and strong points, which were connected up to form a continuous trench the following night. It is of the greatest value to have a definite pattern of trench, and definite patterns of strong points, which R.E., Pioneers and Infantry are all trained to lay out and dig. An adequate supply of tracing tape is most necessary.

Marking Tracks 14. In heavily shelled areas it is of importance to decide on and mark our tracks for infantry. A large supply of signboards painted white for these tracks should be held in readiness. If these were painted with luminous paint on both sides, one every 50 to 100 yards would probably be sufficient, and they would be invaluable for working parties and reliefs.

Communications. 15. The value of well laddered telephone communications was well demonstrated throughout.

It was impossible to find the necessary working parties to bury cables, to any great extent, but it might be possible to select a German communication trench beforehand (where sufficient exist) to ear-mark this as a cable trench; to lay the cable and fill in the trench at once. Dug-outs could be constructed along this trench which would be used first as Battalion Headquarters and then for Brigade and Divisional Headquarters as the advance progressed.

Communication between Coy. & Bn. Hdqrs. 16. A message thrower, capable of propelling the container of a message 500x to 600x would be invaluable. It is understood that the 4th Division use a Stokes Mortar with

/n

a specially prepared projectile for this purpose. The value of such device cannot be overestimated.

Dug-outs.   17. Many German dug-outs in a partially finished condition were found in captured trenches. It would save much time and labour if frames of the standard German pattern were prepared and kept ready for use, so that the work might be continued directly the trenches were captured.

Code A.   18. Practically no use was made of Code "A". It was too complicated under the existing conditions, when the code was changed every day. It is very unlikely that the Germans could decipher the code even if messages were overheard in conditions similar to those that existed in September. If the code were changed not more frequently than once a fortnight it might be so. At present no one has sufficient confidence in the deciphering powers of the recipient to use the code at all.

Major-General,
Commanding 56th Division.

Head Qrs. 56th Divn.
29th October, 1916.

C A S U A L T I E S.

PERIOD.	DIED OF WOUNDS.		KILLED.		WOUNDED.		MISSING.		TOTALS.	
	Off.	O.Rs.	Off.	O.Rs.	Off.	O.Rs.	Off.	O.Rs.	Off.	O.Rs.
JUNE 24th to JUNE 30th, 1916.	1.	-	3.	66	23	405	-	26	27	497
JULY 1st to JULY 4th, 1916.	1.	3	30	347	87	2277	40	1497	158	4124
JULY 5th to AUGUST 20th, 1916	-	1	3	83	20	412	1	22	24	518
SEPTEMBER 6th to OCTOBER 11th, '16	8	2.	81	1148	258	4943	30	1580	377	7773
TOTALS	10.	6	117	1344	388	8037	71	3225	586	12912.

B.M.28.

Headquarters.

56th. Division.

With reference to O.G.59. Account of Operations.

1.   On page 2 para.7 - where it is stated that the attack of the 169th. Bde. failed to make much progress. The whole of the objective assigned to this Bde. was captured with the exception of 100 yards of the northern end of LOOP TRENCH, which although seized at the outset could not be consolidated.   As the 2nd. Londons captured COMBLES Trench down to the track at T.27.b.34.94. and ¾ of the LOOP TRENCH it would seem that the wording of O.G.59 does not adequately describe their success.   The same applies to page 3 line 10 - "had only obtained a portion of their objective".

2.   On page 3 para. 9 - line 26.

The statement that the 169th Bde. attack again failed to make good its objective would imply that the 169th Bde. had attacked the SUNKEN ROAD TRENCH before. This was however the first time that the SUNKEN ROAD TRENCH had been allotted to this Bde. as an objective.

3.   Page 5 para. 10 - Events of the night 25th/26th. September.

The following events and the times they occurred have since been established.

    4.15 a.m. - officer's patrol of L.R.B. entered COMBLES and met the French who were fighting in the S.E. end of the town.

    5 a.m.   - L.R.B. in possession of LOOP and COMBLES TRENCHES.

                              Brigadier General.

                        Commanding 169th. Infantry Brigade.

2nd. November 1916.

APPENDIX VI

56th DIVISION GENERAL STAFF

OPERATION ORDERS

SEPTEMBER 1916.

SECRET.   Copy No. ....

56th DIVISIONAL ORDER No. 28.

1st September, 1916.

1. The 56th Division will move to the CORBIE Area on the 2nd, 3rd and 4th September as follows:-

    (a). Horse transport by road as detailed in March Table "A".

    (b). Infantry, Pioneers, dismounted portions of Engineers, and Field Ambulances by rail. 168th and 169th Infantry Brigade Groups on the 3rd September. 167th Infantry Brigade Group and Divisional H.Q. Group on 4th September. Details will be issued later.

2. Transport columns marching on 2nd instant are not to enter FLIXECOURT until 5.0 pm. An interval of ½ mile will be maintained between brigade groups.

3. Motor transport will move as under in accordance with instructions to be issued later:-

    168th Brigade Group   on 3rd September.
    169th Brigade Group   on 3rd September.
    167th Brigade Group and H.Q. Group on 4th Sept.

4. Application for billets will be made to Town Majors

Date	Village	Town Major.
2nd Sept.	LA CHAUSSEE	Captain MAUNSELL.
" "	ST. SAUVEUR	Captain HUNTER.
3rd Sept.	ARGOEUVES	Captain MAUNSELL.
" "	LONGPRE	Captain HUNTER.

5. Divisional Headquarters will close at ST. RIQUIER at 10.0 am on 4th September and open at the same hour in CORBIE.

6. Acknowledge.

Hdqrs. 56th Divn.

1st September, 1916.

                                    A.S. Bayley Major
                                    for Lieut. Colonel,
                                        General Staff.

        Issued at 6.0 pm, 1.9.16.

Copy Nos:-

    1. G.O.C., 56th Divn.   9. Train.
    2. 167th Inf. Bde.   10. A.P.M.
    3. 168th Inf. Bde.   11. Div. Signals.
    4. 169th Inf. Bde.   12. War Diary.
    5. 5th Ches. Regt.   13. "G"
    6. C.R.A.   14. "Q"
    7. C.R.E.   15. Div. School.
    8. A.D.M.S.   16. Xth Corps.
                                 17. XIVth Corps.
                                 19. Comdnt. Training Area.

MARCH TABLE ISSUED with 56th DIVISIONAL ORDER No. 28 of 1.9.16.

Date.	Group Commander	Units	Starting Point.	To	Route	Remarks.
2nd Sept.	168th Inf.Bde. Transport Group. O.C. - Field Officer to be detailed by 168th Inf. Bde.	168th Inf.Bde.Transport. 2/1st Lon.Fd.Co. No. 3 Co. Train. 2/2nd Lon.Fd.Amb.	Cross roads on ABBEVILLE - ST.RIQUIER Rd. 1 mile S. of CAOURS. Time 10.0 am.	ST.SAUVEUR.	VAUCHELLES AILLY FLIXECOURT.	This column will not make a long halt West of AILLY.
2nd Sept.	169th Inf.Bde. Transport Group O.C. - Field Officer to be detailed by 169th Inf. Bde.	169th Inf.Bde.Transport 2/2nd Lon.Fd.Co.* No. 4 Co. Train 2/3rd Fd.Amb.	Cross roads ¾ mile N. of MILLENCOURT Time 10.0 am. *2/2nd Lond. Fd. Co. to meet column in ST. RIQUIER at 10.45 am. by cross roads at church.	LA CHAUSSEE	ST. RIQUIER AILLY	To pass through AILLY in rear 168th Inf.Bde. Transport Group.
2nd Sept. 3rd Sept.	2/1st Fd. Amb. and No. 2 Co. Train to move in their own time to NEUF MOULIN					
3rd Sept.	167th Inf.Bde. Transport Group. O.C. - Field Officer to be detailed by the 167th Inf. Bde.	167th Infantry Bde. Transport.	Cross roads 1 mile East of COULINVILLERS Time 10.0 am.	ARGOEUVES.	DOMQUEUR - GORENFLOS - VAUCHELLES - FLIXECOURT - LA CHAUSSEE.	
3rd Sept.	Major Dove Park 1/1st Ed.Fd.Co.	1/1st Ed.Fd.Co. No. 2 Co. Train. 2/1st Fd. Amb.	Cross roads on ABBEVILLE - ST.RIQUIER Road 1 mile S.of CAOURS. Time 9.0 am.	ARGOEUVES	VAUCHELLES AILLY FLIXECOURT.	
3rd Sept.	H.Q. Group. C.C.- Field Officer to be detailed by O.C. 5th Ches. Regt.	Div H.Q.Transport Div.R.E.H.Q. " Train H.Q. " Mob.Vet.Sec. " San. Sec. " 5th Ches.Regt."	Cross roads YAUCOURT 9.30 am.	LONGPRE		

Hdqrs. 56th Divn.
1st September, 1916.

A.A.Bayly Major
Lieut. Colonel,
for General Staff.

Appendix VI

SECRET.   COPY No...12..

56th Divisional Order No. 29.

Ref. 1/100,000.
AMIENS SHEET.   2nd Spetember 1916.

1.   March Table of units of the Division into the CORBIE Area is given on attached March Table.

2.   Attention is called to Provisional Billeting Areas CORBIE Area A.Q.S./146.

   Officers in charge of Artillery Columns and Transport Groups should report to Captain Hartley, c/o Town Major DAOURS, to enquire if any changes have been made in the destination of their units.

3.   Acknowledge.

Head Qrs.56th Division.
2nd Spet.1916.

A.R. Barker Major for
Lieut.Colonel,
General Staff, 56th Divn.

Issued at 8 p.m. 2/9/16.

Copy Nos.-

1.	G.O.C.56th Divn.	11.	Div. Signals.
2.	167th Inf.Bde.	12.	War Diary.
3.	168th ,,	13.	"G"
4.	169th ,,	14.	"Q"
5.	5th Ches.Regt.	15.	Div.School.
6.	C.R.A.	16.	Xth Corps.
7.	C.R.E.	17.	XIVth Corps.
8.	A.D.M.S.	18.	Comd.Traing Area.
9.	Train.	19.	Lt.Col.Bendall.
10.	A.P.M.	20.	Major Harding.
		21.	Camp. Condt.
		22.	A.D.V.S.

MOVE of UNITS 56th DIVISION into CORBIE AREA (Issued with 56th DIVISIONAL ORDER No. 29 of 2.9.16.

Date	Group Commander	Units	To	Starting Point & Time	Route	Remarks
3.9.16	Lt.Col. BENDALL, (Attd. "Rangers")	168th Inf.Bde Transport (Less 4th Bn. Fusrs.) 4th Ln. Roy Fusrs.) 2/1st Fd.Co. RE. Transport. 2/2nd Fd. Amb. No. 3 Co. Train.	DAOURS CORBIE DAOURS DAOURS. CORBIE.	Cross roads ARGOEUVES at 8.30 a.m.	AMIENS & VECQUEMENT.	
3.9.16	Major P.E. HARDING (Q.W.R.)	169th Inf.Bde Transport 2/2nd Lon.Fd.Co. 2/2nd Fd.Amb. No. 4 Co. Train.	CORBIE. CORBIE. CORBIE. CORBIE.	Cross roads ½ mile East of LA CHAUSSEE at 8.15 a.m.		
4.9.16	Maj. W.A. CHURTON, 5th Ches.Regt.	Div.H.Q. Transport. Div.R.E.H.Q. 5th Ches.Regt. Train H.Q. Mob.Vet.Sec. Sanitary Sec	CORBIE. CORBIE. BOIS des TAILLE CORBIE. Bivouac at DAOURS. CORBIE.	Railway crossing East of LONGPRE on LONGPRE - AMIENS Road at 8.30 am.		
4.9.16	Major L.R. KING, 7th Middx.Regt.	167th Inf. Bde. H.Q. Transport. 8th Mx.Regt. 3rd Lon. " 1st " " 7th Mx.Regt. 1/1st Ed.Fd.Co. " 2/1st Fd.Amb. " No. 2 Co. Train.	SAILLY-le- SEC. - do - - do - VAUX Sur SOMME BOIS des TAILLES. SAILLY Lo SEC. VAUX Sur SOMME. SAILLY Le SEC.	Road junction ¼ mile East of ARGOEUVES at 9.15 a.m.	AMIENS and VECQUEMENT.	
4.9.16	C.R.A.	H.Q. 56th Div. Arty. 56th Div. Arty.	CORBIE DAOURS.	To be detailed by C.R.A.	Via ALLONVILLE & BUSSY-le- DAOURS.	Tail to be clear of ALLONVILLE by 12 Noon. 20 minutes intervals between brigades.

C.R. Bayly Moir
Lieut. Colonel,
General Staff.

HQrs. 56th Divn.
2nd September, 1916.

SECRET.   Copy No. 12

56th DIVISIONAL ORDER No. 30.

5th September, 1916.

1. The French North of the SOMME have met with considerable success today.

2. 56th Division, less 168th Infantry Brigade (already attached to 5th Division) and R.A. (who are acting under Corps instructions) will be ready to move from 5.0 am. tomorrow (6th September).

3. (a). 167th Infantry Brigade will march at 7.0 am. tomorrow to CITADEL F.21.b. via track North of BOIS des TAILLES and FILIFORM TREE F.25.b.8.7.

   (b). No. 2 Company Train will move by same route to HAPPY VALLEY L.2. and 3.

   (c) 1/1st Edinburgh Field Company, R.E. and 2/1st Field Ambulance will remain at BOIS des TAILLES pending further instructions.

4. 1/5th Cheshire Regiment (Pioneers) will march to BOIS des TAILLES. Starting point - Road Junction at I.35.b.7.8. at 6.0 am. 6th.

5. Headquarters 56th Division closes at CORBIE at 10.0 am. and opens at the FORKED TREE L.2.b.0.9. at the same hour.

6. ACKNOWLEDGE.

Hdqrs. 56th Divn.   Lieut. Colonel,
5th September, 1916.   General Staff.

Issued at 7.30 pm. 5.9.16.

Copy Nos:-

1. G.O.C., 56th Divn.   11. Div. Signals.
2. 167th Inf. Bde.   12. War Diary.
3. 168th Inf. Bde.   13. "G"
4. 169th Inf. Bde.   14. "Q"
5. 5th Ches. Regt.   15. School.
6. C.R.A.   16. 5th Divn.
7. C.R.E.   17. 20th Divn.
8. A.D.M.S.   18. XIVth Corps. G
9. Train   19. Camp Commandant.
10. A.P.M.
                                20 XIV Corps Q

SECRET. Copy No. 12

56th DIVISIONAL ORDER No. 31.

6.9.16.

1. 56th Division relieves 5th Division in the line to-night on the front from the valley S.W. of COMBLES to N. end of LEUZE WOOD.

2. 168th Infantry Brigade, less Kensingtons, will relieve 95th Infantry Brigade under arrangements to be made direct between Brigadiers concerned.

3. 169th Infantry Brigade will relieve the 15th Infantry Brigade under arrangements to be made direct between Brigadiers concerned.

   13th London Regiment (Kensingtons) comes under the orders of the Brigadier General Commanding the 169th Infantry Bde. who will arrange for the relief of the battalion not later than night 7/8th September.
   On relief 13th London Regt. (Kensingtons) will rejoin its own Brigade.

4. Two battalions 169th Infantry Brigade will be temporarily accommodated West of BILLON FARM until the Brigadier General Commanding 169th Infantry Brigade can arrange for their accommodation further forward.

5. 167th Infantry Brigade will be in Divisional Reserve West of BILLON FARM.

6. Relief of R.E. and Pioneers will be carried out under arrangements to be made direct between C.R.Es 5th and 56th Divisions.

7. 167th Infantry Brigade will arrange to send all pack animals of Infantry Battalions and Machine Gun Company to 168th and 169th Brigades. (Half to each Brigade) to be used for carriage of ammunition, water, etc. to the trenches. Details to be arranged direct with Brigades concerned.

8. Lists of code names and code messages already issued will come into force forthwith.

9. Brigadiers will assume command of their sectors on completion of reliefs which will be reported by wire to 5th Div. H.Q. repeated 56th Div. H.Q.

10. Divisional H.Q. will be established at BILLON FARM, F.29.b.9.3. at 9.0 a.m. 7th inst.

11. Acknowledge.

Head Qrs. 56th Divn.
6th September, 1916.

Lieut-Colonel,
General Staff.

Issued at 5.30p.m. 6.9.16.

Copy Nos:-

1. G.O.C., 56th Divn
2. 167th Inf.Bde.
3. 168th Inf.Bde.
4. 169th Inf.Bde.
5. 5th Ches.Regt.
6. C.R.E.
7. C.R.A.
8. A.D.M.S.
9. Train.
10. A.P.M.
11. Div. Signals.
12. War Diary.
13. "G".
14. "Q".
15. School.
16. 5th Divn.
17. 20th Divn.
18. Camp Commandant.
19. XIVth Corps "G".
20. XIVth Corps "Q".

Appendix VI

SECRET.

56th DIVISIONAL ORDER No. 32.   7.9.16.

1.   In view of further offensive operations which will be undertaken on the 9th, the following relief and work will be undertaken at once.

2.   169th Infantry Brigade will extend its left to point where trench issues from N. corner of LEUZE WOOD in relief of 168th Infantry Brigade.

3.   168th Infantry Brigade will take over the front now occupied by the right Brigade of the 16th Division to-night under arrangements to be made direct between Brigadiers concerned.   The line to be held by the 168th Infantry Brigade extends from the N. corner of LEUZE WOOD (inclusive) to a strong point (inclusive) situated about T.20.d.2.5.

4.   The 13th London Regiment (Kensingtons) will be relieved by the 169th Brigade and will rejoin its own Brigade.

5.   The line S.E. of LEUZE WOOD will be pushed forward by 169th Infantry Brigade (within 200 yards of the German trench) running from LEUZE WOOD (T.27.a.5.7.) to COMBLES.

6.   C.R.E. will arrange for two companies 1/5th Cheshire Regiment, Pioneers, to dig communication trench from T.26.a.7.4. to a point S.E. of the E. corner of LEUZE WOOD.   169th Brigade will arrange for a guide who will be ready at their Brigade H.Q. at 6.30 p.m. tonight.

7.   The consolidation of the N.E. and S.E. edges of LEUZE WOOD will be carried out with all possible speed.

8.   Brigadiers will arrange for the construction of assembly trenches with a view to the attack of objectives which will be pointed out to them personally.

9.   Arrangements will be made by both Brigades for visual communication from the S.W. edge of LEUZE WOOD.

10.   Both Brigades will arrange to establish dumps of ammunition and grenades in LEUZE WOOD.

11.   Acknowledge.

Head Qrs. 56th Divn.

A.R. Barker Major
for Lieut-Colonel,
General Staff.

Issued at 1.0 p.m. 7.9.16.

Copy Nos.
1.   167th Infantry Bde.
2.   168th Infantry Bde.
3.   169th Infantry Bde.
4.   C.R.E.
5.   G.O.C.
6.   XIVth Corps
7.   16th Division.
8 & 9   French Liaison Offr.

SECRET.

Appendix VI

167th Infantry Brigade.
168th Infantry Brigade.
169th Infantry Brigade.   C.R.E.

SPECIAL INSTRUCTIONS ISSUED in
CONTINUATION of 56th DIVISIONAL ORDER No. 33.

1. The following instructions are issued in continuation of 56th Divisional Order No. 33 dated 7th September, 1916.

2. (a). One Section 2/1st London Field Company, R.E. will be placed at the disposal of the 168th Infantry Brigade and one Section 2/2nd London Field Company, R.E. at the disposal of the 169th Infantry Brigade from 2.0 pm. tomorrow, at which hour they will report at Infantry Brigade Headquarters.

    (b). Work on dug-outs in the FALFEMONT FARM Line will be discontinued from 12 Noon tomorrow.

    (c). Other R.E. and Pioneer work will continue.

3. Two battalions of the 167th Infantry Brigade will move to DUBLIN and CASEMENT Trenches N.E. of GERMANS WOOD (A.10.a. central) by 3.0 pm. Battalions will march with ten minutes interval between companies.

4. (a). Sketch maps showing the various artillery lifts and barrages are attached (except to C.R.E.)

    (b). The following liaison officers are being attached:-

    To H.Q. 169th Inf. Bde. - One Bde. Commander
                                16th Div. Arty.

    To each Battalion in   )
    front line of 169th Bde.)- One officer 16th Div. Arty.

    To H.Q. 168th Inf. Bde. - One Bde. Commander
                                56th Div. Arty.

    To each Battalion in   ) One officer 56th Div. Arty.
    front line of 168th Bde.)

(c). After the Infantry have started on the attack, if it is essential to turn fire on to any point where the infantry is being held up, or where the enemy is collecting for a counter-attack, the Artillery Liaison Officer with the Brigade concerned may call upon one or more batteries of the Stationary Barrage to turn on to such a point.

5. Prisoners collecting post will be established under Divisional arrangements at CHIMPANZEE (A.5.d.central)

6. Medical arrangements are being notified separately.

7. Acknowledge

Hdqrs. 56th Divn.
8th September, 1916.
    Issued at   8.9.16.

Lieut. Colonel,
General Staff.

SECRET.   Copy No. ....

56th DIVISIONAL ORDER No. 33.
----------------------------   7th September, 1916.

1. The XIVth Corps is renewing the attack on the 9th September in conjunction with Corps to the North.

2. The objective of the 56th Division is the German position from T.27.b.1.5½. - T 21.d.5½.2½. Point 141.7 (1,000 yards East of GINCHY).

The objective of the 16th Division is the trench along the GINCHY - MORVAL road to trench junction T.14.c.5.4½ - T.14.a.4.2., thence to junction of trenches at T.7.d.4.0.

3. The dividing line between divisions will be a line from the GUILLEMENT - LEUZE WOOD ROAD at T.20.d.1.5. to trench junction at T.14.d.8½.4. (inclusive to 56th Division).

The attack of the 56th Division will be carried out by the 169th Infantry Brigade on the right and the 168th Infantry Brigade on the left.

4. The dividing line between Brigades will be the road running N.N.E. from the N. Corner of LEUZE WOOD to the point where the trench crosses the road in T.21.a.

5. (a) The objective of 169th Infantry Brigade is the German trench T.27.b.1.5½. - T.21.d.5½.2½. - T.21.a.8.2½.

(b). The first objective of 168th Infantry Brigade, road from the N. Corner of LEUZE WOOD to T.20.b.4.3., including the capture of the German trench from T.20.d.2.9. to T.20.b.9.1.

(c). The 2nd objective of the 168th Infantry Brigade is the German trench from T.21.a.6.2½. - T.15.c.1.4½. - T.14.d.8½.4.

6. (a). The attack will be preceded by a bombardment of heavy artillery, details of which will be published separately by the General Officer Commanding, R.A., XIVth Corps.

During the bombardment certain trenches may have to be cleared from time to time.

(b). Fifty per cent of the Field Artillery guns covering each Division will be employed for a stationary barrage, and fifty per cent for a creeping barrage.

/ The-

- 2 -

The creeping barrage will in all cases advance at the rate of 50 yards per minute in front of the Infantry.

When the creeping barrage reaches the stationary barrage, the stationary barrage will lift on to the next barrage line.

(c). At zero an intense Field Artillery barrage will open and the Infantry will advance to their first objective.

(d). At zero plus forty the barrage will again become intense, and the Infantry will advance to their second objective.

(e). The objectives when gained will at once be consolidated. The following strong points will be established:-

169th Infantry Brigade.   T.27.b.1.5½. - T.21.d.5½.2½. Edges of BOULEAUX WOOD at T.21.d.2.7. and T.21.d.1.9.

168th Infantry Brigade.   T.20.b.9.1. - T.21.a.6.3. - T.15.c.2.1. - T.15.c.1.5. - T.14.d.9.4.

7.   No. 9 Squadron, R.F.C. will have two contact aeroplanes in the air from zero to zero plus two hours, after that - one contact aeroplane until dark, and one from 5.30 am. to 8.0 am on 10th September.

Flares will be lit as follows:-

(a). On obtaining each objective.
(b). At 6.30 pm. on September 9th.
(c). At 6.0 am on September 10th.

8.   Watches will be synchronised at 6.0 pm. on September 8th and 9.0 am. on September 9th by telephone from Corps H.Q.

9.   Observation on to the MORVAL - LESBOEUFS line is a necessity. Brigades will therefore, on reaching their objectives at once push forward patrols and establish posts from which this observation can be obtained.

10.   ACKNOWLEDGE.

J. Brind

Hdqrs. 56th Divn.   Lieut. Colonel,
7th September, 1916.   General Staff.
          Issued at 9.30 p.m. 7.9.16.
Copy Nos:-
   1. XIVth Corps.   6. 168th Inf. Bde.   12. 5th ChesReg
   2. G.O.C.56th Div.   7. 169th Inf. Bde.   13. Signals.
   3. 16th Div.   8. A.D.M.S.   14. "Q"
   4. G.O.C. Art.Group.   9. C.R.E.   15. R.D.A.
   5. 167th Inf. Bde.   10. French Liaison Offr.   XIV Corps.

SECRET.   Copy No. 19

56th DIVISIONAL ORDER No. 36.

12th September, 1916.

1. The relief of a portion of the 167th Infantry Brigade (as outlined in 56th Divisional Order No. 35) by the 16th Infantry Brigade will be completed tonight.

2. The Composite Infantry Brigade of 5th Division holding the Right Sector of the 56th Divisional front will be relieved by troops of the 56th Division on night 13th/14th September, as follows:-

   (a). 167th Infantry Brigade will take over the Divisional front North of point T.27.a.2.4. Southern Corner of LEUZE WOOD.
   (b). 169th Infantry Brigade will take over the Divisional front South of point T.27.a.2.4.

3. The distribution of troops will be arranged as follows:-

   Right Brigade
   2 Battalions   - Forward area including front line and trenches about FALFEMONT FARM and ANGLE WOOD.
   1 Battalion   - About A.12.b.
   1 Battalion   - About A.10.c.
   Brigade H.Q.   - At CRUCIFIX A.12.b.9.2.

   Left Brigade
   2 Battalions   - Forward area including front line and trenches about WEDGE WOOD.
   1 Battalion   - About A.12.a.
   1 Battalion   - About A.10.a.
   Brigade H.Q.   - H.Q. now occupied by 13th Inf. Bde. at A.5.d.3.3.

4. Details regarding relief will be carried out by Brigadiers concerned direct.

5. Under no circumstances will any troops of the 13th Infantry Brigade be withdrawn until they have been properly relieved and the commander of the relieving unit is satisfied as to the situation.
   -On relief-

6. Composite Infantry Brigade, less two battalions of the 95th Brigade will move to MERICOURT. The two battalions of the 95th Brigade will proceed to VILLE-SUR-ANCRE. Bivouac ground now occupied by 169th Infantry Brigade near BILLON FARM is available to halt in, but must be clear of troops by 11.0 am. 13th inst. Troops will move to MERICOURT, via FILIFORM TREE and cross country tracks - VILLE-SUR-ANCRE - TREUX.

7. 138th Infantry Brigade will remain in their present bivouac near BILLON FARM.

8. ACKNOWLEDGE.

Hdqrs. 56th Divn.

12th September, 1916.

A.R. Barker Major
for Lieut. Colonel,
General Staff.

Issued at 12.30 pm. 12.9.16.

Copy Nos:-
1. XIVth Corps "G".   7. 138th Inf.Bde.   13.) French Liaison
2. XIVth Corps "Q".   8. 169th "   "   14.)   Officer.
3. G.O.C. 56th Div.   9. A.D.M.S.   15. 5th Ches. Regt.
4. 5th Divn.   10. C.R.E.   16. Signals.
5. Composite Bde.5th Div. 11. C.R.A.   17. 6th Division.
6. 167th Inf. Bde.   12. "Q".   18. 1st Cav. Divn.

19 War Diary

SECRET.   War Diary
                                                Copy ....

                 56th DIVISIONAL ORDER No. 37.
                 -------------------------------   12th Sept. 1916.
Reference: Map Sheet 57c. 1:40,000.
           Trench Maps 1:10,000.
           and special map attached.

1. (a). GINCHY and the trenches N.E. of LEUZE WOOD have been
   captured by the XIV Corps, and it is anticipated that the
   situation between LEUZE WOOD and GINCHY will be further
   improved in the near future.

   The XV and III Corps have both advanced their lines.

   (b). The Fourth Army will attack the enemy's defences
   between the COMBLES RAVINE and MARTINPUICH, on "Z" day,
   with the object of seizing MORVAL, LESBOEUFS, GUEUDCOURT
   and FLERS, and breaking through the enemy's system of
   defence. The French are undertaking an offensive
   simultaneously to the south, and the Reserve Army on the
   left of the III Corps.

   (c). The attack will be pushed with the utmost vigour, all
   along the line, until the most distant objectives have
   been reached. The failure of a unit on a flank is not to
   prevent other units pushing on to their final objectives,
   as it is by such means that those units, which have failed,
   will be assisted to advance.

2. The objectives allotted to Divisions of the XIV Corps,
   and the boundaries between Divisions and Corps are shown
   on the attached map. (A)

3. The Infantry will advance to the attack of the green
   line at zero, of the brown line at 0.45 of the blue line
   at 1.30, and of the red line at 4.30.

   The hour of zero and the date of "Z" day will be
   notified separately.

4. (a). The main task of the 56th Division on the right will be
   the clearing of BOULEAUX WOOD, and the formation of a
   protective flank, covering all the lines of advance from
   COMBLES and the valleys running N.E. from COMBLES.

   The capture of MORVAL and LESBOEUFS will be undertaken
   by the 6th and Guards Divisions.

                                                          /5.

5. (a) The tasks of the 167th Infantry Brigade will be:-
   (i). To establish themselves on the green line (vide sketch) by the capture of the German trench running through BOULEAUX WOOD (approximately T.21.d.3.8. to b.3.1.) and the small copse T.21.b.2.8. (which will be known as MIDDLE COPSE) and by forming a strong protective flank one hundred yards S.E. and clear of BOULEAUX WOOD.
   (ii). To establish themselves on the "blue line" This includes the capture and clearing of the remainder of BOULEAUX WOOD, and the establishment of a strong protective flank clear of the S.E. face of the WOOD and from the line of the cutting T.22.a.3.8. along the line of the railway to the point where the road crosses the railway at T.15.d.7.7.

(b) The task of the 168th Infantry Brigade will be to pass through the 167th Infantry Brigade to the "red line" and to secure the right flank of the 6th Division in its attack on MORVAL. Details as to this operation will be issued separately.

(c) The task of the 169th Infantry Brigade (less two battalions)
   (i) is to hold a line from LEUZE WOOD through T.27 central to the railway about B.3.b.3.2.
   (ii) to capture the trenches from T.27.b.1.5. to T.21.d.6.3.

(d) Two Battalions 169th Infantry Brigade will be in Divisional Reserve.

6. Two tanks will be available for the operations of the 167th and 168th Infantry Brigades, and one tank for the operation of the 169th Infantry Brigade.

7. Assembly formations for Brigades are shown on the attached Map (B)
Brigade H.Q. will be established as under :-
   167th Bde.

5.

  167th Bde. in dugouts S. of FALFEMONT FARM
  168th Bde. ANGLE WOOD
  169th Bde. the CRUCIFIX N. of HARDECOURT.

8. (a) General instructions as to the employment of the artillery are issued herewith. Detailed instructions will be issued separately

 (b) The whole of the R.E. and Pioneers will be in Divisional Reserve about   CASEMENT TRENCH   They will be allotted definite tasks under Brigadiers and will be available as soon as the various objectives have been definitely captured.

 (c) Instructions as to the employment of tanks will be issued separately.

9. (a) Dumps of S.A.A. Grenades, water, rockets, etc., will be established as under :-

  By 167th and 168th Brigades in LEUZE WOOD and the FALFEMONT FARM trench line.

  By 169th Brigade in FALFEMONT FARM trench line.

  By the Division at ANGLE WOOD.

 (b). Dumps of R.E. Stores will be arranged by the C.R.E. in direct communication with Infantry Brigades.

10. Instructions as to medical arrangements and signal communications are being issued separately.

11. The Cavalry Corps will be disposed in depth by 10 am. on "Z" day with its head at CARNOY, and will be ready to move to short notice.

 As soon as FLERS, GUEUDECOURT, LESBOEUFS and MORVAL have been captured by the Infantry, the Cavalry will advance, sieze the high ground ROCQUIGNY, VILLERS-AU-FLOS RIENCOURT-Les-BAPAUME, BAPAUME. The XIV and XV Corps will be prepared to support the Cavalry with Infantry on the above line at the earliest possible moment.

 The principle which underlies this operation is to establish a flank on the general line of the SAILLY - SAILLISEL - BAPAUME Road, whilst the bulk of the Fourth

/ and

- 4 -

and Reserve Armies will operate Northwards towards SAPIGNIES, ACHIET-LE-GRAND and MIRAUMONT.

12. The 9th Squadron, R.F.C. will have two contact aeroplanes in the air from Zero to dark on September 15th and again from 6.30 am to 9.0 am. on September 16th.

13. Red / Flares will be lit as follows:-
    (a). On obtaining each objective.
    (b). At 12 Noon and 5 pm. on September 15th.
    (c). At 6.30 am. on September 16th.
Green flares are being used by the Cavalry.

14. Watches will be synchronised at 12 Noon and 6 pm. on September 14th by telephone from Divn. Headquarters.

15. Divisional Headquarters will be established at A.10;b.5.5. at 6.0 pm. on the 14th instant.

16. ACKNOWLEDGE.

(signed) J. Brand

Lieut. Colonel,
General Staff.

Hdqrs. 56th Divn.
12th September, 1916.

Issued at 6.0 pm. 12.9.16.

Copy Nos:-
1. XIVth Corps "G"   7. 168th Inf Bde.   13.) French Liaison
2. XIVth Corps "Q"   8. 169th   "   "   14.)   Officer.
3. G.O.C. 56th Divn.   9. A.D.M.S.   15. 5th Ches. Regt.
4. 5th Division.   10. C.R.E.   16. Signals.
5. Composite Bde.5th Div. 11. C.R.A.   17. 6th Division.
6. 167th Inf Bde.   12. "Q"   18. 1st Cav. Divn.

SECRET.

Issued with 56th Divisional Order No. 37.

ARTILLERY INSTRUCTIONS.

1. Commencing on the 12th September a bombardment by howitzers on the hostile defensive system will take place from 6 a.m. to 6.30 p.m. daily.

2. The preliminary bombardment on the day of the attack will be similar to that of the previous days, there being no further increase of fire previous to zero.

3. At 6.30 p.m. daily night firing will commence, and will be continued until 3 a.m. Lethal shells will be used to increase the effect of night firing.

4. The Field Artillery will carry out wire-cutting and such registration and special bombardment as is necessary by day; otherwise during the day it should remain as quiet as possible, with due regard to its being prepared to take full advantage of favorable opportunities of inflicting losses and preventing all hostile movement.

5. Fifty per cent of the Field Artillery guns will be used for the creeping barrage, and fifty per cent for the stationary barrage, up to the ...... capture of the second objective.

6. (a) At the hour of zero an intensive fire will be opened by the Field Artillery and the creeping barrage will advance at the rate of 50 yards per minute in front of the Infantry, gaps being left open to allow movement of the Tanks, as laid down in the Special Instructions for the Tanks. When the creeping barrage reaches the stationary barrage the stationary barrage will lift on to the next barrage line.

(b) At zero plus 45 minutes the barrage in front of that portion of the XlV Corps, which is to advance to the second objective, will again become intense, to cover the further advance of the Infantry.

(c) For the attack of the third and fourth objectives there will be no creeping barrage immediately in front of the Infantry, but the 50 per cent of the Field Artillery which are employed for the creeping barrage, will creep forward at zero plus one hour, and zero plus 3 hours 45 minutes, and join the stationary barrage on the third and fourth objectives respectively.

7. Gaps of 100 yards will be left in the stationary barrage on the third and fourth objectives from zero plus 1 hour and 25 minutes and zero plus 4 hours 15 minutes.

Head Qrs. 56th Divn.
12th September, 1916.

Lieut-Colonel,
General Staff.

SECRET.

PRELIMINARY INSTRUCTIONS for the EMPLOYMENT of TANKS.

(Issued with 56th Divisional Order No. 37.)

1. Tanks are allotted as follows:-

    9 to Guards Divn. to work partly in the Guards and partly in the 6th Division area.

    3. to the 3th Division to work in their area.

    3 to the 56th Division to assist in the formation of a protective flank.

2. On the nights Y/Z tanks will move during hours of moonlight to positions of departure, routes marked out by tapes. A pace of fifteen yards per minute should be allowed for.

3. Aeroplanes will, if the weather permits, fly over the hostile front lines during the hours of moonlight on the nights W/X, X/Y, Y/Z under Army arrangements so as to cover the noise of the moving tanks as much as possible.

4. The Attack of the First Objective.
    Tanks will start movement at a time so calculated that they will reach their objectives five minutes before the infantry.
    The Infantry will advance as usual behind a creeping barrage in which gaps, about one hundred yards wide will be left for the route of the tanks. The stationary barrage of both heavy and field artillery will be timed to be lifted off the objectives of the tanks some minutes before their arrival at those objectives.

5. After clearing up the first objective a proportion of tanks should be pushed forward a short way to pre-arranged positions as defensive strong points. If necessary a tank may be sent to assist the infantry in clearing such points in the line as may be holding them up.

6. The Attack of the 2nd Objective.
    Tanks and Infantry will advance together under the creeping barrage. Tanks will move as before in column and on well defined routes. The pace will be regulated to tank pace (30 - 50 yards per minute), but infantry must not wait for any tanks that are delayed.
    The action of the tanks will be as for the first objective.

7. The Attack of the 3rd and Subsequent Objectives.
    There will be no creeping barrage.
    The tanks will start sufficiently far in front of the infantry to reach the 3rd and 4th objectives some time before the infantry.
    The tanks will move as before in column.
    Their action will be arranged so as to crush wire and keep down hostile rifle and machine gun fire.
    The infantry must not wait for any tanks that are delayed.

8. The following signals will be used.

    From tanks to Infantry and Aircraft.
    Flag signals. Red flag. - Out of action.
         Green flag- Am on objective.
         Other flags. Are inter-tank signals.

    Lamp signals. Series of T's - Out of action.
         Series of H's. - Am on objective.

    A proportion of the tanks will carry pigeons.

9. If tanks get behind time-table or get out of action infantry must on no account wait for them.

10. If the tanks succeed and the infantry are checked, the tanks must endeavour to help them.

11. <u>General Notes</u>.

Recent trials show that over heavily shelled ground a greater pace than 15 yards a minute cannot be depended on. This pace will be increased to 33 yards over good ground, and down hill on good ground it will reach 50 yards a minute.

12. After the capture of the most distant objectives, tanks will withdraw to just West of GUILLEMONT, where arrangements will be made to replenish them

Hdqrs. 53th Divn.
12th September, 1916.

Lieut. Colonel,
General Staff

War Diary

SECRET.   Copy No........

56th DIVISIONAL ORDER NO.35. 10th September, 1916.

1. The 13th Brigade of the 5th Division is taking over part of the front held by the 167th Infantry Brigade tomorrow evening (11th instant), from junction of trench with road at T.21.a.3.4. (inclusive to 56th Division) to left of Divisional front. Details of relief will be arranged direct between Brigadiers concerned. Reliefs to be completed by 3.30 a.m. 12th instant.

2. Dividing line between 56th and 5th Division will be :- T.21.a.3.4. - N. corner LEUZE WOOD - junction of tracks A.6.d.1.4. - between the N. and S. Brigade H.Q. in CHIMPANZEE TRENCH - thence between DUBLIN and CASEMENT Trenches to A.10.a.0.9. thence through A.9. central.

3. Brigadier Commanding 13th Infantry Brigade will assume command of this Sector on completion of relief, and will come under the orders of the G.O.C. 56th Division until 3.0 a.m. 12th September, 1916, at which hour the command will pass to G.O.C. 5th Division.

4. The 56th Divisional Artillery will continue to cover the front taken over by the 13th Infantry Brigade until the Artillery of the 24th Division is ready to take over.

5. Headquarters of 167th Infantry Brigade, and that portion of the Brigade relieved by the 13th Infantry Brigade, will on completion of relief move to bivouacs at BILLON FARM and DUBLIN TRENCH.

6. That portion of the 167th Infantry Brigade not relieved by the 13th Infantry Brigade will come under the orders of the Brigadier General Commanding 13th Infantry Brigade, whose front will be extended to junction of trench with road at T.21.a.3.4. (inclusive to 56th Division)

7. Under no circumstances will any troops of the 167th Inf. Bde. be withdrawn until they have been properly relieved and the Commander of the relieving unit is satisfied as to the situation.

8. Acknowledge.

                                                    Lieut-Colonel,
Head Qrs. 56th Divn.   General Staff.

10th September, 1916.

Issued at 11.0 p.m. 10.9.16.

Copy Nos.
1. XIVth Corps "G"
2. XIVth Corps "Q"
3. G.O.C. 56th Divn.
4. Guards Divn.
5. 5th Division.
6. Composite Bde.5th Divn.
7. 167th Inf. Bde.
8. 168th Inf. Bde.
9. 169th Inf. Bde.
10. A.D.M.S.
11. C. R. E.
12. C. R. A.
13.) French Liaison Officer.
14.)
15. 5th Cheshire Regt.
16. Signals.
17. "Q"
18. VIth Division.
19. 1st Cavalry Divn.

War Diary

SECRET   Copy No. ....

56th DIVISIONAL ORDER No 34.   10th September, 1916.

1. The following reliefs will be carried out night 10th/11th September on the 56th Divisional front:-

    (a). Composite Brigade of 5th Division to relieve 169th Infantry Brigade on the front S.3.a.8.2. to Corner of LEUZE WOOD at T.21.d.0.4. (In the event of the 169th Infantry Brigade reaching their final objective, point of junction will be T.21.d.2.6.)
    On relief, 169th Infantry Brigade will move to the CITADEL.

    [The COMBLES GINCHY Rd. inclu. to 167th Bde.]

    (b). 167th Infantry Brigade to relieve 168th Infantry Brigade. The front will extend from T.20.d.0.4. (or T.21.d.2.6. if 169th Infantry Brigade reach their final objective) through T.14.d.8.4 to junction with Guards Division.
    The exact point of junction with Guards Division on the left will be notified later
    On relief 168th Inf. Bde. will move to bivouac at BILLON.
    Details of relief to be arranged by Brigadiers concerned direct.

2. Under no circumstances will any troops of the 168th and 169th Infantry Brigades be withdrawn until they have been properly relieved and the Commanders of the relieving units are satisfied as to the situation.

3. 169th Infantry Brigade will arrange that the relief of French Post at S.3.a.8.2. is duly carried out as previously arranged.

4. The pioneer battalion of the 5th Division is placed under the orders of the C.R.E., 56th Division for work on the right sector.
    The 5th Cheshire Regiment will be employed under orders of C.R.E. for work on left sector.

5. Incoming Brigadiers will assume command of their sectors from completion of relief.

6. ACKNOWLEDGE.

                                                T. Bird

Hdqrs. 56th Divn.   Lieut. Colonel,
10th September, 1916.   General Staff.

    Issued at 12.45 pm 10.9.16.
Copy Nos:-
    1. XIVth Corps.   9. A.D.M.S.
    2. G.O.C., 56th Divn.   10. C. R. E.
    3. Guards Divn.   11.) French Liaison Offr.
    4. 5th Division.   12.)
    5. Composite Bde. 5th Div   13. 5th Ches. Regt.
    6. 167th Inf. Bde.   14. Signals.
    7. 168th   "   "   15. "Q".
    8. 169th   "   "   16. C. R. A.

TRENCH MAP.

GUILLEMONT.

Scale 1:20,000.

SECRET.
Copy No. 19
13.9.1916.

56th DIVISIONAL ORDER No. 38.

1. (a). Infantry Brigades will be assembled in their battle areas (shown on map "E") as follows, on the night of Y/Z:-

   167th Inf Bde. will be assembled by 12 midnight.
   169th " " " " " " " "
      (less 2 Bns.)
   168th Inf. Bde. will commence assembling in its battle area at 12 midnight.

   2 Battalions 169th Infantry in divisional reserve will be assembled in their battle area by 4.0 am "Z" day under the command of the senior officer whose name will be reported to Divisional Headquarters and who will send an officer with two runners per battalion to report to Divisional Headquarters at 5.0 am.

   (b). R.E. and Pioneers will be assembled in their battle area by 5.0 am. on "Z" day, under orders to be issued by the C.R.E.

2. (a). The tasks of the 169th Infantry Brigade are defined in Divisional Order No.37, dated 12.9.16.
   The direction of the attack will be from S.W. to N.E. and not as attempted on the 9th instant. The tank (referred to as night tank) detailed to assist this operation will advance from the S.Corner of LEUZE WOOD, and will move up the N.W. side of the trench which runs from T.27.b.2.5. to T.21.d.6.2. During the pause between the capture of the 1st objective and its advance to the 2nd objective, this tank will form a strong point about the corner of the ORCHARD T.21.d.7.1.

   (b). In order to economise men the Brigadier General Commanding the 169th Infantry Brigade will arrange to entrust the defence of that portion of his line on which no advance is being made to a great extent to machine guns, but he will ensure that the liaison with the French on his right is securely established with an adequate number of riflemen in addition to machine gunners.

3. The tasks of the 137th Infantry Brigade are defined in Divisional Order No. 37, para. 5 (a). Two tanks (which will be referred to as Centre and Left Tanks) will co-operate in this attack. Tanks will advance from our front line (about T.21.c.9.9.) along the N.W. edge of BOULEAUX WOOD to the German trench (approximately T.21.b.3.1.) [which runs] through the wood.
   As soon as the first objective has been cleared, tanks will be pushed forward approximately 50 yards to form defensive strong points, until they move forward to the 2nd objective in accordance with time-table.
   In the attack on the 2nd (blue) objective, timed to start at 1 hour 30 minutes, the Right Tank will advance down the edge S.E. side of BOULEAUX WOOD to the cutting T.22.a.3.8., and the Centre and Left Tanks down the N.W. side of the wood to railway cutting T.16.c.5.2. to T.16.c.3.8. There they will be established as defensive strong points until the hour fixed for their advance to the 3rd (red) objective

4. The 168th Infantry Brigade will move forward into the area between BOULEAUX WOOD and the road LEUZE WOOD - B.H.132.6. - MORVAL (head between BOULEAUX WOOD and point 132.6) so as to be formed up by plus 4 hours 15 minutes.

- 2 -

The role of the 168th Infantry Brigade is to protect the advance of the 6th Division in its attack on MORVAL. In order to carry out their role, 168th Infantry Brigade will attack the German 3rd line between the two roads leading from MORVAL to COMBLES and will establish themselves on a line which is shown on attach tracing (of a French Plan directeur 1/10,000).
Tanks will start for the 3rd (red) objective in accordance with time-table. The approximate routes to be followed and the objectives of the tanks are shown on attached sketch in green

5   The time-table referred to in preceding paragraph will be issued separately.

6   The signals laid down in para. 8 of Preliminary Instructions for the Employment of tanks will be made known to all ranks

7   The battalions of the 139th Infantry Brigade in Divisional Reserve will move forward to the trenches on the Southern slopes of MALTZ HORN FARM as soon as they are vacated by battalions of the 168th Inf. Bde.

8   Instructions as to the tasks to be carried out by the Field Companies R.E. and Pioneer Battalion will be issued separately.

9   ACKNOWLEDGE.

J. Bund.

Hdqrs. 53th Divn.   Lieut Colonel,
13th September, 1916.   General Staff.

Issued at 9.0 am. 13.9.26.

Copy Nos:-

1. XIVth Corps "G".   9. 6th Division.
2. XIVth Corps "Q".   10. 1st Cavalry Div.
3. G.O.C. 56th Divn.   11. C.R.E.
4. 167th Infantry Bde.   12. "Q"
5. 168th   "   "   13.) French Liaison
6. 169th   "   "   14.)   Officer
7. A.D.M.S.   15. 5th Ches. Regt.
8. C.R.E.   13. Signals.
   A   17. Tanks.
                           18. Tanks
                           19 War Diary

The following amendments are made to 5?th Divisional Order No. 37:-

Para. 3 - substitute

The infantry will advance to the attack of the green line at Zero, of the brown line at 1.00, of the blue line at 2.00, and of the red line line at 4.30.

Para. 12 - For two contact aeroplanes substitute one contact aeroplane

Artillery instructions.

6   (b). At zero plus 45 read at zero plus one hour.

     (c). In line 4, 5 and 6 read -

will green forward at zero plus one hour and ten minutes and zero plus three hours 30 minutes, and join the stationary barrage on the third and fourth objectives respectively.

ACKNOWLEDGE by wire.

7. All barrages will lift 200 yards clear of the blue and red objectives at zero plus 1.50, and zero plus 4.20, to enable the tanks to move up and join the objectives and destroy wire and obstacles covering them.

Hdqrs. 53th Divn.

14th September, 1916.

A.S. Barker Major

Lieut Colonel,
General Staff

INSTRUCTIONS FOR THE EMPLOYMENT OF R.E. and PIONEERS.

issued in connection with 56th Divl. Order No. 38.

1. With reference to 56th Divisional Order No. 37, para. 8.b. and 38, para. 1.b. units in Divisional Reserve are to be assembled in their battle area as follows :-

    2/1 Field Company R.E. in A.12.a.

    1/5 Cheshire Regiment, Pioneers, in A.11.b.

    One Field Company R.E. A.11.a. (W. of FAVIERE WOOD)

    (Two Battalions 169th Infantry Brigade in Divisional Reserve in trenches in A.10.a. & B. and C. & d.)

    One Field Company R.E. about GERMANS WOOD A.10.a.

2. The 2/1st Field Co. R.E. is placed at the disposal of 168th Infantry Brigade at Zero hour.

3. One Field Co. R.E. and the 1/5th Cheshire Regt. (Pioneers) will move forward under the orders of the C.R.E. immediately the 168th Infantry Brigade have cleared their original assembly area, and will be employed at once on the construction of a track from the neighbourhood of WEDGE WOOD, N.W. of LEUZE and BOULEAUX WOODS to T.16.d.2.8. and MORVAL.

    This route will be reconnoitred as far as possible beforehand.

4. The remaining Field Co. R.E. will be retained in reserve to be used as the situation demands.

Head Qrs. 56th Divn.
13th September, 1916.

Lieut-Colonel,
General Staff.

Positions consolidated
Ens:
Route of Tanks thus:

MORVAL.

SECRET.   Copy No. 2

56th DIVISIONAL ORDER No. 39.

1. The consolidation of the line now held by the 56th Division will be continued. Every effort is to be made to make the line continuous and to connect up with advanced detached posts. Instructions as to minor operations to be undertaken tonight have been issued separately (G.877 and G.881.)

2. Brigades will forward a rough sketch daily showing their exact dispositions and work done.

3. Every effort is to be made to improve the situation by bombing and active patrolling.

4. The following re-organisation of the Divisional line will take place tomorrow:-

   (a). 168th Infantry Brigade with the 5th London Regt. (L.R.B.) and 16th London Regt. (Q.W.R.) attached, will take over the Right Sector of the line, from the railway S.W. of COMBLES to T.27.a.7.8. (point where trench enters LEUZE WOOD). Brigade Headquarters at the CRUCIFIX.

   (b). 167th Infantry Brigade will continue to hold Left Sector of the line from LEUZE WOOD (inclusive) to the track running from the North Corner of the wood to p.132.6. The 167th Brigade will continue to be responsible for the defence of the S.E. face of LEUZE WOOD as far South as T.27.a.7.8, point where trench enters wood.

   (c). 167th Infantry Brigade H.Q. will vacate the battalion H.Q. South of FALFEMONT FARM tonight, which will again be at the disposal of the brigade holding the Right Sector of the line. 167th Infantry Brigade H.Q. will be established in CHIMPANZEE Trench.

   (d). The dividing line between brigade sectors runs from the S. corner of LEUZE WOOD, North of the FALFEMONT FARM enclosure. The Brigade H.Q. at ANGLE WOOD lie within the Southern Brigade area.

   (e). On relief, 169th Brigade H.Q. will move to BILLON FARM and the units of the brigade (less L.R.B. and Q.W.R.) to CASEMENT Trench and the neighbourhood of GERMAN'S WOOD.

5. Brigades are responsible for burying all bodies within their areas.

6. All units are responsible for making every effort to improve the sanitary conditions of their surroundings. Proper latrines must be dug and refuse and other filth must be covered with earth.

7. ACKNO'LEDGE

Hdqrs. 56th Divn.   Lieut. Colonel,
16th September, 1916   General Staff.
     Issued at 9.30 pm. 16.9.16.
Copy Nos:-
       1. G.O.C. 56th Div.   7. 169th Inf. Bde.
       2. "A".   8. C.R.A.
       3. "Q"   9. C.R.E.
       4. War Diary   10. A.D.M.S.
       5. 167th Inf. Bde.   11. 5th Ches. Regt.
       6. 168th Inf. Bde.   12. Signals.

SECRET.   Copy No. 4

56th DIVISIONAL ORDER No. 40.

1. Operations will be continued on the XIVth Corps front to-morrow.
   Objectives of the Corps are as follows :-

   <u>56th Division</u>.- Trench junction T.21.d.7.2. to BOULEAUX WOOD T.21.d.1.5. - S.E. face of BOULEAUX WOOD to T.21.b.7.3. and thence to MIDDLE COPSE inclusive.

   <u>6th Division</u>.- From MIDDLE COPSE exclusive to T.15.a.7.9. where touch will be obtained with the 20th Division.

   <u>20th Division</u>.- Capture of Blue line to T.3.a.2.9.

2. The task given to the 56th Division will be allotted as follows :-

   (a) <u>169th Infantry Brigade</u>.- Objective SUNKEN ROAD TRENCH from T.21.d.7.2. to BOULEAUX WOOD at T.21.d.1.5.
   General direction of attack S.W. to N.E.

   (b) <u>167th Infantry Brigade</u>.- Objective S.E. face of BOULEAUX WOOD to T.21.b.7.3. and thence to MIDDLE COPSE inclusive.
   General direction of attack WEST to EAST.

   The 4th London Regiment is attached to the 167th Infantry Brigade for this operation.

3. Arrangements for artillery barrages will be made by Brigadiers direct in consultation with C.R.A. 56th Division.

   One Section of a medium trench mortar battery has been placed at the disposal of each Brigade.

4. ZERO hour will be 5.50 a.m.

5. A contact aeroplane will be in the air from 7.0 a.m. till 10.0 a.m. and afterwards at intervals throughout the day.
   Flares will be lit at 7.0 a.m. and whenever an aeroplane comes over and sounds its syren.

6. 168th Infantry Brigade, less 4th London Regt., will be in Divisional Reserve.

7. ACKNOWLEDGE.

                                                    J Bird.
Head Qrs. 56th Divn.   Lieut-Colonel,
17th September, 1916.   General Staff.

            Issued at 7.0 p.m. 17.9.16.

Copy Nos :-
   1. G.O.C. 56th Divn.   7. 169th Inf. Bde.
   2. "G"   8. C.R.A.
   3. "Q"   9. C.R.E.
   4. War Diary   10. A.D.M.S.
   5. 167th Inf. Bde.   11. 5th Ches. Regt.
   6. 168th Inf. Bde.   12. Signals.

SECRET.   Copy No. .....

56th DIVISIONAL ORDER No. 41.

1. The 168th Infantry Brigade will relieve the 167th Infantry Brigade in the Left Sector of the Divisional front tonight, under arrangements to be made direct between Brigade Commanders concerned.
    Brigade H.Q. 168th Infantry Brigade will remain at ANGLE WOOD.

2   On relief, two battalions 167th Infantry Brigade will move to the MALTZ HORN RIDGE TRENCHES, and two battalions to CASEMENT TRENCH.
    Brigade H.Q. at CHIMPANZEE TRENCH.

3. 169th Infantry Brigade will continue to hold its present front and will consolidate the ground occupied and push on down the COMBLES TRENCH.

4. The 168th Infantry Brigade will continue the policy of active patrolling and push out advanced posts with the object of establishing a line, if possible, on the S.E. edge of BOULEAUX WOOD, and will get into touch with the post of the 6th Division already established at the N.E. Corner.

5. Completion of reliefs will be reported to this Office

6. ACKNOWLEDGE.

Hdqrs. 56th Divn.   Lieut. Colonel,
18th September, 1916.   General Staff.

        Issued at 2.30 pm 18.9.16.

Copy Nos:-
        1. XIVth Corps "G".   9. 6th Division.
        2. XIVth Corps "Q".   10. 1st Cav. Division
        3. G.O.C., 56th Divn.   11. C. R. E.
        4. 167th Infantry Bde.   12. "Q".
        5. 168th Infantry Bde.   13.) French Liaison
        6. 169th Infantry Bde.   14.)   Officer.
        7. A.D.M.S.   15. 5th Chesh. Regt
        8. C. R. A.   16. Signals.
                                  17. 5th Division.

SECRET.   Copy No. .....

56th DIVISIONAL (WARNING) ORDER No. 42.

1. (a). The Fourth Army will renew the attack on September 21st in combination with the attacks of the French to the South, and of the Reserve Army to the North.

   (b). The objectives of the XIVth Corps include the villages of MORVAL and LESBOEUFS, and those of the XVth Corps GUEUDECOURT.

   (c). The attack will be carried out by the Guards Division on the left and the 5th Division on the right, the 56th Division forming a protective flank facing South

   (d). The boundaries between Corps and between Divisions of the XIVth Corps, and the objectives to be captured are shown on the attached map, which also shows (in red) trenches dug last night by the enemy in T.16., and trenches to be dug by the 168th Infantry Brigade tonight.

   (e). The attack will be made in three stages, details of which are shown on the attached map.

2. The task of the 56th Division is to protect the right flank of the 5th Division, and to effect a junction with the 5th Division about T.16.a.6.6. The actual allotment of tasks to Brigades will be communicated after further reconnaissance. The green line on the attached map merely defines the area in which the defensive flank will lie, and does not indicate the exact line to be occupied by the Division. Personal reconnaissance of the area to be attacked will be made by selected officers of the battalions of the 168th Infantry Brigade.

3. A steady bombardment of the hostile positions will be commenced at 7 am. on the 20th September and will be continued till 6.30 pm. It will be recommenced at 6.30 am. on Sept. 21st.

The ground in front and rear of the German trenches which are being bombarded, will be searched occasionally with 18-pdr. shrapnel and high explosive shell.

There will be no intensive fire previous to the hour of zero.

Night firing will be carried out nightly between the hours of 6.30 pm. and 6.30 am.

The attack in each stage will be carried out under cover of both a creeping and a stationary barrage.

4. 168th Infantry Brigade will tomorrow night (19/20th) take over from the right Brigade of the 5th Division, VICTORIA TRENCH up to and including the cross trench at

T.21.a.20.95. (just South of the QUADRILATERAL) and any
advanced trenches or posts held by the 5th Division South
of the yellow line shown on attached sketch map. Details
of relief will be arranged direct between Brigadier Generals
concerned.

5. ACKNOWLEDGE.

Hdqrs. 56th Divn.   Lieut. Colonel,
19th September, 1916.   General Staff.
      Issued at 5.0 pm. 19.9.16.

Copy Nos:-

    1. XIVth Corps "G".   14. 5th Division.
    2. XIVth Corps "Q".   15. C. R. E.
    3. G.O.C. 56th Divn.   16. "Q".
    4. 167th Inf. Bde.   17.)French Liaison
    5. 168th Inf. Bde.   18.) Officer.
    6. 169th Inf. Bde.   19. 5th Ches. Regt.
    7. A.D.M.S.   20. Signals.
8 - 13. C. R. A.   21. War Diary

SECRET

56th DIVISION ORDER No. 43.

22nd September, 19

(a). The Fourth Army will renew the attack on September 25th in combination with the attacks of the French to the South.

(b). The objectives of the XIVth Corps include the villages of MORVAL and LES BOEUFS. The 56th Division is to form a protective flank for the remainder of the Corps, facing S.E. The 5th Division will be on the left of the 56th Division, and has MORVAL for its objective.

(c). The boundaries between the 5th and 56th Divisions, and between Brigades of the 56th Division, and the objectives to be captured, are shown on attached map (issued to Brigades and C.R.A. only). There is one objective only for the 56th Division (Green line).

2. The tasks of the 56th Division are as follows:-

(a). To secure fire positions about the North Corner of BOULEAUX WOOD from which the valley running N.E. from COMBLES can be swept by fire.

(b). To obtain touch with the 5th Division about T 13.c.4½.7.

(c). To neutralize the German detachments occupying BOULEAUX WOOD. To assist in this, a barrage from smoke mortars will be placed on the area shown on attached map. Details as to the employment of smoke mortars will be issued separately.

3. The following preliminary readjustments of the line will be made:-

On the night of the 24th/25th, the left of the Sector, now occupied by the 167th Infantry Brigade will be taken over by the 168th Infantry Brigade up to MIDDLE COPSE inclusive. Dividing line between Brigades runs S. of MIDDLE COPSE to trench junction at T.21.a.6.3. Arrangements to be made direct between Brigade Commanders concerned.

4. The tasks of the 168th Infantry Brigade are to secure the new German trench running from BOULEAUX WOOD to the tramline about T.16.c.45.55.; to establish a strong point facing South in the North Corner of BOULEAUX WOOD about T.16.c.2.1., and to gain touch with the Right Brigade of the 5th Division at T.13.c.4½.7.

The first wave of the assaulting troops will leave the new trench running through T.15.d.9.4. and T.13.c.1.8. at Zero hour, and will advance under a barrage which will creep Eastwards at 50 yards per minute. (Details of barrage will be issued separately). Zero hour will be notified later, but will probably be after midday.

5. To assist in the operations of the 168th Infantry Brigade and of the remaining Divisions of the Corps, 167th and 168th Infantry Brigades will arrange to bring a heavy fire from machine guns and Stokes Mortars on to the Western edge of BOULEAUX WOOD from Zero Hour onwards.

To prevent the movement of troops, 169th Infantry Bde. will arrange to bring machine gun fire on to the N. and N.E. exits of COMBLES at T.28.a.3.8., T.28.a.8.9. and T.28.b.4.8. from Zero Hour onwards.

A barrage from field guns and howitzers will be maintained on BOULEAUX WOOD as far N. as is consistent with the safety of the 168th Infantry Brigade from Zero hour onwards

- 2 -

6. The attacks on the Green, Brown and Blue objectives by the remaining Divisions of the Corps takes place at Zero, at Zero plus one hour, and Zero plus two hours respectively.

7. A steady bombardment of hostile positions will be commenced at 7 am. on the 24th September and will be continued till 6.30 pm. It will be re-commenced at 6.30 am. on 25th September. The ground in front and rear of the German trenches which are being bombarded, will be searched occasionally with 18-pdr. shrapnel and high explosive shell.
There will be no intensive fire previous to the hour of Zero.
Night firing will be carried out nightly between the hours of 6.30 pm. and 6.30 am.
The attack in each stage will be carried out under cover of both a creeping and stationary barrage.

8. Flares will be lit on obtaining each objective and also at 6 pm. on September 2 rd. 25th
A contact patrol will be in the air from zero till 6.30 pm.

9. 168th Infantry Brigade Headquarters will be established at ANGLE WOOD and 167th Infantry Brigade Headquarters at CHIMPANZEE on the night of 24th/25th. Divisional Headquarters and Headquarters 169th Infantry Brigade will remain as at present.

10. Two tanks have been placed at the disposal of the 56th Division, and will be employed in accordance with instructions which will be issued separately.

11. ACKNOWLEDGE.

J. Burnett.

Hdqrs. 56th Divn.
22nd September, 1916.

Lieut. Colonel,
General Staff.

Issued at 6 - 15pm 22.9.16.

Copy Nos:-
1. G.O.C., 56th Divn.
2. "G".
3. War Diary.
4. XIVth Corps "G".
5. XIVth Corps "Q".
6. 5th Division.
7. French Liaison
8.   Officer.
9.) Special Brigade
10.)   R. E.
11. Heavy Machine Gun
12.   Corps.
13- 20. C. R. A.
21. C. R. E.
22. "Q".
23. Signals.
24. A.D.M.S.
25. 167th Infantry Bde.
26. 168th Infantry Bde.
27. 169th Infantry Bde.

SECRET.   Appendix "A".

INSTRUCTIONS as to EMPLOYMENT of SMOKE MORTARS.
ISSUED in CONJUNCTION with 56th DIVNL. ORDER No. 43, dated
                                                    22.9.16.

1.   A smoke barrage will be placed on BOULEAUX WOOD from zero to zero plus 20 minutes, on the 25th instant.

2.   Eight mortars of No. 4 Special Company, R.E. will be employed for the purpose. These mortars will be placed in GROPI TRENCH, and at other points in BULLY TRENCH and LEUZE WOOD, to be selected under arrangements made by the Officer Commanding No. 4 Special Company, R.E.

3.   Brigades will give every facility to reconnoitring officers and carrying parties of No. 4 Special Company, and will provide any guides required. Carrying will commence early tomorrow morning (24th).

4.   Personnel of No. 4 Special Company will wear Red, White and Green brassards.

5.   Lieut. GRESWELL, R.E. will keep himself in touch with Brigadier General Commanding at ANGLE WOOD, who will be responsible for communicating to him the zero hour and the correct time.

6.   Officers commanding subsections of No. 4 Special Company, R.E. will obtain the zero hour from the Headquarters of Battalions in the line.

7.   The smoke barrage will be employed with a wind in any direction from W.S.W., through W. to N.E. Men in trenches in and South of LEUZE WOOD must be warned that with a wind from N. to N.E. the smoke, which is perfectly harmless, is likely to blow back on them.

8.   The responsibility for deciding whether the wind is in a suitable direction for the firing of smoke bombs or not, rests with Lieut. GRESWELL, No. 4 Company, Special Brigade, R.E., and not with the Brigadier General Commanding the Brigade in the line.

9.   ACKNOWLEDGE.

                                        J. Brind.

Hdqrs. 56th Divn.   Lieut. Colonel,
23rd September, 1916.   General Staff.

SECRET.   Appendix "B"

INSTRUCTIONS AS TO EMPLOYMENT OF TANKS

Issued in connection with 56th Divisional Order No. 43
dated 22nd September 1916.

----

1. Two tanks are placed at the disposal of the 56th Division for the operations of the 25th inst. These tanks will only be employed after the main operations have succeeded.

2. Tanks will rendezvous in the Quarry (T.20.d.2.1.) W. of LEUZE WOOD on the night of the 24/25th inst. Their route to the rendezvous will be taped out -by 10 am. on the 24th- /under arrangements to be made by the Officer Commanding 1/5th Cheshire Regiment (Pioneers)   C.R.A., Brigades and O.C. Signals are responsible for burying wires at any points where they cross the taped route of the tanks.

3. The task of the Tanks is as follows :-

    To proceed by the GUILLEMONT - COMBLES Road between BOULEAUX and LEUZE WOODS, to clear STEW TRENCH, the Northern end of LOOP TRENCH, the orchard about T.22.c. 0.0. and the trenches in T.28.a. and to block the N.E. exits of COMBLES about T.28.a.8.9. and T.28.b.4.7.

4. (a) 167th Infantry Brigade will have bombing parties ready to take advantage of any success obtained by the Tanks N. of the Combles Road, and to occupy STEW TRENCH and the ORCHARD about T.22.c.0.0.

   (b) 169th Infantry Brigade will have bombing parties ready to take advantage of any success gained by the Tanks South of the COMBLES Road, and will occupy the whole of LOOP TRENCH and the Trenches in T.28.a.

5. Lieut. Sir J.L.DASHWOOD, -in command of the two tanks- will keep himself in touch with 168th Infantry Brigade H.Q. at ANGLE WOOD during the afternoon of 25th inst. As soon as information has been received of the success of the major operations, the message "Tanks Advance" will be sent to him through 168th Inf. Bde. H.Q.

                                                            PTO

167th Infantry Brigade will arrange for visual signal communication direct from MALTZ HORN HILL to the Tanks in the QUARRY (T.20.d.2.1.) for use in case of the wires being out.

8. ACKNOWLEDGE.

J Brind

Head Qrs. 56th Divn.
23rd September, 1916.

Lieut-Colonel,
General Staff.

KEY.

APPROXIMATE DEPARTURE LINE. —— —— ——

1st BOUND. ————————

2nd BOUND. ————————

3rd BOUND. ————————

SMOKE BARRAGE. ▨▨▨

DIVIDENG LINE BETWEEN DIVISIONS. ————————

- - - - - - - - - - - - - - - - - - - -

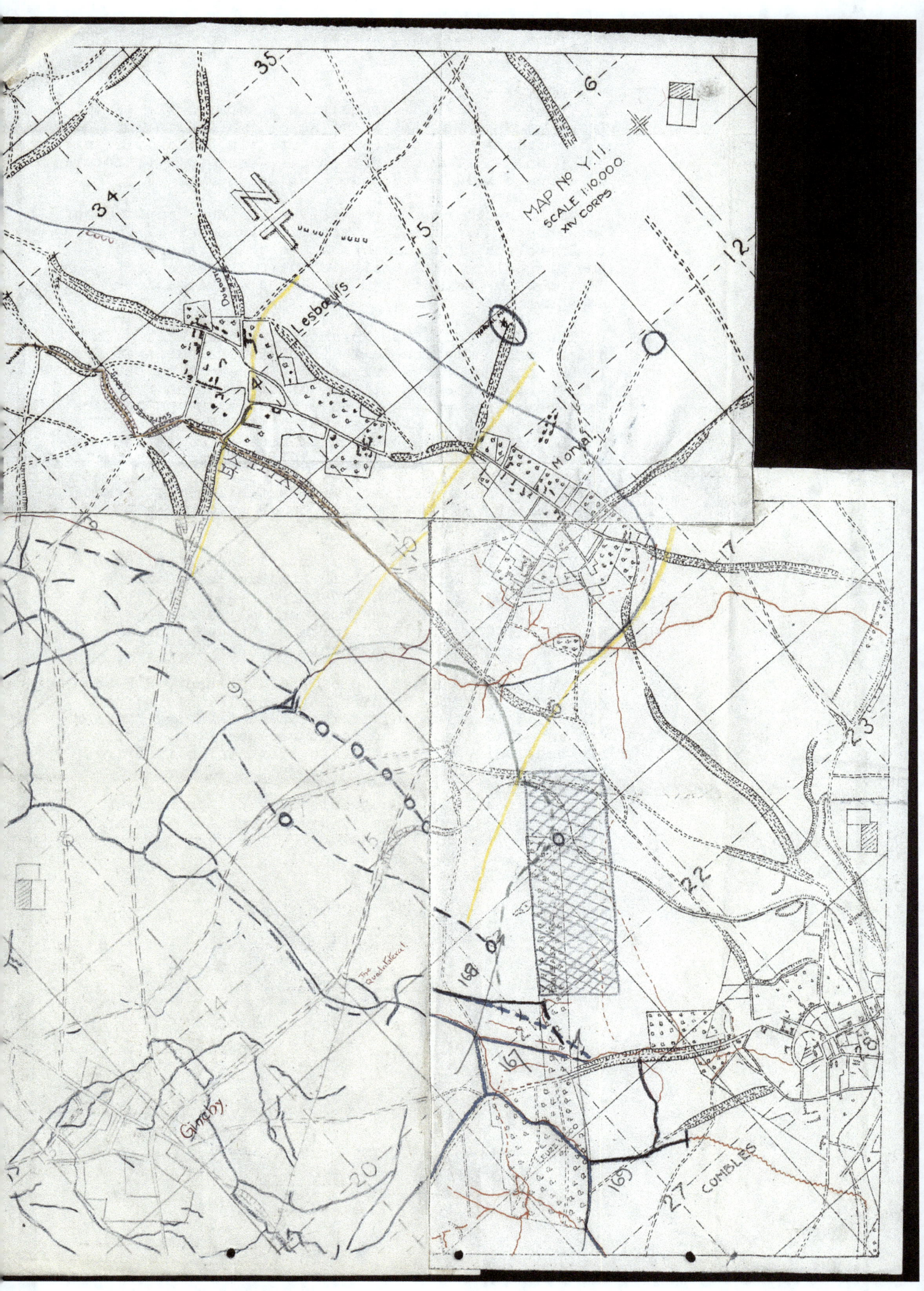

SECRET

56th DIVISIONAL ORDER No. 44.

23rd September, 1916.

1. The time at which assaulting troops of the 168th Infantry Brigade will leave RANGER TRENCH is Zero plus # "A" minutes, not Zero as stated in 56th Divisional Order No. 43 of 22nd September. Amendments to details of barrage will be issued to all concerned.

2. All assaulting troops will be in their positions of assembly by 6 am. on the 25th. Brigades will forward to Divisional Headquarters a sketch or report showing the dispositions of units in their Brigades after 6 am. on the 25th instant, and positions of Battalion Headquarters.

3. The 167th and 169th Infantry Brigades will each detail one battalion to be in Divisional Reserve from 10 am. on the 25th. Brigades will report to Divisional Headquarters the battalions selected and where located. Each battalion will send an officer with two runners to Brigade Headquarters at CHIMPANZEE TRENCH at 12 noon on the 25th. Orders for battalions in Divisional Reserve will be sent through 167th Brigade Headquarters.

4. 168th Infantry Brigade will establish its Advanced Headquarters at the Western Corner of LEUZE WOOD from 10.0 am on the 25th.

5. Visual signal communication will be established between LEUZE WOOD and 139th Brigade Headquarters at the CRUCIFIX. 168th Infantry Brigade will be responsible for the personnel and all arrangements at LEUZE WOOD, and 169th Infantry Brigade for the personnel and all arrangements at the CRUCIFIX.

6. Two sections 2/1st London Field Company, R.E. and one company 1/5th Cheshire Regiment (Pioneers) are placed at the disposal of the 168th Infantry Brigade for consolidation of the captured position. Officers of these units will report to 168th Infantry Brigade for instructions.

7. Watches will be synchronised by telephone from Divisional Headquarters at 6.0 pm. on the 24th and 9.0 am. on the 25th instant.

8. ACKNOWLEDGE.

"A" will be notified later.

Hdqrs. 56th Divn.   Lieut. Colonel,

23rd September, 1916.   General Staff.

Issued at   23.9.16.

Copy Nos:-
1. G.O.C., 56th Div.   11. Heavy Machine Gun
2. "G".   12.   Corps.
3. War Diary.   13 - 20. C. R. A.
4. XIVth Corps "G".   21. C. R. E.
5. XIVth Corps "Q".   22. "Q".
6. 5th Division.   23. Signals.
7. French Liaison   24. A.D.M.S.
8.   Officer.   25. 167th Infantry Bde.
9.) Special Brigade   26. 168th Infantry Bde.
10.)   R. E.   27. 169th Infantry Bde.
    28. 5th Ches. Regiment.

SECRET.   Copy No. 4

56th DIVISIONAL ORDER No. 45.

                                                26th September,
                                                     1916.

1.   The 167th Infantry Brigade will take over the
     front now held by the 169th Infantry Brigade
     tonight 26th/27th September.

       On relief, one battalion will remain at ANGLE
     WOOD, one battalion to move to MALTZ HORN FARM
     TRENCH, and two battalions to CASEMENT TRENCH.
       One battalion of the 167th Infantry Brigade
     will be accommodated at MALTZ HORN FARM TRENCH.

2.   The 167th Infantry Brigade, on taking over the
     line, will obtain touch with the French on their
     right. The dividing line between British and
     French in COMBLES is the railway line.
       The 168th Infantry Brigade will similarly
     obtain touch with the 5th Division on their left.
       Point of junction between   brigades
     will remain as at present, point to be settled
     by Brigadiers concerned direct.
       Boundary between Brigades runs from this point
     to junction of LEUZE and BOULEAUX WOODS at
     T.21.d.1.5. and thence along Southern edge of
     LEUZE WOOD to Northern edge of FALFEMONT FARM
     enclosure.

3.   Headquarters of Brigades will be -

       167th Infantry Brigade   CHIMPANZEE TRENCH.
       168th   "   "   ANGLE WOOD
                                       (Advd. H.Q. LEUZE WOOD.)
       169th   "   "   CRUCIFIX.

4.   Under no circumstances will any troops of the
     169th Infantry Brigade be withdrawn until they
     have been properly relieved and the Commanders
     of the relieving units satisfied as to the
     situation.

     5 acknowledge

Hdqrs. 56th Divn.   Lieut. Colonel,
26th September, 1916.   General Staff.

         Issued at 6.0 pm. 26.9.16.

Copy Nos:-
    1. XIVth Corps   9. A.D.M.S.
    2. G.O.C., 56th Divn.   10. C.R.E.
    3. Guards Division.   11.) French Liaison Offr.
    4. War Diary.   12.)
    5. 167th Inf. Bde.   13. 5th Ches. Regt.
    6. 168th "   "   14. Signals.
    7. 169th "   "   15. "Q".
    8. C.R.A.   16. "G".
                            17. 20th Division

"A" Form. Army Form C. 2121.

MESSAGES AND SIGNALS. No. of Message _____

Prefix....Code....m.	Words	Charge	This message is on a/c of:	Recd. at....m.
Office of Origin and Service Instructions.				
	Sent		....................Service.	Date...........
	At........m.			From..........
	To			
	By		(Signature of "Franking Officer.")	By

TO { War Diary

Sender's Number: 9233 Day of Month: In reply to Number: A A A

27

56th Div. Order No. 48.

1. 168th Inf. Bde. (with 2 Bns. 167th Inf. Bde. attached) will be relieved on the Divnl. front tonight by the French (unit will be notified later)

2. On relief Bns. of 168th Inf. Bde. will be accommodated in DUBLIN and CASEMENT TRENCHES and the area S. of GERMANS WOOD. Bde. H.Q. of 168th Inf. Bde. will be established at CHIMPANZEE for tonight. 3rd Londons and 7th Middlesex will remain attached to the 168th Inf. Bde. until further orders.

3. Details of relief will be arranged by the 168th Inf. Bde. direct with the French units concerned. No unit will be withdrawn until properly relieved and the commanders of the relieving units are satisfied as to the situation. Completion of relief will be reported to Div. H.Q. The relief is to be completed by 6 am. tomorrow (28th).

4. Acknowledge.

From: LONGACRE.
Place
Time

56th DIVISIONAL ORDER No. 47.

Copy No. 13

1. 168th Infantry Brigade with two battalions 167th Infantry Brigade (attached) will move to Ville Sur ANCRE and TREUX to-morrow, 28th inst., under orders to be issued by 168th Infantry Brigade. Head of column to leave GERMANS WOOD at 2.0 p.m. Ten minutes interval between battalions and 100 yards between companies. Route by cross country tracks via the CITADEL.

2. On arrival 168th Infantry Brigade will be accommodated in VILLE SUR ANCRE, and the two battalions 167th Infantry Bde. in TREUX. The Machine Gun detachment of the 167th M.G.Coy. will rejoin its company at the SAND PITS.

3. The 2/1st Field Coy. R.E. will move under orders to be issued by the C.R.E., and after the infantry.

4. On arrival at TREUX the 3rd London Regiment and 8th Middlesex Regiment come under the orders of the Brigadier General Commanding 167th Infantry Brigade

5. Staff Captain and billeting parties will meet the D.A.A. & Q.M.G. at the TOWN MAJOR'S Office at VILLE SUR ANCRE at 12 noon.

6. Completion of moves will be reported to Divisional H.Q.

7. ACKNOWLEDGE.

Head Qrs. 56th Divn.

27th September, 1916.

Lieut-Colonel,
General Staff.

Issued at 9.30 p.m. 27.9.16.

Copy Nos.
1. 167th Infantry Bde.
2. 168th Infantry Bde.
3. 169th Infantry Bde.
4. C.R.A.
5. C.R.E.
6. A.D.M.S.
7. 1/5th Ches. Regt.
8. O.C. Signals.
9. 20th Division.
10. "Q"
11. "G"
12. XIVth Corps.
13. War Diary.

SECRET.   Copy No. 2....

56th DIVISIONAL ORDER No. 48.
                                                  28.9.16.

1. The 56th Division is to relieve the 6th and Guards
    Divisions in the line from approximately T.10.b.9.9.
    to N.34.a.0.5 on the night of the 30th/1st October.
        The 169th Infantry Brigade will relieve the 71st
    Infantry Brigade of the 6th Division in the Sector
    South of the LES BOEUFS - LE TRANSLOY Road. Brigade
    H.Q. at QUARRY T.19.c.1.2.
        The 167th Infantry Brigade will relieve the 2nd Guards
    Bde in the Sector North of that road (inclusive) Brigade
    H.Q. at T.19.a.0.3.
        The 168th Infantry Brigade will be in Divnl. Reserve.
        Further orders as to the relief will be issued
    tomorrow.

2   The following preliminary moves will take place
    tomorrow, 29th instant:-
    (a). 167th Infantry Brigade (less the two battalions
         at MORLANCOURT) will march from SAND PITS at
         1 pm. to TRONES WOOD where they will relieve the
         2nd Bn. Scots Guards and 1st Bn. Welsh Guards.
         Brigade H.Q. will be established in DUMMY TRENCH,
         S.23.d.5.2.
         On arrival 167th Infantry Brigade comes under
         the orders of the General Officer Commanding Guards
         Division, to whom Brigadier General FREETH, C.M.G.,
         D.S.O., will report his arrival.

    (b). The 169th Infantry Brigade will march from MEAULTE
         at 2 pm. tomorrow, 29th instant, to area A.8.a and b.
         and A.3.d., where they will relieve the 18th
         Infantry Brigade of the 6th Division.
         Brigade H.Q. will be established at A.3.d.5.5.
         On arrival, the 169th Infantry Brigade comes under
         the orders of the General Officer Commanding 6th
         Division, to whom Brigadier General COKE, C.M.G.,
         will report his arrival.

3. Route for both Brigades will be by cross-country tracks
    via the CITADEL. Ten minutes interval will be maintained
    between battalions, and 100 yards between companies.
        Rear parties and all details will be clear of billets
    and bivouacs, which will be left clean by 4 pm.

4. Staff Captains and advanced parties will reach their
    destinations by 2 pm. and report to representatives of
    the Brigades they are to relieve.

5. The 168th Infantry Brigade, two battalions 167th
    Infantry Brigade (under the command of Lieut. Colonel
    INGPEN, D.S.O.) and the R.E. and Pioneers all move to
    the forward area about TRONES and BERNAFAY WOODS on
    the 30th instant.

6. Advanced Divisional Headquarters will be established
    East of the BRIQUETERIE ROAD, at A.10.b.3.8. by 6 pm.
    on the 30th instant.

                                                    /7.

- 2 -

7. The General Officer Commanding 56th Division assumes command of the new Divisional front at 9 am. on the 1st October.

8. ACKNOWLEDGE.

J. Broid

Hdqrs. 56th Divn.
28th September, 1916.

Lieut. Colonel,
General Staff.

Issued at 8 p.m. 28.9.16.

Copy Nos:-

1. XIVth Corps."G".
2. G.O.C., 56th Divn.
3. 167th Inf. Bde.
4. 138th " "
5. 169th " "
6. C. R. A.
7. A.D.M.S.
8. C. R. E.
9. Guards Divn.
10. 6th Division.
11. 20th Division.
12. 5th Ches. Regt.
13. "G"
14. "Q".
15. War Diary.
16.) French Liaison
17.) Officer.
18. XIVth Corps "Q".
19 56th Signals

SECRET.   Copy No. 16

56th DIVISIONAL ORDER No. 49.

1. The 169th Infantry Brigade will relieve the 71st Bde. of the 6th Division in the front line from their junction with the French about T.10.b.3½.5 to the junction of the 6th and Guards Divisions at T.4.b.5.4. on the night of the 30th/1st October.

    Details will be arranged direct between Brigadier Generals concerned. Brigadier General Commanding 169th Infantry Brigade will assume command of the Sector on completion of relief. Relief must be completed by 5.30 a.m.

2. The 167th Infantry Brigade will relieve the 2nd Guards Brigade in the Sector T.4.b.5.4. to N.34.a.0.5.(approximately) on the night of the 30th/1st October under arrangements to be made direct between Briagdier Generals concerned.

    The Brigadier General Commanding 167th Infantry Brigade will assume command of the Sector on completion of relief. Relief must be completed by 5.30 a.m.

3. Two battalions 167th Infantry Brigade now at MORLANCOURT will march at 9.0 a.m. to-morrow under the orders of Lieut-Colonel INGPEN, D.S.O., Commanding 8th Middlesex Regiment. These battalions will halt for midday rest at BILLON CAMP, and will move on to trenches T.8 Central and TRONES WOOD under orders to be issued by the 167th Infantry Brigade. Route by cross country tracks.

4. The 168th Infantry Brigade will march from VILLE-SUR-ANCRE at 10.0 a.m. to-morrow to the CITADEL. Two battalions will remain at the CITADEL, and Brigade H.Q. and 2 battalions will move on to the TRONES WOOD - BERNAFAY WOOD area, which is to be vacated by the 16th Brigade of the 6th Division by 4.0 p.m. Brigade H.Q. at the BRIQUETERIE. Advanced parties to reach BRIQUETERIE H.Q. by 2.0 p.m.

5. 1/5th Cheshire Regiment (Pioneers) will march from the SAND PITS at 12 noon. Headquarters and 2 Coys. will relieve the 6th Divisional Pioneers in Northern half of A.4.c. Two Companies will relieve the Pioneers of the Guards Division in trenches running S.E. from C.29 central. These reliefs to be completed by 6.0 p.m.

6. 1/1st Edinburgh Field Coy. R.E. relieves the 73rd Field Coy. at T.9.a.1.5. at 3.0 p.m. 2/2nd London Field Coy. R.E. will relieve a Field Coy. of the 6th Division to-morrow afternoon under arrangements to be made by the C.R.E. 2/1st London Field Coy. R.E. remains at BILLON FARM.

7. All columns will move with intervals of 10 minutes between battalions and 100 yards between companies. Routes by cross country tracks via THE CITADEL.

8. 2nd Echelon Divisional H.Q. will move to H.Q. at A.3.c. 1.6. which are being vacated by the 6th Division by 9.0 a.m. on 1st October. Hour of move will be arranged and notified to all concerned by 56th Division "Q".

/9.

9. The front of the 56th Division will be covered by the Guards Divisional Artillery and one Brigade each of the 4th, 6th and 20th Divisional Artys. under the command of Brigadier-General PRESCOTT-DECIE.
Details as to liaison will be notified to Brigades later.

10. ACKNOWLEDGE.

J. Brind.

Hdqrs. 56th Divn.

29th September, 1916.

Lieut. Colonel,
General Staff.

Issued at 3 pm. 29.9.16.

Copy Nos:-

1. XIVth Corps "G".
2. XIVth Corps "Q".
3. G O.C., 56th Divn.
4. 167th Inf. Bde.
5. 168th " "
6. 169th " "
7. C. R. A. 56th Divn.
8. A.D.M.S.
9. C.R.E.
10. Guards Division.
11. 6th Division
12. 20th Division.
13. 5th Cheshire Regt.
14. "G".
15. "Q".
16. War Diary.
17.) French Liaison
18.)   Officer.
19. Signals.
20 Lt.Col. INGPEN.
21. C.R.A., 4th Divn.

SECRET.   Copy No. 16

56th DIVISIONAL ORDER No. 50.

Ref. 1/20,000 map of Div Front.   30.9.16
(Trenches corrected to 28.9.16) and
Map No. Y.15. 1/20,000

1.   Operations will be continued by certain Corps of the
     Fourth and Reserve Armies on the 1st October.
         A deliberate bombardment of LETRANSLOY line and other
     selected points will commence at 7.0 am. on 1st October.
         At 3.15 pm., the XIVth Corps will co-operate by an
     intense barrage on the enemy's defences on its front.

2.   Advantage will be taken of this barrage to gain as
     much ground as possible towards the brown line shown
     on attached map (issued to Brigades, C.R.A., C.R.E.,
     and Pioneers only)
                                       -and-
3.   Under cover of a standing/creeping barrage (see para.
     5) parties will be pushed forward by the 169th and 167th
     Infantry Brigades and will establish posts at points
     mentioned in following table. Each post will consist of
     at least one officer and 20 other ranks with a Lewis
     Gun detachment. Parties will dig themselves in, covered
     by the Lewis Gun detachments and any other covering
     parties considered necessary by Brigadiers:-

169th Inf. Bde.   Post A - 200 yards due East of South end
                  of FOGGY TRENCH about T.5.c.4.9.
   "   "   "   Post B - Just East of German battery
                  position, approximately T.5.a.7.4.
                  (vide air photo 22 N 1247 of 14.9.16)
   "   "   "   Post C - On track about T.5.a.5.8, (200 yds.
   "   "   "   Post D - On track at N.35.c.2.2. East
                  of RAINY TRENCH

167th Inf. Bde   Post E - On the LES BOEUFS - LE TRANSLOY
                  Road, 200 yards N.E. of point where
                  RAINY TRENCH meets the roads.
   "   "   "   Post F - At S. end of trench N.34.b.5.2.
   "   "   "   Post G - At point where trench meets
                  SUNKEN ROAD at N.34.b.4.8.
   "   "   "   Post H - On track at N.28.d.3.1
                  (200 yards from SUNKEN ROAD)
   "   "   "   Post K - At T.28.d.0.2. (200 yards
                  North of SUNKEN ROAD).

     Points mentioned above are approximate, and must be
     settled exactly by reconnaissance.
         Posts A, B, and C are dependent on   whether the
     trenches about T.5.c. central are occupied by our own
     (or French) troops or not.
167th   Infantry Brigade must be prepared to clear the
     trenches in N.34.b. and SUNKEN ROAD to North of it, of any
     enemy detachments. (attention is called to sketch Y.15.)

4.   The posts dug on the afternoon of the 1st October will
     be connected up by a traversed fire trench on the night
     of the 1/2nd. One company of R.E. and two companies of
     the 1/5th Cheshire Regiment will be placed at the disposal
     of each Brigade to assist in this task.

5.   Details of barrages will be communicated later, but they
     will be so arranged that the parties referred to in para.
     3 can leave our front line trenches (or posts) at 3.15 pm.

                                                            /3.

- 2 -

6. Brigadiers will ensure that the front line and posts are held in normal strength when parties are digging out in front.

7. The next task of the Division will be to dig another trench approximately on the brown line shown on attached map. As this "brown line" will still be on the reverse slope of the ridge (N.35.c. to N.28 Central) it will be necessary to construct posts from which observation of the LE TRANSLOY line can be obtained.

8. ACKNOWLEDGE.

[signed] Brind.

Lieut-Colonel,
General Staff

Head Qrs. 56th Divn.
30th September, 1916.

Issued at 9.30 a.m. 30.9.16

NOTE - The times for the Operation will be normal GREENWICH time. The change from SUMMER time to normal GREENWICH time takes place at 1.0 am. on October 1st, at which hour Clocks and Watches will be put back one hour i e. to MIDNIGHT 30th/1st.

Copy Nos:-

1. XIVth Corps "G".
2. XIVth Corps "Q".
3. G.O.C., 53th Divn.
4. 167th Inf. Bde.
5. 168th " "
6. 169th " "
7. C.R.A. 56th Divn.
8. A.D.M.S.
9. C.R.E.
10. Guards Divn.
11. 6th Divn.
12. 20th Divn.
13. 5th Ches. Regt.
14. "G".
15. "Q".
16. War Diary.
17.) French Liaison
18.) Officer.
19. Signals.
20.-) C.R.A., 4th Divn.
24.)

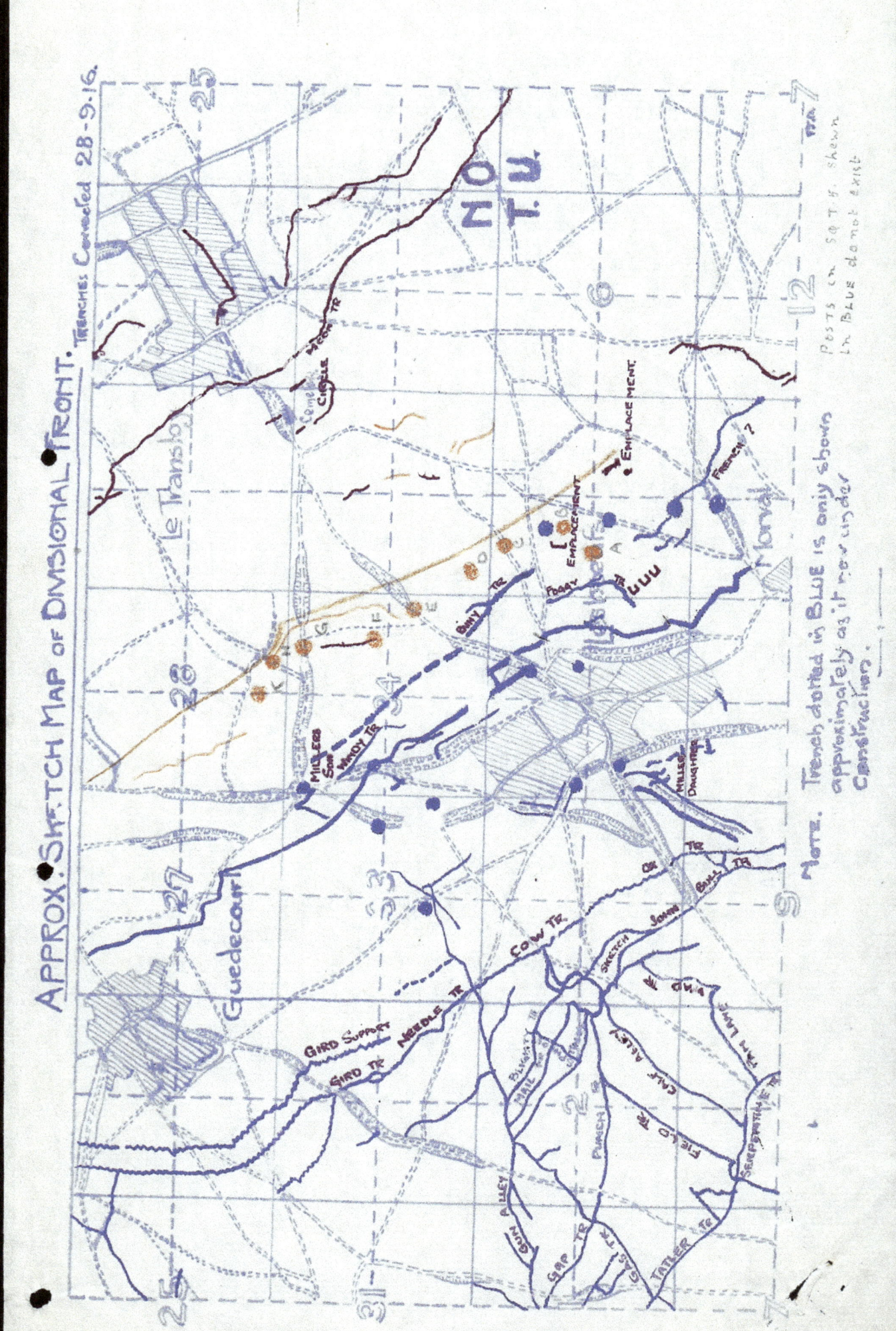

APPENDIX. I.

56th DIVISION GENERAL STAFF

SEPTEMBER 1916.

(a) Scheme for Operation 1st & 2nd.
(b)   "   "   "   3rd.

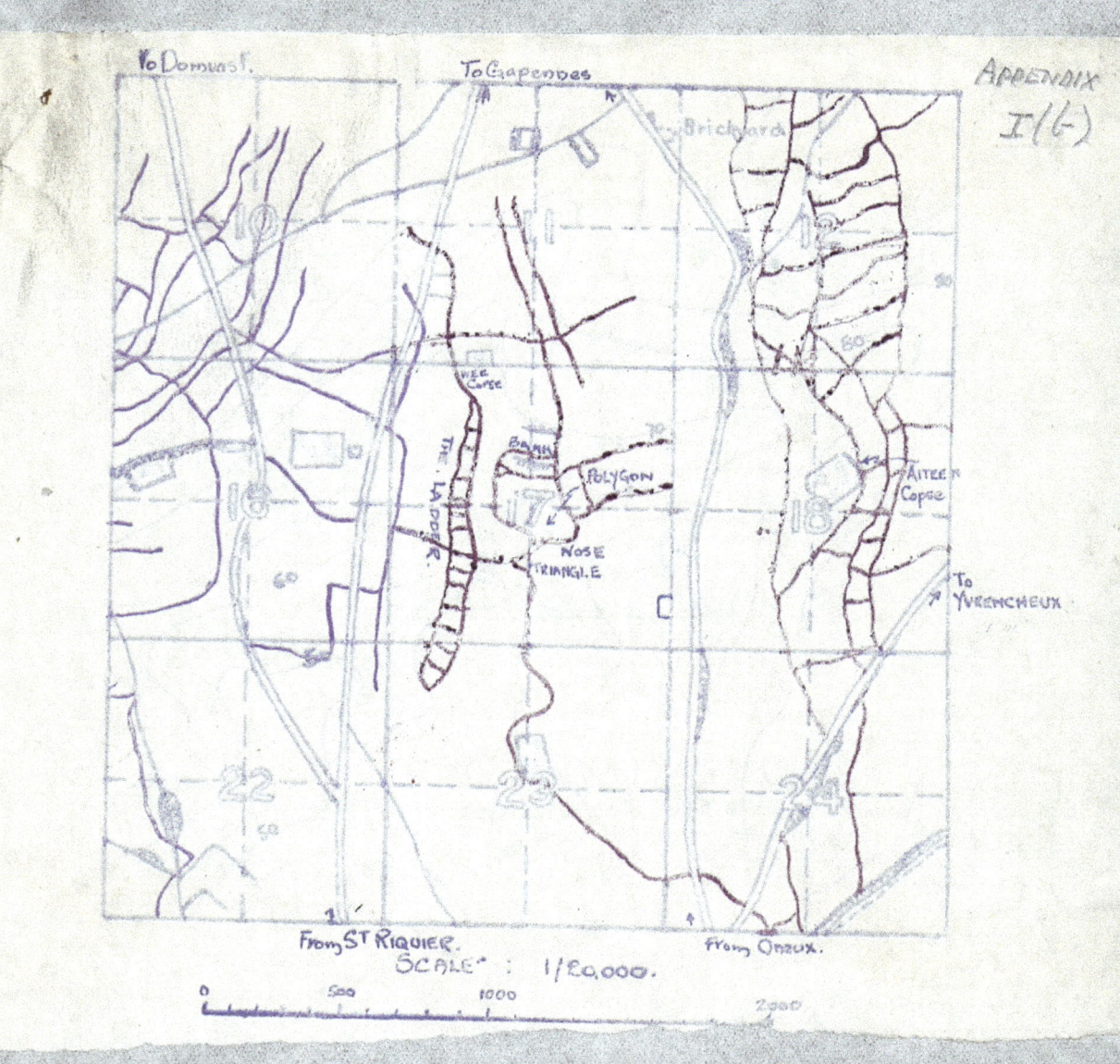

Appendix I (a.)

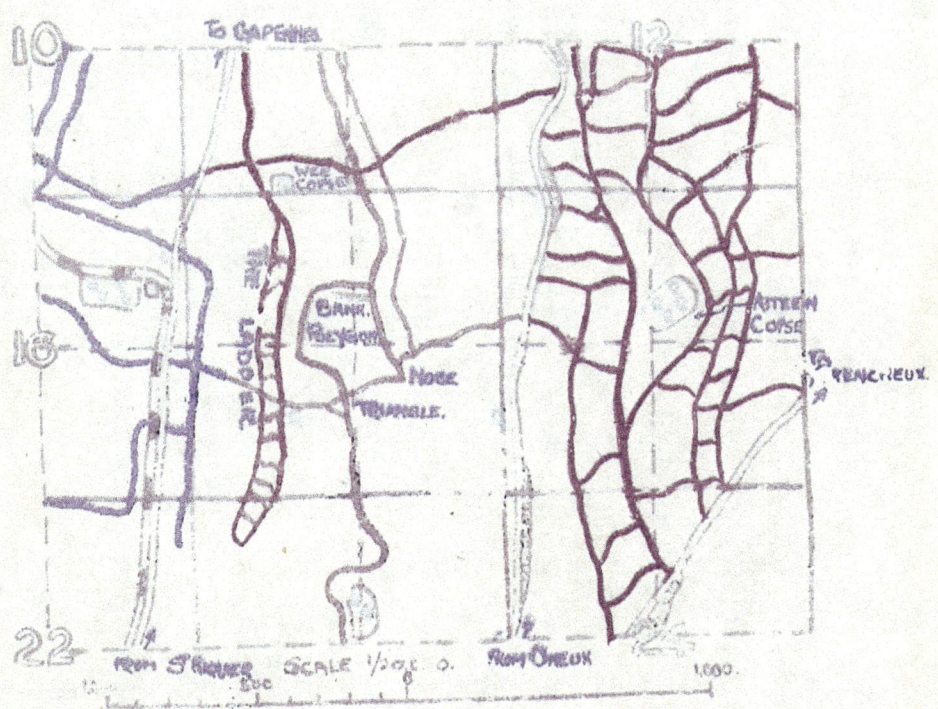

LIST OF APPENDICES

to

56th Divisional WAR DIARY.

September 1916.

APPENDIX I. Schemes for training in co-operation with Tanks at ST.RIQUIER.

" II. Location of Brigades 1st September to 9th October.

" III. Maps.
- Z. = Location map of ST.RIQUIER AREA.
- A. = 5 Sheets shewing area of Operations on the Somme.
- B. = Location Map of Forward area 6th to 26th September, 1916.
- C. = Tracks in area of 56th Division while on the SOMME.
- D. = Route taken by Tanks on night 14/15th Sept. 1916.
- E. = Operation maps for 9th, 15th, 18th and 25th September 1916.
- F. = Map shewing names of trenches in XlVth Corps area and situation on morning of 26th Sept.
- G. = Situation in forward area on afternoon of 27th September before handing over to the French.

" IV. Casualties suffered by 56th Division on the SOMME.

" V. Prisoners and material captured by 56th Division.

" VI. Divisional Orders for September 1916.

" VII. German divisions engaged, French and British Divisions on the flanks of 56th Division during September 1916.

EXTRACT FROM 56th DIVISION ORDER No. 556,

dated 29th August, 1916.

The offensive is to be resumed on the 1st (2nd) inst.

* * * * * * *

The tasks of the 169th (168th) Brigade are :-

* 1st Stage.

    (a) The capture of the German front and support lines (THE LADDER)

    (b) The capture of the system of trenches, about A.17 central (THE POLYGON).

    (c) The consolidation of three strong points at the TRIANGLE (A.17.c.9.6.), the NOSE (A.17.d.3.8.) and the BANK (A.17.b.2.3. to a.8.3.)

* 2nd Stage.

    (a) The capture of the German trench along the road between the tree A.18.c.0.7. (inclusive) to the bank at A.18.a.3.6. (exclusive).

    (b) The capture and consolidation of AITEEN COPSE (A.18.a. and b.), and

    (c) The establishment of an advanced line from trench junction at A.18.d.4.5. to trench junction at A.18.b.6.6.

* * * * * * *

The tasks of the right Brigade (imaginary) of the 56th Division are to capture the Copse in A.23.a. and b. and the Bank about A.24 central.

The tasks of the right Brigade of the 200th Division on our left are to capture WEE COPSE (A.11.c.0.6.) the banks on the road in A.12.c. and A.18.a. and a strong point about A.12.d.0.3.

* * * * * * *

One section H.S.M.G.C. is placed at the disposal of the 169th Brigade on the 1st (168th Brigade on the 2nd). The Officer Commanding the selected section will place himself in communication with the Brigadier General Commanding 169th Brigade on the 31st August (and Brigadier General Commanding 168th Brigade on the 1st September), under arrangements to be made direct.

* * * * * * *

SCHEME for OPERATION to be CARRIED OUT on
September 1st and 2nd in CO-OPERATION with the M.S.M.G. Corps.

GENERAL IDEA.

A British force operating in an Easterly direction has captured the German system of trenches West of the ST. RIQUIER - DOMVAST Road.

SPECIAL IDEA

(Ref. Map of Training Area near ST.RIQUIER and tracing of trenches.)

On 31st August the enemy are occupying their intermediate system running from the ONEUX - GAPENNES Road (at A.24.c.2.5.) West of the copse in A.23.a. and b.; and the line of trenches running from A.23.a.3.8. to the ST. RIQUIER - DOMVAST Road at A.11.a.3.0.

The 56th Division holds the line from the road junction A.22.d.7.9. to the tree at A.16.b.9.5. (inclusive) and has pushed forward and occupied a trench about 100 yards East of the road.

On the morning of 1st September, the 169th Infantry Brigade (2nd September the 168th Infantry Brigade) is on left of the 56th Division front, and holds the front line from trench junction at A.18.d.9.5 to the tree at A.16.b.9.5.

INFORMATION.

The map is known to be somewhat unreliable. Many enemy trenches shown on the map have been practically obliterated by our artillery fire; but the enemy has been working hard, and new trenches have been dug, air photos of which it has been impossible to obtain owing to bad weather.

The following information is considered reliable:-

(a). There is a strong point in the triangle of trenches at A.17.c.9.6.

(b). There is a strong point in a network of trenches about the bank A.17.b.2.3. to A.17.a.8.3.

(c) Hidden Machine Gun Emplacements exist by the tree at A.18.c.0.7.

(d) There is a trench along the line of the road in A.18.a. & c.

(e) The woods in A.18.a. and b. is organised for defence.

Zero hour will be the hour at which the Tanks cross our front line trench, and will be 10.0 a.m. on the 1st and 2nd.

* NOTE.   These two stages would, in reality, be continuous, but for purposes of instruction Brigadiers concerned are authorised to make a pause between the two stages, but the second stage should not start later than 12 noon.

   Reconnaissances must be made from our own front line or West of it.

SCHEME FOR OPERATION TO BE CARRIED OUT ON SEPTEMBER 3rd in CO-OPERATION WITH THE H.S.M.G. Corps.

GENERAL IDEA.

A British force operating in an Easterly direction has captured the German system of trenches West of the ST. RIQUIER - DOMVAST Road.

SPECIAL IDEA.

(Ref. Map of Training Area near ST.RIQUIER and attached sketch)

On the 31st August the enemy are occupying their intermediate system running from the ONEUX - GAPENNES Road (at A.24.c.2.5.) West of the copse in A.23.a. and b., and the line of trenches running from A.23.a.3.8. to the ST.RIQUIER - DOMVAST Road at A.11.a.3.0.

The 56th Division holds the line along the road from A.22.b.8.8. to A.11.c.1.2. and has pushed forward and occupied a trench about 100 yards East of the road, as far North as the trees at A.16.b.9.6.

On the morning of 3rd September the 167th Infantry Brigade holds the 56th Division front, with all four battalions in the front line.

INFORMATION.

The map is known to be somewhat unreliable. Many enemy trenches shown on the map have been practically obliterated by our Artillery Fire; but the enemy has been working hard, and new trenches have been dug, air photos of which it has been impossible to obtain owing to bad weather.

The following information is considered reliable:-

(a). There is a strong point in the triangle of trenches at A.17.c.9. 6.

(b). There is a strong point in a network of trenches about the bank A.17.b.2.3. to A.17.a.8.3.

(c). Hidden Machine Gun Emplacements exist by the tree at A.18.c.0.7. and in a small copse (shown on sketch but not on map) about 100 yards S. of the tree.

(d). The wood in A.18.a. and b. is organised for defence.

(e). There is a system of trenches (which show up owing to the chalk soil) on the N. side of the valley about A.12.d.0.0.

EXTRACTS FROM 56th DIVISIONAL ORDER No. 557,
dated 2nd September, 1916.

* * * * * * *

The tasks allotted to the 167th Brigade are:-

(i). The capture of the German front line trench (THE LADDER) from A.23.a.3.7. to WEE COPSE at A.11.c.6.0 (inclusive).
(ii). The capture of the German second line trench from A.23.b.1.8. to the trench junction at A.11.d.1.1. incl. and the consolidation of strong points at the TRIANGLE A.17.c.9.8., THE NOSE A.17.d.3.8. and the bank A.17.b.1.3. (For 1 platoon each.)
(iii). The capture of AITEEN COPSE and the establishment of a line from the road at A.18.d.5.0. to the North side of the valley at A.12.d.3.4.

The tasks of the 168th and 169th Brigades (imaginary) are to pass through the 167th Brigade and occupy spurs on which BOIS GRAMBUS and BOIS TILLENCOURT stand.

* * * * * * *

Two sections of H.S.M.G.C. are placed at the disposal of the Division and are allotted tasks as under:-

(a). One pair of tanks will cross our front line about A.16.d.9.0. and advance due East to the point where the trench at A.18.d.5.0. joins the ST.RIQUIER - YVRENCHEUX Road.
(b). The objectives of second pair are the TRIANGLE at A.17.c.9.5., the small copse at A.18.c.0.3. to trench junction at A.18.d.4.5.
(c). The third pair will attack the NOSE A.17.d.3.8., and work up the communication trench running Eastwards from the NOSE and attack AITEEN COPSE from the South.
(d). Fourth pair will attack the bank facing North work up communication trench which runs Eastwards from the bank and attack AITEEN COPSE from the North.
(e). Fifth pair will attack the bank facing S. about A.17.a.9.3. and work up the valley to the system of chalk trenches about A.12.d.0.0.
(f). Sixth pair will attack WEE COPSE working up the communication trench running North of the copse and attack the chalk system of trenches from the North (A.12.d.0.0.)

* * * * * *

Tanks will cross our front line at Zero hour and will proceed direct to their ultimate objectives.
The infantry waves will cross our front lines in accordance with following Time Table.

NOTE. Waves may be in one or two lines according to the particular task allotted to them.

1st wave crosses our front line at Zero + 1.
2nd "   "   "   "   "   " Zero + 3.
3rd "   "   "   "   "   " Zero + 5.
4th "   "   "   "   "   " Zero + 6.

The first wave will capture the first objectives
The second wave the second objective, and
The third and Fourth wave the third objective.

* * * * * *

The advance will be conducted by short rushes up to the tanks but not beyond them if the tanks are on the move.
If a tank breaks down, infantry is to proceed as if tanks were not there.

* * * * *

Zero time will be 3.0 pm.

APPENDIX II

56th DIVISION GENERAL STAFF

SEPTEMBER 1916.

LOCATIONS.

SECRET.

APPENDIX II (a)

A.Q.S/146.

PROVISIONAL BILLETING AREAS.
CORBIE AREA - From night
3/4th September, 1916.

Issued with 56th Divisional Order No. 28.

UNITS.	BILLETS	Billeting parties to report to
Divl. H.Q. Group.		
Div. H.Q. and attached } Div. Artillery Hdqrs. } Div. R.E. Headquarters } Div. Train Headquarters } Sanitary Section	CORBIE	Lieut. KING, C/o Town Major.
1/5th Cheshire Regt.	BOIS DES TAILLES	Town Major
Divl. Artillery	Bivouac at DAOURS }	Capt. HARTLEY, C/o Town Major.
No.1 Company, Train	" " "	
Mobile Veterinary Sect.	" " "	
Divl. Supply Column	CORBIE.	Lieut. KING, C/o Town Major.
168th Brigade Group.		
168th Inf. Brigade } (less 1 Battalion) } 2/1 London Fd. Coy. R.E. } 2/2 London Fd. Ambce. }	DAOURS.	Capt. HARTLEY, C/o Town Major.
1 Battalion } No. 3 Company, Train. }	CORBIE	Lieut. KING, C/o Town Major.
169th Brigade Group.		
169th Inf. Brigade } 2/2 London Fd. Coy. R.E. } 2/3 London Fd. Ambce. } No. 4 Company, Train. }	CORBIE.	Lieut. KING, C/o Town Major. Town Major.
167th Brigade Group.		
Bde. Hdqrs. & 2 Battalions } 1/1 Edin. Fd. Coy. R.E. } No. 2 Company, Train } 1 Bn, M.G.Coy. & T.M.B. }	SAILLY LE SEC	Town Major.
2/1 London Fd. Ambce. }	VAUX SUR SOMME	Town Major.
1 Battalion	BOIS DES TAILLES	Town Major.

The above areas are liable to alteration. A Staff Officer of the Division will meet Trains on arrival at CORBIE and will notify any changes to Brigade or Unit Commanders.

Officers in charge of Transport Groups who are moving by road should report to Captain HARTLEY, C/o Town Major, DAOURS, to enquire if any changes have been made in the destination of their Units.

[signature] for Lieut. Colonel,
A.A. & Q.M.G., 56th Division.

2nd September, 1916.

Copies to :-
167th, 168th, 169th Inf. Brigades.
5th Cheshire Regt. (2 copies - 1 for O.C.
H.Q. Transport Group)
A.D.M.S., A.D.V.S., D.A.D.O.S.,
Camp Commandant, Capt. HARTLEY, Lt. KING.
'G' (3 copies) 'Q' (3 copies)

Div. Arty.
Divl. R.E. (2 copies - 1 for Major Dove Park)
Divl. Train (5)
Divl. Supply Column.
167th, 168th, 169th Brigade Transport Groups.

APPENDIX II

DISPOSITION of UNITS in 56th DIVISION.

Unit	1st to 3rd September	4th & 5th	6th September	Night of 6th & 7th Sept.	2.0 pm.7th September	8th September	9th September	10th September	11th September
DIVISIONAL HDQRS.	ST.RIQUIER		FORKED TREE	FORKED TREE	BILLON COPSE	BILLON COPSE	BILLON COPSE	BILLON COPSE	BILLON COPSE
167th Bde. H.Q.	GAPENNES		CITADEL	BILLON FARM	BILLON FARM	BILLON FARM	BILLON FARM	BILLON FARM	CHIMPANZEE TR. } L. Bde.
1st Lond.Rgt.	NOYELLE-en-CH.		CITADEL	BILLON WOOD	BILLON WOOD	BILLON WOOD	BILLON WOOD	BILLON WOOD	(MALTZHORN HILL Trs. Res. R.Front Line.
3rd " "	CONTEVILLE		CITADEL	BILLON WOOD	BILLON WOOD	BILLON WOOD	BILLON WOOD	(WEDGE WOOD (GINCHY Rd.	(Sup.N.of WEDGE WOOD.
7th Midx. "	GAPENNES		CITADEL	BILLON WOOD	BILLON WOOD	BILLON WOOD	BILLON WOOD	FALFEMONT FM.	L.Front Line.
8th " "	MAISON PONTHIEU	Division moving to CORBIE Area. See Appendix II(a)	CITADEL	BILLON WOOD	(BILLON WOOD (See Note.169 Bde.from 7 pm	BILLON WOOD less 1 Coy. and Hqrs. I.B	BILLON WOOD less 1 Coy. and Hqrs. I.B	BILLON WOOD	Trenches.
167th M.G. Coy.	MAISON PONTHIEU		CITADEL	BILLON WOOD	BILLON WOOD	BILLON WOOD	BILLON WOOD	BILLON WOOD	Trenches.
167th T.M. Bty.	QUESNOY Fm.		CITADEL	BILLON WOOD	BILLON WOOD	BILLON WOOD	BILLON WOOD	BILLON WOOD	Trenches.
168th Bde. H.Q.	DRUCAT		MARICOURT Sdg.	CHIMPANZEE Tr.	CHIMPANZEE TR.	CHIMPANZEE TR.	CHIMPANZEE TR.	CHIMPANZEE TR.	BILLON FARM } Sup. Bde.
4th Lond.Rgt.	LE PLESSIEL		Res. Trs.	BILLON WOOD.	WEDGE WOOD (S)	R. Front Line.	R.Front Line.	R.Front Line.	BILLON WOOD.
12th " (Rangers)	NEUILLY L'HOPITAL		Res. Trs.	BILLON WOOD.	MALTZHORN FM.(RES)	L.Front Line	L.Front Line.	(Centre Front Line.	BILLON WOOD.
13th " (Ken'tons)	MILLENCOURT		Sup. Trs.	Trenches L.	(L.of Front Line (Attd.169.I.B.	Res.A.4.d.4.0.	Res.A.4.d.4.0.	Sup.Front Line	BILLON WOOD.
14th " (Lon.Scot)	DRUCAT		Sup. Trs.	Trenches R.	R.of Frontline.	Sup.A.5.d.9.9.	Sup.A.5.d.9.9.	L.Front Line	BILLON WOOD.
168th M.G. Coy.	NEUILLY L'HOPITAL			Trenches.	Trenches	Trenches.	Trenches.	Trenches.	BILLON WOOD.
168th T.M. Bty.	DRUCAT			Trenches.	Trenches	Trenches.	Trenches.	Trenches.	BILLON WOOD.
169th Bde. H.Q.	ARGENVILLERS		HAPPY VALLEY	{R.Bde.V.15 I.B. (CHIMPANZEE Tr.	CHIMPANZEE TR.	CHIMPANZEE TR.	CHIMPANZEE TR.	CHIMPANZEE TR.	THE CITADEL } Res. Bde.
2nd Lond. Regt. (R.F.)	CANCHY		HAPPY VALLEY	Trenches.	R. of Front Line.	Sup.B.2.c.2.2.	Sup.B.2.c.3.3.	R. Front Line.	THE CITADEL.
5th " " (L.R.B)	CANCHY		HAPPY VALLEY	Trenches.	CHIMPANZEE TR.(S)	R. Front Line.	R. Front Line.	Centre Front Line	THE CITADEL.
9th " " (Q.V.R)	ARGENVILLERS		HAPPY VALLEY	W.of BILLON FM.	GERMANS WOOD, Res.	L. Front Line.	L. Front Line.	L. Front Line.	THE CITADEL.
16th " " (Q.W.R)	DOMVAST		HAPPY VALLEY	W.of BILLON Fm.	GERMANS WOOD, Res.	Res.A.5.d.5.5.	Res.A.5.d.9.5.	LEUZE WOOD	THE CITADEL.
169th M.G. Coy.	ARGENVILLERS		HAPPY VALLEY	Trenches.	Trenches.	Trenches.	Trenches.	Trenches.	THE CITADEL.
169th T.M. Bty.	ARGENVILLERS		HAPPY VALLEY	Trenches.	Trenches.	Trenches.	Trenches.	Trenches.	THE CITADEL.
5th Ches. Regt.	ST.RIQUIER.		BOIS des TAILLES	CITADEL.	BILLON COPSE	BILLON COPSE	BILLON COPSE	BILLON COPSE	BILLON COPSE

R. Bde. (composite Bde. 5th Div. — R.Bde. Hdqrs.
2nd K.O.S.B's. — R.Front line.
14th R.War. Regt. — Centre fr.line
15th " " — CHIMPANZEE Tr.
1st R.W.Kents — L.Front line.
1st Devon Regt.) — S.FALFEMONT
1st E.Surrey ") — FARM.

Unit	8.30am 29th September	8.30am 30th September	1st October	2nd October	8.30am 3rd October	8.30am 4th October	8.30am 5th October	8.30am 6th October
DIVISIONAL HDQRS.	BILLON COPSE	BILLON COPSE	A.10.b.3.8.	A.10.b.3.8.	A.10.b.3.8.	A.10.b.3.8.	A.10.b.3.8.	A.10.b.3.8.
187th Bde. H.Q.	SAND PITS	TRONES WOOD	(GUILLEMONT Stn.)	(GUILLEMONT Stn.)	GUILLEMONT STN.	GUILLEMONT Stn.	GUILLEMONT Stn.	GUILLEMONT Stn.
1st Lond.Regt.	SAND PITS	TRONES WOOD	R.Subsector Front line	R.Subsector Front Line	Res. TRONES WOOD	Res. TRONES WOOD	Res. TRONES WOOD	Res. TRONES WOOD
3rd " "	MORLANCOURT	MORLANCOURT	(Res.TRONES WOOD)	(Res.TRONES WOOD)	Res. TRONES WOOD	Sup. SERPENTINE Tr.	Sup. SERPENTINE Tr.	Res. TRONES WOOD
7th Midx. Regt.	SAND PITS	TRONES WOOD	L.Subsector front line	L.Subsector Front Line	Front Line	Front Line	Front Line	Front Line
8th Midx. Regt.	MORLANCOURT	MORLANCOURT	Sup. FLERS Line	Sup. FLERS Line	Sup. SERPENTINE Tr.	Trenches	Trenches	Sup. SERPENTINE Tr.
187th M.G.Coy.	SANDPITS	TRONES WOOD	Trenches	Trenches	Trenches	Trenches	Trenches	Trenches
167th T.M.Bty.	SANDPITS	TRONES WOOD	Trenches	Trenches	Trenches	Trenches	Trenches	Trenches
168th Bde. H.Q.	VILLE-sur-ANCRE	VILLE-sur-A.	BRIQUETERIE.	BRIQUETERIE	BRIQUETERIE	GUILLEMONT Qu.	GUILLEMONT Qu.	GUILLEMONT Qu.
4th Lond. Regt.	VILLE-sur-ANCRE	VILLE-sur-A.	TRONES - BERNAFAY WOODS.	TRONES-BERAFAY WOODS.	TRONES-BERNAFAY WOODS.	(L.subsector, front line Res.N.E. of GUILLEMONT Sup.T.9.d.	(L.subsector Front line Res.N.E. of GUILLEMONT Sup.T.9.d.	(Res.N.E. of GUILLEMONT L.subsector front line Sup.T.9.d.
12th " "	MORLANCOURT	MORLANCOURT	CITADEL	CITADEL	CITADEL			
13th " "	MORLANCOURT	MORLANCOURT	CITADEL	CITADEL	CITADEL			
14th " "	VILLE-sur-ANCRE	VILLE-sur-A.	TRONES WOOD BERNAFAY WOOD Area.	S.of TRONES WOOD – BERNAFAY WOOD AREA.	S.of BERNAFAY WOOD (S. of TRONES-BERNAFAY WOOD Area.	(R.subsector Front line.	(R.subsector Front line	(R.subsector front line
168th M.G.Coy.	MORLANCOURT	MORLANCOURT	Trenches	Trenches		Trenches	Trenches	Trenches
168th T.M.Bty.	VILLE-sur-ANCRE	VILLE-sur-A.	Trenches	Trenches		Trenches	Trenches	Trenches
169th Bde. H.Q.	MEAULTE	A.3.d.5.5.	GUILLEMONT Qu.	GUILLEMONT QUARRY.	GUILLEMONT STN.	BRIQUETERIE.	BRIQUETERIE.	BRIQUETERIE.
2nd Lond. Regt.	- do -	A.3.a. and b. A.3.d.	Sup. T.8.d.	Sup.T.8.d.	(L.subsector Front line.	(W.of TRONES WOOD and S. of MONTAUBAN)	(W of TRONES WOOD and S. of MONTAUBAN)	(S.of MONTAUBAN. W.of TRONES WOOD.)
5th " "	- do -		Res.S.24.d.	Res.S.24.d	R.subsector front line.			
9th " "	- do -		(L.subsector front line (R.subsector front line	(L.subsector front line (R.subsector front line	(Sup.Ox & BOVRIL Tr. Sup.HOGSBACK - CUTLET Tr.	CITADEL	CITADEL	CITADEL
16th " "	- do -		Trenches	Trenches.	Trenches			
169th M.G.Coy.	- do -		Trenches	Trenches	Trenches			S. of MONTAUBAN.
169th T.M.Bty.	- do -		Trenches	Trenches				S. of MONTAUBAN.
5th Ches. Regt.	SANDPITS	SANDPITS	A.4.c.	A.4.c.	A.4.c.	A.4.c.	A.4.c.	A.4.c.

DISPOSITION of UNITS in 56th DIVISION.

Unit	12th September	13th September	14th September	15th September	16th September	17th September	18th September	19th September	20th September
DIVISIONAL HDQRS.	BILLON COPSE	BILLON COPSE	BILLON COPSE	BILLON COPSE A.10.b.3.8	BILLON COPSE A.10.b.3.8	BILLON COPSE A.10.b.3.8	BILLON COPSE A.10.b.3.8	BILLON COPSE A.10.b.3.8	BILLON COPSE A.10.b.3.8
167th Bde. H.Q.	CHIMPANZEE	BILLON WOOD	CHIMPANZEE	FALFEMONT Fm.	FALFEMONT Fm.	CHIMPANZEE Tr.	CHIMPANZEE Tr.	CHIMPANZEE Tr.	CHIMPANZEE Tr.
1st Lon. Rgt.	Res.BILLON Fm.	BILLON WOOD	Front Line	L.Front Line	L.Front Line	(N.of FALFEMONT FARM	(N.of FALFEMONT FARM	(MALTZHORN Fm. TRENCHES	(MALTZHORN Fm. TRENCHES
3rd " "	R.Front Line	BILLON WOOD	(L.Front line (LEUZE WOOD.	(Res.FALFEMONT FARM	(Res.FALFEMONT FARM	S.LEUZE WOOD	S.LEUZE WOOD	CASEMENT Tr.	CASEMENT Tr.
7th Midx.Rgt.	(S.to Front Line	BILLON WOOD	(Sup.WEDGE WOOD	R.Front Line	R.Front Line	(Res.N.of FALFE- MONT FARM	(Res.N.of FALFE- MONT FARM R.Front Line	(MALTZHORN Fm.Trenches	(MALTZHORN Fm.Trenches
8th " "	L.Front Line	BILLON WOOD	Res.A.12.a	Sup.LEUZE WOOD	Sup.LEUZE WOOD	Front Line	R.Front Line	CASEMENT Tr.	CASEMENT Tr.
167th M.G.Coy.	Trenches	BILLON WOOD	Trenches	Trenches	Trenches	Trenches	Trenches	CHIMPANZEE Tr.	CHIMPANZEE Tr.
167th T.M.Bty.	Trenches	BILLON WOOD	Trenches	Trenches	Trenches	Trenches	Trenches		
168th Bde.H.Q.	BILLON FARM	BILLON FARM	BILLON COPSE	ANGLE WOOD	ANGLE WOOD	ANGLE WOOD	ANGLE WOOD	ANGLE WOOD	ANGLE WOOD
4th Lon. Rgt.	BILLON FARM	BILLON FARM	BILLON COPSE	ANGLE WOOD	ANGLE WOOD	ANGLE WOOD	ANGLE WOOD	S.LEUZE WOOD	S.LEUZE WOOD
12th " "	BILLON FARM	BILLON FARM	BILLON COPSE	ANGLE WOOD	ANGLE WOOD	ANGLE WOOD	CRUCIFIX A.12.b.9.2.	ANGLE WOOD	ANGLE WOOD
13th " "	BILLON FARM	BILLON FARM	BILLON COPSE	ANGLE WOOD	ANGLE WOOD	ANGLE WOOD	- do -	ANGLE WOOD	ANGLE WOOD
14th " "	BILLON FARM	BILLON FARM	BILLON COPSE	ANGLE WOOD	ANGLE WOOD	ANGLE WOOD	(L.Front Line (att'd.167 T.B. ANGLE WOOD	Front Line	Front Line
168th M.G.Coy.	BILLON FARM	BILLON FARM	BILLON COPSE	ANGLE WOOD	ANGLE WOOD	ANGLE WOOD	ANGLE WOOD	Trenches	Trenches
168th T.M.Bty.	BILLON FARM	BILLON FARM	BILLON COPSE	ANGLE WOOD	ANGLE WOOD	ANGLE WOOD	ANGLE WOOD	Trenches	Trenches
169th Bde. H.Q.	THE CITADEL	(CRUCIFIX (HARDECOURT	HARDECOURT	HARDECOURT	HARDECOURT	HARDECOURT	HARDECOURT	HARDECOURT	HARDECOURT
2nd Lon.Regt.	THE CITADEL	BRONFAY Fm.	(Sup.FALFEMONT FARM	L.Front Line	L.Front Line	(Res.S.of FAL- FEMONT FARM.	(Res.S.of FAL- FEMONT FARM	(Res.S.of FAL- FEMONT FARM	R.Front Line
5th " "	THE CITADEL	BRONFAY Fm.	Res.A.10.d.	(Div.Res. FALFE -MONT FARM	(Res.FALFE- MONT Farm.	L.Front Line	- ditto -	L.Front Line	L.Front Line
9th " "	THE CITADEL	BRONFAY Fm.	FrontLine	R.FrontLine.	R.Front Line	R.Front Line	R.Front Line	R.Front Line	L.Front Line
16th " "	THE CITADEL	Res.HARDECOURT	Res.HARDECOURT	(Div.R.FALFE- MONT FARM	(Res.FALFE- MONT Farm.	L.Front Line	L.Front Line	Res.ANGLE WOOD	Res.ANGLE WOOD
169th M.G.Coy.	THE CITADEL	BRONFAY Fm.	Trenches	Trenches	Trenches	Trenches	Trenches	Trenches	Trenches
169th T.M.Bty.	THE CITADEL	BRONFAY Fm.	Trenches	Trenches	Trenches	Trenches	Trenches	Trenches	Trenches
Comp.Bde.(13th) 5th Div.H.Q.	CHIMPANZEE	CHIMPANZEE							
2nd K.O.S.B.	R.Front Line	R.Front Line							
14th R.War.Rgt.	L.Front Line	(Res.FALFEMONT FARM							
15th " " "	(S.to FrontLine (LEUZE WOOD.	- ditto -							
1st R.W.Kent Rgt.	- ditto -	(Res.CASEMENT Tr.							
1st E.Surrey "	Res. FALFEMONT Fm.	S.toR.of Front Line							
5th Devon "		L.of Front Line							
5th Ches. Regt.	BILLON COPSE	BILLON COPSE	BILLON COPSE	BILLON COPSE FAVIERE WOOD	SACMESNIL R'C'y FAVIERE WOOD	FAVIERE WOOD	FAVIERE WOOD	FAVIERE WOOD	FAVIERE WOOD

DISPOSITION OF UNITS IN 56th DIVISION. / DISPOSITION of UNITS in 56th DIVISION.

Unit.	10.a.m. 21st September.	22nd September.	23rd September.	24th September.	9.0 am. 25th September.	8.30am. 26th September.	8.30am. 27th September.	8.30 a.m. 29th September.
DIVISIONAL HQRS.	BILLON COPSE.	BILLON COPSE.	BILLON COPSE	BILLON COPSE	BILLON COPSE	BILLON COPSE	BILLON COPSE	BILLON COPSE.
167th Bde. H.Q.	CHIMPANZEE TR.	CHIMPANZEE TR.	CHIMPANZEE	CHIMPANZEE	CHIMPANZEE Tr.	CHIMPANZEE Tr.	CHIMPANZEE Tr.	SANDPITS.
1st Lond. Regt.	(MALTZHORN FM.TRENCHES Res. Bde.	(MALTZHORN FM.TRENCHES	(MALTZHORN Fm. Trs.	MALTZHORN Fm. Trs.	GROPI,LEUZE WOOD	GROPI,LEUZE WOOD	ANGLE WOOD	SANDPITS.
3rd " "	CASEMENT TR.	CASEMENT TR.	(MALTZHORN Fm. Trs.	MALTZHORN Fm. Trs.	ANGLE WOOD	ANGLE WOOD	(D.Front N. of COMBLES.	CASEMENT Tr.
7th Midx. "	(MALTZHORN FARM TRENCHES Res. Bde.	(MALTZHORN FARM TRENCHES	CASEMENT Tr.	CASEMENT Tr.	MALTZ HORN Fm.	MALTZHORN Fm.	MALTZHORN Fm.	SANDPITS.
8th " "	CASEMENT TR.	CASEMENT TR.	WEDGE WOOD	WEDGE WOOD	D.R.CASEMENT Tr.	D.R.CASEMENT Tr.	R.Front COMBLES	DUBLIN Tr.
167th M.G.Coy.	CASEMENT TR.	CASEMENT TR.	Trenches	Trenches.	TRENCHES	TRENCHES	TRENCHES	SANDPITS.
167th T.M.Bty.	CHIMPANZEE TR.	CHIMPANZEE TR.	Trenches	Trenches.	TRENCHES	TRENCHES	TRENCHES	SANDPITS.
168th Bde. H.Q.	ANGLE WOOD	ANGLE WOOD	CHIMPANZEE	CHIMPANZEE.	(ANGLE WOOD (Avd.LEUZE WOOD)	(ANGLE WOOD Avd.LEUZE WOOD)	LEUZE WOOD	CHIMPANZEE Tr.
4th Lond. Regt.	(Sup.FALFEMONT (Fm.TRENCHES	(Sup.FALFEMONT (Fm.TRENCHES	CASEMENT Tr.	CASEMENT Tr.	RANGER, GROPI, Tr.	RANGER,GROPI.Tr.	BOULEAUX WOOD (R.Support	(CASEMENT Tr. (DUBLIN Tr.
12th " "	L.Front Line	L.Front Line	(MALTZHORN Fm. Trs.	(MALTZHORN Fm. Trs.	BEEF, BULLY Tr.	BEEF,BULLY Tr.	L.Front S. of MORVAL.	- do -
13th " "	R.Front Line	R.Front Line	(MALTZHORN Fm. Trs.	MALTZHORN Fm. Trs.	FALFEMONT Fm.	FALFEMONT Fm.	(L.Sup.BOULEAUX (Wd. PIE & CRUST.	- do -
14th " "	(Res.ANGLE WOOD VALLEY. R.Bde.	Res.ANGLE WOOD VALLEY	CASEMENT Tr.	CASEMENT Tr.	(RANGER,GROPI, PIE & CRUST Trs	(RANGER,GROPI, PIE & CRUST Trs,	ANGLE WOOD	- do -
168th M.G. Coy.	Trenches	Trenches.	Trenches	Trenches	Trenches	Trenches	Trenches	- do -
168th T.M. Bty.	Trenches	Trenches.	Trenches	Trenches	Trenches	Trenches	Trenches	- do -
169th Bde. H.Q.	HARDECOURT	HARDECOURT.	CRUCIFIX	CRUCIFIX	(CRUCIFIX, HARDECOURT, FUSILIER Tr.	(CRUCIFIX, HARDECOURT, FUSILIER Tr.	(CRUCIFIX. HARDECOURT. CASEMENT Tr.	MEAULTE.
2nd Lond. Regt.	R. Front Line	R.FRONT LINE	R.Bn. front	R.Bn.front.	(LOOP Tr. to S. ROAD	(LOOP Tr. to (S. ROAD	MALTZHORN Fm.	- do -
5th " "	Res.ANGLE WOOD VALLEY.	Res.ANGLE WOOD VALLEY.	(ANGLE WOOD (VALLEY	(ANGLE WOOD VALLEY	FALFEMONT Fm.	All COMBLES Tr.	CASEMENT Tr.	- do -
9th " "	(Sup.FALFEMONT FM.TRENCHES	Sup.FALFEMONT FM.TRENCHES.	FALFEMONT Tr.	L.front Bn.	CASEMENT Tr.	CASEMENT Tr.	ANGLE WOOD	- do -
16th " "	L.FRONT LINE	L.Front Line.	L.front Bn.	FALFEMONT Fr.				
169th M.G. Coy.		Trenches.	Trenches	Trenches	Trenches	Trenches	(Trenches (CASEMENT	- do -
169th T.M. Bty.		Trenches.	Trenches	Trenches	Trenches	Trenches	- do -	- do -
5th Ches. Regt.	FAVIERE WOOD	FAVIERE WOOD	FAVIERE WOOD	FAVIERE WOOD	FAVIERE WOOD	FAVIERE WOOD	FAVIERE WOOD	SAND PITS FAVIERE WOOD

DISPOSITION OF UNITS IN THE 56th DIVISION

Unit.	8.30 am. 7th October.	8.30 a.m. 8th October.	8.30 am. 9th October.
DIVISIONAL HQRS.	A.10.b.3.& 8	A.10.b.3.& 8	A.10.b.3.& 8
167th Inf. Bde. H.Q.	GUILLEMONT STN.	GUILLEMONT STN.	GUILLEMONT STN.
1st Londons	L.Sub-sector front line.	C.Sub-sector ft. line.	Sup. SERPENTINE TR.
3rd Londons	Res.SERPENTINE TR.	2 Coy. front line 2 Coys.Res.SERP.Tr.	Res.TRONES WOOD
7th Middlesex Regt.	R.Sub-sector front line.	L.Sub-sector front line.	Sup. SERPENTINE TR.
8th Middlesex Regt.	Sup.holding original front line.	R.Sub-Sector front line.	R.Sub-Sector front line.
167th M.G.Coy.	Trenches.	Trenches.	Trenches.
167th T.M.Bty.	Trenches.	Trenches.	Trenches.
168th Inf. Bde. H.Q.	GUILLEMONT QY.	GUILLEMONT QY.	GUILLEMONT QY.
4th London Regt.	C.Sub-sector front line.	Res.TRONES WOOD	Res.BERNAFAY - TRONES WOOD area.
12th " "	L.Sub-sector front line.	Res.HOGSBACK TR.	Sup. Right of original front line
13th " "	Sup.T.9.c. and d.	Original front line.	R.Sub-sector front line.
14th " "	R.Sub-sector front line.	Res.TRONES WOOD	Res.BERNAFAY TRONES WOOD area.
168th M.G.Coy.	Trenches	Trenches.	Trenches.
168th T.M.Bty.	Trenches.	Trenches.	Trenches.
169th Inf. Bde. H.Q.	BRIQUETERIE	BRIQUETERIE	BRIQUETERIE.
2nd London Regt.	TRONES WOOD.	Res.SERPENTINE TR.	Res.SERPENTINE TR. attcHd 167thBde.
5th " " (L.R.B.)	W.of TRONES WD.	R.Sub-sector front line.attd.168 Bde	C.Sub-Sect.Front line attd.168th.
9th " " (Q.V.R.)	N.E.GUILLEMONT.	L.Sub-Sect front line attd.168.	do. do.
16th " " (Q.W.R.)	E.of TRONES WD.	Res.S.ofGINCHY.	L.Sub-sect.front line,attd.168th
169th M.G.Coy.			
169th T.M.Bty.			
5th Ches. Regt.	A.4.c.	A.4.c.	A.4.c.

	8.30 am. 7th October.	8.30 a.m. 8th October.	8.30 am. 9th October.

APPENDIX II

APPENDIX III

56th DIVISION GENERAL STAFF

SEPTEMBER 1916.

MAPS B:C:D:E:F:G: & Z.

Map E.2.

MAP E.3.

MAP SHOWING 55th DIVNL. OPERATIONS 18.9.16.

——————— Original line.(from which no progress was made.
- - - - - - Objective (Not gained)

MAP F

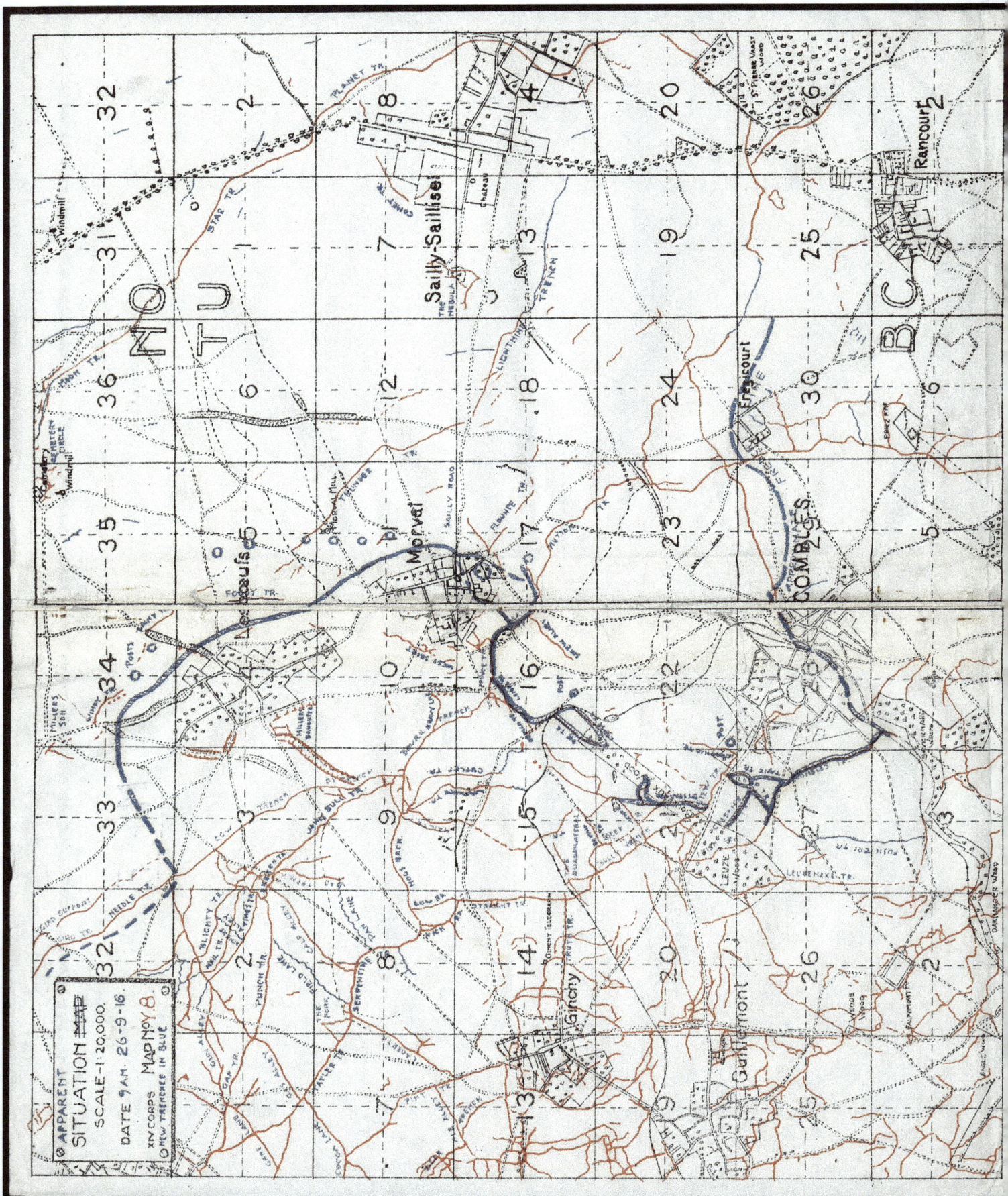

Map G

Situation Map
Afternoon 27.9.16

MAP. E.4.

LOCATION MAP
from 6th to 26th Sept. 1916

TRENCH MAP.
Showing Areas allotted to Units and H.Q.s

GUILLEMONT.

Scale 1:20,000.

MAP B

ROUTE TAKEN by TANKS
NIGHT 14th/15th SEPT. 1916

TRENCH MAP.

GUILLEMONT.

Scale 1:20,000.

MAP D

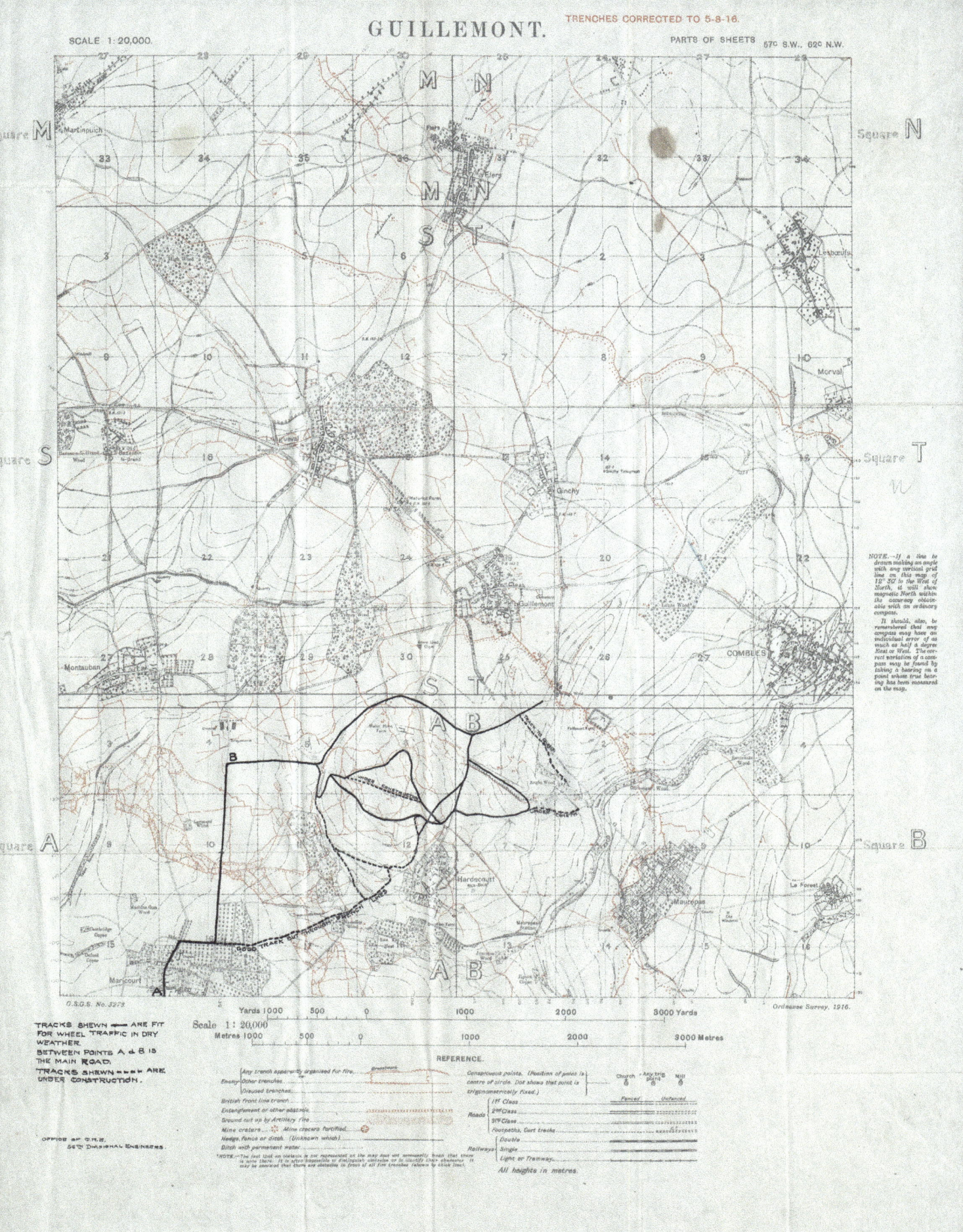

Backs

TRENCH MAP.

GUILEMONT.

Scale 1:20,000

TRACKS in the area occupied by
5th Division from 8th Sept to
9th Oct. 1916

APPENDIX III

56th DIVISION GENERAL STAFF

SEPTEMBER 1916.

MAP "A"

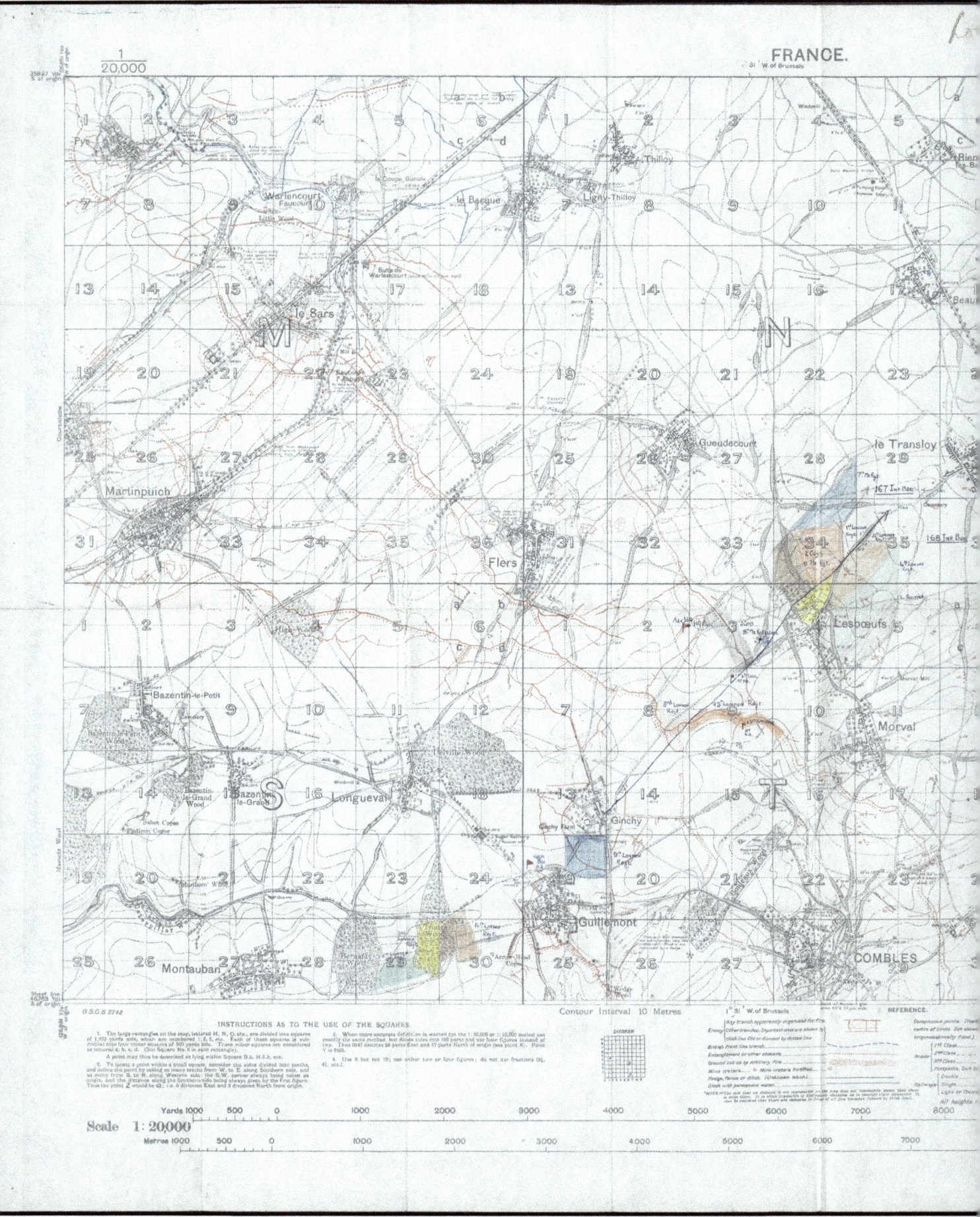

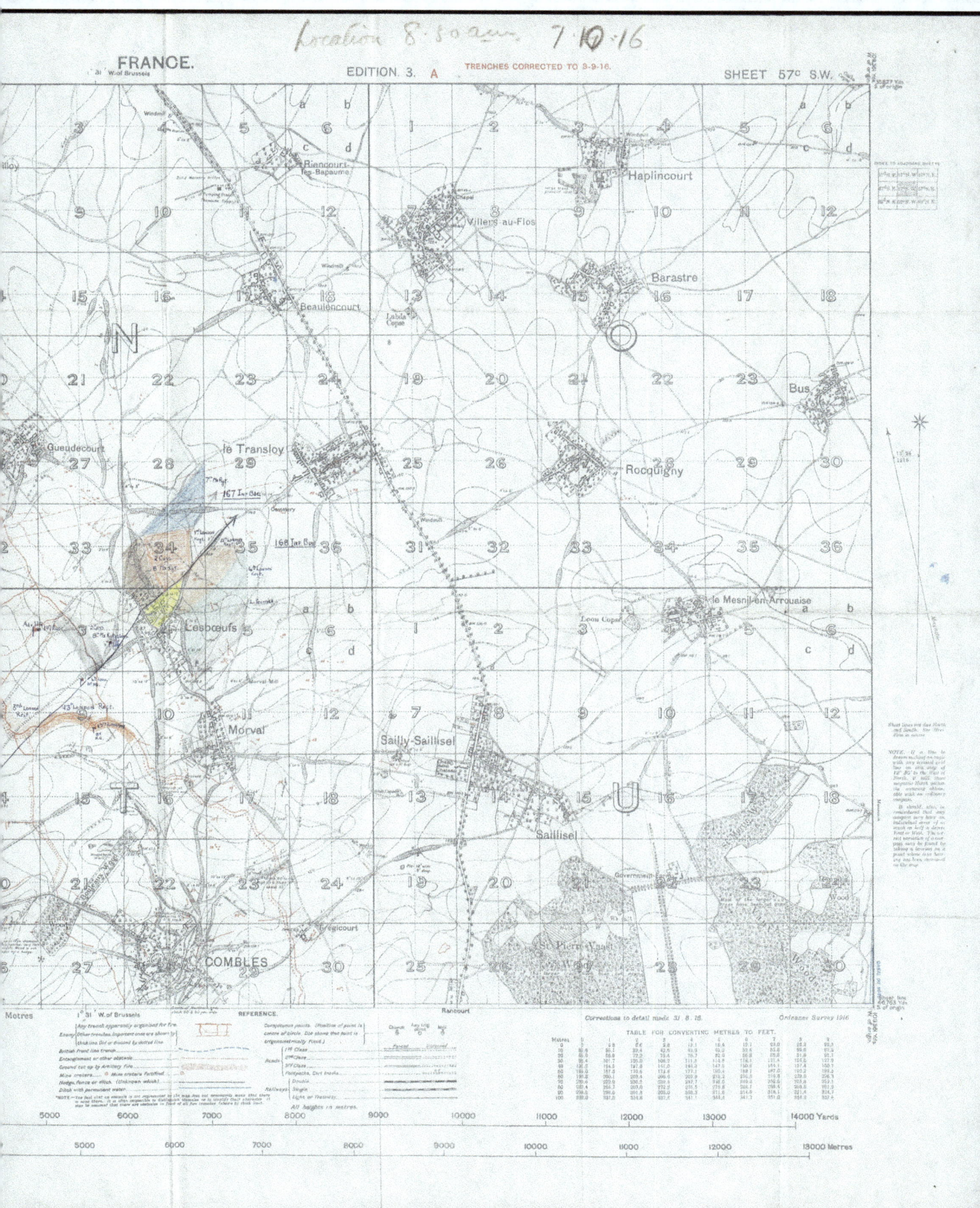

GLOSSARY.

Abbaye, Abbe	Abbey.
Abreuvoir, Abr	Watering place.
Abri de douaniers	Customs-shelter.
Aciérie	Steel works.
Aiguille	Point (Ry.)
Allée	Alley, Narrow road.
Ancien, -ne, Anc	Old.
Aqueduc	Aqueduct.
Arbre	Tree.
" éventail	fan-shaped
" décharné	bare.
" fourchu	forked.
" isolé	isolated.
" penché	leaning.
Arbrisseau	Small tree.
Arc	Arch.
Ardoisière, Ard	Slate quarry.
Arrêt	Halt.
Asile	Asylum.
" des aliénés	Lunatic asylum.
" de charité	
" des pauvres	Asylum.
" de refuge	
Auberge, Aube	Inn.
Aune	Alder-tree.
Bac	Ferry.
" à traille	
Bains	Baths.
Place aux bains	Bathing place.
Balise	Boom, Beacon.
Banc de sable	Sand-bank.
" vase	Mud-bank.
Baraque	Hut.
Barrage	Dam.
Barrière	Gate, Stile.
(Machine à) Bascule	Weigh-bridge.
Bassin	Dock, Pond.
" d'échouage	Tidal dock.
Bassin de radoub	Dry dock.
Bateau phare	Light-ship.
Blanchisserie	Laundry.
B.M. (borne milliaire)	Mile stone.
B (borne kilométrique)	
Boulonnerie	
Fab de boulons	Bolt Factory.
Bouée	Buoy.
Brasserie, Brass	Brewery.
Briqueterie, Briq	Brickfield.
Brise-lames	Breakwater.
Bureau de poste	Post office.
" de douane	Custom house.
Butte	Butt, Mound.
Cabaret, Cab	Inn.
Câble sous-marin	Submarine cable.
Calvaire, Calv	Calvary.
Canal de désséchement	Drainage canal.
Canal d'irrigation	Irrigation canal.
Fab de caoutchouc	Rubber factory.
Carrière, Carr	Quarry.
" de gravier	Gravel-pit.
Caserne	Barracks.
Champ de courses	Race-course.
" manœuvres	Drill-ground.
" tir	Rifle range.
Chantier	Building yard. Ship yard. Dock yard.
Chantier de construction	Slip-way
Chapelle, Ch	Chapel.
Charbonnage	Colliery.
Château d'eau	Water tower.
Chaussée	Causeway.
Chemin de fer	Railway.
Cheminée, Ch	Chimney.
Chêne	Oak tree.
Cimetière, Cim	Cemetery.
Clocher	Belfry.
Clouterie	Nail factory.
Colombier	Dove-cot.

Coron	Workmen's dwellings.
Cour des marchan	Goods yard.
" aux dises	
Couvent	Convent.
Crassier	Slag heap.
Croix	Cross.
Darse	Inner dock.
Démoli-e, Dé	Destroyed.
Déversoir	Weir.
Digue	Dyke, causeway.
Distillerie, Dist	Distillery.
Douane	
Bureau de douane	Custom-house.
Entrepôt de douane	Custom warehouse.
Dynamitière, Dynam	Dynamite magazine.
Dynamiterie	Dynamite factory.
Écluse	Sluice, Lock.
Écluette, Ecl	Sluice.
École	School.
Écurie	Stable.
Église	Church.
Émaillerie	Enamel works.
Embarcadère, Emb	Landing-place.
Estaminet, Estam	Inn.
Étang	Pond.
Fabrique, Fab	Factory.
Fab de produits chimiques	Chemical works.
Fab de faïence	Factory.
Faïencerie	
Ferme, F	Farm.
Filature, Fil	Spinning mill.
Fonderie, Fond	Foundry.
Fontaine, Font	Spring, fountain.
Forêt	Forest.
Forme de radoub	Dry dock.
Forge	Smithy.
Fosse	Mine, Pit.
Four	Kiln.
" à chaux	Lime-kiln.

Four à coke	Coke oven.
Ganterie	Glove Factory.
Gare	Station.
Garenne	Warren.
Garnison	Garrison.
Gazomètre	Gasometer.
Glacerie	
Fab de glaces	Mirror Factory.
Glaisière	Ice factory.
Grue	Crane.
Gué	Ford.
Guérite	Sentry-box, Turret.
" à signaux	Signal-box (Ry.)
Halte	Halt.
Hangar	Shed, Hangar.
Hôpital	Hospital.
Hôtel-de-Ville	Town hall.
Houillère	Colliery.
Huilerie	Oil factory.
Imprimerie, Impr	Printing works.
Jetée	Pier.
Laminerie	Rolling mills.
Ligne de haute	
Laisse marée	High water mark.
" de basse marée	Low
Maison Forestière	Forester's house.
M on f re	
Malterie	Malt-house.
Marbrerie	Marble works.
Marais	Marsh.
Marais salant	Saltern, Salt marsh.
Marché	Market.
Mare	Pool.
Meule	Rick.
Minière	Mine.
Monastère	Monastery.
Moulin, M	Mill.
" à vapeur	Steam mill.
Mur	Wall.
" crénelé	Loop-holed wall.

Nacelle	
Orme	
Orphelinat	
Ouraise	
Ouvrage	
Ouvrages hydrauliques	
Papeterie	
Parc	
" aéronautique	
" aux charbon	
" à pétrole	
Passage à niveau P.N.	
Passerelle, Pas	
Pépinière	
Peuplier	
Phare	
Pilier, Pil	
Phare d'exercice	
Pompe	
Ponceau	
Pont levis	
Poste de garde	
Station côte	
Poteau P	
Poterie	
Poulinière, Poud	
Magasin à poudre	
Prise d'eau	
Puits	
" artésien	
" d'étayage	
" ventilateur	
" de sondage	
Quai	
" aux bestiaux	
" aux marchandises	
Raccordement	
Raffinerie	
" de sucre	
Râperie	

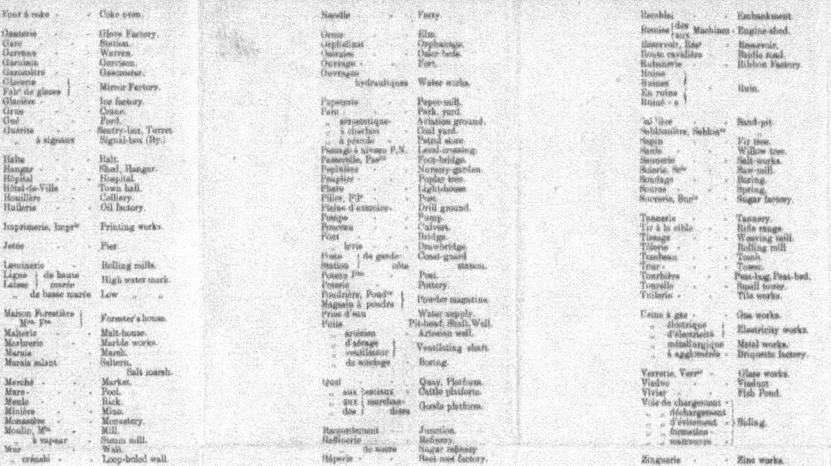

TRENCH MAP
FRANCE.
SHEET 57° S.W.
EDITION 3. A

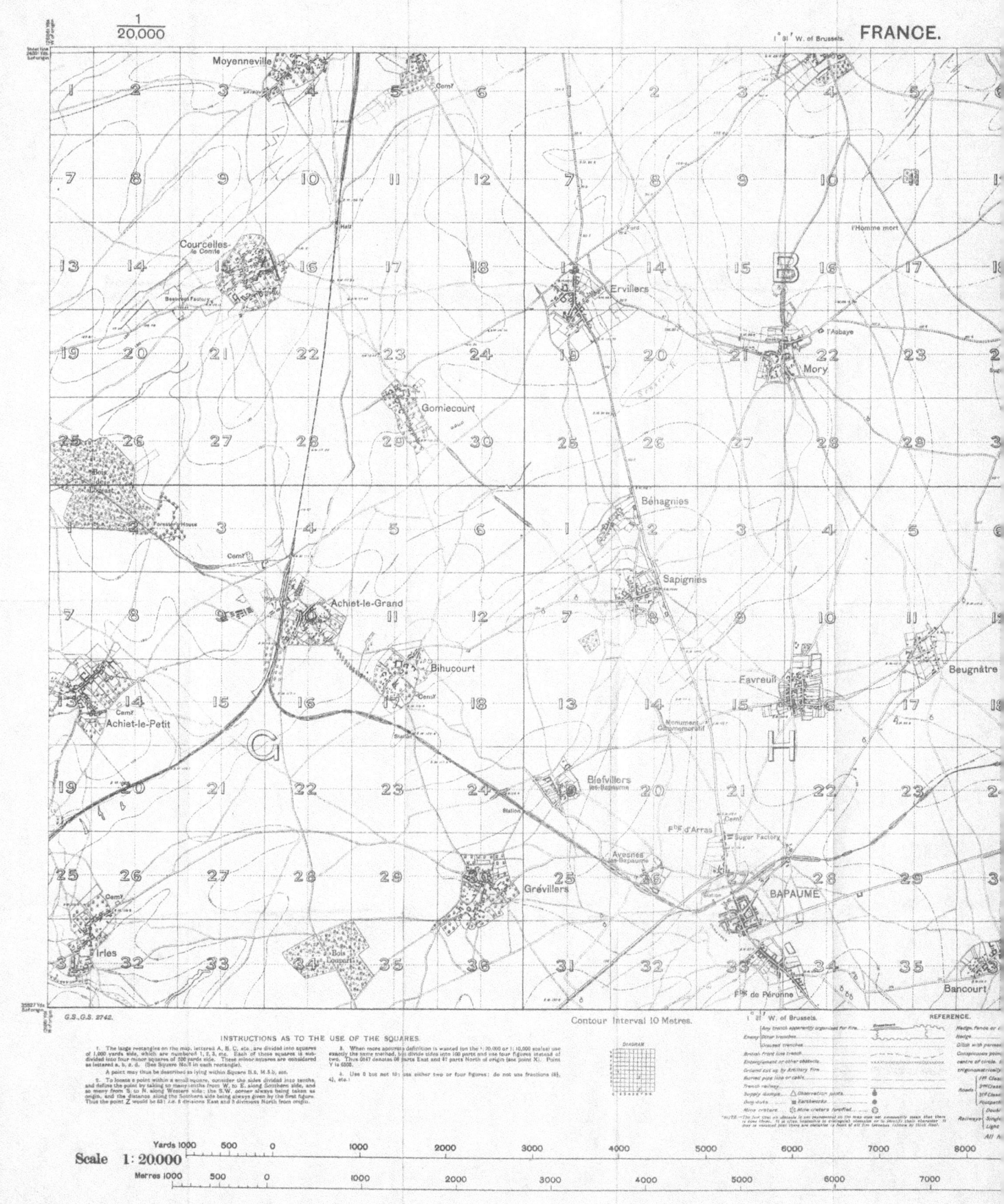

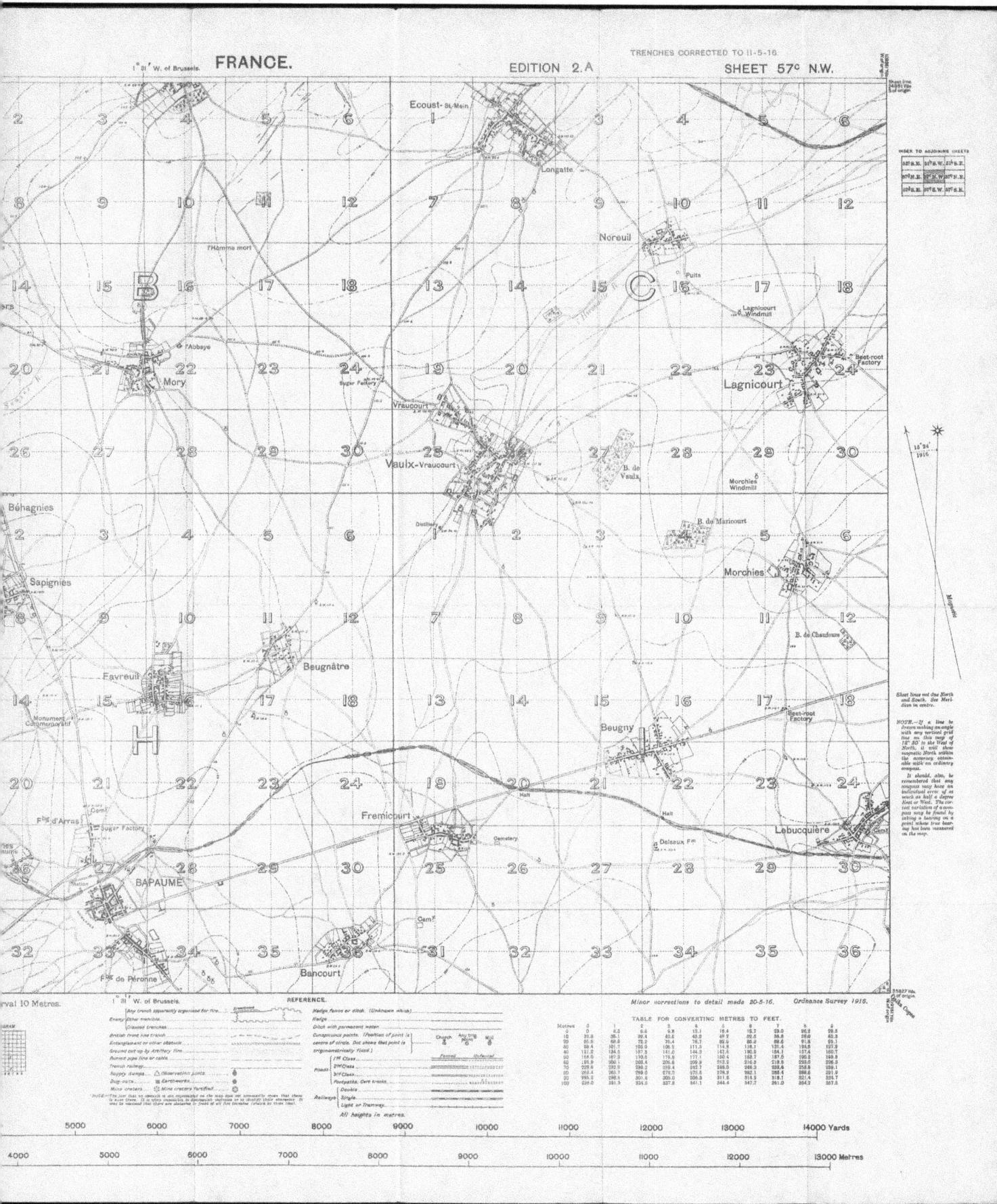

GLOSSARY.

Abbaye, Abb^e	Abbey.
Abreuvoir, Ab^r	Watering place.
Abri de douaniers	Custom-shelter.
Aciérie	Steel works.
Aiguilles	Pointe (Ry.)
Allée	Alley, Narrow road.
Ancien - ne, Ancⁿ	Old.
Aqueduc	Aqueduct.
Arbre	Tree.
,, éventail	,, fan-shaped.
,, déchargé	,, bare.
,, fourchu	,, forked.
,, isolé	,, isolated.
,, penché	,, leaning.
Arbrisseau	Small tree.
Arc	Arch.
Ardoisière, Ard^{re}	Slate quarry.
Arrêt	Halt.
Asile	Asylum.
,, des aliénés	Lunatic asylum.
,, de charité	
,, des pauvres	Asylum.
,, de refuge	
Auberge, Aub^{ge}	Inn.
Aune	Alder-tree.
Bac	Ferry.
,, à treille	
Bains	Baths.
Place aux bains	Bathing place.
Balise	Beacon, Beacon.
Banc de sable	Sand-bank.
,, ,, vase	Mud-bank.
Baraque	Hut.
Barrage	Dam.
Barrière	Gate, Gate.
(Machine à) Bascule	Weigh-bridge.
Bassin	Dock, Pond.
,, d'échouage	Tidal dock.
Bassin de radoub	Dry dock.
Bateau phare	Light ship.
Blanchisserie	Laundry.
B.M. (borne militaire)	Mile stone.
B^k (borne kilométrique)	
Boulonnerie Fab^e de boulons	Bolt Factory.
Bouée	Buoy.
Brasserie, Brass^{ie}	Brewery.
Briqueterie, Briq^{ie}	Brickfield.
Brise-lames	Breakwater.
Bureau de poste	Post office.
,, de douane	Custom house.
Butte	Butt, Mound.
Cabane, Cab^e	Hut.
Cabaret, Cab^t	Inn.
Câble sous-marin	Submarine cable.
Calvaire, Calv^{re}	Calvary.
Canal de dessèchement	Drainage canal.
Canal d'irrigation	Irrigation canal.
Fab^e de caoutchouc	Rubber factory.
Carrière, Carr^{re}	Quarry.
,, de gravier	Gravel-pit.
Caserne	Barracks.
Champ de courses	Race course.
,, ,, manœuvres	Drill-ground.
,, ,, tir	Rifle range.
Chantier	Building yard.
,, Ship yard.	
Chantier de construction	Dock yard.
Chapelle, Ch^{lle}	Slip-way.
Chapel.	
Charbonnage	Colliery.
Château d'eau	Water tower.
Chaussée	Causeway.
Chemin de fer	Highway. Railway.
Cheminée, Ch^{ée}	Chimney.
Chêne	Oak tree.
Cimetière, Cim^{re}	Cemetery.
Cloches	Belfry.
Cloîterie	Nail factory.
Colombier	Dove-cote.

Coron	Workmen's dwellings.
Cour des marchandises	Goods yard.
Couvent	Convent.
Cranier	Sing hosp.
Croix	Cross.
Darse	Inner dock.
Démoli - e	Destroyed.
Déversoir	Weir.
Digue	Dyke, causeway.
Distillerie, Dist^{ie}	Distillery.
Douane	Custom-house.
Entrepôt de douane	Custom warehouse.
Dynamitière, Dynam^{re}	Dynamite magazine.
Dynamiterie, Dynam^{ie}	Dynamite factory.
Écluse	Sluice, Lock.
Écluette, Écl^{te}	Sluice.
École	School.
Église	Church.
Émaillerie	Enamel works.
Embarcadère, Emb^{re}	Landing-place.
Estaminet, Estam^t	Inn.
Étang	Pond.
Fabrique, Fab^e	Factory.
Fab^e de produits chimiques	Chemical works.
Fab^e de faïence	Pottery.
Faïencerie	
Ferme, F^{me}	Farm.
Filature, Fil^{re}	Spinning mill.
Fonderie, Fond^{ie}	Foundry.
Fontaine, Font^{ne}	Spring, fontein.
Forêt	Forest.
Forme de radoub	Dry dock.
Forge	Smithy.
Fosse	Mine, Pit.
Fossé	Moat, Ditch.
Four	Kiln.
,, à chaux	Lime-kiln.

Four à coke	Coke oven.
Ganterie	Glove Factory.
Gare	Station.
Garenne	Warren.
Garnison	Garrison.
Gazomètre	Gasometer.
Glacerie	Mirror Factory.
Fab^e de glaces	
Glacière	Ice factory.
Grue	Crane.
Gué	Ford.
Guérite	Sentry-box, Turret.
,, à signaux	Signal-box (Ry.)
Halte	Halt.
Hangar	Shed, Hangar.
Hôpital	Hospital.
Hôtel-de-Ville	Town hall.
Houillère	Colliery.
Huilerie	Oil factory.
Imprimerie, Impr^{ie}	Printing works.
Jetée	Pier.
Laminerie	Rolling mills
Ligne de haute Laisse marée	High water mark.
,, de basse marée	Low
Maison Forestière M^{on} for.	Forester's house.
Malterie	Malt-house.
Marbrerie	Marble works.
Marais	Marsh.
Marais salant	Saltern.
,, ,,	Salt marsh.
Marché	Market.
Mare	Pool.
Meule	Rick.
Minière	Mine.
Monastère	Monastery.
Moulin, Mⁱⁿ	Mill.
,, à vapeur	Steam mill.
Mur	Wall.
,, crénelé	Loop-hole wall.

Nacelle	
Orme	
Orphelinat	Orphanage
Ossuaire	
Ouvrage	
Ouvrages hydrauliques	
Papeterie	Paper
Parc	
,, aéronautique à ballons	
,, ,, à pétrole	
Passage à niveau	
Passerelle, Pass^{le}	
Pépinière	
Peuplier	
Phare	
Pilier, Pil^r	
Plaine d'exercice	
Pompe	
Ponceau	
Pont	
,, levis	
Poste de garde	
Station	
Poteau ind^r	
Poterie	
Poudrière, Poud^{re}	
Magasin à poudre	
Prise d'eau	
Puits	
,, artésien	
,, d'aérage	
,, ventilateur	
,, de sondage	
Quai	
,, aux bestiaux	
,, ,, marché	
,, aux	
Raccordements	
Raffinerie	
,, de sucre	
Râperie	

MAP A

TRENCH MAP

FRANCE.
SHEET 57° N.W.
EDITION 2. A

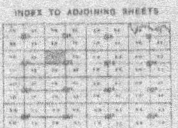

INDEX TO ADJOINING SHEETS

SCALE 1/20,000

FRANCE.

1:20,000

1° 31′ W. of Brussels

Places visible on map:
Pys, Warlencourt Eaucourt, Butte de Warlencourt, le Sars, le Barque, Ligny-Thilloy, Thilloy, Beaulencourt, Rien... les Bapaume, Gueudecourt, le Transloy, Martinpuich, Flers, Lesbœufs, Morval, Bazentin-le-Petit, Bazentin-le-Grand Wood, Delville Wood, Longueval, Ginchy, Guillemont, Combles, Montauban, Bernafay Wood, Trônes Wood, Arrow Head Copse

Grid squares labelled: M, N, S, T

G.S.G.S 2742

Contour Interval 10 Metres

INSTRUCTIONS AS TO THE USE OF THE SQUARES.

1. The large rectangles on the map, lettered M, N, O, etc., are divided into squares of 1,000 yards side, which are numbered 1, 2, 3, etc. Each of these squares is sub-divided into four minor squares of 500 yards side. These minor squares are considered as lettered a, b, c, d. (See Square No. 8 in each rectangle).

   A point may then be described as lying within Square S.5. M.5.b. etc.

2. To locate a point within a small square, consider the sides divided into tenths, and define the point by taking so many tenths from W. to E. along Southern side, and so many from S. to N. along Western side; the S.W. corner always being taken as origin, and the distance along the Southern side being always given by the first figure. Thus the point Z would be 6.8; i.e. 6 divisions East and 8 divisions North from origin.

3. When more accurate definition is wanted (on the 1:10,000 or 1:10,000 scales) use exactly the same method, but divide sides into 100 parts and use four figures instead of two. Thus 6847 denotes 68 parts East and 47 parts North of origin (see point X). Point Y is 6520.

4. Use 0 but not 10; use either two or four figures; do not use fractions (8½, 4¼, etc.).

DIAGRAM

REFERENCE.

Any trench apparently organized for Fire.
Enemy Other trenches. Important ones are shown by their line OR or disused by dotted line.
British front line trench.
Entanglement or other obstacle.
Ground cut up by Artillery fire.
Mine craters ...... Mine craters fortified.
Hedge, fence or ditch. (Unknown which).
Ditch with permanent water.

Conspicuous points (Position, centre of circle. Dot shown by trigonometrically fixed.)
1st Class
2nd Class
3rd Class
Roads
Footpaths, Cart tracks
Double
Railways Single
Light or Tramway

All heights in

*NOTE— ...

Scale 1:20,000

Yards 1000 500 0 1000 2000 3000 4000 5000 6000 7000 8000

Metres 1000 500 0 1000 2000 3000 4000 5000 6000 7000

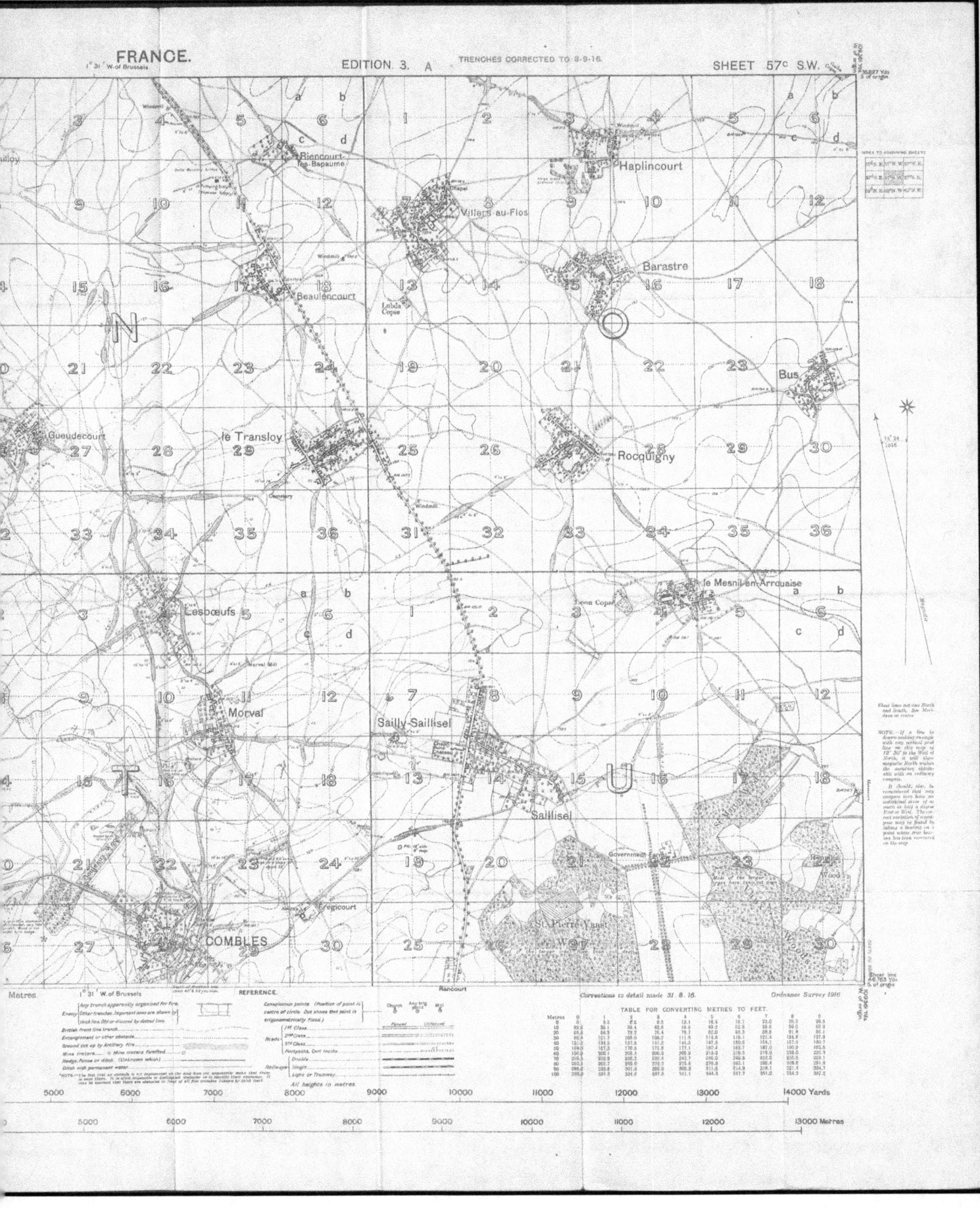

GLOSSARY.

Abbaye, Abb⁶	Abbey
Abreuvoir, Abr	Watering place
Abri de douaniers	Custom-shelter
Aciérie	Steel works
Aiguilles	Points (Ry.)
Allée	Alley, Narrow road
Ancien - ne, Anc⁶ⁿ	Old
Aqueduc	Aqueduct
Arbre	Tree
,, éventail	,, fan-shaped
,, déchiré	,, torn
,, fourchu	,, forked
,, isolé	,, isolated
,, penché	,, leaning
Arbrisseau	Small tree
Arc	Arch
Ardoisière, Ard⁶	Slate quarry
Arrêt	Halt
Asile	Asylum
,, des aliénés	Lunatic asylum
,, de charité	
,, des pauvres	Asylum
,, de refuge	
Auberge, Aub⁶	Inn
Aune	Alder-tree
Bac	Ferry
,, à treille	
Bains	Baths
Place aux bains	Bathing place
Balise	Boom, Beacon
Banc de sable	Sand-bank
,, vase	Mud-bank
Baraque	Hut
Barrage	Dam
Barrière	Gate, Stile
(Machine à) Bascule	Weigh-bridge
Bassin	Dock, Pond
,, d'échouage	Tidal dock
Bassin de radoub	Dry dock
Bateau phare	Light-ship
Blanchisserie	Laundry
B.M. (borne militaire)	Mile stone
B⁶ (borne kilométrique)	
Boulonnerie	Bolt Factory
Fab⁶ de boulons	
Bouée	Buoy
Brasserie, Brass⁶	Brewery
Briqueterie, Briq⁶	Brickfield
Brise-lames	Breakwater
Bureau de poste	Post office
,, de douane	Custom house
Butte	Butt, Mound
Cabane	Hut
Cabaret, Cab⁶	Inn
Câble sous-marin	Submarine cable
Calvaire, Calv⁶	Calvary
Canal de desséchement	Drainage canal
Canal d'irrigation	Irrigation canal
Fab⁶ de caoutchouc	Rubber factory
Carrière, Carr⁶	Quarry
,, de gravier	Gravel-pit
Caserne	Barracks
Champ de courses	Race course
,, manoeuvres	Drill-ground
,, tir	Rifle range
Chantier	Building yard
	Ship yard
	Dock yard
Chantier de construction	
Chapelle, Ch⁶	Chapel
Charbonnage	Colliery
Château d'eau	Water tower
Chaussée	Causeway
	Highway
Chemin de fer	Railway
Cheminée, Ch⁶ⁿ	Chimney
Chêne	Oak tree
Cimetière, Cim⁶	Cemetery
Clocher	Belfry
Clouterie	Nail factory
Colombier	Dove-cot
Coron	Workmen's dwellings
Cour des marchandises	Goods yard
Couvent	Convent
Crassier	Slag heap
Croix	Cross
Dans	Inner dock
Démoli - e	Destroyed
Détruit - e, Dét⁶	
Déversoir	Weir
Digue	Dyke, causeway
Distillerie, Dist⁶	Distillery
Douane	
Bureau de douane	Custom-house
Entrepôt de douane	Custom-warehouse
Dynamitière, Dynam⁶	Dynamite magazine
Dynamiterie	Dynamite factory
Écluse	Sluice, Lock
Échouoir, Éch⁶	Shrine
École	School
Écurie	Stable
Église	Church
Émaillerie	Enamel works
Embarcadère, Emb⁶	Landing-place
Estaminet, Estam⁶	Inn
Étang	Pond
Fabrique, Fab⁶	Factory
Fab⁶ de produits chimiques	Chemical works
Fab⁶ de faïence	Pottery
Fauconnerie	
Ferme, F⁶ⁿ	Farm
Filature, Fil⁶	Spinning mill
Fonderie, Fond⁶	Foundry
Fontaine, Font⁶ⁿ	Spring, fountain
Forêt	Forest
Forme de radoub	Dry dock
Forge	Smithy
Fosse	Mine, Pit
Fossé	Moat, Ditch
Four	Kiln
,, à chaux	Lime-kiln
Four à coke	Coke oven
Ganterie	Glove Factory
Gare	Station
Garenne	Warren
Garnison	Garrison
Gazomètre	Gasometer
Glacerie	
Fab⁶ de glaces	Mirror Factory
Glacière	Ice factory
Gros	Crane
Gué	Ford
Guérite	Sentry-box, Turret
,, à signaux	Signal-box (Ry.)
Halte	Halt
Hangar	Shed, Hangar
Hôpital	Hospital
Hôtel-de-Ville	Town hall
Houillère	Colliery
Huilerie	Oil factory
Imprimerie, Impr⁶	Printing works
Jetée	Pier
Laminerie	Rolling mills
Ligne de haute	High water mark
Laisse marée	
,, de basse marée	Low
Maison Forestière, M⁶ⁿ F⁶ⁿ	Forester's house
Malterie	Malt-house
Marbrerie	Marble works
Marais	Marsh
Marais salant	Saltern, Salt marsh
Marché	Market
Mare	Pool
Meule	Rick
Minière	Mine
Monastère	Monastery
Moulin, M⁶ⁿ	Mill
,, à vapeur	Steam mill
Mur	Wall
,, créneté	Loop-holed wall

MAP A

TRENCH MAP.

FRANCE.
SHEET 57C S.W.
EDITION 3. A

INDEX TO ADJOINING SHEETS

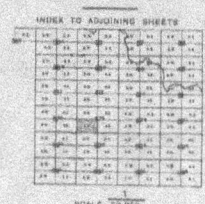

SCALE 1/20,000

Four à coke	Coke oven.
Ganterie	Glove Factory.
Gare	Station.
Garenne	Warren.
Garnison	Garrison.
Gazomètre	Gasometer.
Glacerie, Fabr. de glaces	Mirror Factory.
Glacière	Ice factory.
Grue	Crane.
Gué	Ford.
Guérite	Sentry-box, Turret.
" à signaux	Signal-box (Ry.)
Halte	Halt.
Hangar	Shed, Hangar.
Hôpital	Hospital.
Hôtel-de-Ville	Town hall.
Houillère	Colliery.
Huilerie	Oil factory.
Imprimerie, Imp^{ie}	Printing works.
Jetée	Pier.
Laminerie	Rolling mills.
Ligne de haute	High water mark.
Laisse marée	
" de basse marée	Low "
Maison Forestière, M^{on} F^{re}	Forester's house.
Malterie	Malt-house.
Marbrerie	Marble works.
Marais	Marsh.
Marais salant	Salzern, Salt marsh.
Marché	Market.
Mare	Pool.
Meule	Rick.
Minière	Mine.
Monastère	Monastery.
Moulin, Mⁱⁿ	Mill.
" à vapeur	Steam mill.
Mur	Wall.
" crénelé	Loop-holed wall.

Nacelle	Ferry.
Orme	Elm.
Orphelinat	Orphanage.
Oseraie	Osier-beds.
Ouvrage	Fort.
Ouvrages hydrauliques	Water works.
Papeterie	Paper-mill.
Parc	Park, yard.
" aromatique	Aviation ground.
" à charbon	Coal yard.
" à pétrole	Petrol store
Passage à niveau, P.N.	Level-crossing.
Passerelle, P^{elle}	Foot-bridge.
Pépinière	Nursery-garden.
Peuplier	Poplar tree.
Phare	Light-house.
Pilier, Pil^r	Post.
Plaine d'exercice	Drill ground.
Pompe	Pump.
Ponceau	Culvert.
Pont	Bridge.
" -levis	Drawbridge
Poste de garde-côte	Coast-guard station.
Poteau Ire	Post.
Poterie	Pottery.
Poudrière, Pud^{re}	Powder magazine
Magasin à poudre	
Puits d'eau	Water supply. Pit-head, Shaft, Well.
" artésien	Artesian well.
" d'airage	Ventilating shaft.
" ventilateur	
" de sondage	Boring.
Quai	Quay, Platform.
" aux bestiaux	Cattle platform.
" aux marchandises	Goods platform.
Raccordement	Junction.
Raffinerie	Refinery.
" de sucre	Sugar refinery.
Râperie	Beet-root factory.

Remblai	Embankment.
Remise des Machines	Engine-shed.
Réservoir, Rés^r	Reservoir.
Route cavalière	Bridle road.
Rubanerie	Ribbon Factory.
Ruine	
Ruines	Ruin.
En ruine	
Ruiné-e	
Sablière, Sablon^{re}	Sand-pit.
Sapin	Fir tree.
Saule	Willow tree.
Saunerie	Salt-works.
Scierie, Sc^{ie}	Saw-mill.
Sondage	Boring.
Source	Spring.
Sucrerie, Suc^{ie}	Sugar factory.
Tannerie	Tannery.
Tir à la cible	Rifle range.
Tissage	Weaving mill.
Tôlerie	Rolling mill.
Tombeau	Tomb.
Tour	Tower.
Tourbière	Peat-bog, Peat-bed.
Tourelle	Small tower.
Tuilerie	Tile works.
Usine à gas	Gas works.
" électrique	Electricity works.
" d'électricité	
" métallurgiques	Metal works.
" à agglomérés	Briquette factory.
Verrerie, Verr^{ie}	Glass works.
Viaduc	Viaduct.
Vivier	Fish Pond.
Voie de chargement	
" déchargement	
" d'évitement	Siding.
" formation	
" manoeuvre	
Zingerie	Zinc works.

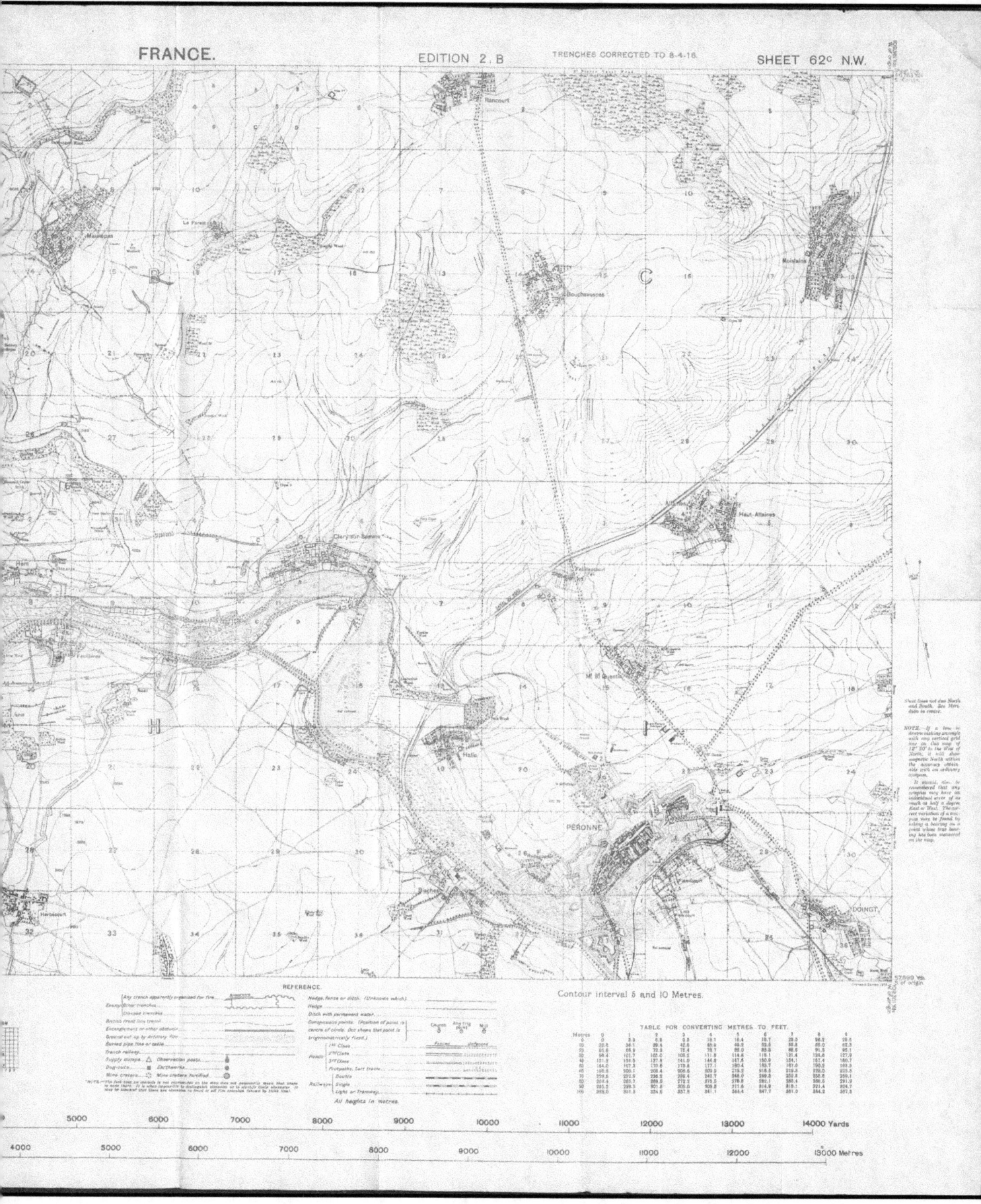

GLOSSARY.

Abbaye, Abbⁿ	Abbey.
Abreuvoir, Abⁿ	Watering-place.
Abri de douaniers	Customs-shelter.
Aciérie	Steel works.
Aiguilles	Points (Ry.)
Allée	Alley, Narrow road.
Ancien - ne, Ancⁿ	Old.
Aqueduc	Aqueduct.
Arbre	Tree.
éventail	fan-shaped.
décharné	bare.
fourchu	forked.
isolé	isolated.
penché	leaning.
Arbrisseau	Small tree.
Arc	Arch.
Ardoisière, Ardⁿ	Slate quarry.
Arrêt	Halt.
Asile	Asylum.
des aliénés	Lunatic asylum.
dⁿ de charité	Asylum.
des pauvres	
de refuge	
Auberge, Aubⁿ	Inn.
Aune	Alder-tree.
Bac	Ferry.
à treille	
Bains	Baths.
Place aux bains	Bathing place.
Balise	Boom, Beacon.
Banc de sable	Sand-bank.
vase	Mud-bank.
Baraque	Hut.
Barrage	Dam.
Barrière	Gate, Stile.
(Machine à) Bascule	Weigh-bridge.
Bassin	Dock, Pond.
d'échouage	Tidal dock.
Bassin de radoub	Dry dock.
Bateau phare	Light-ship.
Blanchisserie	Laundry.
B.M. (borne militaire)	Mile stone.
Bⁿ (borne kilométrique)	
Boulonnerie	Bolt Factory.
Fabⁿ de boulons	
Bouée	Buoy.
Brasserie, Brasⁿ	Brewery.
Briqueterie, Briqⁿ	Brickfield.
Brise-lames	Breakwater.
Bureau de poste	Post office.
de douane	Custom house.
Butte	Butt. Mound.
Cabine	Hut.
Cabaret, Cabⁿ	Inn.
Câble sous-marin	Submarine cable.
Calvaire, Calvⁿ	Calvary.
Canal de dessèchement	Drainage canal.
Canal d'Irrigation	Irrigation canal.
Fabⁿ de caoutchouc	Rubber factory.
Carrière, Carrⁿ	Quarry.
de gravier	Gravel-pit.
Caserne	Barracks.
Champ de courses	Race-course.
manœuvres	Drill-ground.
tir	Rifle range.
Chantier	Building yard. Ship yard. Dock yard.
Chantier de construction	Slip-way.
Chapelle, Chⁿ	Chapel.
Charbonnage	Colliery.
Château d'eau	Water tower.
Chaussée	Causeway. Highway.
Chemin de fer	Railway.
Cheminée, Chⁿ	Chimney.
Chêne	Oak tree.
Cimetière, Cimⁿ	Cemetery.
Clocher	Belfry.
Clouterie	Nail factory.
Colombier	Dove-cot.
Cocon	Workmen's dwellings.
Cour des marchandises	Goods yard.
Couvent	Convent.
Crassier	Slag heap.
Croix	Cross.
Darse	Inner dock.
Démoli - e, Démⁿ	Destroyed.
Déversoir, Dévⁿ	Weir.
Digue	Dyke, causeway.
Distillerie, Distⁿ	Distillery.
Douane	Custom-house.
Bureau de douane	
Entrepôt de douane	Custom warehouse.
Dynamitière, Dynamⁿ	Dynamite magazine.
Dynamiterie	Dynamite factory.
Écluse	Sluice, Lock.
Écluette, Eclⁿ	Sluice.
École	School.
Écurie	Stable.
Église	Church.
Émaillerie	Enamel works.
Embarcadère, Embⁿ	Landing-place.
Estaminet, Estamⁿ	Inn.
Étang	Pond.
Fabrique, Fabⁿ	Factory.
Fabⁿ de produits chimiques	Chemical works.
Fabⁿ de faïence	Pottery.
Faïencerie	
Ferme, Fⁿ	Farm.
Filature, Filⁿ	Spinning mill.
Fonderie, Fondⁿ	Foundry.
Fontaine, Fontⁿ	Spring, Fountain.
Forêt	Forest.
Forme de radoub	Dry dock.
Forge	Smithy.
Fosse	Mine, Pit.
Fossé	Moat, Ditch.
Four	Kiln.
à chaux	Lime-kiln.
Four à coke	Coke oven.
Ganterie	Glove Factory.
Gare	Station.
Garenne	Warren.
Garnison	Garrison.
Gazomètre	Gasometer.
Glacerie	
Fabⁿ de glaces	Mirror Factory.
Glacière	Ice factory.
Grue	Crane.
Gué	Ford.
Guérite	Sentry-box, Turret.
à signaux	Signal-box (Ry.)
Halte	Halt.
Hangar	Shed, Hangar.
Hôpital	Hospital.
Hôtel-de-Ville	Town hall.
Houillère	Colliery.
Huilerie	Oil factory.
Imprimerie, Imprⁿ	Printing works.
Jetée	Pier.
Laminerie	Rolling mills.
Ligne de haute marée	High water mark.
Laisse de basse marée	Low water mark.
Maison Forestière, Mⁿ Fⁿ	Forester's house.
Malterie	Malt-house.
Marbrerie	Marble works.
Marais	Marsh.
Marais salant	Saltern. Salt marsh.
Marché	Market.
Mare	Pool.
Meule	Rick.
Minière	Mine.
Monastère	Monastery.
Moulin, Mⁿ	Mill.
à vapeur	Steam mill.
Mur	Wall.
crénelé	Loop-holed wall.
Nacelle	Ferry.
Orme	Elm.
Orphelinat	Orphanage.
Ouche	Osier-bed.
Ouvrage	Fort.
Ouvrages hydrauliques	Water works.
Papeterie	Paper-mill.
Parc	Park, yard.
aérostatique	Aviation
à charbon	Coal yard.
à pétrole	Petrol store.
Passage à niveau P.N.	Level cros.
Passerelle, Pasⁿ	Foot-bridge.
Pépinière	Nursery.
Peuplier	Poplar tree.
Phare	Light-house.
Pilier, Pilⁿ	Post.
Plaine d'exercice	Drill ground.
Pompe	Pump.
Poteau	Post.
Pont	Bridge.
levis	Drawbridge.
Poste de garde-côtes	Coast-guard station.
Poterie Potⁿ	Pottery.
Poudrière, Poudⁿ	Powder magazine.
Magasin à poudre	
Prise d'eau	Water supply.
Puits	
artésien	Artesian.
d'aérage	Ventilating.
ventilateur	
de sondage	Boring.
Quai	Quay.
aux bestiaux	Cattle platform.
aux marchandises	Goods platform.
Raccordement	Junction.
Raffinerie de sucre	Sugar refinery.
Râperie	Beet-root factory.

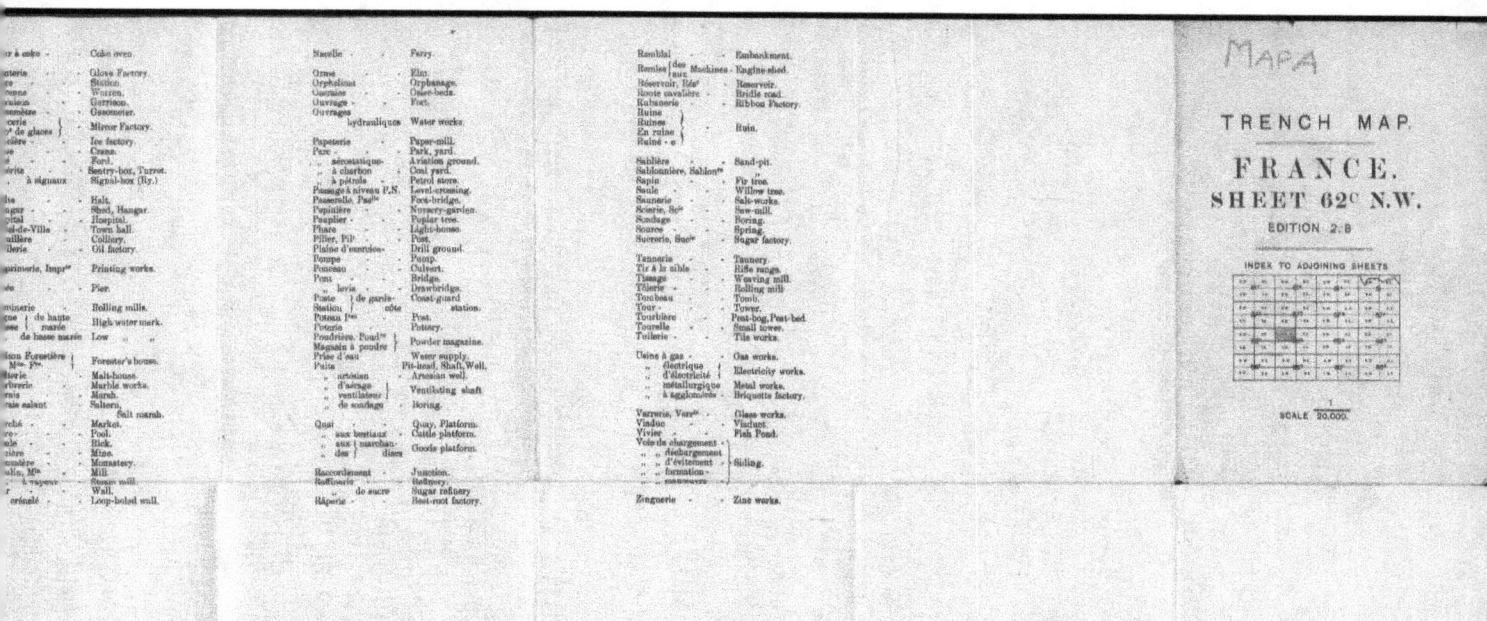

MAPA

TRENCH MAP.

FRANCE.
SHEET 62c N.W.
EDITION 2.B

INDEX TO ADJOINING SHEETS

SCALE 20,000.

GUILLEMONT.

LOCATION MAP Oct 1916
TRENCHES CORRECTED TO 5-8-16.
SCALE 1:20,000.
PARTS OF SHEETS 57c S.W., 62c N.W.

30th Sept. to 9th Oct. 1916

TRENCH MAP.

MAP A

GUILLEMONT.

Scale 1:20,000.

LOCATION

MAP.

SHOWING AREAS ALLOTTED TO UNITS AND H.Q.s

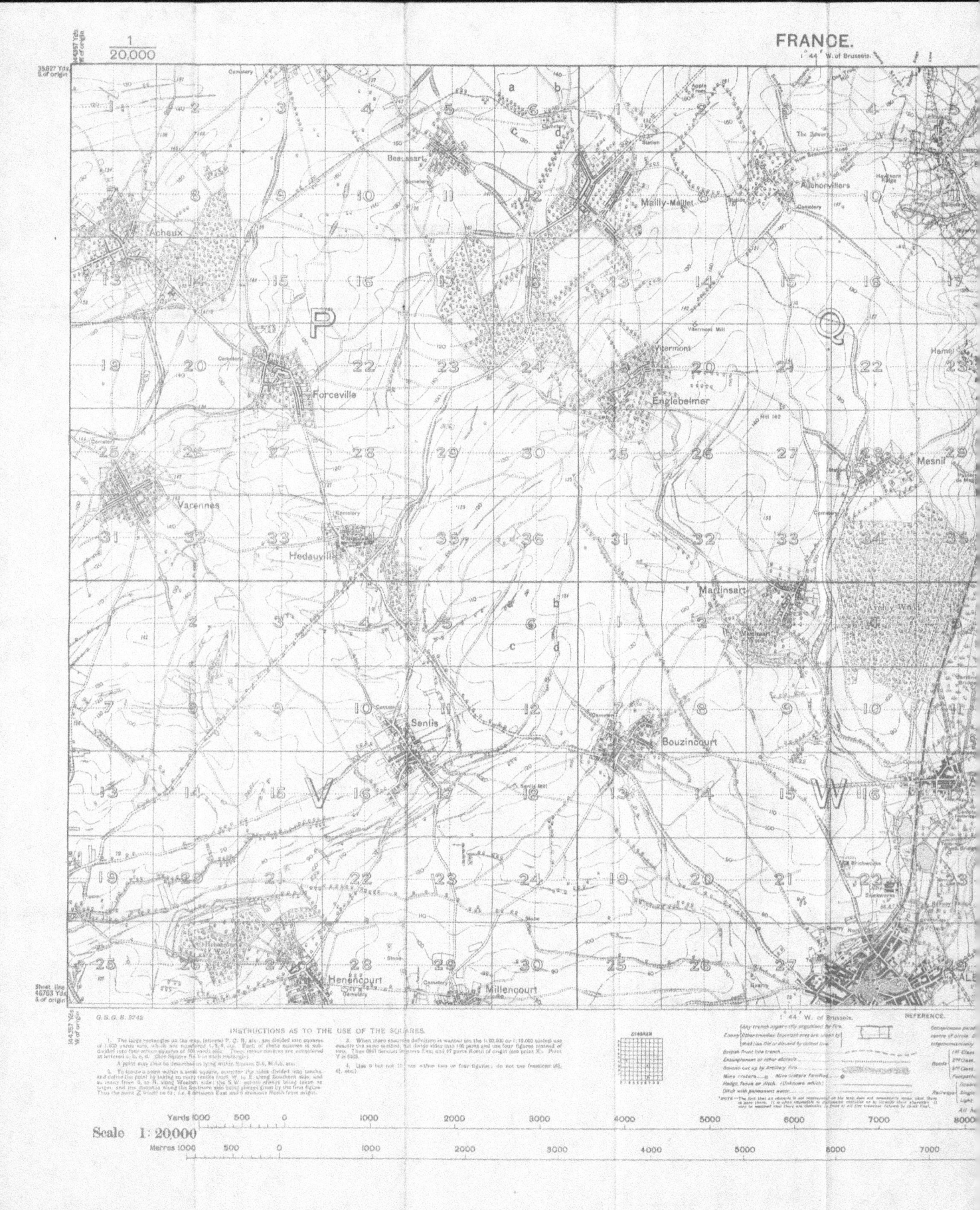

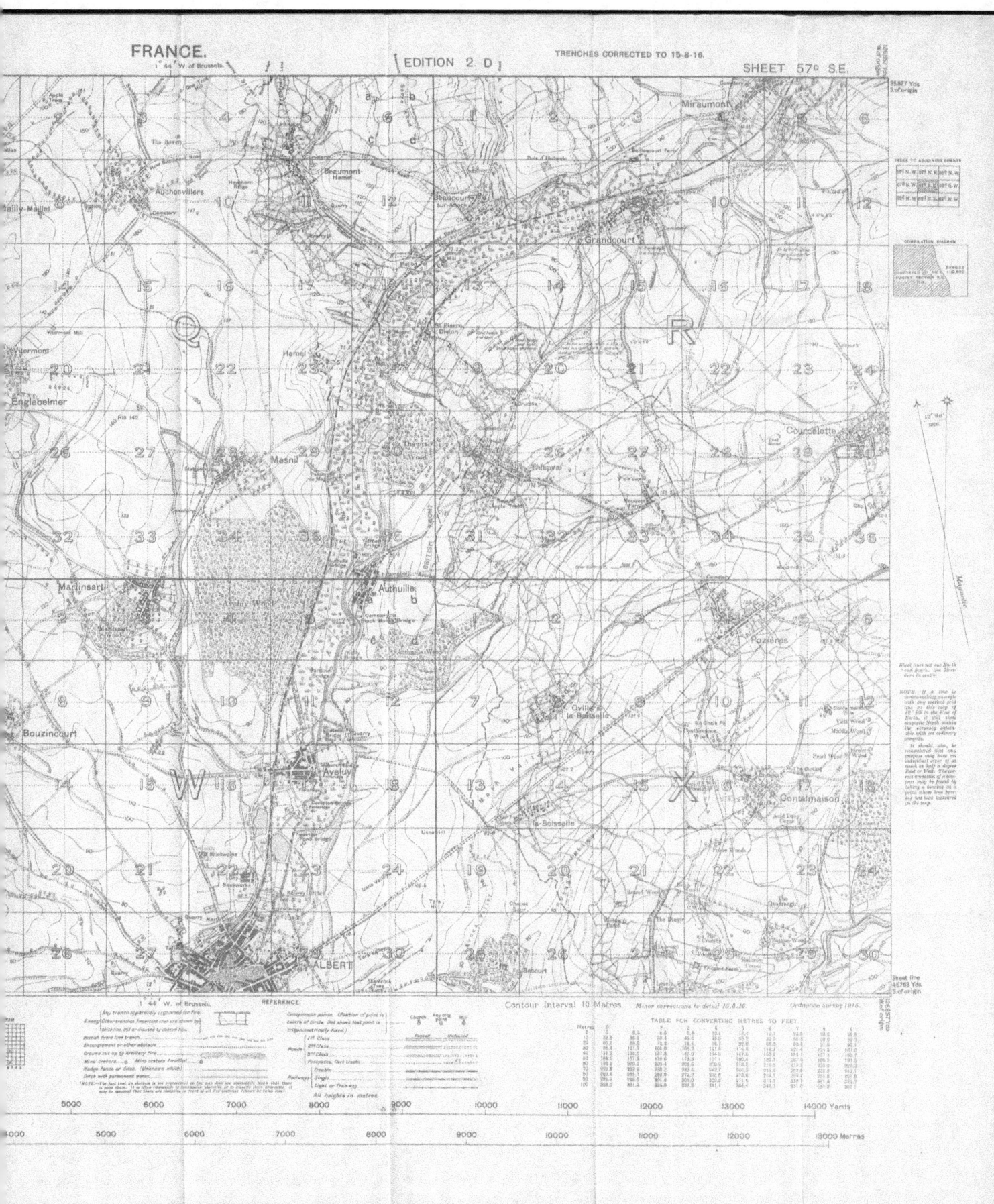

GLOSSARY.

Abbaye, Abb^e	Abbey.
Abreuvoir, Ab^r	Watering-place.
Abri de douaniers	Customs-shelter.
Aciérie	Steel works.
Aiguilles	Points (Ry.)
Allée	Alley, Narrow road.
Ancien - ne, Anc^{ne}	Old.
Aqueduc	Aqueduct.
Arbre	Tree.
,, éventail	,, fan-shaped.
,, décharné	,, bare.
,, fourchu	,, forked.
,, isolé	,, isolated.
,, penché	,, leaning.
Arbrisseau	Small tree.
Arc	Arch.
Ardoisière, Ard^{re}	Slate quarry.
Arrêt	Halt.
Asile	Asylum.
,, des aliénés	Lunatic asylum.
,, de charité	
,, des pauvres	
,, de refuge	Asylum.
Auberge, Aub^{ge}	Inn.
Aune	Alder-tree.
Bac	Ferry.
,, à traille	
Bains	Baths.
Place aux bains	Bathing place.
Balise	Boom, Beacon.
Banc de sable	Sand-bank.
,, vase	Mud-bank.
Baraque	Hut.
Barrage	Dam.
Barrière	Gate, Stile.
Machine à Bascule	Weigh-bridge.
Bassin	Dock, Pond.
,, d'échouage	Tidal dock.
Bassin de radoub	Dry dock.
Bateau phare	Light-ship.
Blanchisserie	Laundry.
B.M. (borne milliaire)	Mile stone.
B^k (borne kilométrique)	
Boulonnerie	
Fab^e de boulons	Bolt Factory.
Bouée	Buoy.
Brasserie, Brass^{ie}	Brewery.
Briqueterie, Briq^{ie}	Brickfield.
Brise-lames	Breakwater.
Bureau de poste	Post office.
,, de douane	Custom house.
Butte	Butt, Mound.
Cabane	Hut.
Cabaret, Cab^t	Inn.
Câble sous-marin	Submarine cable.
Calvaire, Cal^{re}	Calvary.
Canal de dessèchement	Drainage canal.
Canal d'irrigation	Irrigation canal.
Fab^e de caoutchouc	Rubber factory.
Carrière, Carr^{re}	Quarry.
,, de gravier	Gravel-pit.
Caserne	Barracks.
Champ de courses	Race-course.
,, manœuvres	Drill-ground.
,, tir	Rifle range.
Chantier	Building yard. Ship yard. Dock yard.
Chantier de construction	Slip-way.
Chapelle, Ch^{le}	Chapel.
Charbonnage	Colliery.
Château d'eau	Water tower.
Chaussée	Causeway.
Chemin de fer	Railway.
Cheminée, Ch^{ée}	Chimney.
Chêne	Oak tree.
Cimetière, Cim^{re}	Cemetery.
Clocher	Belfry.
Clouterie	Nail factory.
Colombier	Dove-cot.
Coron	Workmen's dwellings.
Cour des marchandises	Goods yard.
,, aux marchandises	
Couvent	Convent.
Crassier	Slag heap.
Croix	Cross.
Darse	Inner dock.
Démoli - e, Détⁱ	Destroyed.
Déversoir	Weir.
Digne	Dyke, causeway.
Distillerie, Dist^{ie}	Distillery.
Douane	Custom-house.
Bureau de douane	
Entrepôt de douane	Custom warehouse.
Dynamitière, Dynam^{re}	Dynamite magazine.
Dynamiterie	Dynamite factory.
Ecluse	Sluice, Lock.
Ecluzette, Ecl^{te}	Sluice.
Ecole	School.
Ecurie	Stable.
Eglise	Church.
Emaillerie	Enamel works.
Embarcadère, Emb^{re}	Landing-place.
Estaminet, Estam^t	Inn.
Etang	Pond.
Fabrique, Fab^e	Factory.
Fab^e de produits chimiques	Chemical works.
Fab^e de faïence	Pottery.
Faïencerie	
Ferme, F^{me}	Farm.
Filature, Fil^{re}	Spinning mill.
Fonderie, Fond^{ie}	Foundry.
Fontaine, Font^{ne}	Spring, fountain.
Forêt	Forest.
Forme de radoub	Dry dock.
Forge	Smithy.
Fosse	Mine, Pit.
Fossé	Moat, Ditch.
Four	Kiln.
,, à chaux	Lime-kiln.
Four à coke	Coke oven.
Ganterie	Glove Factory.
Gare	Station.
Garenne	Warren.
Garnison	Garrison.
Gazomètre	Gasometer.
Glacerie	
Fab^e de glaces	Mirror Factory.
Glacière	Ice factory.
Grue	Crane.
Gué	Ford.
Guérite	Sentry-box, Turret.
,, à signaux	Signal-box (Ry.)
Halte	Halt.
Hangar	Shed, Hangar.
Hôpital	Hospital.
Hôtel-de-Ville	Town hall.
Houillère	Colliery.
Huilerie	Oil factory.
Imprimerie, Impr^{ie}	Printing works.
Jetée	Pier.
Laminerie	Rolling mills.
Ligne de haute laisse	High water mark.
,, marée	
,, de basse marée	Low ,,
Maison Forestière M^{on} F^{re}	Forester's house.
Malterie	Malt-house.
Marbrerie	Marble works.
Marais	Marsh.
Marais salant	Saltern, Salt marsh.
Marché	Market.
Mare	Pool.
Meule	Rick.
Minière	Mine.
Monastère	Monastery.
Moulin, Mⁱⁿ	Mill.
,, à vapeur	Steam mill.
Mur	Wall.
,, crénelé	Loop-holed wall.
Nacelle	
Orme	
Orphelinat	
Oiseraie	
Ouvrage	
Ouvrages hydrauliques	
Papeterie	
Parc	
,, aérostatique	
,, à charbon	
,, à pétrole	
Passage à niveau P.N.	
Passerelle, Pas^{le}	
Pépinière	
Peuplier	
Phare	
Pilier, Pil^r	
Plaine d'exercice	
Pompe	
Puceaux	
Pont	
,, levis	
Poste de garde côte	
Station	
Poteau Ier	
Poterie	
Poudrière, Poud^{re}	
Magasin à poudre	
Prise d'eau	
Puits	
,, artésien	
,, d'aérage	
,, ventilateur	
,, de sondage	
Quai	
,, aux bestiaux	
,, aux marchandises	
Raccordement	
Raffinerie	
,, de sucre	
Râperie	

MAP A

TRENCH MAP.

FRANCE.
SHEET 57ᴅ S.E.
EDITION 2. D

INDEX TO ADJOINING SHEETS

SCALE 1/20,000

Coke oven.	Nacelle	Ferry.
Glove Factory.	Orme	Elm.
Station.	Orphelinat	Orphanage.
Warren.	Oseraie	Osier-beds.
Garrison.	Ouvrage	Fort.
Gasometer.	Ouvrages hydrauliques	Water works.
Ice factory.	Papeterie	Paper-mill.
Orme.	Parc	Park, yard.
Fort.	,, aérostatique	Aviation ground.
Sentry-box, Turret.	,, à charbon	Coal yard.
Signal-box (Ry.)	,, à pétrole	Petrol store.
Halt.	Passage à niveau P.N.	Level-crossing.
Shed, Hangar.	Passerelle, Pss^lle	Foot-bridge.
Hospital.	Pépinière	Nursery-garden.
Town hall.	Peuplier	Poplar tree.
Colliery.	Phare	Light-house.
Oil factory.	Pilier, Pil^r	Post.
	Plaine d'exercice	Drill ground.
Printing works.	Pompe	Pump.
	Ponceau	Culvert.
Pier.	Pont	Bridge.
	,, levis	Drawbridge.
Rolling mills.	Poste de garde	Coast-guard station.
	Station côte	
High water mark.	Poteau P^au	Post.
Low ,, ,,	Poterie	Pottery.
	Poudrière, Poud^re	Powder magazine.
Forester's house.	Magasin à poudre	
Malt-house.	Prise d'eau	Water supply.
Marble works.	Puits	Pit-head, Shaft, Well.
Marsh.	,, artesien	Artesian well.
Salters.	,, d'aérage	
Salt marsh.	,, ventilateur	Ventilating shaft.
Market.	,, de sondage	Boring.
Pool.	Quai	Quay, Platform.
Rick.	,, aux bestiaux	Cattle platform.
Mine.	,, aux marchan-	Goods platform.
Monastery.	,, dises	
Mill.		
Steam mill.	Raccordement	Junction.
Wall.	Raffinerie	Refinery.
Loop-holed wall.	,, de sucre	Sugar refinery.
	Râperie	Beet-root factory.

Remblai		Embankment.
Remise {des Machines / aux}		Engine-shed.
Réservoir, Rés^r		Reservoir.
Route cavalière		Bridle road.
Rubanerie		Ribbon Factory.
Ruine	}	Ruin.
Ruines		
En ruines		
Ruiné ,,		
Sablière		Sand-pit.
Sablonnière, Sablon^re		
Sapin		Fir tree.
Saule		Willow tree.
Saunerie		Salt-works.
Scierie, S^ie		Saw-mill.
Sondage		Boring.
Source		Spring.
Sucrerie, Suc^rie		Sugar factory.
Tannerie		Tannery.
Tir à la cible		Rifle range.
Tissage		Weaving mill.
Tôlerie		Rolling mill.
Tombeau		Tomb.
Tour		Tower.
Tourbière		Peat-bog, Peat-bed.
Tourelle		Small tower.
Tuilerie		Tile works.
Usine à gaz		Gas works.
,, électrique		Electricity works.
,, d'électricité		
,, métallurgique		Metal works.
,, à agglomérés		Briquette factory.
Verrerie, Verr^ie		Glass works.
Viaduc		Viaduct.
Vivier		Fish Pond.
Voie de chargement		
,, de déchargement		
,, d'évitement		Siding.
,, formation		
,, manœuvre		
Zinguerie		Zinc works.

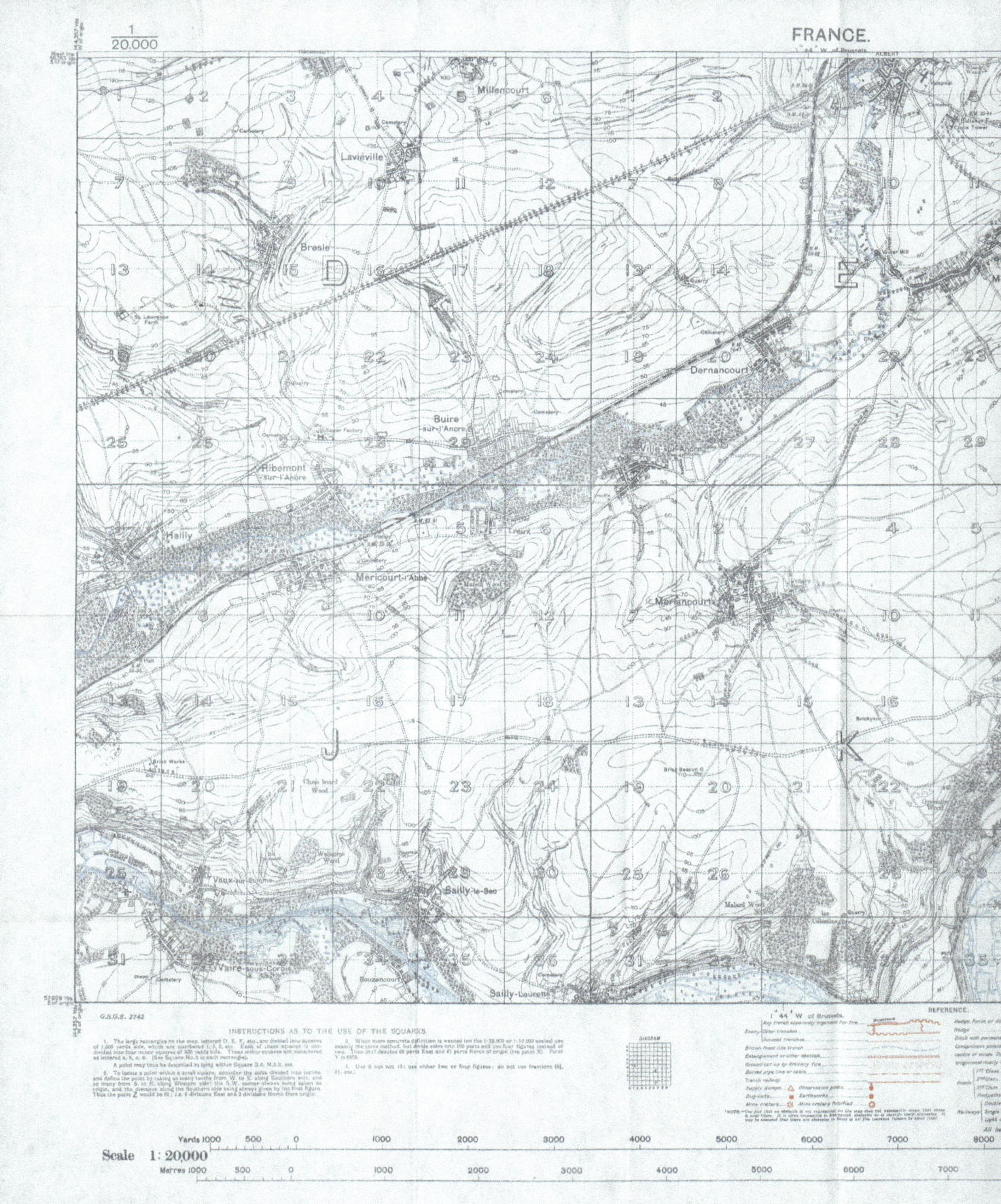

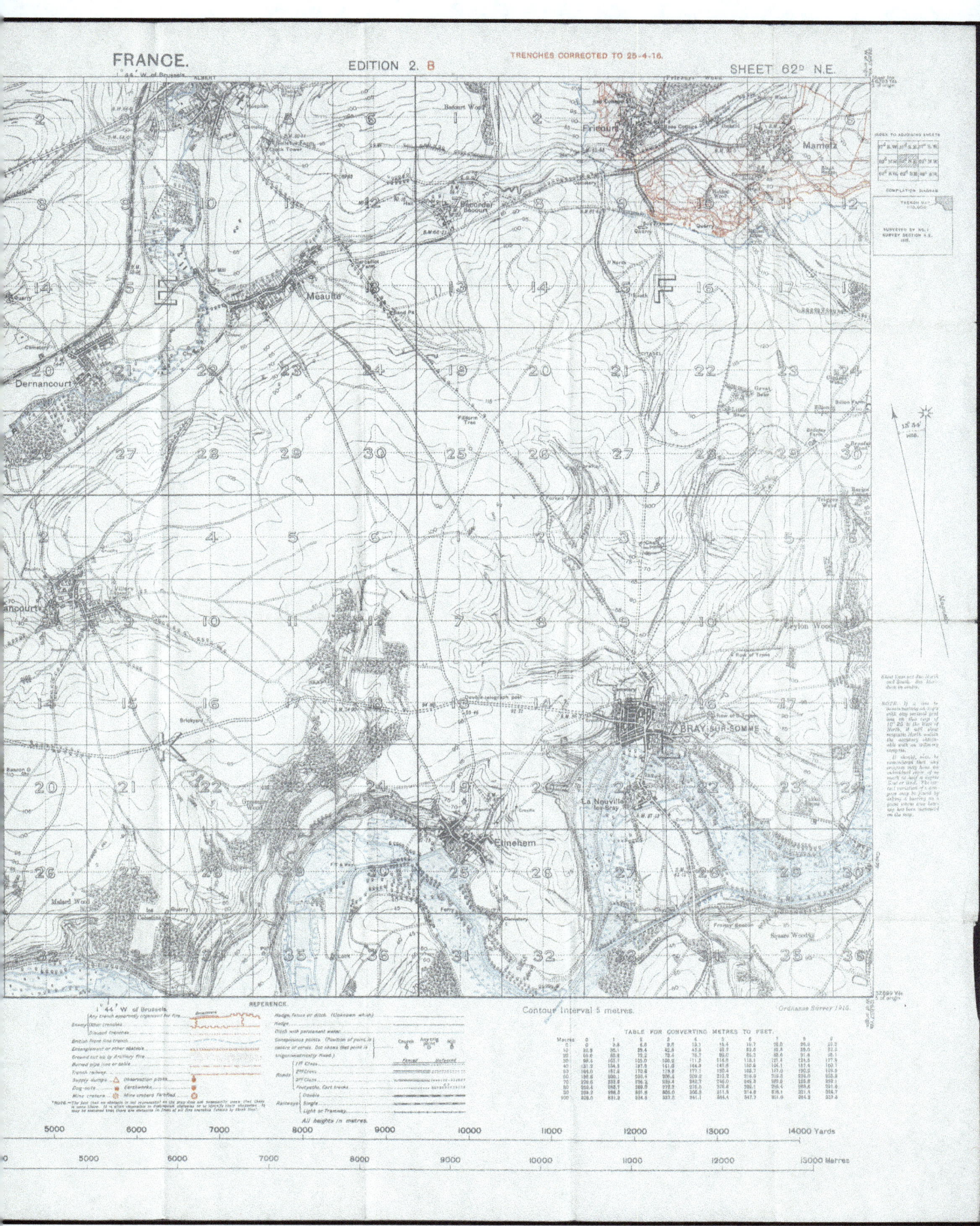

GLOSSARY.

Abbaye, Abbᵉ	Abbey.
Abreuvoir, Abʳ	Watering-place.
Abri de douaniers	Customs shelter.
Aciérie	Steel works.
Aiguillon	Points (Ry.)
Allée	Alley, Narrow road
Ancien -ne, Ancⁿ	Old.
Aqueduc	Aqueduct.
Arbre	Tree.
— éventail	fan-shaped
— dechiré	bare.
— fourchu	forked.
— isolé	isolated.
— penché	leaning.
Arbrisseau	Small tree.
Arc	Arch.
Ardoisière, Ardⁱᵉ	Slate quarry.
Arrêt	Halt.
Asile	Asylum.
— des aliénés	Lunatic asylum.
— de charité des pauvres de refuge	Asylum.
Auberge, Aubᵍᵉ	Inn.
Aune	Alder-tree.
Bac	Ferry.
— à traille	Ferry.
Halles	Halls.
Place aux bains	Bathing place.
Balise	Boom, Beacon.
Banc de sable	Sand-bank.
— vase	Mud-bank.
Baraque	Hut.
Barrage	Dam.
Barrière	Gate, Stile.
Machine à Bascule	Weigh-bridge.
Bassin	Dock, Pond.
— d'échouage	Tidal dock.
Bassin de radoub	Dry dock.
Bateau phare	Light-ship.
Blanchisserie	Laundry.
B.M. (borne milliaire)	Mile stone.
Bⁿᵉ (borne kilométrique)	
Boulangerie	
Fabᵗ de boulons	Bolt Factory.
Bouée	Buoy.
Brasserie, Brassᵉ	Brewery.
Briqueterie, Briqᵗ	Brickfield.
Brise-lames	Breakwater.
Bureau de poste	Post office.
— de douane	Custom house.
Butte	Butt, Mound.
Cabane	Hut.
Cabaret, Cabᵗ	Inn.
Câble sous-marin	Submarine cable.
Calvaire, Calʳᵉ	Calvary.
Canal de dessèchement	Drainage canal.
Canal d'irrigation	Irrigation canal.
Fabᵗ de caoutchouc	Rubber factory.
Carrière, Carʳᵉ	Quarry.
— de gravier	Gravel-pit.
Caserne	Barracks.
Champ de courses	Race-course.
— de manœuvres	Drill-ground.
— de tir	Rifle range.
Chantier	Building yard.
— Ship yard.
— Dock yard.
Chantier de construction	Ship-way.
Chapelle, Chᵉˡˡᵉ	Chapel.
Charbonnage	Colliery.
Château d'eau	Water tower.
Chaussée	Causeway. Highway.
Chemin de fer	Railway.
Cheminée, Chᵉᵉ	Chimney.
Chêne	Oak tree.
Cimetière, Cimᵉ	Cemetery.
Clocher	Belfry.
Clouterie	Nail factory.
Colombier	Dove-cot.

Corons	Workmen's dwellings.
Cour des marchandises, aux diers	Goods yard.
Couvent	Convent.
Crassier	Slag heap.
Croix	Cross.
Darse	Inner dock.
Démoli	Destroyed.
Détruit -e, Détʳ	Destroyed.
Déversoir	Weir.
Digue	Dyke, causeway.
Distillerie, Distᵉ	Distillery.
Douane	Custom-house.
Bureau de douane	Custom-house.
Entrepôt de douane	Customs warehouse.
Dynamitière, Dynamᵗ	Dynamite magazine.
Dynamiterie	Dynamite factory.
Ecluse	Sluice, Lock.
Ecluette, Eclᵗᵗᵉ	Sluice.
Ecole	School.
Ecurie	Stable.
Eglise	Church.
Emaillerie	Enamel works.
Embarcadère, Embʳᵉ	Landing-place.
Estaminet, Estamᵗ	Inn.
Etang	Pond.
Fabrique, Fabᵗ	Factory.
Fabᵗ de produits chimiques	Chemical works.
Fabᵗ de faïence	Pottery.
Faïencerie	Pottery.
Ferme, Fᵐᵉ	Farm.
Filature, Filᵗʳᵉ	Spinning mill.
Fonderie, Fondᵉ	Foundry.
Fontaine, Fontⁿᵉ	Spring, fountain.
Fonts	Fonts.
Forme de radoub	Dry dock.
Forge	Smithy.
Fosse	Mine, Pit.
Fossé	Moat, Ditch.
Four	Kiln.
— à chaux	Lime-kiln.

Four à coke	Coke oven.
Ganterie	Glove Factory.
Gare	Station.
Garenne	Warren.
Garnison	Garrison.
Gazomètre	Gazometer.
Glacerie	
Fabᵗ de glaces	Mirror Factory.
Glacière	Ice factory.
Grue	Crane.
Gué	Ford.
Guérite	Sentry-box, Turret.
— à signaux	Signal-box (Ry.)
Halle	Hall.
Hangar	Shed, Hangar.
Hôpital	Hospital.
Hôtel-de-Ville	Town hall.
Houillère	Colliery.
Huilerie	Oil factory.
Imprimerie, Impʳⁱᵉ	Printing works.
Jetée	Pier.
Laminerie	Rolling mills.
Ligne de haute	
Laisse marée de basse marée	High water mark. Low
Maison Forestière Mⁿ Fʳᵉ	Forester's house.
Malterie	Malt-house.
Marbrerie	Marble works.
Marais	Marsh.
Marais salant	Salines. Salt marsh.
Marché	Market.
Mare	Pond.
Moule	Rick.
Minière	Mine.
Monastère	Monastery.
Moulin, Mⁿ	Mill.
— à vapeur	Steam mill.
Mur	Wall.
— crénelé	Loop-holed wall.

Nacelle	Ferry.
Orme	Elm.
Orphelinat	Orphanage.
Ouacaies	Osier-beds.
Ouvrage	Fort.
Ouvrages hydrauliques	Water works
Papeterie	Paper-mill.
Parc	Park, yard.
— aéostatique	Aviation grⁿᵈ
— à charbon	Coal yard.
— à pétrole	Petrol store.
Passage à niveau P.N.	Level-crossing.
Passerelle, Passᵉˡˡᵉ	Foot-bridge.
Pépinière	Nursery-garden.
Peuplier	Poplar tree.
Phare	Light-house.
Pilier, Pᵉʳ	Post.
Plaine d'exercice	Pasp.
Pompe	Pump.
Ponceau	Culvert.
Pont	Bridge.
— levis	Drawbridge.
Poste de garde	Coast-guard station.
Station côtière	station.
Poterie	Pottery.
Poudrière, Poudʳᵉ	Powder magazine.
Magasin à poudre	
Prise d'eau	Water supply
Puits	Pit-head, Shaft.
— artésien	Artesian well.
— d'arrage	
— ventilateur	Ventilating.
— de sondage	Boring.
Quai	Quay, Platform.
— aux bestiaux	Cattle platform.
— aux marchandises	Goods platform.
Raccordement	Junction.
Raffinerie	Refinery.
— de sucre	Sugar refinery.
Râperie	Beet-root

MAP 2

DUNL: AREA
1st to 3 2nd SEPT 1916

A P P E N D I C E S

IV & V

56th DIVISION GENERAL STAFF

SEPTEMBER 1916.

CASUALTIES.
CAPTURED MATERIAL: PRISONERS.

XIV Corps.
5th Divn. Composite Brigade
167th Infantry Brigade
168th Infantry Brigade
169th Infsntry Brigade
A.D.M.S.
C.R.E.
C.R.A.

56th Division G/393

"Q"
French Liaison Officer
5th Cheshire Regt.
6th Division.

Reference 56th Divisional Order No.36, para 6 line 5, for 13th instant amend 14th instant.

Head Qrs. 56th Div.

12th September, 1916.

A.S.Bayley, Major
for
Lieut.-Colonel,
General Staff.

AMENDMENTS TO OPERATION ORDER NO.1.

by BRIGADIER-GENERAL R.J.G. ELKINGTON, C.M.G.

COMMANDING RIGHT ARTILLERY.

Insert Reference 1/10,000 Trench Map
and Special Sketch Map.

Para 3.   For "at zero" read 'at + 7 minutes'

Para 4.   is cancelled and the following substituted:-

4.   In support of the 56th Division the action of the Right Divisional Artillery from Zero onwards will be as follows:-

FROM Zero onwards.

WILSON'S GROUP (18, 18-pdrs and 4 4.5" Hositzers)

(i) From a standing barrage B.4.a.2.8. to T.27.b.90.95 to T.21.d.4.3. to T.21.d.45.75.
(ii) The howitzers will fire on trenches and trench junctions in the Orchard and Sunken Road and the trenches just South of the road about T.27.b.95.80.

16th DIVISIONAL ARTILLERY.

from Zero onwards

(i) 6 18-pdrs. Standing barrage T.21.d.45.75. to T.21.b.central
(ii) 6 18-pdrs. will enfilade German trench T.16.d.2.2 to T.16.d.90.95.
(iii) 1 4.5-inch Howitzer battery will fire on Bouleaux Wood between the line T.21.b.central to T.21.b.8.4. and the line T.21.b.65.70 to T.21.b.90.95 but not further N.E. than the latter line.

At Zero.

(v) 12 18-pdrs. will establish a creeping barrage T.15.d.8.0. to T.16.c.4.7.
(vi) 6 18-pdrs. will establish a standing enfilade barrage T.21.b.central to T.16.c.4.6.
(vii) 1 4.5-inch Howitzer battery will establish a creeping barrage T.21.b.9.8. to T.16.c.central.

At + 7 minutes.

The creeping 18-pdr. and 4.5-inch Howitzer barrages will move S.E. 50 yards and will continue to move S.E. at the rate of 50 yards a minute until the line T.22.a.20.35 to T.16.c.85.30 is reached when they will stand.
The standing 18-pdr. barrage will lift from the line T.21.b.central - T.16.c.4.6. on to the line T.22.a.20.35 - T.16.c.85.30 - T.16.c.9.8.

2.

At + 14 mins. and onwards.

> The creeping 18-pdr. barrage on T.22.a.20.35 - T.16.c.85.30 will be adjusted to distribute fire equally over the line T.21.b.90.55 to T.22.a.20.35 to T.16.c.85.30 to T.16.c.9.8.
> The Howitzer battery forming the creeping barrage will fire on Cross roads and Trench junctions on the N.W. end of Combles, and on selected cross roads & strong points in Combles N.W. of a line T.28.c.3.4. - Combles Church to T.22.d.5.0.

At + 2 hours

> The Hoqitzer battawy on cross trench T.16.b.6.3. - T.16.d.95.90 will stop firing and await further orders.

From + 2 hours 30 minutes onwards

> The 18pdr. battery on Enfilade German Trench T.16.d.2.2. - T.16.d.90.95 will onlt fire on that portion of the trench T.16.d.2.2. - T.16.d.6.8.

RATE OF FIRE.

Zero to + 14 mins.

> All 18-pdr. and Howitzer batteries shooting north of East and West line through T.21.central to T.22.central INTENSE.
> Other Batteries .. .. ORDINARY

From + 14 mins. until further orders.

> All batteries ORDINARY unless the situation requires an increase rate.

Para 5 is cancelled and the following substituted:-

No fire will be brought to bear S.E. of the line Combles Church to T.18.a.3.9. - Rocquigny Church.

PLEASE ACKNOWLEDGE:

                                                                                  J. A. DON,
                                                                  Major R.A.,
                                                              Brigade Major,
September 24th 1916.   Right Divisional Artillery.

Copies distributed as before with the addition of:-

> FRENCH LIAISON OFFICER   2 copies.
> HEAVY ARTY. LIAISON OFFICER.1 copy.

OPERATION ORDER NO. 1.

BY BRIGADIER-GENERAL R.J.G.ELKINGTON, C. M. G.

COMMANDING RIGHT DIVISIONAL ARTILLERY.

23rd September 1916.

1. (a) Fourth Army will renew the attack on September 25th, in conjunction with the attacks of the french to the south.

   (b) The objectives of the XIV Corps include the villages of Morval and Lesboeufs. The 56th Division is to form a protective flank for the remainder of the Corps facing S.E.
   The 5th Division will be on the left of the 56th Division and has Morval for its objective.

   (c) A map will be forwarded showing boundary between 5th and 56th Divisions, objectives, and other formations.

2. The tasks of the 56th Division are as follows:-

   (a) To secure fire positions about the North corner of Bouleaux Wood from which the valley running N.E. from Combles can be swept by fire.

   (b) To obtain touch with the 5th Division about T.16.c.45.70.

   (c) To neutralise the German detachments occupying Bouleaux Wood. To assist in this a barrage from smoke mortars will be placed on the area to be shewn on Maps which will be forwarded.

3. At Zero 168th Brigade will assault from the new trench T.15.d.9.4. - T.16.c.1.8. with the object of securing the new German Trench running from Bouleaux Wood to tramline about T.16.c.45.55., establishing a strong point facing south in the N.W.(?)corner of Bouleaux Wood about T.16.c.2.1. and gaining touch with the right of the 5th Division about T.15.c.45.70.
   They will advance under close cover of a creeping barrage.

4. In suppprt of the 56th Division the action of the Right Divisional Artillery from Zero onwards will be as follows:-

   At Zero.

   WILSON'S GROUP. (18 18-pdrs. and 4 4.5" Hows.)

   Form a standing barrage B.4.a.2.8.-T.27.b.90.95 - T.21.d.4.3. - T.21.d.45.75.
   The Hoqitzers will fire on the trenches and Trench Junctions in the orchard and Sunken road and on the Trench just south of the Road, about T.27.b.95.80.

16th DIVISIONAL ARTILLERY.

(i) 6 18-pdrs. standing barrage T.21.d.45.75 - T.21.b.central.
(ii) 6 18-pdrs. will enfilade German trench T.16.d.2.2. - T.16.d.90.95.
(iii) 1 4.5" Howitzer Battery will fire on Cross Trench T.16.b.6.3. - T.16.d.95.90.
(iv) 1 4.5" Howitzer Battery will fire on Bouleaux Wood between the line T.21.b.central - T.21.b.8.4. and the line T.21.b.65.70 - T.21.b.90.55. but not further N.E. than the latter line.
(v) 12 18-pdrs. will establish a creeping barrage T.15.d.8.0. - T.16.c.4.7.
(vi) 6 18-pdrs. will establish a standing enfilade barrage T.21.b.central - T.16.c.4.6.
(vii) 1½ 4.5" Howitzer will establish a creeping barrage T.21.b.8.9. - T.16.c.central.

At 1.

The creeping 18-pdr. and 4.5" Howitzer barrages will move S.E. 50 yards and will continue to move S.E. at the rate of 50 yards a minute until the line T.22.a.20.35 - T.16.c.85.30 is reached when they will stand.

The standing 18-pdr. barrage will lift from the line T.21.b.central - T.16.c.4.6. on to the line T.22.a.20.35 - T.16.c.85.30. - T.16.c.9.8.

From 8 onwards.

The creeping 18-pdr. barrage on T.22.a.20.35. - T.16.c.25.30. will be adjusted to distribute fire equally over the line T.21.b.90.55. - T.22.a.20.35. - T.16.c.85.30. - T.16.c.9.8.

The Howitzer battery forming the creeping barrage will fire on cross roads and trench junctions on the N.W. end of Combles.

At 2 hrs. 30 mins.

The Howitzer battery on Cross Trench T.16.b.6.3. - T.16.d.95.90. will stop firing and will await further orders.

From 2 hrs. 30 mins. onwards.

The 18-pdr. batteries on enfilade German trench T.16.d.2.2. - T.16.d.90.95. will only fire on that portion of the trench T.16.d.2.2. - T.16.d.6.8.

RATE OF FIRE.

ZERO to 6.

All 18-pdr. and Howitzer batteries shooting N. of an East and West Line through T.21.central - T.22.central -- INTENSE.

Other Batteries -- ORDINARY.

6 until further orders.

All Batteries - ORDINARY - unless the situation requires an increased rate.

5. No fire will be brought to bear S.E. of the line Combles Church - T.28.central - T.17.d.5.0. - T.18.central - U.7.central.

6. Zero hour will be notified later.

7. ACKNOWLEDGE.

                              J. A. DON,

                                   Major,
                              Brigade Major,
                         Right Divisional Artillery.

SECRET.   56th Div. No. O.G.29.

French Liaison Officer.

   With reference to 56th Divisional Order
No. 44 dated 23rd instant:-

1.   ZERO hour will be at 12.35 p.m. on September
     25th.   The French are attacking at the same hour.

     This hour is only to be communicated to those
     who, it immediately concerns, and in no case
     should it be communicated by tekephone.

2.   Reference para: 1 of Divisional Order, "A"
     minutes will be plus 7 minutes. Assaulting
     troops of 168th Infantry Brigade will therefore
     leave RANGER trench at zero plus 7 minutes.

3.   Acknowledge by wire.

                                    J. BRING.

                                       Lieut.-Colonel.
Hqrs. 56th Divn.   General Staff.

24th September 1916.

SECRET.   56th Division.

                                           O. G. 30.

French Liaison Officer.

      With reference to instructions for smoke mortars (Appendix "A" issued with 56th Divisional Order No. 43, dated 22.9.16) para. 1, the smoke barrage will commence at zero plus 5 minutes instead of zero.

                           J. BRIND.

Hqrs. 56th Divn.   Lieut.-Colonel.

24th September. 1916.   General Staff.

SECRET.

Headquarters,
56th Divisional Artillery,

No. S/CRA/344/15.

24. 9. 16.

Captain Boillot,
   French Liaison Officer,
      attached 5th Division.

      With reference to the letter of Colonel Masselin, copy of which is attached,

2 (a)   Will be done by 4.5" Howitzers (2 batteries) during the preparation and attack, until Right Artillery hear from you that the French G.O.C. wishes fire to be lifted off it.

      No shelling will be done East of the railway.

(b)   Noted. This fire may continue as far as we are concerned throughout the attack.

(c)   Brigadier-General RA. XIV Corps says "The Heavy "Artillery of the Corps will shell Sailly Saillisel "up to Zero on the 25th as agreed with the French."

   It therefore appears that they do not continue on Sailly Saillisel after Zero. This you might ascertain for certain through your Heavy Artillery Liaison Officer.

(d)   Brigadier-General RA XIV Corps says "The Heavy "Artillery will shell Tranchee de Morval down "to 641 (the boundary with the French) up to "Zero and throughout the attack.

                ~~xxxxxxxx~~ J.A.DON.

                Major,
                Brigade Major,
24th September 1916.   Right Divisional Artillery.

Copy of letter received from Captain Boillot by C.R.A.
Right Artillery, at 12.45 p.m. 23rd September, 1916.

Translation of letter addressed to Captain Boillot by
Colonel MASSELIN.

                                                  22.9.16.

1.   Herewith copy of instructions just received.

2.   I should like you to submit the following proposal to such C.R.A's as it may concern:-

(a)   The British artillery which is to shoot on Combles might shoot on the part of the village W. of Railway line during the whole of the preparation and attack.

(b)   I will undertake the summary destruction and neutralisation of Tranchee de Morval during the attack up to 641 inclusive. I intend going on with this shoot right through the attack or up to time selected by British Artillery.

(c)   I propose to entrust the British artillery with the task of carrying out the destruction of the Northern part of Sailly Saillisel N. of Cross-Roads East of Chateau (11.½-92). This destruction may begin now and continue during the attack.

(d)   Moreover, I should like the British artillery to deal with Tranchee de Morval thoroughly from 640 - 641 during the whole of the attack.

                                        (sd) J. Masselin.

                                              Colonel.

COPY.

1st French A.C.
    656/S
 97. A.D./1.

E X T R A C T.

After agreement between 1st Fr. A.C. and XIVth British A.C., it has been settled that the limit of areas in which the respective divisional artilleries will carry out their destructions and barrages runs roughly along the line - Centre of Combles - 8177(300 M. N of station) - 641 (Tranchee de Morval, 400 m N. of Bois de la Haie) - 9791 - (600 m. S.W. of Bois Tripot).

However, the artillery of the XIVth British Corps will support the French artillery by turning some batteries on Sailly Saillisel, and some on Combles for destructive purposes.

The latter batteries will shoot on Combles not only during the preparation of the attack, but also during the attack proper (even after Zero hour) up to the moment when G.O.C. de Fonclare shall require the British artillery to stop the firing on Combles or to lift off the barrage on to the West in the event of same becoming dangerous for assaulting troops under his command.

                                     (sd) GUILLAUMAT.
                                        G.O.C., 1st Fr. A.C.

SECRET.   5th Division
                                                 S.586/22.

Reference 5th Division Operation Order No. 127.

1.   Zero hour will be at 12.35 p.m. on September 25th.
The French are attacking at the same hour.
        This hour is only to be communicated to those whom
it immediately concerns, and in no case should it be
communicated by telephone.

2.   Reference para. 12 of Operation Order:
            for "From zero to zero plus 20 minutes"
            read "From zero plus 5 minutes to zero plus 25 minutes".

ACKNOWLEDGE.

                                         R.A.(?) CURRIE

                                                  Lt.-Colonel.
5th Division   General Staff, 5th Division.
24th September.

To: Captain BOILLOT, 2nd French Div.

Senders Number.	Day of Month.
G. 302.	30th

AAA

    Air photos just received are of little value as regards operation of Longacre aaa Divnl. Order No. 50 is modified as follows aaa Small patrols under officers and approximately ten other ranks will be pushed out close under the creeping barrage and occupy any points vacated by enemy aaa Creeping barrage will commence at hour notified in O.O. 50 one hundred and fifty yards in front of trenches occupied by us aaa Barrage will start creeping at plus two minutes at rate of fifty yards a minute to line two hundred yards East of Brown Line where it will stand aaa After plus sixty minutes rate of fire will be reduced to moderate aaa Points to be secured by patrols if possible are as follows aaa By Loft (169) the two trenches in T.5.c. aaa By Ladder Rainy Trench and trench from T.34.b.5.2. to T.34.b.4.8. and Sunken Road T.34.b.4.8. to T.34.a.1.8. ~~xxxSunkenxRoadx~~ aaa Front line is to be thinly held during the operation and particular attention paid to position of hostile barrage for future guidance aaa ACKNOWLEDGE aaa Addressed Ladder Loft and Redoust repeated Nerve Trumpet and Boillot.

From: Longacre

Time: 10.45 p.m.

E.A.BECK

Major, for
Lt.Colonel,
General Staff.

PRIORITY.

To: French Liaison Officer.

Sender's Number.   Day of Month.

G. 785.   3rd   AAA.

Attack by FACT on FALFEMONT FARM line is held up aaa
FRAY will assist by advancing from his third objective
across valley in T.26.a. and c. and endeavouring to capture
and consolidate south edge of LEUZE WOOD aaa One
battalion of FALLOW is placed at disposal of FRAY for this
purpose aaa It is clear that FALFEMONT FARM is still
strongly held by enemy aaa A fresh bombardment of this
front from Point 48 to WEDGE WOOD will open at once and
will continue until 6.30 p.m. aaa Last ten minutes of
this bombardment will be as intense as possible aaa
FACT will organize a fresh attack which will be launched
at 6.30 p.m. against above line aaa Two battalions of
FALLOW are placed at disposal of FACT aaa Acknowledge aaa
Addsd Fact and Fray Fallow 3rd Div. Arty. and French
Liaison Officer.

From: FAMED

Time: 4.55 p.m.   R.A. CURRIE

                                            Lt.-Colonel G.S.

SECRET. 56th Divn.

O.G. 47.

167th Inf.Bde.
168th Inf.Bde.
169th Inf.Bde.
C.R.A., 56th Div.
5th Ches. Regt.
C. R. E.
56th Divl.Signals.
French Liaison Officer.
----

1. Reference para. 1 of 56th Divisional Order No. 53 dated 5.10.1916, zero time will be 1.45 p.m.

2. ACKNOWLEDGE.

Hqrs. 56th Divn.
6th October 1916.

E.A.BECK

Major, for
Lieut.-Colonel,
General Staff.

To: Capt. Boillot.

Sender's Number.   Day of Month.

   G. 456.   6th.   AAA.

      Reference Div. Order No. 52 and 53 creeping barrage moves as follows aaa From T.5.c.8.5. to T.5.a.4.1. at ZERO aaa Thence to T.35.c.15.0. at plus 2 minutes aaa Thence to N.34.d.7.7. - N.34.b.7.5. - N.28.d.55.0. - N.28.d.0.20. - N.28.c.8.5. at plus 5 minutes aaa Infantry start right battalion LATCH at ZERO aaa Centre battalion LATCH at plus 2 minutes aaa Left Battalion LATCH from Rainy Trench at plus 4 minutes aaa Right battalion LADDER from Trench N.34.d.0.4. - N.34.c.7.7. - N.34.a.9.5. at ZERO aaa Left Battalion Ladder from N.34.b.4.5. to 3.6. to 3.8. to 2.9. to 7.9. at plus 4 minutes aaa Artillery will deal with sap reported by airman from N.34.b. 7.4. to N.34.b.55.20. from ZERO to plus 3 minutes aaa Acknowledge aaa Addressed LADDER, LATCH, LUMBER, repeated NERVE, TRUMPET, and Capt. Boillot.

From   LONGACRE.

Time.   3.40 p.m.   J.Brind.

                                      Major. G.S.

To:
    Capt ain BOILLOT.

             Sender's Number.   Day of Month.

                G. 447.   6th.   AAA.

      Ref: Div: Order No. 53, para.2 aaa Left of French
Green Line is Pt. 9109 not 9106 aaa   This is approximately
T.5.b.9.6. aaa French attack on Green Line takes place
at zero hour and that on their brown line at zero plus
30 minutes aaa Acknowledge aaa   Addressed Latch
repeated Lumber, Loft and Capt. Boillot.

                              (sgd) ..... ?? ....
                                         Lt.-Colonal. G.S.

From: Longacre.
Time: 12.25 p.m.

56th Div.

S.G. 158/5.

XIVth Corps "Q"
4th Division.
168th Inf.Bde.
C.R.A. 56th Div.
C.R.A. 4th Div.
Captain Boillot.

      As there has been some difference of opinion as to the exact dividing line between the French and English divisions in advance of our present front line, the line shown in attached table was agreed upon today by the General Officers Commanding the French 56th Division and British 56th Division through their Liaison Officers.

(sgd) J.BRIND.

Lt.-Colonel for,
Major - General,
Commanding 56th Division.

Hqrs. 56th Divn.

6th October 1916.

To: Ladder.   Lumber.
    Latch.   Nerve.   Capt. Boillot.
    Loft.   Trumpet.

Senders Number.	Day of Month
G. 496.	7th. AAA.

     Situation is as reported in G.494 aaa LADDER will during night (a) push out one company through RAIMBOW to establish strong post at N.35.a.3.9. and round up Germans in SPECTRUM and connect up with post at N.35.a.central aaa (b) dig a trench 200 yards west of SPECTRUM from which fresh attack can be carried out if necessary in morning aaa One battalion LOFT is placed at disposal of LADDER but will not be used for digging tonight aaa LATCH will ascertan and report if DEWDROP is held by enemy or not aaa If it is not held by enemy strong posts will be established to connect post at N.35.a.central and Hazy Trench tonight aaa Battalion of LOFT may be used for this purpose aaa If DEWDROP is held by enemy LATCH will dig new trench 200 yards West of DEWDROP to admit of bombardment before attack in morning aaa In this latter case Bn. LOFT may be used for attack but not for digging aaa Orders for re-bombardment and attack will be issued as soon as LATCH reports definitely as regards DEWDROP aaa Addressed LADDER, LATCH, LOFT, reptd. LUMBER, NERVE, TRUMPET, CAPT. BOILLOT.

                            (sgd) E.A.BECK.

                                 Major. G.S.

From: Longacre.

Time: 6.35 p.m.

To: LADDER.
     LUMBER.
     LATCH.
     NERVE.
     Capt. BOILLOT.

Sender's Number.	Day of Month.	
G. 508.	7th.	AAA

    Latest report indicated that German counter-attack against HAZY trench gun pits in T.5.a. and against French left has succeeded and that right of LATCH and French left are back in their departure trenches aaa LATCH will ensure that new trench connecting FOGGY and BURNABY is dug without fail tonight and LADDER will make certain of digging fresh departure trench 200 yards West of SPECTRUM Trench aaa As much ground down SPECTRUM as possible should be made by bombing aaa Orders as regards reinforcing post at N.35.a.4.4. hold good aaa Report regarding French not yet confirmed by French division.

                      (sgd) E.A.Beck.

                              Major, G.S.

From:

Time.   9.0 p.m.

Copy of Wires.

Nerve.
Capt. Boillot.

      G. 516.   8th   AAA

    Location Repirt aaa Right Brigade LATCH T.19.a.1.4. aaa LEGION in line T.5.c.4.1. to T.5.a.½.4. aaa LENT in line T.4.b.9½.2. to T.4.a.9.9. aaa LAWN in Shamrock Trench aaa LAVA in Hogs Back and LAUNCH and Leak Trones Wood aaa.

    LEFT Brigade LADDER GUILLEMONT STN? aaa LACE in RAINBOW and SPECTRUM aaa LAMB in original front line and Sunken Roads aaa LAKE in SPECTRUM and front line aaa LAMP 2 coys. believed to be in assembly trenches and 2 in FLERS Line aaa LETTER S. of Ginchy aaa LEG in Serpentine trench as Div. Reserve.

From: LONGACRE

Time: 6.51 a.m.

                      (sgd) E.A.BECK,
                                Major.G.S.

. . . .

Capt. Boillot.

      G. 531.   8th   AAA.

    Left Bn. LATCH reports Right Coy. digging in on ridge and all going well aaa This is not quite clear as to whether objective is reached or not aaa Right bn. reports having advanced 600 yards to objective aaa this is not yet confirmed by written message from front aaa No confirmation from LATCH of hostile counter-attack on French left.

FROM: LONGACRE.

Time: 5.10 p.m.

                      (sgd) E.A.Beck.
                                Major, G.S.

. . . .

To: Captain Boillot.

      G. 528.   8th   AAA

    3.55 p.m. report from Art. states aaa Enemy counter-attacking from T.5.d. and firing 2 guns into Les Boeufs aaa Addst. LATCH repeated Capt. Boillot.

From: LONGACRE.

Time: 4 p.m.

                      (sgd) E.A.BECK.
                                Major, G.S.

Copy of Messages.

To: Capt Boillot.

G. 529.   8th   AAA.

Left Bn. LATCH reports from their forward H.Q. that at 3.40 p.m. their attack was going well aaa F.O.O. from LIGHT reports that our troops are in Hazy Trench and French in continuation on their right.

From: Longacre.   E.A.BECK
Time: 4.20 p.m.   Major. G.S.

. . . .

To: Capt. Boillot.

G. 530.   8th.   AAA

Following from Bde. Major LADDER aaa Art did not reach SPECTRUM Trench with their bombardment aaa at 3.30 p.m. LAMP advanced on southern portion, of Spectrum and were met by a very severe German barrage almost immediately aaa M.gun-fire was to be heard on right aaa LAMP did not reach crest.

From: LONGACRE.   (sgd) E.A.Beck.
Time: 4.40 p.m.   Major G.S.

. . . .

To: Capt. Boillot.

G. 540   8th   AAA

Situation of L.R.B. as discovered by personal reconnaissance of C.O. is that they are digging in just west of HAZY Trench and parellel to it with their left in touch with Q.V.R. presumably about T.5.a.9.5. and their right about T.5.a.7.3. aaa Germans are holding Hazy Trench and there are still Germans with machine guns in gun pits T.5.a.3.6. aaa O.C. Q.V.R. not yet returned from personal reconnaissance aaa not having gained touch with the French LATCH are digging trench from T.5.a.7.3. to trench running S.E. from T.5.a.5.5. aaa Ladder are now joining WINDY Trench to Pt. T.4.b.45.92.

From: Longacre

Time: 10.15 p.m.   (sgd) E.A.Beck,
                                              Major   G.S.

OPERATION ORDER NO. 3.

BY BR.-GENERAL R. J. G. ELKINGTON, C. M. G.

COMMANDING RIGHT ARTILLERY.

October 8th 1916.

1. Situation as given in 56th Divisional Order No.54.

2. Our troops have been withdrawn from RAINY Trench.

3. The attack will be supported by a CREEPING and a STANDING BARRAGE.

4. CREEPING BARRAGE will start at zero on the line

   T.5.c.8.5. - T.5.a.35.15. - T.5.a.20.55.
   N.34.d.50.35. - N.34.d.15.85. - N.34.b.3.6.

   At plus minute it will commence to creep at a rate of 50 yards a minute, by increases of 25 yards until it reaches the line T.5.b.5.2. - N.35.d.1.1. - N.35.c.3.6. - N.29.c.1.0.

5. (a) STANDING BARRAGE will commence on line

   T.5.d.0.8. - T.5.a.25.70. - N.34.d.85.20 - N.34.d.7.7. - N.34.b.6.0. - N.34.b.85.20. - N.34.b.65.65. i.e. on the gun pits in T.5.a. DEWDROP TRENCH as far as N.34.b.65.65.

   (b) One battery will also fire on the sap from SPECTRE to about N.34.b.60.25.
   Special attention will be paid to old gun pit in DEWDROP about N.34.d.9.2. and to the Northern gun pits in T.5.a.

6. (a) The STANDING BARRAGE from T.5.d.0.8. - T.5.a.25.70. will lift at plus three minutes on to HAZY TRENCH from T.5.b.2.0. - T.5.a.85.35. - T.5.a.8.8. - T.5.a.80.95.
   At plus five minutes it will again lift on to the line T.5.b.6.3. - N.35.d.1.1. and will then stand.

   (b) A standing barrage from T.5.a.25.70. - T.34.d.7.7. - will lift on to the line N.35.d.1.1. - N.35.c.3.6. - N.35.a.25.00. at plus three minutes and will then stand.

7. RATES OF FIRE.
   Zero to plus ten minutes .. .. INTENSE.
   Plus ten minutes onwards .. .. ORDINARY.

8. Tasks for 4.5" howitzers after Zero are attached.

9. Zero hour is at 3.30 p.m.

10. ACKNOWLEDGE.

(sgd) J.A.DON.
Major,
Brigade Major, R.A.
Right Division.

APPENDIX NO. 1. to RIGHT ARTILLERY OPERATION ORDER NO.3.

Tasks of Grouos 56th Divisional Artillery are as follows:-

1. SEARCH.

Zero to plus 1 minute.   CREEPING BARRAGE on T.5.c.8.5. - T.5.a.20.55, with special thickening of barrage opposite NORTHERN Gunpit.

At plus 1 minute.   Commence creeping and creep as far as line:- T.5.b.5.2. - N.35.d.1.1. where it will stand.

2. LINK.

Zero to plus 3 minutes.   STANDING BARRAGE on line T.5.d.0.8. - T.5.a.25.70, with special thickening of barrage on Northern Gunpit.

At plus 3 minutes.   Lifts on to HAZY TRENCH (T.5.b.2.0. - T.5.a.85.35 - T.5.a.8.8. - T.5.a.80.95.)

At plus 5 minutes.   Lifts off HAZY TRENCH on to line T.5.b.6.3. - N.35.d.1.1. when it will stand.

3. LUCRE.

Zero to plus 3 minutes.   STANDING BARRAGE T.5.a.25.70. - N.34.d.85.40. (Centre of DEWDROP TRENCH), particularly attention to be paid to old gunpit forming a strong point at N.34.d.85.20.

At plus 3 minutes.   Lifts to line N.35.d.1.1. - N.35.c.3.6. and then stands.

4. LIFE.

At Zero.   Places a STANDING BARRAGE on the line N.34.d.85.40. - N.34.d.7.7. - N.34.b.6.0. - N.34.b.85.20.

At plus 3 minutes.   That portion of the barrage south of N.34.d.7.7. will lift.

At plus 5 minutes.   That portion of the barrage NORTH of N.34.d.7.7. will lift, both to the line N.35.c.3.6. - N.35.a.25.25. when they will stand.

. . . .

4.5" HOWITZERS.

1. SEARCH.

Zero to plus 2 minutes.   Intense on gunpit in T.5.a.

Plus 2 to plus 5 minutes.   Intense on HAZY TRENCH (Northern portion).

Plus 5 minutes.	Lift to STRONG POINT (old gun pits) at N.36.c.0.0. and SLEET TRENCH N.35.d.7.1. - N.35.d.55.60. (Marked slightly wrongly in Hectograph map).

2. **LINK.**

Zero to plus 2 minutes.	Intense on DEWDROP at STRONG POINT N.34.d.85.20, thence to area N.35.d.3.8. - N.35.d.70.85. - N.35.b.6.2. - N.35.b.2.1.

3. **LUCRE.**   Intense Zero to plus 4 minutes on HAZY TRENCH.

At plus 4 minutes.	Lift on to same objective as SEARCH Howitzers.

4. **LIFE.**

Zero to plus 3 minutes.	Intense on old gunpit and new work not shewn on map:- T.5.a.85.25. - N.35.c.1.2.
At plus 3 minutes.	Lift to road junctions at N.30.c.9.1. and N.30.d.1.1.

Amendment to RIGHT ARTILLERY OPERATION ORDER NO.3.

Para. 6, (a) line 6, for T.5.b.6.3. substitute T.6.a.2.9. -
                                                             T.5.b.7.8. -

Para 4, Line 7.   for T.5.b.5.2. substitute T.6.a.2.9. -
                                                           T.5.b.7.8. -

....

Amendment to APPENDIX 1 of RIGHT ARTILLERY OPERATION ORDER NO. 3.

1.   SEARCH.   Line 5.

       for T.5.b.5.2. substitute T.6.a.2.9. - T.5.b.7.8. -

2.   LINK.   Line 5.

       for T.5.b.6.3. substitute T.6.a.2.9. - T.5.b.7.8. -

....

N O T E.

Owing to recent information that our Infantry have not withdrawn from the Northern end of SPECTRUM and are still as far South as N.34.b.7.6. no fire will be brought to bear on SPECTRUM North of N.34.b.70.45.

..;......

COPY of wire.

TO:
XIV Corps
    56th Div.
        Capt. BOILLOT.

Senders Number.   Day of Month.
    G.535.   8   AAA

Left Bn. LATCH report they believe all their assaulting companies to have got past DRWDROP aaa there is no written confirmation of this from front line.

From: LONGACRE.
Time: 6 p.m.   (sgd) M.....Stopps (?)
                                        Captain.G.S.

SECRET.

4TH DIVISION OPERATION ORDER NO. 68.

11th October 1916.

Ref: 1/40,000. ALBERT Sheet.

1. The 11th Infantry Brigade will be in Divisional Reserve tomorrow the 12th inst. and from Zero hour onwards the Brigade will be in readiness to move at short notice from Camps now occupied.

2. All Prisoners of War will be taken under Brigade arrangements to the Advanced Divisional Compound at T.8.d.5.6. where they will be handed over to an escort of XIV Corps Cyclists attached to the Division. These cyclists, who are under the orders of the A.P.M. 4th Division, will be responsible for providing the necessary escorts to conduct batches of prisoners to the Intermediate Divisional Cage at South end of BERNAFAY WOOD.

From the Intermediate Divisional Cage prisoners will be sent in batches to the Adcanced Corps Cage at A.8.a.6.8. on the MONTAUBAN - CARNOY Road under arrangements to be made by the A.P.M. who will superintend the arrival and departure of batches.

3. Instructions as to Medical arrangements are being issued by "Q" Branch of the Staff.

4. ACKNOWLEDGE.

(sgd) ...Bartholomew

Lt.-Col.
General Staff, 4th Division.

Issued at 11 p.m.

Ref: 1/20,000 Map 57.c., S.W. & Map A.

SECRET.

4TH DIVISION OPERATION ORDER NO. 67.

1. (a) On October 4th the Fourth Army will renew the attack on the Brown Line as shown on "Map A" simultaneously with an attack by the French on the 4th Division right. Zero hour will be communicated later.

(b) Boundaries of the XIV Corps objective are marked in RED.

2. The task of the XIV Corps will be carried out in two stages, shewn respectively by a Green and Brown Line. The 4th Division will attack on the Right and the 6th Division on the Left - boundary between 4th and 6th Divisions is marked in YELLOW.

3. The first objective of the 4th Division includes the portion of SPECTRUM TRENCH which is not in our possession, DEWDROP TRENCH and HAZY TRENCH and the establishemnt of a line along the Western crest of the ridge from SPECTRUM to HAZY TRENCH up to the boundary with the French.
   The second objective of the 4th Division is to establish a line on the general line running from N.28.b.8.1. where junction will be obtained with the 6th Division through N.35.a.7.8. - N.35.d.4.8. - T.6.a.5.8. where junction will be obtained with the 18th French Division. The object of the attack is to obtain a line from which the Transloy Line can be seen and assaulted at a later date.

4. (a) The 10th Infantry Brigade will attack on the right and the 12th Infantry Bde. on the Left, boundary between Brigades - a line ~~running~~ drawn from N.34.d.0.0. to junction of road and tracks at N.34.d.6.6. and thence along the Les Boeufs - Transloy Road inclusive to 12th Infantry Brigade.
   (b) The 9th Field Company RE. and 1/1st Durham Field Coy. R.E. will be attached respectively to the 10th and 12th Inf.Bdes.
   These units will be allotted definite tasks but will not leave their positions of assembly before the objectives are definitely captured.

5. The infantry will advance to the attack on the First Objective at Zero. At Zero plus twenty minutes they will advance to the attack of the Second Objective.
   At Zero and Zero plus twnety minutes respectively a standing barrage will be placed on the objectives to be attacked and a creeping barrage will be opened in front of the attacking infantry which barrage will advance at the rate of 50 yards per minute.
   Details of barrages will be communicated later.

6. Bombardment of the objectives to be attacked will be carried out from 7 a.m. to 5 p.m. on October 11th and will be continued from 7 a.m. to Zero on the 12th inst. There will be no period of Intense fire prior to Zero.
   As there may be difficulty in bombarding SPECTRUM TRENCH near the point at which the German and English lines meet, preparation must be made by the 12th Inf.Bde. to bombard the Northern portion of this trench with Stokes Mortars.

7. Strong Points will be established as under:-

By the 10th Inf. Bde.
(T.5.central.
(T.5.b.9.9.
(N.35.c.5.5.

By the 12th Inf. Bde.
(N.35.a.5.4.
(N.35.a.4.9.
(N.28.d.8.8.

8. A contact patrol will be in the air from Zero till dark, flares will be lit on reaching each objective and at 5 p.m.

9. An officer from Divl. Hqrs. will synchronise watches at 10th Inf. Bde. Hqrs. at 7 p.m. on October 11th and again at 9 a.m. on October 12th. Representatives from 10th and 12th Inf. Bdes. and R.F.A. Groups will attend at 10th Inf. Bde. Hqrs. at these hours.

10. ACKNOWLEDGE.

(sgd) W.H. BARTHOLOMEW

Lt.-Col.
General Staff.
4th Division.

Issued at 7 p.m.

10th October 1916.

SECRET

<u>XIV Corps No.S.76/134</u>					<u>56th Division O G5</u>

167th Inf. Bde.					French Liaison Officer
168th Inf. Bde.					5th Cheshire Regt.
169th Inf. Bde.					O.C.Signals.
G.O.C.Artillery Group, Ballon Fm.			"Q"
A.D.M.S.						C.R.A. 56th Division.
C.R.E.

    Reference 56th Divisional Order No.33, the hour of Zero to-morrow the 9th instant will be 4.45 p.m.

    Acknowledge by wire.

Head Qrs. 56th Divn.				(Sd.) A.S.Bayley, Major
												for
8th September, 1916.					Lieut-Colonel
												General Staff.

SECRET

Headquarters
56th Divisional
Artillery
No. S/CRA/344/5
Date. 11.9.16.

56th Division "G" (For Liaison Officer
French Army)

1. At 12.30 p.m. to-morrow September 12th the French on our Right are making an attack.

2. Right Divisional Artillery will assist as follows:-

   1. Barrage by 2 18-pdr Batteries on the French running from T.27.b.1.5 to T.27.d.8.4.

   2. Fire on selected points in that portion of Combles situated west of the Railway by 2 4.5" Howitzer Batteries.

3. Fire will be opened at 12-30 pm and will continue intense until 12-45 pm.
   It will then drop to medium, with short intense periods until further orders.

4. A proportion of P.S. and S.K. Lethal Shells will be employed by the 4.5" Howitzers.

11.9.15

(Sd.) H.G. Fisher

Major
for Brigade Major R.A.
56th Division.

Appendix IX

CASUALTIES.

PERIOD.	DIED OF WOUNDS		KILLED		WOUNDED		MISSING		TOTALS	
	Off.	O.Rs.	Off.	O.Rs.	Off.	O.Rs.	Off.	O.Rs.	Off.	O.Rs.
JUNE 24th to JUNE 30th, 1916.	1	-	3	66	23	405	-	26	27	497
JULY 1st to JULY 4th, 1916.	1	3	30	347	87	2277	40	1497	158	4124
JULY 5th to AUGUST 20th, 1916.	-	1	3	83	20	412	1	22	24	518
September 6th to October, 11th, 1916.	8	2	81	1148	258	4943	30	1680	377	7773
TOTALS.	10	6	117	1644	388	8037	71	3225	586	12912

Captain,
D.A.A.& Q.M.G. 56th Division.

17th October, 1916.

APPENDIX V.

Prisoners and material captured by 56th Division.

1. The following number of unwounded prisoners were captured by 56th Division from the commencement of the offensive on 1st July 1916 up to 30th September. Owing to prisoners having in some cases been evacuated through cages other than the Divisional cages these numbers are not absolutely accurate.

	Officers.	O.Rs.
1st July		186.
6th September to 30th September	7.	133
TOTAL.	7.	319.

2. The following material was captured by the Division between 6th September and 30th September :-

		Where taken.
Machine Guns	4.	N. end of BOULEAUX WOOD and dugouts T.16.c.5.6.
Minenwerfer	8.	(3 at N. end of BOULEAUX WOOD and dugouts T.16.c. 5.6. 5 in COMBLES.
Bomb throwers	2.	Railway embankment T.16.c.
FLAMMENWERFER (large)	1.	COMBLES.
(small)	7.	
Grenades	9,000.	(approximately) COMBLES.
Rifles	1,800.	(approximately) COMBLES and SUNKEN ROAD to LEUZE WOOD from COMBLES

In addition to the above several hundred rounds of field gun ammunition were found in MIDDLE COPSE and COMBLES also a large number of Very lights, rockets, S.A.A. in the latter place.

As the Divisional front was handed over to the French on the evening of 27th Sept. the day following the taking of COMBLES, there was not sufficient time to remove all material captured, but the relieving units of the French were informed of the position of such material as was left behind.

APPENDIX VII

56th DIVISION GENERAL STAFF

SEPTEMBER 1916.

BRITISH: FRENCH & GERMAN DIVISIONS
ENGAGED IN OPERATIONS BETWEEN 6th
& 30th SEPTEMBER 1916.

APPENDIX VII.

The following shows the German Divisions engaged, the French Divisions on the right and the British Divisions on the left of the 56th Division at various times between 6th and 30th September, 1916.

Germans Divisions engaged by 56th Division.

5th Bavarian Division.
51st Reserve Division.
185th Division.
18th Reserve Division.

French Divisions on the right of 56th Division.

1st Division.
2nd Division.
56th Division.

British Divisions on the left of 56th Division.

16th (Irish) Division.
6th Division.
5th Division.
Guards Division.
20th (Light) Division.

Army Form C. 2118.

WAR DIARY
or
INTELLIGENCE SUMMARY.
(Erase heading not required.)

Instructions regarding War Diaries and Intelligence Summaries are contained in F. S. Regs., Part II. and the Staff Manual respectively. Title pages will be prepared in manuscript.

Place	Date	Hour	Summary of Events and Information	Remarks and references to Appendices
	1st Oct.	9.a.m.	Location of Units was as follows :- 169th Inf. Brigade in the right sub-sector of the Div. front with Q.W.R. on the right and Q.V.R. on the left of the front line. 2nd Londons in support and the 5th Londons in reserve at S.24.d. 167th Brigade on the left with 1st Londons in on the reserve right and 7th Middlesex on the left in the front line, 8th Middlesex in support in SERPENTINE Trench and 3rd Londons in support TRONES WOOD. Headquarters of 169th Brigade at GUILLEMONT QUARRY, Headquarters 167th Brigade at GUILLEMONT STATION. 168th Brigade in reserve with H.Q. at the BRIQUETERIE on the MARICOURT - MONTAUBAN Road, with the 4th Londons and London Scottish at TRONES WOOD - 12th and 13th Londons at the CITADEL.	See Appendix II Map B
		12.15 p.m.	A report was received from the 167th Brigade that a reconnaissance carried out by Brigade Major showed that the SUNKEN ROAD running East from N.34.a.1.8. was clear as far as the top of the crest, but patrols pushed forward beyond this point drew fire at once. The trenches near N.34.b.8.8. were held by the enemy. The whole of the Western face of the ridge opposite the 167th Brigade as far as N.34.d.3.0. had been patrolled without interference from the enemy. A few of the enemy had been seen in N.28.c. This information was repeated to the XIVth Corps.	See Appendix I Map D
		5.0 p.m.	XIVth Corps was informed that patrols had left our trenches as ordered and had advanced apparently without difficulty. Their actual position was uncertain and the airman's report showed that our occupation of RAINY TRENCH was doubtful. The enemy had placed a heavy barrage on FOGGY TRENCH.	
		5.15 p.m.	Message was received from the 20th Division on our left showing that the contact aeroplane at 4.20 p.m. stated that their patrols had not met with very much success. There was a heavy hostile barrage on LES BOEUFS. FOGGY TRENCH, portions of RAINY TRENCH and WINDY TRENCH had been occupied.	
		6.25 p.m.	This was confirmed by 167th Brigade who stated that their right battalion had occupied RAINY TRENCH with one platoon with posts pushed forward to the crest. The left battalion had gained all its objectives and was digging in. The right battalion of the division on our left (20th) was reported to have gained its objectives. XIVth Corps was informed of the situation.	
		8.0 p.m.	XIVth Corps informed that the situation as ascertained by the Brigade Major of the 167th Brigade was as follows:- We had occupied the trench 100 yards W. of RAINY TRENCH but were not actually in RAINY itself. Posts of the Left Battalion were believed to be approximately along the 120 contour, and thence along the SUNKEN ROAD; digging parties had gone forward to join up the line of posts. It was asked that aeroplane photographs might be provided as soon as possible to confirm this.	
	2nd Oct.	5.20 p.m.	Location of Units was the same as on the 1st. The Right Brigade reported a comparatively quiet night.	/5.30

T.134. W₁. W708-775. 500000. 4/15. Sir J. C. & S.

Army Form C. 2118.

WAR DIARY
or
INTELLIGENCE SUMMARY

(Erase heading not required.)

Instructions regarding War Diaries and Intelligence Summaries are contained in F. S. Regs., Part II and the Staff Manual respectively. Title Pages will be prepared in manuscript.

Place	Date	Hour	Summary of Events and Information	Remarks and references to Appendices
	3rd Oct.	5.30 a.m.	167th Infantry Brigade reported that the situation in RAINY TRENCH was not clear. The enemy's Artillery had been very active during the night, but had not interfered with the work of joining up the posts.	
		10.0 a.m.	167th Brigade reported that the following posts had been joined up during the night 1/2nd:- N.28.c.6.0., N.28.d.0.0., N.34.b.2.7., N.34.b.2.4., N.34.b.3.0. During the morning hostile aeroplanes were very active over our lines. In some cases they flew low over the trenches firing machine guns without being molested; one, however, was brought down by one of our field batteries and fell behind the ridge at N.36.central. Major BAYLEY's G.S.O.2, left the Division to proceed to England to take up an instructional appointment being replaced on the Divnl: Staff by Major E.A. Beck. D.S.O. R. Scots Fus.	See appendix II Map 2
		1.20 p.m.	Orders were issued to 167th and 169th Brigades to carry out the following work during the night:- 2/3rd:- Consolidation of posts gained and connection of posts commenced last night, particular attention to be paid to strengthen posts at inter-brigade boundaries. One good communication trench to be dug in each brigade sector. Brigades instructed to endeavour to round up isolated parties of the enemy about RAINY TRENCH and T.5.c. respectively, by working round them. During the afternoon Divisional Order No. 51 was issued, detailing 169th Brigade to take over the front occupied by the Right Battalion of the 167th Brigade during the night 2/3rd. 168th Brigade to relieve the 169th Brigade in the right sub-sector on the night 3/4th. The dividing line between Brigades to run from M.30.c.0.0., M.35.a.0.0., N.34.d.0.6 along the track to N.34.c.0.0.	See appendix III See map attd. to Div.Order No. 51.
		5.30 p.m.	The following order was issued to C.R.A., and Hy. Artillery XIVth Corps:- "Reference Map Y15 corrected up to 9.0 am. 2nd instant. The following will be dealt with by 4.5" howitzers of the 56th Divnl. Arty. - Portion of RAINBOW TRENCH within our zone, SPECTRUM TRENCH, DEWDROP TRENCH, Battery posts T.5.a.5.5. to 2.6. and HAZY TRENCH. Portions of above where our trenches are close only if observation can be obtained and at times to be settled by liaison officers with Brigades. The following can be dealt with by XIVth Corps Heavy Artillery provided observation can be obtained:- RAINBOW TRENCH from N.28.d.0.2. to Road at N.34.b.6.9. and HAZY TRENCH." Location of units on the morning of the 3rd on completion of relief detailed in Divisional Order No. 51, was as follows:- 169th Brigade on the right with 5th London Regt. in the right subsector and the 2nd London Regt. in the left subsector of the front line - Q.V.R's in OX TRENCH and BOVRIL TRENCH - Q.W.R's in HOGS BACK TRENCH and CUTLET TRENCH in support. 167th Brigade on the left with 7th Middlesex in the front line - 8th Middlesex in support in SERPENTINE TRENCH - 1st and 3rd Londons in Reserve in TRONES WOOD. 168th Brigade in Reserve as before.	See appendix II Map 2
		/5.30 a.m.		

Army Form C. 2118.

WAR DIARY
or
INTELLIGENCE SUMMARY

(Erase heading not required.)

Instructions regarding War Diaries and Intelligence Summaries are contained in F. S. Regs., Part II. and the Staff Manual respectively. Title Pages will be prepared in manuscript.

Place	Date	Hour	Summary of Events and Information	Remarks and references to Appendices
		5.30 a.m.	Situation report shewed that the night passed quietly in front of the 167th Brigade, but on the front of 169th Brigade, the right battalion sector had received considerable shelling which had delayed reliefs. Left Battalion sector had been fairly quiet. It was confirmed that the enemy were occupying trench immediately East of RAINY TRENCH.	
		11.20 a.m.	Work report received from 169th Brigade shewed that the following work had been done during the night. The trench held by us had been deepened and cleared. Communication trench through LESBOEUFS and the communication trench along the track South of LESBOEUFS had been improved. The gap in the front line about T.5.c.2.4. had been joined up.	See Appendix II Map D
		12.25 p.m.	Warning Order was issued stating that the relief of the 169th Brigade by 168th Brigade detailed in Divisional Order No. 51 would probably be postponed for 24 hours. The afternoon passed uneventfully except for hostile shelling of LESBOEUFS.	See Appendix III
		6.0 p.m.	Divisional Order No. 52 issued stating that the Fourth Army would renew the attack on October 5th. The task of the XIVth Corps being to establish itself on a line from which the main LE TRANSLOY system of trenches could be attacked at a later date. The operation was to be carried out in two stages - the first stage of the task allotted to the 56th Division included the capture of the disconnected trenches HAZY, DEWDROP, SPECTRUM and part of RAINBOW Trenches. The second task of the Division was to establish a line along the Western crest of the ridge from which the LE TRANSLOY trench system could be seen. The operation was to be carried out by the 169th Brigade on the right and the 167th Brigade on the left.	
4th Octr.			According to a scheme arranged by the G.O.C., 169th Brigade, the 5th London Regiment occupied the enemy's trenches in T.5.c. during the latter part of the night of the 3rd instant before handing over to the 168th Brigade. One company of this regiment had remained behind a dig a communication trench from the newly captured AEROPLANE Trench to T.10.b. This was reported to be dug through except for forty yards by 3.30 a.m., at which time an almost continuous front line existed from T.11.a.2.9. to a track at T.5.a.1.5. The communication trench which was shallow at some places had been dug through - T.4.c.6.3., T.4.c.9.8. to T.5.c.1.7.	See Appendix D Map D
		3.30 a.m.	Relief of 169th Brigade by 168th Brigade was reported to be complete.	
		5.30 a.m.	Situation on the front of the 167th Brigade could not be ascertained owing to all wires being cut. The location of units was as follows:- 168th Brigade on the right with 14th London Regt. holding the right subsector, 4th London Regt. holding the left subsector, 13th Londons in support in HOGS BACK and CUTLET Trenches, 12th London Regt. in reserve in trenches N.E. of GUILLEMONT - Hdqrs. of the Brigade at GUILLEMONT QUARRY. 167th Brigade on the left with 8th Middlesex in the front line, 3rd London Regt. in support in SERPENTINE TRENCH, 1st Londons	See Appendix IV Map B

/and

Army Form C. 2118.

WAR DIARY
or
INTELLIGENCE SUMMARY

(Erase heading not required.)

Place	Date	Hour	Summary of Events and Information	Remarks and references to Appendices
	5th Oct.	5am.	1st Londons and 7th Middlesex in reserve at TRONES WOOD. 169th Brigade in reserve with Hdqrs. at the BRIQUETERIE. 2nd and 5th London Regts. in TRONES WOOD Area, 9th and 16th London Regts. at the CITADEL.	
			Information was received from the XIVth Corps that owing to the wet weather the operation originally ordered to take place on the 5th October had been definitely postponed for 48 hours. Owing to the state of the weather it had been impossible for aeroplane photographs to be taken, consequently it was very difficult to ascertain the exact position of our troops. During the day the enemy shelled LES BOEUFS and the vicinity almost continuously; also GINCHY and the area immediately N. of it.	
			Morning situation reports showed that the hostile shelling had continued during the night, on LES BOEUFS and our trenches in the vicinity which had interfered with working parties in front of 168th Brigade who reported that enemy movement in RAINY TRENCH drew hostile rifle fire as the enemy had the advantage of observation from DEWDROP.	See Appendix II Map D
		2.30 p.m.	Report received from 168th Brigade that in spite of hostile activity considerable work had been done during the night 4/5th - RAINY TRENCH had been joined up to the post at T.4.c.9.6. with the exception of a gap of 50 yards in the middle. Considerable work was also reported to have been done on several communication trenches. In spite of orders issued the 13th London Regt. had failed to join up from FOGGY TRENCH to RAINY TRENCH. Orders had been issued for this to be done during the night 5/6th and had not fail.	
		2.55 p.m.	Report was received from 167th Brigade with reference to the wire in front of enemy's trenches. Patrol from No. 5 post reported wire in front of the enemy's trenches 350 yards E. of the post. Officers patrol from No. 7. No. 6 post went out for 100 yards beyond the top of the ridge and reported wire about 20 to 30 yards in front of the German trench which was 250 yards E. of the crest. A patrol from No. 7 post reported enemy's lines 200 yards distant with new wire in front of it, which appeared to have been hastily put up. These reports showed that the whole of SPECTRUM and RAINBOW Trenches were wired throughout. Remainder of the day passed without incident, except for the usual shelling of our posts.	
	6th Oct.	5.0 am.	Morning reports shewed that the situation was unchanged on our front. There had been usual hostile shelling and an increase in hostile sniping during the night of the 5/6th.	
		10.30 am.	An order was issued to 169th Inf. Bde. for the two battalions at the CITADEL. to be clear of the camp by 12 noon on the 7th instant to make room for incoming units of the 6th Division.	
		11.30 am.	Patrol reports and reconnaissances showed that HAZY Trench was held by the enemy but appeared to have posts in front of it. This trench was lightly wired as was also a trench from T.5.a.2.8. to N.34.d.9.2. The enemy was holding the gun pits at T.5.a. central. /6.30am.	

WAR DIARY
or
INTELLIGENCE SUMMARY

Army Form C. 2118.

(Erase heading not required.)

Place	Date	Hour	Summary of Events and Information	Remarks and references to Appendices
		6.30 am.	Divnl. Order No. 53 issued notifying units that the operations previously ordered to take place on the 5th instant had been definitely postponed until the 7th. This order also contained full instructions with regard to the operations.	See Appendix III
		1.0 pm.	167th Inf. Bde. reported that assembly trenches of the left battalion had been dug at the following points:- N.34.a.7.9., N.34.a.9.5., N.34.b.2.9., N.34.b.3.8., N.34.b.4.5. and for the right battalion through N.34.b.3.6., N.34.c.7.7., N.34.d.0.4. A creeping barrage was required 150 yards in front of the departure trenches of the left battalion, to continue due South in front of the right battalion. This barrage to start creeping at plus 5, so that the right battalion would advance at Zero, and the left battalion at zero plus 4. 167th Brigade reported that the sap running from N.34.b.7.6. to N.34.b.5.2. was suspected to contain machine guns and an Artillery O.P. and a request made for it to be destroyed by our Artillery. Excellent observation of this trench could be obtained from the Headquarters of the 8th Middlesex Regt. from T.2.b.9.0. During the morning hostile aircraft had been active over our lines and apart from being fired on with rifles and machine guns from our trenches, they had been unmolested. Brigades in the line were ordered to detail two Vickers guns specially for anti-aircraft duty, and a section of four guns from the 169th Brigade was placed at the disposal of the C.R.A. for anti-aircraft duties with batteries.	See Appendix II Map D
		5.30 p.m.	Evening reports shewed that hostile artillery had been active during the day, and had retaliated on the W. of LES BOEUFS and MORVAL in reply to heavy shelling which had been carried out by our own guns.	Appendix II (See map B.
	7th	5.0 am.	Units were in position in their assembly trenches	
		9.0 a.m.	Patrols which had been out from the 167th Infantry Brigade during the night 6/7th reported that wire in front of the enemy trenches still remained strong in some parts though lanes had been cut through at places. On the right, wire was on the whole well cleared. Patrol also reported that the enemy's trench appeared to be lightly held.	
		9.30 a.m.	In view of a report from a contact patrol aeroplane which had been out late in the evening of the 5th instant orders were issued to the C.R.A. to bring the barrage back to the line N.34.d.4.7. to N.34.b.4.3., as enemy was reported to be consolidating a line of shell holes between these points.	
		10.20 am.	Report received from the 169th Brigade stated that from information obtained by patrols and direct observation, it appeared that there was no wire on the front of DEWDROP or HAZY TRENCHES. 250 yards of new assembly trench had been laid out and dug by the centre battalion of this Bde. during the night 6/7th; about half of this trench running N.W. from FOGGY, the other half being in front of and parallel to FOGGY Trench. During the early part of the night digging had been disturbed by a hostile barrage and in the latter part by sniping.	

Army Form C. 2118.

WAR DIARY
or
INTELLIGENCE SUMMARY

(Erase heading not required.)

Instructions regarding War Diaries and Intelligence Summaries are contained in F. S. Regs., Part II. and the Staff Manual respectively. Title Pages will be prepared in manuscript.

Place	Date	Hour	Summary of Events and Information	Remarks and references to Appendices
		1.45pm.	The assault commenced.	
		2.0 p.m.	The G.O.C., 167th Inf. Bde. telephoned that reports from the front line stated that our men started well and that enemy could be seen retiring. It was thought that there was a gap between the two Brigades. This was shortly afterwards confirmed by an F.O.O. who stated that the infantry appeared to have gained their first objective and that battalion of the left brigade had been seen advancing to their second objective. Message received from the 20th Division on our left was that their attack was also progressing favourably. Hostile rifle and machine gun fire was not very heavy, but there was a strong artillery barrage E. of LES BOEUFS.	
		2.30 p.m.	Germans were reported to be counter attacking in N.35.b. An aeroplane report timed 2.30 p.m., which was received at this hour, showed our troops apparently in RAINY TRENCH with the Germans in DEWDROP and SPECTRUM Trenches. O.C. 13th London Regt. reported that at 2.5 p.m. he had seen the right of his battalion advancing from HAZY trench towards the second objective.	
		3.9 p.m.	F.O.O. reported seeing Germans on the track in T.6.a. which was opposite the left flank of the French. He also stated that the German counter-attack on HAZY TRENCH had failed and that the enemy had fallen back four or five hundred yards. A report from the Advance Head-quarters of the 167th Brigade stated that the attack of their left Battalion had been successful, and that apparently about 70 prisoners had been taken. Opposite their right battalion a few Germans were still in shell holes in the first objective but it was not certain whether they were prisoners or not.	
		3.25 p.m.	A more detailed report was received from 167th Brigade saying that the 7th Middlesex and the left of the 1st Londons had advanced very close under our barrage, and had disappeared over the skyline. There appeared to be a gap between the 1st Londons and the 168th Brigade and the right and left Company of this battalion. The support Company of the 1st Londons had moved forward to the 2nd objective on the LE TRANSLOY - LESBOEUFS Road without opposition on the West side of the ridge. Between 50 and 70 German prisoners taken by the 7th Middlesex Regiment were coming back. A party of the enemy was visible in shell holes and was working towards our line in the gap between the two Brigades. Reserve Company of the 1st London Regiment had been ordered to deal with this party. Both Brigades were ordered to make every endeavour to close the gap between their flanks.	
		3.45 p.m.	Brigades informed that aeroplane report timed 2.40 p.m. shewed the Germans occupying trench from N.28.d.1.3. to T.5.a.2.5. 167th and 168th Brigades ordered to ascertain if this was correct, and if so orders would be given to bring back barrage on DEWDROP and SPECTRUM Trenches	/if

2449 Wt. W14957/M90 750,000 1/16 J.B.C. & A. Forms/C.2118/12.

Army Form C. 2118.

WAR DIARY
or
INTELLIGENCE SUMMARY

(Erase heading not required.)

Instructions regarding War Diaries and Intelligence Summaries are contained in F.S. Regs., Part II. and the Staff Manual respectively. Title Pages will be prepared in manuscript.

Place	Date	Hour	Summary of Events and Information	Remarks and references to Appendices
		4.3 p.m.	if required. An aeroplane report received from XIV Corps shewed that the situation in HAZY TRENCH was doubtful but it was believed that this trench was in our hands. This same report stated that the attack on DEWDROP and SPECTRUM TRENCHES had failed. RAINBOW TRENCH was in our hands from N.28.d.6.0. to N.27.b.7.6. - from this latter point the enemy were occupying trench. 20th Division on our left were holding MISTY and CLOUDY Trenches. In spite of this report it was considered that the situation on the front of the 56th Division was more satisfactory than the aeroplane observer stated.	
		4.25 p.m.	167th and 168th Brigades informed that the situation on the left of the 168th Brigade was not clear and that reserve companies and if necessary reserve battalion must be employed to clear up the situation before dark.	
		4.35 p.m.	168th Brigade reported that the left Battalion of the 4th London Regt. was held up by two machine guns in the gun pits at T.5.a.4.7. G.O.C. 168th Brigade had ordered forward the reserve companies of the 12th and 4th London Regiments and two companies of the 13th London Regiment had been sent forward to take their place in the front line.	
		4.50 p.m.	169th Brigade ordered to send forward their leading battalion (9th London Regt.) to appoint to be indicated by the G.O.C. 168th Brigade at whose disposal this battalion was placed. This battalion was not to be used without reference to Headquarters (Divisional), and G.O.C. 169th Brigade was to replace the 9th London Regt. by moving forward another battalion	
		5.13 p.m.	Orders received from the XIV Corps for the Division to keep under shell fire during the night those portions of SPECTRUM and DEWDROP trenches which were not in our possession. From aeroplane photographs taken during the day RAINY TRENCH appeared to be too close to these trenches to allow of an adequate artillery preparation. Our troops were, therefore, to withdraw from RAINY and dig a new assembly trench for the assault on SPECTRUM and DEWDROP. Lastly the 56th Division was ordered to make a fresh attack on SPECTRUM and DEWDROP trenches at an hour to be decided by the G.O.C. who was to arrange the necessary bombardment. 20th Division on our left was ordered to clear up the situation in N.27.b.; to form a defensive flank on the Western end of CLOUDY TRENCH, and to join up CLOUDY and MISTY Trenches if the second objective - MISTY Trench had not been reached.	
		5.50 p.m.	Telephone message from 168th Brigade stated that we definitely held HAZY TRENCH. 169th Brigade ordered to be ready to send forward one battalion to SERPENTINE TRENCH to be at the disposal of 167th Brigade.	
	6.0	6.15 p.m.	Report from Advanced Headquarters 167th Brigade shewed that the 7th Middlesex had taken their /first	

Army Form C. 2118.

WAR DIARY
or
INTELLIGENCE SUMMARY

(Erase heading not required.)

Place	Date	Hour	Summary of Events and Information	Remarks and references to Appendices
			objective and at 3.30 p.m. were consolidating. The left assaulting Company of the 1st London Regiment was also at its first objective. The right Company of this Battalion was established at a bombing post about N.34.b.7.6. The 1st London Regiment's attack on the remainder of their objective had been broken by machine gun fire. Their support company which had been moved forward to make a strong point in the SUNKEN ROAD was reported to have failed to reach its objective. Their Reserve Company had been ~~employed~~ with by machine gun fire before reaching our own front line. The enemy appeared to be holding the first objective on the front of this Brigade southwards from the sap at N.34.b.5.2. G.O.C. 167th Brigade did not consider that a further attack could be made until the situation as regards DEWDROP had been ascertained. It was his intention to move two companies of the 3rd London Regt. into position during the night of the 7/8th with a view to attacking that portion of SPECTRUM trench still in the enemy's hands if necessary. Also to establish a strong point at the end of SUNKEN ROAD at N.35.a.2.9. and to join up with the strong point at N.35.a. Central.	
		6.45 p.m.	The following order was issued to Brigades :- "167th Brigade will during the night (a) Push out 1 Company from RAINBOW Trench to establish a strong post at N.35.a.3.9. and round up Germans in SPECTRUM and connect up with post at N.35.a.Central. (b) Dig a trench 200 yards West of SPECTRUM from which a fresh attack ~~can~~ be carried out if necessary in the morning. One Battalion of 169th Brigade was placed at the disposal of 167th Brigade but was not to be used for digging during the night. 168th Brigade to ascertain and report if DEWDROP is held by enemy or not. If it is not held by enemy, strong post will be established to connect up post at N.35.a.central and HAZY TRENCH tonight. A battalion of 169th Brigade may be used for this purpose. If DEWDROP is held by the enemy 168th Brigade will dig a new trench 200 yards W. of DEWDROP to admit of bombardment before attack in the morning. In this latter case battalion of 169th Brigade may be used for digging tonight. Orders for re-bombardment and attack will be issued as soon as 168th Brigade reports definitely as regards DEWDROP."	
		7.0 p.m.	167th Brigade ordered to arrange for their left battalion to connect up from about N.28.d.2.2. to the S.E. end of MISTY TRENCH which was occupied by the 20th Division.	
		7.25 p.m.	167th Brigade reported that progress was being made by bombing down SPECTRUM Trench and that a machine gun had been captured. Total number of prisoners which had reached the Divisional cage up to this hour was 64 84th R.I.R. and 3 of the 64th R.I.R.	
		7.30 p.m.	167th Brigade informed that both assaulting battalions of the right brigade of the 20th Division had gained their second objective about six hundred yards beyond the German 1st line. Left battalion of 167th Brigade was to be ordered to establish touch with the forward line of the 20th Division by ~~pushing out~~ a post at N.28.d.9.8. / 9.0 pm.	

WAR DIARY
or
INTELLIGENCE SUMMARY.
(Erase heading not required.)

Army Form C. 2118.

Place	Date	Hour	Summary of Events and Information	Remarks and references to Appendices
		9.0 p.m.	Latest reports indicated that a German counter attack against HAZY TRENCH, the gun pits in T.5.a. and the French left had succeeded and that the right of the 168th Brigade and the left of the French were back in their departure trenches. 168th Brigade ordered to make certain that the new trench was dug to connect FOGGY TRENCH and BURNABY during the night. This message was shortly afterwards confirmed by the 168th Brigade who stated that the London Scottish had been counter attacked from HAZY TRENCH and the gun pits and had been driven back to their departure trenches, enemy definitely holding DEWDROP. No news had been received of the post at N.35.a. central. The remaining two companies of the 13th London Regiment had been ordered to the S. end of SHAMROCK Trench.	
		9.30 p.m.	Warning order issued to Brigades that the attack would be renewed on HAZY, DEWDROP, and that portion of SPECTRUM Trench in our hands, on the 8th. Two battalions of 169th Brigade were placed at the disposal of G.O.C. 168th Brigade and one battalion at the disposal of G.O.C. 167th Brigade. The remaining battalion of 169th Brigade to be in Divisional reserve in SERPENTINE TRENCH. Assaulting troops to be in position by 5.0 a.m. on the 8th. Unless DEWDROP was ascertained to be definitely in our possession no troops would be assembled within 200 yards of it so that it might be thoroughly bombarded before assault. Accommodation in the TRONES WOOD Area was placed at the disposal of the 168th Brigade for two battalions and 167th Brigade for one battalion.	See Appendix III
		11.0 p.m.	About this hour Divnl. Order No. 54 was issued containing detailed orders of the attack to be carried out on the morning of the 8th.	See Appendix II Map B
	8th Oct.	12.15 a.m.	All three brigades notified with reference to Divnl. Order No. 54 that the battalion of the 169th Inf. Brigade in Divisional Reserve (2nd London Regiment) was to be assembled in SERPENTINE TRENCH by 10.0 a.m.	
		5.0 a.m.	Morning report showed a fairly quiet night along the Divisional front. 168th Brigade reported that the extension of FOGGY TRENCH had been joined to BURNABY TRENCH during the night of the 7/8th by a trench at least three feet deep.	See Appendix E Map D
		8.0 a.m.	The 4th London Regiment reported that two German machine guns were situated in the Northern end of DEWDROP Trench. These were reported to have held up the attack of the 168th Brigade yesterday and application was made for them to be specially dealt with by the Artillery.	
		8.10 a.m.	Report was received from the 167th Brigade that the 7th Middlesex Regiment on the left stated that the line captured yesterday was held by about 200 men including machine guns and that their left flank was in touch with the 20th Division at N.28.c.7.4. and their right in touch with the 1st London Regt. about 200 yards South of the SUNKEN ROAD. The trench they were in was reported to be unoccupied, it was good, and they were not crowded.	"

/Report

Army Form C. 2118.

WAR DIARY
or
INTELLIGENCE SUMMARY.
(Erase heading not required.)

Instructions regarding War Diaries and Intelligence Summaries are contained in F.S. Regs., Part II. and the Staff Manual respectively. Title pages will be prepared in manuscript.

Place	Date	Hour	Summary of Events and Information	Remarks and references to Appendices
		10.12 a.m.	Report was received from the 168th Brigade that the enemy had steel machine gun emplacements in front of HAZY TRENCH at approximately T.5.a.2.7.. These guns had caused heavy casualties yesterday and it was essential that they should be knocked out if possible. 2nd London Regt. reported ___ (1st Regt one) in position in SERPENTINE TRENCH in Divisional reserve.	
		1.0 p.m.	Midday situation reports showed considerable hostile artillery and machine gun activity on our front and it was reported that the enemy was holding an almost continuous line opposite 168th Brigade. 167th Brigade reported that the 18th London Regiment, who had been placed at their disposal, had been ordered to move at 1.15 p.m. to occupy that portion of the FLERS line which had recently been held by the 3rd London Regt. and that they would move up later in the afternoon to take over the front line. Orders were issued that all battalions of 167th and 168th Brigades arriving in the area W. of GUILLEMONT on withdrawal from the front line, would come under the orders of the 169th Brigade. Warning order received from the XIVth Corps that the Division would probably move out of the Corps area on the 10th, 11th and 12th inst., one brigade group moving out each day. Destination Area. "D". W. of AMIENS. Move of dismounted personnel and infantry to be by bus.	
		2.20 p.m.	7th Middlesex reported that many of our own heavy shells were falling in N.34.a. and b., behind the SUNKEN ROAD, and also in rear of SPECTRUM TRENCH.	
		3.30 p.m.	The assault commenced.	
		3.50 p.m.	The G.O.C. 167th Brigade telephoned that report from the Advanced Brigade Headquarters stated that our barrage had been very feeble at Zero, but that the infantry had advanced. German barrage was extremely heavy and that attack of the 3rd London Regt. was seen to have failed.	
		3.55 p.m.	An F.O.O. reported that the Germans were counter attacking from T.5.d. and firing machine guns into LES BOEUFS. 168th Brigade informed.	
		4.5 pm.	A message received from 168th Brigade stated that a report from the forward H.Q. of their left battalion timed 3.40 p.m. showed our attack as progressing favourably. Shortly afterwards another report from the 167th Brigade confirmed the information received at 3.50 p.m. that throughout the bombardment fire of heavy artillery had been short of SPECTRUM TRENCH. At 3.30 p.m. the 3rd London Regt. had advanced under a very feeble barrage and were met by heavy fire from hostile artillery almost immediately. They had failed to reach the crest. A message from an F.O.O. stated that HAZM TRENCH had been occupied by us and that the French continued the line on our right.	
		4.25 p.m.	Reports from Advanced H.Q. 167th Bde. showed that the attack of the 3rd London Regt. had been caught by fire from machine guns which held up the 1st London Regt's attack on the 7th. /Irrespective	For most reference in connection with the situation on the day see Appendix II Nof C 3

T.134. W. W708-776. 500000. 4/16. Sir J.C.&S.

Army Form C. 2118.

WAR DIARY
or
INTELLIGENCE SUMMARY.
(Erase heading not required.)

Instructions regarding War Diaries and Intelligence Summaries are contained in F.S. Regs., Part II. and the Staff Manual respectively. Title pages will be prepared in manuscript.

Place	Date	Hour	Summary of Events and Information	Remarks and references to Appendices
		5.0 p.m.	Irrespective of the condition of the troops, it was considered useless to try a further attack at this point under the same conditions.	See appendix III
		5.10 p.m.	Definite orders received from the Corps regarding the withdrawal of the Division from the line. Divisional order No. 55 was issued. XIVth Corps informed of the situation and that the right company of 168th Brigade was digging in on ridge, but it was not quite clear as to whether the objective had been reached or not. The right battalion of this brigade reported having advanced 600 yards towards the objective but this was not yet confirmed by written message from the front line. There was no confirmation of hostile counter attack against the French left.	
		5.40 p.m.	169th Brigade ordered to send two sections of machine guns to relieve the guns of the 168th Machine Gun Company.	
		6.0 p.m.	XIVth Corps informed that the left battalion of the 168th Brigade reported that they believed all their assaulting companies to have got beyond DEWDROP TRENCH.	
		6.40 p.m.	Orders were issued to the 167th and 168th Brigades to consolidate all ground gained and take every precaution against a possible hostile counter attack which, if delivered would probably be in strength. That portion of SPECTRUM TRENCH in the enemy's hands would not be attacked again.	
		8.20 p.m.	168th Brigade stated that the company commander of the left company of the 5th London Regiment reported that he had seen his company reach HAZY TRENCH and occupy it. They were in touch with the 9th London Regiment on their left. This was considered as a definite confirmation of the *going of the* objective as far as the centre of the 168th Brigade *was concerned*. Situation of the right battalion of the 168th Brigade was discovered by a personal reconnaissance by their C.O. to be as follows:- Battalion was digging in just W. and parallel to HAZY TRENCH; that their left was in touch with 9th London Regiment about T.5.a.5.9. and their right about T.5.a.7.3.. The Germans were holding HAZY TRENCH and there were still parties of them with machine guns in gun pits at T.5.a.7.6. 9th London Regt. appeared to be E. of DEWDROP TRENCH a The position of the French on our right was unknown. The G.O.C. 168th Brigade had ordered pioneer company to assist the 13th London Regiment in joining up the right of the 5th London Regt. with GERMANS TRENCH. 167th Brigade were joining up WINDY TRENCH to Pt. T.6.a.45.92. O.C. 9th London Regt. had also gone out to make a personal reconnaissance of the situation of his battalion but had not returned at this hour.	
		9.30 p.m.		

T.134. Wt. W708-776. 500000. 4/15. Sir J. C. & S.

Army Form C. 2118.

WAR DIARY
or
INTELLIGENCE SUMMARY.
(Erase heading not required.)

Instructions regarding War Diaries and Intelligence Summaries are contained in F. S. Regs., Part II. and the Staff Manual respectively. Title pages will be prepared in manuscript.

Place	Date	Hour	Summary of Events and Information	Remarks and references to Appendices
	9th Oct.	12.10 a.m.	Corps informed that personnel reconnaissance by O.C. 9th London Regiment confirmed the Report that neither DEWDROP or RAINY Trenches were held by us and that his battalion was back in line of FOGGY and BURNABY Trenches having been counter attacked at dusk from the direction of DEWDROP. One Company of 9th London Regiment had been sent to hold the trench immediately East of FOGGY. Shortly afterwards the Corps were informed that the 5th Londons who had been digging in in prolongation of HAZY TRENCH had been forced to withdraw at 10.30p.m. owing to enfilade and machine gun fire from the gun pits in T.5.a. Central, and they were now back in their departure trenches and had brought in a German machine gun captured earlier in the morning 8th.	
		4.15 a.m.	167th Brigade ordered not to move the 2nd Londons Forward until further orders.	
	5.0 a.m.		Morning Report from left brigade shewed that an Officers patrol which had approached SPECTRUM TRENCH had been fired on and saw Germans occupying the trench. No report had been received from the battalions of the right brigade but the situation appeared to be quiet on their front.	
		10.15 a.m.	The Section of the 169th M.G.C. attached to the artillery for anti-aircraft duties was ordered to rejoin its Brigade at 12 noon.	
		11.30 a.m.	Report shewed that 17 prisoners of the 31st Regiment had been taken by the 5th London Regt. and passed back through the Corps cages.	
		11.45 a.m.	Report shewed that a number of hostile aeroplanes had been active over our lines during the morning. Application was made to the Corps for special anti-aircraft precautions to be taken in view of the movement of troops in SERPENTINE and HOGS BACK Trenches which was necessitated by relief. During the morning XIV Corps wired that the Pioneer Battalion (5th Cheshire Regt.) would remain in the XIV Corps area after the withdrawal of the Division.	
		2.30 p.m.	XIV Corps informed that the situation on the front of the 167th Brigade appeared to be as follows :- We were holding Spectrum Trench down to the bend approximately at N.34.b.8.2. G.O.C. 167th Brigade was confident that this was correct as a strong party of 16th Londons was holding South of the SUNKEN ROAD and was not crowded. Enemy had been endeavouring to dig a trench back from SPECTRUM to the SUNKEN ROAD and the troops in SPECTRUM TRENCH claimed to have shot a large number of Germans both on the 8th and during the morning of the 9th. No aeroplane confirmation of this situation was possible owing to the weather. Divisional Order No. 56 issued with reference to the move of the Division to Area D.	See appendix II Map 9
		2.45 p.m.	Evening situation report shewed that the day had passed quietly on our front. Hostile batteries from a N.E. direction had shelled our battery positions in T.16.a. and T.15.h. heavily during the morning. One of our batteries (A.280) claimed to have caught in its fire a party of about 30 Germans that were in the open from O.31.a.2.8. to N.30.d.5.8. - their fire appeared to have been effective. The total captures during the operations on the 8th now amounted to 17 prisoners of the 31st R.I.R. and one machine gun. /During	See appendix III and Appendix II Map E

Army Form C. 2118.

WAR DIARY
or
INTELLIGENCE SUMMARY.
(Erase heading not required.)

Place	Date	Hour	Summary of Events and Information	Remarks and references to Appendices
			During the night 9/10th the 56th Division, less Artillery, was relieved in the line by 4th Division in accordance with Divisional Order No. 55. The 168th Brigade was relieved by the Xth Infantry Brigade and the 167th Brigade by the 12th Infantry Brigade. This relief was carried out without incident. During the operations between the 1st and 9th October great difficulty was experienced in ascertaining the exact positions of troops and new trenches dug, both by us and the enemy owing to lack of aeroplane photographs which could not be taken owing to the bad weather. It was not until the evening of the 7th inst. that photographs were procured which gave accurate information as to the situation of our troops. During this period 84 prisoners and two machine guns were captured. The majority of the prisoners belonged to the 84 R.I.R. and 31 R.I.R. of the 18th Reserve Division. The total number of prisoners taken by the Division since the commencement of the offensive on 1st July 1916 amounted to over 400 with six machine guns. For other captured material see Appendix V for September.	

WAR DIARY
or
INTELLIGENCE SUMMARY
(Erase heading not required.)

Army Form C. 2118.

Instructions regarding War Diaries and Intelligence Summaries are contained in F. S. Regs., Part II. and the Staff Manual respectively. Title Pages will be prepared in manuscript.

Place	Date	Hour	Summary of Events and Information	Remarks and references to Appendices
???	Oct 10		Bgde Hqrs closed at A.10.b.1.8 at 10 a.m. and reopened at the CITADEL. At this hour G.O.C. (mdg) over command of the Bde to G.O.C. 4th Division. Moves detailed in Bgde Order No 58 issued on. The Corps Commander saw ?Pt. the props & radio commanders during the morning	
BERTOT sur SOMME	Oct 11		Bgde Hqrs. closed at the CITADEL and opened at BERTOT-SUR-SOMME at their hour. Continuation of the division to D area WEST of AMIENS. The Bgde left XIV Corps and came under com of I Corps from midnight 11/12.	
BERTOT sur SOMME	Oct 12		Completion of move 18.6 Bde being the last to arrive in the area.	
BERTOT sur SOMME	Oct 13, Oct 14	}	Spent in using the troops and cleaning up.	
BERTOT sur SOMME	Oct 15		Commenced training a class of Bn. Scouts. Company and Platoon training under brigade arrangement. Leave suspension received from 1st Corps. Later that the Division would probably in appendix II move to the VRAIGNECOURT area on Oct 19th, 20th and 21st with a view to employment at LONGPRÉ and PONT RÉMY after probably not F midnight 23/24th. for 1st Army. G.O.C. proceeded on 10 days leave to England. Brig. Genl. Field c/o G. assumed temporary command of the Division	
BERTOT sur SOMME	Oct 16, Oct 17	}	Training as on 15th Orders received from 10th Corps for Bn. to be clear of their area (area D) by 21st inst.	

Army Form C. 2118.

WAR DIARY
or
INTELLIGENCE SUMMARY

(Erase heading not required.)

Instructions regarding War Diaries and Intelligence Summaries are contained in F. S. Regs, Part II. and the Staff Manual respectively. Title Pages will be prepared in manuscript.

Place	Date	Hour	Summary of Events and Information	Remarks and references to Appendices
BELLOY SUR SOMME	18:Oct	8.30am	Gen: Order No. 57 issued to move of the division to the No.5" (HALLENCOURT) area. Notification received from 10: Corps HQrs. that the division would proceed to XI Corps 1st Army entraining after midnight 23/24.	See Appendix III
BELLOY SUR SOMME	19:Oct	—	Move of 167: Inf. Bde. to No.5" area in accordance with Divn: Order No.57. XI Corps advised that entrainment for 1st Army would commence after midnight 22/23 2nd instead of as previously ordered.	
BELLOY SUR SOMME	20:Oct	11 am	G.S.O.1 and A.A. & Q.M.G. motored to HQrs XI Corps to ascertain particulars of move to XI Corps area. 168: Bde and Divn: Trench HQrs moved to No.5" area. Divn: HQrs. closed at BELLOY-SUR-SOMME at 11 am.	
HALLENCOURT	21st Oct	1pm	Divn: HQrs opened at HALLENCOURT.	Appendix I
HALLENCOURT	21st Oct		Completion of move to No.5" area. 169 Bde and 5th Cheshire Regt. marched to their billets in the afternoon. Divn: train No. 5.0 issued containing instruction for the move of the division to XI Corps area.	See Appendix III
HALLENCOURT	22nd Oct		Party partly consisting of D.A.A. & Q.M.G., Camp Commandant and 4 other officers left for XI Corps area to make preliminary arrangements for taking over from 61st (2nd Midland) Divn in the line from about RICHEBOURG L'AVOUÉ to E of LAVENTIE	

2449. Wt. W14957/Mg0 750,000 1/16 J.B.C. & A. Forms/C.2118/12.

Army Form C. 2118.

WAR DIARY
or
INTELLIGENCE SUMMARY

(Erase heading not required.)

Instructions regarding War Diaries and Intelligence Summaries are contained in F. S. Regs., Part II. and the Staff Manual respectively. Title Pages will be prepared in manuscript.

Place	Date	Hour	Summary of Events and Information	Remarks and references to Appendices
~~ESTREM~~ HALLENCOURT	23rd Oct	11 am	"J" Branch 3rd Echn: closed at HALLENCOURT at this hour. "Q" Branch remaining until completion of the move & entrainment of units for XI Corps Area.	I
LESTREM		p.m.	Adv. Hqrs: with the Exception of "J" & "Q" Branch opened at LESTREM at this hour. 163rd and 169th Bdes. entrained for XI Corps area from PONTREMY and ONS PAR.	
LESTREM	24th Oct		Remainder of Bord. Stfn. moved to LESTREM and movers of units to XI Corps area completed. G.O.C. returned from leave. S.T.O. traveled night reports & the time. Bord. Aston w. 509 w (w) re relief of 61st Div.	See Appendix II. Appendix I
LESTREM	25th Oct		To location of units on this date see appendix. S.O.2 and G.T.O's visited the left and a portion of the centre subsections of the frontage of 56th Div. to arrange reconnaissances of the line to be taken over by them & units and B. officers of 61st Division.	
LESTREM	26th Oct		Reconnaissances as on 25th. Unusual heavy shower from about the day. Corps' Commander visited J.O.C.	

2449 Wt. W14957/M90 759,000 1/16 J.B.C. & A. Forms/C.2118/12.

Army Form C. 2118.

WAR DIARY
or
INTELLIGENCE SUMMARY
(Erase heading not required.)

Instructions regarding War Diaries and Intelligence Summaries are contained in F. S. Regs., Part II. and the Staff Manual respectively. Title Pages will be prepared in manuscript.

Place	Date	Hour	Summary of Events and Information	Remarks and references to Appendices
LESTREM	27th Oct.	—	Commencement of relief of 61st Division. Two battalions from each brigade relieved battalions of 61st Division in brigade reserve in each sector. The battalions will move into the line tomorrow. Rain throughout the day.	See appendix Bvt. Orders 59 and Appendix I Divisional Trace
LESTREM	28th Oct.		G.S.O.I. completed reconnaissance of the line with G.S.O.I. 61st Division. During the morning the battalions for the right sub-sector from each brigade moved into the trenches and in the afternoon the left battalions moved up. The battalions of 61st Division which moved back take B.s. Relief.	See appendix Bvt. Orders 59
LA GORGUE		5:30 pm	Bvt. Hqr.: closed at LESTREM and opened LA GORGUE G.O.C. assumed command of the sector. Considerable hostile activity with T.M.s and artillery against LAMP SALIENT about 4:30 pm to 6 pm. The artillery replied. According to a report received from 3rd Aus. Batten. Bunny boy. The Enemy raided our trenches on the RAILH SALIENT about 7 pm and forced him undershaft. No definite information on the point has been received from 168 Bt. but enquiries are being made.	See appendix Location sheet
LA GORGUE	29th Oct.		A quiet day on the Divisional front. Very wet. Casualties during the 24 hours according to 5/s O.R. amounted to 2 O.R. Bvt. Keppel Stifling and Thrying having leave, spent at LA GORGUE.	
LA GORGUE	30th Oct.		Saw Barney Flew a mine just S.E. MACQUISSANT N.2 crater about M.30.C.22.2.8. Slight damage was done to our gallery but none to the trenches. The enemy of 257 Tunnelling Coy. burned. Heavy rain during the afternoon.	

Army Form C. 2118.

WAR DIARY
or
INTELLIGENCE SUMMARY
(Erase heading not required.)

Instructions regarding War Diaries and Intelligence Summaries are contained in F. S. Regs., Part II. and the Staff Manual respectively. Title Pages will be prepared in manuscript.

Place	Date	Hour	Summary of Events and Information	Remarks and references to Appendices
LA GORGUE	Oct 31st		A quiet day on the Divisional front as regards hostile activity. 2.30pm to 3.30pm our T.M's of all calibres, artillery field and heavy and rifle grenadier coys put on organised bombardment of the WICK SALIENT. The bombardment was satisfactory and the enemy's reply feeble.	
	Nov			

APPENDIX III
DIVNL: ORDERS for OCTOBER 1916

SECRET.　　　　　　　　　　　　　　　　　　　　　Copy No ......

56th DIVISIONAL ORDER No 51

1. The 169th Infantry Brigade will take over the front occupied by the right battalion of the 167th Infantry Brigade (including posts in RAINY TRENCH) tonight under arrangements to be made direct between brigades concerned.

2. The 168th Infantry Brigade will relieve the 169th Infantry Brigade in the Right Sector of the Divisional front tomorrow night 3rd/4th under arrangements to be made direct between brigades concerned All maps and air photos will be handed over.

3. Brigades and battalions being relieved are responsible for the work on the night of relief. Working parties will not be withdrawn until tasks are completed or too light to continue

4. On relief, 169th Inf. Bde. will be disposed as under:-
   Brigade H.Q. at BRIQUETERIE H.Q.
   Two battalions in Divisional area West of TRONES WOOD and S. of MONTAUBAN.
   Two Battalions - CITADEL.

5. The dividing line between brigades in the line will be a line drawn from N.30.c.0.0. - N.35.a.0.0. - N.34.d.0.6 along track to N.34.c.0.0., track inclusive to Northern Bde.
   The dividing lines between Brigade areas behind the front line is shown on attached map.

6. A digging party, strength 500 (exclusive of officers) will be found by 169th Infantry Brigade from 6 am. on October 4th for digging cable trenches under the direction of XIVth Corps Signals.
   A field officer will be detailed by 169th Infantry Brigade to report to an officer of XIVth Corps Signals tomorrow, 3rd instant, at a time and place to be notified later to ascertain details as to rendezvous, time, work to be performed and tools required for work on the 4th.

7. The 2/1st London Field Company, R.E. will relieve the 2/2nd London Field Company, R.E. on the night of the 3/4th under arrangements to be made by the C R E., but work will not be interfered with owing to the relief (vide para. 3.)

8. Completion of reliefs will be reported to Divnl. H.Q.

9. ACKNOWLEDGE.

Braid.

Hdqrs. 56th Divn.　　　　　　　　　　　　　　Lieut. Colonel,
2nd October, 1916.　　　　　　　　　　　　　　General Staff.
　　　　Issued at　　　　2.10.16.

Copy Nos:-
- ✗ 1. XIVth Corps "G".
- 2. XIVth Corps "Q".
- 3. G.O.C. 56th Div.
- ✗ 4. 4th Divn. R.A.
- 5. 20th Divn.
- ✗ 6. 167th Inf. Bde.
- ✗ 7. 168th Inf. Bde
- ✗ 8. 169th Inf Bde
- ✓ 9. C.R.A.56th Div.
- ✓ 10. A.D.M.S.
- ✓ 11. C.R.E.
- ✗ 12. 5th Ches. Regt.
- # 13. XIVth Corps Signals
- ✓ 14. 56th Div. Signals.
- ✓ 15. "G"
- ✓ 16. "Q"
- 17. War Diary.
- 18) French Liaison
- 19)　Officer.

SECRET.   Copy No. 20

56th DIVISIONAL ORDER No. 62.

3rd October 1916

1. (a) The Fourth Army will renew the attack on October 5th at an hour Zero which will be communicated later.

   (b) The task of the XIVth Corps is to establish itself on a line from which the LE TRANSLOY system of trenches can be attacked at a later date.

   (c) The operation will be carried out in two stages which are shewn on the attached map by a green and a brown line respectively. (Issued to Bdes. only).

   (d) The 20th Division will be on the left of the 56th Division.

2. The first task of the 56th Division (green line) includes the capture of the disconnected trenches and emplacements known as HAZY, DEWDROP, SPECTRUM, and part of RAINBOW Trenches, and the establishment of a line along the Western crest of the ridge from SPECTRUM to HAZY TRENCHES.

   The second task of the Division is to establish a line —on the forward slope of the ridge— from which the LE TRANSLOY Trench system can be seen. This line is approximately shewn by the brown line on attached map, and runs from N.28.b.7.2. - N.28.d.9.9. - N.35.a.4.9.- N.35.d.7.½., thence a defensive flank to T.5.b.3.0. where touch will be obtained with the 56th French Division.

3. At zero the infantry will advance to the attack of the Green Line. At zero plus 20 minutes the infantry will advance to the attack of the Brown Line.

4. The operation will be carried out by the 168th Infantry Brigade on the right and the 167th Infantry Brigade on the left.
   The dividing line between brigades will be a line drawn from N.34.d.0.0. to the junction of road and track at N.34.d.6.5., and thence along the LES BOEUFS - LE TRANSLOY Road (inclusive to the 168th Infantry Brigade).

5. Every effort will be made to establish at least two departure trenches, with communication trenches, in front of the existing continuous line E. of LES BOEUFS.

6. The attack will be preceded by a steady bombardment of the hostile positions, details of which will be communicated separately.
   The ground in front and rear of the German trenches which are being bombarded will be searched occasionally with 18-pdr. shrapnel and high explosive shell.
   There will be no intensive fire previous to the hour of zero.
   Night firing will be carried out nightly between the hours of 6 pm. and 8 am.
   The attack in each stage will be carried out under cover of both a creeping and stationary barrage, details of which will be circulated separately.
   There are certain points held by the enemy, such as DEWDROP TRENCH, and possibly a portion of RAINBOW TRENCH, which are too close to be dealt with by our barrage. These points must be dealt with by Stokes Mortars at zero hour if they cannot be captured beforehand.

7. Strong points will be established as under:-

   By 168th Inf. Bde. At bend in trench at
   N.35.d.70.05 and at end of cutting
   about N.35.a.5.4.

   By 167th Infantry Bde. At end of cutting about
   N.35.a.4.9. and on spur about
   N.28.d.9.8.

8. A contact patrol will be in the air from zero to 5.30 pm. Brigades will indicate their positions by means of flares and mirrors on reaching each objective and at 5.0 pm.

9. Watches will be synchronised at 168th Infantry Brigade Headquarters at T.19.c.1.4. at 5.0 pm. on the 4th and 10 am. on the 5th October.
   A watch will be sent from Divisional Headquarters from which the time will be taken by representatives of Infantry Brigades and R.F.A. Groups.

10. ACKNOWLEDGE by wire.

J. Brind.

Hdqrs. 56th Divn.   Lieut. Colonel,

3rd October, 1916.   General Staff.

            Issued at 6.0 pm. 3.10.16.

Copy Nos:-
   1. XIVth Corps "G".   15. C.R.E.
   2. XIVth Corps "Q".   16. 5th Ches. Regt
   3. G.O.C. 56th Div.   17. 56th Div. Signals.
   4. 4th Divn.   18. "G"
   5. 20th Divn.   19. "Q"
   6. 167th Inf. Bde.   20. War Diary.
   7. 168th Inf. Bde.   21 & 22 French Liaison Off.
   8. 169th Inf. Bde
9 -13. C.R.A., 56th Div.
  14. A.D.M.S.

SECRET.

167th Infantry Brigade
168th Infantry Brigade
169th Infantry Brigade
C.R.A. 56th Divn.
A.D.M.S.
C.R.E.
5th Cheshire Regt.
56th Div. Signals.
"Q"
War Diary.
French Liaison Officer.

56th Division O643

    The Operations laid down in 56th Divisional Order No. 52 of 3rd October have been postponed definitely for 48 hours.

    Acknowledge by wire.

Head Qrs. 56th Divn.
4th October, 1916.

Lieut-Colonel,
General Staff.

Secret   Copy No. ......

56th DIVISIONAL ORDER No. 53.

Ref. Brown Line Map
  (Sheets 1 & 2).

   1. The operation referred to in 56th Divisional Order No. 52 will take place on the 7th instant. Zero time will be notified later.
      Watches will be synchronised on the 6th and 7th at the times and place notified in Order No. 52, para. 9.

   2. The 56th French Division is attacking at the same hour.
      Their first objective is a line running S.E. from T.5.b.8.1. (point 9106 in French map).
      Their second objective is a line running S.E. from N.36.c.6.0. (point 9511 in French map) to about U.1.c.6.4. (point 0505 in French map) and thence Southwards East of NORTH COPSE.

   3. In view of the proposed operation of the French, the second objective (Brown Line) of the 56th Division is amended to read as follows:- N.28.b.7.2. - N.28.d.9.9. - N.35.a.4.9. - N.35.d.7.½. - N.36.c.0.0. Touch will be established with the 56th French Division at N.36.c.6.1.

   4. In addition to the strong points ordered in 56th Divisional Order No. 52 (para. 7) strong points will be constructed as follows:-

    By 168th Inf. Bde.   One at German battery position about N.36.c.0.0. and
                                another covering the right flank of the Brigade about T.5.b.6.7.

    By 167th Inf. Bde.   About battery position at N.28.d.1.5.

   5. R.E. and Pioneers are allotted to assaulting brigades as under:-

    To 168th Inf. Bde. - 2/1st London Field Co. R.E.
                         1 Co. 1/5th Ches. Regt. Pioneers.

    To 167th Inf. Bde. - 1/1st Edinburgh Field Co. R.E.
                         1 Co. 1/5th Ches. Regt. Pioneers.

      These units are to be allotted definite tasks in the scheme of consolidation but will not be moved forward until the positions are definitely captured.

   6 169th Infantry Brigade will be in Divisional reserve and will be in position as under by 12 noon on the 7th. All movements to be by companies at 100 yards intervals, and by cross-country tracks.

    169th Inf. Bde. -   H.Q. BRIQUETERIE.
                             1 Bn. S. of GINCHY (T.19.b.)
                             1 Bn. E. of TRONES WOOD (S.24.c.& S.30.a.)
                             2 Bns. TRONES WOOD - BERNAFAY WOOD Area.
                              (S.29.b.,c. & d.)

                                                        / Liaison

- 2 -

Liaison officers of the 169th Infantry Brigade will be at Headquarters 167th and 168th Infantry Brigades from 12 noon onwards, and will keep their Brigadiers informed of the progress of events by report by runner.

7. ACKNOWLEDGE.

J.T. Brind.

Hdqrs. 56th Divn.

6th October 1916.

Lieut. Colonel,
General Staff.

Copy Nos:-   Issued at 6.30 am., 6.10.1916.

1. XIVth Corps "G".
2. XIVth Corps "Q".
3. G.O.C., 53th Div.
4. 4th Division
5. 20th Division.
6. 167th Inf. Bde.
7. 168th Inf. Bde.
8. 169th Inf. Bde.
9 - 13. C.R.A'. 56th Div.
14. A.D.M.S.
15. C.R.E.
16. 5th Ches. Regt.
17. 56th Div. Signals.
18. "G".
19. "Q".
20. War Diary.
21.) French Liaison Offr.
22.)

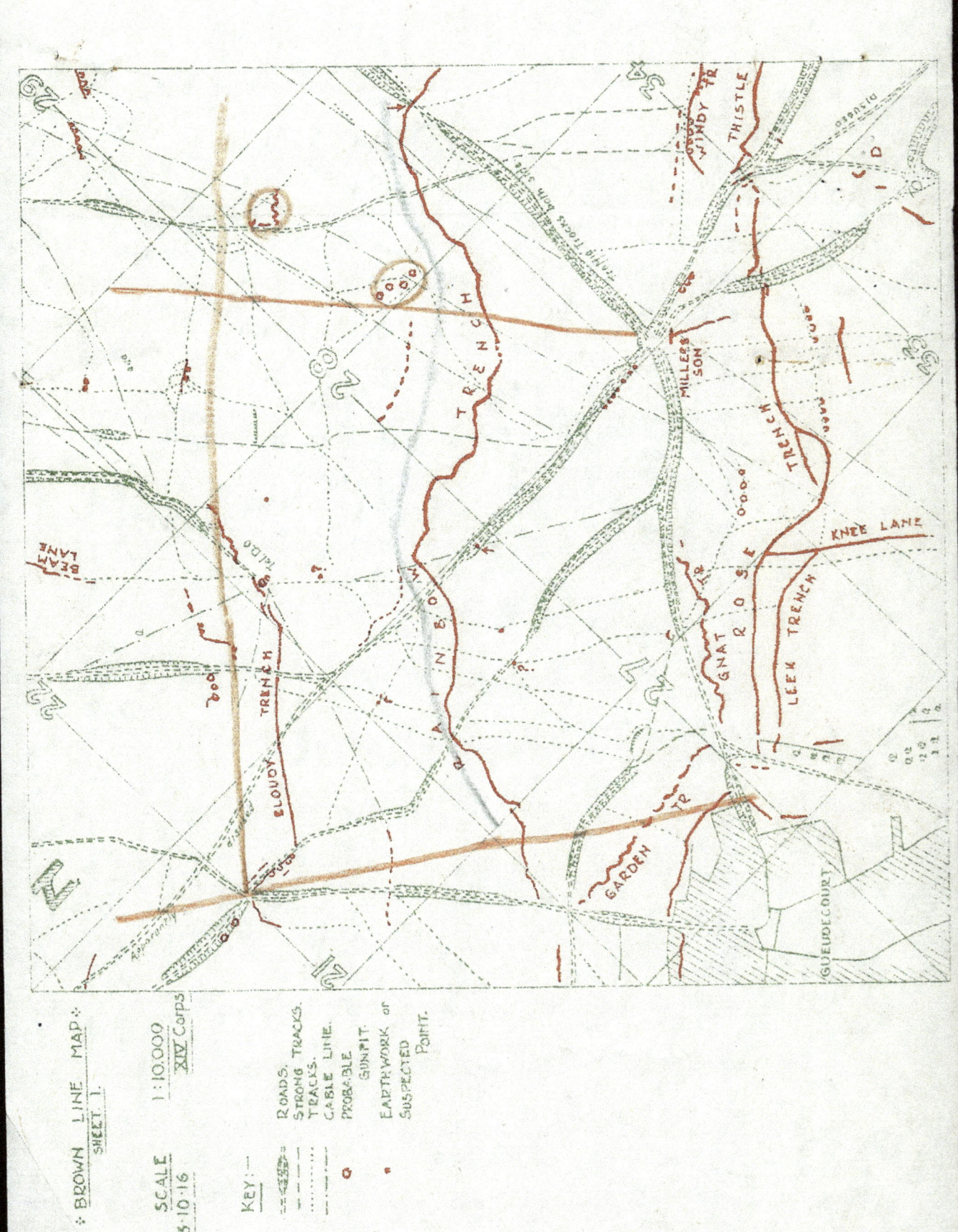

SECRET.   Copy No. 20

56th DIVISIONAL ORDER No 54.

                                                          7.10.1916.

1.   Reports at 9.30 pm. show that our two right
battalions were counter-attacked this evening and are
back in their original departure trench.
      DEWDROP TRENCH is still in German hands.
      The 167th Infantry Brigade secured their first
objective in RAINBOW TRENCH, and in SPECTRUM TRENCH
as far South as N.34.b.6.7.
      An unconfirmed report states that the French left
was driven back to its original departure trench this
evening.

2.   The attack will be renewed tomorrow by the 168th
and 167th Infantry Brigades.
      Two battalions 169th Infantry Brigade are placed
at the disposal of the 168th Infantry Brigade, and one
battalion 169th Infantry Brigade at disposal of 167th
Infantry Brigade.

3.   Trenches are being dug tonight as follows:-

      (a). By 168th Inf. Bde. from FOGGY to BURNABY
                                (T.4.b.5.8.)

      (b). By 167th Inf. Bde. A trench running N. and S.
                              200 yards W. of SPECTRUM TR

4.   Assaulting troops will be in position by 5.0 am.

5.   The objectives of the 168th Infantry Brigade will
be HAZY TRENCH, and the Green Line thence to SPECTRUM
TRENCH.
      The objective of the 167th Infantry Brigade will
be that portion of SPECTRUM TRENCH still occupied by
the enemy.

6.   Troops will be withdrawn from RAINY TRENCH before
dawn so that DEWDROP may be thoroughly bombarded.
      SPECTRUM TRENCH, if not entirely in our hands, will
be blocked and troops withdrawn North of the SUNKEN
ROAD to admit of bombardment.

7.   The bombardment of the trenches to be attacked will
take place during the morning.
      Assaulting troops will leave their departure
trench at Zero and advance close under a creeping
barrage, which will start 100 yards in front of the
infantry and start creeping at Zero at the rate of
fifty yards a minute.

- 2 -

8. The French are attacking at the same hour and the 168th Infantry Brigade will connect up with them South-Eastwards from HAZY TRENCH

9. Zero hour will be 3.30 pm.

10. Accommodation will be available in the TRONES WOOD Area for two battalions 168th Infantry Brigade, and one battalion 167th Infantry Brigade.

11. Brigades will ensure that assaulting battalions are issued with flares, grenades, tools before going into the newly dug assembly trenches.

12. ACKNOWLEDGE.

Hdqrs. 56th Divn.
7th October, 1916.

Lieut. Colonel,
General Staff.

Copy Nos:-

1. XIVth Corps "G".
2. XIVth Corps "Q".
3. G.O.C., 53rd Div.
4. 4th Division.
5. 20th Division.
6. 167th Inf. Bde.
7. 168th Inf. Bde.
8. 169th Inf. Bde.
9 - 13. C.R.A., 56th Divn.

14. A.D.M.S.
15. C.R.E.
16. 5th Ches. Regt.
17. 56th Div. Signals.
18. "G".
19. "Q".
20. War Diary.
21.) French Liaison
22.)   Officer.

SECRET.   Copy No. 20

56th DIVISIONAL ORDER No. 55

8.10.16.

1. The 56th Division, less Divisional Artillery, will be relieved on the night 9th/10th by the 4th Division.

2. The 168th Infantry Brigade will be relieved by the 10th Brigade
   The 167th Infantry Brigade by the 12th Brigade of the 4th Division.
   Details of relief will be arranged direct between Brigadiers concerned. The Commanders of the 167th and 168th Infantry Brigades will hand over command of their fronts on completion of relief.

3. On relief the 167th and 168th Brigade Groups will be accommodated at the CITADEL CAMP, F.21.b., and the 169th Bde. Group at MANSEL CAMP, F.17.b. Moves will take place in accordance with March Table (which will follow).

4. Battalions temporarily attached for the operation to-day to Brigades other than their own will move under the orders of the Brigade Headquarters to which they are attached.

5. Details of relief of the R.E. Coys. and Pioneer Battalion (less 1 Company) will be arranged by the C.R.Es. of the 56th and 4th Divisions.

6. Details of relief of R.A.M.C. Units will be arranged by the A.D.M.S. direct with the A.D.M.S. 4th Division.

7. The relief of all Units not mentioned in this order will be arranged by the A.A. & Q.M.G.

8. (a) All movements will be by cross country tracks, unless the weather is wet, in which case Units will move by the MONTAUBAN - CARNOY Road, and thence Units for the CITADEL will move by cross country track.

   (b) Troops moving by roads must keep following distances :-

      200 yards between Companies
      1000 yards between Battalions

   (c) Troops moving by cross country tracks will keep a distance of 500 yards between Battalions.

   (d) A distance of 500 yards will be maintained between Units and their transport.

9. On arrival in the Divisional Area all Units of the 4th Division are being placed under the Command of the General Officer Commanding 56th Division.

10. The General Officer Commanding the 56th Division will hand over Command of the Divisional Front at 10.0 a.m. on the 10th instant - at which hour Divisional Headquarters will close at the BRIQUITERIE H.Q. (A.10.b.3.8.) and will open at the CITADEL.

11. ACKNOWLEDGE by wire.

J. Brind.

Head Qrs. 56th Divn.   Lieut-Colonel,
8th October, 1916.   General Staff.

Issued at 5.0 p.m. 8.10.16

Copy Nos :-

1.	XIV Corps "G"	7.	168th Inf. Bde.	17.	56th Div. Sigs.
2.	XIV Corps "Q"	8.	169th Inf. Bde.	18.	"G"
3.	G.O.C. 56th Div.	9-13.	C.R.A. 56th Div.	19.	"Q"
4.	4th Division.	14.	A.D.M.S.	20.	War Diary.
5.	20th Division.	15.	C.R.E.	21.	French
6.	167th Inf. Bde.	16.	5th Chos. Regt.	22	Liaison Offr.

SECRET

MARCH TABLE 9th OCTOBER.

Issued with 56th Divisional Order No. 55, dated 8.10.1916.

Group	Units	From	to	Time	Remarks.
169th Bde. Group.	169th Bde. H.Q. 169th M.G.Co.(less 2 Secs.) 169th T.M. Battery. 2/2nd Lond Fld. Co. R.E.	} BRIQUETERIE	CITADEL MANSEL Camp. F.17.b.	1 pm	(a). All movements will be by cross-country tracks, unless the weather is wet, in which case units will move by the MONTAUBAN - CARNOY Rd. and thence units for the CITADEL will move by cross-country track (b) Troops moving by roads must keep following distances 200 yds. between companies 1000 " between battalions. (c). Troops moving by cross-country tracks will keep a distance of 500 yds. between Bns. (d). A distance of 500 yds. will be maintained between units and their transport. *Instructions for moves of these units on 10th will be issued tomorrow. All moves E. of GUILLEMONT will be by platoons at a 100 yds. Interval.
	3rd Lond. Regt. (less 2 cos.) 4th Lond. Regt. 14th "(Lond.Scot.) 2nd Lond. Regt. will march with 169th Bde. Group if situation permits.	} BERNAFAY - TRONES WOOD Area.	} CITADEL Camp. F.21.b.		
167th Bde. Group.	167th Bde. (less H.Q. & 2 coys.3rd Londs) 16th Lond. Regt. (Q.W.R.)	} Left } Sector.	↑ Battns. in FLERS line to CITADEL Camp, on relief, commencing probably about 2 pm. * Battns. in front line & support to TRONES WOOD Area on relief.		
168th Bde. Group.	168th Bds. (less 4th Londs. & Lond. Scot.) 5th Lond. Regt. (L.R.B.) 9th " " (Q.V.R.) 2 Secs.169th M.G.Coy.	Right Sector. " " " " " "	- ditto -		

Hdqrs. 56th Divn.
8th October, 1916.

Lieut. Colonel,
General Staff.

SECRET.   Copy No. 17

56th DIVISIONAL ORDER No 56.

1. The 56th Division (less Royal Artillery) moves to Area D (N.W. of AMIENS) on the 10th, 11th and 12th instant (dismounted personnel by bus, transport by road)

2. Para. 3 of 56th Divisional Order No. 55 and the March Table issued with Divisional Order No 55 are cancelled.

3. Brigade Groups are formed and will remain as under until completion of movement to Area D:-

167th Bde. Group.	168th Bde. Group	169th Bde. Group
167th Bde. H.Q.	168th Bde. H.Q.	169th Bde. H.Q.
167th M.G.Coy.	168th M.G.Coy.	169th M.G.Coy.
167th T.M.Bty.	168th T.M.Bty.	169th T.M.Bty.
7th Middx. Regt.	12th Lond.Regt.(Rangs)	2nd Lond.Regt.
8th Middx. Regt.	13th Lond.Regt.(Kens.)	3rd Lond.Regt.
1st Lond. Regt.	5th Lond.Regt (LRB)	4th Lond.Regt.
16th Lon.Regt.(QWR)	9th Lond.Regt.(QVR)	14th Lond.Regt. (Lond.Scot)
1/1st Edin.Fd.Co.R.E.	2/1st Lond.Fd.Co R.E	2/2nd Lon.Fd.Co RE
One Field Ambnce.	One Field Ambnce.	One Field Ambnce.

4. (a). 169th Brigade Group will move to CITADEL today, starting from BERNAFAY Area as soon as leading units of 4th Division arrive.
    (b). 168th Brigade Group will move to MANSEL CAMP tonight and tomorrow, units relieved in front line halting at BERNAFAY WOOD Area till tomorrow. Hour of move thence to MANSEL CAMP depends on time of completion of relief.
    (c). 167th Brigade Group will move to CITADEL today and tomorrow, units relieved in front line will halt at BERNAFAY Area till tomorrow. Hour of move thence to CITADEL depends on time of completion of relief tonight.

    Routes and intervals for all Brigade Groups are as laid down in para. 8 of 56th Divisional Order No. 55.

5. Moves from MANSEL and CITADEL CAMPS to Area D will take place in accordance with attached Table "A".

6. Brigades moving by bus will be drawn up on a sufficiently broad front to embark simultaneously, and embussing will be carried out under arrangements to be made by "Q" 56th Division. (Busses usually carry either 25 or 30 men.

7. Headquarters 56th Division will move to BELLOY-sur-SOMME and will be established there by 12 noon on the 11th inst.

8. The 1/5th Ches.Regt. will remain at the CITADEL under the orders of XIVth Corps

9. ACKNOWLEDGE.

Hdqrs. 56th Divn.   Lieut. Colonel,
9th October, 1916.   General Staff.

                    Issued at 2.45 pm 9.10.16.

Copy Nos:-
1. XIVth Corps "G"   7. 167th Inf.Bde.   13. 5th Ches.Regt.
2. XIVth Corps "Q"   8. 168th Inf.Bde.   14. 56th Div.Sigs.
3. Xth Corps.   9 169th Inf.Bde.   15. "G".
4. G.O.C. 56th Div.   10 C.R.A.56th Div   16. "Q".
5. 4th Division.   11. A.D.M.S.   17. War Diary.
6. 6th Division.   12. C.R.E.   18. French Liaison
                                              19.   Officer.

TABLE "A"

MARCH TABLE ISSUED WITH 56th DIVISIONAL ORDER No. 56.

Unit.	Date.	Road or bus.	Destination.	Route.	Remarks.
A. Personnel of 169th Bde. Group.	10th Oct.	Bus. en-bus at VILLE-sur-ANCRE.	Area D.	VILLE-CORBIE-AMIENS.	Route to en-bussing place via MEAULTE. Busses arrive at VILLE-sur-ANCRE at 1.30 p.m.
B. Transport of 169th Bde. Group.	10th Oct.	Road.	BUSSY les DAOURS	MEAULTE-VILLE-TREUX-MERICOURT-CORBIE-LANEUVILLE.	Not to enter VILLE before 2.15 p.m. To use tracks alongside road if possible.
D. Personnel of 167th Bde. Group.	11th Oct.	Bus. en-bus at VILLE-sur-ANCRE.	Area D.	VILLE-CORBIE-AMIENS.	Route to en-bussing place via MEAULTE. Busses arrive at VILLE 8.30 a.m. and must be clear of DAOURS by 11.30 a.m.
D. Transport of 139th Bde.Group.	11th Oct.	Road.	Area D.	BUSSY-H.25.a.5.9.-ALLONVILLE-COISY.	To be clear of main AMIENS-QUERRIEU Road by 11.0 a.m.
E. Transport of 167th and 168th Bde.Groups.	11th Oct.	Road.	DAOURS and VECQUEMONT.	MEAULTE-VILLE-TREUX-MERICOURT-CORBIE.	Not to enter MEAULTE until 10.0 a.m.

P.T.O.

Unit.	Date.	Road or bus.	Destination.	Route.	Remarks.
F. Transport of 167th and 168th Bde. Groups.	12th Oct.	Road.	Area D.	VECQUEMONT- AMIENS thence N. of SOMME.	Head to pass VECQUEMONT at 12 noon.
G. Personnel of 168th Bde. Group from MANSEL CAMP.	12th Oct.	Bus.	AREA D.	VILLE - CORBIE - AMIENS.	Details as to hour of on-bussing and route to en-bussing place will be notified later.

[signature] Lieut-Colonel,
General Staff.

Head Qrs. 56th Divn.
7th October, 1916.

SECRET.

War Diary.

56th DIVISIONAL ORDER No. 57.   Copy No. 13.

1.   The 56th Division will move to the HALLENCOURT area on the 19th, 20th and 21st inst. (in accordance with attached MARCH TABLE) and will be prepared to entrain at LONGPRE and PONT REMY any time after midnight 23rd/24th October.

2.   The 5th Australian Division is moving forward to the 15th Corps area on the same dates - personnel by bus and transport by road to ARGOEUVES and LONGPRE. Transport is timed to reach BELLOY, not before 10.0 a.m., and on 19th should be clear of La CHAUSSEE by 12 noon. In case of necessity all units of 56th Division will give way to units of 5th Australian Division on the march.

3.   Divisional H.Q. closes at BELLOY at 11.0 a.m. on the 20th and re-opens at HALLENCOURT at 1.0 p.m.

4.   ACKNOWLEDGE.

                          J. Brind.

Head Qrs. 56th Divn.   Lieut-Colonel,

18th October, 1916.   General Staff.

                 Issued at 6.30 am. 18.10.1916.

Copy Nos :-

     1.   Xth Corps.
     2.   G.O.C. 56th Divn.
     3.   167th Inf. Bde.
     4.   168th Inf. Bde.
     5.   169th Inf. Bde.
     6.   C.R.A.
     7.   A.D.M.S.
     8.   C.R.E.
     9.   5th Ches. Regt.
   10.   56th Div. Signals.
   11.   "G"
   12.   "Q"
   13.   War Diary.
   14.   41st Division.
   15.   5th Australian Divn.
   16.   Camp Commandant.
   17.   A.P.M.

MARCH TABLE ISSUED WITH 56th DIVISIONAL ORDER i.O. 57, dated 17.10.1915.

Date	Group	Units	From	To	Route	Remarks.
19th	167th Bde.	167th Inf. Bde. 1/1st Edin.Fd.Coy 1 Sec.2/2 Lon.Fd.Amb. No. 2 Coy. Train.	FLESSELLES Area. (R.E.at YZEUX)	AIRAINES - BETTENCOURT Sec.Fd Amb.to LIERCOURT Bde.H.Q. to VIEULAINE.	ST.VAST-en-CHAUSSEE. PICQUIGNY. LONGPRE. HANGEST.	To pass cross roads at LA CHAUSSEE TIRANCOURT at 12 FLESSELLES area to be cleared by 12 noon.
20th	168th Bde.	168th Inf. Bde. 2/1st Lond.Fd.Coy.	TIRANCOURT Area YZEUX.	SOREL - WANEL - GRANDSART - HOCQUINCOURT MERELESSART - CITERNE.	PICQUIGNY. HANGEST LONGPRE.	To be clear of PICQUIGNY by 10 am
		H.Q.& No.3 Co.Train Divnl. H.Q. Divnl. Sig.Co.	BELLOY	Bde.H.Q. to YONVILLE HALLENCOURT		Div.H.Q. to march in rear of and under orders of B.G.C. 168th Inf Bde.
21st		1/5th Ches.Regt.	CONDE	HALLENCOURT	FONTAINE SOREL.	March from CONDE at 9.0 am.
21st	169th Bde.	169th Inf. Bde. No. 4 Co. Train. 2/2nd Fd.Co. R.E.	PICQUIGNY Area. YZEUX	HUPPY - LIMEUX BELLIFONTAINE-DU-CQ. ERONDELLE-HUCHENNEVILLE. Bde.H.Q. HUPPY (Ch.VALKA).	HANGEST LONGPRE LIERCOURT.	To be clear of PICQUIGNY by 10 am.
		2/1st Lon.Fd.Amb. 2/3rd " " " 2/2nd " " " (less 1 sec.)	PICQUIGNY VAUX	2/1st Fd. Amb. to AIRAINES. 2/3rd " " to HUPPY. 2/2nd " " to LIERCOURT.		

Hdqrs. 56th Divn.

17th October, 1915.

Lieut. Colonel,
General Staff

SECRET   Copy No 15

56th DIVISIONAL ORDER No. 58

Ref 1/100,000
HAZEBROUCK Sheet.

1. The 56th Division (Less Artillery) will entrain at PONT REMY and LONGPRE on the 23rd and 24th inst. under instructions that are being issued by 56th Division "Q".

2. Units of the Division will detrain at BERGUETTE and MERVILLE, and will be concentrated in the area FOSSE - LESTREM - LA GORGUE - ESTAIRES - MERVILLE by October 25th.
   On arrival in the new area the Division comes under the orders of the XIth Corps

3. Details as to Brigade billeting areas will be issued to units on detrainment. Staff Captains and advanced parties will proceed to the new area tomorrow, 22nd, under arrangements already communicated

4. The Division (less Artillery) will relieve the 61st Division (less Artillery) in the NEUVE CHAPELLE - MOATED GRANGE and FAUQUISSART Sections (Left Sector) commencing on October 27th
   Detailed orders for relief will be issued later.

5. Railhead will be at LA GORGUE from October 24th inclusive.

6. Divisional Headquarters closes at HALLENCOURT at 12 noon 23rd, and opens at LESTREM at 4.0 pm. the same day.

7. ACKNOWLEDGE.

                                            J. Burnd.

Hdqrs. 56th Divn.   Lieut. Colonel,
21st October, 1916   General Staff
            Issued at 6.0 pm. 21.10.16.
Copy Nos:-
   1. Xth Corps.   10. XIth Corps.
   2 G.O.C., 56th Div.   11. 61st Division.
   3. 167th Inf. Bde.   12. 56th Div. Sigs.
   4. 168th   "   "   13. "G"
   5. 169th   "   "   14. "Q"
   6. C.R.A.   15   War Diary.
   7. A.D.M.S.   16. Camp Commandant.
   8. C.R.E.   17. A.P.M.
   9. 5th Ches. Regt.   18. Train.
                                19. A.D.V.S.

SECRET.   Copy No. 13

56th DIVISIONAL ORDER No. 59.

24th October, 1916.

1. The 56th Division, less Divisional Artillery, will relieve the 61st Division on 27th and 28th October in the LEFT SECTOR, XIth Corps.

169th Inf.Bde. will relieve 183rd Inf.Bde. in the NEUVE CHAPELLE Section.
167th   "   "   "   184th   "   "   "   MOATED GRANGE Section.
168th   "   "   "   182nd   "   "   "   FAUQUISSART Section.

2.(a). On 27th instant "A" and "B" Battalions (i.e. battalions destined for the front line) of each brigade, will relieve the two battalions in Brigade Reserve in each Section

  (b). On 28th instant - "A" and "B" Battalions of each Brigade will relieve the front line battalions of each section which, on relief will move into Brigade Reserve.

  (c). On 29th instant - "C" and "D" Battalions of each Brigade will relieve the two battalions in Brigade Reserve in each Section.

The disposition of Brigade Headquarters and Battalions on the nights of 26th/27th to 29/30th October are shown in attached Table "A"

3. All arrangements for relief will be made between Brigade Commanders concerned

Right Battalions in front line in each Section will relieve in the morning, and Left Battalions in the afternoon

Brigadiers will at once get into touch with the Commanders of the Brigades they are to relieve, and arrange for all reconnaissances to take place on the 26th and 27th instant.

Brigadiers of the 56th Division will take over command of their Section on completion of relief of Battalions in the front line

4. The C.R.E. will arrange for the relief of Field Companies and Pioneer Battalion on the 28th instant, when all workshops, dumps and stores will be taken over.

5. The A.D.M.S. will arrange the taking over of all medical arrangements on 28th October, and for the move of Field Ambulances.

6. Lewis Gunners.
   Battalion Observers.
   Battalion Snipers
   Light Trench Mortar Batteries
and portion of Bde. Machine Gun Companies occupying positions in front and reserve lines will be sent up on the 27th instant.

7. The following troops will come under orders of the General Officer Commanding 56th Division from 28th instant (5.30 pm):-

   61st Divisional Artillery.
   No. 1 Coy., 61st Divisional Train.
   257th Tunnelling Company, R.E
   3rd Australian Tunnelling Company.

/ 8

- 2 -

8. (a). All movements in front of the line BELLE CROIX - FOSSE will be by companies or groups of ten wagons at 200 yards distance.
   In front of the line LAVENTIE - Road Junction in M.14.b - LES HUIT MAISONS all movements will be by platoons or two wagons at 200 yards distance.

   (b). When hostile aeroplanes are in sight, troops will halt and clear the road as far as possible.

9. All billet and trench stores
        maps.
        records
        defence schemes
        log books
will be taken over and receipts given. A copy of receipts to be forwarded to Divisional Headquarters.

10. Completion of reliefs will be reported by wire to 61st Division, and repeated to 56th Division.

11. The General Officer Commanding 56th Division will assume command of the LEFT SECTOR, XIth Corps at 5.30 pm. on 28th October, at which hour Divisional Headquarters will close at LESTREM and re-open at LA GORGUE.

12. Acknowledge.

J. Burd.

Hdqrs. 56th Division,   Lieut. Colonel,

24th October, 1916.   General Staff.

   Issued at 9.30pm 24.10.1916.

Copy Nos:-

1. XIth Corps.   10. "G".
2. 167th Inf. Bde.   11. "Q".
3. 168th   "   "   12. G.O.C., 56th Div.
4. 169th   "   "   13. War Diary.
5. C.R.A., 56th Div.   14. 61st Division.
6. C.R.E., "   "   15. 257th Tunnelling Coy. R.E.
7. 5th Ches Regt.   17. 3rd Aust. T. C.
8. A.D.M.S.   18. 56th Div. Train.
9. A.P.M   19. Camp Commandant.
                              20. 5th Division.
                              21. N.Z. Division.

Table "A"

DISPOSITIONS OF BRIGADE H.Q. and BATTALIONS on NIGHTS 26/27th to 29/30th October
issued with 56th Divisional Order No. 59.

Brigade.	Night 26/27th.	Night 27/28th.	Night 28/29th.	Night 29/30th.
159th	Bde. H.Q. CALONNE 1 Bn. FOSSE. 1 Bn. LESTREM 1 Bn. L'EPINETTE PARADIS 1 Bn. CALONNE.	Bde. H.Q. CALONNE. 1 Bn. FOSSE. 1 Bn. LESTREM. 1 Bn. CROIX BARBEE 1 Bn. BOUT DEVILLE.	Bde. H.Q. LES HUIT MAISONS (R.30.c.5.9.) 1 Bn. FOSSE. 1 Bn. LESTREM. 2 Ens. line NEUVE CHAPELLE.Sct.	Bde. H.Q. LES HUIT MAISONS. 2 Ens. line NEUVE CHAPELLE Section. 1 Bn. CROIX BARBEE. 1 Bn. BOUT DEVILLE.
167th	Bde. H.Q. LA GORGUE. 2 Ens. LA GORGUE. 1 Bn. ROBERMETZ 1 Bn. to Gd.PACAUT.	Bde. H.Q. LA GORGUE. 2 Ens. LA GORGUE. 2 Ens. RIEZ BAILLEUL.	Bde. H.Q. COCKSHY HOUSE M.9.b.8.9. 2 Ens. LA GORGUE. 2 Ens. line MOATED GRANGE Sect.	Bde. H.Q. COCKSHY HOUSE. 2 Ens. line MOATED GRANGE Section. 2 Ens. RIEZ BAILLEUL.
168th	Bde. H.Q. ESTAIRES. 4 Ens. ESTAIRES.	Bde. H.Q. ESTAIRES. 2 Ens. ESTAIRES. 2 Ens. LAVENTIE.	Bde. H.Q. LAVENTIE. M.4.b.2.6. 2 Ens. ESTAIRES. 2 Ens. Line FAUQUISSART Section.	Bde. H.Q. LAVENTIE. 2 Ens. line FAUQUISSART Sect. 2 Ens. LAVENTIE.

Head Qrs. 56th Divn.
24th October, 1915.

J. Burnel
Lieut-Colonel.
General Staff.

LIST of APPENDICES
to
56th DIVISIONAL WAR DIARY
October 1916.

Appendix I Location of units 21st and 25th October.

" II Maps.

    A = Location Map of forward area 30th Septr; 1st & 9th October.

    B = Daily Location Maps 1st to 9th Octr. (9 maps).

    C = Operation maps for 1st, 7th and 8th October.

    D = Map showing names of trenches.

    E = "D Area", 11th to 20th October, 1916.

    F = "Area 5", 20th to 23rd October, 1916.

" III Divisional Orders for October 1916.

" IV Tactical progress reports for October 1916.

APPENDIX IV

TACTICAL PROGRESS REPORTS
OCTOBER 1916

TRENCH MAP.

GUILLEMONT.

Scale 1:20,000.

56th DIVISION TACTICAL REPORT No. 1.
from 8.0 a.m. 28th October to 8.0 a.m. 29th October.

Part 1. OPERATIONS.

NEUVE CHAPELLE SECTION.

Our Lewis Guns fired on the German lines throughout the night. Listening and reconnoitring patrols in the right sub-sector neither saw nor heard signs of enemy movement in front of his trenches.

MOATED GRANGE SECTION.

Our T.M: and Artillery carried out bombardment of enemy's front line in reply to his T.M. fire between 4.0 p.m. and 5.30 p.m. Our machine guns fired on gaps in the enemy's wire during the night.

A patrol of 1 N.C.O. and 2 men from the right sub-sector reported seeing a hostile patrol about 9.0 p.m. but did not open fire owing to the enemy's superiority of numbers.

FAUQUISSART SECTION.

Between 4.0 and 5.30 p.m. the enemy replied vigorously to our rifle grenade fire with rifle grenades, L.T.Ms, 77mm. guns and 4.2 Hows. His fire was principally directed on front line and C.Ts. in LAMP SALIENT. Back area near ESQUIN POST also shelled.

Our patrols reported enemy working on his front line during the night.

PART 11. INTELLIGENCE.

NEUVE CHAPELLE SECTION.

Movement was observed at dump S.25.b.85.30 which appears to have been enlarged. Men, thought to be linesmen, were seen on the road at T.2.b.6.5.

MOATED GRANGE SECTION.

A new canvas screen has been put up at N.25.c.8.5. blinding the PIETRE-RUE D'ENFER ROAD.

FAUQUISSART SECTION.

Snipers post reported at N.13.c.85.15. L.T.M. emplacement suspected at N.13.c.8.1½. Enemy's front line between N.19.a.5.8. and N.13.d.5.0. is badly damaged. The wire opposite this portion of the line is thick but damaged in several places.

Movement seen on AUBERS - PAS POMMEREAU Road and in trench between N.26.c.8.5. and N.26.d.2.0.

During the morning of the 28th a considerable amount of smoke was seen issuing from German front line in WICK SALIENT.

Head Qrs. 56th Divn.

29th Oct. 1916.

Captain,
for Lieut-Colonel,
General Staff.

56th DIVISION TACTICAL REPORT No. 3.
from 8.0 am. 29th October to 8.0 am. 30th October.

PART I OPERATIONS.

NEUVE CHAPELLE SECTION.

Patrols which were out during the night found no sign of the enemy. During the afternoon of 29th, Artillery shoot on the Dump at S.23.b.8.3. was successful, timber etc. being thrown up in the air.

A working party at S.17.a.3.½. was also dispersed.

Our batteries also obtained direct hits on a hostile T.M. emplacement at S.11.c.7.3. Our T.M's considerably damaged the enemy's parapet at S.11.a.2.2

MOATED GRANGE SECTION.

Enemy was quite during the day, but there was more sniping and M.G. fire than usual during the night.

A mine was blown by the enemy in front of M.29.1. at 5.0 am. this morning, slight damage was done to our galleries but none to our trenches. Patrols which visited the BIRD CAGE (M.30.a. central) and craters in the vicinity, also craters about M.30.a.1.9. reported no signs of the enemy.

The enemy wire in front of the right company right subsection was visited and found to be in good condition.

Our machine guns were active against the hostile trenches, wire and communications during the night.

FAUQUISSART SECTION.

Our artillery and trench mortars fired on enemy T.Ms. and O.Ps. during the afternoon doing considerable damage. Our snipers had many good targets. Patrols out during the night were undisturbed.

PART II INTELLIGENCE.

NEUVE CHAPELLE SECTION.

At 2.45 pm. 10 heavy trench mortars and some rifle grenades were fired and two direct hits obtained on our front trench. Considerable movement in trench at S.10.d.6.6. The spot was fired on by our Artillery. Several small parties of the enemy were seen on the main road in S.23.b. also at S.17.a.½.0. The party seen at the latter point disappeared into a trench about S.16.d.9.7. when a trench about S.10.d.9.7. when a trench mortar was seen to fire. This point was engaged by our Artillery.

MOATED GRANGE SECTION.

It is thought that hostile artillery was registering our C.T's during the day. Two small hostile patrols seen near the DUCKS BILL CRATER at 10 pm. retired when fired on.

Work was being done in the German trench at M.30.b.15.65. A sergeant who lost his way in NO MANS LAND near the DUCKS BILL on night 28/29th fell in the German wire. A bomb was immediately thrown which wounded him slightly. He reports that the enemy was very nervous and that whenever he touched the wire while trying to find his way back, bombs were thrown. He finally waited for daylight and crawled back yesterday without drawing fire.

FAUQUISSART SECTION.
Enemy trench mortars fairly active. 4 aerial darts fired on S. end of MASSELOT St. between 8 am. and 10 am. An enemy patrol of 2 or 3 men seen in front of BODMIN Trench at 12.30am : they dispersed when fired on.

Head Qrs 56th Divn.
30th October, 1916.

Captain
for Lieut Colonel,
General Staff.

58th DIVISION TACTICAL PROGRESS REPORT No. 3.
from 8.0 am. 30th October to 8.0 am. 31st October.

PART I OPERATIONS.

NEUVE CHAPELLE SECTION.

Our T.M's of all calibres had an organised shoot on enemy's front line between 2.30 and 3.30 p.m. Much damage was done, the parapet being badly knocked about for 30 yards at S.11.a.2.2. A gap was made in the wire at this point and at S.5.d.2.3½. Our Artillery co-operated with covering fire. The enemy's retaliation was feeble

At 5.30 p.m. an infantry party attempting to repair the damage was dispersed by Lewis gun fire.

An enemy working party in communication trench at T.1.b. was dispersed by our Artillery. Our patrols went out along the whole front and found no trace of the enemy. Our snipers accounted for two of the enemy.

MOATED GRANGE SECTION.

Our light trench mortars co-operated with M.T., M.G. and Artillery on targets in enemy front line in M.30.a. Enemy retaliation feeble. Our patrols reconnoitred the new crater M.30.c.1½.2½, and beyond and found no trace of the enemy. The far lip of the crater was wired by us. Patrols on other parts of the front found no trace of the enemy except at enemy's sap at M.24.d.8.4. The patrol was fired on at close range, when it reached the enemy's wire.

FAUQUISSART SECTION.

Our trench mortars and machine guns carried out offensive operation against the German wire and parapets.

No enemy were encountered by our patrols during the night. An officer in charge of a patrol which left our lines at N.13.c.½.2. found a rope leading towards the enemy's trench, broken by shell fire about 70 yards out. He listened for a time from a point about 120 yards from our lines, and then visited the German wire about N.14.c.2.9. which was not in good condition. He gathered the impression that the enemy's line was not strongly manned.

PART II INTELLIGENCE.

NEUVE CHAPELLE SECTION.

A large quantity of new wire has been put up by the enemy and in several places stacks of wire are on the ground ready to be put up. The heads of two Germans could be seen at S.6.a.5.3½. and work seemed to be proceeding at this spot. Artillery fire was opened, the third round landing at the exact spot where the heads were seen.

Movement was again seen on the LA BASSEE Road at S.23.b. and also between S.17.a.2½.0. and S.16.d.9.7. PIANO HOUSE S.24.c.4.0. is suspected of being an O.P. There is a boarding in front of it with a rectangular gap and also a brick wall with a small hole in it.

MOATED GRANGE SECTION.

At 7.15 am. 2 men were seen crawling from a sentry post at M.30.c.55.20.

FAUQUISSART SECTION.

The enemy's artillery and T.M's have been inactive on the whole. Work was in progress on the front line of the WICK SALIENT about midday as earth was seen to be thrown over the parapet at N.13.d.1.6. and N.13.d.5½.5½.

During the afternoon a hostile M.T.M. was reported to be firing from N.13.d.8.6½. on to our trenches at LAMP CORNER. There is a gap in the enemy's wire at N.13.d.6½.3. Smoke was seen rising at the following points, which may be living places:- front line N.13.d.6½.5½. N.13.d.1.6. about N.20.b.3½.3½. and N.14.c.6.2.

Edge, 58th Divn.

Captain,
for Lieut. Colonel.

MAP E

DVNL: AREA "AREA D"
11ᵗʰ to 20ᵗʰ OCT: 1916

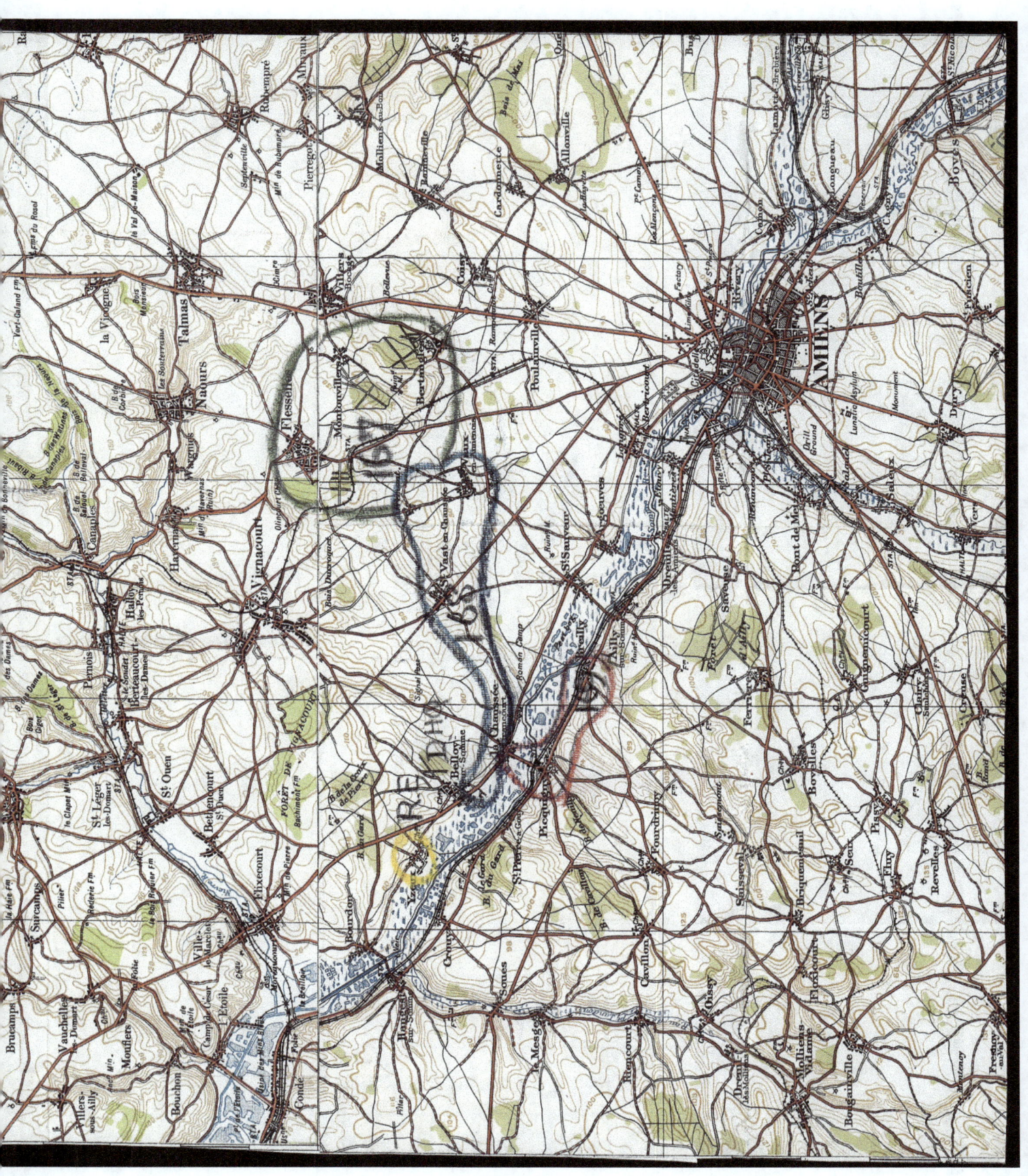

MAP C1

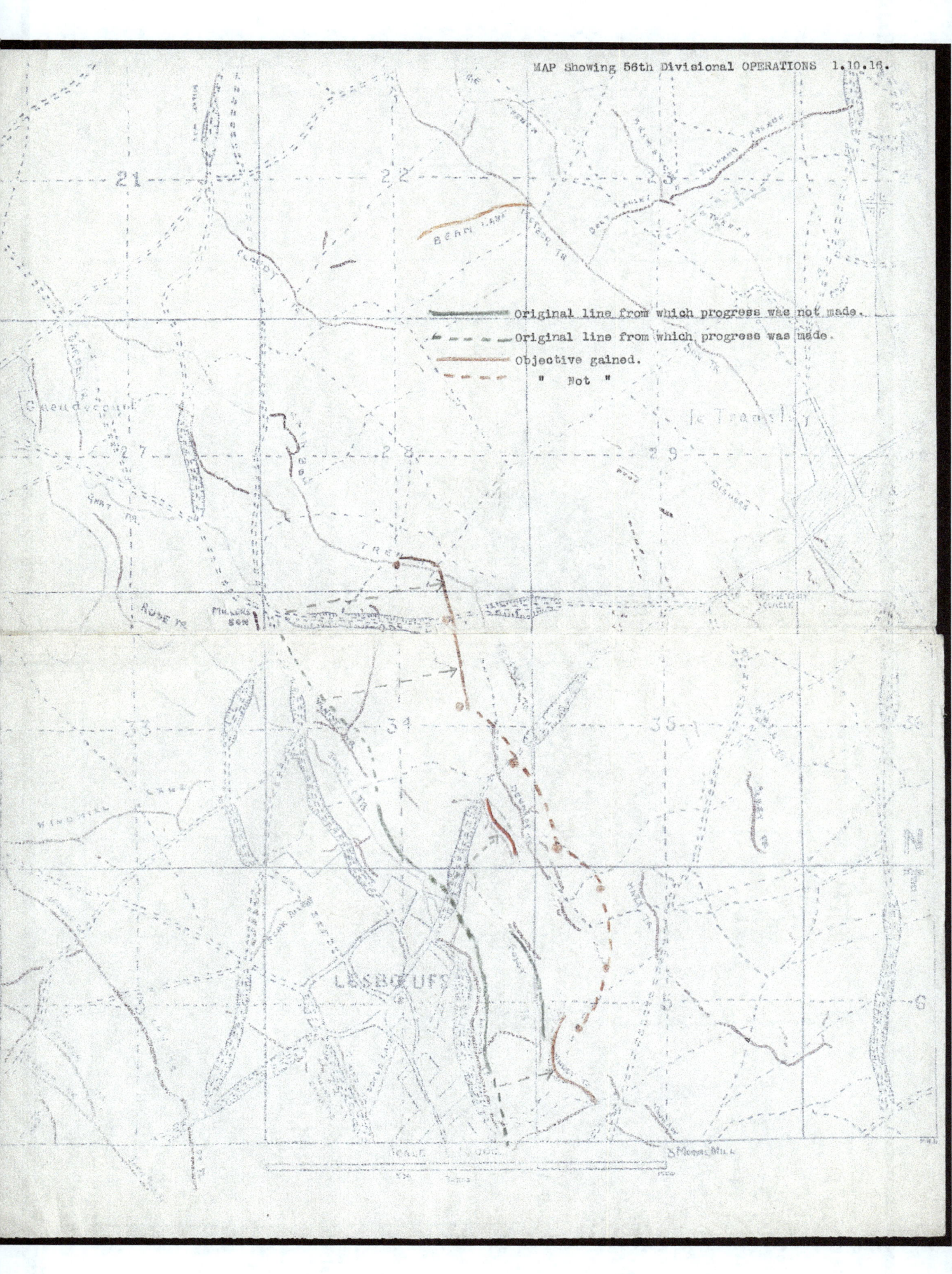
MAP Showing 56th Divisional OPERATIONS 1.10.16.

Map B

Location Map 9 A.M. 1.10.16

Situation Map

167 Inf. Bde:
HQ: Guillemont Stn
Res: 3rd London R.
   Trones Wd.

169 Inf. Bde:
HQ: Guillemont Quarry
L.R.B.
Reserve S.24.d

168 Inf Bde
HQ: Briqueterie
4 London R. — Trones Wd
Rangers — Citadel
Kensingtons — Citadel
Scottish — Trones Wd

Location map
1-10-16

2

MAP B

LOCATION MAP. 8.30 A.M. 2.10.16

167 INF BDE:	
HQ	GUILLEMONT STN
3rd London	
Res: TRONES WD	

169 INF. BDE:	
HQ	GUILLEMONT QUARRY
L.R.B.	
Res: S.24.d. GATE LANE	

168 INF: BDE:	
HQ	BRIQUETERIE
4th London	S of BERNAFAY WD
Rangers	CITADEL
Kensingtons	CITADEL
L. Scottish	S of BERNAFAY
	W.D:

SITUATION MAP

Flers
Bns Mddx
Rainy Tr.
3rd London
Q.V.R.
Q.W.R.
Windy Tr.
Gird Support
Gird Tr.
Needle Tr.
Rutland
Cow Tr.
Bn HQ
Punch Tr.
Gas Alley
The Fork
Tatler Tr.
Serpentine Tr.
8th Mddx
Hogs Back
2nd Lon 2 Coy
Q.V.R. Bx Tr.
Bn HQ
Bovril Tr.
Gueudecourt
Mince Tr.
Meat Tr.
Ginchy Road
Ginchy

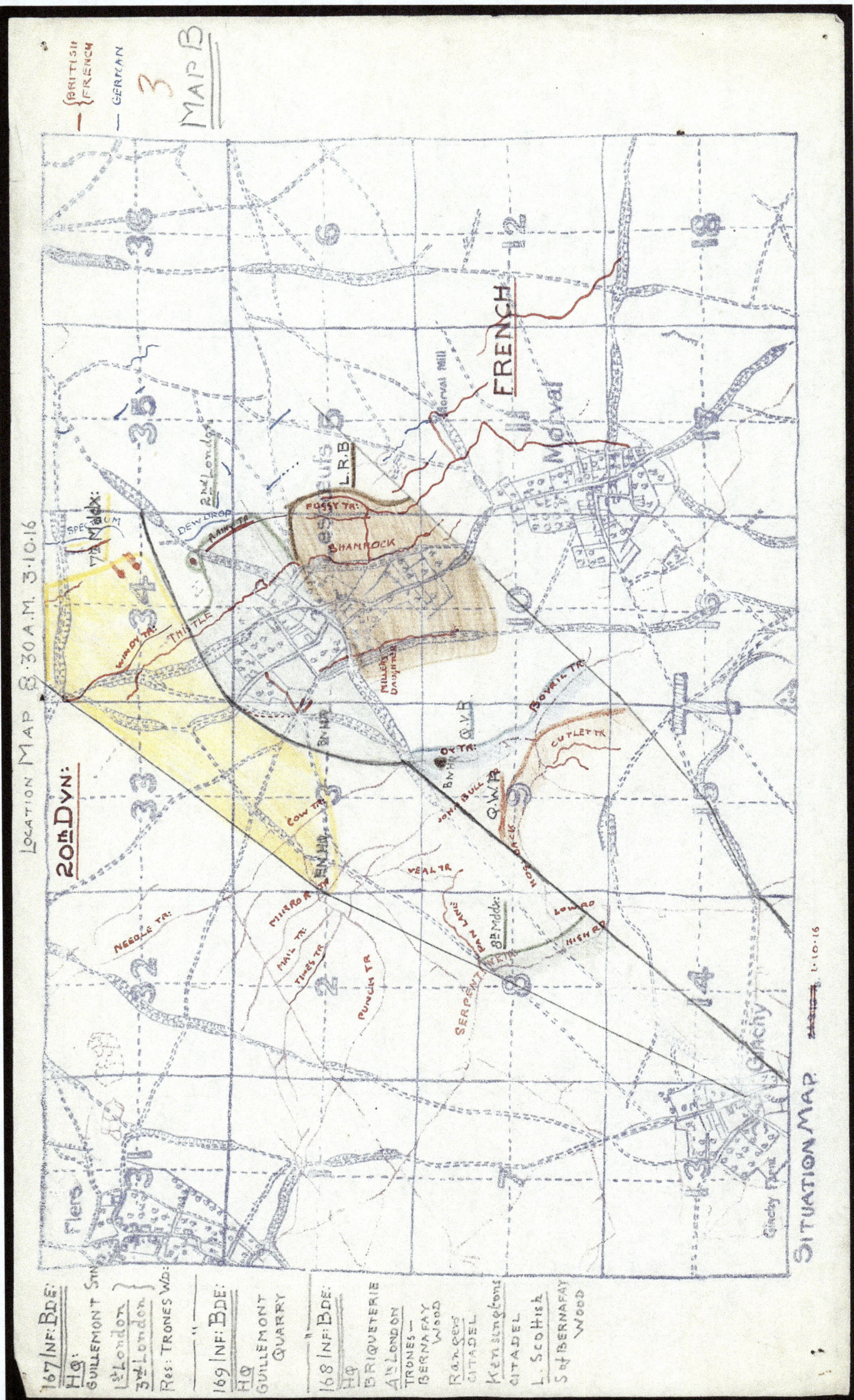

Map B

Situation Map 8.30 A.M. 4.10.16

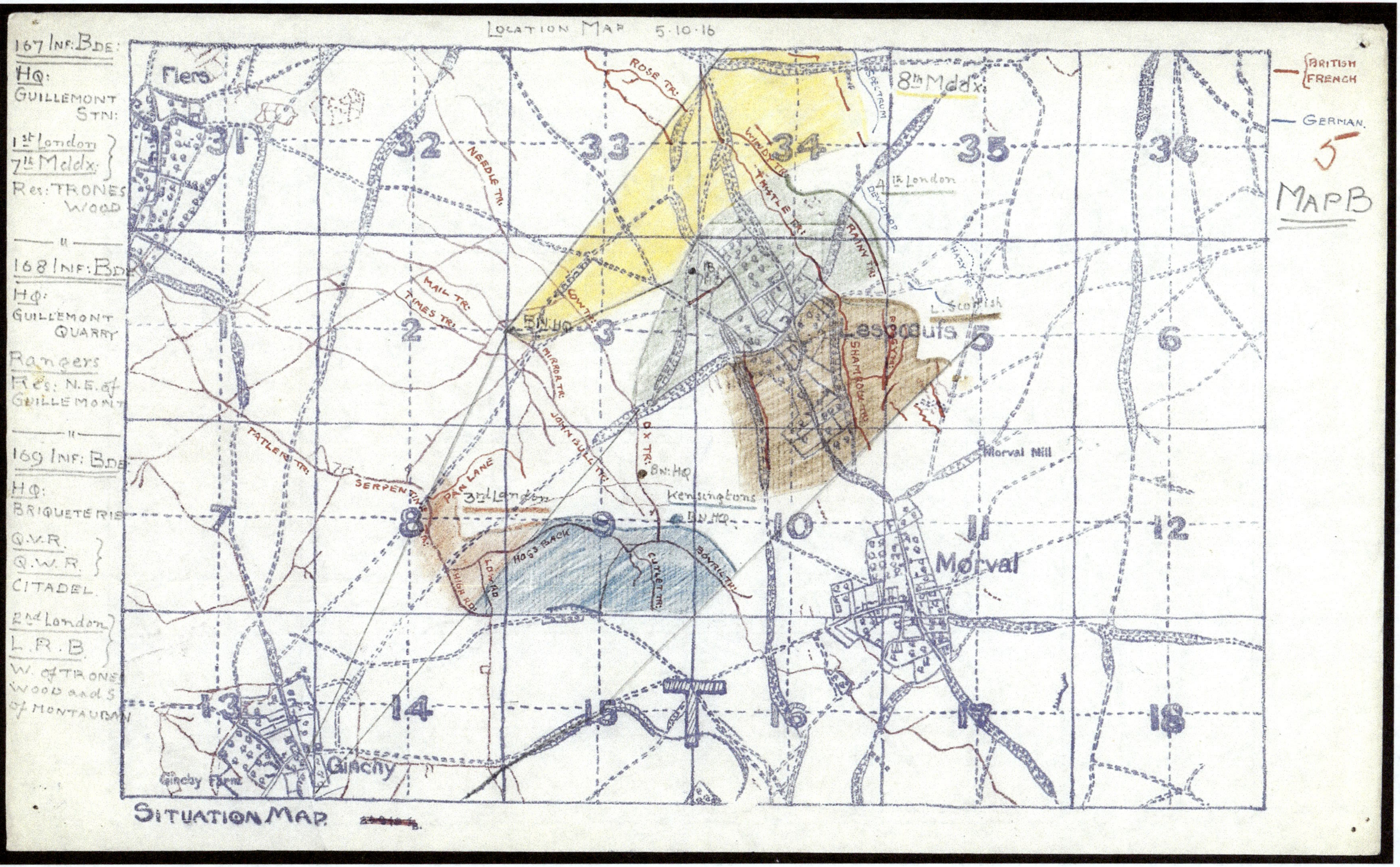
LOCATION MAP 5·10·16
167 INF: BDE:
HQ: GUILLEMONT STN:
1st London
7th Mddx:
Res: TRONES WOOD
168 INF: BDE
HQ: GUILLEMONT QUARRY
Rangers
Res: N.E. of GUILLEMONT
169 INF: BDE
HQ: BRIQUETERIE
Q.V.R.
Q.W.R.
CITADEL
2nd London
L.R.B.
W. of TRONES WOOD and S of MONTAUBAN
BRITISH
FRENCH
GERMAN
5
MAP B
Flers
Ginchy
Ginchy Farm
Lesboeufs
Morval
Morval Mill
ROSE TR.
NEEDLE TR.
MAIL TR.
TIMES TR.
COW TR.
MIRROR TR.
JOHN BULL TR.
TATLER TR.
SERPENTINE TR.
PAN LANE
OX TR.
HOGS BACK
LOW RD
HIGH RD
CUTLET TR.
BOVRIL TR.
WINDY TR.
THISTLE TR.
RAINY TR.
SHAMROCK TR.
SPECTRUM
DEWDROP
HAZY TR.
8th Mddx
4th London
L. Scottish
3rd London
Kensingtons
Bn HQ
SITUATION MAP

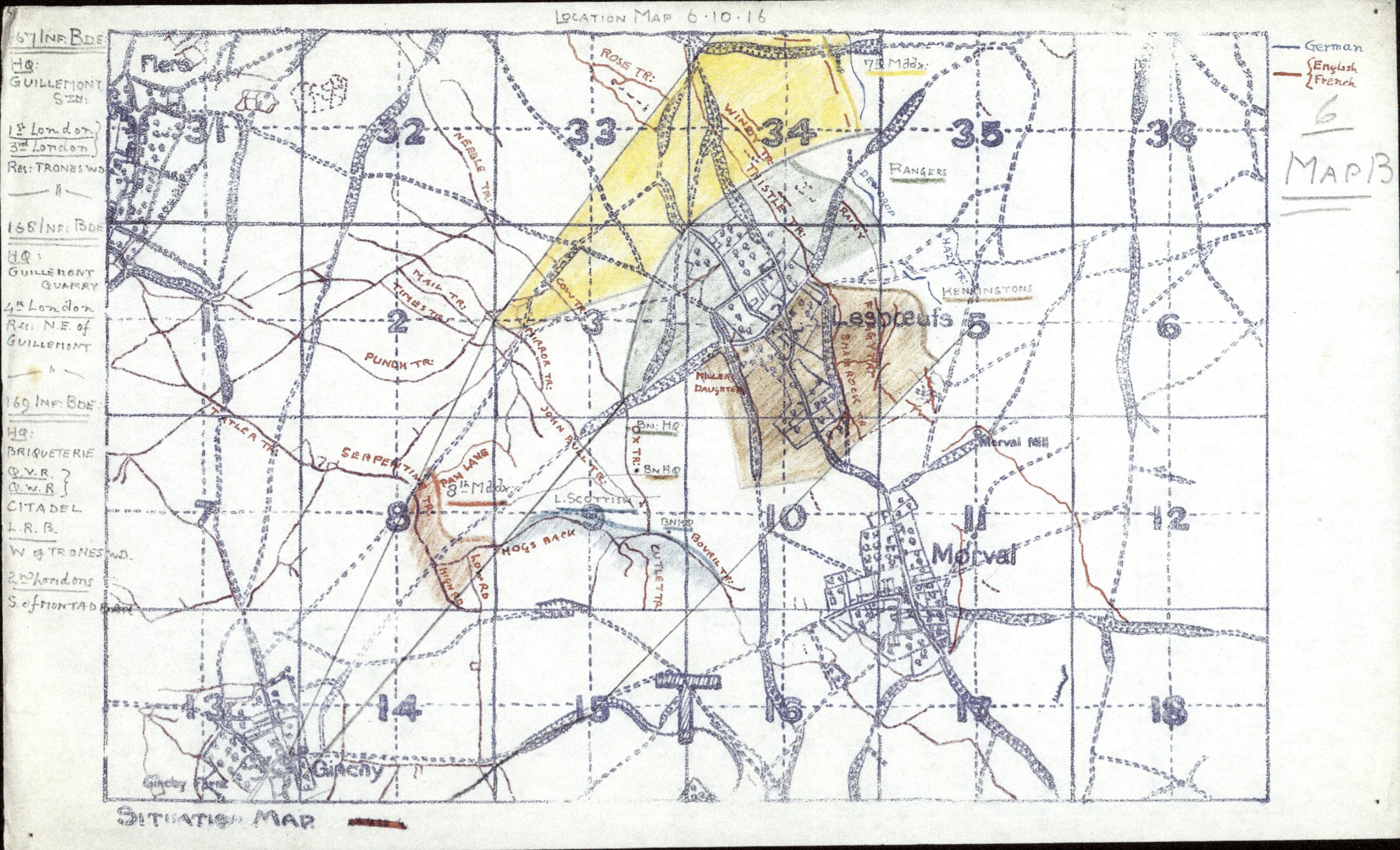

LOCATION MAP 6·10·16
German
English
French
6
MAP B
67 INF. BDE:
HQ: GUILLEMONT STN:
1st London
3rd London
Res: TRONES WD
168 INF. BDE
HQ: GUILLEMONT QUARRY
4th London
Res: N.E. of GUILLEMONT
169 INF. BDE:
HQ: BRIQUETERIE
Q.V.R.
Q.W.R.
CITADEL
L.R.B.
W of TRONES WD.
2nd Londons
S. of MONTADBAN
Flers
Lesboeufs
Morval
Morval Mill
Ginchy
ROSE TR.
WINDY TR.
THISTLE TR.
RAINY
DEWDROP
HAZY TR.
7th Mddx.
RANGERS
KENSINGTONS
SHAMROCK TR.
MILLERS DAUGHTER
NEEDLE TR.
MAIL TR.
TIMES TR.
PUNCH TR.
COW TR.
MIRROR TR.
JOHN BULL TR.
OX TR.
Bn. HQ
TATLER TR.
SERPENTINE TR.
RAIN LANE
8th Mddx.
L. SCOTTISH
HOGS BACK
LOW RD
HIGH RD
CUTLET TR.
BOVRIL TR.
31
32
33
34
35
36
1
2
3
5
6
7
8
9
10
11
12
13
14
15
16
17
18
SITUATION MAP

SITUATION MAP

FOURTH ARMY AREA
ADMINISTRATIVE MAP.
SHEET 2.

MAP F

DVNL: AREA.   "AREA 5"
20th to 23rd OCT: 1916

Map C 3

MAP showing 56th Divisional OPERATIONS 8.10.16.

Original Line from which no attack was made.
     "   "   "   "   "   progress   "   "
Objective gained.
    "   NOT "
    "   gained but retaken by enemy.

FAILED

Gueudecourt

le Transloy

LESBOEUFS

SCALE 1:10000

MAP C 2

MAP showing 56th Divisional OPERATIONS 7.10.16

Original line from which progress was made
" " " " " NOT "
1st Objective gained.
" " NOT "
2nd " gained.
" " NOT "
Objectives gained but retaken by enemy.

MAP D

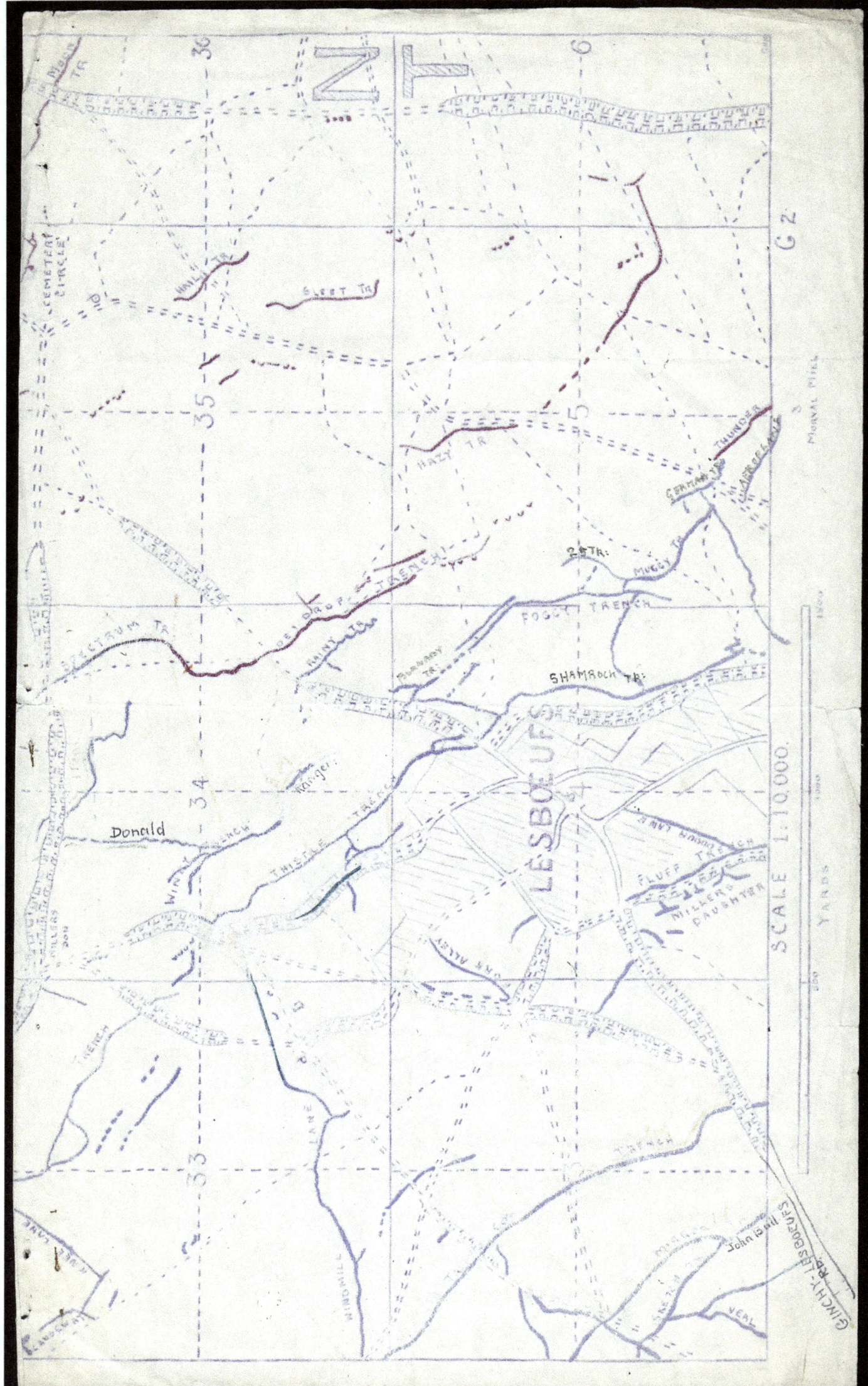

Approx. SITUATION MAP SECRET G2 corrected to 8.10.16

FOURTH ARMY TRENCH MAP B

LEEK

29-9-16. / 9.30.A.M.
Trenches corrected to 28-9-16.

1st Printing Coy R.E. IV Army. Scale 1:20,000.
Thick Blue Line Represents British Front.
New Trenches in Blue.

Places labelled: Beaulencourt, Lubra Copse, Gueudecourt, Le Transloy, Morval, Ginchy, Combles, Frégicourt.

Somme
1916
XXIII
10

LEEK

SECRET

ACCOUNT OF OPERATIONS CARRIED OUT BY 56th DIVISION

DURING SEPTEMBER and OCTOBER, 1916.

1. On the 23rd August the 56th Division arrived in the St. RIQUIER Training area and remained there until September 3rd, when the Division moved partly by road and partly by rail to CORBIE.

   During the stay of the Division at St. RIQUIER information was received that the Division would take part in offensive operations in co-operation with the Heavy Section Machine Gun Corps, and each Brigade had an opportunity of practising with the Tanks during its stay at St.RIQUIER.

   On the arrival of the Division at CORBIE orders were received for the Division to proceed at once to the forward area with a view to going into the line to relieve the 5th Division on the extreme right of the British front.

   On the afternoon of the 5th September the 168th Infantry Brigade proceeded to MARICOURT SIDING and came under the orders of the 5th Division, the remainder of the Division moving up to the CITADEL and HAPPY VALLEY.

   Divisional Headquarters opened at the FORKED TREE (L.2 b.0.9.) at 10 a.m. on 6th September.

   On the night of the 6th/7th the 56th Division relieved the 5th Division in the line in accordance with 56th Divisional Order No. 31. Divisional Headquarters was established at BILLON FARM on the morning of the 7th September.

2. On the 6th September a Warning Order was received from the XIVth Corps that it was intended to renew the offensive with the 16th and 56th Divisions on the line T.27.b.3½.4½ - 141.7 East of GINCHY. This operation was to be carried out in co-operation with the XVth Corps, and was originally intended to take place on the 8th but was postponed to the 9th September.

3. In view of the offensive operations mentioned in the preceding paragraph, 56th Divisional Order No. 33 was issued ordering the attack to be carried out by the 169th Infantry Brigade on the right and the 168th Infantry Brigade on the left with the 167th Infantry Brigade in Divisional Reserve.

   The 169th Infantry Brigade assembled in LEUZE WOOD and the 168th Infantry Brigade in assembly trenches that were dug just South of the LEUZE WOOD - GINCHY ROAD. The hour for the assault was fixed for 4.45 p.m. By 6.0 p.m. the 168th Infantry Brigade were reported to have reached all their objectives also the left battalion (Q.V.R.) of the 169th Infantry Brigade. The situation as regards the 5th Londons (L.R.B.) on the extreme right was obscure. Information was also received that the left Brigade of the 16th Division had reached its final objective East of GINCHY, but that the right brigade had not made progress and was approximately on the line of the road from T.29.a.1.4. T.20.c.1.5. to T.20.d.3.2. where they connected up with our own troops. It was also reported that there was a fair number of Germans still about T.20 central.

   The 169th Infantry Brigade was instructed to clear up the situation on its right flank by putting in its reserve battalion if necessary, and the 168th Infantry Brigade was ordered to put in its reserve battalions from about the Northern corner of LEUZE WOOD in a North Westerly direction so as to surround the Germans in T.20 central by joining up with the left brigade of the 16th Division along the GINCHY - 141.7 road.

   In order to carry this out the 168th Brigade ordered the Kensingtons to reinforce the Rangers and the London Scottish to move forward on their to the line of the GINCHY - 141.7 road.

4. **10th SEPTEMBER.**

   Reports were received during the morning that the left brigade had occupied all its final objectives and that consolidation was proceeding; also that the London Scottish had
   /succeeded

succeeded in reaching the GINCHY - 141.7 road and were extending Westward so as to obtain touch with the Guards who had relieved the 16th Division and were supposed to be in position in trenches due East of GINCHY.

The day was misty and no confirmation of our situation could be obtained from the air. The London Scottish reported that they had failed to obtain touch with the Guards about T.14.c.. On the right of the divisional front the Q.W.R's carried out an attack at 7.0 am with the object of gaining the QUADRILATERAL due East of LEUZE WOOD, but this attack failed.

5. On the evening of the 10/11th, arrangements were made for the 167th Infantry Brigade to take over the line held by the 168th Infantry Brigade, and a composite brigade of the 5th Division relieved the 169th Infantry Brigade on the Southern half of the 56th Divisional front. During the morning of the 11th, reports were received that our troops holding the QUADRIKATERAL had been driven out previous to the relief taking place, and that the Northern extremity of our line now rested at T.21.a.4.8. It also transpired that the London Scottish were not holding the line of the GINCHY-141.7 road but that they had on the previous day apparently lost direction in the mist and were occupying the trench facing North East in T.21.a. This situation was definitely confirmed by air reconnaissance during the afternoon which showed that the QUADRILATERAL in T.15.c. was in German hands. The 167th Bde. made several attempts to gain a footing in the QUADRILATERAL but met with no success, chiefly owing to machine gun fire from T.20.b.

As the efforts to surround the Germans in T.20 had not proved successful, the Corps decided that an attack against the enemy in this neighbourhood would be carried out as a separate operation by the 6th Division on the 13th instant, and the front held by the Division was consequently altered in accordance with 56th Divnl. Order No. 35. This operation however, did not meet with success. On the night of the 13/14th the Composite Brigade of the 5th Division was relieved by the 169th Infantry Brigade.

6. Orders were now received from the Corps that the main offensive would be renewed on the 15th instant, and that the main task of the 56th Division on the right would be the clearing of BOULEAUX WOOD and the formation of a protective flank covering all the lines of advance from COMBLES and the valleys running N.E. from COMBLES. The capture of MORVAL and LESBOEUFS was to be undertaken by the 6th and Guards Divisions.

7. Orders and instructions for the attack on the 15th instant were contained in 56th Divisional Orders No. 37 and 38 which included instructions for the use of tanks, three of which were allotted to this Division. The 169th Infantry Brigade were again formed up on the right with the 167th Brigade on the left and the 168th Brigade in the rear, with orders to pass through 167th Brigade and to secure the right flank of the 6th Division in its attack on MORVAL. The attack was fixed for 5.50 am. and was carried out according to time-table. As regards the three tanks allotted to the Divisions, the male tank broke down on its way to the point of assembly owing to engine trouble, and this tank never came into action One female tank rendezvoused at the S.W. corner of LEUZE WOOD and got as far as T.27.b.4.7., but was unable to proceed any further. The third tank cruised about the Northern side of BOULEAUX WOOD, but finally stuck at T.21.b.2.2.

The attack of the 169th Infantry Brigade failed to make much progress, and the bombing attacks of the 167th Infantry Brigade on the same objective were also held up. The attack of the 167th Infantry Brigade was successful as regards its first objective, but the 7th Middlesex, who were ordered to advance to the second objective were held up in BOULEAUX WOOD by hostile machine gun fire.

/All

- 3 -

All efforts to make further ground were without avail. About 8.30 am. reports from our patrols indicated that the attack of the Division on our left was not progressing favourably. Consequently, orders were sent to thee 168th Infantry Brigade that they would not keep to the time-table issued with Divisional Orders, but would await instructions from Divisional H.Q. before attempting to pass through the 167th Brigade.

The situation on the evening of the 15th September was, therefore, that the 169th Brigade had only obtained a portion of their objective. They had progressed up the LOOP TRENCH as far as T.27.b.8.8., and they were in possession of the COMBLES TRENCH from LEUZE WOOD down as far as the track at T.27.b.4.4.

The 168th Infantry Brigade were holding the main German line running through BOULEAUX WOOD from T.21.b.2.2. to T.21.d.2.7., and had joined up with the 6th Division on our left on the LEUZE WOOD - MORVAL track at T.21.d.8.8.

The 167th Brigade had pushed forward posts into MIDDLE COPSE at T.21.b.2.8.

8. **16th SEPTEMBER.** Was spent in consolidating our present position, and beyond a few isolated bombing attacks, no attack on any large scale was carried out to gain further ground.

Owing to the considerable success attained by the Fourth and Reserve Armies on the 15th instant, further attacks were carried out by the Guards Division and by the XVth Corps against LES BOEUFS and GUEUDECOURT. Attacks were timed to start at 9.25 am.

9. **17th SEPTEMBER.** Instructions were received from the Corps that minor operations were to be carried out on the following day with a view to obtaining a satisfactory line for a further advance in the near future. The 56th Division were to capture the line T.21.b.7.3. - MIDDLE COPSE, where touch was to be obtained with the 6th Division. This attack was to be carried out at 5.50 am. on the 18th instant. The objectives of the 56th Division were allotted as follows. 169th Infantry Brigade to complete the capture of the QUADRILATERAL East of LEUZE WOOD. General direction of attack, S.W. to N.E. The 167th Infantry Brigade were to make good the S.E. face of BOULEAUX WOOD up to T.21.b.7.3., and secure a line thence to MIDDLE COPSE inclusive. The general direction of attack was to be from W. to E. The 4th Londons and the 14th London Scottish were attached to the 167th Infantry Brigade for this operation.

Rain started to fall on the evening of the 17th instant, so that the whole country very soon became a mass of mud, and progress over the ground near LEUZE WOOD, which was badly pitted with "crump" holes, became a matter of extreme difficulty

The result was, that by 5.50 am., the time arranged for the attack, the troops of the left (167th) Brigade attack had failed to reach their rendezvous. This attack, accordingly never materialised. The right (169th Brigade) attack was carried out under an artillery barrage but it again failed to make good its objectives. The attack was not renewed. The attack of the 6th Division on the QUADRILATERAL was completely successful.

On the evening of the 18th, the 167th Brigade was relieved by the 168th Brigade, while the 169th Brigade continued to hold its present front with orders to consolidate the ground gained and to push down the COMBLES Trench.

A Warning Order had now been received from the XIVth Corps that the general offensive would again be resumed on the 21st September, and that the task of the 56th Division was again to form a protective flank on the line from the N.E. Corner of BOULEAUX WOOD to the Southern end of MORVAL.

/ With

With this object in view the ground in the vicinity of MIDDLE COPSE was reconnoitred, and instructions were issued for a trench to be dug on the night 19/20th running from the tramline at T.15.d.8.7. through MIDDLE COPSE on to BEEF TRENCH in the vicinity of the Tank at T.21.b.2.2. This trench was successfully dug by the 1/5th Cheshire Regiment and was occupied by troops of 168th Infantry Brigade on the 20th instant, and on the night of the 20/21st strong points at T.16.c.1.8., T.15.d.9.4., and T.15.d.8.2. were connected up, and this system of trenches was used as assembly trenches for the next offensive.

Information was now received from the Corps that the attack arranged for the 21st inst. had been put off until the 22nd; it was again postponed until the 23rd, and finally postponed until the 25th September.

During this time the Division was busily employed in consolidating the line. On the 23rd instant, a change in the weather occurred, and the ground rapidly dried in the fine weather that ensued.

Orders for the attack on the 25th September were issued in 56th Divisional Order No. 43, which also contained instructions for the employment of two tanks, and instructions to the Special Brigade R.E., who had orders to create a smoke barrage across the Northern end of BOULEAUX WOOD.

On the 25th September, the task allotted to the 56th Division was the capture of the trench running from the Northern corner of BOULEAUX WOOD up to the tram line at T.16.c.4.6., and the construction of a strong post at the Northern extremity of BOULEAUX WOOD. This was carried out successfully by two battalions of the 168th Infantry Brigade - London Scottish on the left, 4th Londons on the right, who were assembled in RANGER and GROPI Trenches.

The assault of the 168th Brigade was timed seven minutes after zero to allow the troops on our left to come up into line, as we occupied trenches well in advance of the Division on our left. The Royal Fusiliers on the right and the London Scottish on the left advanced to their objectives close under a most efficient enfilade artillery barrage. The Royal Fusiliers reached their objective and cleared the Northern end of BOULEAUX WOOD without great opposition, but they killed a number of Germans who were occupying shell craters on the Western side of the Wood. This battalion suffered from snipers in the Southern part of the Wood, while they were establishing and consolidating the two strong points allotted to them. The London Scottish captured their objective the first German trench running N.E. from the end Corner of BOULEAUX WOOD without much opposition. The Germans were very strongly posted in the railway embankment N. of this trench, and for some time a hot bombing fight took place here. The left assaulting company put out of action and captured four hostile machine guns, but in spite of this suffered severe losses from the enemy posted in the embankment. This was finally cleared by 1.30 pm. and 80 prisoners were taken and sent back. Meanwhile, the leading company of London Scottish found the trench objective to have a poor field of fire, and also observed Germans driven out of BOULEAUX WOOD by the Royal Fusiliers withdrawing to a second trench running N.E. from the Eastern corner of BOULEAUX WOOD. This was captured, being cleared with the bayonet.

At a low estimate 150 Germans were killed in these operations a certain number escaped in the direction of COMBLES.

Eight prisoners were taken with four machine guns and five medium Minnenwerfer.

The strong points ordered to be made were sited further S.E. to conform with the greater extent of ground captured.

At 5.50 pm. the 2/1st Field Company, R.E. and "C" Company, 5th Cheshire Regiment were ordered forward to consolidate the ground won. Each section R.E. and each platoon of pioneers had a definite job allotted to it, and the details of stores required had been worked out, and forward dumps

had been formed at BILLON COPSE and at North end of GROPI Trench.
Touch was obtained with the 5th Division on our left after the embankment was cleared at 1.30 p.m., the 5th Division having exactly obtained the objectives allotted to them. The forward trench captured by the London Scottish was of great value in that it commanded a good view of the valley between MORVAL and COMBLES. Patrols were ordered to move Eastwards but could not at first be pushed far forward owing to our own barrage in this valley, but in spite of the barrage our patrols moved several hundred yards East and cleared some dug-outs and captured a few more prisoners.
The Lewis Guns were invaluable in those operations as the dugouts and caves in the embankment were cleared by bombs, the Lewis Guns obtained many good targets as the Germans strived to escape eastwards.
At 10.40 p.m. orders were issued for the blocking of the COMBLES - MORVAL Road to prevent the exit of the garrison of COMBLES. One Officer, 40 O.R. and two Lewis Guns of the London Scottish were moved South along the tram line and established themselves at T.22. Central before dawn. Other posts were established to support them. At dawn our patrols moved down to COMBLES and met French patrols in T.22.d. coming from the Town. From this time on touch was maintained with the French North of COMBLES, and with the 5th Division in the MORVAL-LESBOEUFS Trench line.

10. 26th SEPTEMBER.

During the night of the 25/26th information was received from the French that the enemy proposed to evacuate COMBLES during the night. Brigades were directed to keep constant pressure on the enemy wherever they were in touch, and to patrol actively towards COMBLES from the S.W. N.W. and N. 168th Brigade was directed to block the roads leading from COMBLES towards MORVAL. A heavy barrage was placed across the valley N.E. of COMBLES and the French were asked to continue the barrage to the South, in their own barrage area.

The events of the night can be traced from the following :-

at 12.30 a.m. the enemy was working at his end of LOOP TRENCH.
at 3.0 a.m. his bombing blocks opposite our right Bde. were still active.
at 2.55 am. the enemy evacuated his post behind the derelict tank at T.21.b.2.1. and the 1st Londons had established a post there.
at 3.0 am. patrols from our centre brigade entered the ORCHARDS West of COMBLES.
at 5.30 am. The London Rifle Brigade who had worked down COMBLES TRENCH, obtained touch with the French on the railway.
at 7.0 am. the French occupied the portion of COMBLES south of the railway.
at 7.20 am. reports were received that BOULEAUX WOOD was clear of the enemy.
at 8.0 am. reports were received at 167th Brigade H.Q. that our patrols were in touch with the French along the railway through COMBLES.

It is thought that the bulk of the garrison of COMBLES escaped by the trench running through T.29.a. and b. and N. of FREGICOURT which was not in French hands until early on the 26th. A few small parties who tried to break away north were shot and dispersed by the posts of the London Scottish about T.22 central.
The trophies found in COMBLES were very few -
3 small Minnnworfer
7 small Flammenworfer
1 large do.
Large quantities of rifles, grenades and ammunition were abandoned there by the enemy.
Progress was made throughout the 26th by all Brigades and the situation on the evening of the 26th was that the 168th and 169th Brigades kept touch with the 5th Division at about T.15.d.9.9.

/and

and were holding the line of the road from that point through T.22.b.1.9. joining up with the French at T.22.d.9.2. Two Companies of the Rangers were situated in SUNKEN ROAD between T.22.b.9.0 and T.22.d.9.0 ready to seize MUTTON TRENCH which runs through T.17.c. and d. as soon as that trench had been dealt with by Tanks. The situation in this trench was that the French were reported at T.23.b.8.3. and that the 5th Divn. were as far down as T.17.c.8.6. This trench in between, which was strongly wired on its Western side, was held by the Germans.

Instructions were issued for two Tanks to proceed to MORVAL on the afternoon of the 26th with orders to work down in front of MUTTON TRENCH and destroy the wire, and the Rangers who were in the SUNKEN ROAD were to occupy the trench, as soon as the Tanks were seen to have accomplished their object. One tank, however, stuck at the southern corner of MORVAL and the second tank stuck near the tram line in T.16.c. so the attack of the Rangers from the SUNKEN ROAD never materialised.

On the 27th inst., another three tanks were allotted to the 20th Division for the purpose of clearing up the situation as regards MUTTON TRENCH. This task was, therefore, handed over to the 20th Division and the 56th Division took no further part.

On the evening of the 27/28th the whole of the front was taken over by troops of the 1st and 2nd French Divisions and the 56th Division withdrew to the MEAULTE - SAND PITS and TREUX area.

- 7 -

11. On the morning of the 29th September, Brigades were disposed as follows:-

167th Inf. Bde.   In the area of SAND PITS & MORLANCOURT.
168th   "   "   " "   "   VILLE-sur-ANCRE & MORLANCOURT.
169th   "   "   " "   "   MEAULTE.
Divnl. Hdqrs.   BILLON COPSE.

There was a conference of Brigadiers and Commanding Officers at H.Q. 169th Inf. Bde. MEAULTE during the morning.

In the afternoon, the preliminary moves as detailed in 56th Divnl. Order No. 48 were carried out, the 167th and 169th Brigades moving up into the forward area.

A warning order had been received from the XIVth Corps stating that the Fourth Army would renew the attack on the line LE TRANSLOY - THILLOY - WARLENCOURT - FAUCOURT on or about October 10th, and to enable this to be carried out successfully it was necessary to gain by the 5th October, certain tactical points from which observation of the enemy's main positions could be obtained.

During the afternoon Divisional Order No. 48 was issued for the relief on the night of the 30/1st October of the 6th and Guards Divisions in the Sector E. of LESBOEUFS.

12. On the 30th September moves detailed in Divisional Order No. 49 were carried out, and at 6.0 pm. Divnl. Hdqrs. closed at BILLON COPSE and opened at A.10.b.3.8. on the MARICOURT - BRIQUETERIE Road.

On the night of the 30/1st relief was carried out as ordered without incident, and on the morning of the 1st October Brigades were disposed as follows:-

169th Inf. Bde.   holding the right subsector, with
                  H.Q. at GUILLEMONT QUARRY.
167th   "   "   holding the left subsector, with
                  H.Q. GUILLEMONT STATION.
168th   "   "   in reserve in the area TRONES WOOD -
                  BERNAFAY WOOD, with two battalions at
                  the CITADEL and the Brigade H.Q.
                  at the BRIQUETERIE

At 7.0 am., with a view to co-operating with operations further N., a heavy bombardment of the LE TRANSLOY line and other selected points commenced and lasted until 3.15 pm. when the XIVth Corps opened an intense barrage on the enemy's defences on its front. Under cover of this barrage patrols were pushed out with a view to establishing themselves on a line running approximately parallel to the Divisional front at a distance varying from 500 to 300 yards from it.

The patrols left our trenches and advanced apparently without difficulty. It was not until the evening that the left battalion of the left brigade reported all objectives gained and parties digging in. The right battalion of the left brigade reported RAINY TRENCH occupied by one platoon with posts pushed forward to the Crest - The report about the posts was not correct. The position of the patrols of the right brigade was obscure because although the patrols got forward, it was definitely reported by airmen that the trenches in T.5.c. central were strongly held by the enemy. A further air report showed our occupation of RAINY TRENCH doubtful, but subsequent events proved that it was undoubtedly in our possession.

13. During the night 1/2nd the 169th Infantry Brigade dug a trench parallel to and E. of FOGGY TRENCH, but it was some days before its position could be accurately determined owing to lack of aeroplane photographs.

14. On the morning of the 2nd October, 167th Brigade reported that they were uncertain as to whether RAINY TRENCH was held by them, but they had joined up a line of posts from N.34.b.0.9. to N.34.d.3.7.

During the night 2nd/3rd the right brigade took over 500 yards of the front line from the left brigade so that on the morning of the 3rd the Divisional front was held by 2 Battalions of the right brigade and 1 Battalion of the left brigade. This move was preparatory to relieving the 169th Brigade by the 168th during the night of the 3rd/4th the intention being to reduce the left brigade to a one battalion front in order to avoid the necessity for relief.

15. <u>3rd October</u> By this time it had been ascertained definitely that we were in occupation of RAINY TRENCH, and that DEWDROP immediately East of it was strongly held by the enemy.

During the night 3rd/4th the relief of the 169th Brigade by the 168th Brigade was carried out. Before the relief took place, the London Rifle Brigade seized and occupied at 8.30 p.m. the length of isolated trench T.5.c afterwards known as GERMAN TRENCH. This was connected up the same night by a communication trench to the trench immediately West of it (MUGGY TRENCH), and thence to our front line at FOGGY TRENCH.

16. <u>4th October</u>. GINCHY and the area immediately North of it were frequently shelled throughout the day. A flight of 5 Hostile Aeroplanes over our lines preceded the commencement of the shelling.

On account of the extremely wet weather the renewal of the attack which had been arranged to take place on the 5th was definitely postponed for 48 hours

17. <u>5th October</u> - was unoventful except for the usual shelling of our trench system and valleys to the West of LESBOEUFS.

18. <u>6th October</u> - intermittent shelling of our front line trenches by the enemy with occasional heavy bursts of 77 mm. fire. No enemy movement was observed but his snipers were active throughout the day. During the evening, a flight of four enemy aeroplanes reconnoitred over LE TRANSLOY LESBOEUFS and MORVAL, and were fired on by our anti-aircraft guns and infantry.

From the 1st up to this date a considerable amount of digging had been done by our troops, so as to make a connected trench system which was necessary for launching the attack due to take place on the 7th. This work was greatly impeded by the wet weather which also prevented the taking of aeroplane photographs. Consequently it was exceedingly difficult to obtain correct information as to the position of our own troops and those of the enemy. It was known that the latter was occupying a number of short lengths of trench and gun pits between his main line in front of LE TRANSLOY and our own front system. Reports received from patrols indicated that the whole of RAINBOW and SPECTRUM TRENCHES were wired through; this was contradicted by a special aeroplane reconnaissance. The only definite positions known to be held by the enemy were RAINBOW, SPECTRUM, DEWDROP, Gun Pits in T.5.a. and HAZY TRENCH. It was suspected that DEWDROP and SPECTRUM had been connected by a trench.

The wet weather made living conditions extremely bad, this added to the length of time the troops had been engaged in offensive operations, and the hostile shelling had considerably lowered the fighting efficiency of the Division.

During the night 6th/7th the Divisional front had been readjusted to allow of two battalions of 167th Brigade and three battalions of 168th Brigade being in the front line.

19. <u>7th October</u> - shewed improved weather conditions. The task of the 56th Division in the attack which was to take place at 1.45 pm. was divided into two portions, the first objective was the capture of the Southern portion of RAINBOW TRENCH, SPECTRUM, DEWDROP and HAZY TRENCHES; the second was to push forward a further 500 yards and establish a line within assaulting distance of the enemy's main TRANSLOY line. This second position was to be strengthened by numerous strong points, communication was to be obtained with the 20th Division on the left, and our right flank slightly advanced to gain and keep touch with the 56th French Division on the right.

A heavy bombardment of the enemy's position was maintained throughout the morning; this was not to be increased before zero hour for fear of disclosing our intention to attack. The assault under cover of a standing and a creeping barrage was so arranged that troops which were farthest away from their objectives started at Zero hour and the remainder at varying times according to the distances to be covered so that all assaulting waves should reach their first objectives simultaneously along the Divisional front. This expedient was necessary owing to the fact that it had been impossible to construct a continuous line parallel to that held by the enemy, and a barrage conforming exactly to our irregular line of departure trenches would have been dangerous.

The first reports received showed that the infantry went forward well, and it was shortly afterwards reported that they had gained their first objective However, this later proved to be incorrect. The left battalion of the left brigade (7th Middlesex Regt.) having reached its first objective and occupied it after some minutes of hand to hand fighting in which they succeeded in capturing a number of prisoners (70 off) The right battalion (1st London Regt) of the left brigade was not so successful although it was repeatedly reported that it had taken SPECTRUM trench. Actually the left company of the 1st London Regt reached its objective in SPECTRUM, bombed up to the left, where it obtained touch with the 7th Middlesex Regiment. Several Germans were killed and a machine gun captured. The right brigade were reported as having captured all their first objectives and at 2.15 pm. observers reported seeing troops move forward to their final objective. The first definite information received was from an aeroplane report at 4.3 pm. which stated that the situation at HAZY TRENCH was doubtful but it was thought that this trench was in our hands. The enemy could be seen in occupation of the gun pits at T.5.a.4.7. The attack on DEWDROP and SPECTRUM TRENCHES had failed, but we had gained and were holding RAINBOW TRENCH. The observer stated that owing to the strong wind that was blowing he was unable to vouch for the accuracy of his report. Shortly afterwards the right brigade reported that the advance of their left battalion was being held up by two machine guns in the gun pits T.5.a.4.7. Reserve companies were pushed forward with a view to assisting the advance, but they in their turn failed to dislodge the enemy from this point. Up to nightfall, no further definite information was received. At 6.45 pm the following orders were issued:- Right Brigade (i) to push out a company from RAINBOW TRENCH and establish a strong point at N.35.a.3.9. and round up the enemy occupying SPECTRUM and connect up with a post which was reported to have reached N.35.a. central (ii) to dig a trench 200 yards W. of SPECTRUM from which a further attack could be launched if necessary. One battalion from the reserve brigade (169th Infantry Brigade) was placed at the disposal of the 167th Brigade. 168th Brigade was to ascertain whether or not DEWDROP was held by the enemy. (1) If found empty it was to be occupied and posts established to connect between N.35.a. central and HAZY TRENCH. The battalion from the reserve brigade which had been sent up earlier in the afternoon could be used for this purpose. (ii) If DEWDROP was held by the enemy a new trench was to be dug 200 yards to the West to admit of bombardment should a new attack be launched. The organisation of a fresh attack was to depend on the reports received from the 168th Brigade as to whether DEWDROP was held by the Germans.

On receipt of information as to the position of the right
/flank

flank of the 20th Division our left brigade was ordered to obtain touch with it about the Southern end of MISTY TRENCH. About 7.30 pm. a report was received that we had a footing in the Northern end of SPECTRUM TRENCH where a machine gun had been captured and further progress was being made by bombing.

At 9.10 pm. a message was received stating that the French on our right had fallen back to their line of departure, that the right battalion of the right brigade had been counter-attacked and forced to withdraw from HAZY TRENCH, and the gun pits in T.5.a. central to the trenches from which they had delivered their assault in the morning. By this hour it was definitely ascertained that the Germans were in occupation of DEWDROP.

20. On receipt of instructions from Corps Headquarters orders were issued for the attack to be renewed on HAZY, DEWDROP and that portion of SPECTRUM not in our hands on the morning of the 8th. The night which was comparatively quiet was spent in digging the necessary trenches and re-organising troops for the attack on the forthcoming day.

Owing to our proximity to the objective it was necessary to withdraw from the Northern end of SPECTRUM TRENCH and from RAINY TRENCH so as to allow of the bombardment of SPECTRUM and DEWDROP Trenches.

21. To enable the attack to be carried out, two battalions of the reserve brigade were placed at the disposal of 168th Brigade and one battalion at the disposal of 167th Brigade. These were to be employed either for carrying out the attack or for assisting in the digging of the necessary trenches. As it was unavoidable that the order should be issued very late at night, great difficulty was experienced in getting the troops into position and it was not until daylight that the last battalion reached its assembly trenches. Arrangements for the bombardment and the artillery support were similar to those of the previous day except as regards the barrage. On the 7th RAINY TRENCH was occupied by our troops, and the barrage on DEWDROP was provided by Stokes Mortars. On the 8th in order to allow the artillery barrage to reach DEWDROP, RAINY TRENCH had to be evacuated. Several adjustments of the barrage had to be made, as many batteries owing to the short range were unable to clear LESBOEUFS and hit DEWDROP TRENCH. This readjustment of lines of fire may have been responsible for the thinness of the barrage on the 8th. The assaulting troops, however, left their assembly trenches at Zero hour irrespective of the distances from their objectives. The bombardment by the heavy artillery was not successful, chiefly owing to the difficulty of observation caused by the weather conditions, and many shells were reported to be falling very short. Shortly after Zero a report from an F.O.O. stated that our infantry were advancing along our whole front and that the enemy could be seen leaving their trenches and running back over the rise. This, however, was not the case and at 3 55 pm. a message was received from the left brigade which stated that their attack had been held up by heavy German barrage and machine gun fire and had definitely failed. On the other hand, the left battalion of the right brigade were reported to be progressing favourably. No definite reports were received as to progress of the right and centre battalions of the right brigade until later in the afternoon when a report was received from a wounded officer of the battalion on the extreme right that he had seen his company go through the gun pits in T.5.a. central and enter HAZY TRENCH. At this time reports from wounded tended to show that the extreme right had got to its final objective. No definite news, however, was to hand as regards DEWDROP TRENCH until a message was received that the situation of the right battalion as discovered by the personal reconnaissance of the Commanding Officer was as follows :- His battalion were digging in just West of HAZY TRENCH which was held by the Germans. His left was in touch with the centre battalion about T.5.a.5.9. and his right at T.5.a.7.3. The centre battalion appeared to be East of DEWDROP. The position of the French on the right was unknown.

11.

22. <u>9th October.</u> At 12.10 am. the O.C. of the centre battalion returned from personal reconnaissance and reported that DEWDROP and RAINY TRENCHES were held by the enemy and that his battalion was back in its departure line having been heavily counter-attacked at dusk from the direction of DEWDROP. It was also ascertained that this same counter-attack succeeded in dislodging the right battalion which appeared to have been digging in in prolongation of RAINY TRENCH, in a Southerly direction, bringing back with them 17 prisoners and a machine gun.

On the morning of the 9th the situation was that with the exception of our gains in SPECTRUM trench, we were back in our departure line, RAINY TRENCH apparently having been occupied by the enemy during our bombardment of the 8th.

During the early hours of the morning 167th Brigade had succeeded in digging a continuation of WINDY TRENCH for several hundred yards in a S.E. direction thus forming a more or less continuous line along the Divisional Front.

23. During the night of the 9th/10th the Division was relieved in the line by the 4th Division and withdrawn to the back area.

Head Qrs. 56th Divn.
29th October, 1916.

C. Hull

Major-General,
Commanding 56th Division.

NOTES on OPERATIONS of 56th (LONDON)
DIVISION on the SOMME 7.9.16 to 10.10.16.

The results of the operations carried out by the Division during September and October 1916 have led to the following deductions:-

Direction of Advance.

1. To give an attack a fair chance of success it must be launched from departure trenches as nearly as possible parallel to the objectives. Complicated manoeuvres, such as a wheel or change of direction during an assault prejudice the chances of success of present-day troops.

Distance of departure trenches from objective.

2. The system of departure trenches should not be nearer than 200 yards from the first objective; otherwise trenches may have to be evacuated to enable the Artillery to bombard. An evacuated trench may be occupied by the enemy; and even if it is not, it is liable to be mistaken during an assault for the enemy's first line.

In order to ensure the success of an assault, a proper scheme of assembly trenches must be thought out, and sufficient time must be given for their construction. To enable this to be done, accurate information must be available as to the position of our own troops and trenches, and the enemy's troops and trenches.

Woods.

3. An attack through or from a wood is to be avoided, if it is possible to work round it. If the wood has been heavily shelled it is impossible to dig assembly trenches in it, and troops get disorganised directly they try to move in it.

Selection of Objective.

4. The selection of objectives should be as definite as possible - i.e. they should be recognisable on the ground. Considering the heavy casualties which occur among officers, and the partially trained state of many of the N.C.O's and men, it is seldom of any use leaving the site of the objective to the judgment of the assaulting troops.

Flank in the Air.

5. Too much attention is apt to be paid to the "bogey" of the flank in the air. Commanders should never be deterred from seizing and occupying valuable ground for fear of having a flank exposed. Such a flank is comparatively easily protected, at any rate for a time, by machine or Lewis Guns, or a bombers post, and one knows from experience that it is no easy matter, and usually a costly one, to attack an enemy trench in flank. For example, the left flank of the 56th Division was entirely in the air from September 9th until the QUADRILATERAL was captured by the 6th Division on the 18th; and again (in GROPI and RANGER Trenches in T.15.d. and T.15.c.) from the night of the 20th to the 24th September. The right flank of the Division in the COMBLES, BULLY and BEEF Trenches was continuously in touch with the enemy.

Information as to Situation.

6. Experience has shown that the first reports received from units and from F.O.O's as to the position of advanced troops are generally unreliable. Air photos and air reports are the only reliable sources of information, and both are dependent on the weather. Airmen also complain that troops in the front line frequently neglect to show their positions when called on. This is due to ignorance and want of training. It is suggested that a time should be fixed at which troops in the front line should always indicate their position, on fine days by flares or mirrors, to air observers, and on dull or cloudy days by shutter or some other signal to F.O.O's. In active operations a fixed board is dangerous as it is apt to be left on the parados when our troops advance or withdraw

/7.

- 2 -

Air Photos and Maps.

7. The air photos are excellent but the issue is so small that they scarcely ever reach units below brigades.

The Army, Corps, Divisions and Brigades all produce sketch maps, all of which vary considerably. A clear and reliable map is wanted, in sufficient numbers to be issued down to platoon commanders. It is of course impossible to issue sufficient maps showing daily changes on this scale. A weekly issue of a 1/10,000 map (on paper and similar in style to the GUILLEMONT Trench Map) in sufficient numbers to allow of all commanders down to battalion commanders issuing them with their orders, would meet the case, provided the periodical corrections were issued on a sufficiently large scale to reach battalions and batteries. At present there are too many different maps. Fewer maps and a larger issue would improve matters.

Liaison with R.F.C.

8. It would be an advantage if rather closer liaison could be established between the R.F.C. and Divisions. If the observer detailed to reconnoitre a divisional front were in personal touch with the G.S. of the division concerned, particular points about which further information is wanted could be discussed with the observer overnight.

It is understood that duplicate copies of reports to divisions by contact patrols are always dropped at Corps Headquarters. It would save unnecessary congestion of the telephone and telegraph lines if observers could state on their reports when similar reports are dropped at neighbouring divisions.

Barrages

9. All battalions have realised the importance of working close up under the creeping barrage. The simpler the task set to the Artillery, the more effective will be the barrage. The task for the Artillery is simple when the front departure trench of our own troops is parallel to the enemy's first line trench, and not less than 200 yards from it. An enfilade creeping barrage is most effective, and should be employed whenever possible.

To avoid complications for the Artillery, it is most important after the capture of a village or wood to push troops forward well beyond it; otherwise the trees will interfere with the creeping barrage when the next advance is attempted (e.g. it was difficult to arrange a good creeping barrage on the German trenches just E. of LESBOEUFS on October 7th and 8th)

The system of dividing the barrages into a creeping and standing barrage is sound; but the standing barrage must stand on something definite, such as a line of trenches, or a road known to be held. A standing barrage on an indefinite system of defended shell holes, gun-pits, and short lengths of trench, is likely to result in waste of ammunition unless very careful registration can be carried out beforehand. Under these circumstances it is better to have two creeping barrages.

An effective creeping barrage in a wood is very difficult to arrange, and unobserved bombardment by howitzers is frequently very disappointing. In spite of considerable bombardment GRAPHIC Trench in BOULEAUX WOOD was found to be almost untouched. The same cannot be said of IRISH Trench in LEUZE WOOD, which was most effectively and accurately bombarded by the German Artillery. This was partially due to the fact that IRISH Trench was originally dug by the Germans and was no doubt accurately marked on their maps

Liaison with Hy Artillery.

10. The liaison between Heavy Artillery and units of the Division is not sufficiently close. Many batteries of Heavy guns are newly raised and more than one case has occurred of our Heavy Artillery shelling our own trenches. It is quite realised that an occasional short round is unavoidable, but the delay that occurred in discovering

/and

and stpping the offending battery is avoidable. The present procedure is cumbrous when a message from a company commander that his trenches are being shelled by our own guns has to pass through battalion, brigade, Divisional H.Q., thence from the Heavy Artillery Liaison Officer to Corps Heavy Artillery H.Q., and down through similar channels to the offending battery. It is not suggested that Liaison Officers should be multiplied, as trained officers are too valuable. I think, though, that matters would be improved whenever a heavy battery was detailed to bombard any points in the enemy's line in close proximity to our own trenches, if that battery were placed (temporarily) under the orders of the Field Artillery Group Commander who was responsible for that sector of the front. The battery would then be in close liaison with the infantry brigade, through the Group Liaison Officer, and would have better information regarding, and access to, the best positions from which to observe.

Bombing Attacks.
11. Bombing attacks should not be undertaken lightly. An unsuccessful bombing attack is very wasteful of specially trained men. They are frequently necessary in order to gain some tactically important point, and every means must then be employed to ensure the success of the operation. This means obtaining the co-operation of the Artillery, who must know the exact point the bombers are to start from, and the point they are expected to reach, and the operation must be conducted according to the time table. The bombers must work up close to the barrage, and be able to indicate their position to the supporting guns.
Stokes Gunners, Lewis Gunners and Bombers, must be trained to work together. The training of bombers in the Mills Rifle Grenade is most important.

Patrols.
12. Considerable ground was made on occasions by patrols, who were ordered to work their way forward and dig themselves in. A definite "objective" for these patrols is most essential; otherwise it is most difficult to arrange a suitable defensive barrage.

Digging.
13. Much ground was made at night by digging lines of trenches; and strong points, which were connected up to form a continuous trench the following night. It is of the greatest value to have a definite pattern of trench, and definite patterns of strong points, which R.E., Pioneers and Infantry are all trained to lay out and dig. An adequate supply of tracing tape is most necessary.

Marking Tracks
14. In heavily shelled areas it is of importance to decide on and mark our tracks for infantry. A large supply of signboards painted white for these tracks should be held in readiness. If these were painted with luminous paint on both sides, one every 50 to 100 yards would probably be sufficient, and they would be invaluable for working parties and reliefs.

Communications. 15. The value of well laddered telephone communications was well demonstrated throughout.
It was impossible to find the necessary working parties to bury cables, to any great extent, but it might be possible to select a German communication trench beforehand (where sufficient exist) to ear-mark this as a cable trench; to lay the cable and fill in the trench at once. Dug-outs could be constructed along this trench which would be used first as Battalion Headquarters and then for Brigade and Divisional Headquarters as the advance progressed.

Communication between Coy.& Bn. Hdqrs.
16. A message thrower, capable of propelling the container of a message 500ˣ to 600ˣ would be invaluable. It is understood that the 4th Division use a Stokes Mortar with

/a

4.

a specially prepared projectile for this purpose. The value of such device cannot be overestimated.

[margin note: Have seen this working it was not a success]

Dug-outs. 17. Many German dug-outs in a partially finished condition were found in captured trenches. It would save much time and labour if frames of the standard German pattern were prepared and kept ready for use, so that the work might be continued directly the trenches were captured.

Code A. 18. Practically no use was made of Code "A". It was too complicated under the existing conditions, when the code was changed every day. It is very unlikely that the Germans could decipher the code even if messages were overheard in conditions similar to those that existed in September. If the code were changed not more frequently than once a fortnight it might be u.s. At present no one has sufficient confidence in the deciphering powers of the recipient to use the code at all.

[margin note: Code is not changed now oftener than once in 10 days]

Major-General,
Commanding 56th Division.

Head Qrs. 56th Divn.
29th October, 1916.

CASUALTIES.

PERIOD.	DIED OF WOUNDS.		KILLED.		WOUNDED.		MISSING.		TOTALS.	
	Off.	O.Rs.	Off.	O.Rs.	Off.	O.Rs.	Off.	O.Rs.	Off.	O.Rs.
JUNE 24th to JUNE 30th, 1916.	1.	-	3.	66	23	405	-	26	27	497
JULY 1st to JULY 4th, 1916.	1.	3	30	347	87	2277	40	1497	158	4124
JULY 5th to AUGUST 20th, 1916	-	1	3	83	20	412	1	22	24	518
SEPTEMBER 6th to OCTOBER 11th, '16	8	2	81	1148	258	4943	30	1380	377	7773
TOTALS	10.	6	117	1644	388	8037	71	3225	586	12912.

Vol 10

WAR DIARY

General Staff. 56th Division

1st to 30th November 1916

Vol: X

CONFIDENTIAL

GENERAL STAFF,
56th DIVISION.

WAR DIARY
or
INTELLIGENCE SUMMARY

Army Form C. 2118.

Place	Date	Hour	Summary of Events and Information	Remarks and references to Appendices
LA GORGUE	1st Nov.		Inter battalion reliefs in 168 Infy. Bde sector completed by 1pm. A quiet day in the front line. Carried out the usual T.M. bombardment of the North Trench. Conference at 4pm. IIth Corps at which B.O.C. & G.S.O. were present.	See Appendix III
LA GORGUE	2nd Nov.		Inter battalion reliefs in 167 Infy. Bde sector. An uneventful day on the front.	"
LA GORGUE	3rd Nov.		Inter battalion reliefs in 169 Infy. Bde sector. A Divisional experience was held at Appx 167. Infy. Bde FAYETTE at 8pm. Report received at 11pm that German of 19th Res. Infy. 5th Bav. Div. had been killed inside our trenches at LAHIR CORNER.	"
LA GORGUE	4th Nov.		Report received from 168 Infy. Bde that 3 Germans had been found in our lines about 7.30pm 3-11-15. Lieut. the V. HATIP SALIENT was had been picked and the other two had escaped. A very quiet day on the Divisional front.	
LA GORGUE	5th Nov.		GOC accompanied by C.E. VI Corps inspected the Corps park. An O.P and forward trenches of the Laventie salient. NEUF NEUVE CHAPELLE was carried out by 169. Infy. Btt. No hostile retaliation. Inter battalion reliefs of 168 Infy. R.E.	"
LA GORGUE	6th Nov.		The 1st Army Commander & XI Corps Commander inspected the park in that portion of the Corps Md. which lies in the front. Area during the morning. The E.S.D. & an E.R.E. accompanied them. A very wet and windy day. Quiet on the observed front.	
LA GORGUE	7th Nov.	11p.m	Owing to a strong gusty wind the activity of our T.M's was somewhat curtailed during the night, however, our howitzer guns kept gaps in enemy parapet under fire and at 11p.m. dispersed a large body of the enemy working at their wire at M.36.a.5.0.	

2449 Wt. W14957/M90 750,000 1/16 J.B.C. & A. Forms/C.2118/12.

WAR DIARY or INTELLIGENCE SUMMARY

Army Form C. 2118.

Place	Date	Hour	Summary of Events and Information	Remarks and references to Appendices
LA GORGUE	8th Nov.		187 Inf. Bde. carried out internal reliefs. In the NEUVE CHAPELLE SECTION a combined Artillery and T. Mortar bombardment of the enemy's line was carried out. Good results were reported by an observing aeroplane. At 12.15 a.m. the 2.5/7th (T) Coy R.E. exploded a mine about M.30.c.2.4.21. were just previously the enemy had been heard working 10 feet away. The crater formed was immediately occupied (near lip) by a party of 8 min rifle a Lewis gun, and the far lip was wired. Abnormal movement throughout the day behind the enemy's line indicated a relief in progress. This was further made probable by a lack of sniping and Trench Mortar activity.	See Appendix I.
LA GORGUE	9th Nov.		A bright day which made observation excellent and enabled air photos to be taken. Internal reliefs were carried out by 188 & 189 Inf. Bdes. Combined Art. & T. Mortar Bombardments were carried out by all 3 Brigades during the afternoon when considerable damage was caused to the enemy's defences. There was no hostile retaliation. The enemy's trenches are evidently flooded and his communication in a very wet state as reported stated individuals and small parties were seen throughout the day crossing the open. Our snipers took full advantage and claim several kills.	"

WAR DIARY or INTELLIGENCE SUMMARY

Army Form C. 2118.

Place	Date	Hour	Summary of Events and Information	Remarks and references to Appendices
LA GORGUE	10th Nov		Another bright clear day. Trench mortars in all 3 sections carried out pre-arranged bombardment of German defences in cooperation with artillery. Light and Medium Trench mortars were engaged considerably particularly between the enemy's front trenches and believed Pts M.2.d.7.4 & M.2.2.d.9.8. Pts M.2.d.4.1 and M.30.c.2.8. and between Pts M.24.d.7.4. his garrison the night. Wire breaches back were kept under fire throughout the night. Patrolling at night was difficult owing to a bright moon and the flooding of the ditches in No Man's Land. A patrol however discovered an enemy working party at N.14.a.7.3 returned and divided and Lewis guns & rifle fire on the spot caused wood to cease & the party to disperse. Our photos show enemy trades flooded in places, particularly about WIEK Salient.	
LA GORGUE	11th Nov		A fine day though dull with bad observation. Combined Trench Mortar and Artillery bombardments were carried out by 2nd ID Brigades on NEUVE CHAPELLE and FAUQUISSART sections respectively. The former Section the bombardment aimed at the blocking of the main drain and Bm's players the enemy's trenches in the front line between Pts.S.5.d. 5.9. and 0.5.f. 6.3. which always is the enemy's front line. It was obvious that it's object was attained was done & there is reason to suppose that the artillery was quickly placed by the hostile reply was made to the the FAUQUISSART section no bombardment.	

Army Form C. 2118.

WAR DIARY
or
INTELLIGENCE SUMMARY

(Erase heading not required.)

Instructions regarding War Diaries and Intelligence Summaries are contained in F. S. Regs., Part II. and the Staff Manual respectively. Title Pages will be prepared in manuscript.

Place	Date	Hour	Summary of Events and Information	Remarks and references to Appendices
LA GORGUE	12th Nov		Weather fine but rather overcast, making observation difficult. There was a little casualty shelling in the NEUVE CHAPELLE sector when S.9.S. The enemy was extra reliant with guns after dawn. Two completed T.M. & Artillery barrages (1 by 168 Bde in the FAUQUISSART Section failed to produce any retaliation. Considerable damage was done to the enemy's parapet South of the WICK. The front state of No Mans Land due to the overflowing of the drains still continues to make quiet progress of patrols impossible in most localities. An officer of the left Batt'n finding the mud presented no obstacle, pushed the enemy's line at about N.13.d.1.6 during the night. The patrolled 3 days where were full of water but unsuccessful, though he heard enemy working parties in the vicinity.	
LA GORGUE	13th Nov		Our Medium & Light Trench Mortars were again active co-operating with the Artillery in bombarding the enemy's huts during much material damage. During the night the guns carried in the Trenches did not reply. 4in 9's at intervals through out this night. There was little or no hostile retaliation.	
LA GORGUE	14th Nov		A fine clear day. Our trench mortars and Artillery were again active. Our trench mortars and artillery were again active. The enemy's Artillery was a little more active. Some 4.2 shells being fired into the MOATED GRANGE & FAUQUISSART redoubt. Our aeroplanes flying over the enemy's lines about mid-day drew considerable machine gun fire. During the night but encountering no hostile patrols. Our patrols were active beyond N.19.d.2.0 was dispersed by our rifle fire. An enemy raiding party seen about	

2449 Wt. W14957/M90 750,000 1/16 J.B.C. & A. Forms/C.2118/12.

Army Form C. 2118.

WAR DIARY
or
INTELLIGENCE SUMMARY

(Erase heading not required.)

Instructions regarding War Diaries and Intelligence Summaries are contained in F. S. Regs., Part II. and the Staff Manual respectively. Title Pages will be prepared in manuscript.

Place	Date	Hour	Summary of Events and Information	Remarks and references to Appendices
LA GORGUE	15th Nov.		A clear frosty day with a cold N.E. wind which shifted into the East towards the night, when gas alert was ordered. Our NEUVE CHAPELLE and FAUQUISSART Sections Medium and Light Trench Mortars co-operated with the Artillery in bombarding the enemy's trenches without observation retaliation. Much damage was caused to the enemy's parapets at M.36.a, 4.9. – M.30.a. 85.60 and M.24.d. 45.10 by a T. Mortar bombardment carried out by the Right L the MOATED GRANGE Section. Our Patrols were active throughout the night along the front. Several wiring parties were discovered by Lewis gun fire. One hostile patrol of about 20 men was encountered by a patrol of 1 Officer and 5 in our out from RED LAMP (N.13.7). As our patrol had been seen out without any support the hostile patrol was allowed to pass unmolested. Patrols were carried out in the Right Section during the afternoon.	
LA GORGUE	16th Nov.		A fine day with good visibility & a cold East Wind. In MOATED GRANGE Section our T.M's were active & bombarded the enemy's trenches at M.36.a. 40. 65. & M.30.a. 6.1. The enemy retaliated with a few light T.M. bombs and rifle grenades. In the FAUQUISSART Section a Combined Artillery & Trench Mortar bombardment was carried out at 2p.m. on enemy's trenches at N.19.a. 35. 65. where much damage was done and the parapet crushed. Our patrols were active during the night. The G.O.C. XI Corps visited 164 Inf. Bde. in the afternoon.	

Army Form C. 2118.

WAR DIARY
or
INTELLIGENCE SUMMARY

(Erase heading not required.)

Instructions regarding War Diaries and Intelligence Summaries are contained in F. S. Regs, Part II. and the Staff Manual respectively. Title Pages will be prepared in manuscript.

Place	Date	Hour	Summary of Events and Information	Remarks and references to Appendices
LA GORGUE	17th Nov.		A clear fine day, but a cold East wind. A quiet day on the divisional front. Combined Trench Mortar and Artillery Bombardment to be carried out causing damage to enemy defences.	
LA GORGUE	18th Nov.		A thaw set in after a hard frost at night. Rain followed and low clouds made observation very difficult. T.M's were very quiet and searches upheld to the combined Art. Enemy's Artillery & T.M's were very quiet and searches carried out by us. & T.M Bombardment to carried out by us.	
LA GORGUE	19th Nov.		A wet day. The enemy was very quiet on our front during the morning but commenced the front J.19.c. left site with M.T.M's, rifle grenades and 77M/m from 2.15pm to 3pm. A sharp Artillery duel (chiefly Mainly) but little damage was done. 168: Inf. Bde R.E. carried out inter-battalion relief.	In appendix [iii]
LA GORGUE	20th Nov.		167: Inf. B. E. carried out inter-battalion relief during the afternoon. Relief of 61st Gen'l Artillery by 6" Gen'l Artillery was completed by 9am.	"
LA GORGUE	21st Nov.		Considerable improvement. A gas alert was proclaimed about 9.80am on the divisional front but was cancelled during the afternoon. A Quiet day. 169: Inf. Bde. carried out inter-battalion relief during the afternoon.	"

Army Form C. 2118.

WAR DIARY
or
INTELLIGENCE SUMMARY
(Erase heading not required.)

Instructions regarding War Diaries and Intelligence Summaries are contained in F. S. Regs., Part II. and the Staff Manual respectively. Title Pages will be prepared in manuscript.

Place	Date	Hour	Summary of Events and Information	Remarks and references to Appendices
LA GORGUE	22nd Nov.		A very quiet day on the divisional front. Weather fine.	
LA GORGUE	23rd Nov.		Information received from 11th Corps that the 6th Bavarian Reserve take over approx. 3000x front around the Rets by two brigades with one brigade in reserve. Conference at 11th Corps HQ HINGES 10.30 a.m. C.R.E and C.R.A 76 Divl. Arty. were present. The question of the readjustment of the divisional eastern front was discussed.	
			A raiding party of 3 officers and 12 London Regt. (Rangers) raided the enemy trenches at the WICH SALIENT N.13.d.42.57½ and captured them to 130 yds. on each side of the point of entry. 20 gunmen were seen and the hostile wire in very bad condition. See Tactical Report.	See Appendix II
LA GORGUE	24th Nov	12 n.	Fine was in evidence of hostile artillery firing during the day especially on the front of 168 Inf. Brigade.	
		4 pm	Divl. Order No. 60 issued containing instructions for the readjustment of the divisional front	See appendix
LA GORGUE	25th Nov.		A quiet day on the divisional front. Last night of the 2nd & 3rd Inf. Battalion reliefs carried out in 16 & 8. Inf Bde. area.	
LA GORGUE	26th Nov.		Readjustment of the divisional front commenced in accordance with Divl. Order No. 60 117 Inf. Bde now a portion of the front of 169 Inf. Bde. Firing the day until artillery showed considerably more activity than usual expect the right section of the left brigade	

Army Form C. 2118.

WAR DIARY
or
INTELLIGENCE SUMMARY

(Erase heading not required.)

Instructions regarding War Diaries and Intelligence Summaries are contained in F.S. Regs., Part II. and the Staff Manual respectively. Title Pages will be prepared in manuscript.

Place	Date	Hour	Summary of Events and Information	Remarks and references to Appendices
LA GORGUE	27th Nov.		The relief of the right section of the divisional front by 5th Division was completed without incident by 3 p.m. A fine day. No special activity in the trenches.	
LA GORGUE	28th Nov:		A very misty day which received observation of the enemy's lines very difficult. The enemy bombarded the right Lebisson of 167/B9. Rew ones replied with TM's during the early morning and afternoon. Appx: 169 - Inf: B.D. Closed at HUITS MAISONS and opened at LESTREM dump the afternoon.	
LA GORGUE	29th Nov:		The misty weather continued but during the night our aeroplanes were very busy over enemy lines behind their lines advantage. There was little activity on the front except in Telling of the back area behind the left battalion S.B. at 8.30 p.m. what appeared to be a joint between the 5th Div: who had not closed up to the boundary and ourselves. Though this was rectified during the evening. Since the morning our artillery KTM and 17 TM's bombarded the enemy's trenches in S.F.L opposite the N.W. corner of BIEZ WOOD causing considerable material damage. At 6.30 p.m. a telephone message was received from 167th Inf. B.D. stating that the enemy had entered the DUCKS BILL crater held by us at N.35.d.95.95 about 6 p.m. after a heavy trench mortar bombardment lasting for two hours. Our telephone message VC. W-W about 9.45 p.m. states that our casualties were 2 O.R. killed, 8 O.R. wounded, 1 officer and 5 O.R. missing. Further details are expected later. Report stated that the enemy had been driven out of the crater and sap immediately leaving no identification, but of our casualties accounted for except two who were believed to have been buried. B. TULLEDY C.T. bore the bombardment had been heaviest all the morning but	

2449 Wt. W14957/M90 750,000 1/16 J.B.C. & A. Forms/C.2118/12.

LOCATION TABLE FOR INFANTRY BRIGADES

	12.	13.	14.	15.	16.	17.	18.	19.	20.	21.	22.	23.	24.	25.	26.	27.
			November								November					
167th Infantry Bde.				MOATED GRANGE or CENTRE SECTION.												
Bde. H.Q.																
1st London Regt. (R.F.)		RIEZ BAILLEUL →	L	L	L	L	L	L	←	→ RIEZ BAILLEUL	BR.	L	L	PONT DU HEM		
3rd London Regt. (R.F.)			R R	R	R R	R	R	R	R	R	R	R R	BR.	R	→ PONT DU HEM	
7th Middlesex Regt.		RIEZ BAILLEUL →	R	R	R R	R	R	R	R	→ RIEZ BAILLEUL	BR	R	R	R L		
8th Middlesex Regt.		L	L L	BR	L	BR	L	L	L L	BR	L L	BR	L L			
168th Infantry Bde.				FAUQUISSART or LEFT SECTION.												
Bde. H.Q.																
4th London Regt. (R.F.)	LAVENTIE →	R	R	R	R	R	R	←	→ LAVENTIE	BR	→ R	R	→ R			
12th London Regt. (Rangers)		L	← LAVENTIE	L	L	L	L	L	L	L	← LAVENTIE	BR	L	L		
13th London Regt. (Kens)		R	LAVENTIE (Works)	R	R	R	→	→	R	R	LAVENTIE	BR	R	R		
14th London Regt. (L.Scot.)	LAVENTIE →	L	L	L	L	L	L	L	L	L	L	L	L	L		
169th Inf. Bde.				NEUVE CHAPELLE or RIGHT SECTION.												
Bde. H.Q.																
2nd London Regt. (R.F.)	BOUT DEVILLE →	R	R	R	→ BOUT DEVILLE	BR	R	R	R	→	CROIX BARBEE	BR	R	R		
5th London Regt. (L.R.B.)		R	R	R	R	R	R	R	R	R	R	R	R	R		
9th London Regt. (Q.V.R.)		L	L	L	← CROIX BARBEE	BR	L	L	L	L	L	L	L	L		
16th London Regt. (Q.W.R.)	CROIX BARBEE	L	L	L	L	L	L	L	← BOUT DEVILLE	BR	L	L	L	L		

NOTE :
- D.R. = Divisional Reserve.
- B.R. = Brigade Reserve.
- R. = Right Sub-Section } marked in red.
- L. = Left Sub-Section }

MOATED GRANGE SECTION. M.24.d.1½.6. (LONELY ERITH ST.) to M.35.d.5½.7½ (SIGN POST RD.) Bn. Boundary M.29.d.9.8.
FAUQUISSART SECTION N.8.d.2.8½ (BOND ST.) to M.24.d.1½.6. (LONELY ERITH ST.) Battalion Bndry. N.13.c.7½.8.
NEUVE CHAPELLE SECT. M.35.d.5½.7½ (SIGN POST LANE) to S.10.c.3½.1. (BOND ST.) Battalion Bndry. S.5.c.5½.4.
(OXFORD ST)

	27.	28.	29.	30.	31.	1.	2.	3.	4.	5.	6.	7.	8.	9.	10.	11.
		COCKSHY		HOUSE		MOATED		GRANGE		or		CENTRE		SECTION		
167th Infantry Bde.																
Bde. H.Q.	LA GORGUE	RIEZ BAILLEUL	LA GORGUE	RIEZ BAILLEUL	RIEZ BAILLEUL	RIEZ BAILLEUL	RIEZ BAILLEUL	RIEZ BAILLEUL	RIEZ BAILLEUL	RIEZ BAILLEUL BR.						
1st London Regt. (R.F.)	R	R	R	R	R	R	R	L	L	L	L	L	←	RIEZ BAILLEUL BR	R	R
3rd London Regt. (R.F.)	LA GORGUE	LA GORGUE	RIEZ BAILLEUL	RIEZ BAILLEUL	RIEZ BAILLEUL	RIEZ BAILLEUL								RIEZ BAILLEUL BR	R	R
7th Middlesex Regt.	L	L	L	L	L	L	R	R	R	R	R	R	←		RIEZ BAILLEUL BR	
8th Middlesex Regt.																
		ESTAIRES		LAVENTIE		FAUQUISSART		or		LEFT		SECTION.				
168th Infantry Bde.																
Bde. H.Q.	LAVENTIE	LAVENTIE	LAVENTIE	LAVENTIE	LAVENTIE	LAVENTIE	LAVENTIE	LAVENTIE	LAVENTIE	LAVENTIE	LAVENTIE	LAVENTIE BR	LAVENTIE BR	LAVENTIE BR	LAVENTIE BR	LAVENTIE BR
4th London Regt. (R.F.)	ESTAIRES	ESTAIRES	LAVENTIE	LAVENTIE	LAVENTIE	LAVENTIE	←									
12th London Regt. (Rangers)	ESTAIRES	ESTAIRES	LAVENTIE	LAVENTIE	LAVENTIE	LAVENTIE	L	L	L	R	R	R	R	L	L	R
13th London Regt. (Kens.)	LAVENTIE	LAVENTIE	LAVENTIE	LAVENTIE	LAVENTIE	LAVENTIE	R	R	R	L	L	L	L	R	R	L
14th London Regt. (L.Scot.)							←				LAVENTIE BR					
		CALONNE		HUITS MAISONS		NEUVE		CHAPELLE		or		RIGHT		SECTION.		
169th Inf. Bde.																
Bde. H.Q.	FOSSE	CROIX BARBEE	CROIX BARBEE	CROIX BARBEE	CROIX BARBEE	CROIX BARBEE	CROIX BARBEE	CROIX BARBEE BR	BOUT DEVILLE	BOUT DEVILLE	BOUT DEVILLE BR	BOUT DEVILLE BR	BOUT DEVILLE	BOUT DEVILLE	BOUT DEVILLE	CROIX BARBEE
2nd London Regt. (R.F.)	CROIX BARBEE	CROIX BARBEE	R	R	R	R	R	R	R	R	R	R	R	R	← BOUT DEVILLE	
5th London Regt. (L.R.B.)	BOUT DEVILLE	BOUT DEVILLE	R	R	R	R	R	←	CROIX BARBEE				→	R	R	R
9th London Regt. (Q.V.R.)	LESTREM	LESTREM	L	L	L	L	L	BOUT DEVILLE	BOUT DEVILLE	BOUT DEVILLE			→	L	L	L
16th London Regt. (Q.W.R.)																

NOTE :
D.R. = Divisional Reserve.
B.R. = Brigade Reserve.
R. = Right Sub-Section.
L. = Left Sub-Section) marked in red.

MOATED GRANGE SECTION M.24.d.1½.6. (LONELY ERITH St.) to M.35.d.5½.7½ (SIGN POST RD.) Bn. Boundary M.29.d.9.8.
FAUQUISSART SECTION   N.8.d.2.8½ (BOND St.) to M.24.d.1½.6. (LONELY ERITH ST.) Battalion Bndry. N.13.c.7½.8.
NEUVE CHAPELLE SECT. M.35.d.5½.7½ (SIGN POST LANE) to S.10.c.3½.1. (BOND ST.) Battalion Bndry. S.5.c.3½.4.
(OXFORD ST.)

○ □ ◇ ▷
○ □ ◇ ▷
○ □ ◇ ▷

SECRET

War diary   copy No 13

56th DIVISIONAL ORDER No. 60.

Reference Maps
1/40,000, Sheets 36 & 36.a.
And 1/10,000 Secret Map
36.SW.3. and 36 SW.1.

24th Novr. 1916.

1. There will be a redistribution of the XIth Corps line.

2. The 56th Division will hand over to the 5th Division the portion of the line between BOND STREET (S.10.c.28.05.) and CHURCH Road (S.5.a.92.22.).
   The Southern boundary of 56th Division will be Point S 5.a. 92.22. - thence along CHURCH Road (incl. to 56th Div.) - to S.5.a.41.65. - M.34.c.8.7. - thence to CROIX BARBEE (incl. to 5th Division) - HUIT MAISONS (incl. to 56th Division, but present H.Q. of 169th Infantry Brigade will be at disposal of 5th Division) - thence to FOSSE (incl. to 5th Division) and across to old boundary at R.13.d.4.1. CHURCH Road communication trench will be used by both 56th and 5th Divisions.

3. The Division will hold the new front with two Brigades in the line and one in reserve. The boundary line between Brigades will be a line through points M.24.c.8.2. - M.24.c.35.75. to a point M.23.b.8.5., where it joins and follows the existing inter-brigade boundary.

4. Reliefs will take place as follows:-
   (a). Night of 26/27th November.
       167th Brigade will take over from 169th Brigade the part of the line from SIGN POST LANE to CHURCH Road (inclusive).
   (b). 168th Brigade will take over from 167th Brigade the part of the line from ERITH ST. to the new brigade boundary.
   (c). Night of 27/28th November.
       The 15th Infantry Brigade, 5th Division, will relieve the 169th Brigade in the part of the line between BOND Street and CHURCH Road.

5. Posts will be handed over as follows:-
   By 169th Infantry Brigade to 15th Infantry Brigade of 5th Div:
   COPSE, PORT ARTHUR, HILLS, EDWARDS, HENS, LANSDOWNE, ST. VAAST, CROIX BARBEE, VIEILLE CHAPELLE and LA FOSSE Group. LORETTO
   By 169th Infantry Brigade to 167th Infantry Brigade:-
   CHURCH, CHATEAU, CURZON,-   EUSTON, RUE DU PUITS,
   By 167th Infantry Brigade to 168th Infantry Brigade:-
   ERITH.

6. Details of relief will be arranged between Brigade Commanders concerned. Trench stores, log books, aeroplane photographs etc. will be handed over to incoming units.
   No official issues of maps will be handed over. The Secret maps in possession of 169th Infantry Brigade will be kept at the Brigade and Battalion Headquarters of the Reserve Brigade and handed over on each relief to incoming units, and a copy of receipts forwarded to Divisional Headquarters.

7. Progress of reliefs will be notified to this office.

8. Orders as to distribution of Reserve Brigade and Reserve Battalions of Brigades in the line will be issued later.

/9.

- 2 -

9. That part of the Artillery of 6th Division (including trench mortars) at present covering the front to be taken over by 5th Division will remain in position until further orders and will come under command of the General Officer Commanding 5th Division on completion of reliefs.

10. The General Officer Commanding 5th Division will assume command of the front handed over by 56th Division at 6.0 am., November 28th.

11. ACKNOWLEDGE.

A. Bryant.

Hdqrs. 56th Divn.
24th November, 1916.

Lieut. Colonel,
General Staff.

Issued at 4.0 p.m. 24.11.16

Copy Nos.
1. XIth Corps
2. 167th Inf. Bde.
3. 168th "   "
4. 169th "   "
5. C.R.A., 6th Div.
6. C.R.E.
7. 1/5th Ches. Regt.
8. A.D.M.S.
9. A.P.M.
10. "G"
11. "Q"
12. G.O.C., 53th Divn.
13. War Diary.
14. 257th Tunnelling Co. R.E.
15. 56th Div. Train.
16. Camp Commandant.
17. 5th Division.
18. N.Z. Division.
19. O.C., Signals.
20. Div. School.

War Diary.

SECRET   56th Division S.G.331

Addressed to all recipients of 56th Div. Order No. 60
dated 24th November, 1916.

With reference to para. 8 of 56th Divisional Order No. 60 dated 24th November, 1916, the Reserve Brigade and Reserve Battalions of Brigades in the line will be distributed as follows :-

(a) <u>Reserve Brigade.</u>

   Head Qrs. LESTREM.
   1 Battalion   "
   1 Battalion ROBERMETZ
   1 Battalion LE GRAND PACAUT
   1 Battalion LA GORGUE

   M.G. Coy.)   Not yet
   T.M.Batty.)   decided.

(b) <u>Reserve Battalions of Right Brigade</u>

   1 Battalion PONT DU HEM area
   1 Battalion RIEZ BAILLEUL (South)

(c) <u>Reserve Battalions of Left Brigade</u>

   1 Battalion RUE BACQUEROT
      (as soon as necessary accommodation can be provided)
   1 Battalion LAVENTIE.

Head Qrs. 56th Divn.

25th November, 1916.

J.A.Beck. Major
for Lieut-Colonel,
General Staff.

58th DIVISION TACTICAL PROGRESS REPORT No. 4.
from 8.0 am. 31st October to 8.0 am. 1st November.

PART I OPERATIONS.

NEUVE CHAPELLE SECTION During the afternoon two trench mortar shoots were carried out against the German trench junction at S.10.d.9½.8½. The shooting is reported to have been excellent and a number of direct hits were obtained. The gaps in the wire at S.11.a.2.2. and S.5.d.2.3½. were widened by M.T.M fire. These operations drew retaliation from the enemy in the form of heavy rifle grenade fire and some L.T.M. bombs, but no damage was done.

Patrols which went out during the night report that the gap in the enemy's wire at S.11.a.2.2. is about 15 yards wide, but the loose wire was sufficient to prevent a noiseless passage to the enemy's trench.

MOATED GRANGE SECTION. A successful shoot was carried out against hostile trench system in M.30.a. ; also the MOULIN DUPIETRE, L.T.M's and field artillery co-operating while M.G's fired on C.T's running back from the front line in M.30.a. and on the RUE DENFER. Considerable damage was done to the enemy's front line and much woodwork was seen to fly about M.30.a.4.4. Our patrols found no trace of the enemy during the night. Enemy wire in M.30.c. was inspected and found to be very thick and heaped up about 6 feet in height.

FAUQUISSART SECTION. During the afternoon an organised shoot was carried out on the enemy's trenches from N.14.c.4.9. to the WICK Salient. The following ammunition exclusive of artillery was fired - 10 rounds H.T.M., about 200 rounds M.T.M., 560 rounds L.T.M. and over 100 rifle grenades. Great material damage was done, a large amount of timber and loose earth being thrown up. Hostile retaliation practically Nil. In addition to this shoot, our M.G's and rifle grenades were active in other parts of the Section.

PART II INTELLIGENCE.

NEUVE CHAPELLE SECTION. At 4.30 p.m 25 - 77 mm. shells fell near the front line at S.10.2.; the guns appeared to be firing from S.12.d.9.8. A hostile battery was observed to fire from about S.24.d.6.0.

Between 4.0 am. and 5.20 am. stakes were heard being driven in near the S.W. edge of the BOIS de BIEZ.

About 50 Germans were reported by the Artillery to come from H.T. POMMEREAU WOOD and walk across the C.T's in T.2.a. & c.

MOATED GRANGE SECTION. About 30 L.T.M. shells were fired in reply to our bombardment: no damage was done.

A small hostile patrol near the DUCKS BILL was fired on and dispersed by a m.g.

Smoke was seen coming from behind a farmhouse at M.30.b.55.40.

Wiring on DUCKS BILL Crater and Sap was continued by us, and also round the NEW CRATER. A hostile working party was heard opposite the latter point. L.G. fire was opened and the sound ceased. A path and listening post in No.1 MAUQUISSART Crater has been prepared and trench boards put down.

FAUQUISSART SECTION. Enemy fired a few M.T.M's from about N.14.c.05.25. and N.14.c.45.80. on to our front line in RED LAMP Salient. A machine gun is suspected to fire from N.8 d.5.1½.

One patrol of 6 men were seen examining their wire in N.13.c.

Our artillery dispersed a working party at N.20.b.5.9. A working party was heard at N.14.b.1.8. believed to be wiring.

Enemy working around N.19.d.2½.7. - revetting and repairing CLARA Trench. Enemy wire has been repaired at N.14.b.2.9.

About 7.30 pm. hostile transport was plainly heard - thought to be on RUE DELEVAL in N.14.d.

Hdqrs. 58th Divn.

1st November, 1916.

Captain,
for Lieut Colonel,
General Staff.

56th DIVISION TACTICAL PROGRESS REPORT No. 5,
from 8.0 a.m. 1st November to 8.0 a.m. 2nd November.

PART 1 OPERATIONS.

NEUVE CHAPELLE SECTION.

A patrol which examined the disused trench running forward from our lines at S.11.a.1.7. found some white tape which appears to have been laid by the enemy from the farther end of this trench in an Easterly direction; this was brought in.

A telephone wire was found running along the trench with both ends made fast, but the patrol was unable to trace it for any distance.

This trench was visited by our patrols during the night 31st/1st and found to be very shallow and containing some destroyed dugouts. The wire in the trench has been strengthened by us.

Our Light and Medium T.Ms. were active throughout the day doing damage to the enemy's parapet and wire. During the night our M.Gs. fired on the W. edge of BIEZ WOOD.

MOATED GRANGE SECTION.

The enemy's trenches were bombarded with L.T.M. and M.T.M. at intervals during the day apparently with good results. The only reply was a few Field Gun Shells on WINCHESTER STREET.

A patrol sent out to reconnoitre the sap at M.24.d.5.5. got within 30 yards of it when they were fired on. As they were up to their knees in water and the ground was very swampy, quiet progress was impossible and they withdrew.

FAUQUISSART SECTION.

Our Trench Mortars carried out ranging during the day. At 11.40 p.m. M.Gs. caught a hostile working party near the WICK, apparently causing casualties.

Patrols which were out over the whole front during the night encountered no enemy.

PART 11 INTELLIGENCE.

NEUVE CHAPELLE SECTION.

The enemy replied to our T.Ms. with about 40 rounds L.T.M., 24 rounds M.T.M., and a few heavy T.Ms. Five direct hits were obtained on our parapet and a portion of trench was blocked.

Transport was heard during the night behind BIEZ WOOD.

Work is proceeding on the C.T. from S.16.a.65.55. to S.16.b.00.65
New wire has been put out at S.16.a.6.8.

Movement was seen about H.T. POMMERAU.

A wooden ladder resting against the enemy's trench and a weather vane behind the ladder were seen at S.5.d.40.45.

A light was seen at intervals during the night N.E. of the houses in S.11.a.

MOATED GRANGE SECTION.

Slight increase of hostile Field Gun fire on our front line.
A T.M. was located firing from M.24.d.45.10.

New work is in progress at M.30.c.5.9. where much new earth can be seen. An old dug-out has previously been reported at this point. Clouds of smoke were seen coming from M.30.a. 4.1. which may be a living place or cookhouse.

2.

FAUQUISSART SECTION.

Enemy transport heard at 3.30 p.m. apparently in AUBERS.
Hostile working parties were seen and dispersed at N.19.d.25.30 and in front of the WICK.
Much work has been done on the C.T. at N.14.c.8.3.
An O.P. is suspected at N.20.c.50.85.
The point of the WICK SALIENT N.13.d.05.55. is badly damaged as the result of our T.M. bombardment.
A large volume of white smoke was seen rising from behind the hedge at N.27.b.95.90 on the afternoon of 1st.
At 8.50 a.m. smoke was seen rising from the WICK SALIENT N.13.d.37.55.

Head Qrs. 56th Divn.
2nd November 1916.

Captain,
General Staff "I".

38th DIVISION TACTICAL PROGRESS REPORT No. 6

from 8.0 am 2nd November to 8.0 am. 3rd November.

PART I OPERATIONS.

NEUVE CHAPELLE SECTION.

An officers patrol reconnoitred the enemy's wire in M.30.a.; it appeared to be about 30 yards in depth put out on no particular system but with a large amount of loose wire into which gates and railings have been entangled. The enemy was alert, but no patrols were met. Some effective shooting was carried out by our Artillery against various targets behind the enemy's lines. Two L.T.M. shoots were carried out during the day, 50 rounds being fired on the enemy's C.T. at S.10.d.55.30. where timber was soon blown up in the air, and 50 rounds on C.T. at S.10.d.95.85. with excellent results, much damage was done to the trench and a dense cloud of smoke was seen to rise at one point. Machine guns co-operated during these shoots. Successful rifle grenade fire was carried out at various points.

MOATED GRANGE SECTION.

M.T.M's and L.T.M's co-operated in a shoot on the trenches in M.30.a. and M.36.a., and craters and wire in front of these trenches. L.T.M's fired bursts of rapid fire during the night on the points damaged.

A patrol which left our lines on the N. side of the DUCKS BILL Sap reached the wire in front of the enemy's craters when a dog barked and fire was opened from the near side of the crater which the enemy were holding.

A patrol reached the near side of the craters at M.30.a.4.5. and report that there was no wire, but sounds of wiring could be heard behind the craters. Another patrol reports hearing hostile movement inside the near lip of the crater at M.24.d.3.1.

FAUQUISSART SECTION.

During the afternoon our Artillery in conjunction with T.M's of all calibres carried out an organised shoot on the enemy's defences from N.19.a.25.50. to N.19.a.40.75. and the trenches in rear. Much material damage was done, the enemy front line being breached in places. In addition to this shoot, our L.T.M's destroyed enemy wire in front of the SUGER LOAF and damaged the parapet on a front of about 100 yards.

Our machine guns were active during the night against enemy wire, trenches and communication.

PART II INTELLIGENCE.

NEUVE CHAPELLE SECTION.

During the night hostile machine guns fired short bursts of high angle fire over the right subsection. A rifle battery fired from about M.35.d.75.20. Hostile retaliation for our T.M. shoots was weak. The enemy's tramways were heard in use behind BIEZ WOOD during the night. A party heard about S.11.a.85.30. was dispersed by our L.G. fire. Another party about S.10.c.8.0. was fired on and immediately after three double green flares were sent up by the enemy. Enemy rifle grenades were active along the left subsection front. At 3.0 p.m., hostile bi-plane passed over our lines and disappeared in an S.E. direction. An observation balloon ascended at 3.15 p.m on a line bearing of 127° from FACTORY O.P. Movement on the LA BASSEE - ESTAIRES Road has decreased considerably. The house at S.6.a.8½.3½. is suspected to be used as an O.P. and a telescope is thought to have been seen in the roof.

/ MOATED GRANGE SECT

- B -

MOATED GRANGE SECTION.

Slight hostile retaliation with field guns and T.M's on our front line in reply to our T.M. shoot. At 8.30 p.m. a hostile patrol, strength 15 - 20 men, was seen moving at right-angles to our line from opposite TILLELOY SOUTH C. T. towards COLVIN Craters, it was fired on with rifles and Lewis guns. Later one of our patrols saw a large party take up a position on the far side of COLVIN Craters. This was probably the same hostile patrol. At 4.0 pm. a hostile aeroplane came over our lines and was engaged by A.A. guns.

FAUQUISSART SECTION.

Hostile M.T.M's fired effectively on the extreme right of our line during the afternoon. Hostile machine gun active during the early part of the night. Transport was heard on AUBERS - BAS POMMEREAU Road at 7.30 p.m. Work is still in progress on the new C.T. about N.14.c.5.5.; also at N.14.b.8.6½. Three hostile aeroplanes patrolled our lines about 3 pm. A snipers post is suspected at N.14.a.7.2½. Considerable amount of work appears to have been done on the new C.T. running N.E. from CLARA Trench at N.19.a.95.25. as fresh earth can be seen along its entire length. During a burst of T.M. fire yesterday, the following three hostile T.M's were located:- M.T.M. about N.19.a.8.8. Our artillery replied, several shells bursting round the position, one of which sent up a large amount of debris and it was thought the body of a man. L.T.M's about N.13.c.9.1. and N.13.b.9.5. These 3 T.M's were silenced by our Artillery whose fire was very prompt and accurate. The following loopholes have been located:- A small house N.20.b.35.25. Two bricks have been removed from the wall, possibly an O.P. A very small loophole in the front line parapet at N.13.d.12.63. facing W.; a large loophole in parapet of front line at N.13.d.30.55. facing W.; a loophole amongst sandbags in front line at N.13.b.45.75. facing W.

A dug-out is suspected at N.20.b.14. During the day much smoke was seen coming from chimney in FROMELLES. During the early morning four men were seen carrying planks from the direction of LE PIETRE, entering CLARA Trench close to the trench at N.19.a.95.25.
Movement was seen on FROMELLES - AUBERS Road.

Hdqrs. 56th Divn.

3rd November, 1916.

Captain,
for Lieut. Colonel,
General Staff.

56th DIVISIONAL TACTICAL PROGRESS REPORT No.7

from 8.0 a.m. November 3rd to 8.0 a.m. November 4th.

PART 1 OPERATIONS.

NEUVE CHAPELLE SECTION.

Our patrols were out along the whole front but found no trace of the enemy. An Officers patrol reported that the sap running out from our lines at S.11.a.1.7. is well wired and has a stream in front of it making a sound obstacle.

A party of Germans seen carrying timber to the dump at S.6.a.3.2. was fired on by our artillery and hit. The dump was also damaged.

MOATED GRANGE SECTION.

During the afternoon our T.Ms. carried out a shoot in co-operation with the Artillery on enemy's trenches. Considerable damage done. Retaliation insignificant.

Our patrol came into contact with the enemy at several points. An enemy wiring party was observed by our patrol at M.30.a.7.7. in front of the crater. M.G. fire was opened. Another patrol visited this place afterwards and all was quiet. Shots were fired from the listening post in the crater at M.24.d.3.1, our patrol attempted to reach it but could not owing to water being over knee deep.

An enemy wiring party was observed outside number 3 crater (M.36.c.03.85) they evidently employ a dog as sentry as it started barking when our patrol approached.

A hostile patrol which tried to get out to the COLVIN CRATER was dispersed by our Lewis Gun fire.

FAUQUISSART SECTION.

During the afternoon our T.Ms co-operated with the artillery in bombarding enemy trenches about WICK SALIENT. Considerable damage was done, much material including lengths of tramline were seen in the air. Patrols out during the night were undisturbed.

PART 11 INTELLIGENCE.

NEUVE CHAPELLE SECTION.

A wiring party was heard opposite S.10.5 and was dispersed by L.G. fire.

MOATED GRANGE SECTION.

From close observation it would appear that enemy front line opposite the CHORD is unoccupied by day. It is in a very bad state of repair. Bombing Post at M.30.a.0.0. reports sounds of underground work between midnight and 4.0 a.m.

FAUQUISSART SECTION.

An enemy patrol of three entered our line at RED LAMP about N.13.d.7.9½. This was at once driven out leaving 1 killed. He was identified as being EMIL LERNER, 3rd Coy. 1st Bn. 19th BAVARIAN INFANTRY REGIMENT.

A hostile working part at N.20.a.90.89 was dispersed by our artillery.

It is suspected that the enemy is constructing a new line from N.14.c.3.3. to join up with the unfinished trench running in a North East direction from CLARA at N.19.a.95.25.

/A loophole

- 2 -

A loophole was located at N.12.d.93.25. and an O.P. is suspected in the house at N.20.d.d.47.98.
A hostile machine gun was located firing from enemy first line at N.13.d.85.70.
The following is a list of suspected "LIVING" places:-

N.20.d.50.85.	....	red-tiled house.
N.20.a.90.75.	....	BERTHA TRENCH.
N.13.d.95.70.	....	Front line.
N.13.d.67.53.	....	" "
N.13.d.65.88.	....	" "
N.20.b.4.3.	....	14 Tree clumps.

[signature: L.Y.L.Stopford]

Hdqrs. 56th Divn.
4th November, 1916.

Captain,
Intelligence, General Staff.

56th DIVISIONAL TACTICAL PROGRESS REPORT No. 8.

from 8.0 a.m. 4th November to 8.0 a.m. 5th November.

PART I OPERATIONS.

NEUVE CHAPELLE SECTION. A patrol from the left of the left subsection found the body of a German who had evidently been dead for some time. No badges or identification could be found on him. The patrol got into a trench running towards the enemy's lines, which appeared to have been recently used by the enemy. The wire close to the enemy's trenches was very thick and about 3.6" high. Some effective shooting was carried out by our artillery during the day, T.M.s at S.16.b.8½.0. and S.11.a.7¼.2¼. being silenced. Our L.T.M.s fired with good results on enemy C.T. between S.10.d.5½.1. and S.10.d.7½.3. Wire cutting was also carried out at several points. Our M.G.s kept the tracks in LA RUSSE under intermittent fire throughout the night.

MOATED GRANGE SECTION. Patrols reported no signs of the enemy in NO MANS LAND. A party of six men working on the German wire opposite trench M.24.3. was fired on by our Lewis guns.
Our M.T.M.s and artillery fired in co-operation on German trenches in M.30.a. The hostile retaliation was rather greater than usual. During the evening our L.T.M.s and Lewis guns fired on those parts of the enemy's trench damaged during the afternoon.

FAUQUISSART SECTION. Several hostile wiring parties were seen by our patrols who informed machine gunners. Fire was opened and the parties dispersed. During the afternoon our artillery, M.T.M.s and L.T.M.s. fired most effectively on the enemy's C.T. running E. and W. through N.14.a. & b. L.T.M.s fired on several other parts of the German front line doing damage to the parapets. Our M.G.s were very active during the night firing over 8,500 rounds mainly on the enemy's communications.

PART II INTELLIGENCE.

NEUVE CHAPELLE SECTION. A hostile M.G. fired during the night from about S.11.a.8.9. Our T.M. shoot was replied to by a few H.T.M.s. A German was seen working on the roof of a shelter at S.11.a.8.1. Artillery fire was opened on the spot and damage done. At 8.30 a.m. a trail of white smoke was seen behind LORGIES CHURCH, thought to be a train moving in the direction of LA BASSEE

MOATED GRANGE SECTION. At 11.30 p.m. our post in the MAUQUISSART CRATER reported that they expected to be attacked. On Very lights being sent up a hostile patrol was seen advancing to the S. of the NEW CRATER. Our post opened fire and the enemy withdrew. At the same time a strong patrol was seen lying out to the N of the CRATER which did not approach. During the night the enemy covered up with earth the loophole plates which our snipers had fired on the 5th. A gap in the enemy's wire about 10 yards wide observed at M.30.c.5.8½. was fired on at frequent intervals by a Lewis gun during the night.

FAUQUISSART SECTION. Signs are visible of new work having been done on BERTHA TRENCH in N.14.c. and N.20.a. At 10.30 a.m. on 4th, puffs of smoke were seen from the direction of the AUBERS - FROMELLES Railway. Our artillery fired on the spot. Movement was seen round the house at N.25.b.7.5.; also a party walking from the cottage at N.20.b.90.55. to the RED HOUSE at N.20.b.9.4. On two occasions lights are reported to have been seen at 5.30 pm. about N.20/7.6. They had the appearance of being old lamps giving a dull yellow light. The house at N.26.d.0.4 is apparently occupied as smoke was seen at this point. Smoke was also seen issuing from the chimney of the red roofed house at N.20.d.7.4. and at N.13.d.3.6. It is probable that there is a dug-out at this latter point as an machine gun is suspected in the vicinity

/ The

The loophole previously reported at N.13.d.45.57. was being used by a sniper yesterday. A M.T.M. fired on to N.13.7. from N.14.c.05.25. A mortar has previously been reported at this point. L.T.M.s., 77 mm. and 9 cm. guns fired against our C.T's and front line of the right subsection during the day.

Hdqrs. 56th Divn.
5th November, 1916.

Captain,
Intelligence, General Staff

56th DIVISIONAL TACTICAL PROGRESS REPORT, No. 9
from 8.0 a.m. 5th November to 8.0 6th November 1916.

PART 1 OPERATIONS.

NEUVE CHAPELLE SECTION.

Our patrols were very active from the right sub-section.
One patrol discovered a snipers post between the lines about S.10.d.75.95. A second patrol brought in some telephone wire found in the trench running forward from our line at S.11.a.1.7. - it was loose and not earthed. It is thought to be German wire 7 strand and recently put out (sample herewith).

A third patrol examined the sap running from the German line S.10.d.35 to S.10.d.2.6. There was no sign of it having been used for some time.

Our artillery and T.Ms. co-operated in bombarding the enemy's front and support lines, much damage being done especially to wire at S.10.c.95.30.

MOATED GRANGE SECTION.

Our Artillery and T.Ms. were active during the afternoon and evening, and our machine guns co-operated at night sweeping the enemy parapets. Enemy's retaliation did no damage. The strong head wind made accurate shooting difficult, many of our shells falling short.

The whole front was systematically patrolled throughout the night and no enemy was seen.

The enemy wire in front of the CHORD line was inspected. It is much damaged by T.M. fire about M.30.a.4.3. but has no gaps. About M.30.b.4.8. it is very thick.

A patrol got close to the Crater at M.30.a.5.5. and was fired on from N.E. of this point. The patrol reported that the nearest Crater to them was not occupied and its front was not wired.

FAUQUISSART SECTION.

Our patrols were out as usual covering the whole front but no enemy was seen.

Our artillery and T.Ms. co-operated in a shoot on enemy tramway at N.14.b. and N.8.d. Damage done not yet ascertained.

During the night our machine guns were very active firing nearly 5,000 rounds on enemy's communications and wire.

PART 11 INTELLIGENCE.

NEUVE CHAPELLE SECTION.

Hostile artillery was rather more active than usual during the morning but did little damage to our trenches. Hostile M.Gs. are suspected at S.11.a.4.3. and S.11.a.75.90. Small parties were seen near LARUSSE, thought to be laying cables. Movement was seen on the LA QUINQUE Road at S.16.d. and on the LA BASSEE Road at S.23.b.

MOATED GRANGE SECTION.

At 7.0 p.m. two Germans were seen on the further lip of the DUCKS BILL CRATER (M.36.a.05.00) and were fired on. No trace of them could be found by our patrol.

An enemy party working on their parapet at M.30.a.65.60 were dispersed by L.G. fire.

A round iron cupola, possibly a machine gun emplacement, can be seen at M.30.c.57.15. under an isolated tree.

What looks like a large black box can be seen in a tall tree about N.25.b.5.6. It is thought to be an O.P.

/FAUQUISSART SECTION.

FAUQUISSART SECTION.

An enemy working party was seen at N.26.c.8.3. and was dispersed by our artillery.

A new loophole was located at N.14.a.8.4. Smoke was seen to rise from a house at N.21.c.1.4. Our artillery dealt with this successfully.

Smoke has again been seen coming from Red Tiled House at N.20.d. 50.85.

Movement was seen at the following places :- near house at N.21.a.65.50 - 6 men with slung rifles were seen to leave 14 TREE CLUMP and walk to BERTHA Trench - a party on RUE DELEVAL walking towards BERTHA Trench; they were dispersed by our artillery and ran into the trench.

During the night trains were twice heard on the AUBERS - FROMELLES line moving N.E.

A signal office is suspected at N.13.d.43.57 - several wires can be seen meeting at a small T shaped erection which can be seen over the parapet at this point. The wires are visible running back on standards as far as N.20. central. Two loopholes are visible at the point in the front line (N.13.d.43.57) where the wires meet. A previously suspected M.G. at N.13.d.30.53 has now become active.

At N.26.c.70.65 close to small house, a stack of large black boxes similar to those used on enemy C.Ts. can be seen. This is suspected to be a dump.

Head Qrs. 56th Divn.
6th November, 1916.

Captain,
General Staff "I"

56th DIVISIONAL TACTICAL PROGRESS REPORT No. 10,
from 8.0 a.m. 6th November to 8.0 a.m. 7th November.

PART 1 OPERATIONS.

NEUVE CHAPELLE SECTION. A patrol from the right subsection reported enemy's wire in good condition. Our T.Ms. damaged enemy front line and wire at M.35.d.95.40. to M.35.d.85.25. Lewis guns fired on the damage at night.
   At 1.40 p.m. a sniper from our right battalion killed a German opposite S.11.a.0.7. shooting him through the head.

MOATED GRANGE SECTION. Our T.Ms. co-operated with the Artillery during the afternoon in bombarding the enemy's trenches about M.30.c., M.30.a. and M.24.d. Much damage was done especially in the CHAPIGNY CRATER (M.24.d.25.15.) where much timber was thrown in the air.
   Our patrols found no sign of the enemy.

FAUQUISSART SECTION. Much damage was caused to enemy's defences N.14.b.1.8.- N.8.d.5.2. and N.14.a.75.25. by our combined shoot of artillery and T.Ms. at 2.15 p.m. yesterday. Our L.T.Ms. were active today firing 204 rounds.
   Our patrols on right saw no enemy during the night, but on the left one patrol reported seeing a hostile patrol East of crater about N.13.d.9.9.

PART II INTELLIGENCE

NEUVE CHAPELLE SECTION. During the early part of the night the enemy opened indirect M.G. fire on HUN STREET. Very little hostile T.M. fire during the day. A party of the enemy in S.11.a. was dispersed by our Lewis gun fire. Movement was again seen at LARUSSE. At 6.30 p.m. a wiring party on our extreme left was fired on by a German patrol of about 8 men who were concealed in a shell hole. A sergeant with the wiring party is missing. An officers patrol which went out to look for him reports a shallow trench protected by wire 50 yards outside our wire and also an old dug-out about 30 yards from our wire, submerged in the stream which runs parallel to SIGN POST LANE. Movement was seen in the enemy's reserve line which appears to be in bad condition. At 10.0 p.m. the enemy placed lighted braziers on his parapet opposite trench .10.4. These were fired on and taken down immediately.

MOATED GRANGE SECTION. Hostile patrol which fired on one of our wiring parties was engaged with a Lewis gun from the right subsection apparently with good results as the enemy could be distinctly seen running back in single file (see NEUVE CHAPELLE SECTION). On several occasions our Lewis guns and rifle grenade fire effectively silenced hostile parties working on their trenches and wire.

FAUQUISSART SECTION. Work has been progressing on the new C.T. N.E. of and parallel to BERTHA TRENCH and many new revetting posts have appeared. Transport was plainly heard during the night, thought to be on AUBERS - LE PIETRE Road. Movement seen round 14 TREE CLUMP N.20.b.3½.3½. An active machine gun has been located at N.13.c.96.34. Another gun is suspected in the sap at N.14.a.9.7. Smoke was seen issuing from the chimneys of houses at N.26.d.33.64., and N.25.b.50.45. Also near house at N.21.b.36.16. The sap at N.13.c.90.35. is apparently occupied by night as a Very light was fired from it at 2.40 a.m. The house at N.27.a.5.3. is probably an O.P. as the light flashing on a glass was seen through the wall.
   New enemy wire is visible between N.13.c.9.4½. to N.13.d.2½.6½.

Hdqrs. 56th Divn.

7th November, 1916.

Captain,
Intelligence, General Staff.

56th DIVISIONAL TACTICAL PROGRESS REPORT No.11,
from 8.0 a.m. 7th November to 8.0 a.m. 8th November.

PART 1 OPERATIONS.

NEUVE CHAPELLE SECTION.

An Officers' patrol reported that the ground in front of S.5.4. and S.5.5. was dry and cut up by many shallow trenches. No enemy were encountered and no tracks leading to enemy's wire. A patrol from the right battalion could not find any trace of the sniper reported to fire from S.10.d.75. 95. Our machine guns were active firing on the enemy's communications during the night.

MOATED GRANGE SECTION.

Our M.T.Ms. obtained several direct hits on the enemy's mine shaft at M.36.a.35.40. Enemy snipers were unusually active in the early part of the night but a liberal spraying of their parapet with Lewis Guns stopped them.

An Officers' patrol covered the whole of the right battalion front and discovered no signs of the enemy. The patrols from the left battalion found the ground impassible the ditches having overflowed.

FAUQUISSART SECTION.

Owing to strong and gusty wind our L.T.Ms. only fired 35 rounds. Our machine guns continually fired during the night on to the gaps made in the enemy's parapet by our T.Ms. Our patrols were out during the night but no signs could be found of the enemy.

PART 11 INTELLIGENCE.

NEUVE CHAPELLE SECTION.

About 10 M.T.M bombs fell on the extreme right of the front line. The position of the mortar was observed by our artillery. At the same time about 20 L.T.M bombs fell in rear of the front line about S.10 central.

Sounds of stakes being driven in were heard from S.10.d. 7.7. but ceased on rifle fire being opened on the spot.

Just before 11.0 a.m. a party of Germans were seen to walk in pairs at 100 yards interval from the small wood in S.6.b. to LA RUSSE. At 2.45 p.m. two men walked rapidly from LA RUSSE to the wood, returning at 3.0 p.m. with heavy sacks.

MOATED GRANGE SECTION.

At 11.0 p.m. a large working party was seen in enemy wire about M.30.a.5.0. This was dispersed by Lewis Gun fire. Enemy were seen pumping water over their parapet opposite M.24.2. and were fired on.

At 11.0 a.m. two men, one wearing a peaked cap, and one a helmet, were seen looking through a loophole. A sniper pierced their plate with an A.P. bullet and the loophole was not used again.

The enemy have put fresh wire out opposite MAUQUISSART Crater at M.30.c.5.3.

FAUQUISSART SECTION.

Fresh earth and sandbags seen in enemy's front line at N.13.d.8.6½ and N.13.d.1.6. New wire visible at N.14.a. 7.3.

The suspected new trench running from BERTHA TRENCH at N.14.c.3.3. in a S.W. direction has been repaired where damaged by our Artillery. New work is visible on the new communication trench at N.14.c.95.15.

Two.

FAUQUISSART SECTION (Contd.)
    Two planks were thrown up on the parapet at N.13.d.5.6.
The enemy's parapet is much worn and there is also a gap in the
wire N.13.d.72.70.   This is thought to be a spot used by
outgoing and incoming patrols.
    A small black and white flag on a short stake can be seen
in front of the enemy's first line at N.13.d.48.65. There
is a large black box in the top of the most Northwesterly
tree of the AUBERS CLUMP at N.26.d.6.2.   This is suspected
to be an O.P. hitherto hidden by foliage.
    Last night the enemy fired several rounds (77 mm.) on to
the RUE DU BACQUEROT at its junction with MASSELOT St. All
were duds.   The gun fired from the direction of AUBERS STACK.
Smoke was seen coming from the house at N.20.b.30.35 and from
the trench running N.E. from BERTHA TRENCH at N.20.b.30.55.
which is suspected to be a dug-out.

Head Qrs. 56th Divn.   Captain,
8th November, 1916.   General Staff "I"

56th DIVISIONAL TACTICAL PROGRESS REPORT No. 12.
from 8.0 a.m. 8th November to 8.0 a.m. 9th November.

PART I OPERATIONS.

NEUVE CHAPELLE SECTION

During the afternoon our artillery and T.Ms. carried out a combined bombardment of the enemy's lines. Our observing aeroplane reports that the shooting on the house at LA RUSSE was particularly effective, volumes of smoke issuing from the house. Much damage was done to a T.M.E. at S.16.b 65.00, and the enemy's parapet breached at M.35.d.85.30.: trench boards were seen in the air.

Our machine guns were again active during the night on the point where our T.Ms. had cut wire about S.5.d.2.4., and at the track leading from LA RUSSE. Difficulty was experienced in firing owing to guns sinking in wet emplacements. Bright moonlight hindered active patrolling.

MOATED GRANGE SECTION.

At 12.15 a.m. we exploded a mine about M.30.c.24.21. charged with 800 lbs. ammonal. The enemy had been working ten feet away. We immediately occupied the crater with a party consisting of one officer, one N.C.O. and a Lewis Gun. Our wiring party then started wiring towards the nearest COLVIN CRATER (M.33.c.3.2.). The enemy did not show any activity. The new crater is about 25 yards from the nearest COLVIN CRATER and touches the last crater blown by the enemy. It measures about 70 feet in diameter. We had no casualties. The underground damage has not yet been investigated.

A patrol from our left battalion reports that the ground is impassible owing to swamps.

FAUQUISSART SECTION.

One of our patrols investigated the enemy sap at M.24.d.5.5. and reported it unoccupied and full of water. Another patrol reported a hostile working party opposite N.13.1. It was dispersed by Lewis Gun fire. Other patrols neither saw nor encountered the enemy.

One of our snipers claims to have hit a German seen at N.13.c.9.2½. at 10.30 a.m.

Between 7.0 a.m. and 4.0 p.m. many enemy parties were dispersed by our artillery at N.21.a.95.30.

PART II INTELLIGENCE.

NEUVE CHAPELLE SECTION.

Movement was seen in T.1.a.& b. and at cross roads at LA TOURELLE. This was checked by our artillery. Smoke was seen at S.11.c.0.0.; also from houses at HALPEGARBE.

A hostile machine gun was located at S.11.a.07.05. about 10.0 p.m. The Artillery was informed and in 12 minutes had obtained six direct hits. Nothing further was heard of the M.G. A hostile working party opposite our left battalion was heard and fired on by a Lewis Gun. It is believed casualties were caused, because shouts and groans were heard. It seems that enemy trenches in this section are flooded. A shell falling on this front line caused a big splash.

MOATED GRANGE SECTION.

Yesterday morning a man wearing a grey helmet without a spike and with the figure 10 marked on the front in pencil was seen looking over the parapet.

There was much movement seen behind the enemy line during the day; parties of men in full pack were seen running across the open. A relief is suspected. One man was seen to be hit in the shoulder by one of our snipers.

/ FAUQUISSART SECTION

FAUQUISSART SECTION.
Fresh earth has been thrown up between N.19.a.65.85. and N.19.a.5.7½. The parapet between N.13.d.C0.55. and N.14.d.75.60. has been repaired. There is some new wood showing over the parapet at N.13.c.95.25.

The hostile machine gun at N.13.c.96.34. was very active during the night.

There was abnormal movement behind the line and a relief was apparent. The absence of T.M. fire and sniping confirms this. During the morning small parties of the enemy were seen entering and leaving BERTHA Trench about N.20.a., where it is evidently full of water. In many cases the men carried packs and cloth grey caps. Very few wearing shrapnel helmets. Two parties of from 15 - 20 men were seen walking in single file in an S.W. direction on road from N.21.central to LE PIETRE. The first half at noon, the second half at 4.30 p.m. Much movement was also seen about 14 TREE CLUMP.

The roof of a dug-out can be seen through hedges at N.20.b.1.4. (point where BERTHA Trench cuts hedge) and smoke was seen issuing from a chimney in this roof.

Hdqrs. 56th Divn.

9th November, 1916.

Captain,
Intelligence, General Staff

56th DIVISIONAL TACTICAL PROGRESS REPORT No. 13,
from 8.0 a.m. 9th November to 8.0 a.m. 10th November.

PART 1 OPERATIONS.

NEUVE CHAPELLE SECTION.

Parties of Germans were seen moving over the open during the morning from S.11.d.7.5. to S.11.d.95.85. These were fired on by our artillery.

During the afternoon our artillery and T.Ms. co-operated in a shoot on the front and support lines North of the BOARS HEAD, on the LA BASSEE Road and on the N.W. corner of the BOIS DE BIEZ. Much damage was done. Our T.Ms. damaged wire at S.5.b.7.9. and S.5.b.4.1.

Our patrols reported no hostile encounters. Moonlight prevented active patrolling.

MOATED GRANGE SECTION.

Our M.T.Ms and L.T.Ms. bombarded enemy trenches about M.24.b. and M.30.a. during the afternoon, our field guns providing a covering fire. The bombardment which lasted 40 minutes was very successful, the enemy parapet being breached in several places and his wire damaged. This area was subjected to frequent bursts of Lewis Gun fire at night.
The enemy's reply was feeble.
Our patrols found no sign of the enemy.

FAUQUISSART SECTION.

Our artillery and T.Ms. carried out a very successful bombardment of enemy defences between M.24.d.65.45 and M.24.d.80.50. during the afternoon in co-operation with the brigades on our right. His trenches were badly damaged but he did not retaliate.

Our M.Gs. were very active on the enemy's communications during the night, about 10,000 rounds being fired.

Our usual patrols were out during the night. One enemy patrol seen near RHONDDA SAP (N.8.d.0.6.) was dispersed. An enemy party was reported by one of our patrols to be working at N.14.a.9.5. It was fired on by Lewis Guns and scattered.

PART 11 INTELLIGENCE.

NEUVE CHAPELLE SECTION.

The enemy was more active yesterday with his artillery and T.Ms., the districts from S.5 2 to S.5 6 receiving particular attention. He obtained two or three direct hits, but caused no casualties.

The H.T.M. at S.16.b.0.7. which was shelled yesterday by our artillery was again active yesterday.

Opposite our right battalion much pumping was heard.

At 5.30 p.m. 4 green flares were fired by the enemy from S.E. corner of BOIS DE BIEZ followed by 5 double red and 3 double green from the same place.

A snipers post is suspected about S.5.c.8.1.

MOATED GRANGE SECTION.

A party of men pumping behind their front line at M.36.a.4.4. was fired on by our snipers. It disappeared. A party was heard working behind COLVIN CRATER so Lewis Gun fire was opened on it.

At 6.0 p.m.

- 2 -

MOATED GRANGE SECTION (Contd.)

At 6.0 p.m. a hostile working party was seen leaving their trench. They were turned back by our fire. The enemy then sent up 3 green lights in quick succession followed by a red one bursting into 6 stars. No apparent action followed.

A light has been seen for the last two nights at M.19.c.3.2. The enemy's parapet at M.30.a.4.1. has been rebuilt and wire repaired.

The enemy's trenches are evidently very wet, T.M shells were sending up large columns of water and Germans have been seen walking outside their trenches.

At M.30.c.5.7. the trench is very bad and men were continually seen doubling across the open at intervals.

A party of 6, two of whom were thought to be officers, walked across at 8.40 a.m. Our snipers got in four shots and 1 officer and 1 man were seen to fall.

A man was seen with his head above the parapet watching an aeroplane. He was hit.

FAUQUISSART SECTION.

A small party was seen at 10.0 a.m. at N.19.c.3.9. It was dispersed by our artillery. A party heard working at N.14.a.9.5. was dispersed by our Lewis gun fire.

A hostile aeroplane when returning over the enemy lines about 4.15 p.m. dropped a red light signal.

Smoke was seen coming from the following places, which are suspected to be inhabited - House at N.21.c.2.5. - dug-out at N.20.b.1.4. - first line at N.13.c.96.34. The latter is also a suspected M.G. emplacement. Air photos show this part to be flooded. An O.P. is suspected at N.27.a.8.3. It is a long wooden box in a tall tree and has hitherto been hidden by foliage.

Transport was heard on the AUBERS - LE PIETRE Road.

Hdqrs. 56th Divn.

10th November, 1916.

Captain,

Intelligence, General Staff.

56th DIVISIONAL TACTICAL PROGRESS REPORT NO. 14
from 8.0 a.m.10th November to 8.0 a.m. 19th November

PART 1 OPERATIONS.

NEUVE CHAPELLE SECTION.

Our T.Ms. were active and considerable damage was done to the enemy's trenches, especially at S.10.d.1.4. where the wire was cut and trench breached. Firing was difficult owing to the guns sinking into the mud.

Our patrols did not go out as the moonlight was too bright: the enemy's wire was clearly visible all night.

As usual our M.Gs. sprayed the enemy's dumps, tracks and cross roads during the night.

MOATED GRANGE SECTION.

Our T.Ms. combined both morning and afternoon in shooting on enemy's trenches traversing between M.24.d.4.1. and M.30.b.2.8. Much damage was done a suspected snipers post at M.30.b.1.6., being demolished. The enemy made no reply.

Our patrols reported that ground very wet, making quiet progress impossible. No sign of the enemy was seen.

FAUQUISSART SECTION.

Between 11.15 a.m. and 12.15 p.m. our artillery and T.Ms. co-operated in a shoot on enemy lines M.24.d.75.45. to M.24.d.9.6.

The dug-out at M.24.d.7.4. was totally destroyed by M.T.M. fire and the parapet was much damaged.

One of our patrols discovered an enemy party working at N.14.a.7.3. where our T.Ms. had damaged his works. The patrol returned and Lewis gun and rifle fire was opened. The patrol went out again and could find no sign of the enemy. Another patrol reported enemy pumping at WICK Salient.

PART II INTELLIGENCE.

NEUVE CHAPELLE SECTION.

Several H.T.M. bombs were dropped on our lines in S.5.c. - most of these fell short. Several "aerial torpedoes" were fired but did no damage.

The enemy was heard hammering and sawing all night in the front line opposite our right battalion. Our Lewis guns fired to disturb this and to keep open the gaps made by our T.Ms.

Three Germans were seen on the LA BASSEE Rd. at 11.0 p.m. They were fired at, but got away.

At 11.30 p.m. a searchlight was observed some distance behind N.E. end of BOIS de BIEZ.

Considerable movement of men and horses was observed between the barns at L'AVENTURE (T.3.b.) and the wood at HAUT POMMEREAU (T.1.b.)

New wire has been observed at S.5.d.4.0.

The gaps in the enemy's parapet at M.35.d.95.45. lets through a stream of water which runs under our parapet.

Smoke or steam has been seen rising from trenches around LES BRULOT (S.5.d.). It is thought that there is a pumping engine there.

/ MOATED GRANGE SECTION.

MOATED GRANGE SECTION.

The enemy was working opposite the left battalion at 6.0 p.m. last night. He was dispersed with Lewis gun fire.

At 7.30 a.m., a working party of 20 men was working at M.36.a.4.4. They were fired on and ceased work.

At 2.30 p.m. wood was being carried along the trench to the same place.

The enemy were still showing themselves owing to the flooded trenches, but were always moving too quickly for our snipers to report any hits for certain.

The new crater (M.30.c.20.25) is rapidly filling with water and the lips falling in. The water is now nine feet from the top of the lip.

FAUQUISSART SECTION

Fresh work was visible on BERTHA Trench, fresh earth and planks being visible at N.14.c.45.10.

Several large black boxes used for building C.T's have been placed on the parapet of CLARA Trench at N.19.d.70.25. Four men carrying a box about three feet square left BERTHA Trench at N.20.b.00.55. entering again at N.20.b.3.2. A man was seen to enter the trench running N.E. from BERTHA at N.20.b.35.50.

The light railway running parallel to BERTHA Trench was used last night.

A pair of glasses were being used in a loophole at N.13.d.40.58.

Smoke was seen from the front line at N.13.d.5.6. - house at N.20.b.30.25. and at 10.35 a.m. from FROMELLES Station.

Hdqrs. 56th Divn.

11th November, 1916.

Captain,

Intelligence, General Staff.

56th DIVISIONAL TACTICAL PROGRESS REPORT No. 15,
from 8.0 a.m. 11th November to 8.0 a.m. 12th November.

PART 1 OPERATIONS.

NEUVE CHAPELLE SECTION.

Our T.Ms. of all calibres co-operated in a bombardment of the enemy's front line from S.5.d.5.9 to S.5.b.6.3. with the object of destroying a portion of the line running alongside the main drain thus causing a block and flooding his trenches. Much damage was done, woodwork being seen in the air; quantities of water were thrown up and there is every reason to believe we achieved our object.

Our patrols were very active last night each battalion sending out two. An Officers' patrol examined hostile wire at S.10.d.10.45 and found it low and loose, but no gaps. Three Germans were seen working on this wire at S.10.d.0.3. Another patrol reported that the old trench in front of our line at S.5.1. is 2 ft. wide by 18" deep and overgrown with grass. A patrol investigated the German wire at SIGN POST LANE (M.35.d. 9.4.). It was found to be good. They could find no sign of the trench reported on the night of the 6th/7th November. A patrol which visited the SEVEN SISTERS (S.11.a.8.6.) reported ground swampy, and that the SEVEN SISTERS are not held by enemy, but judging from flashes and flares it is thought that the enemy hold a small trench 50 yards behind.

MOATED GRANGE SECTION.

Our M. and L.T.Ms. damaged the enemy's trenches about M.24.d. yesterday. The snipers post at M.30.b.1.6. also received attention and has not p. since been used.

Our patrol in COLVIN CRATERS (M.30.c.2.0.) report no signs of the enemy. At 9.15 p.m. our listening post in No. 3 MAUQUISSART CRATER (M.30.c.2½.2½) fired on an enemy patrol of 5 men approaching No. 2 MAUQUISSART CRATER (M.30.c.2.3.). Another patrol reported that the crater about M.30.a.4½.5. is held by a small post. Very lights were seen to issue from there. The enemy sap at M.24.d.5.5. is reported to be occupied and work preceeding there.

FAUQUISSART SECTION.

Our artillery and T.Ms. carried out a combined shoot on enemy's defences from M.24.d.8.5. to M.24.d.9.6.

The dugout at M.24.d.75.45 and M.G. emplacement at N.17.a.30. 45. being damaged, Much water was thrown up.

Our patrols found no signs of the enemy.

An enemy periscope was seen at N.14.a.7.3. It disappeared on being fired at. Enemy makes no reply to our firing.

PART 11 INTELLIGENCE.

NEUVE CHAPELLE SECTION.

Enemy's T.Ms. retaliated on our lines at S.5.b.0.3. but little or no damage was done and they were quickly silenced by our artillery.

Enemy wiring parties were located all along our right subsection. They were dispersed by M.G. fire.

New wire seen at S.5.d.5.8.

Boards have been put across enemy's parapet at M.35.d.95.45.

At S.11.a.7.05 there is a green mound with a slit in it. This is suspected to be a M.G. emplacement. Movement was again noticed between POMMEREAU WOOD (T.1.b.) and L'AVENTURE (T.3.c.)

- 2 -

PART II INTELLIGENCE (Contd.)

MOATED GRANGE SECTION.

There has been practically no retaliation by the enemy to our T.M. or artillery fire. The enemy evidently is fairly fully occupied in repairing his trenches which are still very wet, one being seen to get out and double across the open. Our snipers have taken full advantage of this

FAUQUISSART SECTION.

A party of 4 Germans was seen at 7.0 a.m. working about N.13.c.9.3. It was fired on and dispersed by M.G. fire.

The new trench at N.14.b.8.3. has been continued; also the trench running in a Westerly direction from BERTHA Trench at N.14.c.3.3. BERTHA Trench at N.20.a. has been worked upon, the base of the parapet being banked up with fresh earth.

Fresh sandbags have been added carelessly to the parapet of the front line at N.13.d.80.65. Also yesterday afternoon shovel fulls of mud were thrown over at this point, but many parts breached by our T.Ms. are not yet repaired.

Smoke was seen coming from red roofed house at N.21.a.7.4.

Houses at N.20.d.50.85. and N.26.b.84.15 and from 14 TREE CLUMP (N.20.b.4.4.).

A two horsed wagon was seen on road in AUBERS at N.26.d. 50.55.

Head Qrs. 56th Divn.
12th November, 1916.

Captain,
Intelligence, General Staff.

56th DIVISIONAL TACTICAL PROGRESS REPORT No. 18.
from 8.0 a.m. 12th November to 8.0 a.m. 13th November.

PART I OPERATIONS.

FAUQUISSART SECTION.

Our artillery and T.Ms. combined in shooting on enemy defences at N.1z.c.75.10.& M.24.d.central. Much material damage was done. Our machine guns were active during the night on enemy's communications.

An officer of left battalion finding the wire presented no obstacle entered the enemy front line at about N.13.d.1.6. He patrolled three bays and found the trenches in a very bad condition, being half full of mud and water. He did not see any enemy, but heard them working not far off. The enemy directed a small searchlight upon one of our patrols when returning to our lines on the extreme left. Enemy machine guns opened fire, but no casualties ensued.

MOATED GRANGE SECTION.

Our M.T.Ms. and L.T.Ms. were active on following targets:- emplacement at M.30.c.5½.1. - M.30.b.5½.9. and crater at M.24.d.3½.1. At about M.24.d.5.1½ a dug-out appeared to be blown up and at another point a body is reported to have been seen in the air. Very slight retaliation. Our machine guns were active during the night.

An officers patrol went out from M.29.1 with the object of examining hostile wire and attacking any hostile patrol They were heavily fired on on leaving the crater, the enemy's trenches being thickly manned. Later when the fire died down the wire was examined and found to be very thick.

NEUVE CHAPELLE SECTION.

Patrol from our left battalion searched the ground out in front of NEUVE CHAPELLE but could find no trace of the enemy. A patrol from our right spent 4½ hours reconnoitring the enemy's defences about S.10.c.9.1. It passed out from our lines at S.10.c.6.2., went through two lines of old trenches now about three foot deep and very broad. At S.10.c.75.00. there is a large shell hole 30 foot broad filled with water; twenty yards further on is the German wire which was very deep and thick. The patrol watched 1½ hours from here but no sound or flare came from the enemy's trenches.

PART II INTELLIGENCE.

FAUQUISSART SECTION.

About dozen rounds of 5.9" howitzer fell around ELGIN St. otherwise very quiet. (M.24.5.)

Machine guns are suspected at N.13.d.8.7., N.13.d.3.5., and snipers loopholes at N.14.a.8.4., and N.8.d.2.1½

There is new work at N.14.b.37.80. also on BERTHA Tr. (N.20.a.8.8.), and the trench running in a Westerly direction from BETHA Tr. (N.14.c.3.3.).

Smoke was seen rising from the red-roofed house at N.21.a.7.4 At N.14.a.7½.3½. are four poles apparently carrying a hose pipe The absence of movement generally was most noticeable.

MOATED GRANGE SECTION.

Enemy fired about 16 rounds H.E., possible 4.2" howitzer. which dropped near the tramway behind GRANTS Post (M.23.d.3.3. causing no damage. Otherwise no retaliation at all.

/NEUVE CHAPELLE S

NEUVE CHAPELLE SECTION.

Hostile artillery more active. A few rounds of 5.9" howitzer falling near WINTER POST O.P. (S.10.b.2.5.) There was much movement of vehicles between POMMEREAU WOOD and L'AVENTURE. A carrying party of about 15 was twice observed near dump at S.23.b.35.70.

Enemy were seen in C.T. at S.6.a.3.2. and S.11.d.55.80.

The following working parties were located - at S.11.a.0.0. ; digging and earth thrown up about 7.30 a.m. at S.11.a.6.7. - baling at S.11.a.30.25.

New woodwork is visible at S.13.a.9.6. A T.M. has been located at S.16.b.50.05. Snipers posts are suspected at S.16.a.88.90. and S.11.a.35.25. (where there is a blue sandbag over the loophole.

Judging from the amount of rifle fire drawn by an allied aeroplane from the enemy's trenches at about 3.0 p.m., the line is not strongly held opposite S.10.3.

At. 9.30 p.m. the enemy seen to be bombing his own wire at M.35.d.75.40.

Two Germans ran from their support line to a black mound at foot of tree stump at S.10.d.28.20. Machine gun flashes were seen coming from here.

Hdqrs. 56th Divn.

13th November, 1916.

Captain,

Intelligence, General Staff.

56th DIVISIONAL TACTICAL PROGRESS REPORT No. 17
from 8.0 a.m. 13th November to 8.0 a.m. 14th November.

PART I OPERATIONS.

NEUVE CHAPELLE SECTION.

Our L.T.Ms. operated on the junction of the enemy's trench and drain at S.10.d.20.25 with the object of blocking the latter and flooding his trench. Considerable damage was done, wood and water being thrown up. The enemy's retaliation was heavy.
Our patrols were out along the whole front but found no sign of the enemy.

MOATED GRANGE SECTION.

Our T.Ms. bombarded enemy trenches from M.30.c.5.6. to M.30.c.72.70 good results being obtained. The enemy's retaliation was feeble.
One of our patrols located an enemy wiring party about M.30.c.5.6.- our Lewis Guns dealt with them successfully and work ceased.
Our snipers were again active; they claimed to have hit two Germans. One offered an excellent target at M.36.a.4.7. He was hit and fell back into the trench. The other was hit in the arm. He was one of a party of six carrying spades and walking behind the front line at M.36.a.4.8.

FAUQUISSART SECTION.

Our artillery, Medium and Light T.Ms. co-operated in bombarding the enemy's lines about N.13.c.70.05 at 3.45 p.m. and again at 7.30 p.m. Much material damage was done, bits of trench being thrown into the air and the wire cut about. Our M.Gs. sprayed these points during the night.
Our patrols recconncitred the whole front and discovered no signs of the enemy.

PART II INTELLIGENCE.

NEUVE CHAPELLE CHASECTION.

A German was seen in the sniping post at S.11.b.70.93 wearing a light blue uniform and soft hat with a white badge.
The enemy's T.Ms. retaliated for our L.T.M. shoot by expending much ammunition on our L.T.M. positions. The damage was not great considering the rounds fired, S.11.1, S.5.1 and HUN STREET (S.5.c.3.1.) receiving direct hits, the latter being blocked for 20 yards.
Transport was heard on the LA BASSEE - ESTAIRES Road from 2.0 to 4.0 a.m.
A loophole has been located at S.11.a.18.20. There appears to be a snipers post or O.P. at S.11.b.70.93, a platform being visible in a tree in the edge of the BOIS DE BIEZ.
The C.T. at S.16.a.90.45. is apparently flooded, men were seen to get out, walk along in the open and get in again further on.
At 7.15 a.m. two dummies were placed on the enemy's parapet at M.35.d.8.3. Shortly afterwards three men started work on the parapet. They were fired on and the dummies were then taken in.
Sentries from our left sub-section reported what appeared to be an airship or observation balloon passing overhead from the rear at 1.30 p.m.

/MOATED GRANGE SECTION.

PART 11 INTELLIGENCE (Contd.)

MOATED GRANGE SECTION.

Movement was seen behind a concrete emplacement at M.30.d.9.7. probably a working party repairing it. Our artillery dropped three shells within 10 yards after which movement ceased.

A periscope has been located at M.36.a.4.4.

Hostile artillery fired a few 77mm. shells on to the head of S.TILLELOY C.T. (M.35.b.8.8.) but little damage was caused.

FAUQUISSART SECTION.

At midnight a party was heard working behind the front line at WICK SALIENT about N.13.b.3.6. - stakes were being driven in.

At 1.30 a.m. a bell was heard to ring in enemy's trenches about N.13.d.6.5.

New work is visible on the C.T. at N.20.a.9.9. also on the trench running West from BERTHA TRENCH at N.14.c.3.3. and on the trench running N.E. and parallel with BERTHA at about N.20.b.15.85.

Horse transport was heard on the RUE D'ENFER (N.25.b.)

At N.20.b.90.45 two men were seen walking S. along the track and later two men walking N.

A 4.2" Howitzer was suspected to fire from N.28.a.4.1.

Head Qrs. 56th Divn.
14th November, 1916.

Captain,
Intelligence, General Staff

56th DIVISIONAL TACTICAL PROGRESS REPORT No. 18.
from 8.0 a.m., 14th November to 15th November, 1916.

NEUVE CHAPELLE SECTION.   PART I OPERATIONS.

Our artillery was active throughout the day, the targets including hostile T.Ms, movement, dumps and machine guns, which were firing at our aeroplanes. Our M.Gs. fired on enemy's communications to trench mortar emplacements during the night with the view of stopping their supply of ammunition.
Our patrols were out on the whole front, but found no signs of the enemy.

MOATED GRANGE SECTION.

At 2.0 pm. our T Ms. co-operated in firing on enemy's trenches at M.24.d.52.20. and M.30.a.45.05. Much damage was done, a gap 5 yards wide being made at the first point, and a smaller one at the latter. Their retaliation was feeble.
One of our patrols reconnoitred the sap at M.24.d.5.5. and the crater at M.24.d.3.1. Owing to water it was difficult to reach these points; both were reported unoccupied. Another patrol reported the enemy's wire to be very thick and strong about M.30.a.4.1.

FAUQUISSART SECTION.

At 2.0 p.m. our T.Ms. and artillery co-operated in damaging the enemy's trenches at N.13.c.9.2., N.13.d.0.6., and N.14.c.5.5. (where new work is visible). Much damage was done, the parapet being breached at several points.
Our patrols were out along the whole front, but no enemy were encountered. An enemy wiring party seen about N.19.a.2.0. was dispersed by our rifle fire

PART II INTELLIGENCE.

NEUVE CHAPELLE SECTION.

Hostile machine guns were very active against our aeroplanes from front line trenches. One of our aeroplanes was soon to retaliate on enemy from a low altitude with a Lewis Gun.
Transport heard on LA BASSEE Road between 11.0 p.m. and 2 a.m.
Four men were seen to pass down C.T. at S.18.a.7.5. at 3.15 p.m. Parties of Germans passed down the road at S.23.b.6.3. (dump) at 9.0 a.m.
An enemy wiring and covering party was seen about S.11.a.2.2. at 9.30 p.m. It was dispersed by L.G. fire It was soon again later and again dispersed. Sentries reported movement later so an officers patrol went out but did not encounter anyone.
Two other working parties at S.10.d.1.4. and M.35.b.8.3. were dispersed by our Lewis guns.
An aeroplane flew over our lines at 1.0 am. in an easterly direction. It was showing two white lights. When over enemy territory, green and red lights were dropped and answered (presumably) by a red and white signal flare from well behind their front line. This was repeated again a few minutes later.
The enemy bombed his own wire about S.10.d.0.4. at 9.15 p.m. A sheet of whitish metal with a hole in the centre has been placed over the shelter in enemy advanced trench at M.35.d.8.3.
Smoke was seen from house at S.11.b.3.0.

MOATED GRANGE SECTION.
Enemy's artillery was slightly more active, some 4.2" shells falling about M.23.d.9.1.
The enemy was working hard behind his parapet during the night, sounds of pickets being driven in and pumping being heard.
A Very light fired by us into one of the WINCHESTER CRATERS (M.30.a.central) set fire to smething which burned with a blue
/flame

flame six feet high for twenty minutes. This crater was afterwards visited by a patrol but found unoccupied.

FAUQUISSART SECTION.

Hostile artillery and trench mortars were more active today. A few 4.2" shells falling on MASSELOT POST (M.18.a.3.7.) RUE TILLELOY and RUE BACQUEROT during the afternoon. Possibly retaliation.

The enemy is firing Very light from his support trench, these often falling in his front line.

Movement was seen behind HAYSTACK O.P. in N.21.d.

A hostile 4.2" battery has been located to fire from N.28.d.15.50. This was verified by cross bearings on flashes and the oblique air photographs show mounds resembling gun pits at this point.

Smoke was seen from N.14.c.17.75. and N.32.a.8.6.

New work and repairs at N.14.b.2.9.

T.l.Heald

Hdqrs. 56th Divn.

15th November, 1916.

Captain,

Intelligence, General Staff.

56th DIVISIONAL TACTICAL PROGRESS REPORT No. 19,
from 8. 0 a.m. 15th November to 8. 0 a.m. 16th November.

PART 1 OPERATIONS.

NEUVE CHAPELLE SECTION.

Our patrols were very active on this section last night, much useful ground information being obtained, viz : the ground round houses in S.11.a.. A hostile working party was seen here and dispersed by Lewis Gun fire from our trench. Also the ditch running to the German lines from S.10.3. is reported to be full of water but not much wire. The German wire here is close to their parapet, low, but not very thick. No gaps could be found.

Our T.Ms. co-operated with our artillery in a shoot on various targets, the latter's objective being LES BRULOT. Our Stokes guns fired 300 rounds on S.5.b.6.3. with the idea of blocking the drain. This combined action of Heavy Group and Trench Artillery undoubtedly caused much damage, and since the areas chosen as targets have shown considerable activity lately, casualties were probably caused. Our M.Gs. sprayed LES BRULOT during the night.

At midnight a platoon on our left opened rapid rifle fire with the object of drawing the enemy's fire and thus disclosing his sentry group positions. He did not, however, reply.

MOATED GRANGE SECTION.

Our T.Ms. damaged the enemy's parapets at M.36.a.4.9.- M.30.a. 85.60 and M.24.d.45.10. The shooting was good as much material was seen in the air.

At midnight rapid fire was opened by all in front line of right sub-section, the object being as stated above. This brought forth no retaliation, only an increase of Very Lights.

Our patrols were out along the whole front but no hostile patrols were encountered. They, however, located several wiring parties who were duly dispersed.

FAUQUISSART SECTION.

At 3. 0 p.m. our artillery and T.Ms. co-operated in a shoot on enemy defences at N.13.c.80.15 and N.13.c.62.02. At the first point the parapet was breached for 10 yards. Some bombs appeared to go very deeply into the earth as if dropping into a deep dug-out. When this happened large unusual clouds of white smoke arose.

Our Stokes Guns caused much damage to enemy's front line at N.14.c. Our M.Gs. fired about 8,000 rounds on enemy's communications during the night.

A patrol reported enemy working at N.13.d.05. They were sent back by our Lewis Guns and rifle fire. Our patrol reconnoitred the spot later and reported all quiet. A patrol of 1 Officer and 5 O.Rs. left RED LAMP (N.13.7.) at 6.0 p.m. with the intention of entering the enemy's lines about N.13.d.3.6.

After proceeding about 160 yards an enemy patrol of about 20 strong was encountered. Our patrol remained observing/enemy until his withdrawal.

PART 11 INTELLIGENCE.

NEUVE CHAPELLE SECTION.

Several "Minnies" were fired by the enemy in retaliation for our afternoon shoot. Most of these fell short but four dropped in our trench. The enemy was seen working in front of his trenches at S.11.a.20.25. Fire was opened and work ceased.

Hammering was again heard in the enemy's front line about S.10.d.0.4.. A large number of flares were sent up from this

/area

P.T.O.

NEUVE CHAPELLE SECTION (Contd.)

area both from the 1st and 2nd lines. Sounds of work were also heard opposite S.10.4.

An aeroplane observer reports that dugouts and camouflage sheets can be plainly seen in BOIS DU BIEZ S.6.c. especially at the N. end. Movement was seen at LA RUSSE S.6.d.5.9. at 10.15 a.m.

MOATED GRANGE SECTION.

Germans have been seen opposite this section wearing soft caps, mostly with red bands round them. Some, however, had white and one black.

Two men were seen dropping down from trees close behind the enemy's front line at "Stand to" this morning. These are probably the snipers who have been worrying us lately at night. Their trees will be dealt with tonight.

A party of 5 men were seen at T.1.b.2.1. walking towards HT.POMMEREAU. A hostile T.M. fired from M.30.a.7.5. (about).

FAUQUISSART SECTION.

At 11.0 p.m. sounds of driving in of stakes was heard from N.14.a.8.5. Lewis gun fire was opened and it ceased. A M.T.M. is reported to fire from M.30.a.7.5. The woodwork screen at N.14.a.8.5. has been replaced after being shelled by us the day before.

A hose pipe can be seen over the parapet at N.13.c.93.48.

Birds are now often seen hovering over and moving about enemy front line at N.13.d.1.8. which confirms the belief that the apex of this salient is not occupied by day.

The enemy used a searchlight from the direction of ROUGES BANCS between 7.0 and 9.0 p.m.

Our Field guns have done considerable damage to BERTHA C.T.

A Gas Alert was proclaimed on our front at 8.30 p.m. All Units were informed, also the Division on our left. The Division on our right had previously ordered the same.

Head Qrs. 53th Divn.
16th November, 1916.

M C Heald
Captain,
Intelligence, General Staff.

56th DIVISIONAL TACTICAL PROGRESS REPORT No. 20
from 8.0 a.m. 16th to 8.0 a.m. 17th November, 1916.

PART I OPERATIONS

NEUVE CHAPELLE SECTION.

Our patrols were very active. An officers patrol investigated the snipers post reported at S.5.c.8.1. No trace could be found of this. A combative patrol of one officer and nine other ranks searched the area from SIGN POST LANE M.35.d.7.4., where the ground was very wet, to the "FIVE TREES" M.35.d.6½.0. where the ground was dry, and back again, but could find no sign of the enemy. A patrol examined the trench running from S.11.a.35.95. through S.11.a.4.7. to S.11.a.1.4. It is 3'6" deep, overgrown with grass and a foot of stagnant water in the bottom. Telephone wire was found leading to the trench S.11.a.1.5. where wire was found on 2.11.16.

Another patrol went out from S.10.c.8.4. and examined the German wire at S.10.d.0.3. It is waist high and thick. This patrol was fired at and bombs were thrown from the trench, but no casualties ensued.

Another small patrol left our line at S.10.d.4.8. and keeping the drain on their right proceeded to the German wire. The grass provides good cover for forty yards. The wire was in good condition and 15 yards deep with no gaps. Two sentries were firing, one thirty yards to the right and one twenty yards to the left of the drain.

Our Artillery carried out a Group concentration at 3.45 p.m. on S.11.b.22.05.

A working party at S.10.d.5.6. was dispersed by our Artillery at 10.15 a.m.

MOATED GRANGE SECTION.

Our T.Ms. were active shooting on the enemy's trenches at M.36.a.40.65, M.30.a.6.1. where much new woodwork was thrown in the air, and M.30.b.3.9. parapet damaged. The enemy retaliated with a few Light T.Ms. and rifle grenades. An officers patrol visited the Crater at M.36.c.0.9. and reported it unoccupied. It was thought that it is occasionally used as a listening post. The COLVIN Craters at M.30.c.2.0. was also found unoccupied. Other patrols could find no trace of the enemy.

One of our snipers killed a German about M.30.c.5.4. at 1.30 a.m.

FAUQUISSART SECTION.

At 2.0 p.m. our Artillery and T.Ms. co-operated in a shoot on enemy's trenches at N.19.a.35.65. Much damage was done, the parapet being breached in several places.

Our machine guns fired about 7,750 rounds on the enemy's communications during the night.

One of our patrols located a German working party repairing wire at M.24.d.8.4½. Lewis gun fire was turned on and the party dispersed.

PART II INTELLIGENCE.

NEUVE CHAPELLE SECTION.

Hostile T.Ms. were inactive, a few rounds falling behind S.10.6. A good deal of transport was heard last night. Horse transport was heard behind BOIS du BIEZ at 7.15pm. A sound which suggested a caterpillar tractor was heard at the same place.

At 11.0 a.m. a German appeared behind the first line opposite S.10.2. Twelve men were seen on the road at T.25.a.65.40, moving North at 12.50 p.m. At 1.25 a small party was noticed near LORGIES carrying timber. At 3.15 p.m., 12 men passed down C.T. at S.17.a.45.55. to front line. At 3.30 p.m. movement was seen at S.11.d.5.6. and S.10.d.3.5. Two men were seen to leave

/ruined

- 2 -

ruined house at S.6.a.9.8. carrying planks, disappearing into the trench at M.36.c.85.15. This house may possible be a dump, but it is also suspected to be an O.P.

MOATED GRANGE SECTION.

A considerable amount of work is going on in the enemy's trench about M.36.a.3.5. Men were seen carrying boards along the front line to this point.
A man was seen to leave the O.P. in the tree at N.31.d.3.0.
Some timber in one of the craters about M.30.a.central was set alight by one of our Very lights; it burned with a crackling noise for some minutes.
The enemy snipers have ceased work in this section.

FAUQUISSART SECTION.

At 11.0 am., the enemy shelled our O.P. at N.13.a.9.9. with 4.2's, of which many were blind.
A loophole has been located at N.14.a.8.4. A M.G. appeared to fire from here on to our aircraft.
Enemy is busy repairing his support line.
At 11.34 a man was seen to leave the HAYSTACK O.P. at N.21.d.4.2. and walk to road at N.21.d.9.35. which is screened.
On several occasions three of four men were seen in new C.T. at N.20.b.3.6., but no actual work was seen in progress.

T.C.Heald

Hdqrs. 56th Divn.
13th November, 1916.

Captain,
Intelligence, General Staff.

56th DIVISIONAL TACTICAL PROGRESS REPORT No. 21,
from 8. 0 a.m. 17th November to 8. 0. a.m. 18th November.

PART 1 OPERATIONS.

NEUVE CHAPELLE SECTION.

An Officers' patrol set out to investigate hostile wire about S.11.a.22. but owing to the ice cracking they were discovered. they got back safely. A later patrol examined the German wire at S.11.a.15.15; it was found to be 20 yards deep 2.6" high, and it runs up to the parapet. Another patrol reconnoitred the wire opposite S.10.3. No gap could be found. Another patrol found the German wire at S.11.a.05.07. in good condition. The ground between the lines affords easy going. A patrol of two men worked out to the SEVEN SISTERS - S.5.c.7.0. thence left to the German wire. They found a T shaped trench running out about 100 yards from the main trench. They located a wiring party and a hostile patrol, so they returned quickly with this information and Lewis guns dealt with these parties.

Our L.T.Ms. bombarded the trench junction S.5.b.7.85. Several dug-outs being reported as damaged. Our M.T.Ms. carried out a shoot on M.35.d.8.2. and S.5.d.35.44. Duckboards and timber were thrown up.

MOATED GRANGE SECTION

Officers patrols visited DUCKS BILL (M.36.c.0.9.) COLVIN and MAUQUISSART (M.30.a.2.0.) Craters, and inspected the enemy wire S. of DUCKS BILL. These patrols saw no signs of the enemy and were not fired upon in spite of the noise made in moving about over the ice.

Another patrol located a hostile wiring party at M.30.b.2.8. On their return Lewis gun fire was opened.

The enemy's wire opposite ERITH STREET (M.24.d.5.5.) was examined and found to be low and in bad repair. One of our snipers claim to have killed a man on the right sub-section.

Our T.Ms. co-operated in bombarding the enemy's trench about M.36.c.00.55. to M.33.c.20.85. An Officers' patrol examined the wire at this point later and reported considerable damage. Our Lewis guns and L.T.Ms. kept up an intermittent fire during the night on the damaged parts.

A small explosion was heard at 9.0 p.m. which may have been an enemy grenade store. Our M.Gs. were very active in harrasing the enemy during the night.

FAUQUISSART SECTION.

Our patrols were out covering the whole front but beyond locating a covering party who were then dispersed by our Lewis guns and a small patrol who hurriedly withdrew, they had nothing to report.

Our T.Ms. co-operated with the artillery in shooting on to enemy lines about N.14.a.75.30, considerable damage being done and the tramway destroyed for about 100 yards.

Our M.Gs. expended nearly 8,000 rounds on selected targets behind the enemy's lines, including an aeroplane.

PART 11 INTELLIGENCE.

NEUVE CHAPELLE SECTION.

Several men in small parties were seen to leave the front line trench at S.5.b.85.25 and double along behind the parados for 20 yards before re-entering the trench which appears to be impassable. The men were wearing equipment and carried rifles.

/Four

P.T.O.

2.

NEUVE CHAPELLE SECTION (Contd.)

Four small parties were soon walking across the open from HT. POMMEREAU towards HALPE GARBE. Movement was seen between BOIS DE BIEZ and the second line at S.5.b.9.3. and on the track at S.6.b.3.1.

In reply to our bombardment 8 rounds from a hostile H.T.M. were fired on the end of CHURCH ST. which was blocked. At 4.p.m. there was some hostile activity with 77 mms. and M.T.Ms. on the extreme right.

A patrol of 7 men was encountered near the SEVEN SISTERS in S.11.a. Work was seen in progress outside LES FRULOT. Four men were seen pushing a trolly load of timber near LA RUSEE.

Shortly after 4. 0 p.m. a brilliant light was seen far back in the BOIS DE BIEZ, it disappeared possibly into a dug-out about S.6.c.90.35. Smoke was seen continuously issuing from house at S.17.a.85.70. Movement was seen on the road running N.W. from FME DU BIEZ.

MOATED GRANGE SECTION.

Opposite the right sub-section a man was again seen wearing a helmet with figure 10 marked on the cover. Other men wearing soft caps with red bands were also seen. A hostile M.G. from due East of the DUCKS BILL fired on one of our wiring parties without causing casualties.

Opposite the left sub-section there was more hostile rifle and M.G. fire than usual during the night.

A M.G. emplacement is reported at M.36.c.1.6.

Movement was observed between the East end of DA C.T. at N.31.c.95.20 and the road at N.31.d.10.15.

FAUQUISSART SECTION.

Puffs of smoke were seen coming from house at N.21.b.0.1. and it is thought that some kind of engine was working there. New work has been done on BERTHA TRENCH at N.14.c.3.3.

A party carrying planks was seen to leave trench at N.21.d. 5.3. and walk in a westerly direction.

At 2.10 p.m. smoke was seen as from a train moving S.W. on AUBERS - FROMELLES Railway. It is thought that this may have been from an engine of some kind on the road as no train could be seen. At 4.5. p.m. smoke, which appeared to be from a stationary engine was seen near FROMELLES STATION.

The N.E. face of IRMA C.T. has been repaired at N.14.b.0.2.

New work is visible on C.T. at N.14.c.25.65., also at N.13.d.2.2.

Wooden screen in rear of the front line at N.14.b.2.9. has been repaired. Woodwork is being erected along the line from N.14.a.35.20. to N.14.a.9.5. Hostile aircraft was active but in most cases returned to their own line on being engaged by our A.A. guns and M.Guns.

Captain,
Intelligence, General Staff.

Head Qrs. 56th Divn.
18.11.16.

56th DIVISIONAL TACTICAL PROGRESS REPORT No. 22
from 8.0 a.m., 18th to 8.0 a.m., 19th November, 1916.

PART I OPERATIONS.

NEUVE CHAPELLE SECTION.

Our patrols were very active last night, especial attention being paid to the enemy's wire. From S.16.a.5.7½. to about 100 yards N. of that point it was found to be ten to fifteen yards deep and fairly thick, no gaps could be found. At S.10.d.08.42., where a gap was suspected, the patrol saw a man throw a few coils of loose wire into position and run back to the trench. This point will be examined in daylight. At S.10.d.55.70. it was found to be thick and no gaps could be discovered. A contact patrol patrolled the area in front of S..10.1. and S.10.2. between the drains running towards the German lines. They went up to his wire, but did not meet any opposition. A patrol went along the right hand side of the road to the ruined houses at S.11.a.75.90. but heard no sounds of occupation although they lay out for an hour. They heard the tramway being used at the rear of the re-entrant. Patrol suits were worn and found very useful.

A patrol proceeded along the right of the LA BASSEE Road to the German wire about S.11.a.2.2. They heard a tramway being used and the sound suggested it ran just behind the front line.

A contact patrol covered the ground in front of S.5.2. along to S.5.5. The going was bad and they found the ditch running from S.5.b.50.25 to S.5.c.6.6. with willows on the bank, a serious obstacle. They were forced to wade through waist deep. No sign of the enemy was encountered.

Our M.T.Ms. searched the German front line from S.5.d.5.9. to S.5.b.70.35. Wire and trench were damaged, a floor board being seen in the air. The L.T.Ms. brought a cross fire to bear on the front line from S.11.a.05.15. to the LA BASSEE Road. The high wire made accurate shooting difficult, but most of the shots were well placed and much damage was done. Our M.Gs. showed their usual activity.

MOATED GRANGE SECTION.

An officers patrol when approaching the enemy's wire about M.36.c.0.7. had some bombs thrown at them, but took no casualties. Another patrol was examing the ditch which leaves our line at M.36.a.0.9., When they got close to the enemy's sap at M.30.c.4.0. a bell was heard to ring and a light was put up. From half way down the sap. A M.G. from about M.36.a.4.9. immediately opened fire. Our patrol waited for the enemy for 20 minutes, but he did not come out. Our patrol returned with casualties.

Patrols from our left subsection located enemy wiring parties which were fired on by our Lewis guns. Our snipers hit one of three men who were crossing the field about M.36.a.2.9. Our M.T.Ms. damaged the enemy's parapet at M.36.a.57.57 and M.36.a.4.32., whilst our L.T.Ms. in co-operation with machine guns fired 210 rounds at M.24.d.4.0. A gap was blown in the parapet and the wire badly damaged. Lewis gun fire was directed on these points during the night. Slight retaliation.

FAUQUISSART SECTION.

Our patrols report enemy's wire very bad, in places only patches of wire found 15 to 20 yards apart, and no sign of life in the enemy first line.

Our T.Ms. in co-operation with the Artillery considerably damaged with their fire the enemy's front and support lines at N.14.a.90.57. and N.14.b.0.65. Our L.T.Ms. in addition further destroyed the WICK SALIENT at N.13.c.05.

/ PART II.

PART II INTELLIGENCE.

NEUVE CHAPELLE SECTION.

S.5.c.3.0.   The hostile T.Ms. retaliated energetically with M.T.Ms. on HUN St, and LANSDOWNE St. (S.10.b.7.2) and the the front line between, but only obtain two direct hits and no casualties.

Much movement was seen; the enemy is/working hard to repair damages and clear drains.

At 1.0 p.m., a green flare which burst into two green lights was fired from S.10.d.00.30. (Approximately). This was immediately followed by two others. After a moment's pause, a small shrapnel shell burst over S.10.1. trench, evidently a test. At 2.0 a.m., a red light was sent up from the same place. No action followed.

MOATED GRANGE SECTION.

The enemy retaliated to our T.M. shoot with some rifle grenades. A few 77 mm. shells fell on RUE TILLELOY about M.23.d.8.2. No casualties. The enemy were reported to be working in the crater at M.33.c.15.90. between 5 and 6 p.m.

Two red lights were put up opposite our right battalion during the night, but no action ensued.

Smoke was seen issuing from house at N.26.d.7.7. Four men all carrying sacks walked across the open from trench at N.26.c.35.80. to hedge at N.26.c.20.15. Two men were seen examing the wire at N.32.c.40.95.

FAUQUISSART SECTION.

Enemy's T.Ms. and Artillery showed some activity; a few light shells falling about N.8.c.5.4. At 9.0 a.m. an enemy M.G. opened fire from N.13.c.85.15. This spot was afterwards bombarded by T.Ms. and M.G. has not fired since. A motor horn was heard from DE LA PORTE FARM N.15.a.6.6. at 9.45 p.m.

Smoke seen rising from N.13.d.2.4. and second line at N.13.d.92.52.

Hdqrs. 56th Divn.

19th November, 1916.

T.C.Heald
Captain,
Intelligence, General Staff.

56th DIVISIONAL TACTICAL PROGRESS REPORT No.23.
from 8.0 a.m. 19th to 8.0 a.m. 20th November, 1916.

PART I OPERATIONS.

FAUQUISSART SECTION.

Our T.Ms. co-operated in bombarding the enemy's defences at N.14.b.1.7. and N.14.b.1.8. about 4.0 p.m. Much material damage was caused. Our M.Gs. during the night, fired on to the portions damaged.

One of our patrols discovered a track leading through the enemy wire at N.19.a.3½.3½., but there was no obvious gap. Other patrols found no sign of the enemy.

We carried out some concerted bursts of rapid fire along the whole front line. The enemy replied with M.Gs. firing from N.13.c.9½.3. and N.19.a.3.4. on to our right sub-section.

MOATED GRANGE SECTION.

Our T.Ms. did considerable damage to enemy trenches at M.36.a.5.2½, M.36.a.5.2. and M.24.d.4.0. This brought more retaliation than usual but little damage was done.

At 5.25 a.m. this morning 100 rounds L.T.M. were fired on WINCHESTER CRATERS at M.30.a.60.85 and M.30.a.40.45 followed by 100 rounds (air bursts) over enemy front line behind those points. Rapid rifle fire also was opened. The enemy made no retaliation.

Our M.Gs. sprayed the enemy's communications very liberally last night, nearly 8000 rounds being fired.

An Officers' patrol saw a small hostile patrol near the northern-most COLVIN Crater N.30.c.25.25. In attempting to cut off this patrol our party was seen by the enemy who threw a bomb at them and ran away our patrol being unable to overtake them. Another patrol located a large working party at M.36.c.20.75. which was then dispersed by Lewis and Machine Gun fire. Another patrol reported work in progress on Crater at M.30.a.3.5.4.

NEUVE CHAPELLE SECTION.

A fighting patrol left our lines at S.11.a.17.70 walked towards the LA BASSEE Road and turned along it to the German wire. Then they turned to the left and reached point S.11.a.40.35 when the wire turned sharply away to the East. They suspected a listening post here but after listening for two hours they found no sign so returned. The wire was good and no gaps could be found.

Another fighting patrol reached the enemy wire at S.10.d.9.9. Footsteps were heard in the trench, also a pump which squeaked. The wire was examined for 40 yards to the left and found to be good, going right back to the parapet.

Another fighting patrol reported the German wire S.10.d.15.45 to S.10.d.35.55. to be 15 yards deep consisting of a curtain wire in front about 3 ft high with a thick low entanglement behind which reached to the parapet. A pump was heard working at S.10.d.3.5.

A further fighting patrol found a gap in the enemy's wire at M.35.d.8.3. They then patrolled down the wire to the South as far as S.5.b.7.9. At M.35.d.85.30 a new bit of apron entanglement was found. An officer and another man got through and found the wire beyond to be about 3.6" high and 30 ft. deep, largely concertina barbed wire. Many large holes were found caused by our T.Ms. and at S.5.b.70.95. it was possible to crawl through to the borrow pit. No signs of the enemy were seen and the trench was quiet..

Our T.Ms. carried out a combined shoot on enemy's line from S.5.d.25.35 to S.5.d.8.0. Much damage was done, floor boards being seen in the air. During the night Lewis Guns fired on the damage.

P.T.O. /PART II.

PART II INTELLIGENCE.

NEUVE CHAPELLE SECTION.

During the afternoon hostile T.T.Ms., 77 mm. guns and rifle grenades bombarded our front line for half an hour obtaining several direct hits.

Movement was observed round LA TOURELLE (S.17.a.87.60.) and N.E. of BOIS DU BIEZ where a party was seen working on trolly tracks. Work has been done on the enemy's parapet opposite trench b.10.5.

A M.G. was located firing from S.11.a.15.15. Our Artillery were informed. Four rounds were fired and the M.G. ceased.

MOATED GRANGE SECTION.

At 3.45 p.m. about 10 men were seen near the Shrine at N.20.c.35.92. carrying white bags. This was reported to our artillery who opened fire and dispersed the party.

Another party was seen walking behind the screens on the AUBERS - BAS POMMEREAU Road towards AUBERS.

The enemy was working hard on his front line opposite the right sub-section during the night, and two of his wiring parties were dispersed by M.G. and L.G. fire. Enemy snipers were more active than usual yesterday. A Sally Port has been located at M.36.a.35.60 and a distinct path can be seen leading from this spot.

There was some hostile artillery retaliation on the front of the right Sub-section in reply to our T.M. fire.

FAUQUISSART SECTION.

Movement was seen at several points especially near the house at N.21.b.0.1., in C.T. North of and parallel to BERTHA C.T. at N.20.b.34.66. This trench was fired on by our artillery and damaged considerably. Two men were seen on track in N.21.d. and two others wearing long grey overcoats and peak caps walked over the open from N.20.a.85.65 to N.20.b.1.2. Smoke was seen issuing from the dug-out chimney in the hedge at N.20.b.1.4. also from houses at N.27.a.40.05.- N.21.c.20.45.

Early this morning transport was heard on the LE PIETRE Road. A German sniper was located firing from N.13.d.1.7. during the night.

Sounds of pumping were heard in the WICK SALIENT (N.13.d)

A small white flag flying from a black and white pole can be seen at the S.W. end of AUBERS in N.26.c.

Head Qrs. 56th Divn.

20th November, 1916.

Captain,
Intelligence, General Staff.

56th DIVISIONAL TACTICAL PROGRESS REPORT No. 24,
from 8.0 a.m. 20th November to 8.0 a.m. 21st November, 1916.

PART 1 OPERATIONS.

NEUVE CHAPELLE SECTION.

One of our patrols moved out along the left side of the LA BASSEE Road - S.11.a.0.3. for about 80 yards, and then went half left to enemy's wire. A hostile wiring party about 15 strong was soon so our patrol remained in position hoping to get a prisoner. The enemy fired several Very lights from his trench and on each occasion the wiring party lay down. On return of their patrol, Lewis Gun fire was opened and it is thought good results were obtained.

Other patrols examined the German wire at S.10.c.95.35., S.10.c.9.0. and at S.10.d.5.8. It was reported good and no gap could be found. The ditch running from S.10.c.7.3. to S.16.a.0.9. can be crossed at any point.

An officers patrol searched the ground between the lines in S.5.d. for two hours, but encountered no one. Work on the parapet at S.5.d.35.35. could be heard. The going was good.

Our M.Gs. fired on the enemys dumps, tracks and railways during the night.

MOATED GRANGE SECTION.

Our L.T.Ms. fired about 200 rounds during the afternoon on prearranged targets. Slight enemy retaliation.

An officers patrol examined No. 3 DUCKS BILL CRATER M.36.a.1½.0. It was unoccupied but heavily wired. There was a gap in the wire at the Northern end. A standing patrol occupied the COLVIN CRATER M.30.c.2½.0. all night and had nothing to report. WINCHESTER CRATER M.30.a. central was patrolled and found unoccupied: most of them are dry except the most Northerly. Ground between the Crater and the enemy's wire is fairly good going. Another patrol examined the ground round the Crater at M.24.d.3.2. It was very wet and flooded. The Crater is believed to be unoccupied.

FAUQUISSART SECTION.

Our T.Ms. co-operated in firing on the enemys lines at N.14.b.2.9., N.14.b.30.95. and N.13.c.85.70. Much damage was done, but the retaliation was slight.

An officers patrol reported that there is no wire between N.13.d.3.6. and N.13.d.½.3. unless it be concealed in the ditch. This part of the line appeared to be held by one M.G. at N.13.d.1.6.

The enemy's wire between N.13.d.0.4. and N.19.a.3.8. is reported to be fairly strong. A working party was heard about N.13.d.7.7. and fired on Organised bursts of rifle and Lewis Gun fire at morning and evening "stand to" only drew reply from one M.G. firing from about N.8.d.3.0.

PART II INTELLIGENCE.

NEUVE CHAPELLE SECTION.

The hostile T.Ms. were more active than usual. A "minnie" which fired from S.11.c.45.15. was silenced by our artillery.
The following parties were seen:-
8.30 a.m. baling party at S.16.a.8.8.
9.15 a.m. three men at S.17.b.25.90.
10.35 a.m. five men at S.11.c.3.6.
10.15 a.m. two men at S.17.b.10.85.
10.30 a.m. A party at S.17.b.3.9. carrying timber and dugout frames.

Several small parties at S.23.b.8.3.
11.45 a.m. man walking on fire stop at S.5.b.8.7.
1.55 p.m. six men walked in the FERME du BOIS.
3.0 p.m. man at S.11.a.43. wearing a woollen cap
11.45 movement at S.5.b.5.1.
/Much

- 2 -

Much work and movement was observed round LA RUSSE. A searchlight was seen behind BOIS DE BIEZ, coloured lights were being used.

MOATED GRANGE SECTION.

At 4.0 p.m. three men were seen working in the trench at M.30.c.6.2. A pump was heard working here at midnight.

At 12.15 p.m. a party of six men were seen to walk slowly from AUBERS CLUMP at N.28.d. to BAS POMMEREAU.

Movement was seen on the edge of the H.T. POMMEREAU Wood at MT.1.b.25.90. and also one man was seen for a few moments looking over parapet of second line at M.30.b.2.5. holding a white object.

FAUQUISSART SECTION.

Hostile M.Gs. were observed to fire from N.13.d.4.3. and N.13.d.4.4. at 11.30 p.m.

New wire has been erected at N.14.a.8.5. and patrols report that much of the enemy wire is now.

Much fresh earth is visible on AUBERS Defences at N.26.d.25.90. Three long mounds, probably possibly dug-outs can be seen at N.26.c.75.65.

Four men were seen looking at our trenches and frequently pointing at them from N.26.d.32.95.

A man was seen using the O.P. at N.27.a.8.3.

Several wires are seen to meet on an upright pole close to dug-out at N.20.b.30.55. - a suspected H.Q. Smoke was seen issuing from its chimney.

The FARM de la FAVEILLE in N.22.d. is suspected as a H.Q. as a small flag can be seen flying at entrance.

There is a suspected O.P. at N.27.a.4.6. in a tree.

A green mound can be seen at the foot, possibly a dug-out.

Smoke was seen from dug-out at N.20.b.3.6., small chimney at N.2?.c.45.50. and AUBERS Defences at N.26.d.05.85.

Hdqrs. 56th Divn.

21st November, 1916.

Captain,

Intelligence, General Staff.

58th DIVISIONAL TACTICAL PROGRESS REPORT No. 25,
from 8.0 a.m. 21st November to 8.0 a.m. 22nd November '16

PART 1 OPERATIONS.

NEUVE CHAPELLE SECTION.

Our patrols were active along the whole front. The enemy's wire at S.10.d.35.50 is about 12 yards deep and 5 feet high. There is good cover in shell holes at this point. No signs of the enemy were seen opposite the right sub-section.

A patrol from the left sub-section left our line at M.35.d.3.1. with a view to reconnoitring the enemy's wire. On approaching the wire a German working party was seen repairing it protected by two strong covering parties. Our patrol was too small to engage the enemy so withdrew, and directed Lewis Gun fire on the point where work was in progress.

Our L.T.Ms. fired 100 rounds on the German trenches - S.10.d.55.80 and S.10.d.95.85. Good results and several direct hits were obtained.

Our M.T.Ms. cut a gap in the enemy's wire at S.10.d.07.40 and caused considerable damage to wire about S.10.c.95.70.

Machine Guns sprayed enemy's tramways and roads during the night.

MOATED GRANGE SECTION.

A patrol which went out through No. 3 MAUQUISSART CRATER saw a patrol of about 4 of the enemy which withdrew. Patrols which examined the enemy's wire found it strong round the crater at M.24.d.3.2. The front line appeared to be unoccupied and Very lights were being sent up from the second line. The Craters in M.30.a. were visited and found unoccupied.

Parties working on the enemy's wire at M.30.c.50.97 and M.30.b.1.3. were dispersed by our Lewis Gun fire. Our L.T.Ms. fired with good effect on the enemy's trenches opposite the left Sub-section. The German L.T.Ms. replied slightly.

FAUQUISSART SECTION.

At 9.0 p.m. one of our patrols heard an enemy working party driving in stakes about M.14.a.7.4. A covering party was also seen. The patrol returned and reported the position of the enemy, who was then dispersed with Lewis Gun fire. Our L.T.Ms. co-operated with M.T.Ms. causing damage to the enemy's parapet and throwing up stakes, coils of wire and trench boards. There was no hostile retaliation.

Organised shoots of rapid rifle fire and Lewis Gun fire were carried out in both sub-sections at morning and evening "Stand to".

PART 11 INTELLIGENCE.

NEUVE CHAPELLE SECTION.

Hostile H.T.Ms. fired on both sub-sections during the afternoon. M.T.Ms. and L.T.Ms. retaliated on the right-sub-section for our bombardment.

At 6.35 p.m. and 6.40 p.m. red lights were sent up by the enemy opposite the centre of the right sub-section. Star shells bursting into rain were fired at the same time. Opposite trenches S.10.5 and 7 the enemy was firing lights from his second line. A few rounds of light shrapnel were fired over OXFORD ST. about S.5.c. during the afternoon.

/MOATED GRANGE SECTION.

P.T.O.

PART II INTELLIGENCE (Contd.)

MOATED GRANGE SECTION.

A new loophole has been located at M.24.d.55.20. Hostile M.Gs. fired a few high bursts of fire during the night. A few T.M rounds fell near ERITH POST M.24.d.75.95 during the afternoon.

FAUQUISSART SECTION.

A few rounds 77 mms. fell between RUE TILLELOY and RUE BACQUEROT in the right sub-section at 7.30 p.m. also some H.E. about N.14.a.3.7.

A hostile M.G. is reported to have fired during the night from N.14.b.05.80.

The enemy's tramway was heard working in rear of the SUGAR LOAF.

Very lights continue to be fired from the enemy's support line by night.

Our T.Ms. appear to have pierced the roof a dug-out at N.13.d.0.5. Jagged edges of sheet iron and several logs can be seen at this point.

GENERAL.

Observation beyond the German front line was very difficult on 21st owing to the thick mist.

On receipt of current copy of Divisional Tactical Progress Report in the trenches, previous copy to be destroyed.

Head Qrs. 56th Divn.
22nd November, 1916.

Captain,
Intelligence, General Staff.

56th DIVISIONAL TACTICAL PROGRESS REPORT No. 26.
from 8.0 a.m., 22nd November to 8.0 a.m. 23rd November, 1916.

PART I OPERATIONS.

NEUVE CHAPELLE SECTION.

A Bangalore torpedo was successfully exploded in the enemy's wire at M.35.d.3.1. The enemy opened a little rifle fire when the explosion took place. A patrol which left our lines at S.5.c.6.6. reconnoitred towards the SEVEN SISTERS - S.11.a.8.3. without finding any trace of the enemy. The going is good for 150 yards from our trench, after which there are a number of large shell holes full of water.
Our Artillery engaged a hostile T.M. and checked movement on the LA BASSEE Road near the DISTILLERY.
During the day and night, our M.Gs. fired on enemy's dumps, C.Ts. and tramways; also on LA TOURELLE cross roads.

MOATED GRANGE SECTION.

No signs of the enemy were seen by our patrols who thoroughly reconnoitred NO MAN'S LAND and the various crater systems. The route to the WINCHESTER Craters in M.30.a. is difficult and wet with much loose wire lying about.
L.T.Ms. fired on the enemy trenches and a snipers post at M.24.d.5½.2. during the day and on M.30.b.1.4., where work was in progress on night 21/22nd, during the night
Our M.Gs. were active during the night firing over 4,000 rounds on various points behind the enemy's line.
One of our snipers caused a German behind the front line opposite left sub-section to cease work.

FAUQUISSART SECTION.

A patrol from the right subsection reports a path leading through the enemy's wire from a SALLY PORT at N.19.a.3.1. where the wire is weak. A patrol from the left subsection located an enemy working party at N.8.d.4.3. The patrol returned at once and directed M.G. fire on the enemy who was dispersed.
L.T.Ms. fired on enemy's defences about N.13.d.1.6. (where an M.G. emplacement is suspected) Also E. & S.W. of the SUGAR LOAF. Much wood and corrugated iron was thrown up and the breastwork damaged. Our M.Gs. fired over 8,000 rounds between dusk and dawn

PART II INTELLIGENCE.

NEUVE CHAPELLE SECTION.

Parties were seen on the LA BASSE Road in S.17.d. and S.23.d. wearing marching order. Movement was seen at S.6.b.15.85. and at the dump S.23.b.35.70. A party was heard working on the enemy's wire about S.10.d.0.3½. Our Lewis guns kept up bursts of fire on this point during the night. At 6.0 p.m. nine red lights breaking into "rain" were again seen on our right. No action appeared to follow, A German using field glasses over the parapet at S.16.a.63.78. was fired at and got down. Dummies were put up at S.13.a.60.70. for 15 minutes and then withdrawn.
Four men wearing white fatigue dress were seen to walk from the ruins at S.6.a.65.50. to the ruins at S.6.a.75.60.

MOATED GRANGE SECTION.

In reply to our L.T.M. shoot the enemy fired a number of aerial torpedoes and H.T.M. shells on the front of the right subsection. All fell very short of or well over our trenches. During the night more aerial torpedoes were fired into and S of MAUQUISSART Craters M.30.c.20.25. A hostile T.M. is reported to have been firing from M.24.d.53.20. Pumping was heard in the German lines about M.30.c.6.1. This spot was kept under bursts of fire during the night.

Hostile M.Gs. fired occasional bursts during the night. A gun opposite the left subsection was firing from the German second line, shots going high over our trenches. Three men were soon outside the house at N.28.c.8.3. Smoke was soon rising from trench at M.30.a.95.55.

FAUQUISSART SECTION.

A few T.M. shells fell in NO MANS LAND in front of the extreme right of the section during the afternoon and early morning. An hostile M.G. fired occasional bursts from WICK Salient N.13.d.20.54. during the night. At 6.30 p.m. a train was heard in the direction of FROMELLES. A working party seen at N.8.d.4.3. was dispersed by M.G. fire.

Very lights were being sent up from N.14.a.80.45. during the night.

Movement was seen in BERTHA Trench at N.14.c.45.10.

Hdqrs. 56th Divn.

23rd November, 1916.

Captain,
Intelligence, General Staff.

56th DIVISIONAL TACTICAL PROGRESS REPORT No. 27
from 8.0 a.m. November 23rd to 8.0 a.m. November 24th.

On receipt of current copy of Divisional Tactical Progress Report in the trenches, previous copy to be destroyed.

PART 1 OPERATIONS.

NEUVE CHAPELLE SECTION.

Patrols found no sign of the enemy. An old trench or snipers post was found where the ditch meets the enemy's wire about S.10.d.91.81.

From 1.0 p.m. to 4.0 p.m. a prearranged bombardment with Artillery and T.Ms. was carried out on the enemy's trenches and communications. Our guns engaged hostile T.Ms. which retaliated. During this shoot our L.T.Ms. fired 400 rounds on S.10.c.96.22 and S.10.d.00.35 with excellent results. Large quantities of wire were destroyed while planks and stakes were blown back into our own trenches. During the afternoon M.Gs. fired on enemy's dumps, communications and O.P. at S.12.c.½.2. Lewis Guns fired on the spot where we exploded a Bangalore Torpedo during night 22/23rd.

MOATED GRANGE SECTION.

One of our patrols found an enemy's patrol opposite the CHORD in M.29.b. The enemy withdrew on our approach and fire was opened from his trenches. Enemy's wire round the BIRDCAGE M.30.a.4.5 is reported good and without gaps.

Patrol from the right sub-section found the CRATER at M.33.c.1½.8. heavily wired and occupied by the enemy.

In the left sub-section three T.M. shoots were carried out in conjunction with rifle and M.G. fire. Wire was cut from M.24.d.4.0 to M.24.d.6.3., in front of the Crater at M.24.d.3.1., the trench in rear of this crater was also damaged.

A further 200 rounds L.T.M. were fired along the enemy's front line (traversing fire) from M.33.a.4.0. to M.33.c.2.7. There was no retaliation except some fire from snipers in reply to our Machine Guns.

FAUQUISSART SECTION.

The only enemy seen by our patrols was a working party at N.14.a.95.50. which was dispersed with Lewis Gun fire. A small raiding party of three officers and 27 O.Rs. left our lines at N.13.d.5.9. at midnight and entered the enemy's trenches about N.13.d.½.5½. The trenches were searched for about 150 yards to the East and 150 yards to the S.W. from the point of entry, but no enemy were seen or heard. The trenches were in a very bad condition, being full of mud and water, revetment broken down and no fire stops to be seen. A snipers post was found at the point of entry, built into the parapet. It was constructed of wood, corrugated iron and sandbags. An old M.G. emplacement was found about 10 yards S.W. of the point of entry facing N.E. It was built of stout beams and provided with overhead cover of sandbags. Both of these positions were in a bad state of repair, and were further damaged by our party. After 1 hour the party withdrew. The German wire was practically non-existent and presented no obstacle. The enemy was firing Very lights from his second line.

Our T.Ms. damaged the enemy's parapet at N.13.d.1.6. during the afternoon. Our M.Gs. were active during the night.

/ PART II INTELLIGENCE.

P.T.O.

PART II INTELLIGENCE.

NEUVE CHAPELLE SECTION.

Hostile Artillery co-operated with T.Ms. in reply to our T.M. bombardment. Three shells reported to be 5.9" fell in HUN STREET. About 60 H.T.M. bombs were fired mostly on the right sub-section, M.T.Ms, aerial torpedoes co-operated. The enemy was quickly silenced by our artillery. Movement was seen at L'AVENTURE and MT.POMMEREAU. Flares were fired behind the enemy's lines at 10.0 p.m. and 12.15 a.m. No action was observed. A hostile aeroplane flew over our lines at 4 p.m.

Hostile M.Gs. fired on our aeroplanes during the day.

A man was seen looking over the German second line at S.T. b.9.9.

MOATED GRANGE SECTION.

Opposite the right subsection a man was seen at M.36.c.2.7. wearing a dark blue tunic with brass buttons and an old blue peaked cap. He was hit by our snipers. Activity of hostile artillery and T.Ms. was normal. The left subsection report enemy sending up more Very lights than usual during the night. Movement was seen at MIN DUPIETRE M.30.d.85.85.

FAUQUISSART SECTION.

Hostile artillery was slightly more active than usual, a number of rounds being blinds. A hostile M.T.M. is suspected to have fired from N.19.c.02.64.; the rounds fell short of our trenches.

Hostile M.Gs. are reported to have fired from N.14.a.8.5. and N.14.c.5.9.

A train was heard in FROMELLES Station at 7.30 p.m.

A party seen working on tramways at N.14.c.5.5. was dispersed. Several men were seen on track in N.21.a.55.35. A man was seen to walk from the direction of LE CLERCQ FARM and inspect the trenches at N.21.d. and N.27.b. after which he disappeared into the trench at N.21.d.3.1.

The following points are suspected to be living places:-
House in AUBERS N.26.d.45.30. a
Suspected dug-out at N.26.d.15.30.
House in AUBERS N.27.a.55.15.
House in AUBERS N.21.b.28.12.

A small white wind vane on a pole is visible about N.27.a.4.1. at 1.30 p.m. large clouds of white smoke were seen from direction of AUBERS Station and later a whistle resembling that of an engine was heard from the same point. At 10.0 a.m. an enemy observation balloon ascended from the direction of BAS POMMEREAU. It descended after half an hour.

Thick black smoke was seen rising from chimney at N.23.c.15.55.

(signed)

Hdqrs. 58th Divn.   Captain,

24th November, 1916.   Intelligence, General Staff.

56th DIVISIONAL TACTICAL PROGRESS REPORT No. 28.
from 8.0 a.m. 24th November to 8.0 a.m. 25th November, 1916.

(On receipt of current copy of Divisional Tactical Progress Report in the trenches, previous copy to be destroyed).

PART I OPERATIONS.

NEUVE CHAPELLE SECTION.

A patrol which left our lines at trench S.10.5. to examine a suspected trench at S.10.b.81.92. was unable to reach its objective owing to a party working on German wire. This party could not be fired on from our trenches owing to our own working parties being out. Patrol reports the going to be good in NO MANS LAND. Another patrol examined enemy's wire from S.5.b.45.20. to M.35.d.3.1. and reports it to be thick with a trip wire in front of the main entanglement. The cart full of sandbags at S.5.b.40.05. was examined and showed no signs of being used by the enemy.

During the afternoon our Artillery and T.Ms. carried out a bombardment programme of the enemy's trenches, communications, dumps, tramways and second line positions. The BOIS DU BIEZ was throughly searched. Shooting was good and much damage was caused. H.T.Ms. obtained six direct hits about S.5.d.5.6. and M.T.Ms. cut wire at S.10.d.05.35. and S.10.c.95.25. Our machine guns fired during the morning and afternoon.

MOATED GRANGE SECTION.

A patrol from the left company, left subsection, reports that enemy's front line opposite this point appears to be uninhabited. Another patrol located an enemy working party which was fired on with M.Gs. and Lewis guns and dispersed. A patrol which went out later reported that work had ceased. WINCHESTER Craters M.30.a. were examined and found unoccupied. No enemy patrols were encountered.

Our T.Ms. were active during the day. Snipers post at M.30.c.55.92. was demolished and suspected T.M. emplacement at M.24.d.53.20. was bombarded with 50 rounds L.T.M. A small bomb store is thought to have been blown up opposite the left subsection as one burst was followed by several explosions. During the night short bursts of fire were opened on M.30.b.2.8. to prevent repair of damage caused in the afternoon.

FAUQUISSART SECTION.

No enemy were seen or encountered by our patrols. During the evening several salvoes of 18-pdrs. were fired on enemy's front line between N.14.b.0.7. and N.14.a.8.3. Our T.Ms. and rifle grenades engaged targets in the enemy's front line about the DEVILS JUMP N.19.a. and SUGAR LOAF N.8.d. damaging and breaking down the parapet in several places. Hostile retaliation was slight. Our M.Gs. fired at intervals during the night searching the enemy's front line, wire, C.Ts. roads roads and cross-roads.

PART II INTELLIGENCE.

NEUVE CHAPELLE SECTION.

Hostile artillery was again more active than usual, a number of rounds 77 mm. being fired at NEUVE CHAPELLE and C.Ts. in the right subsection. Hostile T.Ms. retaliated freely to our bombardment, most of the bombs falling about S.5.b.1.5. Hostile M.Gs. fired on our aeroplanes, one gun opened fire on the LA BASSEE - ESTAIRES Road at 5.0 p.m. and another at 10.45 p.m. in co-operation with a searchlight from the centre of the West edge of BOIS DU BIEZ. A machine gun which fired on one of our patrols was thought to be in the sap about M.35.d.80.35.

/ MOATED GRANGE SECTION.

MOATED GRANGE SECTION.

Hostile Artillery and M.G. activity was normal. Opposite the right subsection hostile T.Ms. showed considerable activity at 7.0 a.m., 1.10 p.m., 1.45 p.m. and 2.5 p.m. Later in the afternoon aerial torpedoes were fired at our front line on the right and into the FAUQUISSART Craters (M.30.c.15.30.) New earth has been thrown out of C.T. at M.30.b.85.25. At 6.30 a.m. two men were observed lying out in front of the enemy's wire; they were fired at and disappeared. Our snipers in the loft subsection claim to have hit a German who was forced to move by our T.M fire.

FAUQUISSART SECTION.

Hostile Artillery was active against RUE TILLELOY, FAUQUISSART and C.Ts. in the loft subsection during the day. Hostile T.Ms. both heavy and light, were active on the right of our line. An M.G. firing from SUGAR LOAF N.8.d. swept our parapet between N.14.a.3.7. and N.13.b.9.1. at dusk. An M.G. which fired at our aeroplanes appeared to be located at N.14.c.9.2.. Another gun was seen to fire from N.13.d.2.3. Considerable movement was seen at TRAMWAY CORNER N.26.c.8.3., 80 men in all being counted on the AUBERS - BAS POMMEREAU Road moving in both directions, including one party of 30 and another of 12. They were dressed in the usual grey uniform with soft caps and without packs. Other details could not be distinguished. A few men were seen leaving AUBERS, turning N.W. at TRAMWAY CORNER and disappearing about N.26.c.7.5. Men were frequently seen entering and leaving the red tiled house at N.26.c.80.45. Movement seen on LIGNY - H.T. POMMEREAU Road at T.2.a. A very obvious O.P can be seen at N.31.b.45.45. It consists of a square brick built tower with a slit 5 to 6 feet long facing N.W. (The house at this point has previously been reported as a suspected H.Q.) Three men were seen to enter the AUBERS Defences from road at N.21.d.40.15. Smoke was seen rising from ruins at N.20.d.5.8. and from the chimney of a small house on RUE D'ENFER at N.26.c.15.82.

Hdqrs. 56th Divn.
25th November, 1916.

Captain,
Intelligence, General Staff.

56th DIVISIONAL TACTICAL PROGRESS REPORT No. 29,
from 1.0 a.m. 25th November to 8.0 a.m. 26th November.

(On receipt of current copy of Divisional Tactical Progress
Report in the trenches, previous copy to be destroyed).

PART I OPERATIONS.

NEUVE CHAPELLE SECTION.

Patrols encountered no signs of the enemy. The state of the ground in "NO MAN'S LAND" was very bad after the recent rain. Our artillery silenced hostile T.Ms. at 1.0 p.m. and 4.0 p.m. Rifle grenades were fired with good effect on to the enemy's trenches from M.35.d.25.00. Rapid rifle fire was opened from both sub-sections for short periods during the night.

MOATED GRANGE SECTION.

An Officers' patrol heard sounds of movement in the Crater at M.36.c.1.8½. The enemy appeared to be nervous as he continually fired Very lights and sniped from this Crater. He also threw a number of hand grenades which fell short of our position. During the day our T.Ms. fired on about M.36.c.1.8. and a T.M. emplacement about M.24.d.5.1. Hostile retaliation was slight. Our snipers smashed a periscope at M.30.c.55.90. Our M.Gs. fired on various targets including a hostile patrol.

FAUQUISSART SECTION.

Our L.T.Ms. fired on N.19.a.4.8. to N.13.c.6.0. with good effect also on N.14.c.25.00 and N.14.a.6.0. in support of M.T.Ms.
An officer and N.C.O. examined the enemy's wire and parapet at N.19.a.3½.3 and N.13.a.3.5. Wire was found to be satisfactorily destroyed in places and no difficulty was experienced in getting through. Enemy's parapet was observed but no movement was seen. As the patrol was leaving considerable splashing was heard in the enemy's front line. The patrol returned to the parapet and 8 Mills Grenades were thrown into the trench, whereupon a star shell was immediately fired from the enemy's front trench on to our left.
Our M.Gs. fired at intervals during the night and dispersed a small working party opposite N.13.3.

PART II INTELLIGENCE.

NEUVE CHAPELLE SECTION.

Hostile artillery was fairly quiet except for about 25 rounds of 4.2" which fell round COPSE ST. about 4 p.m. A M.G. from about S.10.d.6.6. traversed our parapet in the right sub-section at 5.15 p.m. in reply to two or three rifle shots. It is thought that this gun was waiting for our usual burst of rapid rifle fire which has taken place shortly after 5.0 p.m. for the last two days. On this occasion we had altered the hour. Fire from 2 M.Gs. was directed on M.35.d.25.10 and the gun which fired from M.35.d.80.35 on night 24/25th was again active. Transport was heard behind the enemy's lines in S.11.d. during the night. Hostile working parties were engaged by our Lewis Guns and dispersed. At 5.0 p.m. a party seen at M.35.d.8.1. carrying coils of wire was dispersed with L.G. and rifle fire. The enemy appeared to be very nervous during the night, bombing his wire on several occasions, and at 1.20 a.m. opening rapid fire and sending up a large number of flares.

MOATED GRANGE SECTION.

Hostile artillery and T.Ms. showed normal activity. A few small shells fell near CHAPIGNY FARM and some T.M. bombs on the right sub-section. At 8.0 p.m. a small group of the enemy was seen in front of their wire about M.30.a.7.3. They were fired on by Lewis Guns and it is believed casualties were caused. Opposite the left company of the right sub-section unusual movement was observed at 1.45 p.m. as though a relief were taking place. This may account for the enemy's change of attitude during the night. Our artillery fired on the enemy where movement was seen.

P.T.O. /FAUQUISSART SECTION.

FAUQUISSART SECTION.

Movement was again seen at Tramway Corner N.26.c.8.3. Smoke was seen issuing from houses at N.27.a.40.05 (suspected O.P.) and at Redtiled house N.20.d.50.85 (previously reported). About 5.0 a.m. a party of the enemy appeared to dump some material in the WICK SALIENT N.13.d.

Head Qrs. 56th Divn.
26th November, 1916.

Captain,
Intelligence, General Staff

56th DIVISIONAL TACTICAL PROGRESS REPORT No. 30.
(from 8.0 a.m. 26th to 8.0 a.m. Novr. 27th, 1916.)

PART I OPERATIONS.

NEUVE CHAPELLE SECTION.

Patrols which were out all along the section during the night had two hostile working parties opposite our right which were dispersed by L.G. fire. Artillery co-operated with our T.Ms. and silenced a hostile T.M.

M.T.Ms. fired with good effect on enemy's front line at S.5.b.75.80.

MOATED GRANGE SECTION.

Our L.T.Ms. fired a series of bursts at irregular intervals during the morning on the enemy's front line opposite trench M.35.3. and also 70 rounds into the crater at M.36.c.1.8½.; much wood and wire debris being thrown up. The enemy replied to the latter shoot with L.T.Ms. Later in the morning our M.T.Ms. fired on suspected M.G. and T.M. emplacements about M.30.c.55.05. Our M.Gs. fired at parties of the enemy seen on PIETRE Road. Listening posts in the MAUQUISSART Crater M.30.c.1½.3½. report seeing smoke from several fires in the enemy's front line during the night. One of our snipers claims a hit at M.30.b.5.9¾. A hostile party of about ten men seen moving towards the COLVIN CRATERS M.30.c. was dispersed by L.G. Fire.

FAUQUISSART SECTION.

Our L.T.Ms. co-operated in a shoot with H.T.Ms. on DEVIL'S JUMP N.19.a. and the enemy's front line parapet N.14.a.5.0. The shooting was successful, the breastwork and wire being damaged. There was slight hostile retaliation on our front line. Our M.Gs. fired at intervals during the night traversing hostile parapet and searching C.Ts. Patrols which were out during the night encountered no hostile parties.

A small hostile party seen in the early morning about N.13.c.9.4. was fired on.

PART II INTELLIGENCE.

NEUVE CHAPELLE SECTION.

At intervals during the day the enemy fired a few rounds 4.2" and some shrapnel over our C.Ts. Hostile T.Ms. inactive. Small working parties were observed at the following points S.11.c.55.15.; S.16.b.40.35.; S.23.b.35.70. Considerable movement was observed in the direction of L'AVENTURE and H.T.POMMEREAU. Two officers and several men were seen in trench at S.11.a.25.20. Several parties of men, each about 12 strong, in marching order, were seen moving along C.T. at S.11.c.35.30. between 8 a.m. and 9 a.m. New wire has been put out from S.5.b.8.4. to S.5.b.8.5.; also at S.10.c.99.10. and the trench at S.11.a.45.30. has been repaired. From recent hostile movement it is thought that a relief may have taken place opposite this section.

MOATED GRANGE SECTION.

The enemy fired a few rounds 4.2" on to S.TILLELOY ST. A T.M. from about M.30.c.55.05. fired on to the crater at M.30.c.1.3½. During the morning movement was observed at M.30.b.5.9¾., sentries appearing for a short time and then disappearing. An officer was also observed wearing a soft cap with three silver bands, each with a twist in front. One of the sentries was shot by our snipers.

/FAUQUISSART SECTION.

FAUQUISSART SECTION.

Hostile artillery was more active than usual especially on the right subsection. 4.2" and 5.9" shells were fired on RUE TILLELOY M.18.d.25.20., and in rear of front line just E. of M.24. central. A 77 mm. gun from the direction of AUBERS CHIMNEY fired on C.T. at N.13.c.7.8.. Hostile M.GS. fired occasional bursts during the night and were very active against our aeroplanes. An enemy observation balloon was seen at 12.45 p.m. over AUBERS on a true bearing of 136° from N.13.a.5½.3¾. A party of men were seen repairing N. face of C.T. at N.20.b.1.9. Our Artillery were informed and shelled the spot with H.E. causing movement to cease.

On two occasions a man was seen to leave DORA C.T. N.25.a. and enter the ruins of LES MOTTES FARM from the rear. A man was seen to leave AUBERS - FROMELLES Road at N.27.b.9.9., run across the open and disappear behind hedge at N.27.b.8.9. A man was observed pushing a trolley towards N.13.d.0.3.

Smoke was seen at the following points:-
From behind screen on AUBERS - BAS POMMEREAU Rd. N.26.d.05.38.
" house in AUBERS N.26.d.69.70.
" trench at N.14.c.10.05. (Trench shown on map as old or disused).
" house in LE PIETRE N.20.b.32.25.
" enemy's second line N.15.a.50.85.

Hdqrs. 56th Divn.   Captain,

27th Novr, 1915.   Intelligence, General Staff.
(On receipt of current copy of Divisional Tactical Progress Report in the trenches, previous copy to be destroyed).

56th DIVISIONAL TACTICAL PROGRESS REPORT No. 81,
from 8.0 a.m. 27th November to 8.0 a.m. 28th Nov.'16.

On receipt of current copy of Divisional Tactical Progress Report
in the trenches, previous copy to be destroyed.

PART I OPERATIONS.

RIGHT SECTION.- Our artillery fired on various targets during the day and also on cross roads at M.31.b.8.1½ where transport was heard during the night. Our H.T.Ms. carried out a bombardment of the enemy's defences at M.24.d.47.12 and M.30.b.2.8. during the morning causing damage to dumps and parapet. L.T.Ms. fired on Crater M.30.a.40.35 and trench junction in rear of M.30.a.35.30. The enemy retaliated to all our fire. Our M.Gs. searched the PIETRE ROAD during the night.

Patrols from the left sub-section which visited WINCHESTER CRATERS - M.30.a. several times during the night reported them unoccupied and full of water. There is no sign of work having been done on them. It is practically certain that the enemy neither holds nor patrols these craters by night. A patrol reports that the enemy's wire M.30.c.5.3. to M.30.a.35.40. is very thick and consists of two rows of concertina wire about 20 yards wide. No signs of work or occupation were seen at the Craters M.36.a.15.95 but the enemy was heard talking in his front line.

Our snipers claim one hit at M.36.b.1.1.

LEFT SECTION.- Our L.T.Ms. fired on the enemy's parapet at several points. Very good results were obtained by one L.T.M. firing on the line N.13.c.3.0. to N.13.c.9.7. much damage was done to the enemy's breastwork, sheets of iron and rails being thrown into the air. Our M.Gs. swept the enemy's parapet at intervals during the night.

An Officers patrol from the left sub-section approached to within about 40 yards of the enemy's wire at N.13.d.7.8. The enemy was working on his front line and parties were heard patrolling in front. Shots were fired occasionally apparently from fixed rifles.

A patrol from the right sub-section examined the enemy's wire about N.13.c.9.3. It was found to be much damaged but a new line was being erected diagonally from the trench to a small sap at N.13.c.9.3.

Sniping was carried out whenever any possible targets were offered.

PART II INTELLIGENCE.

RIGHT SECTION.- The enemy fired a number of 4.2" shells against our front line at M.30.c.1.3½ and trench M.35.2. during the day. L.T.Ms. and rifle grenades fell between S.5.b.2.9. and S.5.a.9½.2½ also some shells from a L.T.M. located about M.30.c.5.3. were fired at M.29.b.5.2. Hostile M.Gs. traversed our parapet at dusk and dawn. An enemy patrol of about 14 men was seen near the DUCKS BILL CRATER at 1.45 a.m. but quickly disappeared to the N. when fired at from the left sub-section. The enemy has strengthened his wire at M.36.a.4.1. and M.36.a.35.50.

A light appeared behind the German line from 3.0 a.m. to 4.0 a.m. on a true bearing of 77° from M.30.a.3.8. It resembled a powerful searchlight at a distance flashing S-I-T-E in morse code slowly and continuously.

Two of the enemy were seen at M.36.a.4.7. but disappeared before they could be fired on.

/LEFT SECTION.

2.

LEFT SECTION. - Light shells fell in the area held by the centre coy. of the left Sub-section, on the RUE TILLELOY and near ERITH ST. during the day. Several L.T.Ms. fell on the extreme right of the section. Hostile M.Gs.were active during the night. No hostile patrols were seen during the night but two were heard on our left keeping close to the own wire.

Sounds of transport were heard opposite the right of the section during the night. The enemy appeared to be repairing the North edge of the WICK at N.13.d.0.5.

A little new wire has been added at N.13.d.46.60.

What looked like glasses were seen flashing from the N.W. end of the roof of house at N.26.d.75.75. Movement was seen round 14 TREE CLUMP N.20.b.4½.4. and AUBERS DEFENCES at N.21.d. 40.15.

During the day 30 men were seen to pass tramway corner N.26.c.8.3. including a party of 20 moving towards AUBERS at noon. The artillery were informed.

Smoke was seen at the following points :- AUBERS DEFENCES N.21.d.40.15 and N.21.d.1.0. also from houses at N&21.c.55.60. and N.21.a.70.65.

A hostile observation balloon was up during the afternoon on a true bearing of 102° from N.8.a.2.3½.

[signature]

Head Qrs. 56th Divn.
28th November, 1916.

Captain,
Intelligence, General Staff.

56th DIVISIONAL TACTICAL PROGRESS REPORT No. 32.
from 8.0 a.m., 28th to 8.0 a.m., 29th November, 1916.

On receipt of current copy of Divisional Tactical Progress in the trenches, previous copy to be destroyed.

PART I OPERATIONS.

RIGHT SECTION. Our T.Ms. were active during the early morning and afternoon. 60 rounds were fired with success at crater M.36.a.2½.2½. and a further 60 rounds into the wire at M.30.a.4.½. The mist prevented accurate observation. Hostile retaliation was heavy.

Our M.Gs. fired intermittently during the day on AUBERS, PIETRE CROSS ROADS, LES MOTTES FARM, RUE DENFER and C.Ts. Patrols visited the crater systems in this section, but found no signs of the enemy. The wire round WINCHESTER CRATERS in M.30.a. is very thick.

At 2.0 p.m., during a lift in the mist, a party of the enemy was seen at M.30.c.35.00. Our snipers and Lewis Guns opened fire immediately and it is believed that three of the enemy were hit.

LEFT SECTION. M.T.Ms. fired on enemy's front line between N.14.c.1.7. and N.14.a.7½.3. Water was thrown up indicating the flooded condition of the trench. Our M.Gs. were very active during the night. A hostile patrol of about 8 men was encountered about N.8.c.7½.2½. and fired on with a Lewis Gun. A patrol reports that the sap at N.13.c.7½.3½. is in a bad state of repair and unoccupied.

Two of the enemy were fired on by our snipers and seen to dro[p]

PART II INTELLIGENCE. Hostile Artillery quiet.

RIGHT SEC. At 8.0 a.m. and 12.45 p.m., enemy bombarded front of right subsection with heavy, medium, light T.Ms. and rifle grenades. At 3.55 p.m. a similar bombardment was commenced, but was promptly checked by our Artillery. Twice during the day, hostile M.T.Ms. from about M.36.a.4.7. fired on the front line of the left 3 c subsection. A hostile M.G. is reported to have fired from M.35.d.9.3. M.Gs. and fixed rifles fired on the left subsection during the night from the enemy's line opposite the COLVIN and MAUQUISSART CRATERS in M.30.c. The activity of the enemy in the MAUQUISSART Area has increased recently.

LEFT SECTION. Hostile Artillery quiet. T.Ms. fired on our trenches between M.24.d.1.7½. and M.24.d.2.6½.; also on M.24.d.2.7., unusual M.G. activity is reported from rear of the enemy's front line opposite the centre of the left subsection, but the target at which they were firing is unknown. A hostile working party was suspected about N.14.b.1.8. at 10.30 a.m., and was fired on. A small party was discovered during the afternoon working on the wire at the DEVIL'S JUMP N.19.a. under cover of the mist and was dispersed by fire.

It is believed that the enemy's line about N.14.a.9.5. is unoccupied and in a very bad state of repair. During the morning smoke was observed at M.24.d.6.3.; th The front line at N.14.c.1.7., junction of BERTHA C.T., and the front line, has the appearance of being badly damaged.

Hdqrs. 56th Divn.
29th Novr. 1916.

Captain,
Intelligence, General Staff.

56th DIVISIONAL TACTICAL PROGRESS REPORT No. 33,
from 8.0 a.m. 29th November, to 8.0 a.m. 30th November.

On receipt of current copy of Divisional Tactical Progress Report
in the trenches, previous copy to be destroyed.

PART 1 OPERATIONS.

RIGHT SECTION. Our T.Ms. cut a passge through enemy's wire about M.30.a.4½.1 - Retaliation nil. A T.M. shoot was carried out on the enemy's second line starting at M.30.a.9½.4½ and traversing to M.30.a.8.4½. Retaliation slight. One M.Gs were active firing accord to programme. A patrol visited the enemy's wire to inspect damage done by our T.M. shoot. No new wiring had been commenced. The whole system of the WINCHESTER CRATERS M.30.a. was thoroughly searched and no trace of enemy occupation or work was discovered. Patrols also visited the COLVIN CRATERS M.30.c. without finding any trace of the enemy.
Our snipers fired at a few targets which were soon during the day. Three of the enemy were thought to be hit. Opposite the Left Sub-section the enemy shows no enterprise and apparently never leaves his lines.

LEFT SECTION. Our L.T.Ms. and M.T.Ms. caused considerable damage to the enemy's parapet during the day. At 1.15 a.m. two of our L.T.Ms. fired on and dispersed a hostile working party. The usual M.G. activity was carried out during the night. In the Right Sub-section patrols were out from each Company during the night. A German wiring party was at work opposite the right Company until 3.30 a.m. A large wiring party protected by covering parties was located at N.13.c.9.2. Lewis Guns and T.Ms. opened fire on the spot. Patrols from the Left Sub-section reported no hostile movement. Our snipers took advantage of a number of targets disclosed by the lifting of the mist during the day and scored several hits. Three men were soon to pass a gap in the WICK SALIENT and were fired on. Five minutes later only two of them were seen. About ten men were soon in twos and threes approaching their front line in N.14.c; they were fired at and two fell. In the Right Sub-section a periscope was smashed at N.13.d.¼.4½ and a man walking behind the front line was hit. A working party at M.24.d.4¾.0. was fired at, one man being seen to fall. The remainder took cover and were fired at with rifle grenades. Infantry Observers noticed smoke behind the German line opposite our right and reported it to the artillery, who opened fire successfully on the spot.

PART II INTELLIGENCE.

RIGHT SECTION. Enemy shelled the area between M.36.a.0.9 and M.35.b.80.05. with H.E. and shrapnel. During the afternoon about 20 shrapnel were fired which burst over S.TILLELOY ST. about 300 yards in rear of the front line, M.29.d.5.0. Hostile M.T.Ms. and L.T.Ms. at M.35.d.9.4. and M.35.d.8.0. fired on the front line of the Right Sub-section; most of the rounds fell short. At 8.0 a.m. and 4.0 p.m. T.Ms. fired on our line just North of MAUQUISSART CRATER M.30.c.1.3½. M.Gs. also paid special attention to this point during the night. A patrol of 12 men was seen near the COLVIN CRATERS M.30.c. during the night and dispersed by M.G. and rifle fire. The enemy showed unusual nervousness opposite the left Sub-section firing many more Very Lights that usual.

LEFT SECTION. Hostile T.Ms. fired on our parapet at M.24.b.3.1. and M.24.d.15.65. A hostile M.G. was active during the morning from in rear of the SUGAR LOAF firing towards the LAMP SALIENT.

/Several

PART II INTELLIGENCE. (continued)

LEFT SECTION.

Several parties of the enemy were seen moving in both directions in trench at N.20.b.32.65 and N.14.c.9.3. Our artillery were informed and fired on them. About 15 men were seen to leave trench from point N.14.b.80.85., walk along tramwa tramlines to N.14.b.8.6. then turn S.W. along C.T. to N.14.b.65.20. They were full marching order and great coats. Our artillery was informed.

Smoke was seen at the following points :-
    AUBERS DEFENCES N.21.d.40.15. (previously reported)
    RUINS N.20.d.9.1.
    HOUSE IN AUBERS N.27.a.45.10.
    TRENCHES N.8.d.40.15.
    Near DUGOUTS N.20.b.30.55.
    Hostile M.T.M. was located about N.19.c.35.00.

From patrol reports there was apparently more activity than usual in the enemy's lines during the night 29/30th, and many more than the normal number of Very lights were fired. It is thought that the enemy's line was more strongly manned than on previous nights. Very lights were fired from the small salient at N.14.c.3.9.

Hdqrs. 56th Divn.
30th Novr. 1916.

Captain,
Intelligence, General Staff.

CONFIDENTIAL VOL. II

Vol XI

War Diary

General Staff 56th Division

December 1916

WAR DIARY or INTELLIGENCE SUMMARY

Army Form C. 2118.

Place	Date	Hour	Summary of Events and Information	Remarks and references to Appendices
LAGORGUE	1st Dec.		Weather continued to be very misty. About a German patrol was dispersed opposite our left and an officer of 19th Hav: Inf: Regt: ran into our trench mistaking them for his own. He was captured. We carried out mutual trench mortar shoots against the enemy's trenches being favourable. The hostile retaliation was in nine cases feeble. Min drew at the point before he was hit.	
LA GORGUE	2nd Dec.		No change in the weather. A quiet day along the whole of the divisional front. We carried out our usual T.M. activities.	
LA GORGUE	3rd Dec.		Shortly after midnight 2/3rd Dec. a raiding party of 1/8th London Regt: entered the German trenches at N.13.9.9.5 "THE DEVIL'S JUMP" and (claimed) that for two hours without seeing a hearing any signs of the enemy. A covered trench and two other main entrances suspected were found. An Officer was put into the former but the fire failed to detonate the charge. The raiding party returned to our lines without casualties. Our report that the former trenches were badly damaged and very shallow and it appeared that no attempt had been made to repair the breastwork. The Wound course at the Divisional School assembled as MERVILLE. A quiet day.	
LA GORGUE	4th Dec.		Improvement in the weather, mist lifted. An uneventful day on the divisional front.	

Army Form C. 2118.

WAR DIARY
or
INTELLIGENCE SUMMARY

(Erase heading not required.)

Instructions regarding War Diaries and Intelligence Summaries are contained in F. S. Regs., Part II. and the Staff Manual respectively. Title Pages will be prepared in manuscript.

Place	Date	Hour	Summary of Events and Information	Remarks and references to Appendices
LA GORGUE	5th Dec.		Our front was actively patrolled during the night & enemy's trenches entered in three places. No enemy were encountered & there were no signs of recent occupation. A certain amount of medium & heavy T.M. bombardment of enemy works in N1.a. was carried out. Enemy established bombs on our front line in M24.c, causing some damage to trench work & tramway. A very quiet day & some rounds of evacuation were carried out. Relief of 6th Div. Artillery & T.M. by 56th Div. Artillery reported complete.	
	6th Dec.	4.40 p.m	A quiet night along the whole front. Enemy bombarded our front line at M24.a. between 2 & 3 pm the rifts little damaged. At Tilleloy Rd. our heavy artillery retaliated vigorously – A midday. A small raiding party entered the German line at N13.d.37 at 2 a.m. Only 2 Germans were seen & they ran away. A small bottle patrol was sent out.	
	7th Dec.		DUCKS BILL + JIND in. One man was relieved & have been lost. A very quiet day. There was present any observation. 168th I.P. Bde. carried out a battalion relief during the day.	

Army Form C. 2118.

WAR DIARY
or
INTELLIGENCE SUMMARY
(Erase heading not required.)

Place	Date	Hour	Summary of Events and Information	Remarks and references to Appendices
ESTDE LA GORGUE	8th Decr.		A quiet night. Patrols were active all day, tho' frost, but no signs of the enemy were seen. There was some hostile shelling of area about SIGN POST MAPLE ends in the evening. During the day observation was impossible owing to mist, which accounted for a very inactive period.	
	9th Decr.		A quiet night. The day was again bad for observation but our artillery carried out a small bombardment of LES MOTTES FME. (N.25.a.65) — Otherwise nothing to report. 164th Brigade relieved 167th Brigade with little action during the day without incident, according to Div. O.O. No.64.	APPENDIX I
	10th Decr.		During the day hostile artillery and T.M's were active as known on front Rue du Marais to Ottomar Keep.	
	11th Decr.		Strong enemy working parties were reported by patrols opposite RED LAMP CORNER and effectively dealt with by our artillery & T.M's. Enemy T.M's (incl periste) through the night in spite of artillery retaliation especially one on our extreme right.	

WAR DIARY or INTELLIGENCE SUMMARY

Army Form C. 2118.

Place	Date	Hour	Summary of Events and Information	Remarks and references to Appendices
LA GORGUE	11th Decr (cont)		There was considerable hostile T.M. activity distributed along the whole front during the day and our O.P.s were apparently registered by hostile artillery. Our fire in M24 was answered by rifle fire. A fine day.	
	12 Decr.		Enemy T.M.s were active against the night section during the night – Rumball and Hostile H.T.M.s bombarded the extreme left of the section during the morning. A certain amount of Artillery + T.M. shots were carried out against suspected T.M. emplacements. The night section was ably harassed by T.M. fire during the night, but the day passed quietly along the front. 16 & 14 Bde carried out the battalion relief during the day.	
	13th Decr.		The XI Corps Commander inspected the 8th Middlesex Regt at 10am, the 3rd London Regt at 11.15 and at LA GORGUE. During the day 1140 reinforcements arrived for the division, mainly returned wounded.	

Army Form C. 2118.

WAR DIARY
or
INTELLIGENCE SUMMARY
(Erase heading not required.)

Place	Date	Hour	Summary of Events and Information	Remarks and references to Appendices
LAGORGUE	14th Decr.		Against night. During the day hostile artillery + T.M.s were active opposite MAUQUISSART. We arranged artillery + T.M. programme effectually silenced them. The G.O.C. XI Corps inspected 1st MIDDLESEX Regt at 10 am & GRAND PACQUT and the 1st LONDON Regt at 11.15 am at ROBERMETZ. The reinforcements received by the division were organised into three large companies to prepare for training.	
	15th Decr		Against night. Except for some hostile artillery registration an uneventful day. 168th + 169th Coys of the Training Battalion assembled at LE SART under the command of Major PARNELL, 13th LONDONS, + the 164th Coy. at BOUT DEVILLE under Major STOWELL, 3rd LONDONS. Conference at Div. H.Q. Present – Brigadier M.G. Major – XI Corps. A quiet period. We carried out artillery + T.M. bombardment & in both sectors XI Corps Order No. 89 received for shortening the divisional lines wing to a raid of the 39th Division.	
	16th Decr		193rd M.G. Coy. joined the Division in the Truth M.G. Coy.	

WAR DIARY or INTELLIGENCE SUMMARY

Army Form C. 2118.

Place	Date	Hour	Summary of Events and Information	Remarks and references to Appendices
LAGORGUE	Dec 17th		Enemy TMs were active in front of NEUVE CHAPELLE during the night. April day site patrols quite uneventful to the left. barrage without incident.	
	Dec 18th		G.O.C. XI Corps inspected the training. battn in LESART and BOUT DEVILLE.	
			Hostile TM + artillery were again active in the night radius. We carried out organised shots during the day, which puzzled slightly hostile retaliation.	
	Dec 19th		Our patrols were active during the night. Located enemy working parties which were effectively dealt with. Successful TM bombardments were carried out during the day.	
	Dec 20th		There was some hostile T.M. activity during the night. About 6.30 am one of our patrols met a hostile patrol of 5 men. Shot the patrol leader + took the remainder four prisoners. The Army Commander and G.O.C. XI Corps inspected the divisional relief during the morning.	
	Dec 21st		During the night hostile TMs were active again. The night section strove activity continued during the day. On the ne of the line, the patrol paired with instead.	
	Dec 22nd		A patrol of our troops who replied meeting 37 Inf. + 167 Rds relieved 168th according to night. During the day hostile TMs of all calibres bombarded 2nd Bn. Depot battalion of the night section.	APPENDIX I

WAR DIARY
or
INTELLIGENCE SUMMARY.

Army Form C. 2118.

Place	Date	Hour	Summary of Events and Information	Remarks and references to Appendices
LA GORGUE	Decr. 23rd		During the night, the Rifle bombardment of the left battalion of the right brigade became intense + under cover of this, the enemy effected an entrance into trenches immediately N. of the MAUQUISSART crater (M 30 c 14) and took 5 prisoners, as of whom 2 were wounded. Considerable damage was done to our trenches, but casualties were slight. During the day there was some T.M. fire on these men, + on the rear of the front line the day passed quietly.	
December 24th Decr. 24th		The G.O.C. XI Corps examined candidates for commissions at Divisional H.Q. The night was unusually quiet. During the day there was more Rifle shelling of the front line in the left sub-section + about OPs on RUE TILLELOY	
Decr. 25th		Bombardment of enemy lines + batteries was carried out according to programme. Hostile artillery was weak, until 2.30 pm, when about 60 heavy shells were fired into M 12 c.	
Decr. 26th		The enemy lines were entered in three places opposite the left section during the night – on each occasion were found unoccupied, fully damaged, full of water.	
Decr. 26th		Bombardment was continued + enemy reply was slight except on extreme right. Enemy lines were entered during the night again and found unoccupied in four places	

Army Form C. 2118.

WAR DIARY
or
INTELLIGENCE SUMMARY.
(Erase heading not required.)

Instructions regarding War Diaries and Intelligence Summaries are contained in F.S. Regs., Part II. and the Staff Manual respectively. Title pages will be prepared in manuscript.

Place	Date	Hour	Summary of Events and Information	Remarks and references to Appendices
LA GORGUE	Decr. 27th		The artillery + T.M. programme was completed without drawing any considerable retaliation. The Rotten Row opposite the right section was found to be occupied, but patrols from the left section again entered the enemy front line in three places + found it unoccupied + in very bad condition.	
	Decr. 28th		The G.O.C. proceeded on leave + Bde-Genl. LOCH, C.M.G. assumed temporary command. A very quiet period. Our patrols again entered the enemy lines without finding any trace of occupation.	
	Decr. 29th		The German lines in the left section were entered in three places + found to be fully damaged + unoccupied. A quiet day.	
	Decr. 30th		Efforts made by patrols to raid the hostile support line were prevented by its flooded state + the ground was known not to be practicable. Hostile artillery was rather more active during the day, shelled O.P.s + was carefully dealt with by our own fire.	
	Decr. 31st		A quiet night. During the day hostile artillery was active as against our front line, C.T.s + support line, while but little was done in reply. Hostile attack.	

J.H. Crosthwaite (?)
Captain,
(Intelligence) General Staff,
56th Division.
4th Jan. 1917.

SECRET.   Copy No. 18

56th DIVISIONAL ORDER No. 61.

Ref. Map   5th Decr. 1916.
1/40,000
Sheet 36A.

1. The 169th Infantry Brigade will relieve the 167th Infantry Brigade in the NEUVE CHAPELLE SECTION on the 9th December. Relief to be complete by 6.0 a.m. on the 10th December.

    Machine guns and light trench mortars will relieve on the 8th December. Nos. 1 of outgoing gun teams will remain in the line until 9th December or until their services can be dispensed with.

2. All arrangements for relief will be made between Brigade Commanders concerned.

3. On relief, the 167th Infantry Brigade will move into Divisional Reserve as follows:-

    Bdo. Hdqrs.)
    1 battalion)   at LESTREM.
    & L.T.M Bty)

    1 battalion   at LA GORGUE.

    1 battalion   at LE GRAND PACAUT.

    1 Battalion   at ROBERMETZ.

    M.G. Coy.   at REGNIER Le CLERC.

4. Completion of relief will be reported by wire to Divisional Headquarters and repeated to the Brigades on either flank.

5. Acknowledge.

                                        A P Bryant.

Hdqrs. 56th Divn.   Lieut. Colonel,

                                        General Staff.

Issued at 6.30 a.m.
through Signals.

Copy No. 1. XIth Corps.   10. Divnl Signals.
        2. 5th Divn.   11. Divnl. School.
        3. New Zealand Div.   12. Divnl. Train.
        4. 167th Inf. Bde.   13 A.D.M.S.
        5. 168th Inf. Bde.   14. A. P. M.
        6. 169th Inf. Bde.   15. G.O.C., 56th Div.
        7. 6th Divnl. Arty.   16. 257th Tunnelling Co. R.E.
        8. C. R. E.   17. War Diary.
        9. "Q".   18 & 19 File.
                                20. C.R.A., 56th Divn.

SECRET.   Copy No 19

56th DIVISIONAL ORDER No. 62.
                                                                17.12.16.

1.   The following reliefs will take place on 21st December:-

   (a). Portion of 169th Inf.Bde. in NEUVE CHAPELLE
        Section between CHURCH ROAD (exclusive)
        and SIGN POST LANE (exclusive), by "A" Bde. 37th Divn.

   (b). Portion of 168th Inf. Bde. in FAUQUISSART Section
        between present Brigade boundary and ERITH STREET
        (inclusive) by 169th Infantry Brigade.

   (c). Portion of 168th Inf. Bde. in FAUQUISSART Section
        between ERITH STREET (exclusive) and BOND STREET
        (inclusive) by 167th Infantry Brigade.

   Machine guns and Light Trench Mortars of 167th Infantry
   Brigade will relieve on the 20th December. Nos.1 of
   outgoing gun teams will remain in the line until 21st
   December or until their services can be dispensed with.

2.   All arrangements for reliefs (b) and (c) above will be
   made between Brigade Commanders concerned. All trench stores,
   log-books, defence schemes, air photos etc. will be handed over.
   Instructions regarding relief (a) will be issued later.

3.   On relief, 168th Infantry Brigade will move into Divisional
   Reserve as follows:-

        Brigade H.Q.   MERVILLE.
        1 Bn. &   )   Billets to be
        L.T.M. Bty.)   notified later.
        1 Bn.   at   LA GORGUE.
        1 Bn.   at   LE GRAND PACAUT.
        1 Bn.   at   ROBERMETZ.
        M.G. Coy.   at   REGNIER le CLERC.

4.   On completion of reliefs, the Division will hold the
   following sections:-

        MOATED GRANGE Section   from SIGN POST LANE (inclusive)
                                  to ERITH STREET   (inclusive)

        FAUQUISSART Section   from ERITH STREET   (exclusive)
                                  to BOND STREET   (inclusive).

5.   New boundaries will be as follows:-

   Between 37th Division and 56th Division.
   Junction of SIGN POST LANE with front line. SIGN POST LANE
   (inclusive to 56th Division) M.27.h.35.25. and thence as
   shown on map issued to Brigades, "Q", Divnl. Artillery,
   C.R.E. and Divnl. Signals.

   Between MOATED GRANGE and FAUQUISSART Sections.
   ERITH ST. (inclusive to MOATED GRANGE Section) along
   LONELY ERITH   "   "   "   "   "
   to RUE du BACQUEROT and thence along existing boundary.

6.   Artillery covering the NEUVE CHAPELLE Section will remain
   in position and will come under the orders of the G.O.C.,
   37th Division on completion of relief.

7.   No. 2 Section, 15th M.M.G. Battery will continue to be
                                                    /attached to

2.

to the M.M.G.Coy.of the Right Brigade.

8. Completion of relief will be reported by wire to Divnl. H.Q. and repeated to the Brigades on either flank.

9. ACKNOWLEDGE.

CV Bryant.

Head Qrs. 56th Divn.   Lieut-Colonel,
                                                               General Staff.

        Issued at 3.30 p.m.

Copy No.
1. XIth Corps.   11. Divnl. Schools.
2. 5th Divn.   12. Divnl. Train.
3. New Zealand Divn.   13. A.D.M.S.
4. 167th Inf. Bde.   14. A.P.M.
5. 168th Inf. Bde.   15. G.O.C. 56th Divn.
6. 169th Inf. Bde.   16. 257th Tunnelling Co. R.E.
7. 56th Divnl. Arty.   17. 37th Division
8. C.R.E.   18. 15th M.M.G. Coy.
9. "Q"   19. War Diary.
10. Divnl. Signals.   20.& File.
                               21

SECRET.

56th Divn.
S.G. 378.

All recipients of 56th Div. Order No. 62.

In continuation of 56th Div. Order No. 62 dated 17.12.16 -

1. Reference para. 1 (a) for "A" Brigade 37th Division read 111th Infantry Brigade.

    Reference para. 2, the relief of a portion of the 168th Infantry Brigade by 111th Infantry Brigade will be carried out under arrangements made between Brigade Commanders concerned.
    All trench stores, log books, defence schemes, air photos etc. for the area in question will be handed over.

2. The following posts will be handed over to the 111th Infantry Brigade:-

    CHATEAU REDOUBT.
    CURZON POST.
    EUSTON POST.
    RUE du PUITS.
    (HUIT MAISONS.
    (WELLINGTON.
    LESTREM.
    L'EPINETTE.
    PARADIS N.

3. The General Officer Commanding 37th Division will assume command of the NEUVE CHAPELLE Section at 9.0 a.m. December 22nd.

4. On relief, 1 battalion and L.T.M. Battery of 168th Infantry Brigade will be accommodated in the BOUT DEVILLE Area. The 2/2nd London Field Company, now at HUIT MAISONS, will, on relief, move to billets in LAVENTIE.

5. ACKNOWLEDGE.

Hdqrs. 56th Divn.
19th December, 1916.

A. Bryant.
Lieut. Colonel,
General Staff.

LOCATION TABLE FOR INFANTRY BRIGADES.

	15.	16.	17.	18.	19.	20.	21.	22.	23.	December. 24.	25.	26.	27.	28.	29.	30.	31.
167th Infantry Bde.																	
Bde. H.Q.	LESTREM						LAVENTIE M.4.b.2.b										
1st London Regt.	ROBERMETZ						LAVENTIE.B.R.										
3rd " "	LA GORGUE					R	R	R	R	R	R	R	L	L	L	L	L
7th Middlx. "	GRAND PACAUT								LAVENTIE.B.R.								
8th " "	LESTREM												LAVENTIE B.R				
168th Infantry Bde.																	
Bde. H.Q.	LAVENTIE M.4.b.2.b						MERVILLE										
4th London Regt. (Rangers)	LAVENTIE B.R	L	R	R	R	R	BOUT DEVILLE										
12th " "	L	L	L	L	L	L	ROBERMETZ	R	R	L	L	L	L	L	L	L	L
13th " " (Kens.)	R	R	L	L	L	L	GRAND PACAUT										
14th " " (Lon.Sc.)	LAVENTIE B.R	L	R	R	R	R	LA GORGUE										
169th Infantry Bde.																	
Bde. H.Q. (R.F.)	LAVENTIE, COCKSHY HOUSE					L	L	L	L	L	L	L	L	L	L	L	L
2nd London Regt. (LRB)	RIEZ BAILLEUL					L	RIEZ BAILLEUL						RIEZ BAILLEUL				
5th " " (QVR)	PONT DU HEM					R	R	R	R	R	R	R	R	R	R	R	R
9th " " (QWR)	R	R	R	R	R	L	PONT DU HEM						PONT DU HEM				
16th " "	R	R	R	R	R	R											

NOTE:— B.R. = Brigade Reserve.
       S. = Support
       R. = Right subsection) (in RED)
       L. = Left subsection)
       Res. Bde. = Reserve Brigade (in GREEN).
Left Section N.8.d.2.8½. (BOND ST.) to M.24.c.8½.1½.   Bn. Boundary N.13.c.7.8½.
Right Section M.24.c.8½.1½. to S.5.a.9½.2½. (CHURCH RD.)   Bn. Boundary M.35.b.8⅓.7¼.

From 21st December :-
LEFT SECTION N.8.d.05.85 to M.24.d.15.65   Bn. Boundary N.13.c.7.9.
RIGHT SECTION M.24.d.15.65 " M.35.d.55.65   Bn. Boundary M.29.d.95.80.

LOCATION TABLE FOR INFANTRY BRIGADES.

	Nov 25	26	27	28	29	30	Dec 1	2	3	4	5	6	7	8	9	10	11	12	13	14	15
167th Infantry Bde.																					
Bde. H.Q.		LAVENTIE. COCKSHY HOUSE M.9.c.8.9.													LESTREM						
1st Lond. Regt.		L	L	L	L	L	L	L	←RIEZ BAILLEUL B.R.→						→ROBERMETZ						
3rd " "	R	R	R	R	R	R	R	R	←PONT DUHEM. S						→LA GORGUE						
7th Midx. "	R	R	R	R	R	R	R	R	←PONT DU HEM. S.→						→GD. PACAUT						
8th " "	←RIEZ BAILLEUL.B.R.→														→LESTREM						
168th Infantry Bde.																					
Bde. H.Q.	LAVENTIE M.4.c.2.6.																				
4th Lond. Regt.	R	R	R	R	R	R	R	←LAVENTIE B.R.→							R	R	R	R	LAVENTIE.B.R.		
12th " (Rangers)	←LAVENTIE B.R→							L	L	L	L	L	L	L	←AVENTIE B.R.→						
13th " (Kens.)	←LAVENTIE B.R.→							R	R	R	R	R	R	R	←LAVENTIE.B.R.→						
14th " (Lon.Sc.)	L	L	L	L	L	L	L	←LAVENTIE B.R.→							L	L	L	L	LAVENTIE.B.R.		
169th Infantry Bde.																					
Bde. H.Q.	HUIT MAISONS CROIX BARREE		HUIT MAISONS GRAND PACAUT			LESTREM									COCKSHY HOUSE						
2nd Lond.Regt.(RF)	R	R	LESTREM												→RIEZ BAILLEUL B.R.						
5th " (LRB)	L	L	LA GORGUE						L	L	L	L	L	L	L	L	L	L			
9th " (QVR)									R	R	R	R	R	R	R	R	R	R			
16th " (QWR)	←BOUT DEVILLE ROBERMETZ														→PONT DU HEM. S.						

NOTE:—
- B.R. = Brigade Reserve.
- S. = Support.
- R. = Right subsection.) (in RED).
- L. = Left subsection.)
- Res.Bde. = Reserve Brigade (in GREEN).
- Left Section N.8.d.2.8½. (BOND ST.) to M.24.c.8½.1½.
- Right Section M.24.c.8½.1½. to S.5.a.9½.2¼. (CHURCH RD.)
- Bn. Boundary N.13.c.7.8½.
- Bn. Boundary M.35.b.8¾.7¼.

56th DIVISIONAL TACTICAL PROGRESS REPORT No. 34.
from 8.0 a.m. 30th November to 8.0 a.m., 1st December, 1916.

On receipt of current copy of Divisional Tactical Progress Report in the trenches, previous copy to be destroyed.

PART I OPERATIONS.

RIGHT SECTION. During the morning of 30th Novr. an organised bombardment of the enemy's defences in S.5.b. was carried out; heavy artillery, field artillery M.T.Ms. and L.T.Ms. co-operating. The enemy's trenches and works were considerably damaged, parapets being breached and quantities of timber and wire thrown up. The enemy retaliated. Our M.Gs. fired over 4,000 rounds during the day and night. Patrols which were out during the night met no enemy. A number of rifle grenades were fired on to the enemy's lines about M.30.c.6.1., damaging the parapet.

LEFT SECTION. Our T.MS. carried out several short bombardments of the SUGAR LOAF N.8.d. doing considerable damage to the parapet and throwing up timber. Our machine guns fired according to programme during the night, paying special attention to the road between N.20.b.4.1. and N.21.c.0.3. A strong patrol consisting of 2 officers and 20 O.R. from the left company of the right subsection entered the enemy's front line between N.13.c.95.35. and N.13.d.0.5. remaining there for 45 minutes. The trench was found to be badly damaged by our fire and unoccupied. There appeared to have been no recent occupation of this portion of the front line and the ground in rear of it was flooded. No signs of the enemy were seen or heard. A patrol which left our lines on the extreme left reported everything quiet on that front, but observed what appeared to be a German wiring party to the South. The patrol returned to our lines and brought Lewis Gun fire to bear on the place where the enemy had been seen.

PART II INTELLIGENCE.

RIGHT SECTION. Between 3 p.m. and 5 p.m. the enemy opened a heavy bombardment of our lines between the DUCKS BILL M.35.d.95.93. and S.TILLELOY C.T. M.35.b.85.75., both inclusive. Heavy, medium and light T.Ms. and also 5.9" and 4.2" howitzers co-operating, while M.Gs. from the enemy's support line swept our parapet. At 5.0 p.m. a hostile patrol entered the DUCKS BILL CRATER and SAP but was ejected leaving a number of bombs and a steel helmet in the crater. The only marks on the helmet are the figures "62" and what appears to be "AK" both painted inside the lining.

Pumping was heard in the enemy's front line about M.35.d.8½.3.; also between midnight and 1.0 a.m. sounds of work in the crater at M.30.c.4.0. During the night a wiring party heard at M.30.c.5.6. was dispersed by rifle and Lewis gun fire. At 6.7 p.m. and 6.12 p.m. the enemy fired a rocket breaking into two red lights and at 6.13 p.m. another rocket which broke into two green lights. These appeared to be fired from about M.30.c.9.9. or on the line of the road running N.W. from here. No action appeared to follow the firing of these rockets. At M.30.c.52.80. a dummy head was placed on the parapet over snipers post. At noon yesterday, a man looked over the parapet at this point, but disappeared immediately.

LEFT SECTION. About midday several H.E. shells fell at about N.13.c.5.4. and on our front line at N.13.c.60.75. Later a few shells were fired on RIFLEMAN'S AVENUE and RUE TILLELOY in N.13.a. Hostile M.Gs. were more active that usual sweeping RUE TILLELOY at dawn; fire appeared to come from behind the enemy's lines in the direction of FERME DELEVAL. A M.G. is suspected to be located at N.13.d.3.4½.

/A

A working party was again seen behind the enemy's lines opposite the right of the right subsection and was fired fired on New work has been done on the trench about N.8.d.35.15. Much new wire has been put out between N.24.d.5.2½. and N.30.b.2.7. At the latter point there appears to be a box about 6 feet long by 4 feet wide, covered with a sheet. About 10 feet to the left of this, behind the enemy's parapet is a large yellow tarpaulin.

Smoke was seen at the following points:-

    N.20.b.30.55.
    N.19.c.15.75.
    N.20.c.80.85.
    N.25.b.8.9.

The ruins at N.14.b.90.35. are suspected to conceal a dugout.

[signature: W.G.L. Stopford]

Hdqrs. 55th Divn.　　　　　　　　　　Captain,

1st December, 1916.　　　　　　　　Intelligence, General Staff.

56th DIVISIONAL TACTICAL PROGRESS REPORT No. 35,
from 8.0 a.m., December 1st to 8.0 a.m. December 2nd 1916.

On receipt of current copy of Divisional Tactical Progress Report
in the trenches, previous copy to be destroyed.

PART 1 OPERATIONS.

RIGHT SECTION. Our T.Ms. fired 80 rounds on to enemy's trench and
tramway between M.24.d.50.05. and M.24.d.40.00 causing much damage.
70 rounds were also fired on enemy's parapet and wire at M.30.a.
4½.½. and a further 50 rounds breached the parapet at M.30.a.9.6.
Our M.Gs. were active during the day and night.

A patrol visited the enemy's front in the Northern part of
M.30.c. without seeing or hearing signs of the enemy. Work was
heard from the Craters about M.36.a.20.90 but on the approach of
one of our patrols work ceased and no party could be seen.

Our snipers claim several hits on targets revealed during
lifts in the mist. We fired a number of rifle grenades at a
prominent mound resembling a dugout about M.30.c.77.22. This
drew rifle grenade retaliation from the enemy. Our Lewis Guns
fired on this point during the night.

LEFT SECTION. Our artillery fired several rounds on men walking along
RUE DELEVAL about N.20.b.1.9. Our T.Ms. were active during the
day damaging the enemy's parapet and wire at the DEVILS JUMP N.19.a.
parapet at N.8.d.5.2. and tramway in rear of the trench at this
point. A T.M. shoot was carried out against a M.G. which had
been seen to fire from N.8.d.5.2. When the mist cleared it was
seen that this portion of the trench had been demolished. Our
M.Gs. were more active than usual firing on the enemy's front
line system and communications. An Officers' patrol visited the
German wire about N.19.a.25.30. and found it satisfactorily cut
and easily approached. Another patrol examined the wire from
N.8.d.3.1. to a point about 150 yards S.W. The wire here was very
thick and formed a good obstacle. Other patrols which were out
during the night reported no signs of hostile movement. Our
snipers caused a party to cease work on the front line just S. of
the DEVILS JUMP and claim a hit about N.14.d.2.4.

PART II INTELLIGENCE.

RIGHT SECTION. Hostile T.Ms. fired a few rounds on trench M.29.2 and
in the neighbourhood of the MAUQUISSART CRATER M.30.c.1.3½. Hostile
M.Gs. were active during the night sweeping our parapets. A train
was heard behind the enemy's lines at 3.0 p.m. in the direction of
the MIN DU PIETRE. Transport thought to be on the roads in N.23.c.
sounded unusually loud and heavy, our M.Gs. at once swept those
roads. At 9.0 a.m. a party of about 10 men seen in rear of the
WINCHESTER CRATERS - M.30.a. carrying planks was dispersed by our
fire. At 7.45 p.m. a working party opposite point M.29.2 was seen
and dispersed by Lewis Gun. The enemy was busy during the day
working under cover of the mist but at intervals good targets were
disclosed of which we took advantage.

LEFT SECTION. At 6.5 p.m. a German Officer was taken prisoner in our
front line. He was in charge of a patrol which we dispersed and
ran into our trenches thinking they were his own. He is a Lieutenant
(Company Commander) 19th Bavarian Infantry Regiment (normal).
Hostile artillery has been very quiet during the last 24 hours.
T.Ms. retaliated to our T.M. shoots against the extreme right of the
section. At 5.40 p.m. a party of about 8 of the enemy was seen
outside our wire at LAMP CORNER - N.13.d.40.85. It was immediately
dispersed by our gun fire.

Sounds of transport thought to be on the AUBERS-FROMELLES Road,
were heard between 3.0 and 4.0 p.m.

/During

PART II INTELLIGENCE (Continued)

LEFT SECTION.- During the night VERY LIGHTS were fired from the enemy's front line at the DEVILS JUMP - N.19.a. and from the second line behind and South of the WICK SALIENT N.13.d.

At 8.30 a.m. a man was seen to leave trench at about N.14.c.00.25. and walk across the open to N.20.b.15.35 where he became lost to view. Shortly afterwards much smoke was seen coming from this spot where a dugout is suspected.

Smoke was also observed from chimney of house at N.27.a.3.0.

[signature]

Head Qrs. 56th Divn.
2nd December, 1916.

Captain,
Intelligence, General Staff.

56th DIVISIONAL TACTICAL PROGRESS REPORT No. 56,
from 8.0 a.m., December 2nd to 8.0 a.m. December 3rd, 1916.

On receipt of current copy of Divisional Tactical Progress Report in the trenches, previous copy to be destroyed.

PART I OPERATIONS

RIGHT SECTION. Our L.T.Ms. fired bursts at intervals during the night on to the COLVIN CRATER and sap in M.36.a. There was slight hostile retaliation with L.T.Ms. after each shoot.

Our M.Gs. carried out their usual offensive programme during the night.

Patrols were out all along the whole front during the night, but encountered no enemy.

Several targets revealed by lifts in the mist were taken advantage of by our snipers.

LEFT SECTION. A combined shoot of Artillery and T.Ms. was carried out at midday against the enemy's defences between M.30.b.35.95 and TRIVELET. Much damage was done to the enemy's breastwork, and a bomb store is believed to have been blown up as there was a big explosion followed by a quantity of smoke. Our M.Gs. were active during the night. A raiding party of 1 officer and 20 O.R. entered the enemy's trenches at the DEVIL's JUMP about N.19.a.3.5. on the night 2/3rd. After staying there for two hours they returned having seen no signs of the enemy. Explosive was laid in a concrete dug-out at N.19.a.3.5. but the fuze failed to explode the charge. Two other uninhabitable dug-outs were also found. The front line trench itself is fairly dry, but very shallow and much damaged. No attempt appears to have been made to repair the breastworks. In front of the enemy's second line there appears to be a strong wire entanglement and the trench seems to be in good repair.

Several hits are claimed by our snipers opposite the left subsection. One man of a party of five was hit walking towards the front line trench at N.14.a.95.60.

PART II INTELLIGENCE.

RIGHT SECTION. Hostile M.T.Ms. fired a few rounds at long intervals during the night on to the area about S.5.b.00.15. During the day hostile T.Ms. were less active than they have been recently. One of our patrols located an M.G firing from a sap, the emplacement being low down and close in front of the enemy's parapet at M.35.d.7.0. It is about ten yards to the North of the clump of willows. A M.G. emplacement is suspected at M.30.a.5½.⅔. (see aeroplane photograph 25.J.411. 25.7.16.) Two of the enemy were seen at M.30.a.4.3. at 8.15 p.m. They were fired on and disappeared. Heavy wheeled transport was again heard behind the enemy's line in M.30.b. Our M.GS. swept roads on which it was thought to be moving. The enemy was heard working persistently during the day between M.30.c.5.6. and M.36.a.4.0. A fire was seen in wood at N.25.a.½.½. there is probably a dug-out at this point.

LEFT SECTION. Hostile T.Ms. made little reply to our bombardment. There was increased activity on the part of hostile M.Gs. which appeared to be firing mostly from the enemy's second line. One gun is thought to be located at N.8.d.4.1. and another which fired on one of our patrols, at N.13.d.4.7.

Enemy working parties were located by our snipers at N.14.c.7.4. and N.8.d.30.13.

At N.14.c.2.7. and N.14.a.67.27. there are now loopholes and a strongly built opening can be seen in the parados at N.14.c.07.70. Smoke was seen from two fires at N.14.d.1.5. also from houses at N.20.d.50.85. and N.20.b.30.35.

The enemy has apparently been repairing the trench junction at N.14.c.10.40 as fresh earth and timber can be plainly seen.

Hdqrs. 56th Divn.

3rd Decr. 1916.

Captain,
Intelligence, General Staff.

56th DIVISIONAL TACTICAL PROGRESS REPORT No. 37
from 8.0 a.m. 3rd December to 8.0 a.m. 4th December, 1916.

On receipt of current copy of Divisional Tactical Progress Report
in the trenches, previous copy to be destroyed.

PART I OPERATIONS.

RIGHT SECTION. Our artillery replied to hostile shelling at 11.30 a.m. During the early morning 100 rounds T.M. were fired on the enemy's front line, and suspected sap opposite trench M.29.4. The results were satisfactory and hostile retaliation was slight. A further 30 rounds were fired on the trench and sap at M.35.d.80.35. causing much damage. The enemy replied to this shoot with Medium and Light T.Ms. and rifle grenades. Our Machine Guns fired as usual during the night. Our patrols which went out from both Sub-sections encountered no enemy.

LEFT SECTION. Our T.Ms. fired about 100 rounds on DEVILS JUMP - N.19.a.3.5. A dump apparently was hit as 4 large coils of wire were thrown into the air. The parapet was breached. Retaliation very slight. Our M.Gs. showed their usual night activity and a hostile M.G. at N.14.a.65.20 was silenced.
    Two patrols went out from our right battalion at 8.0 p.m. and after searching the intervening ground they united and 2 N.C.Os. and 3 men entered the enemy's trench about N.19.c.0.7. They walked along for several bays without being challenged. The trench is reported to be 3 to 4 ft. deep in water, but otherwise in good condition. Another patrol entered enemy's front line just S. of WICK N.13.c.95.30 and found no sign of occupation. Other patrols reported work being carried on in enemy's second line about N.13.d.0.0.
    Another patrol inspected enemy's wire from N.8.d.3.2. for 250 yards S.W. of that point and reported it to be low and thick.
    Our snipers were active and fired on small parties coming along RUE d'ENFER N.25.a.6.9. causing them to run.

PART II INTELLIGENCE.

RIGHT SECTION. During the morning the enemy fired 15 4.2" shells on our front line about S.5.a.9.8. There was some hostile T.M. fire during the day, shells falling at about M.30.a.4.8.-M.29.d.9½.7½ and S.5.a.9.3. During the morning a few rifle grenades fell about S.5.a.9.5.
    Hostile M.Gs. fired at our parapet during the night especially on points where their T.M. shells had fallen during the day. The enemy was heard working in his trenches opposite the right Sub-section during the night. Dogs were heard barking in the enemy's trenches about M.30.c.7.7. also opposite CHORD TRENCH - M.29.B.

LEFT SECTION. Hostile T.Ms. again fired on our breastwork and wire between M.24.b.3.2. and M.24.d.1½.6½. A patrol seen near the LAMP SALIENT - N.13.d. was dispersed by L.G. fire. Fresh earth and new sandbags are visible at N.14.c.2.7. Infantry Observers saw three Germans, two of them wearing full marching order, rush across the open from their front trench at N.14.a.95.65. The artillery were at once informed and opened fire. The head and shoulders of a man were seen over the parapet of the enemy's second line trench at N.13.d.73.40. He appeared to be measuring the trench. Smoke was observed at the following points:-
    N.20.b.15.35
    N.20.b.30.55   Close to dugout at this point. Smoke continuous.
    N.21.d.40.15   Aubers defences. Previously reported.
    N.20.b.30.28   Close to house at this point.
    N.25.b.35.08   From suspected dugout.
    N.14.c.7.0.
    N.14.b.55.10   Trench within clump of trees.
    A snipers post is visible near N.14.b.05.75 where a M.G. is suspected.

Head Qrs
4th December, 1916.

Captain,
Intelligence, General Staff

56th DIVISIONAL TACTICAL PROGRESS REPORT No. 38
from 8.0 a.m. 4th December to 8.0 a.m., 5th December, 1916.

On receipt of current copy of Divisional Tactical Progress Report
in the trenches, previous copy to be destroyed.

PART I OPERATIONS.

LEFT SECTION. An officers patrol examined the German wire about N.8.d.3.2.: the wire was low, and in front of it was a small ditch filled with wire. Patrols entered enemy's trenches at N.19.a.3.3. and M.24.d.7.4. and found no sign of the enemy. They reported an enemy M.G. firing from a house behind TRIVELET. The enemy wire in N.13.c. was examined and found to be good with no gaps.
  An officers patrol entered the German trench at N.13.d.70.55. No enemy were seen, but shots were fired from the front line at about N.13.d.90.75. They reported the wire at N.13.d.8.6. to be badly knocked about.
  Our T.Ms. demolished a snipers post at N.8.d.3.2., which has not been used since; whilst our M.Gs. sprayed the enemy's breastworks and supports lines during the night. Our snipers dispersed a small party entering the second line about N.19.c.5.6.

RIGHT SECTION. An officers patrol examined the enemy's wire opposite M.29.2. It is about 20 yards thick and stands 50 yards from the trench. The disused trench running S.W. from M.30.a.40.15. is very strongly wired, but the craters at M.30.a.35.30. are unwired. No enemy were seen or heard. The ground is very swampy.
  Our T.Ms. during the afternoon fired 150 rounds on to the enemy's second line at M.30.b.5.8½. Good results were obtained and the enemy's retaliation was feeble. Our M.Gs. were very active, nearly 10,000 rounds being fired on the enemy's communications during the night. Our snipers fired at a German in the front line at M.30.c.5¼.9¼.: he disappeared. They claim to have hit one of two officers seen about M.30.c.5¼.9¼.

PART II INTELLIGENCE.

LEFT SECTION. About 30 rounds light H.E. were fired in co-operation with T.Ms. on our front line about RED LAMP CORNER, and about 20 on salient in M.24.c. Some damage was caused to breastworks, and hostile M.Gs. were very active on these points during the night.
  During the night, the enemy were heard hammering corrugated iron about N.13.d.2.4. Fresh work appears to have been done at N.14.c.25.70. Material can be seen above the parapet here.
  Smoke was seen at the following points:-
  N.20.b.4.4. rising from 14 TREES CLUMP.
  N.20.b.30.55. from a dug-out yesterday and again this morning; a suspected H.Q.
  N.25.a.55.85. from DORA C.T.
  There was considerable movement observed throughout the day at the bend in C.T. at N.20.b.30.65. 37 men were observed to pass this point, many of them being single men.
  The Artillery were got on to several targets during the day with satisfactory results.
  On three occasions a light truck was seen to cross the sky-line near LA CLIQUETERIE Farm.
  Four men wearing greatcoats were seen to get out of disused trench at N.14.c.96.82. and walk along parados for a short distance and re-entered trench.

RIGHT SECTION. During the morning the enemy fired about 20-4.2's. on CHAPIGNY FM. and front line at M.29.4. At the same time a few L.T.M. shells fell on the front line. About 4.30 p.m. about 30 L.& H.T.M. shells were fired at M.29.1. There was also some trench mortaring of the front line in front of NEUVE CHAPELLE at intervals during the day. A hostile patrol was seen opposite M.30.2. during the night and dispersed by L.G.fire. Wiring and other working parties were heard at intervals through the night, and L.G. fire invariably caused work to cease.

Hdqrs. 56th Divn.
5th Decr. 1916.

T.C.Heald
Captain,
Intelligence, General Staff.

56th DIVISIONAL TACTICAL PROGRESS REPORT No. 39
from 8.0 a.m. 5th December to 8.0 a.m. 8th December 1916.

On receipt of current copy of Divisional Tactical Progress Report in the trenches, previous copy to be destroyed.

PART I OPERATIONS.

RIGHT SECTION.- Patrols examined enemy wire opposite MAUQUISSART CRATERS where our T.Ms. had fired, and found it badly damaged. The going here was good. Another patrol about M.30.a.9.6. was stopped 30 yds. from the hostile wire by the flooded nature of the ground. Wire was also examined for 200 yards North from M.35.d.7.0. and found to be very thick.

M.Gs. carried our programmes on enemy wire, roads and C.Ts. Snipers claim an orderly carrying a dixie and an Officer observing from M.30.c.52.92. where officers were seen observing yesterday.

Our L.T.Ms. fired about 150 rounds on enemy dug-out at M.30.c.65.70. Considerable debris was thrown up and a German seen to be killed. Retaliation heavy.

LEFT SECTION. - A patrol entered enemy front line near BEDFORD ROAD and saw no signs of the enemy or of recent occupation. Another patrol saw an enemy patrol leave his front line at N.13.c.9.3.- strength about 8. An enemy patrol, probably the same one, was soon moving about N.13.d.2.8. and fired on by our listening post. Extensive examinations of the enemy's wire were carried out. A good gap in enemy wire was found at N.13.c.9.3. Wire for 200 yards S.W. from N.8.d.3.2. was found to be low but very thick, while at N.13.d.40.65 it was reported as weak.

Our M.Gs. fired 12,000 rounds on enemy communications during the night.

Snipers had very few favourable targets yesterday but dispersed a working party near the house at N.25.b.8.8.

Our Heavy, Medium and Light T.Ms. combined in a shoot on enemy's front line wire and suspected M.G. Emplacement about DEVIL'S JUMP. Hostile retaliation was heavy, with T.Ms. and artillery and several bays have been blown in at N.24.c. & d.

PART II INTELLIGENCE.

RIGHT SECTION.- About 20 4.2" were fired at CHAPIGNY FARM and GLASS-HOUSE (M.24.c.0.2.) during the day. At noon M.24.1. was heavily shelled with M.T.Ms.

About 50 L.T.M. shells fell in M.29.2. about 3.30 p.m.

Enemy M.Gs. were active against the portions of our line damaged during the day. An enemy Listening Patrol near DUCKS BILL CRATER No. 5 was dispersed by L.G. fire.

LEFT SECTION.- Between 10.30 a.m. and 3.0 p.m. there was considerable hostile shelling of our lines in N.24, and a good deal of damage was done to breastwork. Enemy T.Ms. combined on the extreme right.

Work was seen being done on the new C.T. at N.14.c.95.05. Timber for this work appeared to be drawn from near 14 TREE CLUMP where two parties were seen to disappear.

Movement was seen about house at N.21.a.7.4. and on RUE d'ENFER- the latter parties of two or three.

Smoke was again seen rising from 14 TREE CLUMP.

Head Qrs. 56th Divn.

8th December, 1916.

Captain,

Intelligence, General Staff

38th DIVISIONAL TACTICAL PROGRESS REPORT No. 40.
from 8.0 a.m. 6th December to 8.0 a.m. 7th December, 1916.

On receipt of current copy of Divisional Tactical Progress Report
in the trenches, previous copy to be destroyed.

PART I OPERATIONS.

RIGHT SECTION. Our Artillery carried out registration during the day, and also three times effectively retaliated for hostile T.M. fire. Our L.T.Ms. fired 120 rounds on targets in N.30.a. cross roads. There was no retaliation. Our M.Gs. carried out night firing on PIETRE, RUE D'ENFER and tramways.
    A patrol inspected enemy wire from N.30.a.4.4. to 5.7. and found it very good over the whole stretch; at places it appeared as much as 30 yards thick. An officers patrol went out to try to cut an entrance in enemy wire about N.35.d.7.0. Wire is very thick and high here. About a dozen lines of wire had been cut when our patrol was observed and compelled to withdraw.

LEFT SECTION. A small raiding party consisting of two officers and 33 O.R. entered the enemy line about 2.0 a.m. at N.13.d.75.35. Whilst the covering party was being posted a party of 5 Germans (apparently a working party) were observed about N.13.d.70.60. on the parapet. They opened rapid fire on our covering party and then withdrew. They could not be followed up owing to a wide ditch intervening.
    The trench party established a block of 1 N.C.O, and 3 men thirty yards to the right of point of entry. The remainder of the Trench Party moved along the trench to the left of point of entry. They found mud and water along the whole length of front line between 2 and 3 feet deep. In many places duck boards were afloat. Owing to the state of the trenches, the party had to move along the top of the parapet which is in a fairly good state of repair in most places. On reaching a point 120 yards from point of entry they were challenged by two Germans who came out of a snipers post made of sandbags. These two Germans fired at the officer in charge of the Trench Party and they ran away across the open towards the German second line and were not seen again. They were fired at as they ran. The snipers post was examined and found to be empty. The Trench Party found 2 M.G. emplacements - one at point of entry and another about 50 yards to the left of that point. These emplacements are in good condition and are made of sandbags. They were found to be empty. There is a further snipers post midway between the two M.G. emplacements. Nothing further was discovered and after waiting until 3.20 a.m. to see if any enemy patrols appeared, the party withdrew having been in the enemy lines about 45 minutes. There were no casualties.
    An officers patrol examined the German wire about N.14.a.6.2.: it was found to be thick and strong. Another patrol entered the German trenches about N.24.d.60.25. It was unoccupied and much damaged by shell fire. The sergeant in charge reconnoitred behind the trench and found a truck which had apparently been used on the tramway, but he could discover no trace of the lines. The truck was about 3' by 2' wide. Two Very lights were fired towards the enemy second line, but no movement was observed. Our snipers fired on a man seen through a gap at L.14.a.72.32.

PART II INTELLIGENCE.
RIGHT SECTION. Between 11 and 12 noon about 30 rounds of hostile 4.2" fired from direction of AUBERS fell on area N. of NEUVE CHAPELLE without doing any damage. A few enemy L.T.Ms. were fired on points in our front line during the day. At 11 p.m. a hostile patrol was seen about 50 yards from their wire opposite N.35.b.8.1. Fire was opened on them and 1 man is believed to have been hit.

LEFT SECTION. During the afternoon considerable activity was shown by hostile T.Ms. and Artillery on our extreme right. Our Artillery replied vigourously, and the enemy ceased to fire. A patrol of 50 men in marching order without packs was seen moving in an Easterly direction along track at N.21.a.85.85. at 1.30 p.m. A few minutes later another party of 6 men passed the same spot. Unfortunately our Artillery could not be warned at the moment. Work was being done on trench at N.19.b.50.85. and movement was seen in new C.T. at N.20.b.30.65. A tramway is suspected to be in use about N.30.b. A party of 5 men working at N.13.d.7.6. & another party working on the C.T. about N.14.d.05.10. were dispersed by our Arty. At 11.10 a.m. 9 men in clean fatigue were seen at leave trench at
/N.14.c.95.05.

- 2 -

N.14.c.95.05. passed behind 14 TREE CLUMP and enter house at N.20.d.50.95. A machine gun emplacement is suspected at N.14.a.67.27. At N.14.a.97.67. there is a new steel plate surrounded by sandbags suspected to be used by M.G. at night.

Smoke was observed at the following points:-
- M.35.d.9.2.   Front line.
- N.21.a.65.50. House.
- N.20.b.5.0.   In front of house.
- N.21.d.40.15. From AUBERS DEFENCES.
- N.22.b.4.9.   From small group of houses.

John D. Crosthwaite

Hdqrs. 56th Division.

7th December, 1916.

Captain,
Intelligence, General Staff.

56th DIVISIONAL TACTICAL PROGRESS REPORT No. 41
from 8.0 a.m. 7th December, to 8.0 a.m. 8th December 1916.

<u>ON receipt of current copy of Divisional Tactical Progress Report in the trenches, previous copy to be destroyed.</u>

PART I OPERATIONS.

<u>RIGHT SECTION.</u>- An officers' patrol found DUCKS BILL Craters Nos.1 & 6 unoccupied. The road junction S.W. of No. 4 crater is flooded. Other patrols had nothing to report.

Our M.Gs. carried out a night firing programme on MIN du PIETRE.

At 3. p.m. our L.T.Ms. fired 80 rounds on enemy tramway at M.30. c.8.9. and at 4 p.m. 70 rounds on enemy lines about M.30.b.4.8., where an M.G. emplacement and dug-outs have been reported. Results appeared satisfactory.

<u>LEFT SECTION.</u>- No enemy were encountered by our patrols, who have nothing of interest to report.

Our M.Gs. dispersed three hostile Working Parties during the night, and it is believed that casualties were inflicted.

Our L.T.Ms. were quiet during the day, mist preventing observation.

At 3.15 p.m. five men wearing forage caps without rifles or equipment were seen walking behind front line at N.19.c.5.8. A sniper hit the leading man, who fell, and remainder doubled to cover.

At 3.30 p.m. four men carrying rifles, but without equipment, were seen walking towards their front line. A sniper hit one man and the others dropped into C.T. just by them.

PART II INTELLIGENCE.

<u>RIGHT SECTION.</u>- Enemy artillery was quiet during the day, but between 7 p.m. and 8 p.m. about 25 4.2" and 25 Field Gun shells were fired on area between S.TILLELOY and NEUVE CHAPELLE.

Hostile T.Ms. replying to our L.T.M. shoots were all firing well over our breastwork and doing no damage.

A party of 10 attempted to work on their wire early yesterday morning, under cover of the mist, but they were dispersed by L.G. fire. Two patrols were also fired on by L.Gs.

Two paper flags on which it was written that BUCHAREST had fallen to Bavarian troops, were placed in our wire with a bomb attached to each. These were exploded by snipers, and the flags brought in.

<u>LEFT SECTION.</u>- A few heavy T.M. shells fell about M.24.c.9.2. during the afternoon doing no damage.

A hostile M.G. firing from direction of BERTHA C.T. was very active last night.

A party off RED LAMP SALIENT was dispersed by L.G. fire.

Between 8. and 8.30 a.m. several small parties were seen to leave 14 TREE CLUMP and pass behind the trees to the rear of new C.T.

Movement was seen in a ruined house in RUE DELEVAL about N.14. b.90.35.

Head Qrs. 56th Divn.
8th December, 1916.

Captain,
Intelligence, General Staff.

56th DIVISIONAL TACTICAL PROGRESS REPORT No. 42
from 8.0 a.m. 7th December, 1916 to 9th December, 1916.

On receipt of current copy of Divisional Tactical Progress Report in the trenches, previous copy to be destroyed.

PART I OPERATIONS.

LEFT SECTION. Our M. and L.T.Ms. co-operated in a shoot on enemy's front line wire at N.14.c.6.9.2. to N.13.c.7.4. The light was bad, making observation difficult, but the wire was seen to be much damaged. Later our T.Ms. damaged the enemy's parapet about N.14.a.8.4. and his second line at N.13.d.2.2. Our M.Gs. displayed their usual activity during the night nearly 9,000 rounds being fired on to the enemy's communications

Our patrols reported the enemy to be working hard in his front line at M.24.d.6.2. and the wire to be in good condition there. The wire between N.13.c.9.3. to N.13.c.8.15. is weak with many gaps, and no signs of recent repairs.

Our snipers had many targets during the day. Men were frequently seen walking in the open behind their front line and running past the gaps in their parapet. Our L.Gs. dispersed a party of Germans seen near N.15.a.1.5.

RIGHT SECTION. Our patrols did not encounter any of the enemy, but they discovered recent foot prints in the mud in the ditch running S.E. from crater at M.36.a.1.9. to the German lines. It is thought this is the route used by the enemy who placed the notice on our wire. At 3.30 a.m. one of our patrols bombed DUCKS BILL Crater No. 1, M.36.c.1.9. to which the enemy replied with a few rifle shots.

PART II INTELLIGENCE.

LEFT SECTION. Out of 14 light shells fired by the enemy on to BEDFORD Rd. 12 were blind. A few M.T.M. shells fell on to our wire at M.24.c.80.05. A M.G. was firing during the morning from behind FME DELAVAL and this emplacement is suspected to be at N.14.d.9.95. - several rounds hitting the observers O.P. at N.8.a.2.4. A M.G. was reported as firing from the enemy's front line in M.24.d.

Much movement was again seen in new trench running parallel to BRTHA TR., timber being carried about at N.20.b.3.6.

Two men were seen looking over parapet at N.14.a.85.30. scanning our lines. A piece of white timber appeared over parapet at N.19.a.95.98. for a few minutes. A considerable amount of movement was seen in IRMA Tr: at N.14.b.2.2. A party of about 12 men were seen carrying timber and were evidently working close to here. Small parties were also observed passing gap at N.14.b.35.18.

A man was seen in front line at N.14.b.1.9. at regular intervals throughout the morning. A pole was seen being erected at N.13.d.2.2.

Smoke was seen at the following places:-
New trench at   N.14.b.8.5.
Ruins at   N.25.b.53.15.
House   N.20.b.30.28.
Dugout   N.20.b.15.30.
AUBERS DEFENCES   N.21.d.40.15.

A hostile 4.2" battery has been located at N.27.a.60.25., the flashes being plainly visible. It fires enfilade towards RICHEBOURG L'AVOUE.

RIGHT SECTION. A hostile working party was observed at 1.45 a.m., apparently repairing the parapet of DUCKS BILL Crater at M.36.c.15.85. A few men have been seen running between the front and support lines at M.30.a.5¼.9½.

T.L.C.Hrald
Captain,

Hdqrs. 56th Divn.

9th December, 1916.   Intelligence, General Staff.

56th DIVISIONAL TACTICAL PROGRESS REPORT No. 43,
from 8.0 a.m. 9th December, 1916 to 8.0 a.m. 10th Decr. 1916

On receipt of current copy of Divisional Tactical Progress Report in the trenches, previous copy to be destroyed.

PART I OPERATIONS.

LEFT SECTION.- Our artillery and T.Ms. co-operated in a shoot on enemy's lines between N.13.d.2.2. and N.13.d.5.3. good results being obtained. Our H.T.Ms. fired 8 rounds on to enemy front line at N.19.a.55.90. Our patrols were very active last night covering the whole front. Patrols in front of RHONDDA Sap N.8.d.0.5. observed no enemy movement. A patrol attempting to examine German wire near BEDFORD ROAD N.19.c.3.4. was fired on from several points in the front line, which apparently is now occupied here. A second patrol went out later to the same place along the right of BEDFORD ROAD, and located a large working party putting out new wire, and a strong covering party protecting them. On their return fire was brought to bear on this party. Another patrol reported the wire at N.19.a.55..95. to be in poor condition.

RIGHT SECTION.- Our artillery carried out a small bombardment of LES MOTTES FME. N.25.a.6.5. where much movement has been observed. The shooting was good. During the night our M.'s. fired on selected targets and C.Ts.

Our patrols were out along the whole front, but did not come into contact with the enemy.

The crater at M.30.c.1.3.was examined and no signs of the enemy found.

PART II INTELLIGENCE.

LEFT SECTION.- Enemy artillery and T.Ms. were inactive. Two men were seen outside our wire at about N.13 central. They were fired on disappeared. The enemy has succeeded in putting out about 250 yds. of new wire from BEDFORD ROAD to the South. New timber can be seen in enemy front line at N.13.c.95.35 - M.13.c.80.10 - N.19.a.3.6. (also a sniper's plate) and N.19.a.35.95. It is evident he is making strenuous efforts to repair his front line/reoccupy it at these points. New white planks have been put into CLARA C.T. Timber has been seen being carried along the trench at M.30.b.3.9. and M.30.b.2.8. LE PIETRE about N.20.b.3.5.& 14 TREE CLUMP is a centre of enemy activity, a great deal of movement being reported from here every day. A Headquarters is suspected here, men are continually being seen working here and smoke is seen here every day.

From 7.30 - 9.0 a.m. parties of twos and threes were observed passing in both directions along road from about N.25.b.35.25 to N.20.c.2.5. At 7.45 a.m. a German was seen here with a woman wearing a shawl moving S.W. first appearing about N.20.c.2.5.

A man was seen in trench at N.25.a.3.8.- also a man wearing forage cap seen looking over the parapet at M.30.b.3.9. A small black flag was seen on enemy's parapet at N.14.a.9.6. Two pigeons flew from M.30.b.3.9. at 12.30 p.m. and made off towards AUBERS.

Movement was observed near LA CLIQUETERIE Fm. Smoke was seen at the following points :- N.19.d.5.4.
N.19.a.6.7.
N.19.c.4.9.

OVER

RIGHT SECTION.- Just before 3.0 p.m. 12 L.T.M Shells fell about
M.30.a.4.9.   Enemy horse transport was heard at 1.45 a.m. about
M.30.a.85.70.
        A German Officer probably observing for T.Ms. was seen look-
ing over parapet at M.30.c.50.85.   He was fired at and disappeared.

                                        T.J.C.Heald

Head Qrs. 56th Divn.   Captain,
10th December, 1916.   Intelligence, General Staff.

56th DIVISIONAL TACTICAL PROGRESS REPORT No. 44.
from 8.0 a.m., 10th December, to 8.0 a.m. 11th December, 1916.

On receipt of current copy of Divisional Tactical Progress Report in the trenches, previous copy to be destroyed.

PART I OPERATIONS.

LEFT SECTION. Our M.T.Ms. bombarded the enemy work behind front line at N.13.d.4.5. damaging the parapet and throwing timber and wire into the air. Our L.T.Ms. co-operated and damaged the wire. A working party located by one of our patrols about N.13.d. central was dispersed by our L.T.Ms.

Patrols reported work being carried out in enemy front line at N.19.a.3.5. and a wiring party at N.19.a.2.3. L.G. and M.G. fire was directed at those on the return of the patrols. A patrol went out at 2.0 a.m. from N.13.d.4.9. with the object of entering and damaging the German trenches. An enemy working party was seen at the point chosen for entry; it was at least 30 strong, and there was another working party of similar strength about 70 yards further N. The patrol returned about 2.45 a.m. and our Artillery and T.Ms. opened fire with, it is believed, very successful results.

RIGHT SECTION. Our patrols were out along the whole front and encountered no signs of the enemy. A thorough inspection was made of our own wire.
Our Artillery bombarded points behind the enemy line where movement had been observed whilst our M.Gs. sprayed the road in front of the BOIS du BIEZ in S.5.d. during the night.

PART II INTELLIGENCE.

LEFT SECTION. The hostile artillery has been more active than it has been for some weeks. Their targets being our communication trenches and RUE TILLELOY. The enemy's T.Ms. were also active damaging our trenches at M.24.d.15.65. and at M.24.d.3.8. The heavies appeared to fire from various points in their line. One was located at N.19.c.12.62.

The enemy's parapet is being built up from N.19.a.3.6. to N.19.a.25.50. New sandbags can be seen at N.19.a.35.70.

At 10.0 a.m. 2 pigeons were thrown up from the front line at N.19.a.3.7.

Movement was seen at road junction in AUBERS N.27.a.55.20. LA CLIQUERERIE.Fm. Rd. in T.3.a. - a party of 20 men walking N.E. and 2 limbers and 2 men going the opposite direction.

Three large parties, one of 40 and two of 30 men left trench at N.21.a.9.7. and walk in an S. direction disappearing in clump of trees at N.21.a. A few wearing packs.

A little movement was seen on RUE DELAVAL at N.14.b.7.2 Our Artillery registered on all above points.

A man was seen working on revetment of BERTHA Tr. at N.14.c.37.20. and another on new C.T. at N.14.c.95.15. Two Germans were seen in front of LONG BARN at about N.26.b.80.55. A party of Germans seen in front of the cottage at N.20.b.9.5. was dispersed by shrapnel.

Smoke was seen at:-
AUBERS DEFENCES   N.21.d.40.15. (This is seen every day)
FROMELLES   "   N.22.b.65.35.
Dugout   N.20.b.3.5.   (Usual).
2nd line   N.19.a.85.90.
1st line   M.30.b.30.88.
Also from AUBERS Chimney N.27.c.0.6.

At 1.15 a.m., red flares, two at a time, were seen in enemy's line in direction of ARMENTIERES. Within half a minute enemy guns opened fire on the section opposite those.

RIGHT SECTION. Hostile artillery was more active than usual. 77mm. guns and 4.2" hows. appeared to be registering. Also some retaliation for our shoot on MUSKRAT MOUND (S.6.a.8.5.) Enemy T.Ms. were fairly active all day. A M.G.E. was located at M.30.c.55.80. Also a M.G. appeared to fire from about M.30.c.5.6. at an aeroplane. A hostile working party at M.35.d.8.2. was dispersed by our L.G. fire.

/ About

About M.36.a.central a hostile working party was fired on by our L.Gs. All sentries reported groans and cries of pain. The enemy M.Gs. replied vigorously. Our men at work on wire saw a German working party leave their trench at M.30.c.5.5. L.G. opened fire and the party retired hastily.

Movement in the enemy front line has been observed at M.30.c.55.85. There is a periscope among the tree stumps on enemy parapet at M.30.c.55.80. Smoke was seen at M.30.a.55.10 and N.25.a.65.60. Three Germans were seen opposite M.35.2. wearing soft hats.

Hdqrs. 53th Divn.
11th December, 1916.

T.I.C.Hkald
For. Captain, Lieut
Intelligence, General Staff.

56th DIVISIONAL TACTICAL PROGRESS REPORT No. 45
from 8.0 a.m. 11th December to 8.0 a.m. 12th December 1916.

On receipt of current copy of Divisional Tactical Progress Report
in the trenches, previous copy to be destroyed.

PART I OPERATIONS

RIGHT SECTION.- One of our patrols discovered two German working parties just South of SIGN POST Lane M.35.d.7.4. L.G. fire was directed on them from the trench with good result. Other patrols could find no signs of the enemy.

Our M.Gs. fired along the road in front of the BOIS DU BIEZ in S.3.a. and also on to the tracks in S.6.d. during the evening.

LEFT SECTION.- Our patrols were out on the whole front and report that enemy front line in M.24.d. is occupied, that the new wire between N.19.a.3.4. and N.19.a.35.70. is erected in front of the old wire and similar to our apronwire but not so high, and that the enemy wire in N.13.d. is still in poor condition. A working party 30 strong was located about N.19.a.35.38 on the parapet and on our patrols return L.G. fire was opened on this point.

Our artillery co-operated with our T.Ms. and rifle grenades at midnight in bombarding the new work between N.13.c.95.30 and N.13.c.75.10 - results not yet ascertained.

Our L.T.Ms. fired 60 rounds on the snipers post at N.19.a.3.7. The parapet was breached and wire badly cut. Slight retaliation.

The dug-out at N.14.a.85.45 also received attention. Our M.Gs. were again active during the night. Our snipers claim to have hit a man looking over the parapet at N.19.a.3.8.

PART II INTELLIGENCE.

RIGHT SECTION.- Enemy artillery was inactive, a few 4.2" and 77 mm. shells, however, falling on the front line. No damage was done.

Hostile M.Gs. fired occasional bursts during the night, the following emplacements being reported as used :- M.30.c.5.6., M.30.a.40.15 and M.30.a.5.5.

Hostile T.Ms. were decidedly active yesterday but only one direct hit was obtained. Emplacements were located about M.30. c.5.6. and M.30.a.62.02. A train was heard well behind the enemy's lines between 5.30 and 6.30 p.m. The trolley lines were also being used during the night.

A working party was heard about M.36.a. central, L.G. fire was opened and noise ceased. A party was also heard on the right of DUCKS BILL CRATER about M.36.c.0.9.

A German was seen in the first line at M.30.c.55.75 wearing usual uniform and soft hat. 2 Germans carrying rifles at the trail left MUSKRAT MOUND S.6.a.8.5. and disappeared into the wood at left rear.

Timber and sandbags were thrown up on parapet at M.30.c.53.60. A snipers plate has been placed on the parapet at M.30.c.53.95. New wire has been put out on edge of Crater at M.30.a.55.50. 200 to 300 yards of canvas screen are visible at M.26.b.85.75. Smoke was seen at HAUT POMMEREAU WOOD at T.1.b.3.5. and Chimney in MARQUILLIES.

LEFT SECTION.
Hostile artillery was quieter also their T.Ms. A H.T.M. was quickly silenced by our guns, the emplacement being located at N.19.c.00.55. At 5.30 p.m. sounds of railway activity were heard from AUBERS. Between 5.55 p.m. and 6.30 p.m. transport could be heard N. of AUBERS.

At M.24.d.7.4. new timber is visible above the parapet. Two men wearing equipment and rifles, left trench at N.15.c.10.88 and entered again at N.15.c.0.7. probably because of its bad state.

/Movement

2.

Movement observed at :-

    N.21.a.9.7.   - over open
    N.20.b.30.65 - in new C.T.
    N.14.c.95.10 - along C.T. to 14 TREE CLUMP.
    N.21.d.5.2.   - over open.
    T.3.a.   - LA CLIQUETERIE FARM Road - cyclist moving S.W.
    N.26.c.8.3.   - along road.

Smoke was seen at the following places :-

    N.20.a.85.65 from house in RUE DELEVAL
    N.14.b.60.18 from house
    N.20.b.3.2.   from house
    N.14.b.60.05 from behind trees on RUE DELEVAL.
    N.20.a.95.75 from suspected dug-out behind screen on cross roads.
    N.20.b.15.40 from suspected dug-out.
    Houses in AUBERS viz:- N.27.a.2.0 - N.27.a.3.0 - N.27.a.38.00 - N.27.a.45.10 - N.27.a.6.2.

T.C. Heald Lieut.

Head Qrs. 56th Divn.

12th December, 1916.

Intelligence,
General Staff.

53th DIVISIONAL TACTICAL PROGRESS REPORT No. 36.
from 8.0 a.m. 12th December to 8th/13th December, 1916.

On receipt of current copy of Divisional Tactical Progress Report in the trenches, previous copy to be destroyed.

PART I OPERATIONS.

Right Section. No enemy were seen by our covering parties and patrols last night. During the night we shelled roads, houses and C.Ts. in retaliation for hostile T.M. fire During the day registration was continued. Our M.Gs. carried out the usual night firing and rapid rifle fire was opened twice during the night.

Left Section. On two occasions our patrols saw large enemy working parties at N.19.d.3.0. working in their parapet and wire. On each occasion M.G. and L.G. fire was opened. Our Artillery fired throughout the day in retaliation for hostile T.M. fire. At 2.30 p.m. an organised shoot was carried out by Div.Arty. on suspected T.M. emplacements and silenced hostile T.Ms. till dark. Our L.T.Ms. fired 150 rounds during the day and destroyed a dug-out at N.14.a.85.45. and it is believed obtained direct hits on an M.G.E. near this spot. Our bombardment on night 11/12th of new work about N.13.c.8.2. was very successful, many of the revetments have been blown up and the parapet is breached at N.13.c.9.2.
Our M.Gs. were active on enemy W.Ps., C.Ts. and roads.

PART II INTELLIGENCE.

Right Section. Enemy artillery was inactive, except for 8-4.2" shells N. of NEUVE CHAPELLE and some 77 mm. along the front line. On the other hand, hostile T.Ms. were very active, firing over 50 H.T.M. and 200 L.T.M. bombs against the left battalion front, several direct hits being obtained and the trench blocked in two places. Hostile M.Gs. were also more active than usual, a gun about M.30.a.40.15. sweeping the parapet of the CHORD Line almost continuously between 6 and 8 p.m. Our listening post at M.30.a. reported a party of enemy advancing down ditch in front of this point and L.G. fire was opened.
Artillery observers report the following locations:-
H.T.M. - M.30.c.5.6.
         M.30.a.62.02. a dug-out previously reported here.
M.G.E. - M.30.c.5.3.)
         M.30.a.5.5.) have been previously reported
         M.30.a.50.15.)

Left Section. Enemy artillery was quiet during this period, but H.T.Ms. were active in the morning on the right subsection. New work has been seen at N.13.c.9.2. where revetting posts can be seen. There was again movement near the new C.T. at N.20.b.30.35. and parties seen moving across the open to 14 TREE CLUMP. Enemy trench at N.15.c.10.75. is evidently in a bad state of repair as men were seen to get out here and walk along behind the trench. The house at N.14.d.10.55. is suspected to be a H.Q. Men have been seen going to and from this house at frequent intervals. The track at N.21.a.35.90 was also in use during the day. Infantry observers report the followi locations -H.T.M. N.19.c.05.45. andther independent observer
                  N.19.c.12.62   (giving N.19.c.0.4.
                  M.24.d.9.5.

Smoke was seen at:
          I.15.c.05.70. trench.
          N.14.d.95.55. house.
          N.19.a.94.98. trench junction.
          M.30.b.10.45. support trench.
          M.24.d.84.55. front line.
          N.13.d.15.10. support line.

John D. Crosthwaite

Hdqrs. 56th Divn.   Captain,
13th December, 1916.   Intelligence, General Staff.

55th DIVISIONAL TACTICAL PROGRESS REPORT No. 47
from 8.0 a.m. 13th December to 8.0 a.m. 14th November '16

On receipt of current copy of Divisional Tactical Progress Report in the trenches, previous copy to be destroyed.

PART I OPERATIONS.

LEFT SECTION.- Our L.T..s. fired on the enemy's trenches from N.13.d.15.55 to N.13.d.3.5. with good results. Wire was cut, parapet breached & a sniper's post destroyed. A suspected M.G. emplacement at N.8.d.3.1. was also fired at and destroyed.

Our M.Gs. showed their usual activity during the night.

Patrols were out along the whole front but could discover no signs of the enemy. Our wire was inspected from N.13.c.75.85 to N.13.d.35.95 and reported good.

RIGHT SECTION.- Our Artillery in co-operation with our T..s. carried out a bombardment with over 300 rounds on enemy trenches at N.30.a.55.22 and N.30.c.3.4. from which places hostile T..s. and M.Gs. have been active lately. At the same time our 18 Pdrs. covered the communications to these points with their fire. The shooting was observed to be very effective, and much damage was done. During the night our M.Gs. fired on the points damaged. One gun fired on the Railway Station at HALPEGARBE.

Owing to the large number of men engaged in wiring active patrolling was not possible, but our covering parties did not find any signs of the enemy.

PART II INTELLIGENCE.

LEFT SECTION.- A German working party was seen coming over their parapet at N.13.d.00.55 at 4.15 p.m. It was fired on by our M.Gs. L.Gs. and rifles and it disappeared.

The enemy is evidently not yet fully occupying his front line as last night Very lights were sent up from the 2nd line.

The usual movement was seen about N.20.b.30.65, parties of 3 men were seen continually passing this point, and proceeding in the direction of the AUBERS - LE PIETRE Road. A horse and limber were seen on the LA CLIQUETERIE F..Road in T.3.a.; also clouds of smoke probably from a locomotive on the road.

A heavy hostile battery firing 15 rounds on a target well to our right from 4.45 to 5.0 p.m. last night is suspected to be at T.3.d.90.1.

Large quantities of fresh earth are visible on IR.A C.T. at N.14.b. 2.2. and the gap at N.14.b.24.20 where it was possible to see men pass has been boarded up. The suspected M.G. emplacement at N.14.b.05.85 has been worked upon, fresh earth and boarding being visible. All movement on the RUE DELEVAL is visible between N.14.b.87.27 and N.14.b.75.18. Several men were seen moving along it in both directions but no large parties.

Two men were seen pushing a truck in a S.E. direction on the light railway at N.15.a.10.15. Smoke at :-

N.20.a.75.35.	suspected dug-out.
N.20.b.1.4.	do.
N.20.b.3.3.	dug-out.
N.20.b.25.50	do.
N.20.d.50.95	house (direct hit by our artillery)
N.22.c.40.35	AUBERS defences.
N.23.d.10.85	do.

RIGHT SECTION.- The hostile artillery were inactive. A little work was heard in the enemy's lines at N.36.a.35.45. The enemy is evidently occupying his front line in this Section as much movement has been seen. Two Germans were seen at N.36.a.35.45. Pumping was observed about N.35.d.8.3. at 9.30 a.m. and a rifle was shown over the parapet. Two Germans in soft caps and blue tunics, possibly miners overalls were seen opposite N.35.5. Another seen soon after appeared to be wearing a gas mask. A German wearing a grey forage cap showed himself for a second or two in the Crater at N.30.a.55.55.

New wire has been put out by the Germans at N.30.c.52.92.

/Smoke

2.

Smoke seen at :-

        M.35.d.8.3.   1st line trench
        M.30.a.30.02   2nd do.
        M.30.c.85.75   2nd do.
        M.30.c.80.45   2nd do.

Large dense clouds of smoke were seen at various places yesterday.
White cloud in front of BOIS DU BIEZ.
Red   "   at M.30.c.85.90 from 8.55 to 9.10 a.m.
White " " N.25.a.15.07   " 10.45 " 11.5 a.m.

                                                    T.H.Hiald

Head Qrs. 53th Divn.   Captain,
14th December, 1915.   Intelligence, General Staff.

56th DIVISIONAL TACTICAL PROGRESS REPORT No. 48
from 8.0 a.m. 14th December to 8.0 a.m. 15th December, 1916.

On receipt of current copy of Divisional Tactical Progress
Report in the trenches, previous copy to be destroyed.

PART I OPERATIONS.

LEFT SECTION. Our artillery was active shelling enemy front line in N.14.a. and in co-operation with T.Ms. his second line in N.19.c., where T.M. emplacements are suspected. Our L.T.Ms fired on reserve breastwork in N.19.c. doing considerable damage, breaching the parapet and throwing trench boards and wire into the air.
Our H.T.Ms. also fired 7 rounds effectively on WICK Salient, the parapet being levelled for at least 10 yards at N.13.d.00.55.
Our M.Gs. were active throughout the night on enemy wire, breastworks and communications. Patrols who were out at intervals along the front had nothing to report.

RIGHT SECTION. At 1.30 p.m. we opened an organised bombardment of the enemy trenches about M.36.a.4.9. and the C.Ts. in rear. M.T.Ms. fired 15 rounds and L.T.Ms. 50 rounds, field hows. 155 rounds and 18-prs. 110 rounds. At the same time 50 Stokes shells were fired on enemy line about M.30.a.5.2. and 18 prs. fired on heads of C.Ts. and second line. Considerable damage was done by both these shoots, much material being thrown up from the trenches and the wire badly damaged. Enemy trenches appeared to be very wet, as a considerable amount of water was thrown up. Hostile retaliation was quickly put on, but was weak. Our L.T.Ms. also fired 80 rounds on M.35.d.9.4.
At 12.15 p.m. a hostile T.M. was observed to fire one round from N.19.c.35.05.; a field gun battery fired in conjunction with 6" Hows on this spot, and several direct hits were obtained. Ammunition was exploded and the emplacement was in flames for half an hour.
At night our M.Gs. fired on areas bombarded and on cross roads in rear. A fighting patrol worked Southwards from DUCKS BILL and covered all the ground in M.35.d., but without discovering any sign of the enemy.

PART II INTELLIGENCE.

LEFT SECTION. Hostile artillery was more active than usual and shelled RED LAMP Corner and ROTTEN ROW during the day, but their T.Ms. were very quiet. The enemy kept up heavy M.G. fire from 4.0 p.m. till midnight, one gun firing from about N.13.d.2.6. and another against the extreme right of the Section. A patrol of 10 Germans lying outside our wire at M.24.6.3.7. bombed a covering party to wiring party as they were coming over the parapet and then immediately ran away. Horse transport was heard by several observers on the RUE d'ENFER at 4.45 p.m.
Repairs have been done to the enemy front line at N.14.c.25.75. Earth was thrown over the parapet at N.13.d.05.55. Much movement was again seen about 14 TREE CLUMP and also smoke. Our Artillery fired on the men. Men wearing white overalls were seen at N.27.a.9.9. and the usual movement in C.T. at N.20.b.30.85. Four men were seen using the track at N.21.c.2.5. and linesmen were observed examining wires in IRMA C.T. about N.14.b.55.15.
At 12.45 p.m. parties of 4 to 10 men in clean fatigue passed TRAMWAY CORNER - 40 men in all. A gun was laid on this point, but only one other man was seen to pass. Two men were seen walking on the road at N.26.b.7.1. Movement was seen in the roof of the house at N.26.d.89.54. Smoke was seen at:-

N.21.d.40.15 & N.26.d.10.85. AUBERS DEFENCES.
N.26.d.45.60.	House.	N.20.b.15.40.	Dugout.
N.27.a.40.05.	House.	N.20.a.95.75.	Dugout.
N.20.b.32.26.	Ruins. Our artillery fired on this.	N.23.c.15.60.	Chimney stack.
N.20.b.30.55.	Yesterday & today. Suspected H.Q.	N.21.a.8.6.	Suspected dug-out.

RIGHT SECTION. Hostile artillery was fairly active yesterday. About 80 rounds 4.2" Hows fell in the section; targets appeared to be MIN ST. by day and the MOATED GRANGE by night. Very little damage was done. T.Ms. were quiet. Six heavy rounds fell near M.35.4.

/without

without doing any damage. It fired from M.30.d.80.85. An M.G. swept our parapet at intervals from DUCKS BILL Southwards. Trains were heard at 8.0 p.m. and 10.30 p.m. Men were seen going towards AUBERS over the open just N. of BOIS de BIEZ. A German was again seen in the crater at M.30.a.55.55. and he was believed to be hit by our sniper. A small screen has been put up in enemy front line at M.30.c.55.85 where an officer was seen observing. A crows nest can be seen in a tree at M.30.c.55.95. Work was been done on enemy front line at M.30.c.6.7.

John D. Crosthwaite

Hdqrs. 56th Divn.

15th December, 1916.

Captain,
Intelligence,
General Staff.

56th DIVISIONAL TACTICAL PROGRESS REPORT No. 49
from 8.0 a.m. 15th December to 8.0 a.m. 16th December 1916.

On receipt of current copy of Divisional Tactical Progress Report
in the trenches, previous copy to be destroyed.

PART I OPERATIONS

LEFT SECTION.- Our artillery fired on enemy line about N.8.d.30.15. and the DISTILLERY - N.19.c.3.0., whilst out T.Ms. caused considerable damage to the SUGAR LOAF and to the enemy's wire about M.24.d.5.3. Our M.Gs. expended over 8,000 rounds on enemy's communications during the night.

A patrol from the left sub-section saw five Germans near their parapet at N.14.c.25.85. Fire was opened on their return.

A patrol from the right sub-section saw three Germans examining our wire, a ditch prevented them from rounding these up, so they returned to the trench and dispersed them with L.G. fire.

Our snipers fired two shots at a man seen in a gap in the parapet at N.14.a.65.25.

Four rifle grenades fired on to a hostile M.G. suspected to be firing from N.14.c.0.7. soon silenced it.

RIGHT SECTION.- Our artillery fired 10 rounds H.E. into trench at M.30.d.0.6. doing much material damage.

At 10.30 a.m. our L.T.Ms. fired 30 rounds, slow, on to enemy's front line at M.30.a.3.4. where a gap in the parapet could be seen and movement observed. The parapet was wrecked. They also replied to hostile L.T.M. fire and silenced them.

Our M.Gs. shewed their usual activity firing especially on to communications and points damaged by our shell fire. One of our patrols examined the ditch from M.29.b.9.1. to M.30.a.3.4. The ditch contained 2 ft. of water, the grass around it was long and the ground marshy. No signs of the enemy were encountered. Another patrol examined the crater at M.30.a.5.6. and found it full of water. The small crater to the left of it was thinly wired round the lip, but there was no recent work, and neither crater shewed signs of occupation.

PART II INTELLIGENCE.

LEFT SECTION.- Enemy artillery fired intermittently on RUE TILLELOY about FAUQUISSART Village, and on the reserve line between ELGIN and STRAND C.Ts., but their T.Ms. were again quiet.

A M.G. was located at N.13.d.2.6. firing on RED LAMP corner and another gun is suspected at N.19.b.00.55.

An enemy Working Party at N.14.a.75.50 was dispersed by L.G.fire.

A platform in a tree at N.20.b.25.10 can be seen.

MOVEMENT.
2 men carrying shovels and wearing no equipment passed a gap in enemy parapet at N.14.b.07.75. There was the usual movement in C.T. N.20.b.30.65. One party of 8 were seen. They disappeared into the willows East of this point.

15 men in 2's and 3's left trench at N.21.a.9.7. and walked S. disappearing into low wood. A few men passed TRAMWAY CORNER during the day.

RIGHT SECTION.- About a dozen 4.2" on end of MOATED GRANGE and CHAPIGNY FM. and some 77 mm. on front line on our extreme right was the only hostile artillery activity.

MOVEMENT.
A man was seen walking along the track in N.32.d. and there was some movement on the CRIQUETERIE FM. road in T.3.a.

Parties of 20 men and over were seen in and around MOULIN du PIETRE.

/Smoke.

P.T.O.

SMOKE

N.20.b.15.40	Dugout.
N.20.b.30.55	Dugout - suspected H.Q.
N.20.b.30.02	BERTHA C.T.
N.21.d.40.15	AUBERS Defences.
N.22.b.7.4.	FROMELLES "
N.20.d.50.85	house.
N.20.b.32.36	ruins
N.27.a.3.0	house
N.26.c.80.45	house
N.26.d.7.8.	house
N.20.d.4.9.	ruins
N.36.c.1.6.	front line

Head Qrs. 53th Divn.

16th December, 1916.

T.L.C.Hoald
Lieutenant,
for Lieut-Colonel,
General Staff.

56th DIVISIONAL TACTICAL PROGRESS REPORT No. 59
from 8.0 a.m. 16th December to 8.0 a.m. 17th December, 1916.

PART I OPERATIONS.

Left Section. Our Artillery and T.Ms. of all calibres co-operated in bombarding the enemy's line from DEVILS JUMP to WICK SALIENT causing considerable damage especially in the vicinity of N.13.d.30.55. Two Germans observed blown up at DEVILS JUMP. Our L.T.Ms. also fired at an enemy M.G.E. and snipers post at N.13.d.05.70. and N.13.d.85.70. The parapet was blown in and what seemed to be a small light trolley was thrown in the air, two wheels being distinctly seen. Our L.T.Ms. later fired on N.13.c.95.50. where work had been observed. Our M.Gs. kept the damaged points under their fire during the night. Our patrols did not encounter any of the enemy: they report that the enemy's wire from N.13.d.0.6. to N.13.d.65.65 is non-existent.

Right Section. Our Artillery and T.Ms. co-operated in a shoot (a) on dug-outs, M.G.Es. and T.M.Es. round M.36.b.2.8.; the shooting of the Artillery was very effective, the ROTUNDA at M.30.c.5.5. was badly damaged. The T.Ms. were troubled with attacking base plates and consequently were not so effective (b) on drains round M.35.d.85.35. The enemy retaliation was silenced by our L.T.Ms. and we finished up with 100 rounds on drains at junction of drains at M.30.a.90 55. Our M.Gs. showed their usual activity during the night.

One of our patrols proceeded N.E. from M.29.b.0.2. as far as the road. Patrol observed aerial torpedoes and rifle grenades fired from about M.30.a.4.0. No enemy encountered. Another patrol examined the three small craters at M.30.a.65.85. All were flooded: they were thinly wired, but wire was old and much damaged. The enemy opened M.G. fire from about M.30.a.85.55. but caused us no casualties. Another patrol examined ground in front of post at M.30.c.08.47. It was wet and marshy, and the post could not be approached without noise.

PART II INTELLIGENCE.

Left Section. The hostile artillery was inactive, there being no retaliation to our combined shoot. A hostile M.G. is reported to have fired from N.14.c.3.8. A barricade is being erected across the road by ruined house at N.25.b.8.9. The enemy fired some rifle grenades at RED LAMP Corner which appeared to come from N.13.d.8.65. The usual smoke and movement were seen from the vicinity of 14 TREE CLUMP viz:- N.20.b.15.40., N.20.b.30.55. (H.Q.).

Right Section. The hostile retaliation to our bombardment was not strong. There was a quick reply on the left from hostile M.T.Ms. and aerial torpedoes, but little damage was done. During the afternoon there was a small bombardment of the N. end of NEUVE CHAPELLE and CHATEAU REDOUBT (M.35.c.9.4.). About 30 "minnies" fell about M.35.1. The hostile M.Gs. were fairly active last night. About 12 noon, smoke was observed apparently from a train on the railway in T.2.a. There seems to be a gap in the enemy parapet at M.36.c.15.70. and movement is seen through this.

F. I. Oldfield
Lieutenant.

Hdqrs. 56th Divn.
17th December, 1916.   Intelligence, General Staff.

On receipt of current copy of Divisional Tactical Progress Report in the trenches, previous copy to be destroyed.

56th DIVISIONAL TACTICAL PROGRESS REPORT No. 51
from 8.0 a.m. 17th December to 8.0 a.m. 18th December 1916.

On receipt of current copy of Divisional Tactical Progress Report in the trenches, previous copy to be destroyed.

PART I OPERATIONS.

LEFT SECTION.- Our T.Ms. fired on the M.G. Empl. at N.8.d.30.05. The parapet was blown in and the M.G. has not fired since. Also on N.13.d.20.55 where work had been reported.
　　　Our M.Gs. displayed their usual activity during the night about 6,250 being fired on selected targets in the enemy's lines.
　　　One of our patrols went out from N.13.b.2.1. and located an enemy patrol coming through their wire. They returned with this information, and M.G. fire was opened. Results not ascertained. Other patrols reported no signs of the enemy.
　　　Our snipers fired at 3 men at SUGAR LOAF SALIENT; they disappeared.

RIGHT SECTION.- Owing to mist our artillery were inactive, occasionally firing a few rounds on points where movement had been observed lately. Our M.T.Ms. fired on M.35.d.95.50 where three dugouts had been located. Much damage was observed. Our L.T.Ms. bombarded enemy front line and wire from M.36.a.3.3. to M.36.a.35.55. Our M.Gs. maintained their usual fire during the mist and night.
　　　A small officer's patrol left M.29.d.1.8. at 7.30 p.m. and proceeded on the right of stream running N.E. from this point. After crossing another stream running to the right about 80 yds. from our lines the remains of a light railway were found. On reaching a point M.30.a.35.15 a hostile patrol, 15 strong, was seen emerging from crater M.30.a.3.3. By working to the left and slightly back an encircling movement of the enemy was baulked. The patrol returned safely at 10 p.m. During the reconnaissance a footpath, apparently made by enemy patrol, was observed to run from M.30.c.1.8. to M.30.a.4.2.
　　　A small patrol left M.30.a.2.7. at 7.40 p.m. and proceeded to crater M.30.a.42.49 which bore no signs of occupation. Patrol then visited the outer craters running N.E. until a point M.30.a.45.68 was reached where the patrol listened for 15 minutes. A dog was heard barking in enemy lines due East and transport was also heard in the same direction. The patrol returned at 9.35 p.m.
　　　A patrol of the enemy having been reported cutting our wire at M.35.b.98.70 two patrols were sent out with a view to establishing contact with the enemy and a L.T.M. was got into position to cover them. Patrols proceeded on right and left banks of ditch running S.E. towards enemy lines. None of the enemy were encountered however and the patrol returned to our lines. Enemy flare lights were sent up from behind craters at M.30.d.55.15.
　　　A small patrol under 2nd/Lieut. S.C. YEATES of the Q.W.R. went out at 11.30 p.m. from SUNKEN Rd. C.T. to discover which craters the enemy occupied and examine the wire. Patrol worked along our wire from SUNKEN Rd. to TILLELOY SOUTH C.T.; they then followed a ditch for 100 yards towards the German lines and then turned right till they reached the DUCK'S BILL CRATER M.36.c.0,9 The Northern German crater seemed to be unoccupied, but voices were heard in the centre one, and shots were fired at them from it. Turning half left towards the German lines they found a "snake" trench, 3 ft. 6 in. deep and full of water. Crossing the trench they inspected the German wire and found it very thick. Patrol then returned having been out 3 hours.

PART II INTELLIGENCE.

LEFT SECTION. - Observation yesterday was impossible owing to mist. Hostile Artillery and T.Ms. were inactive. A hostile working party heard at N.13.d.5.5. was fired on by one of our Lewis Guns and sounds of work ceased.

/RIGHT SECTION.

RIGHT SECTION. - A few 4.2" fell round CHATEAU REDOUBT and in
M.35.a. and b. causing no damage.   Hostile T.Ms. replied vigorously
to our fire, about 20 rounds falling in the vicinity of our emplacement.   Our artillery silenced them when they were located.
        The enemy snipers were very active and caused us two casualties
at Stand to.

T. Lithald
Lieutenant,
Intelligence, General
Staff.

Head Qrs. 56th Divn.

18th December, 1916.

56th DIVISIONAL TACTICAL PROGRESS REPORT No. 52.
from 8.0 a.m. 18th December to 8.0 a.m. 19th December, 1916.

On receipt of current copy of Divisional Tactical Progress Report
in the trenches, previous copy to be destroyed.

PART I OPERATIONS.

RIGHT SECTION. A combined Artillery and T.M. shoot was carried out at
11.30 a.m. on enemy lines behind the WINCHESTER Craters and C.Ts. in
rear. 4.5" Hows. fired 300 rounds on trench junctions and M.T.Ms.
fired 30 rounds on their front line. L.T.Ms. co-operated, but
shifting base plates caused great inaccuracies. Fresh emplacements
were constructed and the L.T.M. programme was completed in the afternoon
with good effect. During the night and early morning, our M.Gs. were
active over enemy's roads and tracks. Principle targets, MOULIN de
PIETRE, RUE d'ENFER, LA RUSSE.

An officers patrol found enemy wiring parties at work opposite
S.5.3. and covered by strong and vigilant covering parties. Two Lewis
guns traversed this area on the return of the patrol. The going is
reported to be good here. A second officers patrol attempted to
reconnoitre enemy's wire opposite M.35.3. They examined the road
running parallel to the lines M.35.d.7.6. - M.35.d.95.95 and found it
a foot deep in water and the ditches at the side of the road impassible.
A patrol lay out by the enemy wire at M.24.d.55.15. A T.M. half right
from this position, opened fire on a whistle being blown and a Very
light was sent up as each round was fired. An Officers patrol examined
the COLVIN Craters. Two men were left on the far lip and the patrol
moved to its right front. The enemy were heard talking and pumping
about M.3.a.4.9. Two Germans were seen to get up and return hurriedly
to their lines and rifle grenades were fired into the craters.

LEFT SECTION. 18-pdrs. fired on EVA C.T. and on the DISTILLERY LES MOTTES
Farm breastwork and field hows. on the new trench running N.E. from
MIN du PIETRE. L.T.Ms. and M.T.MS. co-operated in a shoot on enemy
front line and wire at M.24.d.60.35. - 80.50. Considerable damage was
done and hostile retaliation was slight. M.Gs. fired on enemy breastworks and communications during the night. The front was patrolled
throughout the night without meeting any trace of the enemy. The front
line is reported to be held at M.24.d.6.2. A german looking over the
parapet at M.30.b.25.85. was fired at.

PART II INTELLIGENCE.

RIGHT SECTION. Hostile Artillery was less active, but fired 30-4.2's. near
MOATED GRANGE, some near the T.M. emplacement near NEW CUT ALLEY and
along the front line. Hostile T.Ms. fired 45 rounds on head of
WINCHESTER STREET and 50 at bend of NEW CUT ALLEY, and some medium and
light bombs into our wire in M.35.5. and M.29.1. A camouflage tree
is suspected at M.30.c.52.85. Movement was seen near -
                    near HAUT POMMEREAU
           along road at N.25.c.9.7. and N.31.a.4.8., where carrying
parties were seen. Stakes can be seen along the road and it is thought
the screening is in process of extension.

LEFT SECTION. A few shells fell near PICANTIN AV. at 11 a.m. At 3.30 p.m.
ROTTEN ROW was shelled and more than 50% failed to detonate. About 40
shells were fired on our front line about BEDFORD ROAD. Active M.Gs.
are suspected at N.14.c.0.7. and N.15.a.1.5. The listening post at
N.13.d.80.95. reported enemy patrol of 8 - 10 men crossing its front
They were dispersed by L.G. fire. A hostile W.P. on their parapet at
N.13.d.8.3. was also dispersed. A long ladder was seen up a tree at
N.32.a.25.65 (about) The screen at RUE DELEVAL has been extended.
Canvas can be seen in the tree at N.20.a.85.65. There is a dump of
new timber on the parapet of BERTHA TR. at N.14.c.40.15. Work has
been done at N.20.b.30.55. Much new timber revetting can be seen in
CLARA at N.19.d.8.1. Fresh earth has been thrown up from trench at
N.14.b.37.00. There is a small dump covered with tarpaulin at
N.14.c.05.30.

/ Movement

- 2 -

MOVEMENT.

A small party carrying poles at N.32.a.2.5.
A party of 12 moving along the road S. of 14 TREE CLUMP.
Three men were seen working near CLIQUETERIE Farm, probably on the trench at T.3.a.20.55.
Four men were seen working on the wire in front of the AUBERS DEFENCES at N.26.b.05.20. They ceased work at 8.45 a.m. Usual movement at N.20.b.30.65.
There was considerable movement along RUE DELAVAL Artillery were informed and a gun was laid on it.
A party of 30 were seen and also 6 men carrying what looked like a stretcher. Both these parties were dispersed by the Artillery.
Two men were seen pushing a truck along the tramway at N.14.d.80.85.

Smoke.

N.13.d.10.35.	Support Line.
N.19.a.9.5.	Redoubt.
N.21.d.40.15.	AUBERS DEFENCES.
N.20.b.1.4.	Dugout.
N.20.a.75.60.	Trench.
N.20.b.30.55.	H.Q. Dugout.
N.22.c.40.55.	AUBERS DEFENCES.

John W. Crosthwaite

Hdqrs. 56th Divn.

19th December, 1916.

Captain.

Intelligence, General Staff.

56th DIVISIONAL TACTICAL PROGRESS REPORT, No. 54,
from 8.0 a.m. 19th December to 8.0 a.m. 20th December 1916.

On receipt of current copy of Divisional Tactical Progress Report in the trenches, previous copy to be destroyed.

PART I OPERATIONS.

RIGHT SECTION.- Our artillery and Stokes Mortars co-operated in bombarding enemy trench junction at M.35.d.85.35. Firing was successful no base plate trouble being experienced. The enemy's retaliation was heavy, their T.Ms. continuing to fire for some time after our guns opened on them.

Our M.Gs. carried out their usual programme during the night.

Our patrols were very active last night, bringing back much useful information and four prisoners. The details are :- A small patrol examined the old trenches from M.35.b.80.25 to M.36.a.1.5., from M.35.b.95.20 to M.36.a.2.5. and from M.36.a.00.15 to M.36.a.25.50. They were about 5 ft. deep and 4 ft. wide, the second one had a revetted parapet with a few shelters.

At 6.35 p.m. a patrol left the trench at M.29.d.95.80 and followed stream running N.E. for 100 yards. At this point a stream was found to be running S.E. at right angles to the first stream. The patrol followed this up for about 100 yards and then proceeded along another stream running to the left. While reconnoitring this stream a hostile T.M. was observed to be firing from M.30.c.8.9. and the near the emplacement a light railway was heard working. The enemy's wire at this point is thick and in a good state of repair. No enemy patrol was encountered and our patrol returned at 7.40 p.m.

A small officers' patrol left M.35.b.95.78 and proceeded to COLVIN Craters in one of which a dead German was found. The body was in an advanced state of decomposition and had probably been there for 7 or 8 weeks. Patrol then went N. between Craters and the enemy line. No enemy were encountered or seen but sounds of talking and coughing were heard. Enemy wire was found to be thick and high and no gaps could be found in it. Patrol returned by same route having been out for 1½ hours.

At 6.20 a.m. a party of the enemy was reported outside our wire. A contact patrol was sent out under Lance-Corporal WOOLLEY. Our patrol concealed themselves in the Copse just outside the CHORD Tr. M.30.b.1.9. and were able to see the enemy party against the snow. L/Cpl. WOOLLEY shot the biggest German and called upon the rest to surrender, which they did, all four of them being brought back to our lines.

LEFT SECTION. - Our artillery and T.Ms. shelled selected targets round WICK SALIENT, good results being obtained, whilst our M.Gs. fired nearly 10,000 rounds on the enemy's communications during the night.

One of our patrols from the Left Sub-section entered the enemy trench at N.13.d.60.55 and patrolled from N.13.d.37.55 to N.13.d.75.60. The trench was unoccupied and no Germans were seen or heard. Other patrols examined enemy wire at point recently bombarded and found it damaged. A man was heard whistling in front line at M.30.b.35.95.

PART II INTELLIGENCE.

RIGHT SECTION. - The prisoners captured as above appear to belong to the 7th Bavarian Infantry Regiment (Normal) further particulars will be given later.

The hostile artillery and T.Ms. were fairly active, some shrapnel and 4.2" falling round CHATEAU REDOUBT and M.35.b.80.42. Their M.Gs. were active with overhead fire.

Considerable movement was detected in the enemy front line at M.30.a.40.15 during the morning. Also on road at N.25.c.70.35. A working party was seen at M.30.a.40.45 and smoke at M.30.b.10.20. New wire has been put out by the enemy at M.33.a.37.50. A M.G.E. is suspected at M.33.a.53.30. A loophole plate can be seen at M.33.a.47.30.

/LEFT SECTION.

LEFT SECTION.- Hostile artillery and T.Ms. were inactive.

At 9.35 to 10.0 a.m. 12 Germans were seen working on road at N.32.a.20.45, they appeared to be filling sandbags.

Work still continues on new trench from N.14.b.45.10. to N.14.b.40.05., much fresh earth being visible at the latter point. Also on new trench at N.14.b.85.80. New revetting is visible in IRMA Trench at N.14.b.55.10.

The parapet between M.24.d.50.15 and M.24.d.60.23 has been repaired. Fresh earth and new sandbags being visible. New boards are visible in C.T. at M.24.d.50.05. The enemy is working in support line covering WICK SALIENT. Usual movement was observed at N.20.b.30.65. At 11.10 a.m. eight Germans were seen passing along C.T. at N.14.b.45.15 wearing equipment and rifles with fixed bayonets. Five Germans carrying a plank disappeared behind a house in LE PIETRE at N.20.b.25.45. Movement was seen by LA CLIQUETERIE FARM.

Smoke was seen at :-
    N.20.b.30.25   House
    N.14.d.35.95   Trench
    N.27.a.52.13   House
    N.27.a.45.10.   House
    N.27.a.27.37   AUBERS DEFENCES.
    N.21.d.40.15.   do.,

T.C. Heald

Head Qrs. 56th Divn.
20th December, 1916.

Lieutenant,
Intelligence, General Staff.

56th DIVISIONAL TACTICAL PROGRESS REPORT No. 55.
from 8.0 a.m. 20th Decr. to 8.0 a.m. 21st December, 1916.
On receipt of current copy of Divisional Tactical Progress Report
in the trenches, previous copy to be destroyed.

PART I OPERATIONS.
RIGHT SECTION. Between 6.0 p.m. and midnight our Artillery and T.Ms. co-operated in a shoot on enemy trenches about M.30.a.5.8.&M.30.c.5.6. Results not yet ascertained. Our M.Gs. showed their usual activity. Our patrols did not encounter any sign of the enemy.

LEFT SECTION. Our Artillery fired on the enemy's trong point at N.25.b.8.9. with great effect. Our patrols covered our whole front, but could not discover any trace of the enemy.

PART II INTELLIGENCE.
RIGHT SECTION. The hostile Artillery showed very little activity - a few light shells falling about M.35.d. But hostile T.M. fire was almost continuous round about M.30.a. during the night. One fire bay and traverse has been completely destroyed. They were eventually silenced by our Artillery and T.Ms. Considerable movement, including men in full marching order was observed on road about N.25.c.7.3. Movement was again seen at cross roads N.25.c.60.15. where work is going on and at BAS POMMEREAU. A sniping post can be seen in the enemy parapet at M.36.a.35.60., but it does not appear to be used. Also a closed loophole at M.36.a.37.75. A hostile sniper fires at night time from about S.5.b.57.25., this probably indicates the position of a sentry group.

LEFT SECTION. Hostile Artillery and T.Ms. were quiet, a few shells falling on ERITH POST M.24.c.8.8. At 6.10 p.m. a trench railway was heard in use behind WICK SALIENT. A working party of about 20 was seen at M.30.d.75.80. Movement was again observed on track at N.15.c.65.3. Our Artillery were informed. One man was seen pushing a truck on tramway at N.21.b.08.50. moving South. Usual movement was observed in MOSSY C.T. at M.20.b.30.65;RUE DELEVAL about N.20.a.7.45.and LE CLIQUETERIE Emp. Rd. in T.3.a. At 3.0 p.m. two men were seen on track at N.32.d.90.35. One carried a white flag with which he appeared to be signalling. Two men were observed making a screen on AUBERS - BAS POMMEREAU Road at N.26.c.6.1. Much movement was observed on the AUBERS - BAS POMMEREAU Road. Much new work and earth is visible on BERTHA C.T. at N.14.c.40.15., also in IRMA C.T. about N.14.c.6.1. where it is suspected that company H.Q. dugouts are in course of erection. Hostile battery was observed firing and was located about T.14.b.90.45. Two pigeons were sent from the enemy first line at N.19.a.37.77. and flew off in the direction of AUBERS. Smoke was seen at:-

N.21.d.40.15.	AUBERS DEFENCES.
N.26.d.80.89.	" "
N.20.d.7.6.	House.
N.20.b.3.55.	H.Q. dugout.
N.20.c.13.39.	House.
N.14.d.25.95.	Trench.
N.25.b.80.90.	House.
N.20.b.15.40.	Trench.

Hdqrs. 56th Divn.
21st December, 1916.

T.L.C.Hrald
Lieutenant,
Intelligence, General Staff.

56th DIVISIONAL TACTICAL PROGRESS REPORT No. 56
from 8.0 a.m. 21st December to 8.0 a.m. 22nd December 1916.

On receipt of current copy of Divisional Tactical Progress Report in the trenches, previous copy to be destroyed.

PART I OPERATIONS.

RIGHT SECTION.- Our patrols thoroughly reconnoitred our front during the night. They, however, found no signs of the enemy. Our wire in front of M.35.3 and 4 is reported damaged by hostile T.M. fire. Ground generally very wet.

Our M.Gs. showed their usual activity during the night. The arrangements which had been made for co-operation by visual signalling between Brigade Observers and M.Gs. by day proved exceedingly successful. A party of the enemy were seen working near the road M.25.c.8.4. so M.G. fire was directed on them. At the first burst they scattered but came back to their work almost at once. At the second burst of fire, however, they got away hurriedly across country and observers report that two or three men were seen to have been hit.

LEFT SECTION.- Our T.Ms. concentrated on enemy railway at N.14.a.75.25 and trench junction at N.14.a. 9.3. A considerable amount of debris was thrown up. Other points fired on were Railway and C.T. at N.14.c.35.85. - Railway junction at N.13.c.97.30.- Enemy's second line at N.19.a.90.97 to N.19.a.7.8. Our M.Gs. fired chiefly on enemy's front line and wire during the night.

Our patrols were out along the whole front, going was very wet.

The enemy's wire opposite N.14.1 was in good condition. A fire was observed in enemy's second line trench.

PART II INTELLIGENCE.

Right Section - Hostile artillery was generally inactive but LA BASSEE DUMP M.21.c.5.9. and road LA FLINQUE - PONT DU HEM each received a few shells.

Hostile T.Ms. were unusually active, many new emplacements have been located, and they are evidently attempting to silence our T.Ms. which have caused the enemy much damage lately.

Our front line M.35.2,4 & 5 and about M.22.b.6.2. were subjected to a sharp bombardment by Heavy and Medium T.Ms. from 3.0 p.m. to 4.30 p.m. causing a considerable amount of damage. Our 18 pdrs. and 4.2's retaliated but failed to silence them. New emplacements are suspected at M.30.a.5.1. and M.36.a.4.4. Further locations are required, especially of the H.T.Ms. it being very important that reports should come from more than one source in order to fix the exact location of a hostile T.M. Hostile M.Gs. were active during the early part of the night most of the fire being directed on to our front line parapet. A searchlight played on to our parapet from a N.E. direction during this period. A large fire burnt from 2.0 to 4.0 a.m. somewhere about LES MOTTES FME.

Usual movement seen on road from PIETRE to RUE D'ENFER, also at MOULIN DU PIETRE. Smoke was seen coming from N.31.d.

LEFT SECTION.- Considerable movement was seen on track at N.15.c.65.32 Our Artillery registered this point.

Two men carrying sacks were seen on track at N.21.d.6.0. moving N.E.- they entered trench at N.21.d.4.15. where smoke is often seen.

A party of 15 men were seen working on the new trench about N.32.a.58.87, which is already about 3 feet deep. Our artillery fired on them and they dispersed to trench at N.26.c.85.20. They were turned out with H.E. and disappeared in all directions.

The hostile battery reported on 14.12.16. at T.3.d.90.15 was again observed in action yesterday. Movement at N.20.b.30.65 was abnormal. Between 10.45 and 11.15 a.m. parties numbering in all 40 men in full marching order passed this point. Possibly a local relief was taking place.

Movement and work were observed in BERTHA Trench at N.20.a.90.82. A sentry was observed pacing up and down here. Our artillery fired on this point and men were observed to disappear beneath a shelter over this trench.

2.

Two men in white coats were working about N.27.a.8.7. filling sandbags.

What appeared to be a pair of glasses were seen shining in the roof of a house at N.20.d.90.00.

Smoke seen at :-

    N.25.a.7.6.   corrugated iron hut. Direct hit by our Arty.
    N.14.d.39.52   trench thought to be disused.
    N.16.c.10.16   Ruins.
    N.20.b.30.55   H.Q. dugout.
    N.21.d.40.15   AUBERS DEFENCES. Man seen looking over parapet at this point.
    N.20.d.7.6.   house.
    N.27.a.27.37   AUBERS DEFENCES.

T.J.C.Ibald
Lieutenant,
Intelligence, General Staff.

Head Qrs. 56th Divn.
22nd December, 1916.

53th DIVISIONAL TACTICAL PROGRESS REPORT No. 57.
from 8.0 a.m. 22nd December to 8.0 a.m., 23rd December.

On receipt of current copy of Divisional Tactical Progress Report in the Trenches, previous copy to be destroyed.

PART I OPERATIONS.

RIGHT SECTION. One of our patrols reconnoitred the ground in front of our left subsection for three hours, but could discover no signs of the enemy, except noise of pumping was occasionally heard. Progress was difficult owing to water. Another patrol followed the old trench running from M.30.a.20.36. towards enemy first line. The patrol listened near the enemy wire for 20 minutes; no sign of the enemy was seen but work was heard about M.30.a. Our T.Ms. retaliated to enemy T.Ms. but failed to silence them.

LEFT SECTION. Our Artillery was fairly active during the day shelling movement in rear of the enemy's line. Our T.Ms. fired on enemy's works at N.13.d.95.70., N.14.c.3.9. and N.24.d.8.4. Good results were obtained, much material being thrown up into the air. Fire was also brought to bear on N.24.d.7.1½. and N.19.c.½.5. at 6.0 p.m. as a relief was suspected to be taking place. Our M.Gs. showed their usual activity during the night. A patrol which left our lines by RHONDA Sap proceeded to enemy's sap at N.8.d.2.1., which was found to be flanked by a considerable amount of wire. No sounds or signs of the enemy were heard or seen. The enemy sap at N.8.d.5.4. was also patrolled; the wire here was found to be very thick, but damaged in places. Another patrol, when about 30 yards from the enemy's wire at N.13.d.90.75., the patrol returned and Lewis gun fire was directed on this spot. This patrol went out later and examined the crater at N.13.d.90.97.; this was found to be fairly dry. Other patrols did not see any signs of the enemy.

PART II INTELLIGENCE.
RIGHT SECTION. Hostile T.M's., both heavy and other calibre were extremely active. Short bursts on our line, chiefly behind the MAUQUISSART (M.30.c.10.35.) and DUCKS BILL CRATERS (M.35.b.8.1.) took place at 4.30 p.m., 8.30 p.m., and 12.30 p.m. The first two bursts lasted about 20 minutes each and the last about ½ an hour. The bombardment at 12.30 a.m. and extended as far N. as MIN St. (M.29.b.7.0.) but damage caused to left sector was not serious. A large number of enemy mortars were in action at once, two missles were always in the air, and sometimes four could be observed. A lift took place and a raiding party entered our trenches just S. of the MAUQUISSART Crater about 1.0 a.m. Two of our wounded were captured and two bombers cannot be accounted for at present. Our Artillery retaliated heavily within five minutes. When it was ascertained that a raid had been attempted, sharp bursts of fire were opened up by the whole Group on to enemy trenches about M.30.c. central and it is believed that damage to enemy personnel was caused by this. During yesterday, an unusual amount of smoke was seen issuing from the direction of MARQUILLIES, thought to be a train entering and leaving the station at this place. At 11.45 a.m., about 200 men were seen on the LE CLIQUETERIE FME Rd. in T.3.a., these moved along road in an N.E. direction in parties of about 40. The first detachment was preceded by a horse and limber and each was accompanied by one or more mounted men. Four 4-horsed wagons were seen moving S.W. later. Several red, green and white flares were seen at 3.15 p.m. about LE CLIQUETERIE FME. They were visible for about 12 minutes.

LEFT SECTION. Hostile Artillery and T.Ms. on the whole quiet; a few shrapnel fell about M.24.d.35.70. and five M.T.Ms. on N.13.b.30.10. of which three were blinds. Damage was very slight. Enemy M.Gs. fired on our parapets and RUE TILLELOY at intervals. An unusual amount of movement was seen on track at N.21.a.8.6., N.21.a.95.20. Two large parties of 25 and 12 men were seen during the morning and smaller parties during the afternoon. Our Artillery fired on this target several times. Also much movement around AUBERS DEFENCES in N.21.d. and MOSSY C.T., N.20.b.30.65. The HAUT POMMEREAU defensive
/ line

- 2 -

line in N.31.d. is apparently under repair, new material can be seen on the parapets. Movement was seen on track running through N.33.c. (N.E. and S.W.) In all, 16 men passed along track. Also at TRAMWAY Corner (N.26.c.80.25.)

New work is in progress at:-
FROMELLES DEFENCES N.22.d.95.15.
IRMA C.T.   at N.14.d.88.85.
Trench running from IRMA C.T. at N.14.b.4.1. in a S.W. direction.
New trench at N.26.c.96.12.

A white flag can be seen flying from a tree on the RUE de la LOMMERIE in FROMELLES at N.23.a.40.25. Two flags, one black & white and the other red & yellow are flying from a tree at about N.20 d.95.85. A glass was seen shining for a few moments in the HOUSE O.P. at N.27.a.45.25.

Smoke seen at:-
    N.21.b.35.15.   House.
    N.15.c.02.70.   Trench.
    N.26.a.75.65.   Trench.
    N.20.d.50.85.   House.
    N.20.b.30.35.   H.Q. dugout.
    N.25.b.5.5.   House.

Hdqrs. 56th Divn.

23rd December, 1916.

T.C. Heald

Lieutenant, Intelligence,
General Staff.

56th DIVISIONAL TACTICAL PROGRESS REPORT NO.58
from 8.0 a.m. 23rd December, 1916 to 8.0 a.m. 24th Decr.1916.

On receipt of current copy of Divisional Tactical Progress Report in the trenches, previous copy to be destroyed.

PART I OPERATIONS.

LEFT SECTION.- Our artillery fired on several working parties, and our L.T.Ms. fired 110 rounds on enemy works at N.14.c.25.45., N.19.a.6.6., and dump at N.14.c.3.5. Much damage was done especially on the 1st of these targets. There was no hostile retaliation. Our M.Gs. were active during the night.

One of our patrols located a hostile working party of 15 men at N.8.d.1.0. This was dispersed by L.Gs. on their return.

Enemy's wire opposite N.14.1 reported good. Another hostile working party about N.14.c.33.88 was located by a patrol; this was also dispersed by L.G. fire after our patrols returne

RIGHT SECTION.- Our artillery caught several working parties and inflicted casualties near BAS POMMEREAU & MOULIN DU PIETRE. All worked ceased. Our T.Ms. fired on M.36.a.4.9. and considering the strength of the wind good results were obtained, a quantity of timber and wire being thrown into the air.

One of our patrols inspected the ground in front of M.29.2 no signs of the enemy were found. The enemy's wire appeared thick at this point. Another patrols advanced along the ditch from M.30.a.2.7. to the crater at M.30.a.45.55 which was found to be wired but unoccupied. Immediately in front of the crater is a disused trench wired and containing water. No enemy were seen or heard.

A strong defensive patrol patrolled the damaged portion of our front by MAUQUISSART Craters M.29.1 all night to prevent any enemy approaching.

PART II INTELLIGENCE.

LEFT SECTION.- Hostile artillery and T.Ms. were quiet during the day. Short bursts of M.G. fire were opened during the night on our parapets. A gun sweeping RUE TILLELOY about N.7.d.0.0 was located about N.13.d.78.55 and another emplacement is suspected at N.14.b.1.7. A working party seen at 9.0 a.m. working on the S.E. side of the road N.25.b.5.4. to N.25.d.1.9. were reported to R.A. who dispersed them, and a carrying party with planks seen at N.14.d.15.60 at 9.45 a.m. was also fired on by our artillery.

Occupied dugouts and dumps are suspected at N.25.b.8.9.

A man was seen white washing the lower part of the house at N.26.d.70.65. The sentry post in BERTHA C.T. at N.20.a.90.82 was again seen. The sentry was wearing a Balaclava helmet. Part of the roofs of the houses at N.20.d.50.85 and N.26.c.80.35 have been blown away by the wind, and also part of the screen on the AUBERS-BAS POMMEREAU Road.

A working party on the new trench in N.26.c. & N.32.a. was dispersed at 10.15 a.m. and work was not resumed.

The wire in front of HT.POMMEREAU Defences in N.31.d. has been considerably strengthened. A dump of wire can be seen at N.31.d.7.3. Much work has been done in the first line at N.14.a.98.60 - the parapet has been cut away for several yards and replaced by sandbags. New revetting stakes can be seen over the top of the parapet.

Fresh earth can be seen at N.22.c.36.10 and at N.27.a.96.90 where baulks of timber have been carried.

MOVEMENT.

At the X Roads N.25.b.35.20 throughout the day.

In the front line S. of SUGAR LOAF and in the second line at N.14.c.87.10 and N.14.c.30.57.

2 men left BERTHA Trench at 2.30 p.m. at N.20.a.70.85 and walked across the open to RUE DELEVAL at N.20.a.78.62.

Two parties, one of 6 men and the other of 15 disappeared behind the house at N.20.a.87.70.

/The track

The track at N.20.d.4.2. was in use throughout the day.
Usual movement in the trench at N.20.b.30.85.
At 3.0 p.m. our artillery were shelling 14 TREE Clump, and three men were seen to run S.W. along the LE PIETRE-AUBERS Road. A little later 2 men were seen to move down the road carrying a stretcher.
Considerable movement along the track in N.15.c.
Two men carrying sacks on RUE DELEVAL left their sacks at what looked like a dugout at N.14.b.94.33, and then returned to N.14.b.75.18.

RIGHT SECTION. - Hostile artillery and T.Ms. were very much quieter, only firing in retaliation. A T.M.E. has been located at M.30.c.70.07. (No.9.) and confirmed by cross bearings.
A party of 6 men were seen on the edge of one of the Craters to the right of the DUCK'S BILL CRATER - M.36.c.0.8. They disappeared when fired at by our sentries.
A working party of 50 men were seen driving in stakes on road at N.26.c.7.1. Another large party was seen working on the new trench at behind this point. Our artillery dispersed them. 20 cyclists were seen at N.31.b.80.15 going towards AUBERS.
One man in clean fatigue dress passed round corner of sap leading to Crater at M.30.a.65.55.
A Crows Nest O.P. is suspected at N.26.c.20.15 near AUBERS.

SMOKE.-
    N.20.a.87.75   Immediately in front of the house where.
    N.13.d.2.2.   Support line.
    N.20.d.50.85   House
    N.26.b.84.75   BERTHA C.T.
    N.25.b.45.50   House
    N.21.c.55.78   House, where movement was also seen.

John D. Crosthwaite

Head Qrs 56th Divn
24th December 1916.

Lieutenant,
Intelligence, General Staff.

[GENERAL STAFF, 56th DIVISION.]

PART I OPERATIONS.

Right Section. Strong patrols were out between 1 a.m. and 3 a.m. and covered all the front without meeting any of the enemy.
A slow bombardment started last night in accordance with programme and appeared to be effective, considerable damage being observed after dawn. Each of six L.T.Ms. fired over 100 rounds. 13,000 rounds were fired by our M.Gs. on enemy communications, while our L.Gs. and snipers kept up a desultory fire along the hostile wire and parapet.

Left Section. A bombardment of the enemy lines was carried out last night by our Artillery and T.Ms. L.T.Ms. fired 1,150 rounds on targets in N.14., N.19. and N.24. in bursts of 20 to 100 rounds each and also kept up a steady rate of fire throughout the night. Our M.Gs. fired 8,500 rounds on enemy front line, wire and communications. Hostile retaliation was occasional and weak with T.Ms. and M.Gs. During the quiet period the enemy lines were entered at N.24.d.9.6., DEVILS JUMP and N.13.c.95.30. The wire in each place is reported weak and much damaged and the trenches in extremely bad condition, deep in mud and water, and the ground behind covered by large pools of water. No sign of the enemy was seen or heard. A telephone wire was found running towards our lines at N.24.d.75.00. and a sample brought in. The wire was German. The front line was searched from N.13.c.95.30. to N.13.d.05.50.

PART II INTELLIGENCE.

Right Section. Hostile Artillery was quiet during the day and their reply to our bombardment weak. Their T.Ms. which attempted to reply to our T.M. fire and Artillery bombardment were immediately engaged by the Divisional Artillery and silenced. Hostile M.Gs. were active at evening "stand to" but after that quiet. There was some enemy rifle fire from our right up to the DUCKS BILL and some rifle grenades were fired into the same piece of line. An M.G. was seen firing at one of our aeroplanes from N.30.b.2.8. Other emplacements are suspected at N.24.d.4.1., N.31.a.52.90. and about the S. end of the DISTILLERY.
A german was seen using a helio at N.31.b.20.35. The movement on road at N.25.c.9.7. seemed to be more hurried than usual and in smaller parties.

Left Section. A few 77 mm. shells and T.M. bombs have been fired at our lines during the last 24 hours without doing any damage. Hostile M.Gs. were more active than usual, sweeping our parapet and RUE TILLELOY. Flares fired by the enemy were falling about their own front line trenches. At 9.15 p.m., an aeroplane dropped two bombs just in rear of our front line at N.14.1. One of those failed to explode. A Klaxon horn was sounded twice by the aeroplane. At 9.0 p.m., red lights were seen to go up in the enemy lines. Considerable movement was again seen round AUBERS DEFENCES in N.21.d., all men using the track running S.W. from N.21.d.4.2. and entering and leaving the tracks at this point. Much work was being done, and fresh earth and revetting could can be seen in many parts of this line. Between 9.30 and 10.30 a.m., movement on the CLIQUETERIE FME Road - T 3.a. was abnormal. Six parties of fifty men each and six of about ten were seen moving S.W. Some of the larger parties were accompanied by limbers. Movement was also seen on the track N.15.c.65.32. - N.15.c.4.2, and along the road in T.1.b., and men carrying wood along the road at N.21.b.30.13. The thatched cottage at N.21.a.6.4. has collapsed. The C.T. at N.30.d.45.35. has been freshly revetted.

Smoke -   N.20.d.82.52.   House.
          N.26.c.40.74.   House.
          N.26.b.95.00.   House.
          N.21.c.58.78.   House.
          N.27.c.30.98.   House.
          N.20.b.50.55.   Dugout.
          N.21.d.40.15.   AUBERS Defences.
          N.25.b.45.50.   House.

Hdqrs. 56th Divn.
25th December, 1916.

J.D. Crosthwaite Captain,
Intelligence, General Staff.

56th DIVISIONAL TACTICAL PROGRESS REPORT No. 60.
from 8.0 a.m. 25th December to 8.0 a.m. 26th December 1916.

On receipt of current copy of Divisional Tactical Progress Report
in the trenches, previous copy to be destroyed.

PART 1 OPERATIONS.

RIGHT SECTION.- Our patrols were very active last night during the period when our artillery and T.Ms. were quiet, but they were much hindered by water, the ditches being almost impassable.

Our patrol was prevented from entering the German trenches about M.24.d.0.0. by a deep ditch, which was impassible without a bridge. Another patrol located 3 sentries in the German line within 100 yards by hearing them cough, fire and send up flares about M.30.c. central. The Craters further North were found unoccupied and full of water. Another patrol thoroughly examined the the BIRD CAGE CRATERS M.30. a. central, and found no trace of the enemy. The Dyke at M.30.a.8.7. was impassable.

Another patrol examined the enemy's wire at M.30.a.40.13. It is strong and no gaps could be found. The sap there is full of water and wire is impassable. No enemy flares went up in front of the patrol, nor were any enemy seen or heard. Other patrols saw no signs of the enemy.

Our artillery continued their slow bombardment of the enemy defences, and in addition dealt severely with some hostile T.Ms. which were active during the evening. Our T.Ms. had successful shoots in the morning and afternoon, targets being M.30.a.55.85.35 and M.30.c.62.75. Much damage was done to enemy's defences.

LEFT SECTION.- Three of our patrols entered the enemy's lines last night, a fourth was prevented by water. The details are :
An Officers' patrol entered the enemy's line at M.24.d.9.6. at midnight. No sign of the enemy could be seen but coughing was heard about 200 yards away. Trenches are very bad. Two notice boards were brought back one marked "F.2" and one "UNTERSHLUFF"

Another patrol entered at N.19.a.35.30 and worked left. No signs of the enemy were seen or heard. The trench is impassable. The wire has been fairly good but now is poor. Another patrol entered at N.13.c.75.10 and worked left to the WICK SALIENT. The wire is poor being in isolated heaps, and the trenches are full of mud and water.

Our artillery and T.Ms. continued their slow bombardment with short periods of rapid fire. There was no retaliation. Our M.Gs. were very active with their fire during the night.

PART II INTELLIGENCE.

RIGHT SECTION. - The hostile artillery retaliated to our bombardment by firing over our back areas generally and M.12.c. in particular. 60 4.2" H.E. falling in this locality. Our Infantry Observers report that our artillery shooting on M.Gs. at M.30.b.9.8., M.24.d. 4.1. and right edge of DISTILLERY N.19.c.6.0 was very good, the emplacements are probably destroyed, and that our H.T.Ms. considerably damaged the enemy's support line between M.30.a.5.0 and M.30.b.55.70. The enemy could be heard pumping opposite M.20.3 and rifle fire came from the same part. Singing was heard at "Standto" this morning. Smoke was rising from MARQUILLIES CHIMNEY and from trench at M.30.d.7.2. and M.30.d.50.57.

LEFT SECTION. - The hostile artillery was active firing on to our back areas. About 55 5.9" shells fell about M.12.c.2.6. without doing any damage. A base plate was dug up which measured 5.9". A hostile battery was located firing from N.27.c.8.5.on to the above target, flashes from two guns being seen at intervals of 15 seconds.

A man was seen laying out tape in the AUBERS DEFENCES between LE CLERQ FM. N.27.b.70.85 and N.27.a.85.62 A man was seen working at N.21.d.40.15. Smoke is often seen at this point.

A little movement was seen on the track at N.21.a.8.6. - N.21.a.95.20. In all 12 men being seen. Two men were seen pushing a truck on the light railway at N.21.b.1.4. moving N.W.

P.T.O. /The sentry

2.

The sentry over the H.Q. dugout at N.20.b.30.55. was seen looking over the top of the trench. He was wearing his shrapnel helmet.

Men were seen at intervals all day coming and going from the suspected H.Q. at N.25.b.30.25. Much movement and smoke was seen about the house at N.20.a.87.63.

Three men carrying sacks left AUBERS DEFENCES at N.27.a.3.4. moving N.W.

Much movement, both transport and men was seen on LA CLIQUETERIE FM. Road in T.3.a.

The house O.P. at N.27.a.45.25 was again in use a glass being seen at intervals shining through the roof.

A wind vane mounted on a pole can be seen about N.27.a.35.10.

Smoke seen at :-
    N.21.a.70.65 ruins
    N.21.a.98.30 house
    N.15.c.02.70 trench.

Head Qrs. 56th Divn.
26th December, 1916.

          Captain,
       Intelligence, General Staff.

56th DIVISIONAL TACTICAL PROGRESS REPORT No. 31.
from 8.0 a.m. 26th December to 8.0 a.m., 27th December.

On receipt of current copy of Divisional Tactical Progress Report in the trenches, previous copy to be destroyed.

PART I OPERATIONS.

Right Section. A very thorough reconnaissance of the Northern end of the BIRD CAGE Craters (M.30.a. central) was made by one of our patrols. Voices were heard about the right crater of the group of craters. A Boche was heard singing in rear and voices were heard to the left of the craters. Seven or eight flares were sent up from the right portion of the craters. An enemy M.G. was active on the left. The state of the ground made quiet movement impossible. It is thought that the enemy do not occupy the craters, but the trench running in rear of them. Another patrol heard talking in the German trenches about M.36.a.3½.5. They listened again 50 yards further N. and found the trench occupied. They gathered the impression that the enemy were standing to. Other patrols could find no sign of the enemy. The enemy wire about M.36.a.3½.7½ is not put up on any system, but is a tangled mass which gives good protection. The ground generally is in a very sodden state. Our Artillery continued their programme shoot, and, on account of the mist, cross roads and known rendez-vous were shelled by day as well as by night. Our T.Ms. had another successful day and the infantry report that their fire was most effective. Bursts of rapid fire were kept up by L.Gs. and rifles during the night on the enemy's front line.

Left Section. Our patrols in this section again entered the enemy trenches at three points. The WICK Salient in N.13.d. was entered both on the N. side and on the S. It appears to be flooded out and abandoned by the enemy. The wire is practically destroyed. A low trip wire was found, of which a specimen was brought in. Another patrol entered the enemy's trenches at N.19.a.3.5. The trench here is more like a ditch than a trench, and the land behind is a swamp. The wire is almost totally destroyed. Another patrol attempted to enter the enemy trench at N.19.a.3.0. but was prevented by a deep ditch 12' wide and 3' deep. They could not find a crossing although they went 150 yards to the right. An enemy working party was heard driving in stakes well to the left and in rear of his front line. Our Artillery carried out their pre-arranged programme and slow fire was kept up during the night. Our M.Gs. fired on vulnerable points in the enemy's communications. The enemy did not retaliate.

PART II INTELLIGENCE.

Right Section. The hostile Artillery and T.Ms. were quiet, a few light shrapnel shells fell about M.29.2. and a few 4.2" H.E. about M.35.b.6.5. Hostile M.G.s. were more active firing on our wiring parties. A good deal of transport was heard in the evening and a tramway in use opposite M.29.3. A periscope was observed in the sap M.36.a.2.8.26. at 11.0 a.m. A searchlight was operating from the W. end of BOIS de BIEZ and six red lights were fired from the same direction between 3 and 4 a.m. Pumping was heard at M.36.a.5.6. and M.24.d. New wire has been put out at M.30.b.15.70. Smoke was seen at M.36.c.25.20.

Left Section. The hostile Artillery and T.Ms. were generally quiet, a few 4.2" shells fell about M.12.c.2.8. during the night. A hostile T.M. was observed to fire from N.19.a.85.80. Movement was seen there, also a flash at 2.30 p.m. The shot fell short. The enemy has been very quiet during the last 24 hours. An aeroplane was heard early last evening to our left; a green flare was dropped.

T.L.C.Hiald
Lieutenant,
Intelligence, General Staff.

Hdqrs. 56th Divn.
27th December, 1916.

59th DIVISIONAL TACTICAL PROGRESS REPORT No. 62.
from 8.0 a.m.27th December to 8.0 a.m. 28th Decr. 1916.

On-receipt of current copy of Divisional Tactical Progress Report
in the trenches, previous copy to be destroyed.

PART I OPERATIONS.

RIGHT SECTION. - NO MAN'S LAND was thoroughly patrolled during the night, and no trace of the enemy met with. Enemy wire was examined at several places and useful local information obtained.

Our artillery carried out registrations during the day and also silenced hostile T.Ms.

LEFT SECTION.- The hostile front line was entered at N.13.c.10.60 and found to be full of water with no signs of occupation.

Another patrol was not able to find a way through the wire. at N.19.a.2.8. and heard sounds of a large working party in the enemy front line at this spot.

Our L.T.Ms. fired 200 rounds on targets about N.19.a.75.85 and searched the C.T. from N.13.c.8.1. to N.13.c.9.0.

Our M.Gs. were active during the night against enemy wire, parapet and back areas.

A German seen crossing the open about N.20.a.4.9. was hit by one of our snipers.

PART II INTELLIGENCE.

RIGHT SECTION.- Hostile artillery fired a few rounds of shrapnel over S.TILLELOY C.T. during the relief. The H.T.M. at M.36.a. 9.9. fired 30 rounds without doing any damage, before it was silenced.

A working party was heard near the crater at M.30.c.4.0.

Visibility was poor throughout the day.

Work has been done at M.36.c.1.6. and a sentry and periscope could be seen there between 9.30 and 10.30 a.m.

LEFT SECTION.- Enemy showed no signs of activity at all yesterday, and the area of observation was very limited owing to the mist.

The O.P. in the house in AUBERS at N.26.d.60.65 was being used in the afternoon.

John D. Trosthwaite

Head Qrs. 38th Divn.
28th December, 1916.

Captain,
Intelligence, General Staff

56th DIVISIONAL TACTICAL PROGRESS REPORT No. 63.
from 8.0 a.m. 28th December to 8.0 a.m. 29th December, 1916.

On receipt of current copy of Divisional Tactical Progress
Report in the trenches, previous copy to be destroyed.

PART I OPERATIONS.

Right Section. Our Artillery and T.Ms. co-operated in a shoot during the afternoon. The H.T.M obtained one direct hit on the suspected mine shaft at M.36.a.40.85. The M.T.Ms. fired on the short trench at M.30.a.5.5. and M.G.E. at M.30.a.7.1. Much damage was done, two direct hits being obtained on the latter. Our stokes mortars badly damaged the post at M.24.d.65.30. where much work has been done lately.

One of our patrols moved out along SIGN POST Lane M.35.d., crossed the road running parallel to our trenches, which is flooded, at its junction with SIGN POST Lane and proceeded to the German wire about M.36.c.1.7. It was in very good condition. A German sentry saw them and threw a bomb at them; they also heard footsteps in the German trenches at M.36.c.0.6. They returned safely. Another patrol attempted to approach the crater at M.30.c.4.0. Owing to the state of the ground it was impossible to approach silently and when they got near a flare went up and bullets were fired at them so they withdrew. Another patrol examined the German wire at M.24.d.4.1. It was found to be very cut up, but still impassable. The patrol commander is of opinion that this portion of the line is unoccupied. A M.G. emplacement is suspected at M.24.d.68.17. and a sniper was heard to fire from the support line. The ground is a mess of shell holes at this point.

Left Section. Our T.Ms. fired short bursts on to enemy lines at N.13.d.3¼.2¼. and N.13.d.5.8¼. Shooting observed to be effective. Our M.Gs. were active firing on to the enemy's defences during the night. Our patrols entered the enemy lines at three points, viz:- N.13.d.1.6., derelict as before, N.19.a.3.6. unoccupied and badly damaged; Chevaux de frise had been placed along the parapet, and at M.24.d.70.35. trenches derelict. The wire at all these points is destroyed. The patrol which entered WICK Salient penetrated 40 yards towards the support line. Another of our patrols observed a German wiring party just leaving their lines. Our patrols allowed them to get to their work and then returned and L.Gs. and M.Gs. were turned on to the spot. A later patrol reported work still in progress so fire was again brought to bear on them. Subsequent heavy rain made the ditches impassable, but third patrol which was sent out reported they could not hear any sounds of work. Other patrols did not encounter any signs of the enemy. The ground was flooded and impassable.

PART II INTELLIGENCE.

Right Section. The hostile Artillery and T.Ms. retaliated feebly to our shoot without doing much damage. Our wire outside M.35.5. was hit by a L.T.M. bomb which fell in SUNKEN Road C.T. about M.35.b. central. Transport was heard at 6.0 p.m. and 2 p.m. on the MAUQUISSART - PIETRE Road. A party of 15 men at intervals of 10 yards were seen digging about 10.0 a.m. in rear of road from N.25.c.65.15. to N.25.b.35.20. Timber was being carried there also. Work was heard in front line at M.36.c.02.60. L.G. fire was opened. Work was also heard about M.30.c. central. Movement was seen in the front line at M.36.c.02.60.where there is a suspected dug-out with a corrugated iron roof. A very young German, wearing a new cap was seen. Rather more flares were sent up by the Hun. than usual. A red rocket, from the direction of the BOIS DE BIEZ was sent up about 9.45 p.m.

/ Left Section.

- 2 -

Left Section. Hostile Artillery and T.Ms. were quiet.
About 10.20 a.m. what was thought to be the hammering of stakes was heard in the neighbourhood of the WICK Salient and at the same hour 4 men were seen at work about N.19.c.90.30.
New earth was seen on BERTHA Trench at N.14.c.30.40. Usual movement observed at N.20.b.30.65.
Work is in progress on enemy's fron line at N.14.b.25.20., new boards being visible at this point. Work is still continuing at N.14.b.45.10., the mounds of earth on these trenches are much larger. Very lights appeared to be fired from enemy support line during the night.
Smoke was seen at:-
  N.20.b.30.55. H.Q. dugout.
  N.20.d.50.85. Chimney of house.
  N.22.c.4.35. AUBERS Defences.

T.F.C.Heald

Hdqrs. 56th Divn.   Lieutenant,
29th December, 1916.   Intelligence, General Staff.

56th DIVISIONAL TACTICAL PROGRESS REPORT No. 64
from 8.0 a.m. 29th December to 8.0 a.m. 30th D[ecember]

[...] of [...]
[...] day and also fired on hostile T.Ms. T.M. shoots were
carried out on defended locality M.24.d.65.30. and on MINNIE
at M.30.c.70.07. Enemy retaliation was considerable. Small
patrols covered our front during the night, and there were no
signs of enemy in NO MAN'S LAND.

LEFT SECTION.- Our L.T.Ms. cut wire from N.14.b.1.8-2.9 with satisfactory
results.
Our patrols were very active during the night and the hostile
lines were entered at four places :-
1. A patrol went to the junction of DORA C.T. front line
where new work had been reported, but found the trench
derelict.
2. An Officers patrol moved down the RUE d'ENFER with the
intention of finding out whether TRIVELET ruins
are held, but shortly after passing the enemy front
line trench the road disappears under water and becomes
impassable. Enemy Very Lights were being sent up
some hundreds of yards in rear of this and by their
light nothing but a sheet of water could be seen in
front of the patrol.
3. The German lines were entered at N.13.d.05.55 and found
to be derelict.
4. A patrol entered the enemy lines at N.14.a.65.23 and
examined a hundred yards of trench. The going though
wet is not bad and the wire non-existent. The fire
bays were practically destroyed, and the control trench
in very bad state of repair.
5. A patrol left our lines to ascertain results of T.M bombardment at N.14.b.1.8. The wire is reported as
completely destroyed, but the voices of a considerable
working party were heard; no entry was attempted.

PART II INTELLIGENCE.   artillery
RIGHT SECTION. - Hostile/retaliated for our T.M. bombardment and
also fired a few rounds on the front line/supports during the
day.   Two bursts of rapid 4.2" were fired at PUMP HOUSE
KEEP and DEAD HORSE COPSE during our Evening M.T.M. shoot.
A few L.T.Ms. fell rear the head of MIN STREET, and some
M.T.M. shells on the SWITCH Trench near SIGN POST LANE, and on
the head of S.TILLELOY. New work and wire can be seen round
WINCHESTER CRATERS. A searchlight was used last night from
behind enemy front line in M.36.a. Loaded trucks were seen
standing on the railway - N.31.d.90.23 - N.31.a.90.80. A
light railway engine and three trucks was seen in T.2.a.
Parties were seen as follows and dealt with by artillery :-
between 8.0 a.m. and 11.0 a.m.
N.32.a.45.85   15 men on screening
N.32.c.1.3.   8 men working on trench
N.31.a.55.95   7 men digging.
N.25.c.6.2.   50 men wearing greatcoats and carrying
                  rifles and spades.
LES MOTTES FM. 1 men walking about.
NEW TRENCH in   )
N.23.c.-N.32.a.) 24 men fled into AUBERS on being shelled.
                12 men were again working here this morning
                  and artillery were informed.
On CLIQUETERIE Three parties of 40 moving N.E. in column
FM.Road   of route with full equipment at 20 minutes
                  interval.
N.21.a.8.6.   Parties using this track were fired on with
                  good effect.

LEFT SECTION.- Hostile artillery was more active than usual
yesterday.   Some 77 mms. shells fell along RUE TILLELOY and
on front line near RUE MASSELOT. ESQUIN POST and M.10.b. was
shelled with 4.2" about midday. H.E. fell near O.Ps.
at SIEGE HOUSE, FARM (1 direct hit on the new observation
post in course of construction), CONVENT and C.R.As. HOUSE
(3 direct hits) during the day.

Field gun shells were also fired into M.11.c., M.6.a.,
M.18.c.

Hostile T.Ms. and M.G. activity was normal.

A train of five trucks stopped on the light railway in
N.27.c. at 2.30 p.m.

A large carrying party with planks was seen between 10 and
11 a.m. on the road about N.26 central.

At 10 a.m. work was in progress near MIN du PIETRE.

Working party at N.15.c.65.50 was dispersed by our artillery.

Two men standing outside the entrance to a dugout at N.20.b.
30.35. were wearing black bands on the right arms of their
overcoats.

An officer with steel helmet was seen observing our lines
from N.20.b.45.30.

The sentry at N.20.b.30.55 was looking over the top of the
trench here, and a rifle was being fired at intervals from a
loophole by him.   Single men and parties were seen all day
near the house at N.20.a.87.63 and our artillery were informed.

Planks were being dumped at 9.30 a.m. and again at 10.0 p.m.
from a track into trench at N.27.a.88.65.

6. A patrol went out with the intention of entering enemy lines at
N.8.d.3.0. At N.8.c.1.2. patrol became suspicious and waited.
Immediately on starting to crawl forward 3 M.Gs. opened fire from
approximate positions N.8.d.30.15., N.14.b.30.95, N.14.b.1.8.

7. At N.14.b.0.8, N.14.a.90.75 a Working Party was observed by a
patrol and M.G. fire opened. The patrol then went out again to
this same spot, but there was no sign of enemy, but voices
could be heard from the trenches.

A man in enemy second line trench at N.14.b.25.55 was hit by
one of our snipers.

Head Qrs. 56th Divn.
30th December, 1916.

Captain,
Intelligence, General Staff.

56th DIVISIONAL TACTICAL PROGRESS REPORT No. 85
from 8.0 a.m. December 30th to 8.0 a.m. 31st December 1916

On receipt of current copy of Divisional Tactical Progress Report
in the trenches, previous copy to be destroyed.

PART I OPERATIONS.

RIGHT SECTION. - Our Artillery dispersed Enemy Working Parties at
M.36.d.5.7. and M.31.d. and effectively silenced Enemy T.Ms
which attempted to be troublesome before they had got off many
rounds.

Our patrols were out during the night but did not come into
contact with the Enemy. They found the ground very marshy and
silent progress impossible. The Craters about M.30.c.2.2. were
searched but no Enemy were seen. The ground around was much cut
up by 'Minnies'.

Our Snipers claim a hit at M.36.a.4.3.

LEFT SECTION. - Commencing at 12 noon on 39th inst., an organised
bombardment of IRMA TRENCH and the strong point in N.14.b. and C.
was carried out by 6" Howitzers, 4.5" Howitzers, 18 pdrs, Medium
and Light T.M.s. The bombardment lasted for half an hour.
Shooting was reported to be more effective and much timber and
debris was thrown up. A direct hit was obtained on SOUSA'S HOUSE
at N.14.d.95.75.

540 rounds L.T.M. were fired on QUADRILATERAL of Trenches
N.14.a.6½.1½. - 7¾. 2½ - 9.2½ - 8.3¾. in cooperation with above
shoot, traversing and enfilade fire was carried out with good effect.

8000 rounds were fired by our M.G.s during the night, special
attention being paid to the area bombarded by our Artillery.

A patrol which entered the WICK SALIENT at N.13.d.0.4. found
the trenches completely derelict. Very Lights were fired from
some distance behind the "RIV - DES - LAIES" and fell at least
500 yards in front of our patrol. An officers patrol again tried
to reach TRIVELET FARM, moving S. of RUE D'ENFER but was again held
up by a sheet of water in rear of the Enemy's front line trench.

A patrol was sent out to investigate the damage done by
our bombardment to the enemy's front line N.14.a.8.3. This patrol
was accompanied by the same N.C.O. who entered the German Lines
near the same place on night 29th/30th He reports that the
trenches are now quite transformed, the control trench which
previously was comparatively dry now contains from two to four
feet of water. The ground for 50 yards in rear of the trench
is flooded. The fire bays have been destroyed by our shelling
and have fallen in. The patrol tried to reach what was thought
to be an open M.G. Emplacement but failed owing to the depth
of water and mud. Another patrol was sent out to inspect the
Enemy's wire and trench at N.14.b.00.65. which point is slightly
N. of the Left Flank of the area bombarded. The sap head at
N.14.a.94.83. was found to be full of water. The wire at this
point consisted of only loose lengths and a few iron angle stakes,
the fire step in the trench was made of sandbags and the trench
itself was in poor condition. Four other patrols which were sent
out neither saw nor heard any of the Enemy.

PART II INTELLIGENCE.

RIGHT SECTION. Hostile Artillery took advantage of the good light and
fired on targets in the back areas CHAPIGNY FARM and working
parties in C.Ts. A hostile M.G. was firing in bursts from about
M.30.c.45.00.

A green flare was sent up from the BOIS DU BIEZ at 8.p.m. A
dog was heard in the Enemy's lines opposite M.24.2. New work
appears to have been done on Enemy's second line in M.24.d. and
M.30.b. Wire has been strengthened, breastworks erected and
what appears to be a dugout has been put up at M.30.b.1.75.

/New

2.

New earth can be seen at M.36.a.4.8. where our H.T.M. was hitting on the 29th. Movement was seen behind the enemy's front line South of our right boundary.

LEFT SECTION. - The hostile artillery showed more activity than usual many points in our back areas and C.Ts. being lightly shelled, but no damage was done. A few T.M. shells fell on our front line about M.24.4.

Pumping was in progress in the German support line at N.14.d. 4.4. at 8.45 a.m. A party carrying planks was seen moving between N.20.b.8.3. and N.20.b.95.35 at 2.0 p.m. Another party carrying sacks was seen to leave ruins at N.14.d.80.45 and proceed across open to ruins at N.14.d.60.35.

In an embankment at the bottom of the 7th TREE on the left of House at N.20.a.85.65 two slots can be seen. This is believed to be a machine gun emplacement. On the right of the house is a square hole in the wall about 7 ft. from the ground believed to be an O.P. Considerable movement was seen during the day.

Between 10.45 a.m. and 12 noon about 200 men in parties of about 10 were seen to pass along the road from Road Junction at N.26.c.8.3. to Road Junction at N.26.c.6.7. thence across fields, after which they entered CLARA TRENCH. at N.26.a.7.2. They were wearing greatcoats packs, caps and carried rifles. At 1.30 p.m. a few men wearing marching order were seen to leave CLARA TRENCH at the same point and proceed along the Road in the opposite direction. It appears that a local relief may have taken place.

Movement of small parties without rifles or equipment was seen throughout the day at many points in rear of the enemy's lines.

An O.P. is suspected in a tree at N.32.b.9.5. as three men were seen to descent from it and walk away after the enemy's guns had ceased firing.

A great quantity of new wire has been added to that already existing at N.14.d.2.2.

A party of 11 men were seen moving S.W. along track at N.20.b. 9.5.

Usual movement was seen in MOSSY TRENCH at N.20.b.30.65.

The sentry over the H.Q. dugout there was seen using a pair of glasses apparently watching one of our aeroplanes.

Considerably movement was again seen during the day on the LA CLIQUETERIE FM.Road in T.3.a. small parties amounting to 21 men being seen; also 2 G.S. wagons and a motor lorry.

A very big mound of fresh earth is now visible at N.22.b.45.30.

On the AUBERS -FROMELLES ROAD at N.27.b.94.85. there is what may possibly be a sentry shelter. A man was seen working with a shovel on top of the shelter.

Smoke was seen :-

N.20.b.30.55	H.Q. dugout.
N.26.d.72.80	House in AUBERS
N.26.c.80.45	House
N.27.a.12.30	AUBERS Defences.
N.27.a.87.72	do.

Head Qrs. 56th Divn.
31st December, 1916.

T.J.C.Heald
Lieutenant,
Intelligence, General Staff.

56th DIVISIONAL TACTICAL PROGRESS REPORT No. 66
from 8.0 a.m. 31st December to 8.0 a.m. 1st January 1917.

On receipt of current copy of Divisional Tactical Progress Report in the trenches, previous copy to be destroyed.

PART I OPERATIONS.

RIGHT SECTION.- Two bombardments in short bursts were carried out against enemy's C.Ts. and roads at dusk and at 10.55 p.m. last night, with a view to catching enemy W.Ps. moving up and disturbing any New Year celebrations. From 10.a.m. to 4.p.m. a slow observed bombardment by Heavy and Medium T.Ms. was carried out against enemy T.Ms. in M.30.a. and trenches M.30.a.9.3. and M.30.c.6.7.- results were good, much material damage being observed.

Our M.Gs. combined with the artillery bombardments and carried out the usual night firing.

One of our patrols was fired upon from enemy lines about M.36.c.0.5. Enemy wire was inspected for 200 yards opposite GHORD TRENCH and found to be much damaged by our fire. A large hostile working party was located and L.Gs. were brought to bear on it.

A telephone wire buried about a foot deep was found entering our parapet at M.30.a.40.88. The wires were traced into the ditch running from M.30.a.40.94. to M.30.a.90.56. and for about 70 yards along the ditch where the wire was lost.

LEFT SECTION.- At midnight our T.Ms bombarded enemy lines at N.14.c.3.4. without drawing any retaliation.

Our M.Gs were active throughout the night, firing on back areas.

German trenches were entered as follows :-
1. At junction of DORA C.T. and front line and line found in a very bad state.
2. Immediately S. of WICK SALIENT.
3. A standing patrol was established in the German front line in front of TRIVELET. They heard sounds of working near N.19.b.1.5. during the early part of the night.
   All patrols report Very lights were being fired from 300-500 yards in front of them.
4. Snipers have been established in the hostile front line at N.13.c.9.2. to wait for targets today.
5. At N.13.d.8.7. the line was found to be five feet deep in mud and water and water has risen considerably everywhere since the night before.
6. At N.14.c.25.85. enemy line is reported in fairly good condition except that the water is up to the fire step.
7. The wire at N.8.d.2.1. is now reported completely cut and the saps waterlogged.

The opportunity is being taken of sending out all fresh men who have not been on patrol before and much instruction is being given.

A sniper claims a victim who was seen to fall forward and has not moved since.

PART II INTELLIGENCE.

RIGHT SECTION. - Hostile Artillery was fairly active and retaliated with some effect for our T.M. Bombardment. Our front line, C.Ts and B. Line all received some attention. Retaliation for our 10.55pm bombardment was also prompt but no damage was done. Back areas were shelled during the day, the roads round LA FLINQUE and PONT DU HEM being fired over.

Hostile M.Gs were more active than usual traversing our parapets by night. A night emplacement is suspected at M.36.c.4.7. Hostile T.Ms were active in the Right Subsection - the Heavy mortars opening fire twice on M.29.2. Artillery retaliation was vigorous and effective.

PART II INTELLIGENCE (continued)

LEFT SECTION. – Heavy Artillery fired some H.E. on front line without doing any damage. A hostile T.M. was observed to fire 6 rounds from enemy support line at N.14.c.10.55 and another battery was reported in action from N.14.a.70.09. A new M.G. Emplacement is suspected at N.14.b.20.88.

New wood can be seen at N.22.c.8.7. (FROMELLES DEFENCES) and N.27.a.75.60. (AUBERS DEFENCES). Fresh earth has been thrown up in hostile second line at N.13.d.85.50.

Much movement was seen during the day and many parties dispersed by our Artillery.

A party at Road Junction N.26.c.9.7. was dispersed with shrapnel.

A Working Party on the new trench in N.32.a. was dispersed with by Howitzer and Gun fire. The CLIQUETERIE FARM Road was in use during the day and three parties of 30 men and six of 12 men were seen to pass moving N.E. shortly after 11.0 a.m. Artillery was informed.

At 14 TREES CLUMP.
   N.21.a.88.70   small parties moving S.E. along the tramway.
   N.15.c.05.70

TRAMWAY CORNER.
   About AUBERS DEFENCES N.22.c., N.21.d. and N.27.a.   2 men laying lines at N.21.d.2.1.
   N.25.d.7.5.   Party of 12 men carrying brushwood.
   N.20.d.75.32   9 men carrying shovels.
   N.14.d.90.55   9 men.
   several other smaller parties.

ARTILLERY.
At 5. p.m. the flashes of 2 guns were seen and they were thought to be about N.25.c. central.
   N.34.a.50.65   No. 149 Battery reported at 11.30 a.m. firing on N.13.a.
   N.28.d.4.2.   No. 159 was again seen yesterday and is a 77 mm. battery firing N. and N.W.

6 trucks were seen standing on the AUBERS-FROMELLES Rly. E. of FERME DU HOYON and 5 trucks W. of the Farm.

SMOKE.
   N.27.a.55.50)
   N.21.d.05.00) AUBERS DEFENCES.

   N.20.d.7.6.   House.
   N.20.d.5.8.   House.   Direct hits obtained.
   N.20.b.30.55   Trench.
   N.15.a.1.5.   Chimney.

Head Qrs. 56th Divn.
1st January 1917.

Captain,
Intelligence, General Staff.

56th DIVISIONAL TACTICAL PROGRESS REPORT No. 27.
from 8.0 a.m 1st January to 8.0 a.m. 2nd January 1917.

On receipt of current copy of Divisional Tactical Progress Report
in the trenches, previous copy to be destroyed.

PART I OPERATIONS.

RIGHT SECTION.- At 1.p.m. the enemy commenced an organised bombardment which opened with a quarter of an hour's rapid distributed over the whole of our front. It is apparent from the list of targets engaged that the enemy had obtained a fair knowledge of our "tender spots" from observation extending over the last month Our artillery quickly retaliated on to enemy front and support line. When it was evident that the enemy was carrying out an organised "shoot" which local fire was quite powerless to check, a short programme for Group Artillery in conjunction with 6" Hows. and 4.7" was arranged for 3.0 p.m. This succeeded in stopping his fire to a very large extent, but steady fire on back areas was continued till dusk, a large number of lachrymatory shells falling on the line of the RUE BACQUEROT. A retaliatory bombardment has been arranged to take place today.
Our M.Gs. showed their usual night activity.
One of our patrols examined the buildings at M.35.d.8.7. on their S. and W. fronts. They form a hollow square with pit in centre full of water. None of the enemy were encountered. Another patrol examined the enemy wire opposite M.29.3. They heard two or three men walking through water in the enemy trench, halting occasionally for a few moments. It appears, therefore, that this portion of the enemy line is merely patrolled. Other patrols could find no signs of the enemy

LEFT SECTION.- Our artillery replied affectively to the enemy's bombardment during the afternoon, whilst our M.Gs. sprayed the enemy's wire and trenches intermittently throughout the night especial attention being paid to the Cross Roads at N.20.a.8.7. Patrols were sent out last night to investigate the following points:-
(1) Junction of BERTHA TRENCH and front line
(2) Junction of IRMA and front line
(3) SUGAR LOAF
In all 12 patrols went out during the night but only 2 were able to penetrate the enemy's front line owing to the state of the ground although bridging was employed. At N.13.d.9.7. an Officers' patrol entered the German line by the Sap and Crater. Both were found unoccupied, the former in a bad state and the latter full of water but a few bombs were found about Saphead. Very few strands of wire were found at this point. Patrol moved South along parapet to point N.13.d.68.58. - trench was in good condition, wood revetted but water was above fire step which was about 3 ft. high. Wire was quite good here, and three groups of bombs were found. Patrols returned with spade bombs and box periscope. A further patrol under the same officer worked N. from Crater to N.14.c.15. 73. Trench good in most places but same level of water. At N.14.c.10.70. an open M.G. Emplacement was found with a pile of empty cartridge cases. This is the only point so far which has been found to have communication to the rear, duck boards being laid across the water. Sap nearby was unoccupied. Another patrol visited these parts about 2 hours later but nothing was seen or heard of the enemy. Six separate attempts were made to examine trenches at the head of IRMA not a sound was heard of the enemy. Two patrols attempted to enter the S. side of the SUGAR LOAF but failed. They worked with the battalion on our left.
The three snipers who had remained in the German front line at N.13.c.9.2. all day report that the German front line trench is on the far side of the River LAIES running parallel to it from 50 to 100 yards distant. They state that the ground between the old German front line and the River LAIES is like a lake dotted with islands. They could see no points capable of being held by the enemy. No passages across the water could be perceived and no bridges across the LAIES to the RUE D'ENDER.

No movement or targets were seen, but there appeared to be much new work on the trench across the river LAIES.

PART II INTELLIGENCE.

RIGHT SECTION.- During the bombardment mentioned above it is estimated that the enemy fired over 1,300 shells of all calibres. His trench mortars co-operated and a number of Heavy and Medium Shells fell along the front line - damage was not great.

Considerable movement during the day was seen on the screened road AUBERS - BAS POMMEREAU.. Work was being carried on at N.25.c.6.2. and at the Railway at M.30.d.45.60. Two men walked from BAS POMMEREAU to WIRELESS HOUSE T.2.b.2.7. at 12 noon.

LEFT SECTION.- In the afternoon hostile shelling became very heavy reaching its maximum about 2.45 p.m. first on front line then on RUE TILLELOY and Reserve Line lifting to RUE BACQUEROT. The shells fired were mainly 4.2" or 5.9" including a quantity of gas and tear shells. A great number of flashes were observed coming from Wood at N.27.c.8.5. and from behind Wood at N.17.d.5.5. The hostile battery at N.28.d.4.2. was again in action. The hostile T.Ms. were active during the bombardment. At 1.0 p.m. the trench mortar at N.14.c.1.5½. fired 15 rounds, and another trench mortar about 20 yards to its right was also firing. A heavy T.M. was located at N.14.d.95.65.

Fresh earth and timber are reported on CLARA C.T. at N.19.d.15.95. About 8.0 a.m. a party of Germans was seen to dump coils of wire about N.19.b.9.2. They went off in an Easterly direction entering BERTHA C.T. at N.20.b.3.0. At this point a sentry could be seen looking over the top. New work has been done on the emplacement about N.14.b.2.8. New wire and stakes have been erected at N.26.a.3.2. and N.20.d.7.72. About 1.45 a.m. a party of 10 Germans came from behind the hedge at N.14.d.1.4. and disappeared at N.20.a.87.63. A glass was seen moving from side to side in slit in roof of house at N.26.d.60.65. Usual movement was seen at N.20.b.30.65. and AUBERS DEFENCES.

Smoke was seen at N.20.b.35.5. Headquarters Dugout.
N.21.d.40.15. AUBERS DEFENCES.
N.27.a.5.3. House.

Head Qrs. 56th Divn.
2nd January, 1917.

Lieutenant,
Intelligence, General Staff.

Army Form A. 2007.

CENTRAL REGISTRY.

Central Registry No. and Date.

502/122 (G)

Attached Files.

SUBJECT, AND OFFICE OF ORIGIN.

Minor Operations — Raid
carried out by 12th London Regt. against
enemy trenches in FAUQUISSART Section (N.13.d. 8.7½)
on night 6th/7th December 1916.   56th Div

Referred to	Date	Referred to	Date	Referred to	Date
S	9.12.16				
I	11/12/16				
G	12.12.16				
		2982		P.A.	13/12/16

Schedule of Correspondence.

29/6

39

XI Corps.   56th Division O.G.61/15

In accordance with XI Corps RHS.1158/5, dated 14.11.16, herewith report in duplicate on raid carried out by Battalion holding the Left Sub-section of the FAUQUISSART SECTION on night 6th/7th December, 1916.

No special Artillery orders were issued, but the Left Group Commander was informed of the details of the enterprise and asked to stand by, but not to open fire unless called upon to do so.

Head Qrs. 56th Divn.   Major-General,
7th December, 1916.   Commanding 56th Division.

Headqrs First Army
    Forwarded.
The raid was well carried out but the values as regards the destruction of m.g. emplacements don't appear to have been

attended to. I am putting this right.

R. A. K. King Lt Gen
Mdg XI.. Corps.

9.12.16.

Headquarters,
    56th Division.

Herewith a copy of the "Report on a Raid" carried out by the 'RANGERS' at 2 a.m. on the morning of the 7th. Dec.

A copy of the orders for the raid is attached.

It is regretted that apparently no attempt was made to destroy the sniping posts and machine gun emplacements discovered, which is laid down to be one of the objects to be effected in all raids when possible.

Enquiries are being made as to reasons for failure.

7/12/16.

G Shoch
Brigadier General,
Commanding 168th Infantry Brigade.

THE RANGERS.
REPORT on RAID.

1. Officers patrols reconnoitred the proposed point of entry N.13.d.8.6½. on the nights of the 4th and 5th instant and ascertained that the hostile wire presented no serious obstacle - that the enemy trenches were considerably damaged and very wet. No signs of enemy movement were observed, but there appeared to be an enemy post at about N.13.d.90.75.

2. No preliminary wire cutting was required.

3. Detailed orders for the raid are attached.

4. The party left RED LAMP at 2.0 a.m. and entered enemy trench at N.13.d.75.65. Whilst the covering party was being posted, a party of five Germans (apparently a working party) were observed about N.13.d.70.60. on the parapet. They opened rapid fire on our covering party and then withdrew. They could not be followed up owing to a wide ditch intervening.

The trench Party established a block of one N.C.O, and 3 men thirty yards to the right of point of entry.

The remainder of the Trench Party moved along the trench to the left of point of entry. They found mud and water along the whole length of front line between two and three feet deep. In many places duck boards were afloat.

Owing to the state of the trenches, the party had to move along on top of the parapet which is in a fairly good state of repair in most places.

On reaching a point 120 yards from point of entry they were challenged by two Germans who came out of a snipers post made of sandbags. These two Germans fired at the officer in charge of the Trench Party and then ran away across the open towards the German second line and were not seen again.

They were fired at as they ran. The snipers post was examined and found to be empty.

The Trench Party found two M.G. emplacements - one at point of entry and another about fifty yards to our left of that point. These emplacements are in good condition and are made of sandbags.. They were found to be empty. There is a further snipers post midway between the two M.G. emplacements.

Nothing further was discovered and after waiting until 3.20 a.m. to see if any enemy patrols appeared, the party withdrew having been in the enemy lines about 45 minutes. There were no casualties.

Sgd/ A.D. BAYLIFFE, Lieut. Colonel,
Comdg. The Rangers, 12th Lond. Regt.

THE RANGERS

OPERATION ORDER NO 3.

RAID. "B" Company will carry out a small raid on the hostile trenches on the 7th instant. The Raiding Party will leave RED LAMP at 2.0 a.m.

OBJECTS.
(a). Killing enemy.
(b). Secure identifications.
(c). Bring away M.Gs. equipment, etc.

POINT OF ENTRY. N.13.d.8.7½.

PARTIES.

(a). Trench Party.

1 Officer) each
1 N.C.O.) carrying
8 Riflemen) 4 Mills
—   Grenades.
10

(b). Parapet Party

1 Officer (or Warrant Offr.)
1 N.C.O.
4 Riflemen (with wire cutters
—
6

(c). Covering Party.
1 Officer
1 N.C.O.
12 Riflemen
2 Runners
—
16

DUTIES
(a). Trench Party.
Will establish a block of 4 men 30 yards to the right of the point of entry.
(b). Remainder of party will move to their left from point of entry and kill or capture the first enemy post found.
If no post is found this party will endeavour to kill or capture one of his trench patrols.
Parapet Party.
Will line the enemy's parapet at point of entry and deal with any counter-attacks over the open.
Covering Party.
Will be disposed across NO MAN'S LAND to cover the line of withdrawal from flank attacks. This party will remain in position until the Trench Party has returned through it.

EQUIPMENT. Every man will wear belt and side arms and (except the Trench Party) will carry two grenades in addition to whatever else he may be carrying. All ranks will have their faces blacked. All marks of identification will be removed from clothing & equipment and no papers of any description will be carried. Every man will carry 50 rounds in a pouch worn on the belt.

ARTILLERY, M.G. & L.T.M. SUPPORT. This is not desired until called for but it is desired that it should be instantly available. A special telephone will be run to the front line for the purpose of the raid and an Officer placed in charge.

GENERALLY. The raid will be carried out as silently as possible, grenades will only be used if the exigencies of the situation demand them.
The companies in the front line will stand by whilst the raid is being carried out and will not display any abnormal activity.

5.12.16.

(sgd.) H.A.W. BACKHOFF,
Capt. & Adjt. The Rangers

APPENDIX I

LOCATION TABLES

S E C R E T.   A.Q.S/5.

LOCATION TABLE - 56th DIVISION - 21.10.16.

Divisional Headquarters)	
Divisional R.E. Headquarters)	
Divisional Train Headquarters)	
A.D.M.S.)	
Sanitary Section)	HALLENCOURT.
D.A.D.O.S. Store)	
French Mission)	
Divisional Reserve Company)	
1/5th Cheshire Regt. (Pioneers))	

167th INFANTRY BRIGADE HEADQUARTERS	VIEULAINE.
167th Machine Gun Company)	
167th Trench Mortar Battery)	
1st London Regiment)	LONGPRE.
7th Middlesex Regiment)	
3rd London Regiment)	AIRAINES.
8th Middlesex Regiment)	

168th INFANTRY BRIGADE HEADQUARTERS	YONVILLE.
168th Machine Gun Company)	
168th Trench Mortar Battery)	CITERNE.
4th London Regiment)	
12th London Regiment	MERELESSART.
13th London Regiment	SOREL and WANEL.
14th London Regiment	HOCQUINCOURT and GRANDSART.

169th INFANTRY BRIGADE HEADQUARTERS	VAL^{a} CH^{au}. HUPPY.
169th Machine Gun Company)	
169th Trench Mortar Battery)	BELLIFONTAINE.
2nd London Regiment	BAILLEUL.
5th London Regiment	HUPPY.
9th London Regiment	LIMEUX.
16th London Regiment	HUPPY.

1/1st Edinburgh Field Company, R.E.	BETTENCOURT.
2/1st London Field Company, R.E.)	
2/2nd London Field Company, R.E.)	EPONDELLE.

1 Sect. No.1 Company, Divisional Train	HALLENCOURT.
No. 2 Company, Divisional Train.	BETTENCOURT.
No. 3 Company, Divisional Train.	HALLENCOURT.
No. 4 Company, Divisional Train.	CAUMONT.

2/1st London Field Ambulance	AIRAINES.
2/2nd London Field Ambulance	LIERCOURT.
2/3rd London Field Ambulance	HUCHENNEVILLE.

Mobile Veterinary Section	HALLENCOURT.
Divisional Supply Column	FONTAINE-SUR-SOMME.

Divisional Artillery in XIV Corps Area, and No. 1 Company, Train.

19/10/16.

Captain,
D.A.A. & Q.M.G., 56th Division.

SECRET.

LOCATION TABLE - 56th DIVISION - 25.10.16.

56th DIVISION SECRET A.Q.S./6.

Divisional Headquarters.	
Divisional R.E.Headquarters.	LESTREM
Divisional Train Headquarters.	
Sanitary Section.	
D.A.D.O.S. Store.	LA GORGUE (L.34.c.88)
Divisional Reserve Company	LE VERT BOIS.
1/5th Cheshire Regiment.(Pioneers).	CORNET MALO. (K.32.c)
Headquarters, 167th Infantry Brigade.	LA GORGUE.
167th M.G.Company.)	
167th T.M.Battery.)	
1/1st London Regiment.	REGNIER LE CLERC.
1/3rd London Regiment.	ROBERMETZ.
1/7th Middlesex Regiment.	LA GORGUE.
1/8th Middlesex Regiment.	LE GRAND PACAUD.
Headquarters,168th Infantry Brigade.)	LA GORGUE.
168th M.G.Company.	
168th T.M.Battery.	
1/4th London Regiment.	ESTAIRES.
1/12th London Regiment.	
1/13th London Regiment.	
1/14th London Regiment.	
Headquarters, 169th Infantry Brigade.	CALONNE.
169th M.G.Company.)	
169th T.M.Battery.)	
1/2nd London Regiment.	PARADIS-L'EPINETTE.
1/5th London Regiment.	FOSSE.
1/9th London Regiment.	PARADIS-L'EPINETTE.
1/16th London Regiment.	LESTREM.
1/1st Edinborough Field Coy.R.E.	CALONNE.
2/1st London Field Coy.R.E.	CALONNE.
2/2nd " " " "	ESTAIRES.
2/1st London Field Ambulance.	CALONNE.
2/2nd " " "	ESTAIRES.
2/3rd " " "	MERVILLE.(Corps Rest Station). LE SART.(1 section at AHUTZIN).
No.2 Coy.Divl.Train.	GD. PACAUD.
No.3 Coy.Divl.Train.	ESTAIRES.
No.4 Coy.Divl.Train.	CALONNE.
Mobile Veterinary Section.	CORNET MALO.

Divisional Artillery and No.1 Coy.Divl Train in XIV Corps Area.

Railhead.   LA GORGUE.

                                         Captain,
                                    D.A.A. & Q.M.G., 56th Division.

25/10/16.

www.ingramcontent.com/pod-product-compliance
Lightning Source LLC
Chambersburg PA
CBHW080814010526
44111CB00015B/2555